Measurement of Productivity and Efficiency

Methods and perspectives to model and measure productivity and efficiency have made a number of important advances in the last decade. Using the standard and innovative formulations of the theory and practice of efficiency and productivity measurement, Robin C. Sickles and Valentin Zelenyuk provide a comprehensive approach to productivity and efficiency analysis, covering its theoretical underpinnings and its empirical implementation, paying particular attention to the implications of neoclassical economic theory. A distinct feature of the book is that it presents a wide array of theoretical and empirical methods utilized by researchers and practitioners who study productivity issues. An accompanying website includes methods, programming codes that can be used with widely available software like Matlab and R, and test data for many of the productivity and efficiency estimators discussed in the book. It will be valuable to upper-level undergraduates, graduate students, and professionals.

Robin C. Sickles is the Reginald Henry Hargrove Professor of Economics and Professor of Statistics at Rice University. He served as Editor-in-Chief of the Journal of Productivity Analysis as well as an Associate Editor for a number of other economics and econometrics journals. He is currently an Associate Editor of the Journal of Econometrics.

Valentin Zelenyuk is the Australian Research Council Future Fellow at the School of Economics at the University of Queensland, where he was an Associate Professor of Econometrics and also served as Research Director and Director of the Centre for Efficiency and Productivity Analysis (CEPA). He is currently an Associate Editor of the Journal of Productivity Analysis and the Data Envelopment Analysis Journal and an elected member in the Conference on Research in Income and Wealth (CRIW) of the National Bureau of Economic Research (NBER).

Measurement of Productivity and Efficiency

Theory and Practice

Robin C. Sickles
Rice University, Texas

Valentin Zelenyuk
The University of Queensland, Australia

CAMBRIDGE
UNIVERSITY PRESS

CAMBRIDGE
UNIVERSITY PRESS

University Printing House, Cambridge CB2 8BS, United Kingdom

One Liberty Plaza, 20th Floor, New York, NY 10006, USA

477 Williamstown Road, Port Melbourne, VIC 3207, Australia

314–321, 3rd Floor, Plot 3, Splendor Forum, Jasola District Centre, New Delhi – 110025, India

79 Anson Road, #06–04/06, Singapore 079906

Cambridge University Press is part of the University of Cambridge.

It furthers the University's mission by disseminating knowledge in the pursuit of education, learning, and research at the highest international levels of excellence.

www.cambridge.org
Information on this title: www.cambridge.org/9781107036161
DOI: 10.1017/9781139565981

First published 2019

Printed and bound in Great Britain by Clays Ltd, Elcograf S.p.A.

A catalogue record for this publication is available from the British Library.

Library of Congress Cataloging-in-Publication Data
Names: Sickles, Robin, author. | Zelenyuk, Valentin, author.
Title: Measurement of productivity and efficiency theory and practice / Robin
C. Sickles, Rice University, Texas. Valentin Zelenyuk, University of
Queensland, Australia.
Description: New York : Cambridge University Press, [2019]
Identifiers: LCCN 2018035971 | ISBN 9781107036161
Subjects: LCSH: Labor productivity – Measurement. | Industrial
efficiency – Measurement – Mathematical models. | Performance – Management.
Classification: LCC HD57 .S4977 2019 | DDC 658.5/15–dc23
LC record available at https://lccn.loc.gov/2018035971

ISBN 978-1-107-03616-1 Hardback
ISBN 978-1-107-68765-3 Paperback

To my family: Janet, Danielle, and David

—Robin Sickles

To my family: Natalya, Angelina, Kristina, Mary;
my parents: Hrystyna Myhaylivna and Petro Ivanovych;
my brother Oleksiy and sister Elena

—Valentin Zelenyuk

Contents

Figures

Tables

Preface

Cambridge University Press has published a number of successful books that focus on topics related to ours: Chambers (1988), Färe et al. (1994b), Chambers and Quiggin (2000), Kumbhakar and Lovell (2000), Ray (2004), Balk (2008), and Grifell-Tatjé and Lovell (2015). These books – and an increasing number of articles related to production analysis, published in top international journals in economics, econometrics, and operations research – suggest a growing interest in the academic and business audience on the subject.[1]

Our book is meant to complement and expand selected topics covered in the above-mentioned books, as well as the volume edited by Fried et al. (2008) and the edited volume by Grifell-Tatjé et al. (2018), and addresses issues germane to productivity analysis that would be of interest to a broad audience. Our book provides something genuinely unique to the literature: a comprehensive textbook on the measurement of productivity and efficiency, with deep coverage of both its theoretical underpinnings as well as its empirical implementation and a coverage of recent developments in the area. A distinctive feature of our book is that it presents a wide array of theoretical and empirical methods utilized by researchers and practitioners who study productivity issues. Our book is intended to be a relatively self-contained textbook that can be used in any graduate course devoted to econometrics and production analysis, of use also to upper-level undergraduate students in economics and in production analysis, and to analysts in government and in private business whose research or business decisions require reasoned analytical foundations and reliable and feasible empirical approaches to assessing the productivity and efficiency of their organizations and enterprises. We provide an integrated and synthesized treatment of the topics we cover. We have covered some topics in greater depth, some at a broader scope, but at all times with the same theme of motivating the material with an applied orientation.

---

[1] For a remarkable treatment of the history of the US economic growth experience and the sustainability of innovation-induced productivity growth see Gordon (2016).

Our book is structured in such a way that it can be used as a textbook for (instructed or self-oriented) academics and business consultants in the area of quantitative analysis of productivity of economic systems (firms, industries, regions, countries, etc.). In addition, some parts of this book can be used for short, intensive courses or supplements to longer courses on productivity and other topics, such as empirical industrial organization. Another example of the book's application would be to use the first section on production theory as a supplement in a course on advanced microeconomics. We have tried to structure the textbook in such a way as to broaden the audience for the topics we cover, and – just as important – help readers to have a self-contained source for gaining knowledge on the topics we cover with key references for further details.

It is important to note that the many methods we detail in our textbook are meant to be viewed as relative measures to some benchmark. We provide several different benchmarks in our early chapters, based on technical considerations as well as on excess costs, diminished revenues, and lower profits than could be generated were the firm or decision-making unit optimizing with respect to standard neoclassical assumptions. However, we are purposeful in our silence about the type of market mechanism that is adopted by firms or industries that are being analyzed. Reality shows that any country, or industry within any country, or firm within any industry – whether centrally planned or market oriented, or a hybrid of the two – can have inefficiency and low levels of productivity and therefore can be analyzed using the methods we detail in our book. As Thaler and Sunstein (2009, p. 6) have pointed out:

> Individuals make pretty bad decisions in many cases because they do not pay full attention in their decision-making (they make intuitive choices based on heuristics), they don't have self-control, they are lacking in full information, and they suffer from limited cognitive abilities.

Our book speaks to firms or agencies that are privately or state-owned, capitalist or centrally planned economies, developed, developing, or transitional countries – anywhere where the goal is to measure productivity and identify and explain possible inefficiencies. An aim of our textbook is to help a productive entity improve and move to higher levels of efficiency and productivity and a more efficient utilization of valuable and costly resources.

Our textbook also can be viewed as a comprehensive and integrated treatment of both neoclassical production theory and of the broader contextual theoretical and empirical treatment that renders it a special case. Such a treatment of production theory and productivity that explicitly allows and accounts for inefficiency has the advantage of providing researchers with the tools to pursue the production side of theories developed by Robert Thaler, the winner of the 49th Sveriges Riksbank prize in economic sciences (2017 Nobel Memorial Prize in Economic Science). According to the Nobel committee, Thaler provided a "more realistic analysis of how people think and behave when making economic decisions." We feel that allowing for similar realistic possibilities that producers, just like consumers, make decisions that may not reflect optimizing behaviors is warranted on both empirical and theoretical grounds.

Another important distinctive feature of our book is the availability of software. Much of the applied work in productivity and efficiency analysis that we discuss can be implemented using the packages of code for the MATLAB software that can be accessed at https://sites .google.com/site/productivityefficiency/ and is maintained by Dr. Wonho Song of the School of Economics, Chung-Ang University, Seoul, South Korea. The different packages for the MATLAB software were programmed by various scholars – Pavlos Almanidis, Robin Sickles, Léopold Simar, Wonho Song, Valentin Zelenyuk – and then checked, integrated and synthesized by Dr. Song to go along with this book. This MATLAB code is free and can also be integrated into R, Julia, and C++ programming environments. Details on how to access and implement the various estimators we discuss in our book, as well as data sources available to productivity researchers, are in Chapter 17. We anticipate that the availability of such freeware will allow a broad audience of interested scholars and practitioners to implement the methods outlined in our book as well as promote empirical research on the subject of efficiency and productivity modeling. The website has data sets for efficiency analysis, an inventory of the public use data available to researchers worldwide, and various instructional aids for teachers as well as students, including answer keys for selected exercises from the book. Software to estimate several of the Data Envelopment Analysis (DEA) and Stochastic Frontier Analysis (SFA) models that we have considered using cross-section, time series, and panel data can also be found in LIMDEP, R, STATA, and SAS, to mention a few.

Acknowledgments

For both of us, this book is a culmination of professional careers in economics dating back over several decades. It would make sense that there are numerous people we wish to thank for making this book possible. They are our families, our mentors, our collaborators, our students, and our many colleagues who contributed by providing substantive comments and contributions to the book's narrative and technical details. Below we give individual and more specific acknowledgments.

From Robin Sickles I was quite fortunate to have remarkable mentors in my life. My brother Rick, who has given me advice throughout my entire life; my first economics teacher, Carl Biven, whose course in the History of Economic Thought at Georgia Tech inspired my transition from a major and co-op job in aerospace engineering to economics; and Mike Benoit, whose friendship and support was instrumental in my making the career choice to pursue graduate studies. In some cases, an individual or individuals may take on the role of both a mentor and a collaborator. C. A. Knox Lovell and Peter Schmidt are two such people. It is remarkably fortunate that I would be in graduate school at the University of North Carolina at Chapel Hill in the early 1970s at a time when these remarkable scholars' careers were defined by their collaborative efforts that led to the iconic Aigner, Lovell, and Schmidt stochastic frontier paper and many other seminal works, often with each other, with other colleagues at UNC, or with other students at UNC. I have expressed my appreciation and gratitude and have acknowledged my debt to Knox and Peter in many venues – edited special journal issues, volumes, and special awards that I have been honored to present. It is rare indeed for a collaborative enterprise to have lasted such a long time, but we continue to work together on many projects and to attend many of the same professional conferences. Not only have the collaborative efforts among us been long lasting as a professional enterprise, but so has our friendship. That is a rare gift, and I will always know how lucky I have been to have had such mentors, collaborators, and friends.

My career in productivity and efficiency would not have had the longevity it has had were I also not in the right place at the right time in 1976 when

I began my appointment as an assistant professor at the George Washington University. John Kendrick (who received his PhD at UNC) asked me to assist him in developing methods to attribute specific factor productivity growth to particular factors of production in the US airline industry. That work with the Air Transport Association was my first formal endeavor in the field of productivity, and I thank my late colleague and mentor John Kendrick for giving me that opportunity. Lovell and Sickles (2010) have a brief memorial article on John and his seminal contributions to productivity. Later, after I had moved to the University of Pennsylvania, I was lucky enough to have an appointment as a Faculty Research Fellow at the National Bureau of Economic Research. I am indebted to Ernst Berndt and to Zvi Griliches for making that possible, and to Ned Nadiri, Erwin Diewert, and my many other colleagues in the Productivity Program during my time in that position. While at Penn, Jere Behrman, Robert Pollak, Paul Taubman and I worked on a number of productivity-related issues, some of which are referenced in this book. I am indebted to them for their kind support and their most appreciated mentorship.

I have been particularly lucky to have had exceptional graduate students with whom I have worked and who have helped teach me so much. By far and away my best student in productivity has been David H. Good, who was a PhD student of mine while I was at Penn and who is the Director of the Transportation Research Center at Indiana University at Bloomington, as well as a faculty member of the School of Public and Environmental Affairs there. David and I wrote many, many papers together on productivity and efficiency, and our joint research has been some of my very best. Another student of mine at Penn whom I must also thank is Lars-Hendrik Röeller, who stepped down as the founding President of the ESMT Berlin European School of Management and Technology in 2011 to become the Chief Economic Advisor to the Chancellor, Federal Chancellery, Germany.

PhD students at Rice who have taught me much, and with whom I have been engaged in productivity and efficiency work, much of which is detailed in this textbook, include Byeong-Ho Gong, Mary Streitwieser, Purvez Captain, Ila Semenick Alam, Robert Adams, Patrik Hultberg, Byeong Jeon, Lullit Getachew, Wonho Song, Timothy Gunning, Junhui Qian, Pavlos Almanidis, Hulushi Inanoglu, David Blazek, Levent Kutlu, Jiaqi Hao, Junrong Liu, Pavlo Demchuk, Chenjun Shang, Jaepil Han, Deockhyun Ryu, and Binlei Gong.

I have benefited from the assistance of a number of people in preparing the draft materials for the book and for providing technical expertise to make possible the editing of the final manuscript. Among these are Aditi Bhattacharyya, John Paul Peng, Wajiha Noor, my former Rice PhD students and collaborators Jaepil Han, Binlei Gong, and Wonho Song, my current PhD students Shasha Liu and Kevin Bitner, and former Rice PhD students Nigel Soria and Nick Copeland. Rice Economics PhD student Peter Volkmar and Rice Statistics Masters student Jiacheng Liang provided programming expertise to translate the MATLAB code for estimating the various productivity and efficiency estimators discussed in Chapter 17 into compatible R code.

My contribution to this book would not have been possible were it not for these many wonderful students I have learned from over my 32 years at Rice University, and I thank the University and the Department of Economics for the good fortune I have had in working with our remarkable students and with my distinguished Rice colleagues.

I would like to thank Léopold Simar at the Center for Operations Research and Econometrics (CORE) and the Institut de Statistique at the Université Catholique de Louvain for my many summer visits that he sponsored there, that led directly to this book project. In addition to my many research works with Léopold Alois Kneip, and visiting faculty Byeong Park while in Louvain-la-Neuve, I also first discussed this book project with Valentin Zelenyuk while we were both visiting Léopold's Institute of Statistics.

I would like to thank Christopher O'Donnell, Valentin, and the Center for Efficiency and Productivity Analysis at the University of Queensland for providing me the funding during my sabbatical leave at the University in 2014 to work on portions of this manuscript. Seminars at UQ and substantial interactions with leading scholars there made a difference in my approach to writing this book.

I would like to thank Loughborough University's School of Business and Economics, and its former Dean Angus Laing and current Dean Stewart Robinson, who have supported my efforts during visits there that began in 2014. During those times I have been engaged with my co-authors Anthony Glass and Karligash Kenjegalieva in our work on spatial productivity measurement and efficiency spillovers, and also with them and my colleagues David Saal and Victor Podinovski in developing Loughborough's Centre for Productivity and Performance.

Particular thanks are also due to Aditi Bhattacharyya, Will Grimme, Hiro Fukuyama, Levent Kutlu, Young C. Joo, Hideyuki Mizobuchi, Alecos Papadopoulos, Jaemin Ryu, Kien C. Tran, Kerda Varaku, and Yi Yang, who have provided extensive edits and helpful additions and comments on many of the chapters.

From Valentin Zelenyuk Besides thanking my dear family and parents, all my teachers through life, co-authors and students, friends and opponents, I would like to express my sincerest thanks to the two greatest researchers and mentors I had the enormous honor to work with: Rolf Färe and Léopold Simar. Most of the research I have done (and probably will do in the future) is directly or indirectly related to what I learned from them, and has been inspired in a large part by them.

Indeed, my start in this area was largely due to Rolf Färe, and to some extent Shawna Grosskopf, when I set out as their first MSc student in 1998, and then as their PhD student in 1999–2002, at Oregon State University (here I thank the Edmund Muskie program of the US government for sending me there on a fellowship). After giving me a great foundation in production theory and in the theory of DEA and its applications, and helping with developing and publishing several works that were exciting for me, Rolf and Shawna strongly recommended me (at my public PhD defense) to find ways to work with and learn from Léopold Simar. A few weeks later I attended NAPW-2002, where I first met and talked to Léopold and another research era started for me at that point, filled with many other exciting research projects.

The collaboration with Léopold was particularly vital for me in keeping up with research despite the heavy teaching load – eight courses per year – at the EERC program of Kyiv-Mohyla Academy in Ukraine, later renamed as the Kyiv School of Economics (KSE), as well as at IAMO (Germany). Fortunately, three of those courses were related to advanced production theory and productivity and efficiency analysis, and this is where the writing of this book was originated for me. Here, it is worth noting that, being sponsored by various donors (Eurasia Foundation in USA, the World Bank, Soros Foundation, Swedish government, etc.), the EERC/KSE was gathering many of the best students from Ukraine and nearby countries, creating the best motivation for me to prepare hard for my lectures and so I am thankful to this school and its donors, and Ukraine in general, for this opportunity. I especially thank the students who kept me working above my normal pace and in particular those with whom I worked and who gave valuable feedback to my lecture notes: Mykhaylo Salnykov, Vladimir Nesterenko, Oleg Badunenko, Pavlo Demchuk, Bogdan Klishchuk, Alexandr Romanov, Oleg Nivyevskiy, to mention just a few.

I also thank the Center for Russian and Eurasian Studies at Harvard University: the great academic spirit and atmosphere of Harvard fueled my enthusiasm to write the first draft of about quarter of this book during my two months, sabbatical visit there in the winter of 2004. That was a great start to what turned out to be a very turbulent period both in my life and in Ukraine. Indeed, at that time Ukraine was on the verge of either sliding into a dictatorship or having a revolution. As we now know, the latter happened – the Orange Revolution of 2004 – and like many patriotically minded activists, feeling euphoric, I almost made a fatal error – going into politics – and it was the exciting work with and learning from Léopold that literally saved me from it: the Postdoc Fellowship at the Institute of Statistics of the Université Catholique de Louvain (UCL) in Belgium in 2004/2005 was one of the most productive times for me, and I am very thankful to Léopold and the Institute in general for that period and for many fruitful visits I made there afterward, which kept me engaged in the area despite other temptations from businesses or politics, and despite the GFC-related turbulence.

Interestingly, it was also there at UCL that I met Robin Sickles in 2004, and I am very happy we decided to combine our efforts on this book, and I thank Robin for his valuable feedback on my writings. It was also there at UCL, in 2009, that I incidentally learned of, applied to, and eventually got a position at the School of Economics at the University of Queensland (UQ), which for me was (and still is) associated with one of the greatest focal points of research in the area: the Centre for Efficiency and Productivity Analysis (CEPA). It is mainly because of this Centre, or more precisely the people that form and visit it, that I made what at that time seemed to many of my friends a fairly radical decision: to move to Australia. In hindsight, I see it as one of the best decisions I have ever made; it helped me substantially progress in my research endeavors in general and in writing this book in particular. So, I would like to express sincere thanks to Australia in general and the UQ School of Economics and CEPA in particular, and especially my CEPA colleagues: Knox Lovell, Chris O'Donnell, Antonio Peyrache, Alicia Rambaldi, and Prasada Rao, as well as Tim Coelli who was at CEPA's origin: together they created the greatest environment for productivity and efficiency analysis in the world, and I am honored to have joined their efforts, trying to make my own contribution. I also thank Hideyuki Mizobuchi, Hirofumi Fukuyama and Sung-Ko Li, as well as his students (especially Xinju He), for valuable comments on this book and for our joint research that helped in shaping it.

I also thank Per Agrell, Bert Balk, Rajiv Banker, Peter Bogetoft, Robert Chambers, Laurens Cherchye, Erwin Diewert, Finn Førsund, Paul Frijters, Jiti Gao, William Greene, William Horrace, Jeffrey Kline, Dale Jorgenson, Subal Kumbhakar, Flavio Menezes, Byeong Uk Park, Chris Parmeter, Victor Podinovski, John Quiggin, Subhash Ray, John Ruggiero, Robert Russell, David Saal, Peter Schmidt, Rabee Tourky, Ingrid Van Keilegom, Hung-Jen Wang, Paul Wilson, Joe Zhu, among many others who I had great opportunity to interact with and learn from on many occasions and from their works, which directly or indirectly helped me in gaining or synthesizing the knowledge for this book.

Last, yet not least, I also would like to thank the students at UQ who gave valuable feedback and technical assistance on various versions of this book, especially Bao Hoang Nguyen, Duc Manh Pham, Andreas Mayer, and Yan Meng, as well as David Du, Kelly Trinh, and Alexander Cameron. Finally, besides support from the universities that employed me or hosted me for research visits, I also would like to acknowledge the support of my research from ARC DP130101022 and ARC FT170100401, as some of this research directly or indirectly influenced the content of this book.

Both authors would like to thank a number of scholars who have provided needed criticism and suggested additions to earlier drafts that have broadened and enhanced the topics and technical material we develop in our book. These include Robert Chambers, Erwin Diewert, Rolf Färe, William Greene, Shawna Grosskopf, Kris Kerstens, Subal Kumbhakar, Young Hoon Lee, C. A. Knox Lovell, Chris Parmeter, Victor Podinovski, Robert Russell, Peter Schmidt, William Schworm and Léopold Simar.

Finally, we thank our Cambridge University Press editor Karen Maloney and the Cambridge University Press editorial team for their patience, support, and professionalism.

Introduction

In this brief introduction we discuss motivations for the study of productivity, when optimizing behavior is not always practiced by the firm or productive unit under observation, that mostly come from important literatures that we will not cover in depth in our book. We discuss several sets of motivating factors and introduce them under the generic headings of management practices, behavioral economics, and X-efficiency. We purposely introduce the arguments in these literatures without reference to the more recent work in DEA and stochastic frontiers that make up the methodological coverage in the remaining chapters of the book. We do so in order to highlight the broad consensus that has existed since at least the early twentieth century for the persistent and transitory existence of suboptimal behaviors coming from these relatively distinct but very related literatures in management, psychology, sociology, and from classical economics.

Management Practices and Inefficiency in Production

Inefficiency in production, and the approaches to address it that we detail in the chapters to follow, can be linked to the sometimes overlooked but quite important literature on management practices, variations in which are what we almost always interpret as changes in the level of a firm's operating efficiency. Empirical studies have shown large differences in productivity across both firms and countries (Lieberman et al., 1990; Foster et al., 2008; Hsieh and Klenow, 2009; Hall and Jones, 1999), and one of the clear determinants of such differences can be attributed to management practices, as pointed out by Glaister (2014). In a study of microdata from 45 developing countries, Nallari and Bayraktar (2010) found that research and development, capacity utilization, and adoption of foreign technology were clearly related to productivity differences among the micro-units, and these are all determined by the decisions of management, which for all intents and purposes is an unobserved latent variable. In the classic work on variations in management practices, Bloom et al. (2012) find an $R^2 = 0.81$ in their regressions of gross domestic product (GDP) per capita on management practices across 17 countries. Bloom et al. (2013) found similar variations in productivity explained by management practices within India. The exact formal mechanisms that map management skills and practices into a particular firm's productivity advantages is frankly not well understood, and empirical research on the topic has provided little in the way of a consensus on how such a formal linkage can be modeled. We often think of such a linkage in terms of a reduced form model that dispenses with a formal structure for the mediating factors and view the latent management input as being a function of a number of observable factors. There appears to be a consensus on the main factors that influence the effectiveness of management practices and it would appear that innovation is one of them. However, it is often difficult to distinguish between the innovation that is typically identified with technical changes, and the innovations instituted by management practices. Incremental innovations in management practices are ubiquitous throughout market economies (Dodgson and Gann, 2010, p. 15). Such adjustments to management practices may be informal and based on trial by error, involving the marketing of new models of existing products and services, changes in organizational structures and processes, coordination, routine supervision, and many other factors. These changes are incremental and it is their accumulation that triggers measurable productivity impacts (Rosenberg, 1982, p. 62–70; Mokyr, 1985, p. 28; McCloskey, 1985, p. 66; Blaug, 1999, p. 110). Moreover, there would appear to be a growing consensus that small to medium size enterprises are at a disadvantage in providing the resources needed to systematically impact productivity via R&D expenditures vis-à-vis larger enterprises (Haltiwanger et al., 1999; Shane, 2009; Van Praag and Versloot, 2007).

Prices also may drive financial performance just as much as productivity does. As pointed out by Lovell (2013), as well as Grifell-Tatjé and Lovell (2013, 2014, 2015), managers can get lucky and manage at the right time (minerals in Australia during 1995–2005) or the wrong time (minerals in Australia during 2006–2013). However, management practices also can be mitigating factors in response to such demand shocks that are out of the control of the firm. Bloom and Van Reenen (2007) studied 732 firms in the USA, the UK, France, and Germany and found that productivity gaps could be explained by 18 key management practices. Among the most important management practices were (1) shop floor operations (2) monitoring (3) targets (4) incentives. Why do management practices differ? Is it is due to product market competition? Is it due to ownership? What are the consequences of management practices on total factor productivity (TFP), profitability, sales growth, survival, Tobin's Q? In Brea-Solís et al. (2015) they provide counterexamples to the notion that productivity growth is necessary in order for a firm to be successful, based in part on Walmart's remarkable corporate history. This is also echoed in the volume by Grifell-Tatjé and Lovell (2015), which is devoted in part to the topic of business strategy, an expression apparently coined by Drucker (1954). Business strategy is of course connected to productivity but has important differences.

Do entrepreneurs engage in ventures that create value and how is this value captured as profit? Value in this context is the wedge between customers' willingness to pay and suppliers' willingness to sell (Brandenburger and Stuart, 1996). Creating value and capturing it as profit is the function of the business model. Creating value is an outcome of the dynamic interplay of productivity, innovation, and business practices. Value creation may in some cases be facilitated by finance and financial engineering, but these financial enterprises do not, in and of themselves, tend to create value.[1]

Although financial services have a role in intermediation, their role as a casino does raise doubt about their influence on aggregate economic growth. Does the focus on financial services and not on value creation impact income inequality, which it is argued by many puts a damper on productivity growth? In the USA there has been a disconnect since the 1970s between TFP growth and wage growth. This has been pointed out by a number of scholars. Sickles et al. (2016) have assessed counterfactuals based on relinking productivity growth and wage compensation during this period and have provided evidence that income inequality in the USA would be more comparable to present day Sweden than the countries with which it shares its current ranking (e.g., Iran and Bulgaria) had productivity growth been distributed to wage compensation as it had been in the post WWII years through the early 1970s. Income inequality is both a determining factor of productivity growth and a factor determined by it and demands more attention by scholars to measure its impact and disentangle the causal links between productivity growth and income inequality (Jones, 2015).

As creating value and capturing it as profit is the function of the business model, value must be created. The business model is developed to lay out the "the logic of the firm, the way it operates, and how it creates and captures value for its stakeholders" (Brandenburger and Stuart, 1996). Brea-Solís et al. (2015) point out the characterization of business models by Casadesus-Masanell and Ricart (2007, 2010, 2011) models by Casadesus-Masanell and Ricart (2007, 2010, 2011) and Casadesus-Masanell and Zhu (2010). They argue that the business model is grounded in the choices that are under the control of management, such as assets, policies, the governance of those policies and assets, and the consequences of these choices, which cannot be controlled by management. Brea-Solís et al. (2015) use this description of the business model and management's role in executing it in a very insightful case study of the sources of profit variations over time over the tenure of three of Walmart's CEO's: Sam Walton (1970–1988), David Glass (1998–2000), and Lee Scott (2000–2008).

---

[1] Recall the *Economist* article in 1999 heralding Houston as the City of the Twenty-First Century. The Jewel in the Crown was Enron. Enron was a finance company that sold itself as something very different. At the end of the day, when it was liquidated several years later, it was clear that its assets were often somewhat dubious titles to titles of titles to assets. There was no value added.

How does management assess the success of these practices? It typically does so by recognizing that, although innovation is the key aspect of a production process that management can impact, it is innovation in the workplace, or in-process innovation, that is impacted most by effective management. How is this measured?

In our brief discussion of management practices and their linkages to productivity we also can reconsider the debate that occurred during the 1970s between Harvey Leibenstein with his view of X-inefficiency (Leibenstein, 1966) and George Stigler (1976) with his view of internal inefficiency.[2] Stigler's rather condescending comment that "We may sympathize with Leibenstein's desire to associate his X-efficiency with economic behavior, but this shotgun marriage is not fertile" is still a view harbored by many neoclassical economists who stay true to assumptions that market forces result in only short-run divergences between first-order conditions for optimizing behavior and thus can be ignored. Indeed, in his Presidential Address to the American Economic Association, Zvi Griliches (1994), who was then Director of the National Bureau of Economic Research's (NBER) Productivity Program and of course a pioneer in productivity research, commented in regard to NBER's Productivity Program: "Harvey Leibenstein's (1966) ideas about X-efficiency, or more correctly X-inefficiency, did not get much of a sympathetic ear from us." In his address Griliches, foreshadowing the work by Bloom (current Co-Director of the NBER's Productivity and Growth Program) and his colleagues, noted that X-inefficiency gains importance at times when the firm finds itself in disequilibrium or faces unexploited profit opportunities and develops innovative ways to close the gap between its current state and the "frontier." [3]

X-inefficiency, and which management practices directly influence it, is important not when the firm finds itself in "disequilibrium" but also when it finds itself in equilibrium; that is, all of the time. Equilibrium is a factor that posits conditions under which optimizing behaviors should trend, much like the equilibrium concepts of strong attractors and cointegrating long-run and short-run relationships that are represented in error-correction models (Engle and Granger, 1987). Such issues are addressed later in this book in our chapter on dynamics and convergence from a stochastic and deterministic point of view. It is important to remember that management practices as drivers of innovation and efficiency change are important not only when the firm is in equilibrium or disequilibrium but also when the firm faces opportunities and,

---

[2] Much of this discussion is based on Lovell (2013).

[3] It is hard to overstate the influence that the late Zvi Griliches and his Harvard colleague Dale Jorgenson, whose current World KLEMS initiative is refocusing researchers on sector specific productivity issues through the world, have had on the study of productivity. Nerlove (2001), who himself contributed so much to duality theory and to the panel data literature whose approaches are utilized in Chapters 11 and 12, has a particularly insightful treatise on Griliches' particular contributions in his thoughtful and detailed discussion of Griliches' life and contributions to economics.

if unwilling to take advantage of opportunities, may incur the opportunity cost of not undertaking a particular strategy that may generate net value and hence profits.

There is indirect evidence for the presence and for concern by the management of their firm's inefficiency. The existence of a substantial consulting industry devoted to benchmarking analysis (that is, efficiency analysis) would suggest that the notion of inefficiency and its measurement using the techniques discussed in this book have passed the market test. It is clear that businesses and regulators use formal models to measure productivity and focus their attention on mechanisms to incentivize its diminution. Moreover, it is unlikely that anyone involved in a public/government service has not tried to find inefficiency and remove it.

Why are these measures taken by enterprises and their leadership? It is of course to improve performance, that is, to improve productivity. It is why the management consultant exists and is highly paid, it is the reason for cost cutting, rightsizing, etc. Although there is a semantic difference, and a difference that can be developed more fully at a theoretical level, the question of whether or not the presence of inefficiency results in the firm's reoptimizing or trimming the fat, there is little difference in fact. The firm is not doing as well as it could with the resources at its disposal relative to other firms with which it competes.

The evidence for the need for benchmarking/efficiency analyses is also direct. The Journal of Productivity Analysis (Springer) is a case in point. So is the work by Bloom and Van Reenen (2007), Bloom et al. Bloom et al. (2012, 2013). As Bloom et al. (2013) conclude: "improved management practice is one of the most effective ways for a firm to outperform its peers."

Behavioral Economics and Inefficiency in Production

As we discussed in the preface, behavioral economists have provided motivation for allowing nonoptimal allocations in production to be a testable restriction rather than an *a priori* assumption. That firms often operate inefficiently and in markets where inefficiencies can persist, is not a new concept nor a new empirical or theoretical insight. A treatment of production theory and productivity with optimal decisions a testable restriction is consistent with the recent Nobel Prize in Economic Sciences winner Robert Thaler's views on human nature (recalling that managers are the decision-makers on the supply side of the market just as consumers are decision makers on the demand side of the market). Decision making by inefficient firms was studied exhaustively by many economists and sociologists in the 1940s and 1950s. Such scholars as Harvey Leibenstein, George Katona, and Herbert Simon laid the foundation for the more recent cohort of behavioral economists and experimental economists such as George Akerlof, Daniel Kahneman, Richard Thaler, Vernon Smith, and Amos Tversky (Frantz et al., 2017). Efficiency and rationality are the cornerstones of modern neoclassical economics, but these cornerstones have always been fragile and in need of repair. John Maynard Keynes was clear in his views on the subject, devoting the first page of his General Theory of Employment, Interest, and Money (1936) to the fact that the term "General" was meant to question *status quo* beliefs by the classical economists of his time who stifled intellectual developments (Frantz et al., 2017, p. 92). Similar points about "irrational" behavior were made by George Katona (1951) with his psychological economics and by Herbert Simon (1957) with his selective rationality. Such inefficient firm decision-making was treated extensively by Leibenstein and others, as documented in the excellent Routledge Handbook of Behavioral Economics (Frantz et al., 2017). Frantz (1997) notes a revealing and poignant observation made by Leibenstein in his discussion of Lionel Robbins' (1932) book, An Essay on the Nature and Significance of Economic Science in the forward to his X-Efficiency: Theory, Evidence and Applications. In Robbins's book economics is defined as the study of the efficient allocation of scarce resources in their alternative uses. Leibenstein's comment is:

> What got lost... was the businessman's idea and the engineer's idea of efficiency, which signify how well or poorly people and machines are working. Once allocative efficiency is combined with the maximization-of-utility or profits postulate there is no longer any room for the businessman's and the engineer's concept of efficiency. Thus, the idea disappeared that suboptimal operations by the firm and inside the firm are possible... Businessmen, engineers, and psychologists are aware of suboptimal behavior, but standard economic theory somehow does not easily or readily lend itself to the possibility of suboptimal operations.

Leibenstein's major work, X-efficiency theory, was based on an interdisciplinary perspective in efficiency analysis that brings together psychology, management and engineering studies. We also adopt this approach in our book by integrating the fields of operations research, engineering, management science (a field, it has been argued, that was begun at Carnegie Mellon University by Herbert Simon and one of the seminal contributors to the field of DEA discussed in this book, W. W. Cooper), statistics, and economics. Although the classical concept of an idealized rational optimizing agent has scientific merit, allowing for such behavior to be testable instead of assumed *a priori* leads to a research perspective that we hope will broaden the field of productivity analysis and result in a deeper and more meaningful theoretical and empirical body of knowledge that can be brought to bear on its study.

X-Efficiency in Production: Perspectives on Efficiency by Harvey Leibenstein

Before Harvey Leibenstein introduced X-Efficiency (XE) theory in 1966, economists had been studying efficiency, allocative efficiency specifically, based on the assumption that agents are rational and thus are utility maximizers. It was believed that firms could achieve full efficiency in a competitive market in which firms set prices equal to marginal costs. XE theory challenged the well-accepted assumption that firms try to minimize costs in their production. Repeated observations of irrational behavior of firms and individuals have established the foundation of XE theory. The neoclassical theory is one of the cases XE theory considers when firms produce optimally in accordance with their production and cost functions. However, XE theory also incorporates irrationality in firms' behavior and allows for institutional environments that may lead to X-Inefficiency (XIE).

Sources of XIE are prevalent in economics. The agency problem is an important source for XIE. When managers pursue risky investments, or devote resources based on personal benefits rather than on the basis of increasing firms' profits – in the short run and in the long run – XIE occurs even if the firms are allocatively efficient. Market power also gives rise to inefficiency. Since the agency problem is more likely to exist when a firm has market power, monopolistic firms tend to have incentives for non-cost-minimizing behavior. In general, XIE is expected to be higher when government regulation, state ownership, or monopoly exists in the market. Leibenstein (1966, 1975, 1987) argued that inefficiency is persistent in production due to such agency problems in a firm, as well as due to information asymmetry and to monitoring required by regulatory oversight.

XE theory is in line with the ideas in productivity and efficiency literature that we explore in our book wherein total factor productivity growth is decomposed into technological change (innovation) and technical efficiency change (catch-up). XE has been incorporated into technical efficiency in hundreds of empirical studies on firm/industry efficiency. Empirical evidence from various industries, e.g., health care, telecommunications, airlines, and education, are consistent with the implications of XE theory (Frantz, 1997, 2007). XIE has been empirically estimated to be much more significant than allocative inefficiency. Studies (Kwan, 2006; Jiang et al., 2009; Fu and Heffernan, 2009) utilizing stochastic frontier analysis on the Chinese banking system, where periods of government deregulation had a different impact on banks' efficiency levels, estimate an average 25 percent XIE level from 1990 to 2015. Studies (Yao et al., 2008; Rezvanian et al., 2011) have also shown that Chinese banks' XE increased in periods after admission to WTO. Other studies on efficiency of financial institutions in various countries have shown consistent estimates with XE theory. US financial institutions, for example, have an average 20 percent XIE level from 1980s to 1990s, and they tend to have higher XE levels in periods after the banking deregulation (Bauer and Hancock, 1993; Mester, 1993; DeYoung, 1998).

As the literature on XE has flourished since Leibenstein introduced the theory, so has criticism. The most forcefully presented leisure-effort argument, for example, argues that the product of a firm also includes "non-traded" output which can be the health and leisure of employees. A decrease in employees' effort to pursue more leisure changes output rather than inefficiency, and a rational agent would not choose leisure if its cost outweighed its value. Such an argument that XIE does not exist and all inefficiencies are allocative is based on the assumption of complete information in the market for, and prices of, leisure by employees, which would appear to be unrealistic. Different schools of criticisms are essentially tautological in the way that they disprove XE theory by assertion but they can't prove the existence of maximizing behavior. As Frantz (1997) raises the question in his book, "what becomes of the word maximize if non-maximize is not possible? Is the concept of efficiency important if the possibility of inefficiency is ruled out *a priori*?" The importance of efficiency remains as long as economics remains important.

Modeling Inefficiency in Production – A Road Map on How We Synthesize Different Perspectives on the Sources of Productive Inefficiency

The term "frontier firm" is ubiquitous in economics and business. In the relatively recent OECD Report Frontier Firms, Technology Diffusion and Public Policy: Micro Evidence from OECD Countries (Andrews et al., 2015) the term is used 336 times. In the recent *Economist* review of Haskel and Westlake (2018) and the book itself, the term is also used throughout as a key concept in various discussions. It is clear from the brief set of studies we have discussed in this introduction, many of which have not originated in the relatively recent literature on productivity and efficiency on which the remainder of the book is focused, that economists and business analysts have great interest and a large number of ways to approach the modeling and explanations of such production outcomes. It is the purpose of our book to provide the economics and business community with broad methodologies within an operational paradigm to identify such frontier firms, measure deviations from such benchmarks, analyze their sources, and to understand how other firms can improve their performance.

What we attempt to do in the remaining chapters is to provide a sound theoretical grounding in how such outcomes of the production process can be squared with models of optimizing behavior and how suboptimal and optimal production decisions can be measured, estimated, and interpreted. Most of the theoretical foundations are treated in Chapters 1–5. Chapters 6–10 discuss how productivity can be measured empirically, with Chapter 6 focusing on functional forms for estimating the technology and Chapters 7–10 focusing on various methods to estimate production outcomes, technical change, and efficiency levels and changes in them using linear programming methods from the field of operations research and statistics. Chapters 11–16 discuss a number of econometrically motivated topics, beginning with the stochastic production frontier paradigm and ending with methods to build consensus estimates from competing models (model averaging) and to impose regularity constraints on econometrically specified nonparametric representations of technology or its many dual forms. Our final Chapter 17 speaks to the main sources of data that productivity researchers have and are using, and focuses on the World KLEMS initiative and many recent studies using it that have appeared in the literature. We discuss a number of other data sets briefly and also introduce the various linear programming and econometrics software programs that are publicly available to estimate productivity and efficiency.

CHAPTER 1

Production Theory: Primal Approach

One of the key strengths of contemporary efficiency and productivity analysis is that it has the production theory of neoclassical economics at its foundation and provides optimality criteria with respect to which efficiency benchmarking can be done. Consequently, the first few chapters of this text are devoted to outlining the main ideas and results of this theory – to lay out the economic foundation for further discussion of efficiency and productivity analysis techniques. In our discussion, we follow the style set by Shephard (1953, 1970) and Färe and Primont (1995).

1.1 SET CHARACTERIZATION OF TECHNOLOGY

The task of laying out a theoretical foundation for analyzing the production performance of a firm is quite challenging, to say the least. To stay as general as possible, we have to tame a formal expression of production processes and related decisions of a *typical* firm that would fit the context of operation of many possible types of firms. This is needed so that the methodology can be used (with some tuning) to analyze virtually any economic system: a firm, a plant, a department, an industry, a country, etc.

In general, any production process can be viewed as a process whereby some technology transforms inputs (x) into outputs (y). Virtually all firms use more than one input (say, N inputs) and produce more than one output (e.g., M outputs). To account for this multidimensionality in our framework we assume that x is a vector in the nonnegative real (Euclidian) space of some finite dimension N, i.e., denoted as $x = (x_1, \ldots, x_N)' \in \Re_+^N$, and y is a vector in the nonnegative real space of some finite dimension M, i.e., denoted as $y = (y_1, \ldots, y_M)' \in \Re_+^M$.[1] Basically, what we want to analyze can be schematically represented as in Figure 1.1.

---

[1] Note that this implies that all inputs and all outputs are completely divisible, in the sense that they can take all values on the real line (including irrational numbers). Such an assumption is of course for simplicity of modeling and, while it may not hold in practice, it often serves as a good approximation of reality, with a much simpler theoretical framework.

Figure 1.1 A typical production process.

The key, of course, is how to characterize the "technology" of a typical firm that would fit many types of firms. A standard way of doing it in economics is to assume that the technology of a particular firm we want to analyze can be characterized by what we will refer to as the *technology set*, which we will denote with T, and define it in very general terms as

$$T \equiv \{(x, y) \in \mathfrak{R}_+^N \times \mathfrak{R}_+^M \ : \ y \text{ is producible from } x\}. \tag{1.1.1}$$

That is, T is a set composed of all possible pairs (x, y) such that the second vector of the pair, y, is producible from the first vector of the pair, x. The exact conditions implied by the generic statement "y is producible from x" could of course be different for different industries, or even different firms, or even the same firm but in different times or different circumstances – these would need to be specified more precisely in an empirical work (and we will discuss this more, later in the book), but for the theory it is convenient to keep it as general as possible. To fix the ideas with a simple example, imagine a technology that requires one unit of a single input (e.g., labor) to produce up to three units of one output – the corresponding *technology set* that would characterize such a technology can be formally written as $T \equiv \{(x, y) \in \mathfrak{R}_+^1 \times \mathfrak{R}_+^1 : y \leq 3x\}$. Such a technology set is illustrated in Figure 1.2a. Meanwhile, Figure 1.2b gives another example of the technology set – hinting that, in principle, it may have any shape, and our task soon will be to restrict the shape of T so that it reasonably mimics reality.[2]

Figures 1.2a and 1.2b illustrate technology sets consisting of all combinations of inputs and outputs, (x, y), that are to the right of (or down from) the curve denoted by f ("technology frontier"), including this curve f. All points inside this technology set will be called technologically *feasible* and outside of it will be called technologically *infeasible* – given the particular technology T.

Another characterization of technology can be given via the *output sets* corresponding to any particular level of inputs. To do so formally, one can use the mathematical concept of a correspondence, a generalization of the notion of a function, which maps a point to a set rather than a point in a set. Here, we will call it the output-correspondence $P : \mathfrak{R}_+^N \to 2^{\mathfrak{R}_+^M}$ that defines the output (possibilities) sets as[3]

---

[2] One could also imagine a particular structure of T being a network – a static or a dynamic one – with intermediate outputs. Such an approach is a subject in itself and is outside the focus of this book; see Färe and Grosskopf (1996); Färe et al. (1996), Tone and Tsutsui (2010, 2014); and Kao (2009a,b, 2014) for related discussions.

[3] Recall that the notation $2^{\mathfrak{R}_+^M}$ stands for the power set of $\mathfrak{R}_+^M$, i.e., the set of all the subsets of $\mathfrak{R}_+^M$.

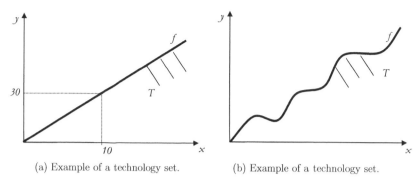

(a) Example of a technology set.   (b) Example of a technology set.

Figure 1.2 Examples of a technology set.

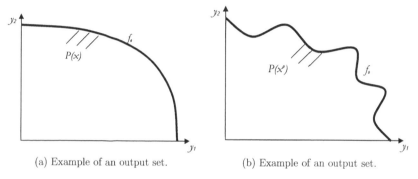

(a) Example of an output set.   (b) Example of an output set.

Figure 1.3 Examples of an output set.

$$P(x) \equiv \{y \in \mathfrak{R}_+^M : y \text{ is producible from } x\}, \ x \in \mathfrak{R}_+^N. \qquad (1.1.2)$$

In words, the correspondence P gives a set of all possible combinations of outputs producible from any particular $x \in \mathfrak{R}_+^N$.

Figures 1.3a and 1.3b illustrate two different output sets, both consisting of all combinations of outputs, y, that are to the left of or down from the curve denoted by f_o, including this curve f_o.[4] Again, all points inside these sets are called technologically *feasible* and outside of it are called technologically *infeasible* – given the particular input levels x and x^o, respectively. It is also worth noting that the two very different-looking output sets may, in principle, characterize the same technology – just at different levels of inputs, x and x^o.

Yet another characterization can be given to the technology via the *input requirement sets*, corresponding to any particular level of outputs. This is done via the input-correspondence $L : \mathfrak{R}_+^M \rightarrow 2^{\mathfrak{R}_+^N}$ that defines the input requirement sets as

---

[4] This curve (a surface in higher dimensions) is usually referred to as *"frontier of output set"* or *"output isoquant"* and we will formally define it later in the chapter.

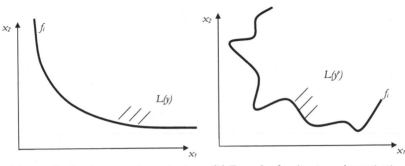

(a)Example of an input requirement set.   (b) Example of an input requirement set.

Figure 1.4 Examples of an input requirement set.

$$L(y) \equiv \{x \in \mathfrak{R}_+^N : y \text{ is producible from } x\}, y \in \mathfrak{R}_+^M. \tag{1.1.3}$$

In words, for each level of output $y \in \mathfrak{R}_+^M$ we have a set (in the input space) of all possible combinations of inputs that can produce this particular level of output. An example of an input requirement set $L(y)$ for a multiple-output–*two*-input case is given in Figures 1.4a and 1.4b.

Figures 1.4a and 1.4b illustrate two different-looking input requirement sets, which may still characterize the same technology – just at different levels of output, y and y^o. Both sets consist of all combinations of inputs, x, that are to the right of or up from (and including) the curves denoted f_i.[5] All points inside (outside) these sets are called technologically feasible (infeasible) – for the particular levels of outputs y and y^o, and with the technology characterized by $L(y)$ and $L(y^o)$, respectively.

An important question now is: how different are the three characterizations of technology given above? By construction, these *three characterizations are equivalent*. To emphasize this (and other) simple but very important result, we will state it as a theorem:

Theorem. The technology characterizations (1.1.1), (1.1.2), and (1.1.3) are equivalent, i.e.,

$$(x, y) \in T \Leftrightarrow y \in P(x) \Leftrightarrow x \in L(y). \tag{1.1.4}$$

Proof. A proof follows directly from definitions (1.1.1), (1.1.2), and (1.1.3):

$$(x, y) \in T \Rightarrow y \in \mathfrak{R}_+^M \text{ is producible from } x \in \mathfrak{R}_+^N$$
$$\Rightarrow y \in P(x) \text{ (by (1.1.2)), } x \in L(y) \text{ (by (1.1.3))}$$
$$y \in P(x) \Rightarrow y \in \mathfrak{R}_+^M \text{ is producible from } x \in \mathfrak{R}_+^N$$
$$\Rightarrow (x, y) \in T \text{ (by (1.1.1)), } x \in L(y) \text{ (by (1.1.3))}$$

---

[5] This curve (a surface in higher dimensions) is usually referred to as *"frontier of input requirement set"* or *"input isoquant"* and we will formally define it later in the chapter.

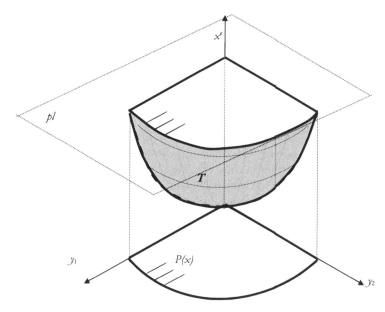

Figure 1.5 Example of the output set as a "slice" of the technology set.

$$x \in L(y) \Rightarrow y \in \mathfrak{R}^M_+ \text{ is producible from } x \in \mathfrak{R}^N_+$$
$$\Rightarrow (x, y) \in T \text{ (by (1.1.1)), } y \in P(x) \text{ (by (1.1.2)).} \qquad \square$$

The practical intuition of this theorem is very simple and encouraging: *we can use any of these characterizations – whichever is more convenient in a given situation.* A theoretical intuition that helps in understanding the relationship between the three objects is as follows. The output sets can be intuitively understood as the "slices" or images of the technology set T at a particular level of input – so if we have all such "slices" at all the $x \in \mathfrak{R}^N_+$, then we have all the information about the technology set T. For the two-output case, this is illustrated in Figure 1.5 – where we "slice" the technology set T at x^o with a plane pl that is parallel to the output space $(y_1, y_2) \in \mathfrak{R}^2_+$ and the resulting slice is then projected onto this output space.

Similar intuition can be given to the input requirement sets. Intuitively, this object can be understood also as a "slice" of the technology set T – but now the "slice" is at a particular level of output y^o. Again, if we have all such "slices" at all the $y \in \mathfrak{R}^M_+$, then we have all the information about the technology set T. We leave it to the reader to imagine and picture this slicing of T to get $L(y)$.

1.2 AXIOMS FOR TECHNOLOGY CHARACTERIZATION

It might seem that the characterization of technology given above is so general that it is practically useless. This would indeed be true were we not imposing some properties on T. These properties must reflect our common sense, or common beliefs of what a typical technology set we analyze should be like. For this reason, these properties are often called *axioms of production theory*. Another common name for them is *regularity conditions* (for the production technology), and the technology satisfying them is often referred to as a regular technology. Let us start imposing and understanding them one by one.

Axiom 1. *"No Free Lunch"*

Even most people who have never attended economic courses must have heard this expression in their everyday lives. In our context, this expression would mean that if a firm (or, more generally, an economic agent) were not to input anything, it would not get any output. How can we state this mathematically? Here is one way:

$$A1. \quad y \notin P(\mathbf{0}_N), \forall y \geq \mathbf{0}_M. \tag{1.2.1}$$

In words, any output vector strictly different from zero cannot be technologically feasible from zero input.

It is a good place to pause here to note that we just used (and will continue to use) conventional notation for vector comparisons: "$\geq$" means at least one element of the vector is greater than zero, "$>$" means that all elements are greater than zero, and finally, "$\geqq$" means that any (even all) elements may be equal to zero or greater than zero. However, for comparison of *scalars,* we will treat "$\geq$" as equivalent to "$\geqq$". Also note that boldface for zero is used to emphasize that this is a vector of zeros, where the dimension of the vector is usually indicated in the subscript.

Axiom 2. *"Producing Nothing is Possible".*

This axiom is desirable for the modeled technology to allow a quite realistic (even if undesirable) phenomenon: some inputs are used, yet no outputs are produced. Formally, this can be stated as:

$$A2. \quad \mathbf{0}_M \in P(x), \forall x \in \mathfrak{R}_+^N, \tag{1.2.2}$$

i.e., zero output (or output-singularity) is always feasible and one can call (1.2.2) as feasibility condition for output-singularity.

Note that an immediate consequence of (1.2.1) jointly with (1.2.2) is that

$$P(\mathbf{0}_N) = \{\mathbf{0}_M\}, \tag{1.2.3}$$

i.e., $P(\mathbf{0}_N)$ has only one element, which is $\mathbf{0}_M$, the vector where each output is zero. It is very intuitive: zero input (or input-singularity) implies zero output (output-singularity). We will refer to (1.2.3) as *full singularity condition* in economics.

Another common sense expectation is that from a finite amount of input one can produce only a *finite* amount of output – we formalize it in the following axiom.

Axiom 3. *"'Boundedness' of the Output Sets"*

$\quad\quad$ A3. $\quad$ $P(x)$ *is a bounded set, for all* $x \in \mathfrak{R}_+^N$.

Throughout the book, we will work with the "upper" boundary of the technology set – the technological frontier – and it is logical to assume that all of this frontier belongs to the set T, i.e., the frontier is technologically feasible. This (and other useful properties) motivates the next axiom.

Axiom 4. *"'Closedness' of the Technology set T"*

$\quad\quad$ A4. $\quad$ T *is a closed set.*

Almost an immediate implication of this axiom is that both $P(x)$ and $L(y)$ are also closed sets. As a result, together with Axiom 3, this axiom implies that $P(x)$ is a compact set (as a subset of Euclidean space). Hence, while optimizing on this set, we can employ the extreme-value theorem in mathematics stating that there exists an optimum of a continuous function on a compact set.[6]

Another regularity axiom which we would employ in one version or another is often called monotonicity or the disposability axiom. Let us come to it through an intuitive way described below.

Naturally, one would expect that an increase in some inputs would allow for the production of more output; or, at least, not less output than before the increase. This common sense argument is incorporated with the next axiom.

Axiom 5. *"Strong (or Free) Disposability of All Inputs"*

$\quad\quad$ A5. $\quad$ $y \in \mathfrak{R}_+^M$, $x^o \in L(y)$, $x \geqq x^o \Rightarrow x \in L(y)$. $\quad\quad\quad$ (1.2.4)

In words, this axiom states that if from x^o the technology was capable of producing y (i.e., $x^o \in L(y)$), then the same technology shall also be capable of producing the same y with *any* other input combination that is not smaller (in any element) than the vector x^o. Figure 1.6a gives an example of a technology that satisfies Axiom 5. On the other hand, Figure 1.6b gives an example that violates Axiom 5 – due to the shaded region in the figure, which, by construction, constitutes the only difference with Figure 1.6a.

Not all technologies we could think of in practice, however, would satisfy this axiom. In agriculture, for example, if such input as seeds (or especially fertilizer) were to be increased while another input, such as land, stayed the same (or not sufficiently increased), it may happen that the output may indeed decrease. Economists often call this phenomenon *"congestion"* and its possibility can be incorporated via the following Axiom (to replace Axiom 5).[7]

---

[6] This theorem (usually attributed to Karl Weierstrass, although apparently it was earlier proven by Bernard Bolzano) also extends to semi-continuous functions.

[7] See Shephard (1974); Färe and Svensson (1980) for more detailed discussion of this and related topics.

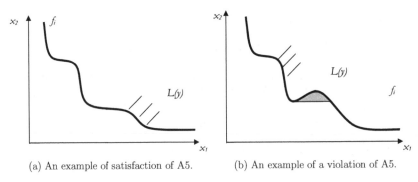

(a) An example of satisfaction of A5.   (b) An example of a violation of A5.

Figure 1.6 Illustrations for the Axiom A5.

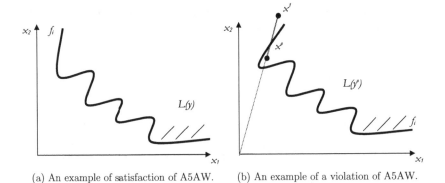

(a) An example of satisfaction of A5AW.   (b) An example of a violation of A5AW.

Figure 1.7 Illustrations for the Axiom A5AW.

Axiom 5AW.   *"Weak Disposability of All Inputs"*

A5AW. $y \in \mathfrak{R}_+^M$, $x^o \in L(y) \Rightarrow \lambda x^o \in L(y)$, $\forall \lambda \in [1, +\infty)$.   (1.2.5)

With this axiom, only equiproportional increases in *all* inputs guarantee no decrease in the outputs. This is quite intuitive: if one is able to produce a certain level of output then it is natural to expect that the same level (if not more) can be produced when *all* inputs are increased by the same proportion, which avoids the congestion of one of the inputs. Equiproportional changes are sometimes also called *radial* changes, because geometrically they are changes along the ray from the origin in a certain space (in the input space here).

An example of a technology that satisfies A5AW (but violates A5) is given in Figure 1.7a. Meanwhile, Figure 1.7b gives an example of a technology that is just slightly different from the technology in Figure 1.7a – the "upper-left" part of the input isoquant is bending a bit more backward than that in Figure 1.7a. Despite such a small difference, the technology in Figure 1.7b violates A5AW – since for a point x^o, for example, not all radial expansions of it belong to $L(y)$, e.g., such as point x^1.

One could also think of a hybrid of the last two axioms – the axiom that allows for free disposability for some inputs but only weak disposability for other inputs. We call it here partially weak disposability.

Axiom A5PW. *"Partially Weak Disposability of Inputs"*

$A5PW.$ $y \in \mathfrak{R}_+^M$, $(x_1^o, x_2^o, \dots, x_j^o, x_{j+1}^o, \dots, x_N^o)' \in L(y)$,

$$x_1 \geqq x_1^o, x_2 \geqq x_2^o, \dots, x_j \geqq x_j^o$$

$$\Rightarrow (x_1, x_2, \dots, x_j, \lambda x_{j+1}^o, \dots, \lambda x_N^o)' \in L(y), \; \forall \lambda \in [1, +\infty).$$

(1.2.6)

In this variant of disposability, the first j elements of the input vector are freely disposable, and the rest are only weakly disposable in the sense that, to maintain the same output, some of the inputs must be increased by the same proportion, e.g., which is typical when some exact chemical composition is required to obtain another chemical. Note that if technology satisfies A5 then it also satisfies A5PW, while if it satisfies A5PW then it also satisfies A5AW, but the reverse is not true.

The reader is probably expecting that similar axioms must apply to output. Indeed, common sense logic might suggest to us that if a firm can produce a certain level of outputs, y^o, then this firm, with the same inputs and the same technology, shall be able to produce a lower level of outputs. At least, the firm can produce y^o and then freely dispose of any portion of it so that the final level is lower than y^o. This argument is formalized in the next axiom.

Axiom 6. *"Strong (or Free) Disposability of All Outputs"*

$$A6. \quad x \in \mathfrak{R}_+^N, \; y^o \in P(x), \; \mathbf{0}_M \leqq y \leqq y^o \Rightarrow y \in P(x). \quad (1.2.7)$$

In words, this axiom states that if from x the technology was capable of producing y^o (i.e., y^o is in $P(x)$), then the same technology with the same level of inputs, x, shall also be capable of producing *any* other output combination that is not larger (in any element) than the vector y^o.[8]

Figure 1.8a gives an example of a technology that satisfies A6. Figure 1.8b gives an example that violates A6 – due to the shaded region in the lower-right part of the set, which is the only difference with Figure 1.8b.

Again, such an assumption is consistent with many technologies, yet not all. In electricity generation, metallurgical and other industries, an undesirable or "bad" output – pollution or other types of environmental degradation – is produced along with the good output. And, unfortunately, technologies may not allow *free* disposal of some of the bad output by decreasing it, say, to zero, while keeping the input, technology, and the good output at the same level. A

---

[8] E.g., one also could achieve this *ex post*: produce y^o and then "dispose" of unnecessary amounts of y, if such disposal is free and so from here comes the name "free disposability."

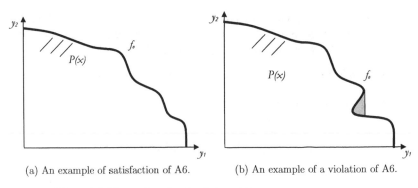

(a) An example of satisfaction of A6.   (b) An example of a violation of A6.

Figure 1.8 Illustrations for the Axiom A6.

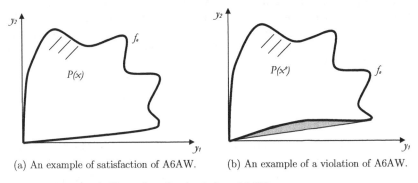

(a) An example of satisfaction of A6AW.   (b) An example of a violation of A6AW.

Figure 1.9 Illustrations for the Axiom A6AW.

trade-off might be required: decreasing the bad output together with decreasing the good output. This possibility is formalized in the next axiom.

Axiom 6AW   *"Weak Disposability of All Outputs"*

$$A6AW. \quad x \in \mathfrak{R}_+^N, \ y^o \in P(x) \Rightarrow \theta y^o \in P(x), \ \forall \theta \in (0, 1]. \quad (1.2.8)$$

Thus, with this axiom, only equiproportional (radial) decreases in all outputs are feasible. An example of a technology that satisfies A6AW (but violates A6) is given in Figure 1.9a. A technology that violates A6AW is given in Figure 1.9b, where for some output combinations that are originally in the output set there exist some radial contractions that are not in the same set, as indicated by the shaded region in the lower part of the set.

Similarly as in the input case, one could also think of a hybrid of the last two axioms – an axiom that allows for free disposability for some outputs but only weak disposability for other outputs. We will call it partially weak disposability of outputs.

Axiom 6PW   *"Partially Weak Disposability of Outputs"*

$$A6PW. \quad x \in \mathfrak{R}_+^N, \ (y_1^o, y_2^o, \ldots, y_m^o, y_{m+1}^o, \ldots, y_M^o)' \in P(x) \quad (1.2.9)$$

$$0 \leq y_1 \leq y_1^o, 0 \leq y_2 \leq y_2^o, \ldots, 0 \leq y_m \leq y_m^o$$
$$\Rightarrow (y_1, y_2, \ldots, y_m, \theta y_{m+1}^o, \ldots, \theta y_M^o)' \in P(x), \ \forall \theta \in [0, 1].$$

In this version of output disposability, the first m elements of the output vector are freely disposable, and the rest are only weakly disposable. Clearly, as in the input case, if technology satisfies A6 then it also satisfies A6PW, while if it satisfies A6PW then it also satisfies A6AW, but the reverse is not true.[9]

It is important to note at this point that all these axioms are intended not to complicate but to enormously simplify our analysis of the very complex phenomena one may intend to study. Without such axioms, the analysis might be very complex or, in some cases, even impossible or formally undefined. Many real-world technologies, of course, do not satisfy some or even all of these axioms (think about examples!). Nevertheless, the imposition of such axioms is often innocent with respect to influencing the main conclusions, yet does a great job of simplifying the immense complexity of the real world.

There are also situations when some of the axioms imposed are unjustified and may influence the final conclusions. Because of this, an applied researcher is encouraged always to start his/her empirical investigation with diagnostics of whether the specifics of the real-world process under study fit the axioms imposed by the theory. If some axioms seem *critically* inconsistent with the reality, then the axiomatic foundation must be "tuned up to fit the reality." The examples above, on how free disposability was tuned up into weak disposability in order to fit the specifics of some technological processes, may serve as a guide to the reader as to how such tuning can be done.

While there is no minimal set of axioms that satisfy all the situations of interest, many (yet not all) theoretical results in production theory typically require Axioms 1–4 and at least the weak disposability of all inputs and/or all outputs, and so we will assume these *hold throughout the book*, referring to them as the *main regularity axioms* (conditions).

1.3 FUNCTIONAL CHARACTERIZATION OF TECHNOLOGY: THE PRIMAL APPROACH

In the preceding section, we have given three different (and equivalent) set-wise characterizations of technology. The axioms that followed have helped us to refine them into simplified mathematical objects that we think (and hope!) reasonably mimic a typical production process. In this section, these set characterizations will help us to employ some rather easier-to-play-with instruments for representing technology: functional characterizations.

---

[9] In practice, certain bad outputs are related to certain good outputs, and such connections can also be modeled. One may also impose the axiom of null-jointness of good and bad outputs, which requires all or some of the good outputs to be zero if the related bad outputs are at zero. We will come back to this topic in Chapter 8.

When a production process involves only one output, then a simple way of characterizing technology with a function is to use the concept of the *production function* $f : \mathfrak{R}_+^N \to \mathfrak{R}_+^1$, defined as

$$f(x) \equiv \max_y \{y \ : \ (x, y) \in T\}$$

$$= \max_y \{y \ : \ y \in P(x)\}. \tag{1.3.1}$$

In words, this is just a function (mapping from the input space into the *single* output) giving the maximal value of output, y, which can be produced at each particular level of input, x. The second equality we can write due to (1.1.4).[10]

Virtually all firms, however, produce more than one output from the set of the same or different inputs. One way to incorporate this would be to think of a separate production function for each output – this, however, would impose a restrictive assumption of independence of the production processes for each output. Some particular structure of dependence may be assumed between production functions for different outputs, but this might be even more restrictive, since such information is rarely available to researchers and is likely to differ from one technology to another.

Another, more appealing, general way to deal with such a situation is to use some *implicit* function as a characterization of technology. Perhaps the most popular of such functions are Shephard's distance functions, which are heavily used in advanced production theory and are invaluable in contemporary efficiency and productivity analysis.

In this book we will start with, and mostly concentrate on, the *output-oriented* distance function thoroughly developed by Shephard (1970), which we define next.

Definition. The Shephard's output distance function $D_o : \mathfrak{R}_+^N \times \mathfrak{R}_+^M \to \mathfrak{R}_+ \cup \{+\infty\}$ is defined as

$$D_o(x, y) = \inf_\theta \{\theta > 0 : (x, y/\theta) \in T\}$$

$$= \inf_\theta \{\theta > 0 : y/\theta \in P(x)\}. \tag{1.3.2}$$

This function is not as enigmatic as it may seem at first glance and is easily explained geometrically. First of all, note that (1.3.2) is a minimization problem.[11] Figure 1.10 gives a pictorial intuition of this function for a

---

[10] Note that since y is continuous on $P(x)$, a compact set, the maximum exists and is unique.

[11] Here and everywhere we use inf, which is a generalization of the min operator, for theoretical convenience – so that the function is well-defined on all its domain (including the singularity points, etc., where min does not exist but inf does), clearly mapping into its defined range. In practice, however, the main value of this function is in the cases when min exists and so, for practical purposes, one may just think of it as min. One can also replace inf with min if more assumptions are added onto technology that guarantees existence of min; see Diewert and Fox (2017) for related discussion.

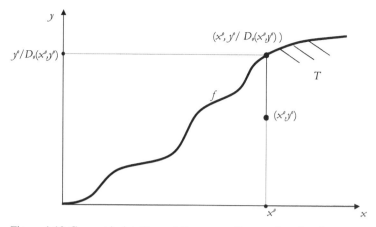

Figure 1.10 Geometric intuition of the output distance function for a one-input–one-output example of T.

single-input–single-output case: for any particular combination (x^o, y^o), this distance function gives the smallest scalar that is needed to *divide* the actual output, y^o, so that it expands to the level just reaching the frontier of T, no more, no less, while keeping the inputs fixed at x^o.

The reader might wonder if there is any relationship between this distance function and the production function that the reader probably has been happy with so far. Indeed, in the single output case, there is a precise and simple relationship between the two: since D_o in this case is merely the ratio of the actual output to the potential (maximal) output that can be produced with the same level of input, we have that $f(x^o) = y^o/D_o(x^o, y^o)$. We will establish this argument formally a bit later. In general – in the multiple-output case – the Shephard's distance function is a very convenient *generalization* of the production function.

Looking at Figure 1.11, we can see that, in the multiple-output case, the Shephard's output distance function is also the smallest scalar that is needed to expand *all* the outputs – in a *radial* fashion – until they reach the frontier of the output set, while keeping the input at its original level. So the trick of the generalization is that no matter what the dimension of the output space is, for any point in this space, there always exists a ray from the origin coming through this point – and thus we can (under quite mild assumptions) relate this point to the output set and, most importantly, to the frontier of this set.

It is a common mistake, however, to think that the Shephard's distance function is defined only for points inside the technology set. Looking at the definition (1.3.2) reveals that it is a mapping from the entire input–output space, $\mathfrak{R}_+^N \times \mathfrak{R}_+^M$, and therefore it also allows the measuring of distances from points outside the output sets, as illustrated in Figure 1.11 for point (x^1, y^1).

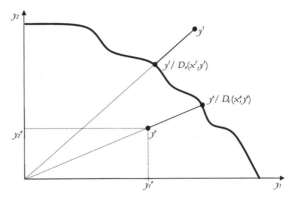

Figure 1.11 Geometric intuition of output distance function for a one-input–two-output example of T.

Since the Shephard's distance functions are the key instruments of efficiency analysis, we need to understand their most important properties. First of all, note that this function is defined at all points of its domain, including the singularity points $((x, \mathbf{0}_M), (\mathbf{0}_N, y)$ and $(\mathbf{0}_N, \mathbf{0}_M))$, as suggested by the next theorem.

Theorem. At the *points of output-singularity,* $(x, \mathbf{0}_M)$, *input-singularity* $(\mathbf{0}_N, y)$ *and full singularity* $(\mathbf{0}_N, \mathbf{0}_M)$, we have

(a) $D_o(x, \mathbf{0}_M) = 0, \forall x \geq \mathbf{0}_N,$ (1.3.3)

(b) $D_o(\mathbf{0}_N, y) = +\infty, \forall y \geq \mathbf{0}_M,$ (1.3.4)

(c) $D_o(\mathbf{0}_N, \mathbf{0}_M) = 0.$ (1.3.5)

Proof.

$$(a) \ D_o(x, \mathbf{0}_M) = \inf\{\theta > 0 : \mathbf{0}_M/\theta \in P(x)\}$$
$$= \inf\{\theta > 0 : \mathbf{0}_M \in P(x)\} = \inf\{0 < \theta < \infty\}$$
$$= 0 \quad \text{(using A2 and then definition of "inf")}.$$
$$(b) \ D_o(\mathbf{0}_N, y) = \inf\{\theta > 0 : y/\theta \in P(\mathbf{0}_N)\}$$
$$= \inf\{\varnothing\} = +\infty, \ \forall y \geq \mathbf{0}_M.$$

Note that the second equality in (b) is due to A1, while the last equality is from the fact that any real number is a bound for the empty set and the greatest of such bounds is positive infinity. Finally, the proof of (c) is similar as for (a).   ☐

This theorem suggests that the use of this distance function will be problematic for the singularity points $((x, \mathbf{0}_M), (\mathbf{0}_N, y)$ and $(\mathbf{0}_N, \mathbf{0}_M))$, e.g., when one wants to use it in defining productivity indexes that take this function as building blocks in ratios. Therefore, in the rest of the book by default (unless emphasized explicitly), we will focus on points other than the singularity points.[12]

A reader might have experienced that it is often convenient to deal with a homogeneous function. This useful property is also pertinent to the distance function – under any technology, as described in the next theorem.

Theorem. D_o is *homogeneous of degree 1 in all outputs*, i.e.,

$$D_o(x, ty) = t D_o(x, y), \forall t \in (0, \infty), \ (x, y) \in \mathfrak{R}_+^{N+M}. \tag{1.3.6}$$

This simple result will be very useful in our future derivations and the reader is advised to tame down the very simple proof given below.

Proof. For all $\forall t \in (0, \infty)$, we have:

$$D_o(x, ty) = \inf\{\theta > 0 : ty/\theta \in P(x)\}$$
$$= t \inf\{(\theta/t) > 0 : y/(\theta/t) \in P(x)\} \equiv t D_o(x, y),$$

where to get to the expression after the second equality we used a trick of "change of variable in the optimization," which we will use frequently. □

Perhaps the most important property of the output distance function is the complete characterization property – as stated in the next theorem.

Theorem. D_o completely characterizes technology set T, in the sense that

$$D_o(x, y) \leq 1 \Leftrightarrow (x, y) \in T. \tag{1.3.7}$$

Proof. (See Färe and Primont, 1995.) □

The meaning of this result is very fundamental: it says that (under the main regularity conditions), we can use the statement on the l.h.s. of (1.3.7) instead of that on the r.h.s., and vice versa, without losing any information. In other words, if we define a new set $\{(x, y) : D_o(x, y) \leq 1\}$, then this set would be equivalent to the set T defined above in (1.1.1), and $\{y : D_o(x, y) \leq 1\}$ would be equivalent to $P(x)$. Also note, since A6 and A6PW imply A6AW, the theorem (1.3.7) can also be stated in terms of A6 or A6PW.

Let us immediately apply the two last properties we have proven above to obtain the promised relationship between the Shephard's output distance function and the production function, in the single output case.

Theorem. For all $(x, y) \in \mathfrak{R}_+^N \times \mathfrak{R}_+$, we have

$$D_o(x, y) = y/f(x). \tag{1.3.8}$$

---

[12] This is a fairly modest restriction. Indeed, even many advanced models in physics have certain problems in their singularity points/regions.

Proof.

$$f(x) \equiv \max\{y : (x, y) \in T\} = \max\{y : D_o(x, y) \le 1\} \quad \text{(using (1.3.7))}$$
$$= \max\{y : yD_o(x, 1) \le 1\} \quad \text{(using (1.3.6))}$$
$$= \max\{y : y \le 1/D_o(x, 1)\} = 1/D_o(x, 1) \quad \text{(by maximization)}$$

Thus, $f(x) = 1/D_o(x, 1) = y/D_o(x, 1)y = y/D_o(x, y)$ (again using (1.3.6)). $\square$

The main reason we talk about this function in this book is that it is particularly convenient as a criterion for technical efficiency of a firm with technology characterized by $P(x)$ and the relationship between D_o and $f(x)$, proven above, gives a nice intuition for this. In particular, the theorem says that, in the single output case, the Shephard's output distance function is the ratio of actual output to the potential or maximal output (i.e., $f(x)$) that can be produced with the same input level.

In general, for an allocation $(x^o, y^o) \in T$, note that D_o gives a "measure" (or an index valued between 0 and 1) of a distance from y^o in $P(x^o)$ to the "upper" boundary of $P(x^o)$. Such an efficiency criterion also appears in another form, known as the output-oriented Farrell (or Farrell-type) measure of *technical efficiency*, defined (usually only for the technologically feasible combinations) as[13]

$$TE(x, y) \equiv \sup\{\theta > 0 : \theta y \in P(x)\}, \ y \in P(x), \ x \in \mathfrak{R}_+^N \quad (1.3.9)$$
$$= 1/D_o(x, y), \ y \in P(x), \ x \in \mathfrak{R}_+^N.$$

Formally, if we let the *"frontier of the output set"* or the *"output isoquant"* to be the "upper" boundary of $P(x^o)$ defined (in the radial manner) as

$$\partial P(x) \equiv \{y : y \in P(x), \theta y \notin P(x), \forall \theta \in (1, +\infty)\}, x \in \mathfrak{R}_+^N, \quad (1.3.10)$$

then with our main regularity axioms on the technology, we would call (x^o, y^o) *technically* efficient, in the Farrell sense, if and only if

$$D_o(x^o, y^o) = 1 \Leftrightarrow y^o \in \partial P(x^o). \quad (1.3.11)$$

This last property is often referred to as the *indication* or *identification* property, in the sense that it (completely) *identifies the output isoquant* defined in (1.3.10).[14] Next, note that we would call (x^o, y^o) *feasible* but *technically inefficient* from the output orientation if and only if

$$0 < D_o(x^o, y^o) < 1 \Leftrightarrow y^o \in P(x^o), y^o \notin \partial P(x^o), y^o \ne \mathbf{0}_M, \quad (1.3.12)$$

---

[13] Originally, Farrell (1957) focused on the input-oriented version of such efficiency measurement (discussed later), which was inspired by the theoretical concept of Debreu (1951), who referred to it as the *coefficient of resource utilization*. In turn, both concepts are closely related to the concept introduced by von Neumann (1945), who referred to it as the *coefficient of expansion of the economy* (which measures inefficiency when it takes values less than 1).

[14] Note, however, that this is not the same as identification of the so-called Pareto–Koopmans efficiency, as we will discuss in more detail in Chapter 3. Also note that some authors refer to (1.3.7) as the indication property of the distance functions.

and the corresponding *inefficiency* score would be given by $D_o(x, y)$ or by (1.3.9), whichever scale is preferred. We can also characterize points outside the output sets, i.e., such y^o that are *infeasible* for the technology given by $P(x^o)$. Two scenarios are possible here, yielding very different values of the function. The first case is:

$$\text{if } (x^o, y^o) \notin T, \text{ but } \exists \lambda > 0 : (x^o, \lambda y^o) \in T \Rightarrow D_o(x^o, y^o) > 1, \qquad (1.3.13)$$

which corresponds to the situation when we could find a (finite) radial contraction towards the frontier, and the distance function would "measure" this contraction with a value greater than 1 (but less than infinity). The second case is:

$$\text{if } (x^o, y^o) \notin T, \text{ and } \forall \lambda > 0 : (x^o, \lambda y^o) \notin T \Rightarrow D_o(x^o, y^o) = +\infty, \qquad (1.3.14)$$

which corresponds to the situation when there is no finite radial contraction towards the frontier, and the only way to bring the output to the output set is to "contract" it to zero. The distance function, in this case, reflects this by going to positive infinity. The remaining possibility is the following degenerate (yet feasible) case: $D_o(x^o, y^o) = 0$, if and only if $y^o = \mathbf{0}_M$.

Other important properties of this distance function include the fact that $D_o(x, y)$ is lower semi-bounded on $\mathfrak{R}_+^M$ (an implication of Axiom 3), and is lower semi-continuous on $\mathfrak{R}_+^M$ (a manifestation of Axiom 4), as well as non-decreasing in output, i.e., $D_o(x, y') \geq D_o(x, y) \, \forall y' \geqq y$.

A similarly important instrument in efficiency analysis is the *input-oriented distance function* thoroughly explored by Shephard (1953), which we formalize below.

Definition. The Shephard's *input-oriented distance function* $D_i : \mathfrak{R}_+^M \times \mathfrak{R}_+^N \to \mathfrak{R}_+^1 \cup \{+\infty\}$ is defined as:

$$\begin{aligned} D_i(y, x) &\equiv \sup\{\theta > 0 : (x/\theta, y) \in T\} \\ &= \sup\{\theta > 0 : x/\theta \in L(y)\}. \end{aligned} \qquad (1.3.15)$$

First of all, note that (1.3.15) is a maximization problem.[15] Again, some mysteries of this function can be clarified with a picture, and the reader is encouraged to deploy her/his artistic skills to do so. The resulting figure shall reflect the intuition of this function giving the largest scalar that is needed to *divide* all the inputs so that they are changed radially (i.e., or along the ray from the origin and through the point x in the input space) to just reach the frontier of the input requirement set that can still produce the same output level y.

---

[15] Here and below, for theoretical convenience we use the sup (a generalization of max) operator. This helps $D_i(y, x)$ to be well-defined on all its domain clearly mapping into its defined range. As with $D_o(x, y)$, the main value of $D_i(y, x)$ in practice is where max exists and so for practical purposes, one may simply think of it as max . One can also assume more structure on technology that will guarantee the existence of max and then replace sup with max; see Diewert and Fox (2017) for related discussion.

This function is also a natural efficiency criterion, which often appears in another form, known as the Farrell input-oriented measure of *technical efficiency,* defined as

$$TE_i(y, x) \equiv \inf\{\theta > 0 \ : \ x\theta \in L(y)\}, \ x \in L(y), \ y \in \mathfrak{R}_+^M \quad (1.3.16)$$
$$= 1/D_i(y, x), \ x \in L(y), \ y \in \mathfrak{R}_+^M.$$

Both functions, (1.3.15) and (1.3.16), possess properties analogous to those of their output-oriented analogs and we leave their proof as exercises – see Shephard (1953) – while we summarize the key ones below.

Theorem. D_i satisfies the following properties:

   (i) homogeneity of degree 1 in inputs, i.e.,

$$D_i(y, \delta x) = \delta D_i(y, x), \ \forall \delta \in \mathfrak{R}_+;$$

  (ii) monotonicity: nondecreasing in inputs

$$D_i(y, x') \geq D_i(y, x) \, \forall x' \geq x;$$

  (iii) $D_i(\mathbf{0}_M, x) = +\infty, \forall x \geq \mathbf{0}_N;$
  (iv) $D_i(y, \mathbf{0}_N) = 0, \forall y \geq \mathbf{0}_M;$
   (v) upper semi-bounded on $\mathfrak{R}_+^N;$
  (vi) upper semi-continuous on $\mathfrak{R}_+^N.$

1.4   MODELING RETURNS TO SCALE IN PRODUCTION

Many models of economic theory employ the assumption of *constant returns to scale* (CRS) – the state of technology where increases of all inputs by the same proportion lead to increase in all the outputs by the same proportion. Such an assumption is often made for simplicity, as it indeed simplifies a lot of derivations (as we will see). More importantly, it is also coherent with many production processes, at least approximately. For example, if certain levels of ingredients (e.g., chemicals, molecules) are needed to produce or synthesize a certain level of a product (e.g., a cake, petrol, gold), then increasing all the ingredients by the same proportion naturally leads to the increase in that same product by the same proportion. Even if the true technology does not satisfy CRS, considering a counterfactual or a hypothetical CRS technology associated with the true technology can be very useful, e.g., to identify the most efficient scale, which can be viewed as the socially optimal level. Given such importance, we will dedicate this section and the next to CRS and closely related concepts, and will involve them frequently in the next chapters.

In the single output case, CRS boils down to the property of the production function being homogeneous of degree 1. To understand what the

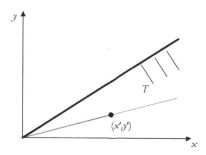

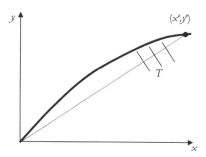

Figure 1.12 A CRS technology.   Figure 1.13 An NIRS technology.

CRS property implies in the multiple output case, let us first view this concept through the set-wise characterization of technology, as in the following definition.

Definition. Technology exhibits *global* CRS if and only if T is a cone, i.e.,

$$\lambda T = T, \forall \lambda \in (0, +\infty). \tag{1.4.1}$$

The word "global" emphasizes that this CRS property is true for all $(x, y) \in T$. Figure 1.12 gives a pictorial intuition of this definition for a single-input–single-output case: it shows that any radial expansion or radial contraction of an arbitrary point in T will always remain in T.

Recalling Theorem 1.1.4, we shall expect some similar implications of this definition for the other set-wise characterizations of technology. This implication is given in the next theorem.

Theorem. The following statements are equivalent

$(a)\ \lambda T = T, \forall \lambda > 0;$

$$(b)\,P(\lambda x) = \lambda P(x), \forall \lambda > 0, x \in \mathfrak{R}_+^N; \tag{1.4.2}$$

$$(c)\,L(\lambda y) = \lambda L(y), \forall \lambda > 0, y \in \mathfrak{R}_+^M. \tag{1.4.3}$$

Proof. We only prove equivalence of (a) and (b) here

$(\Rightarrow)\ P(\lambda x) = \{y : (\lambda x, y) \in T\},\ x \in \mathfrak{R}_+^N$ (by (1.1.4))

$\qquad = \{y : (x, y/\lambda) \in \lambda^{-1}T\},\ x \in \mathfrak{R}_+^N$

$\qquad = \{y : (x, y/\lambda) \in T\},\ x \in \mathfrak{R}_+^N$ (since $\lambda T = T, \forall \lambda > 0$)

$\qquad = \lambda\{\tilde{y} : (x, \tilde{y}) \in T\},\ x \in \mathfrak{R}_+^N$ (where $\tilde{y} = y/\lambda, \forall \lambda > 0$)

$\qquad = \lambda P(x),\ x \in \mathfrak{R}_+^N.$ (by (1.1.4))

$(\Leftarrow)$ $\quad \lambda T = \lambda\{(x, y) : y \in P(x), x \in \mathfrak{R}_+^N\}$ $\qquad$ (by (1.1.4))

$\qquad = \{(\lambda x, \lambda y) : \lambda y \in \lambda P(x), x \in \mathfrak{R}_+^N\}$

$\qquad = \{(\lambda x, \lambda y) : \lambda y \in P(\lambda x), \lambda x \in \mathfrak{R}_+^N\}$

$\qquad (P(\lambda x) = \lambda P(x), \forall \lambda > 0, \ x \in \mathfrak{R}_+^N)$

$\qquad = \{(\tilde{x}, \tilde{y}) : \tilde{y} \in P(\tilde{x}), \tilde{x} \in \mathfrak{R}_+^N\}$ $\qquad$ (change of variable)

$\qquad = T.$ $\qquad$ (by (1.1.4))

A proof of equivalence of (c) with (a) or (b) is similar and is left as an exercise.

$\qquad\qquad\qquad\qquad\qquad\qquad\qquad\qquad\qquad\qquad\qquad\qquad\qquad$ $\square$

Because the distance functions are also (complete) characterizations of technology, certain implications of the CRS assumption must also appear in them through additional properties. This is described in the following theorem.

Theorem. The following statements are equivalent

$\quad$ (a) $\lambda T = T, \ \forall \lambda > 0$;

$\quad$ (b) $D_o(\lambda x, y) = \lambda^{-1} D_o(x, y), \ \forall \lambda > 0, \ (x, y) \in \mathfrak{R}_+^{N+M}$; $\qquad$ (1.4.4)

$\quad$ (c) $D_i(\lambda y, x) = \lambda^{-1} D_i(y, x), \ \forall \lambda > 0, \ (x, y) \in \mathfrak{R}_+^{N+M}$; $\qquad$ (1.4.5)

$\quad$ (d) $D_o(x, y) = 1/D_i(y, x), \ \forall (x, y) \in \mathfrak{R}_+^{N+M}$. $\qquad$ (1.4.6)

Proof. We first prove equivalence of (a) and (b):

$(\Rightarrow)$ $D_o(\lambda x, y) \equiv \inf\{\theta > 0 : (\lambda x, y/\theta) \in T\}$

$\qquad\qquad = \inf\{\theta > 0 : (x, y/(\lambda\theta)) \in \lambda^{-1}T\}$

$\qquad\qquad = \lambda^{-1}\inf\{\tilde{\theta} > 0 : (x, y/\tilde{\theta}) \in T\}$ (use (1.4.1) and let $\tilde{\theta} \equiv \lambda\theta$)

$\qquad\qquad \equiv \lambda^{-1} D_o(x, y).$

$(\Leftarrow)$ $\quad \lambda T = \lambda\{(x, y) : D_o(x, y) \leq 1\}$ $\qquad$ (by (1.3.7))

$\qquad\qquad = \{(\lambda x, \lambda y) : \lambda^{-1} D_o(x, y)\lambda \leq 1\}$

$\qquad\qquad = \{(\lambda x, \lambda y) : D_o(\lambda x, \lambda y) \leq 1\}$ $\qquad$ (use (1.3.6) and (1.4.4))

$\qquad\qquad = \{(\tilde{x}, \tilde{y}) : D_o(\tilde{x}, \tilde{y}) \leq 1\}$ $\qquad$ (where $\tilde{x} \equiv \lambda x, \tilde{y} \equiv \lambda y$)

$\qquad\qquad = T, \ \forall \lambda > 0.$ $\qquad$ (by (1.3.7))

Equivalence of (c) with (a) is similar and left as an exercise, while for (d) we have:

$(\Rightarrow)$ $D_i(y, x) \equiv \sup\{\theta > 0 : (x/\theta, y) \in T\}$

$\qquad\qquad = \sup\{\theta > 0 : D_o(x/\theta, y) \leq 1\}$ $\qquad$ (by (1.3.7))

$\qquad\qquad = \sup\{\theta > 0 : \theta D_o(x, y) \leq 1\}$ $\qquad$ (by (1.4.4))

$\qquad\qquad = \sup\{\theta > 0 : \theta \leq 1/D_o(x, y)\}$

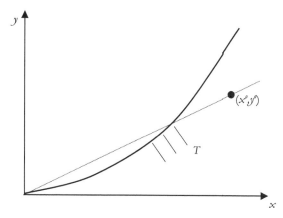

Figure 1.14 An NDRS technology.

$$= 1/D_o(x, y). \qquad \qquad \text{(by optimization over } \theta)$$
$$(\Leftarrow)\ D_o(\lambda x, y) = 1/D_i(y, \lambda x), (x, y) \in \mathfrak{R}_+^N \times \mathfrak{R}_+^M \qquad \text{(by (1.4.6))}$$
$$= 1/(\lambda D_i(y, x)), (x, y) \in \mathfrak{R}_+^N \times \mathfrak{R}_+^M \text{ (by homogeneity of } D_i)$$
$$= D_o(x, y)/\lambda, (x, y) \in \mathfrak{R}_+^N \times \mathfrak{R}_+^M, \qquad \text{(by (1.4.6))}$$

i.e., (1.4.4) must hold, which in turn implies CRS, as was established above.
$$\square$$

In words, the theorem says that if technology exhibits CRS then, and only then, the distance functions are homogeneous of degree (-1) in all inputs for D_o and in all outputs for D_i. The last statement of the theorem is a fundamental one: if technology exhibits CRS then, and only then, the input distance function is the *reciprocal* of the output distance function.

Set characterizations can also be used to define the *non*-CRS technologies as in the definition below.

Definition. T exhibits *global* nonincreasing returns to scale (NIRS) if and only if

$$\lambda T \subseteqq T, \forall \lambda \in (0, 1) \tag{1.4.7}$$

and T exhibits *global* nondecreasing returns to scale (NDRS) if and only if

$$\lambda T \subseteqq T, \forall \lambda \in (1, +\infty). \tag{1.4.8}$$

Figures 1.13 and 1.14 give a pictorial intuition of this definition for a single-input–single-output case. In the NIRS case, any radial contraction (but not necessarily any expansion) of an arbitrary point in T will remain in T, which is illustrated in Figure 1.13. On the other hand, under the NDRS case, any radial expansion (but not necessarily any contraction) of an arbitrary point in T will also remain in T, which is illustrated in Figure 1.14.

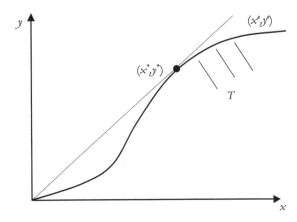

Figure 1.15 A VRS technology.

As in the case of *CRS*, we shall also expect that the *NIRS* and *NDRS* properties can also be viewed through the other set-wise characterizations of technology – this is described in the next two theorems.

Theorem. *The following statements are equivalent:*

(a) $\lambda T \subseteq T, \forall \lambda \in (0, 1)$;

(b) $\lambda P(x) \subseteq P(\lambda x), \forall \lambda \in (0, 1), x \in \mathfrak{R}_+^N$; (1.4.9)

(c) $\lambda L(y) \subseteq L(\lambda y), \forall \lambda \in (0, 1), y \in \mathfrak{R}_+^M$. (1.4.10)

Proof. Left as an exercise. □

Theorem. *The following statements are equivalent:*

(a) $\lambda T \subseteq T, \forall \lambda \in (1, +\infty)$;

(b) $\lambda P(x) \subseteq P(\lambda x), \forall \lambda \in (1, +\infty), x \in \mathfrak{R}_+^N$; (1.4.11)

(c) $\lambda L(y) \subseteq L(\lambda y), \forall \lambda \in (1, +\infty), y \in \mathfrak{R}_+^M$. (1.4.12)

Proof. Left as an exercise. □

Very often the technology may not exhibit one particular type *globally* and in this case imposition of the assumption above would lead to inconsistent estimation. In this case, not assuming any global returns to scale property might be a better solution and *after* estimation, the researcher may measure and/or test for a specific returns to scale, globally or locally.

When none of the global types of returns to scale are satisfied, but each may be true locally (in some regions of the technology set), then the technology is said to exhibit a *variable returns to scale (VRS)* property. An example of the shape of such a technology set for the one-input–one-output case is given in Figure 1.15, where at point (x^*, y^*) such technology exhibits *local CRS*, while to the left of this point it exhibits local *NDRS*, and to the right of this point it exhibits local *NIRS*. In general, the *VRS* technology need not have only one point of *local CRS*, but any number – for example, Figure 1.10 gives another example of a *VRS* technology.

Applied researchers are also often interested in the actual measuring of the returns to scale at various specific points such as observed allocations, average allocation, etc. There are two general ways that have been popular in practice for such measurement. One of them relies on the concept of *scale elasticity* and the other on the concept of *scale efficiency*, and we will consider them both in this book, starting with the scale elasticity in the next section.

1.5 MEASURING RETURNS TO SCALE IN PRODUCTION: THE SCALE ELASTICITY APPROACH

Many readers may be familiar with the concept of elasticity from microeconomics and will probably have seen the following (simplified) definition of scale elasticity based on the production function, f, that is assumed to be differentiable (at least once) at a point of interest x,

$$e_i(x) \equiv \sum_{j=1}^{N} \frac{\partial f(x)}{\partial x_j} \frac{x_j}{f(x)}. \tag{1.5.1}$$

A general version of this concept can be also given in the following expression,

$$e_i(x) \equiv \frac{\partial \ln f(\lambda x)}{\partial \ln \lambda}\bigg|_{\lambda=1} \tag{1.5.2}$$

$$= \sum_{j=1}^{N} \frac{\lambda}{f(\lambda x)} \frac{\partial f(\lambda x)}{\partial (\lambda x_j)} \frac{\partial (\lambda x_j)}{\partial \lambda}\bigg|_{\lambda=1} \quad \text{(by the chain rule)}$$

$$\equiv \sum_{j=1}^{N} \frac{\partial f(x)}{\partial x_j} \frac{x_j}{f(x)} \quad \text{(evaluating at } \lambda=1).$$

Using the conventional gradient notation, $\nabla'_x f(x) \equiv (\partial f(x)/\partial x_1, \ldots, \partial f(x)/\partial x_N)$, we can write (1.5.1) in a more compact way, as

$$e_i(x) \equiv \nabla'_x f(x) x / f(x). \tag{1.5.3}$$

How can this measure now be generalized to the multiple output case? To see this, note the trick used in the general definition (1.5.2) to have *all* the inputs increasing in an equiproportional way: we take the derivative of the scalar λ (in the neighborhood of unity) that multiplies *all* the inputs, so we increase *all* the inputs in the radial fashion or equiproportional way. This same trick can be used in generalizing the notion of scale elasticity to the multiple output case. So, we will be increasing *all* the inputs and record how *all* the outputs would increase along the ray from the origin and through the point at which we want to measure the local scale effect. The reader must have guessed that we are going to use the distance functions for this generalization, as can be seen in the next definition.

Definition. Suppose the input and output distance functions are continuously differentiable with respect to each element of inputs and outputs in a neighborhood of a point of interest; then the *output-* and *input*-oriented measures of scale elasticity are given, respectively, by

$$e_o(x, y) = \frac{\partial \ln \theta}{\partial \ln \lambda}\bigg|_{\theta=1,\lambda=1}, \quad \text{such that } D_o(\lambda x, \theta y) = 1, \qquad (1.5.4)$$

and

$$e_i(y, x) \equiv \frac{\partial \ln \lambda}{\partial \ln \theta}\bigg|_{\theta=1,\lambda=1}, \quad \text{such that } D_i(\theta y, \lambda x) = 1. \qquad (1.5.5)$$

Note that besides evaluating at $\lambda = 1$ and $\theta = 1$, we have additional conditions that, respectively,

$$D_o(\lambda x, \theta y) = 1 \text{ and } D_i(\theta y, \lambda x) = 1. \qquad (1.5.6)$$

These conditions are manifestations of the desire to measure the scale elasticity at the corresponding (input or output) isoquants. After taking derivatives, the elasticity expressions above simplify into the more compact and practically usable forms given in the following theorem.

Theorem. *Given the definitions in (1.5.4) and (1.5.5), we have*

$$e_o(x, y) = -\nabla'_x D_o(x, y)x, \qquad (1.5.7)$$

and

$$e_i(y, x) = -\nabla'_y D_i(y, x)y. \qquad (1.5.8)$$

Proof. Here, we will only sketch a proof for the case of input orientation.[16]

$$e_i(y, x) = \frac{\partial \ln \lambda}{\partial \ln \theta}\bigg|_{\theta=1,\lambda=1}, \quad \text{such that } D_i(\theta y, \lambda x) = 1$$

$$= -\frac{\theta}{\lambda} \frac{\sum_{m=1}^{M} \frac{\partial D_i(\theta y,\lambda x)}{\partial(\theta y_m)} \frac{\partial(\theta y_m)}{\partial\theta}}{\sum_{j=1}^{N} \frac{\partial D_i(\theta y,\lambda x)}{\partial(\lambda x_j)} \frac{\partial(\lambda x_j)}{\partial\lambda}}\bigg|_{D_i(\theta y,\lambda x)=1,\theta=1,\lambda=1}$$

(use the implicit function theorem)

$$= -\frac{\nabla'_y D_i(y, x)y}{\nabla'_x D_i(y, x)x}\bigg|_{D_i(y,x)=1}$$

(evaluated at $\lambda=1, \theta=1$)

$$= -\nabla'_y D_i(y, x)y.$$

[16] It appears that Caves et al. (1982a) were the first to derive (1.5.7), while Färe et al. (1986) were the first to derive (1.5.8). See Section 1.7 for more references.

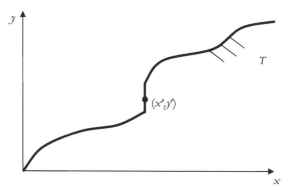

Figure 1.16 An example of technology where $D_i(y, x) = 1 \Leftrightarrow D_o(x, y) = 1$ is not always true.

The last equality is using the property of homogeneity of the distance function and *Euler's rule*, and then we use the "being on the isoquant" condition $D_i(y, x) = 1$.

A proof of $e_o(x, y) = -\nabla'_x D_o(x, y)x$ is very similar and is left as an exercise. ☐

Note immediately that under CRS, both (1.5.7) and (1.5.8) equal unity – recall the property (1.4.4) and (1.4.5) and apply *Euler's rule*. If a technology exhibits increasing returns to scale at some point (x^o, y^o) on the isoquant of $P(x)$, then (and only then) at that point $e_o(x^o, y^o) > 1$ provided that D_o is differentiable at all (x, y). If instead we have decreasing returns to scale then (and only then) at that point we have $e_o(x^o, y^o) < 1$. For the input-oriented measure, the inequality signs are the opposite.

An important question is: "How are the two measures of scale elasticity related?" The answer is very encouraging, and is given in the next theorem.

Theorem. Given (1.5.4) and (1.5.5), we have

$$e_o(x, y) = 1/e_i(y, x) \tag{1.5.9}$$

if and only if

$$\nabla'_x D_o(x, y)x \neq 0 \text{ and } \nabla'_x D_i(y, x)x \neq 0. \tag{1.5.10}$$

Proof. (See Zelenyuk, 2013a,b.) ☐

The meaning of this theorem is important and simple: the two elasticity formulas measure the same thing equivalently and we can get one from the other by just taking the reciprocal. Note that the condition $D_i(y, x) = 1 \Leftrightarrow D_o(x, y) = 1$ of the theorem is critical and some peculiar technologies may not satisfy it. For example, the technology illustrated in Figure 1.16 does not satisfy this condition since for the point (x^o, y^o), located on the portion of the frontier parallel to the output axis, we have $D_i(y, x) = 1$, while $D_o(x, y) < 1$. The theorem, however, will hold for this technology at all other points where this condition is satisfied.[17]

A conceptually different way of measuring scale was proposed within the research on efficiency analysis, which we will discuss in the following chapters in the context of particular efficiency measures.

1.6 DIRECTIONAL DISTANCE FUNCTION

The input and output Shephard's distance functions have been widely used in economics. More recently, a more general characterization of technology has been introduced to economists, which subsumes both Shephard's distance functions as special cases. This characterization of technology can take virtually any *direction* of measurement, predetermined by a researcher, and thus is called the *directional distance function*, which we formally define next.[18]

Definition. For a nonzero direction $d = (-d_x, d_y) \in \mathfrak{R}_-^N \times \mathfrak{R}_+^M \backslash \{0_{N+M}\}$, the directional distance function $D_d : \mathfrak{R}_+^N \times \mathfrak{R}_+^M \to \mathfrak{R} \cup \{\infty\}$ is defined as

$$D_d(x, y | -d_x, d_y) \equiv \sup_{\theta} \{\theta \in \mathfrak{R} : (x - \theta d_x, y + \theta d_y) \in T\}. \quad (1.6.1)$$

Intuitively, for a particular point (x^o, y^o) this measure yields the real number $(D_d(x^o, y^o | -d_x, d_y) = \theta^*$, the solution to optimization problem (1.6.1)), that represents the "portion" of the directional vector $(-d_x, d_y)$ that must be added to this point (x^o, y^o) to bring it exactly onto the frontier of the technology T, by shifting it in the direction $d = (-d_x, d_y)$, as illustrated in Figure 1.17.

Importantly, note that $(-d_x, d_y)$ specifies two aspects: (i) the direction in which the distance between observation (x, y) and the boundary of the technology set T is measured, as well as (ii) the length relative to which the measurement is done (e.g., note that for the same direction, same (x, y) and T, the value of θ depends on how large $(-d_x, d_y)$ is). Thus, $(-d_x, d_y)$ can be understood as a numeraire selected by the researcher to reflect her/his relative valuation of each input and output.

Similarly to the case of Shephard's distance functions, various properties can be derived for this function. Most importantly, it can be shown that the directional distance function completely characterizes the technology (under standard regularity conditions), as is summarized in the next theorem.

---

[17] It might be worth noting that this result resembles Cauchy's lemma in the theory of elasticity in physics (e.g., see Atanackovic and Guran, 2000).

[18] The idea of the directional distance function has its origin in Allais (1943), as noted and elaborated on by Diewert (1983a), and revived and thoroughly developed by Chambers et al. (1996b, 1998). The idea was also employed by Luenberger (1992), who called it shortage/benefit function, in the context of consumer theory.

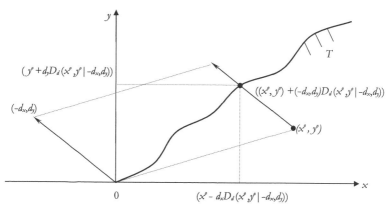

Figure 1.17 Geometric intuition of the directional distance function.

Theorem. D_d provides complete characterization of T, in the sense that, for any $(-d_x, d_y) \in \mathfrak{R}_-^N \times \mathfrak{R}_+^M \backslash \{\mathbf{0}_{N+M}\}$, we have

$$D_d(x, y| - d_x, d_y) \geq 0 \Leftrightarrow (x, y) \in T.$$

The proof of this statement is somewhat similar to the proof of complete characterization of technology by any of Shephard's distance functions and its details can be found in the seminal works of Chambers et al. (1996b).

Moreover, and just as importantly, note that D_d is able to identify a certain type of frontier of technology set T, namely

$$D_d(x^o, y^o| - d_x, d_y) = 0 \quad \Leftrightarrow \quad (x^o, y^o) \in \partial_d T,$$

where

$$\partial_d T \equiv \{(x, y) \,:\, (x, y) \in T, \ (x', y') \equiv ((x, y) + \lambda(-d_x, d_y)) \notin T, \forall \lambda > 0\}.$$

That is, D_d identifies a direction-specific frontier, defined in terms of the particular direction $d = (-d_x, d_y)$, i.e., the d-oriented frontier of T, by yielding zero for points on such a frontier. Such points are called technically efficient (or zero-inefficient), from the perspective of D_d (and for the particular d), while it can be inefficient in the Farrell sense for the input or output orientation, or both.

Meanwhile, note that D_d yields negative numbers for points outside T, reflecting how much should be subtracted from the particular input–output allocation to bring it to the frontier of the technology set T in the specific direction d. This is useful for measuring technology changes.

A few other useful properties are summarized in the next theorem.

Theorem. D_d satisfies ($\forall d = (-d_x, d_y) \in \mathfrak{R}_-^N \times \mathfrak{R}_+^M \backslash \{\mathbf{0}_{N+M}\}$):

(i) *homogeneity of degree -1 in the directional vector, i.e.,*

$$D_d(x, y| - \delta d_x, \delta d_y) = D_d(x, y| - d_x, d_y)/\delta, \ \forall \delta \in \mathfrak{R}_+;$$

*(ii) monotonicity: nondecreasing in inputs and nonincreasing in outputs,
i.e.,*

$$D_d(x', y| - d_x, d_y) \geq D_d(x, y| - d_x, d_y) \, \forall x' \geq x;$$

$$D_d(x, y'| - d_x, d_y) \leq D_d(x, y| - d_x, d_y) \, \forall y' \geq y;$$

(iii) translation by a real scalar:

$$D_d(x, y| - d_x, d_y) - \delta = D_d(x - \delta d_x, y + \delta d_y| - d_x, d_y), \, \forall \delta \in \Re;$$

(iv) upper semi-continuity in (x, y);
(v) upper semi-bounded on $\Re_+^N \times \Re_+^M$;
(vi) homogeneity of degree 1 in (x, y) *under CRS, i.e.,* $\forall \delta \in \Re_+$:

$$D_d(\delta x, \delta y| - d_x, d_y) = \delta D_d(x, y| - d_x, d_y) \iff \delta T = T.$$

We leave the proofs of these properties as exercises (see Chambers et al., 1996b, 1998, for some details).

Besides serving as an efficiency measure, this function can also be used for measuring scale via scale elasticity (e.g., see Fukuyama, 2003, Zelenyuk, 2013a). We will come back to this function on many occasions in the following chapters.

Finally, it is worth noting here that one could further generalize the idea of directional distance function by allowing for different scalars (rather than the same scalar θ) for each output or/and each input, leading to what is called slack-based directional efficiency measure, as we will discuss in more detail in Chapters 3 and 8.

1.7 CONCLUDING REMARKS ON THE LITERATURE

What we covered in this chapter is a relatively brief summary of the primal approach in production theory and so some remarks about more detailed literature are in order. Perhaps the biggest contribution to the neoclassical production theory in economics so far was made by Ronald W. Shephard, mostly due to Shephard (1953, 1970) and so this is the main reference we recommend for a more interested reader. Another important reference is the seminal work on production theory by Fuss and McFadden (1978), as well as by one of McFadden's prominent students, Erwin Diewert (e.g., see Diewert, 1971, 1982, etc.). Fundamental developments in production theory are also due to Charles Blackorby, Robert Chambers, Rolf Färe, Shawna Grosskopf, Daniel Primont, Robert Russell, to mention just a few (e.g., see Dogramaci and Adam, 1981; Dogramaci and Färe, 1988; Grifell-Tatjé and Lovell, 2013; Grifell-Tatjé et al., 2018 for nice reviews and many useful references).[19]

---

[19] This particular chapter (and related material in other chapters) is inspired in large part by the lectures of and joint work with Rolf Färe and Shawna Grosskopf as well as by many of their works.

The notion of elasticity in economics was apparently inspired by the somewhat similar notion in physics, where a much more elaborate theory of elasticity plays a prominent role in explaining many natural phenomena and is frequently used in engineering, including production engineering.[20] The first use of the elasticity of an implicit transformation production function for multiple inputs and multiple outputs is apparently due to Hanoch (1970) and later explored in Hanoch (1975) and Panzar and Willig (1977a). The first derivations of elasticity for a distance function we found is in the classic work of Caves et al. (1982a), in the context of output distance function, while Färe et al. (1986) appears to be the first who used it for the input distance function and established its dual relationship with the elasticity based on cost function. Other important developments on the topic include the seminal works of Banker and Thrall (1992), Førsund (1996) and more recent works of Fukuyama (2000, 2003), Hadjicostas and Soteriou (2006, 2010), Podinovski et al. (2009), to mention a few. Also see Zelenyuk (2013b,a) for more details.

1.8 EXERCISES

1. Can you give a real-world example of a technology that:
   (a) does not satisfy Axiom 1?
   (b) does not satisfy Axiom 2?
   (c) does not satisfy Axiom 3?
   (d) does not satisfy Axiom 4?
   (e) does not satisfy Axiom 5?
   (f) does not satisfy Axiom 6?
2. Show that if T is closed then $P(x)$ and $L(y)$ are also closed.
3. Show that free disposability implies weak and partially weak disposability.
4. Show that $P(x)$ and $L(y)$ can be convex while T is not convex.
5. Show that convexity of T implies convexity of $P(x)$ and $L(y)$.
6. Give an example (pictorial or analytic) of a technology that is convex but not freely disposable.
7. Give an example (pictorial or analytic) of a technology that is freely disposable but not convex.
8. Give a pictorial representation of the input distance function for:
   (a) for 1-input–1-output case,
   (b) for 2-inputs–multiple-outputs case.
9. Define the input isoquant (in a radial fashion).
10. List and prove the properties of the input distance function defined in (1.3.15).

---

[20] E.g., see the classic book of Landau and Lifshitz (1959) or a more recent book of Atanackovic and Guran (2000).

11. Show (pictorially or analytically) that $D_o(x, y) = 1$ does not necessarily imply that $D_i(y, x) = 1$ or vice versa. Explain the intuition.

12. Show what the Shephard's input distance function is equal to if:

    (a) $(x^o, y^o) \notin T$, but $\exists \lambda > 0 : (\lambda x, y) \in T$,
    (b) $(x^o, y^o) \notin T$, and $\forall \lambda > 0 : (\lambda x, y) \notin T$.

13. Note that other general important properties of the Shephard's input distance function include the fact that $D_i(y, x)$ is upper semi-bounded on $\mathfrak{R}_+^N$ and also upper semi-continuous on $\mathfrak{R}_+^N$. These properties are the consequence of which axioms?

14. Show that in the single output case, (1.4.1) is equivalent to the production function being homogeneous of degree 1 in all inputs.

15. Prove that (1.4.3) is equivalent to (1.4.1).

16. Prove that (1.4.5) is equivalent to (1.4.4).

17. Prove that (1.4.7), (1.4.9) and (1.4.10) are equivalent.

18. Prove that (1.4.8), (1.4.11) and (1.4.12) are equivalent.

19. Show that $e_o(x, y) = -\nabla'_x D_o(x, y)x$.

20. Prove that the definitions (1.5.1) and (1.5.4) are equivalent for the single-output case.

21. Prove theorem (1.5.9).

22. Derive properties of the directional distance function (e.g., see Chambers et al., 1996b, 1998).

23. How would you measure the *scale efficiency*? Do you see any conceptual problem (e.g., with respect to orientation)?

CHAPTER 2

Production Theory: Dual Approach

In the previous chapter, we dealt with characterizations of technology that use the input–output information about the production process. This approach is, by convention, referred to as the *primal* approach, while the input–output information that is needed for such analysis (i.e., data on (x, y)) is often referred to as the primal information.

Very often researchers do not have some of the primal information: for example, only input prices, not the inputs themselves, might be available for privacy or other reasons. This situation was one of the motivations for various legendary economists[1] to develop duality theory in economics – a discovery that truly made a revolution in the neoclassical economic theory of production (as well as impacted other areas) and provided foundations for many useful theoretical results with practical values.

Here we will only summarize some of the key results of this theory that we will refer to later on. We will mostly focus on the duality nature of the cost function – perhaps the most popular instrument in economic theory, while similar results for the revenue as well as profit functions must be clear afterwards and so we will be briefer there. In our discussion we will mainly follow Shephard (1953, 1970) as well as Diewert (1974a, 1982), Chambers (1988), Varian (1992), Färe and Primont (1995), to mention a few.

2.1 COST MINIMIZING BEHAVIOR AND COST FUNCTION

Consider a firm that wants to produce a certain level of outputs, $y \in \mathfrak{R}_+^M$, from a vector of inputs, $x \in \mathfrak{R}_+^N$ with the available technology and facing input prices given in the *row* vector $w = (w_1, \ldots, w_N) \in \mathfrak{R}_{++}^N$ (ordered in

---

[1] The list of these economists includes Alexandr Konus, Sergey Byushgens, Ronald Shephard, Paul Samuelson, Hirofumi Uzawa, Daniel McFadden, Erwin Diewert, to mention a few. The roots of duality in economics also appear in the seminal work of Konüs and Byushgens (1926) and von Neumann (1945), originally published in 1938.

the same way as the input vector). We assume that the prices of inputs are given, strictly positive and fixed.[2] Recall from the previous chapter that $L(y)$ is called the input requirement set and is one of the complete characterizations of technology, defined as[3]

$$L(y) \equiv \{x \in \mathfrak{R}^N_+ : y \text{ is producible from } x\}, \quad y \in \mathfrak{R}^M_+$$

and completely characterized by Shephard's input distance function, as

$$x \in L(y) \quad \Leftrightarrow \quad D_i(y, x) \geq 1,$$

where

$$D_i(y, x) \equiv \sup\{\theta > 0 : x/\theta \in L(y)\}.$$

The questions we raise now are: how much shall the firm employ of each input to achieve its production target given by y? What would be the resulting total cost? These two questions are answered by solving the following mathematical formulation of the firm's problem.

Definition. Let $Dom L \equiv \{y \in \mathfrak{R}^M_+ : L(y) \neq \varnothing\}$ be the set of all $y \in \mathfrak{R}^M_+$ that are producible from some $x \in \mathfrak{R}^N_+$, then the function $C : Dom L \times \mathfrak{R}^N_{++} \to \mathfrak{R}^1_+ \cup \{+\infty\}$, defined as[4]

$$C(y, w) \equiv \min_x \{wx : x \in L(y)\}, \tag{2.1.1}$$

will be called the (long run, total) *cost function* and the solution to (2.1.1),

$$x(y, w) \equiv \arg\min_x \{wx : x \in L(y)\}, \tag{2.1.2}$$

will be called the vector of conditional (on y) demand functions for inputs assuming the cost-minimizing behavior.[5]

The geometric intuition of the optimization (2.1.1), the resulting cost function and the conditional demands for inputs are given in Figure 2.1. The cost-minimizing allocation is achieved where the hyperplane $\{x : wx =$

---

[2] Many of the results below also hold for weaker cases when $w \in \mathfrak{R}^N_+$, yet for simplicity and without much loss of generality, it is reasonable to assume that all input prices are strictly positive, as we do here.

[3] We also recall that the main regularity axioms (conditions) of production theory are assumed to hold (see Chapter 1 for details), although some of these results may require weaker conditions.

[4] Use of $Dom L$ instead of all $\mathfrak{R}^M_+$ is needed to simply avoid the irrelevant cases where y is not producible from any x. For such cases, one can also set the cost function to ∞ or simply call it undefined.

[5] Note that the minimum exists here by the extreme-value theorem, because wx is a continuous function optimized on effectively a compact set. Indeed, although $L(y)$ is not compact (because it is not bounded, yet it is closed due to the assumption that T is closed), the optimization (2.1.1) is effectively done on a "compact portion" of $L(y)$: e.g., the intersection of $L(y)$ and $\{x : wx \leq c\}$ for $w > \mathbf{0}_N$ and a large enough constant c (such that $L(y) \cap \{x : wx \leq c\} \neq \emptyset$), which is closed and bounded and so is also compact (in the Euclidean space).

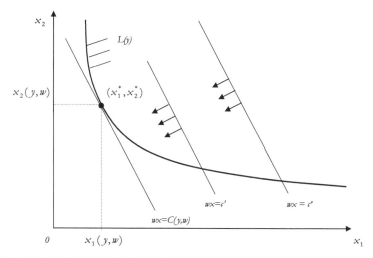

Figure 2.1 Geometric intuition of the cost minimization problem.

$C(y, w)$} is tangential to the frontier of the input requirement set $L(y)$. The point of tangency determines the conditional demand for each input, $x_1(y, w)$ and $x_2(y, w)$.

Note that economists often distinguish two types of time spans: short run and long run. The short run is defined as a time period when something (e.g., some inputs) is fixed, while everything is flexible in the long run. Despite the somewhat pessimistic note often attributed to Sir John M. Keynes about the long run, we will stay optimistic and analyze the long run cost function, while extensions to the short run must be clear most of the time.

To understand a function, it is worth learning about its properties, as we do from the next theorem.

Theorem. *For any* $w \in \mathfrak{R}^N_{++}$, $y \in DomL$, *the cost function* $C(y, w)$ *defined in (2.1.1) possesses the following properties,*

(1) $C(y, w) \geq 0$,   *(nonnegativity)*   (2.1.3)

(2) $C(y, \tilde{w}) \geq C(y, w), \forall \tilde{w} \geq w$,   *(monotonicity in w)*   (2.1.4)

(3) $C(y, tw) = tC(y, w), \forall t > 0$,   *(homogeneity in w)*   (2.1.5)

(4) $C(y, w)$ *is concave in* $w \in \mathfrak{R}^N_{++}$,   *(concavity in w)*   (2.1.6)

(5) $C(y, w)$ *is continuous in* $w \in \mathfrak{R}^N_{++}$,   *(continuity in w)*   (2.1.7)

(6) $C(y, w)$ *is lower semi-continuous*   *(lower semi-continuity in y)*

     in $y \in \mathfrak{R}^M_+$.   (2.1.8)

Proof. (See Appendix.)   □

There is quite an interesting economic intuition behind these properties. The first property says that the cost function never takes negative values, which is fairly obvious, because inputs and their prices are typically assumed to be non-negative.[6] The second property says that the total cost never decreases with an increase in prices of any inputs, which is quite intuitive. The third property says that if all prices were to increase by the same multiple, then the cost would increase by the same multiple as well – quite a natural property too. The fourth property implies that the cost minimizing firm would never react to the increase in some input prices by hiring more of those inputs, but rather would try to substitute part (or all) of those more expensive inputs with the other, relatively cheaper inputs. According to the fifth property, the cost-minimizing firm would react to small changes in input prices with small changes in the total cost. The sixth property states that, in general, some infinitesimal changes in output plans may lead to jumps in the minimal costs, yet these will be finite jumps, with the cost function taking the smallest values at the jumps.[7]

2.2 THE DUALITY NATURE OF COST FUNCTION

It turns out that, under one additional assumption, the cost function can be used as a characterization of technology – alternative to characterizations by the distance functions. Roughly speaking, this is the essence of the duality theory in economics, which we briefly sketch below.[8] A key additional assumption needed for this theory to hold is stated next.

Axiom 7. *"Convexity of Input Requirement Set"*

$$A7. \ L(y) \text{ is a convex set, for any } y \in \mathfrak{R}_+^M. \tag{2.2.1}$$

Convexity is usually motivated by a common observation that averages are usually (though not always) better or at least not worse than extremes. For the case of producing an output, it is also reasonable to expect that an average of input allocations are not worse or even better than these allocations. Another important motivation refers to the fact that convexity of $L(y)$ ensures

---

[6] There are exceptions to this, e.g., in case of subsidies, weak disposability or other peculiar cases, some prices can happen to be negative or zero.

[7] Note that by imposing additional structure one may also attain continuity of $C(y, w)$ in y. In fact, often one also needs to assume differentiability of $C(y, w)$ in y (and sometimes in w), which in turn will imply its continuity in y.

[8] Several chapters can be dedicated to describing duality theory in economics in thorough detail. Here we will focus on the main results and then refer an interested reader for more details to the seminal works on duality by Shephard (1953, 1970); Diewert (1971, 1974a, 1982) and more recent expositions by Chambers (1988); Varian (1992); Färe and Primont (1995).

a nonincreasing marginal rate of technical substitution between any two inputs (formally defined as $\partial x_i / \partial x_j |_{D_i(y,x)=1}$). This axiom allows for obtaining one of the main results of duality theory, summarized below.

Theorem. *Assume $L(y)$ is convex and satisfies strong disposability of inputs,*[9] *then the set of inputs characterized by the cost function is equal to the* input requirement set that this cost function is defined upon, *i.e.*

$$\hat{L}(y) = L(y), \text{ for any } y \in \mathfrak{R}_+^M,$$

where

$$\hat{L}(y) = \{x : C(y, w) \le wx, \forall w > \mathbf{0}_N\}.$$

The proof of this theorem is a bit involved and we refer the reader to Färe and Primont (1995), while an intuitive sketch of the proof can be found in Varian (1992). The implication of this theorem is that not only $C(y, w)$ can be defined in terms of $L(y)$, but also $L(y)$ can be completely characterized in terms of $C(y, w)$, when $L(y)$ is convex. In particular, we can say: $L(y) = \{x : C(y, w) \le wx, \forall w > \mathbf{0}_N\}$. Thus, the theorem says that if we know the firm's minimal cost of operation for *every* possible price vector $w > \mathbf{0}_N$ and output level y, i.e., we know $C(y, w)$, then we know the entire set of technological choices available to the firm (assuming the main regularity conditions, free disposability and convexity of $L(y)$). In other words, under those assumptions, the cost function is another *complete characterization of the technology*! I.e., all the information on technology contained in $L(y)$ (or in $D_i(y, x)$) can be recovered from the cost function.

Theorem. *If the technology satisfies strong disposability of inputs (A5), and $L(y)$ is convex (A7), then*

$$C(y, w) = \min_x \{wx : D_i(y, x) \ge 1\}, w \in \mathfrak{R}_{++}^N, \tag{2.2.2}$$

if and only if

$$D_i(y, x) = \inf_w \{wx : C(y, w) \ge 1\}, x \in \mathfrak{R}_+^N. \tag{2.2.3}$$

Proof. The statement (2.2.2) is derived by using the complete characterization property of the input distance function, saying that

$$D_i(y, w) \ge 1 \Leftrightarrow x \in L(y), y \in \mathfrak{R}_+^M, \tag{2.2.4}$$

and then directly applying it to the definition of the cost function. The second statement, (2.2.3), emerges as follows:

---

[9] Recall that we also assume that the main regularity axioms (conditions) of production theory hold throughout the book (see Chapter 1 for details).

$$D_i(y, x) \equiv \sup_{\theta}\{\theta > 0 : x/\theta \in L(y)\} \qquad \text{(by definition)}$$

$$= \sup_{\theta}\{\theta > 0 : C(y, w) \leq wx/\theta, \forall w > \mathbf{0}_N\} \quad \text{(by previous theorem)}$$

$$= \sup_{\theta}\{\theta > 0 : \inf_{w}\{C(y, w) \leq wx/\theta\}\} \qquad \text{(take inf over } w > \mathbf{0}_N,$$

$$\text{since true for all } w > \mathbf{0}_N)$$

$$= \sup_{\theta}\{\theta > 0 : \inf\{wx/C(y, w)\} \geq \theta\} \qquad \text{(rearranging the terms)}$$

$$= \inf_{w}\{wx/C(y, w)\}, \, w \in \mathfrak{R}^N_{++} \qquad \text{(by maximizing over } \theta)$$

$$= \inf_{w}\{wx : C(y, w) \geq 1\}, \, x \in \mathfrak{R}^N_+.$$

It is worth noting here that the last equality follows from a more general result in mathematics about the ratio of linearly homogeneous functions (see Färe and Primont, 1995 for a proof). $\qquad\square$

Intuitively, this theorem says that the cost function is essentially the "input distance function" but in the input price-space, while the usual input distance function is the "cost function" in the input-space. So the duality exists here between the two spaces – input and input-prices – through the two functions, $D_i(y, x)$ and $C(y, w)$, optimized over these two spaces, respectively. The theoretical result (2.2.2)–(2.2.3) is very important and will be used a number of times in our further derivations.

Now, what if $L(y)$ is not convex? Do we still have $\hat{L}(y) = L(y)$? No. In fact, it must be obvious that $\hat{L}(y)$ is a convex closure of $L(y)$ and therefore

$$L(y) \subseteq \hat{L}(y), \text{ for any } y \in \mathfrak{R}^M_+. \qquad (2.2.5)$$

That is, $L(y)$ is always contained in $\hat{L}(y)$ as can be easily seen geometrically. But, can we still rely on the cost function? Yes! To clarify this point, consider the following auxiliary function:

$$\hat{C}(y, w) = \min_{x}\{wx : x \in \hat{L}(y)\}, \, y \in DomL, \qquad (2.2.6)$$

i.e., this is the cost function which is defined *not* on the original $L(y)$, but on its convex closure, $\hat{L}(y)$. The next theorem clarifies the relationship between the cost function on non-convex $L(y)$ and the cost function on "convexified" version of such $L(y)$.

Theorem. *If technology satisfies the strong disposability of inputs axiom (but not necessarily convexity of $L(y)$), then*

$$\hat{C}(y, w) = C(y, w), \text{ for any } y \in \mathfrak{R}^M_+, w \in \mathfrak{R}^N_{++}.$$

Proof. To sketch a proof, first note that because of (2.2.5), we have $\hat{L}(y)$ being less restrictive than $L(y)$, thus it follows that

$$\hat{C}(y, w) \leq C(y, w), \, y \in \mathfrak{R}^M_+, w \in \mathfrak{R}^N_{++}. \qquad (2.2.7)$$

So, if we prove that $\hat{C}(y,w) \geq C(y,w)$ is also true, the theorem will be proved. To do so, suppose that the statement "$\hat{C}(y,w) \geq C(y,w)$" is not (always) true. If so, then it must be true that for some $\tilde{w}, \exists \tilde{x} \in \hat{L}(y) : \tilde{w}\tilde{x} = \hat{C}(y,\tilde{w}) < C(y,\tilde{w})$, but this should never happen since by definition of $\hat{L}(y)$, we should have $C(y,x) \leq wx, \forall w \geq \mathbf{0}_N$, including $\tilde{w}$. Thus, $\hat{C}(y,w) \geq C(y,w)$ is always true, and combining it with (2.2.7) suggests this can be if and only if $\hat{C}(y,w) = C(y,w)$ is always true – exactly what we had to prove. $\square$

In words, this theorem says that the cost function derived from $L(y)$ is the same as the cost function derived from the "convexified" version of $L(y)$. Intuitively, this means that if, in reality, $L(y)$ is non-convex (but still satisfies the main regularity axioms and free disposability in all inputs) then the axiom of convexity that we impose on $L(y)$ would not be harmful to the information on technology contained in the cost function. This is one of the biggest results of the duality theory in economics, which we can also rephrase as: *The cost function of a cost-minimizing firm summarizes all the economically relevant aspects of technology (characterized via $L(y)$) used by this firm, and does it equivalently whether $L(y)$ is convex or not.*

2.3 SOME EXAMPLES OF USING THE COST FUNCTION

Let us immediately use the duality results to unveil the relationship between the *primal* measure of scale elasticity which we have defined before and its *dual* analog.

Definition. Suppose the cost function is continuously differentiable with respect to each element y in a neighborhood of a point of interest, then the cost-based measure of scale elasticity is defined as[10]

$$e_c(y,w) \equiv \left. \frac{\partial \ln C(y\theta, w)}{\partial \ln \theta} \right|_{\theta=1}. \tag{2.3.1}$$

Intuitively, with (2.3.1) we are measuring how much the total cost would increase (as a percentage) due to an *equiproportional* increase in *all* outputs. After simple rearrangements we arrive at a more simplified form

$$e_c(y,w) = \frac{\nabla'_y C(y,w)y}{C(y,w)}. \tag{2.3.2}$$

More intuition for this measure is unveiled when one looks at the single-output case, where (2.3.1) becomes simply the marginal cost divided by the average cost (so, for positive y, they are equal if and only if technology exhibit *CRS* at that point). The next theorem establishes a relationship of (2.3.1) with the primal scale elasticity measure.

---

[10] The earliest reference to this measure we found is Panzar and Willig (1977b).

Theorem. *Let* $e_c(y, w)$, $e_i(y, x)$ *and* $x(y, w)$ *be defined in* (2.3.1), (1.5.5), (2.1.2), *then we have*

$$e_c(y, w) = e_i(y, x(y, w)), \quad y \in \mathfrak{R}_+^M, \quad w \in \mathfrak{R}_{++}^N. \tag{2.3.3}$$

Proof. To sketch a proof of (2.3.3), we follow Färe et al. (1986), and note that the Lagrangian to the problem (2.2.2) is given by

$$L(x, \lambda | y, w) \equiv wx - \lambda(D_i(y, x) - 1). \tag{2.3.4}$$

Assume an interior solution to (2.3.4) exists, call it $x^* \equiv x(y, w), \lambda^* \equiv \lambda(y, w)$, then it must satisfy the following system of equations, coming from the *f.o.c.*,

$$\nabla_x L(x^*, \lambda^* | y, w) \equiv w - \lambda^* \nabla_x D_i(y, x^*) \overset{set\ to}{=} 0, \tag{2.3.5}$$

$$\frac{\partial L(x^*, \lambda^* | y, w)}{\partial \lambda} \equiv D_i(y, x^*) - 1 \overset{set\ to}{=} 0. \tag{2.3.6}$$

Evaluating the Lagrangian function (2.3.4) at the optimal solution and applying the *envelope* theorem gives

$$\nabla_y' C(y, w) \overset{Env.Th.}{=} \nabla_y' L(x^*, \lambda^* | y, w) = -\lambda^* \nabla_y' D_i(y, x^*). \tag{2.3.7}$$

Now, note that post-multiplying both sides of (2.3.5) by $x^* \equiv x(y, x)$, gives

$$C(y, w) \equiv wx(y, w) = \lambda^* \nabla_x D_i(y, x^*) x(y, w) = \lambda^* D_i(y, x^*) = \lambda^*, \tag{2.3.8}$$

where the second equality is due to applying Euler's rule (due to the homogeneity of D_i) and the third equality is due to the condition that we compute the elasticity at the frontier, i.e., applying (2.3.6). Now, recalling that $e_i(y, x) = -\nabla_y' D_i(y, x)y$ and combining it with (2.3.2), (2.3.7) and (2.3.8) yields

$$e_c(y, w) = \nabla_y' C(y, w)y / C(y, w) = \nabla_y' C(y, w)y / \lambda^*$$
$$= -\nabla_y' D_i(y, x^*)y = e_i(y, x^*).$$

$\square$

Another fundamental implication of the duality theory is the result known as Shephard's lemma, also sometimes called the Hotelling–Shephard lemma, with which we conclude this section.

Lemma. *Let* $C(y, w)$ *and* $x(y, w)$ *be defined in* (2.1.1) *and* (2.1.2), *respectively, and assume* $C(y, w)$ *is continuously differentiable (at least once) with respect to each element* w *in a neighborhood of a point of interest, then*

$$\nabla_w C(y, w) = x(y, w), \quad y \in \mathfrak{R}_+^M, w \in \mathfrak{R}_{++}^N. \tag{2.3.9}$$

Proof. Taking the *Lagrangian* function (2.3.4) from the proof above, evaluating it at the optimal solutions $x^* \equiv x(y, x), \lambda^* \equiv \lambda(y, w)$, and applying the *envelope* theorem (wrt w), we get

$$\nabla_w C(y, w) \overset{env.th.}{=} \nabla_w L(x^*, \lambda^*|y, w) = x(y, w), \quad w \in \mathfrak{R}^N_{++}.$$

$\square$

In words, this important result says that the conditional input demand for an input j can be found by taking partial derivatives of the cost function with respect to w_j, i.e., the price of the corresponding input j.[11]

2.4 SUFFICIENT CONDITIONS FOR COST AND INPUT DEMAND FUNCTIONS

By now the reader must be convinced of how useful the cost function is for analyzing the behavior of a firm. If it is so important, it is worth revisiting the properties of the cost function and its derivatives (the conditional demands for inputs) to make sure they are well understood.

The question we address now is: "What if we are given a function that is non-negative, homogeneous of degree 1 in w, monotonic in w, as well as concave and continuous in w – is it necessarily a cost function of *some* technology?" In other words: "Do the properties of any cost function that we have discussed above give the *complete* list of properties that any cost function must have? That is, are those properties not only necessary but also sufficient for the function to be a cost function of *some* technology?" The answer turns out to be – Yes! We formalize it in the next theorem.

Theorem. *Let $\phi(y, w) \geq 0$ be a function that $\forall w \in \mathfrak{R}^N_{++}$, $y \in DomL$ satisfies the following conditions:*

$\phi(y, w) \geq 0,$

$\phi(y, tw) = t\phi(y, w), \ \forall t > 0,$

$\phi(y, w') \geq \phi(y, w), \ \forall w' \geqq w,$

$\phi(y, w)$ *is concave in* w,

$\phi(y, w)$ *is continuous in* w,

$\phi(y, w)$ *is lower semi-continuous in* y.

Then $\phi(y, w)$ is the cost function for the technology defined by

$$\hat{L}(y) = \{x \ : \quad wx \geq \phi(y, w), \quad for \ all \ w \geq \mathbf{0}_N\}.$$

---

[11] This result is a simplified quintessence of the result from Shephard (1953), while its name appears to be due to Erwin Diewert, who also pointed out that Hotelling, Hicks and Samuelson had derived simplified versions of this important result (see Diewert, 1974a for more details and historical remarks).

A sketch of a proof of this theorem can be found in many books of advanced production theory or microeconomics.[12] Meanwhile, how about a similar question about the conditional factor (input) demand functions? First, note that the conditional factor demand functions satisfy the properties stated in the next theorem.

Theorem. *Let $x(y, w)$ be defined in (2.1.2), then we have*

(i) $x_j(y, w) \geq 0$, *for all* j, $w \in \mathfrak{R}^N_{++}$, $y \in DomL$;

(ii) $x_j(y, tw) = x_j(y, w)$, $t > 0$ *for all* j, $w \in \mathfrak{R}^N_{++}$, $y \in DomL$; *and, if $C(y, w)$ is also a continuously differentiable (at least twice) with respect to each element in $w \in \mathfrak{R}^N_{++}$, then*

(iii) $\nabla_w x(y, w)$ *is a sym. neg. semi-def. matrix,* $\forall w \in \mathfrak{R}^N_{++}$, $y \in DomL$.

Proof. The first property follows from the fact that inputs are nonnegative. The second property becomes clear when we recall Shephard's lemma and the fact that the cost function is homogeneous of degree 1 in w. In general, note that $C(y, w) = wx(y, w)$ and $C(y, wt) = (wt)x(y, wt)$, but also recall that $C(y, wt) = C(y, w)t$, thus, $(wt)x(y, wt) = wx(y, w)t$, so $wx(y, wt) = wx(y, w)$. For the last property, note that the gradient of the (vector of) conditional input demands, wrt w, is simply the Hessian (matrix of second-order derivatives) of the cost function – because of Shephard's lemma. And, it is well known that the Hessian of a concave function (as the cost function is wrt w) is a symmetric negative semi-definite matrix.   □

As with the cost function, it turns out that these properties are not only necessary but also sufficient for a function to be a conditional input demand function for some technology, as we formally state in the next theorem.

Theorem. *Let $g_j(y, w)$ be a continuously differentiable function with respect to each element in $w \in \mathfrak{R}^N_{++}$ and satisfying the following conditions:*

(i) $g_j(y, w) \geq 0$, *for all* $j = 1, \ldots, N$,

(ii) $g_j(y, tw) = g_j(y, w)$, $t > 0$ *(for all* $j = 1, \ldots, N$)*,

(iii) $\nabla_w g(y, w)$ *is a symmetric negative semi-definite matrix.*

Then $g_j(y, w)$, $j = 1, \ldots, N$, are the conditional factor demand functions for the technology characterized by $\hat{L}(y) = \{x : wx \geq \sum_{j=1}^N w_j g_j(y, w), \forall w > 0_N\}$.

A sketch of the proof of this theorem can be found in Varian (1992). In words, the theorem says that the properties of the conditional factor demand functions discussed above make a complete (necessary and sufficient) list of conditions that any such function must satisfy.

2.5 BENEFITS COMING FROM THE DUALITY THEORY FOR THE COST FUNCTION: A SUMMARY

The development of the duality theory by Ronald W. Shephard substantially enriched the state of economic theory and practice. What we have covered so far is just a small part of it, yet before moving further, it is worth synthesizing the knowledge from this chapter so far into a summary of benefits one gets from the duality theory of the cost function and we try to do so in this section (see Färe and Primont, 1995 and Varian, 1992 for further discussion).

First of all, through the cost function, we get another (often easier) representation of technology. For example, think about a multiple output case – we cannot use the production function, only an implicit function, e.g., Shephard's distance functions, yet we still can (and often do) use the cost function, which is quite an intuitive concept and easily comprehended by practitioners.

Second, the cost function representation of technology incorporates optimization behavior of firms with respect to the optimal *allocation* of inputs given their prices, while the primal characterization of the distance or production functions does not do so. In other words, the cost function might be intuitively viewed as a superior characterization of technology, containing more information, relative to what the primal characterizations contain.

Third, if a firm is inefficient in the sense that it does not minimize costs given the market prices, there is still duality between the technology (or its primal characterization) and a cost function with respect to a certain sets of prices, called the shadow prices.

Fourth, the cost function has a precise and *full* list of properties needed to be satisfied to represent the technology of a cost-minimizing firm. These properties are often relatively easy to check, which helps when inquiring whether the firm under study is cost-minimizing or not. This also helps when specifying a proper parametric form of the cost function for *econometric* estimations – the functional parametric form must satisfy (*ex post* or *ex ante*) all the conditions we have listed in the theorem above.

Finally, the data for variables (y, w) together with data on associated costs needed in econometric estimation of the cost function are often easier to obtain than those needed in the estimation of technology requiring the primal data (y, x). For example, think about the estimation of technology for a car manufacturer: information on *all* inputs may be impossible to find for an outside researcher, while information on input prices might be more available, or easier to find via a proxy.[13]

2.6 REVENUE MAXIMIZATION BEHAVIOR AND THE REVENUE FUNCTION

Similar developments on duality can be done for the case when a firm is trying to maximize revenue, for a certain level of inputs and with technological

---

[13] For more discussions, see Shephard (1953); Diewert (1974a); Chambers (1988); Varian (1992); Färe and Primont (1995).

possibilities characterized by $P(x)$ and fixed output prices listed in the *row* vector $p = (p_1, \ldots, p_M) \in \mathfrak{R}_{++}^M$ (ordered in the same way as the output vector).[14] Recall from the previous chapter that the output set $P(x)$ is a (complete) characterization of technology, defined as

$$P(x) \equiv \{y \in \mathfrak{R}_+^M : y \text{ is producible from } x\}, \quad x \in \mathfrak{R}_+^N \qquad (2.6.1)$$

and completely characterized by the Shephard's output distance function as

$$y \in P(x) \quad \Leftrightarrow \quad D_o(x, y) \leq 1, \qquad (2.6.2)$$

where

$$D_o(x, y) \equiv \inf\{\theta > 0 : y/\theta \in P(x)\}. \qquad (2.6.3)$$

In the revenue maximization context, the key question is how much shall this firm produce of each output, according to output prices, given a (fixed) amount of inputs and current technology, to achieve the maximal revenue, and what would be this maximal total revenue? These two questions are answered by solving the following mathematical formulation of the firm's problem.

Definition. The function $R : \mathfrak{R}_+^N \times \mathfrak{R}_{++}^M \to \mathfrak{R}_+ \cup \{+\infty\}$, defined as

$$R(x, p) \equiv \max_y \{py : y \in P(x)\}, \qquad (2.6.4)$$

is called the *revenue function*, while the solution to (2.6.4), denoted as

$$y(x, p) \equiv \arg\max_y \{py : y \in P(x)\}, \qquad (2.6.5)$$

is the vector of conditional (on x) supply functions of each output under the revenue-maximizing behavior.[15]

A geometric intuition of the revenue maximization is presented in Figure 2.2. Here, by maximizing the revenue, we shift the revenue line (or *isorevenue*), say $py = r^o$, upward until it is just tangent to the frontier (*isoquant*) of the output set, before any further shift, however small, would make this line have no common points with $P(x)$. The point of tangency in Figure 2.2 gives a solution to the revenue maximization problem, at $y^* = (y_1^*, y_2^*)$, i.e., when the isorevenue line is given by $R(x, p) = py^* = py(x, p)$.

The properties of the revenue function and of the conditional supply function are stated in the next theorem, the proof of which is analogous to that for the cost function and therefore is left as an exercise.

Theorem. *For any $p \in \mathfrak{R}_{++}^M$ and $x \in \mathfrak{R}_+^N$, the functions $R(x, p)$ and $y(x, p)$ defined in (2.6.4) and (2.6.5) possess the following properties,*

---

[14] Again, many of the results below also hold for a weaker case when $p \in \mathfrak{R}_+^M$, yet for simplicity and without much loss of generality, it is reasonable to assume that all output prices are strictly positive, as we do here.

[15] Note that the maximum exists here by the extreme-value theorem, because py is a continuous function optimized on $P(x)$, which is compact.

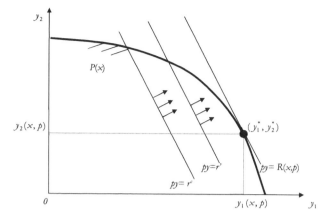

Figure 2.2 Geometric intuition of the revenue maximization problem.

   (i) $R(x, p) \geq 0$;

  (ii) $R(x, \tilde{p}) \geq R(x, p)$, $\forall \tilde{p} \geq p$ *(i.e., nondecreasing in p)*;

 (iii) $R(x, tp) = t R(x, p)$, $\forall t > 0$;

  (iv) $R(x, p)$ *is convex in p*;

   (v) $R(x, p)$ *is continuous in p and is upper semi-continuous in* x;[16]

  (vi) $y_m(x, p) \geq 0$, *for all* $m = 1, \ldots, M$;

 (vii) $y_m(x, tp) = y_m(x, p)$, $t > 0$, *for all* $m = 1, \ldots, M$;

(viii) *if* $R(x, p)$ *is continuously differentiable (at least twice) in p, then* $\nabla_p y(x, p)$ *is a symmetric positive semi-definite matrix.*

The proof of this theorem is similar to the one for the cost function (see Appendix), and can be found in books on production theory so we leave it as an exercise. Furthermore, all the duality results that we have developed for the cost function above have their analogues for the revenue function case. The reader is invited to do the exercises deriving these analogues, while we will only state the main results which we will use in the future.[17] First of all, we need to replace Axiom 7 with an appropriate analogue, which we state next.

Axiom 8. *"Convexity of Output Sets"*

    A8. $P(x)$ *is a convex set, for any* $x \in \Re_+^N$.   (2.6.6)

Theorem. *Assume technology satisfies strong disposability of inputs and* $P(x)$ *is convex, then the set of outputs characterized by the revenue function is equal to the output set that this revenue function is defined upon, i.e.,*

---

[16] By imposing an additional structure one may also attain continuity of $R(x, p)$ in x. In fact, one often needs to assume differentiability of $R(x, p)$ in x, which in turn will imply its continuity in x.

[17] In addition to references cited above, for more details on the revenue function and related duality, see Diewert (1974b); and Diewert and Morrison (1986).

$$\hat{P}(x) = P(x), \text{ for any } x \in \Re_+^N, \tag{2.6.7}$$

where

$$\hat{P}(x) = \{y \ : \ R(x, p) \geq py, \ \forall p > \mathbf{0}_M\}. \tag{2.6.8}$$

Similarly to the cost approach, the implication of this theorem is not only that $R(x, p)$ can be defined in terms of $P(x)$, but also that $P(x)$ can be completely characterized in terms of $R(x, p)$, given the stated assumptions. In particular, we can say that: $P(x) = \{y : R(x, p) \geq py, \ \forall p > \mathbf{0}_M\}$. Thus, intuitively, the theorem says that if we know the firm's maximal revenue for *every* possible price vector p and input level x, i.e., if we know $R(x, p)$, then we know the entire set of technological choices available to the firm, given the main regularity conditions, free disposability and convexity of $P(x)$. That is, the revenue function is another *complete characterization of the technology* and thus all the information on the technology that is contained in $P(x)$ (and thus in $D_o(y, x)$) can be recovered from the revenue function. A consequence of this theorem is the following result.

Theorem. *If technology satisfies the main regularity axioms (A1-4), as well as strong disposability of outputs (A6), and if $P(x)$ is convex (A8), then*

$$R(x, p) = \max_y\{py : D_o(x, y) \leq 1\}, \ p \in \Re_{++}^M, \ x \in \Re_+^N, \tag{2.6.9}$$

if and only if

$$D_o(x, y) = \sup_p\{py : \ R(x, p) \leq 1\}, \ (x, y) \in \Re_+^{N+M}. \tag{2.6.10}$$

Proof. The statement (2.6.9) comes from taking the complete characterization property of the output distance function (2.6.2), and then directly applying it to the definition of the revenue function (2.6.4). The proof of (2.6.10) is analogous to the proof of (2.2.3) and is left as an exercise. □

The intuition of this duality theorem is similar to the duality theorem for the cost function. It says that the revenue function is, in essence, the "output distance function" in the output price-space, while the Shephard's output distance function is the "revenue function" in the output-space. So, the duality here is between the two spaces – the output-space and the space of output-prices – through the two functions, $R(x, p)$ and $D_o(x, y)$, optimizing over those two spaces.

What if $P(x)$ is not convex? Do we still have $\hat{P}(x) = P(x)$? No, but it must be obvious that

$$P(x) \subseteq \hat{P}(x), \text{ for any } x \in \Re_+^N, \tag{2.6.11}$$

i.e., $P(x)$ is contained in $\hat{P}(x)$. Yet, again, we can continue relying on the information contained in this revenue function. To see this, consider the following auxiliary function

$$\hat{R}(x, p) = \max_{y}\{py : y \in \hat{P}(x)\}, \tag{2.6.12}$$

i.e., this is the revenue function defined *not* on the original $P(x)$, but on its convex closure, $\hat{P}(x)$. The next theorem establishes the relationship between this function and the original revenue function.

Theorem. *If the technology satisfies the main regularity axioms and the strong disposability of outputs axiom (but not necessarily convexity of $P(x)$), then*

$$\hat{R}(x, p) = R(x, p), \text{ for any } x \in \mathfrak{R}^N_+, p \in \mathfrak{R}^M_{++}. \tag{2.6.13}$$

The proof of this result is similar to the proof we have sketched for the cost function framework and so is left as an exercise. In words, this theorem states that the revenue function derived from $P(x)$ is the same as the revenue function derived from the "convexified" version of $P(x)$. Intuitively, this means that if, in reality, $P(x)$ is not convex (but has free disposal in all outputs and satisfies the main regularity axioms) then the axiom of convexity (A8) we have imposed on $P(x)$ is not harmful to the key information on technology contained in the revenue function. In summary, *the revenue function of a revenue-maximizing firm summarizes all the economically relevant aspects of the technology (characterized via $P(x)$) used by this firm, and does it equivalently whether $P(x)$ is convex or not.*

Finally, as in the cost framework, we can use the duality theory of the revenue function to establish a relationship between the *primal* measure of scale elasticity based on the output distance function and its *dual* analog, defined below.

Definition. Suppose $R(x, p)$ is continuously differentiable with respect to each element of x in a neighborhood of a point of interest, then the revenue-based measure of scale elasticity is defined as

$$e_r(x, p) \equiv \left.\frac{\partial \ln R(x\theta, p)}{\partial \ln \theta}\right|_{\theta=1}. \tag{2.6.14}$$

Intuitively, with (2.6.14) we are measuring how much (as a percentage) the total revenue would increase due to an *equiproportional* increase in *all* inputs. After simple rearrangements we arrive at a more simplified form

$$e_r(x, p) = \frac{\nabla'_x R(x, p)x}{R(x, p)}. \tag{2.6.15}$$

The next theorem establishes a relationship of (2.6.14) to its primal analogue.

Theorem. *Let $e_r(x, p), e_o(x, y)$ and $y(x, p)$ be given in (2.6.15), (1.5.7) and (2.6.5), then*

$$e_r(x, p) = e_o(x, y(x, p)), \text{ for any } x \in \mathfrak{R}^N_+, p \in \mathfrak{R}^M_{++}. \tag{2.6.16}$$

A proof of this result is analogous to the proof we have outlined for the cost function approach and we encourage the reader to do it as an exercise, while we state another fundamental implication of the duality theory, the results known as Shephard's lemma for the revenue function.

Theorem. *Let $R(x, p)$ and $y(x, p)$ be as in (2.6.4)–(2.6.5) respectively, then*

$$\nabla_p R(x, p) = y(x, p), \quad x \in \Re_+^N, \, p \in \Re_{++}^M. \tag{2.6.17}$$

In words, this theorem says that the conditional output supply function for each output can be obtained by taking partial derivatives of the revenue function wrt the price of the corresponding outputs. Again, a proof of this theorem is left as an exercise since it is analogous to the proof we have given for the cost function approach.

2.7   PROFIT-MAXIMIZING BEHAVIOR

Yet another approach to modeling producer's behavior is based on the assumption that the producer has the goal to maximize profit, given prices of inputs and outputs and certain technology. A mathematical formulation of such behavior can then be characterized via the profit function, given in the next definition.[18]

Definition. The function $\pi : \Re_{++}^N \times \Re_{++}^M \to \Re_+^1 \cup \{+\infty\}$ defined as

$$\pi(w, p) \equiv \sup_{x,y}\{py - wx \, : \, (x, y) \in T\}, \tag{2.7.1}$$

is the *profit function*, while its solution, denoted as

$$(x(w, p), y(w, p)) \equiv \arg\sup_{x,y}\{py - wx \, : \, (x, y) \in T\}, \tag{2.7.2}$$

gives the vectors of demand for inputs $(x(w, p))$ and supply of outputs $(y(w, p))$ under the profit-maximizing behavior.

The geometric intuition of the profit maximization is presented in Figure 2.3. Geometrically, maximizing profit means we shift the profit line (or *isoprofit*), say $py - wx = \pi^o$, till it is just tangent to the frontier of the technology set T – where any further shift would make this line have no common points with T. The point of tangency in Figure 2.3 is a solution to the profit maximization problem that defines the (unconditional) input demand functions $x(w, p)$ and (unconditional) supply functions $y(w, p)$.[19] The next theorem lists the properties of the profit function.

---

[18] In addition to references cited above, for more details on the profit function and related duality, see Diewert (1973).

[19] Note that $\pi(w, p) = +\infty$ for a technology that exhibits increasing returns to scale globally. When technology exhibits CRS, then $\pi(w, p) = +\infty$ or $\pi(w, p) = 0$ depending on the prices (w, p) relative to the shape of technology set T. A "remedy" to such cases is to allow for

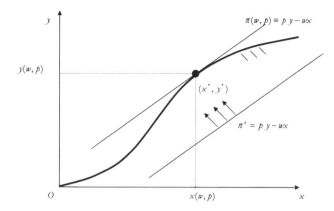

Figure 2.3 Geometric intuition of the profit maximization problem.

Theorem. *For any* $p \in \mathfrak{R}^M_{++}$ *and* $w \in \mathfrak{R}^N_{++}$, *the functions* $\pi(w, p)$, $y(w, p)$ *and* $x(w, p)$ *defined in (2.7.1) and (2.7.2) possess the following properties,*

- *(i)* $\pi(w, p) \geq 0$;
- *(ii)* $\pi(\tilde{w}, \tilde{p}) \geq \pi(w, p)$, $\forall \tilde{p} \geqq p$, $\forall \tilde{w} \leqq w$;
- *(iii)* $\pi(tw, tp) = t\pi(w, p)$, $\forall t > 0$;
- *(iv)* $\pi(w, p)$ *is convex in* p *(for all* $w \in \mathfrak{R}^N_{++}$), *and in* w *(for all* $p \in \mathfrak{R}^M_{++}$);
- *(v)* $\pi(w, p)$ *continuous in* p *(for all* $w \in \mathfrak{R}^N_{++}$), *and in* w *(for all* $p \in \mathfrak{R}^M_{++}$);
- *(vi)* $y_m(w, p) \geq 0$, *for all* $m = 1, \ldots, M$;
- *(vii)* $y_m(w, tp) = y_m(w, p)$, $t > 0$ *for all* $m = 1, \ldots, M$;
- *(viii)* *if* $\pi(w, p)$ *is also continuously differentiable (at least twice) in* p, *then* $\nabla_p y(w, p)$ *is a symmetric positive semi-definite matrix;*
- *(ix)* $x_j(w, p) \geq 0$, *for all* $j = 1, \ldots, N$;
- *(x)* $x_j(tw, p) = x_j(w, p)$, $t > 0$ *for all* $j = 1, \ldots, N$;
- *(xi)* *if* $\pi(w, p)$ *is also continuously differentiable (at least twice) in* w, *then* $\nabla_w x(w, p)$ *is a symmetric negative semi-definite matrix.*

The duality theory for the profit function can be established in a similar manner as duality theories for the cost and revenue functions. One way of doing so is to use the directional distance function, as was done in Chambers et al. (1996b, 1998). To summarize these results, recall from the previous chapter that the directional distance function is defined as

$$D_d(x, y \mid -d_x, d_y) \equiv \sup_{\theta} \{\theta \in \mathfrak{R} : (x - \theta d_x, y + \theta d_y) \in T\}, \quad (2.7.3)$$

additional constraints: e.g., fixed inputs at a given period, maximal amount of inputs available, budget limits, etc. (See Färe et al., 2018 for related discussion and references.)

where $(-d_x, d_y)$ is some nonzero vector in $\mathfrak{R}_-^N \times \mathfrak{R}_+^M$ that specifies the direction in which the distance between observation (x, y) and the frontier of the technology set T is measured.

To establish the duality relationship between this function and the profit function, we would need another assumption.

Axiom 9. *"Convexity of Technology Set"*

A9. *T is a convex set, for all $y \in \mathfrak{R}_+^M$.* (2.7.4)

Theorem. *If T is convex, then for $p \in \mathfrak{R}_{++}^M$, $w \in \mathfrak{R}_{++}^N$*

$$\pi(w, p) = \sup_{x,y}\{py - wx + D_d(x, y| - d_x, d_y)(pd_y + wd_x)\}, \quad (2.7.5)$$

if and only if

$$D_d(x, y| - d_x, d_y) = \inf_{w,p}\left\{\frac{\pi(w, p) - (py - wx)}{(pd_y + wd_x)}\right\}, \quad x \in \mathfrak{R}_+^M, \ y \in \mathfrak{R}_+^N.$$
$$(2.7.6)$$

The intuition of this theorem is quite appealing. Besides telling us that, under certain conditions, the profit function and the directional distance functions are dual to each other, the expression (2.7.6) gives us an intuitive dual explanation of the latter. Specifically, it tells us that the directional distance function is simply the difference between the potential and the actual profits, normalized by some particular value, and optimized over input–output prices. Interestingly, the normalizing value $(pd_y + wd_x)$ can also have a meaning: it is a monetary value that represents a combination of objective and subjective importance of each output and each input relative to each other. The objective importance is reflected in market prices, while the subjective importance is expressed in the researcher's choice of measurement direction. This is fundamentally different from what has been known about Shephard's duality.

The proof of the last theorem, together with more results from duality theory, can be found in Chambers et al. (1996b, 1998). A more complete duality "picture" that synthesizes the "state of the art" of duality in production theory, involving the distance functions and their "indirect" analogues (not considered here) can be found in Färe and Primont (2006) and references cited therein.

It might be also worth noting that, sometimes, the information on inputs is not available, yet researchers might have information on cost function (e.g., estimated by other researchers), then a convenient profit formulation is

$$\pi(w, p) \equiv \sup_{y}\{py - C(y, w)\}, \quad (2.7.7)$$

which is possible whenever $C(y, w)$ can serve as the complete characterization of technology. Moreover, when the output prices are not given or fixed but depend on the level of output, i.e., $p = p(y)$, which is a very common case in theory and practice, then an extension of (2.7.7) would be

$$\pi(w) \equiv \sup_y \{p(y)y - C(y, w)\}, \tag{2.7.8}$$

which is very commonly used in the neoclassical economics theory. Finally, note that the directional distance function and the profit function can be used to measure scale via scale elasticities based on these functions, as was outlined in detail in Zelenyuk (2013a).

2.8 EXERCISES

1. Derive the properties of the revenue function.
2. Derive the properties of the conditional supply of output.
3. Prove the relationship between $e_r(x, p)$ and $e_o(x, y)$.
4. How would you measure "cost efficiency"?
5. How would you measure "revenue efficiency"?
6. Does convexity of $P(x)$ imply convexity of $L(y)$, and vice versa?
7. Does convexity of $P(x)$ and of $L(y)$, together, imply convexity of T, and vice versa?
8. Prove the properties of the profit function stated in the theorem above.
9. Prove that $\pi(w, p) = +\infty$ for a technology that exhibits increasing returns to scale globally.
10. Prove that if technology exhibits CRS, then $\pi(w, p) = +\infty$ or $\pi(w, p) = 0$ depending on the prices (p, w) relative to the shape of technology set T.
11. Derive properties of the unconditional input demand and supply functions.
12. Define the measure of scale based on information about (w, p). Hint: use profit functions (see Zelenyuk, 2013a).
13. Show a relationship of your scale elasticity based on (w, p) with a primal scale elasticity (see Zelenyuk, 2013a).
14. How would you measure "profit efficiency"? (See Färe et al., 2018.)

2.9 APPENDIX

Proof. Proofs of (2.1.3)–(2.1.7) can be found in many books on advanced production theory or advanced microeconomics and we sketch them here for pedagogical purposes (mainly following Varian, 1992).

(1) The nonnegativity is evident, since w and x are nonnegative.

(2) The monotonicity property is true since, $C(y, w) \equiv wx(y, w) \leqq wx(y, \tilde{w}) \leqq \tilde{w}x(y, \tilde{w}) \equiv C(y, \tilde{w}), \forall x \in L(y), w \in \Re_{++}^N$, where $x(y, w) \equiv \arg\min_x \{wx : x \in L(y)\} \Rightarrow wx(y, w) \leqq wx, \forall x \in L(y), w \in \Re_{++}^N$, and $x(y, \tilde{w}) \equiv \arg\min_x \{\tilde{w}x : x \in L(y)\} \Rightarrow \tilde{w}x(y, \tilde{w}) \leqq \tilde{w}x, \forall x \in L(y), \tilde{w} \in \Re_+^N, \forall \tilde{w} \geqq w$.

(3) The homogeneity property is evident, and left as an exercise.

(4) To establish concavity, let $\hat{w} \equiv tw + (1 - t)\tilde{w}$, and define $x(y, \tilde{w}) \equiv$ arg $\min_{x}\{\tilde{w}x : x \in L(y)\}$. We have to prove:

$$t\,C(y, w) + (1 - t)\,C(y, \tilde{w}) \leqq C(y, \hat{w}), \quad \forall w, \tilde{w}, \hat{w} \in \mathfrak{R}_{++}^{N}.$$

This is equivalent to saying that

$$twx(y, w) + (1 - t)\tilde{w}x(y, \tilde{w}) \leqq \hat{w}x(y, \hat{w}), \; \forall w, \tilde{w}, \hat{w} \in \mathfrak{R}_{++}^{N},$$

which is true, since $\hat{w}x(y, \hat{w}) = t\,wx(y, \hat{w}) + (1 - t)\tilde{w}x(y, \hat{w})$ and due to cost minimization behavior, we have

$$wx(y, w) \leqq wx(y, \hat{w}) \text{ and } \tilde{w}x(y, \tilde{w}) \leqq \tilde{w}x(y, \hat{w}), \quad \forall w, \tilde{w}, \hat{w} \in \mathfrak{R}_{++}^{N}$$

(5) and (6). The continuity properties are from a general result from the optimization theory in mathematics, saying that a function $F(a)$ defined as

$$F(a) = \min_{x}\{f(x, a) \quad : \quad x \in G(a)\}, x \in \mathfrak{R}_{+}^{N}, a \in \mathfrak{R}_{+}^{M},$$

is a continuous function if $f(x, a)$ is a continuous function with a compact range and G is a compact-valued, continuous correspondence characterizing a non-empty constraint set that depends on a. In our case: $a = (y, w)$ and $f(x, a) = wx$, so f is a continuous function in w for any x. The role of G here is played by L, a continuous correspondence (due to the assumption that T is closed), but $L(y)$ is not compact (since it is not bounded). Yet, we can just focus on the compact part of $L(y)$, e.g. $\tilde{L}(y, w) = \{x : x \in L(y), wx \leq wx^{o}, \text{ for some } x^{o} \in L(y)\}$. Thus, letting $G(a) = \tilde{L}(y, w)$ would guarantee that $C(y, w)$ is a continuous function in $w > \mathbf{0}_{N}$. Because y is not present in the continuous objective function of the cost optimization, one cannot guarantee that $C(y, w)$ is always continuous, i.e., jumps are possible yet they will be finite by similar reasoning, and since $C(y, w)$ is a minimization problem, the lower values at the jumps will be taken, meaning that $C(y, w)$ is lower semi-continuous in y. $\qquad\square$

CHAPTER 3

Efficiency Measurement

For ages that passed (and probably ages yet to come), economists have had an enormous interest in the ability to measure and analyze the performance of various economic systems and their individual *decision-making units* (often abbreviated as DMUs), such as an employee or a group thereof, a firm, a shop, a public agency, a bank, a hospital, an industry of these units, an entire country or a region of countries, or the entire world.

Only recently has such an interest culminated in a relatively young and fast-growing area of economic and econometric thought – *the efficiency and productivity analysis* – which has become one of the sub-fields of modern economics, as indicated, for example, by its inclusion in the RePEc rankings in economics.[1]

Theoretical research in this area has provided practitioners with various tools for answering such important questions as, for example, which types of management or policy measures or ownership structures or types of regulations of various firms (industries, countries, etc) are associated with greater efficiency and productivity in practice.

Before considering practical estimation issues, however, it is imperative to understand the major underpinnings of the *theory* of efficiency measurement. The goal of this chapter is to outline the essence of this theory, which, as the reader will recognize, is heavily based on the neoclassical production theory and briefly outlined in the previous chapters. In particular, we will consider a few of the most commonly used measures of efficiency, their relationship among each other, and some of their major properties.

3.1 VARIOUS MEASURES OF TECHNICAL EFFICIENCY

In the previous chapter, we tried to tame the functional characterization of technology via the distance functions and noticed that it is a convenient measure of efficiency. In this section, we elaborate on this measure as well as considering a few other alternatives offered in the literature.

---

[1] E.g., see https://ideas.repec.org/top/top.eff.html

The definition of the frontier is very important here. In general, the frontier of a set characterization of technology (T or $P(x)$ or $L(y)$) can be thought of as the intersection of the set itself and the closure of the complement of this set. This general definition, however, is not very functional. One very convenient definition of the "frontier of the output sets" or the "output isoquants" that has been frequently used in practice for measuring output efficiency was already given in Chapter 1, i.e.,

$$\partial P(x) \equiv \{y \ : \ y \in P(x), \quad \theta y \notin P(x), \quad \forall \theta \in (1, \infty)\}, x \in \mathfrak{R}_+^N. \quad (3.1.1)$$

Such a (radial-fashion) definition of output isoquants is very convenient from the point of view of the output-oriented Farrell technical efficiency measure, which we have defined above as

$$TE(x, y) \equiv \max\{\theta \ : \ \theta y \in P(x)\}, \ y \in P(x). \quad (3.1.2)$$

We can think of the "state of full or perfect technical efficiency" of an observation $(x^o, y^o) \in T$ as a situation where this observation belongs to the technological *frontier*. In the Farrell sense under output orientation (i.e., measuring as a radial expansion in the output space), this happens if and only if $y^o \in \partial P(x^o)$. And, whenever this happens, we have $TE(x^o, y^o)$ being equal to unity (indicating 100 percent technical efficiency, in the Farrell sense). Formally,

$$TE(x^o, y^o) = 1 \quad \Leftrightarrow \quad y^o \in \partial P(x^o). \quad (3.1.3)$$

We have called this appealing property the *indication* (or *identification*) property, since we are able to identify the *output isoquant* defined in (3.1.1). Another reason the Farrell measure of technical efficiency seems to have been most popular in practice stems from its quite simple *interpretation*. Specifically, a particular point (x^o, y^o) is *technically* inefficient (in the Farrell sense) *wrt* the isoquant defined in (3.1.1) if and only if

$$1 < TE(x^o, y^o) < \infty, \quad (3.1.4)$$

and the value of $TE(x^o, y^o)$ itself represents the proportion by which *all* outputs of vector y^o must be increased *simultaneously*, while keeping input x^o and technology $P(x^o)$ fixed at the same level. So the quantity $[1 - 1/TE(x^o, y^o)]$ can be called the *percentage* of the (Farrell-type or "*radial*") output "inefficiency" of observation (x^o, y^o) relative to its potential (x^o, y^*), where y^* is the *radial* projection of y^o onto the frontier of $P(x^o)$. In fact, another way to understand $TE(x^o, y^o)$ is to note that,

$$TE(x^o, y^o) = \ \|y^*\| / \|y^o\|,$$

i.e., the Farrell output-oriented measure of technical efficiency at point (x^o, y^o) is a ratio of the Euclidean norm of y^* (the *radial* projection of y^o onto the frontier of $P(x^o)$) to the Euclidean norm of y^o. Similar explanations can be given to the other Farrell-type measures.

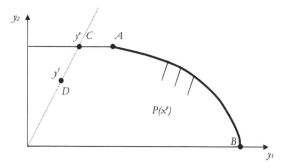

Figure 3.1 An example of the failure of the Farrell measure to identify the efficient subset of the isoquant.

One could ask a natural question: Why must the increase in outputs necessarily be "equiproportionate"? Such a change is clearly allowed by our disposability axioms, yet that does not mean that such an increase would necessarily be the "most reasonable". Figure 3.1, illustrates this argument geometrically: the firm observed at point C, with output $y^o = (y_1^o, y_2^o)$, is on the output isoquant, it is Farrell-type technically efficient, but at that point the firm can produce more of output y_1 – without changing the other output (y_2), with the same inputs and the same technology, e.g., with allocation anywhere on the line segment between C and A. Extending the reasoning further, perhaps a firm with an inefficient allocation such as point D should be compared not to point C, as the Farrell measure would do, but to a point on the "efficient part of the isoquant", e.g., such as point A.

This drawback of the Farrell-type technical efficiency measure was tackled in the seminal paper of Färe and Lovell (1978), who suggested an alternative and called it *the Russell measure of technical efficiency* (hereafter RTE). Here, we redefine RTE for the output-oriented case (for $y \in P(x)$), as following,[2]

$$RTE(x, y) \equiv \max_{\theta_1, \dots, \theta_M} \left\{ \left(\sum_{m=1}^{M} \delta(y_m) \right)^{-1} \sum_{m=1}^{M} \theta_m \delta(y_m) : \right.$$

$$\left. (\theta_1 y_1, \dots, \theta_M y_M) \in P(x), \ \theta_m \geq 1, m = 1, \dots, M \right\},$$

$$(3.1.5)$$

where

$$\delta(y_m) \equiv \begin{cases} 1, & y_m > 0 \\ 0, & y_m = 0 \end{cases}, \ m = 1, \dots, M$$

[2] Färe and Lovell (1978) originally considered only the input orientation. In fact, in the past, just the input-oriented measures were often introduced or presented with statements that developments for the output analogues are similar (which is usually true) and this left some gaps in the literature and we will try to fill some of these gaps in this book, especially because popularity of output-oriented measures in practice has substantially increased.

is a device to ensure that only strictly positive outputs effectively partici-
pate in the scaling towards the frontier (think what happens without it when
some output is zero!). Intuitively, this measure of efficiency takes inputs
and technology as fixed and searches for such an expansion of *any* outputs
$y_m (m = 1, \ldots, M)$ through the individual multipliers θ_m corresponding to
each output $m = 1, \ldots, M$, so that the sum (or average) of these multipliers is
maximized.

Clearly, the Russell measure would not run into the problem illustrated in
Figure 3.1, since it would be identifying another type of frontier – the *efficient
output isoquant*, sometimes called the *efficient subset of the (radial) output
isoquant*, in the sense that

$$RTE(x^o, y^o) = 1 \quad \Leftrightarrow \quad y^o \in eff \; \partial P(x^o),$$

where *eff* $\partial P(x)$ is formally defined as

$$eff \; \partial P(x) \equiv \{y : y \in P(x), \; y^o \notin P(x), \; \forall y^o \geq y\}, \; x \in \Re^N_+, \quad (3.1.6)$$

and, in Figure 3.1, it is highlighted with a thicker curve (from A to B).

Although the Russell measure is appealing, it does not possess some of the
desirable properties (of an efficiency index), such as the homogeneity property (check!). Moreover, it is also harder to interpret the scores of the Russell
measure, unlike in the Farrell case.

To improve upon the Russell measure, Zieschang (1984) suggested another
alternative, which is often referred to as the Zieschang measure of technical
efficiency – it is a *hybrid* of the Farrell measure and the Russell measure, and
we redefine it here for the output-oriented case as follows:

$$ZTE(x, y) \equiv RTE(x, y \times TE(x, y)) \times TE(x, y). \quad (3.1.7)$$

The measure (3.1.7) would be equivalent to the Farrell measure (3.1.2) if the
input isoquant coincides with its efficient subset (i.e., when (3.1.1) and (3.1.6)
are equal). They also would be numerically equal for the points whose radial
expansions project onto the efficient subset. Otherwise, as for point (x^o, y^1)
in Figure 3.1, the Zieschang measure would first make the radial expansion
and then would use the Russell measure to remove what is often referred to
as "slack" from the Farrell-adjusted output to reach the closest point in the
efficient subset, i.e., first go from point D to C and then to A in Figure 3.1.
This measure is clearly homogeneous of degree (-1) in all outputs (check!)
and also identifies the efficient subset of the output isoquant, in the sense
that

$$ZTE(x^o, y^o) = 1 \quad \Leftrightarrow \quad y^o \in eff \; \partial P(x^o).$$

All the measures above also have their input-orientation analogues, some of
which will be discussed in the next section. Meanwhile, note again that, in general, the input-oriented efficiency measures can give very different values than
the output-oriented efficiency measures, even in the case of Farrell measures
(even after conversion to the same scale). Indeed, from Chapter 1 we know
that only in special cases one can establish a one-to-one relationship between

$D_o(x, y)$ and $D_i(y, x)$. E.g., we know that technology is CRS if and only if $D_o(x, y) = 1/D_i(y, x)$, but there is no general explicit relationship between the two. Indeed, in general, we can have $D_o(x, y) = 1$ but $D_i(y, x) \neq 1$ (and possibly very far from 1), which may imply different conclusions and policy implications.[3]

Not surprisingly, the next wave of efficiency analysis research was influenced by a concern that even for non-Farrell-type measures, the orientation was fixed to be either measurement in the input space or in the output space. This was one of the motivations for Färe et al. (1985) to introduce another interesting efficiency measure, which can be viewed as a synthesis of the input and the output distance functions, and is often referred to as the *hyperbolic efficiency measure*. It is based on the *hyperbolic distance function* $HD : \mathfrak{R}_+^N \times \mathfrak{R}_+^M \to \mathfrak{R}_+ \cup \{+\infty\}$ defined as

$$HD(x, y) = \inf_{\lambda} \{\lambda > 0 : (\lambda x, y/\lambda) \in T\}, \tag{3.1.8}$$

i.e., this measure contracts all inputs and expands all outputs by the same proportion, via the scalar λ, until the allocation $(\lambda x, y/\lambda)$ reaches the frontier. The trajectory of such projection towards the frontier in the (x, y)-space appears as a hyperbola, giving rise to its name. It should be clear (check!) that $HD(x^o, y^o) \in [0, 1]$ if and only if $(x^o, y^o) \in T$ and

$$HD(x^o, y^o) = 1 \quad \Leftrightarrow \quad (x^o, y^o) \in \partial_H T,$$

where $\partial_H T$ is yet another definition of the frontier of technology set T, given by

$$\partial_H T \equiv \{(x, y) : (x, y) \in T, (\delta x, y/\delta) \notin T, \forall \delta \in [0, 1]\}.$$

About the same time, Charnes et al. (1985) introduced another concept – the *additive* technical efficiency measure, which we redefine here as

$$AdTE(x, y) \equiv \max_{\substack{\theta_1, \dots, \theta_M, \\ \lambda_1, \dots, \lambda_N}} \left\{ \frac{1}{M + N} \left(\sum_{m=1}^{M} \theta_m + \sum_{j=1}^{N} \lambda_j \right) : \right.$$

$$(x_1 - \lambda_1, \dots, x_N - \lambda_N, y_1 + \theta_1, \dots, y_M + \theta_M) \in T,$$

$$\left. \theta_m \geq 0, \ m = 1, \dots, M, \quad \lambda_j \geq 0, \ j = 1, \dots, N \right\}. \tag{3.1.9}$$

Intuitively, this measure can be understood as an "additive" analogue of the Russell measure (which could also be redefined to simultaneously contract inputs and expand outputs, with individual scalars). It must be also clear that the additive measure is *not* homogeneous of any degree. An important advantage of it is that it identifies the efficient subset of the entire technological frontier in the sense that

$$AdTE(x^o, y^o) = 0 \quad \Leftrightarrow \quad (x^o, y^o) \in eff \partial T,$$

---

[3] Usually, the difference is not very large near smooth parts of the technology frontier or when technology is close to CRS, but these are not always the case in practice.

where

$$eff\,\partial T \equiv \{(x, y) \,:\, (x, y) \in T,\ (x^o, y^o) \notin T, \forall (-x^o, y^o) \geq (-x, y)\}.$$
$$(3.1.10)$$

The efficiency characterized via (3.1.10) is sometimes referred to as the *Pareto–Koopmans efficiency*, which we define in words below.

Definition. A production allocation $(x, y) \in T$ is called *Pareto–Koopmans efficient* for a given technology T if and only if under that technology T it is impossible to increase any of the outputs without decreasing some other outputs or increasing some of the inputs from x, as well as impossible to decrease any of the inputs without increasing some other inputs or decreasing the output y.

Note that while $AdTE$ identifies Pareto–Koopmans efficiency, it does not have such a nice interpretation (e.g., the percentage of inefficiency) as, for example, the Farrell measure. In fact, the unit of measurement of this measure, in its original form, is not clear: Indeed, the objective function is adding expansions of *different* outputs (apples, oranges, etc.) with contractions of *different* inputs (people, cars, etc.) – so the final units of measurement are unclear![4]

Yet another measure of efficiency that can take virtually any direction of measurement predetermined by a researcher is the efficiency measure that is based on the *directional distance function* (DDF), which we already discussed in the previous chapters, defining it as

$$D_d(x, y \,|\, {-}d_x, d_y) \equiv \sup_{\theta}\{\theta \in \mathfrak{R} \,:\, (x - \theta d_x, y + \theta d_y) \in T\}, \quad (3.1.11)$$

where $(-d_x, d_y)$ is a nonzero vector in $\mathfrak{R}^N_- \times \mathfrak{R}^M_+$ stipulating the direction along which the distance between (x, y) and the upper frontier of T is measured.

Intuitively, and as illustrated in Figure 3.2, for a particular point (x^o, y^o), this measure yields the number representing the "portion" of the directional vector $(-d_x, d_y)$ that must be added to this observation (x^o, y^o) to move it to the frontier of T, in the direction $(-d_x, d_y)$. The reader must have also noticed already that this measure may not always identify the *efficient* subset of the technological frontier – only the frontier defined in terms of the particular direction $(-d_x, d_y)$, i.e.,

$$D_d(x^o, y^o \,|\, {-}d_x, d_y) = 0 \quad \Leftrightarrow \quad (x^o, y^o) \in \partial_d T,$$

---

[4] An easy fix of this unit of measurement problem is to normalize each input slack and output slack by their corresponding inputs and outputs (observed for the corresponding firm or their averages or their standard deviations for the analyzed sample), e.g., see Tone (2001) and references therein and our discussion at the end of this chapter.

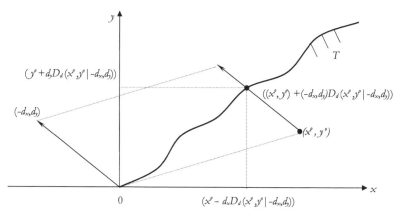

Figure 3.2 Geometric intuition of the directional distance function.

where

$$\partial_d T \equiv \{(x, y) : (x, y) \in T, \ (x', y') \equiv ((x, y) + \lambda(-d_x, d_y)) \notin T, \forall \lambda > 0\}.$$

As we will show in the next section, this last measure is a generalization of both the input and the output distance functions (and Farrell measures of technical efficiency). The advantage of this measure is that it allows for any direction in the output space and/or input space (including the radial directions) – which can be specified by the vector $(-d_x, d_y)$. This same feature, however, also implies a disadvantage – the need to choose a particular direction from the infinity of options. To our knowledge, the question of objective or theoretically well-justified choice of direction has remained largely unresolved before this book was finished. As a result, the practical complication in real-world applications is that the choice of direction for a researcher is usually ambiguous or somewhat *ad hoc*. It must be also clear that the additive measure is *not* homogeneous of any degree, yet satisfies the translation property, as we will notice in the next section. One also must be careful about the interpretation of the unit of measurement of efficiency measure based on the DDF because it may depend on the directional vector, as are results and conclusions.

3.2 RELATIONSHIPS AMONG EFFICIENCY MEASURES

In this section, we show a few key relationships between various efficiency measures. In particular, we will first discuss the relationship between the Shephard and the DDFs. We then discuss the relationship between the Farrell and the Russell efficiency measure and, analogously, between the DDF and the additive measure of efficiency.

3.2.1   Shephard vs. Directional Distance Functions

In this subsection we follow Chambers et al. (1996b, 1998) and Zelenyuk (2002, 2014a). To obtain our main results, let us recall the following useful properties that were discussed above:

$$(x, y) \in T \Leftrightarrow D_o(x, y) \leq 1 \Leftrightarrow D_i(y, x) \geq 1, \tag{3.2.1}$$

$$D_o(x, ky) = kD_o(x, y) \text{ and } D_i(y, kx) = kD_i(y, x), \ \forall k > 0, \tag{3.2.2}$$

$$CRS \Leftrightarrow D_o(kx, y) = (1/k)D_o(x, y), \ \forall k > 0,$$

$$\Leftrightarrow D_i(ky, x) = (1/k)D_i(y, x), \ \forall k > 0, \tag{3.2.3}$$

$$CRS \Leftrightarrow D_o(x, y) = 1/D_i(y, x), \tag{3.2.4}$$

where, recall that CRS means the "technology exhibits constant returns to scale," defined as: $\lambda T = T, \forall \lambda > 0$.

In addition, recall that $D_d(\cdot)$ is also a complete characterization of technology, in the sense that

$$(x, y) \in T \Leftrightarrow D_d(x, y; -d_x, d_y) \geq 0, \ (d_x, d_y) \geq (\mathbf{0}_N, \mathbf{0}_M). \tag{3.2.5}$$

The next theorem shows that, $D_d(\cdot)$ is a generalization of $D_i(\cdot)$ and $D_o(\cdot)$.

Theorem. *Given the main regularity axioms, we have:*

(a) *if the directional vector* $(-d_x, d_y)$ *is* $(-x, \mathbf{0}_M)$, *then*

$$D_d(x, y; -x, \mathbf{0}_M) = 1 - 1/D_i(y, x), \tag{3.2.6}$$

(b) *if the directional vector* $(-d_x, d_y)$ *is* $(\mathbf{0}_N, y)$, *then*

$$D_d(x, y; \mathbf{0}_N, y) = 1/D_o(x, y) - 1. \tag{3.2.7}$$

Proof. To sketch a proof of part (a), note that

$$\begin{aligned}
D_d(x, y; -x, \mathbf{0}_M) &\equiv \sup\{\theta : (x - \theta x, y + \mathbf{0}_M) \in T\} \\
&= \sup\{\theta : (x(1 - \theta), y) \in T\} \\
&= \sup\{\theta : D_i(y, x(1 - \theta)) \geq 1\} \quad \text{(by (3.2.1))} \\
&= \sup\{\theta : D_i(y, x)(1 - \theta) \geq 1\} \quad \text{(by (3.2.2))} \\
&= \sup\{\theta : (D_i(y, x) - 1)/D_i(y, x) \geq \theta\} \quad \text{(rearranging terms)} \\
&= (D_i(y, x) - 1)/D_i(y, x) = 1 - 1/D_i(y, x),
\end{aligned}$$

where the last equation is due to optimization over θ. Part (b) is analogous and so is left as an exercise. $\square$

Note that the relationship described by this theorem requires either y or x direction to be zero. What about a relationship when directions in both x and y are accounted for? In the following theorem we summarize one such relationship for *CRS*. In contrast to (3.2.6) or (3.2.7), note that the relationship holds for a direction $(-d_x, d_y)$ positioned anywhere "in-between" (and including) the directions in (3.2.6) or (3.2.7), in the sense that the direction can be characterized by the linear combination

$$(-\alpha x, \beta y) = \alpha(-x, \mathbf{0}_M) + \beta(\mathbf{0}_N, y), \ \forall (\alpha, \beta) \geq (0, 0).$$

We formalize and prove this claim below (following Zelenyuk, 2002, 2014a).

Theorem. *Let* $(-d_x, d_y) = (-\alpha x, \beta y) \neq \mathbf{0}_{N+M}, \ \forall (\alpha, \beta) \geq (0, 0)$, *then* T *exhibits CRS if and only if*

$$D_d(x, y; -d_x, d_y) = (D_i(y, x) - 1)/(\alpha D_i(y, x) + \beta), \qquad (3.2.8)$$

and

$$D_d(x, y; -d_x, d_y) = (1 - D_o(x, y))/(\beta D_o(x, y) + \alpha). \qquad (3.2.9)$$

Proof. $(\Rightarrow)$: suppose T exhibits *CRS*, then:

$$
\begin{aligned}
D_d&(x, y; -\alpha x, \beta y) \\
&\equiv \sup\{\theta : (x - \theta(\alpha x), y + \theta(\beta y)) \in T\} \\
&= \sup\{\theta : (x(1 - \alpha\theta), y(1 + \beta\theta)) \in T\} \\
&= \sup\{\theta : D_i(y(1 + \beta\theta), x(1 - \alpha\theta)) \geq 1\} \quad \text{(by (3.2.1))} \\
&= \sup\{\theta : D_i(y, x)(1 - \alpha\theta) \geq (1 + \beta\theta)\} \ ((3.2.2) - (3.2.3)) \\
&= \sup\{\theta : (D_i(y, x) - 1)/(\alpha D_i(y, x) + \beta) \geq \theta\} \\
&= (D_i(y, x) - 1)/(\alpha D_i(y, x) + \beta). \text{ (due to opt. over } \theta)
\end{aligned}
$$

By the same logic, it follows that:

$$
\begin{aligned}
D_d&(x, y; -\alpha x, \beta y) \\
&\equiv \sup\{\theta : (x - \theta(\alpha x), y + \theta(\beta y)) \in T\} \\
&= \sup\{\theta : (x(1 - \alpha\theta), y(1 + \beta\theta)) \in T\} \\
&= \sup\{\theta : D_o(x(1 - \alpha\theta), y(1 + \beta\theta)) \leq 1\} \\
&= \sup\{\theta : D_o(x, y)(1 + \beta\theta) \leq (1 - \alpha\theta)\} \\
&= \sup\{\theta : \theta \leq (1 - D_o(x, y))/(\beta D_o(x, y) + \alpha)\} \\
&= (1 - D_o(x, y))/(\beta D_o(x, y) + \alpha).
\end{aligned}
$$

$(\Leftarrow)$: assume (3.2.8) and (3.2.9) are true, then after rearranging terms in (3.2.8) and (3.2.9), we get

$$D_i(y, x) = (1 + \beta D_d(x, y; -\alpha x, \beta y))/(1 - \alpha D_d(x, y; -\alpha x, \beta y)), \quad (3.2.10)$$

and

$$D_o(x, y) = (1 - \alpha D_d(x, y; -\alpha x, \beta y))/(1 + \beta D_d(x, y; -\alpha x, \beta y)). \quad (3.2.11)$$

Clearly, (3.2.8) and (3.2.9) together imply $D_i(y, x) = 1/D_o(x, y)$, which in turn is equivalent to *CRS*, by property (3.2.4).[5]   □

Intuitively, this theorem says that, under *CRS*, one can use Shephard's distance functions to solve explicitly for the DDF (and vice versa) with any direction "in-between" $(-x, 0)$ and $(0, y)$, as described by a linear combination of these extremes. Because the CRS assumption is often used in economics, this theorem may be very useful in many studies involving multi-output technologies where currently Shephard's distance functions are used. As an example, we will see an application of this theorem to productivity measurement, in Chapter 4.

3.2.2   Farrell vs. Russell Measures

This subsection is based on Zelenyuk (2002); Färe et al. (2007). We will focus only on the input-oriented efficiency measures, and it will be relatively clear how to extend the analysis into the output-oriented case.

First of all, recall that the (*radial-type*) input isoquant is defined as

$$\partial L(y) = \{x : x \in L(y), \lambda x \notin L(y), 0 < \lambda < 1\}, \ y \in \Re_+^M, \ (3.2.12)$$

and the efficient subsets of this isoquant would be

$$eff\partial L(y) = \{x : x \in L(y), x' \le x \Rightarrow x' \notin L(y)\}, \ y \in \Re_+^M. \ (3.2.13)$$

Our goal here is to find conditions on the technology, characterized by $L(y)$ for any $y \in \Re_+^M$, such that the Farrell measure is identically equal to the Russell measure for all $x \in L(y)$. This is possible if we *redefine* the original Russell measure into a *multiplicative* version – where the objective function is the geometric rather than arithmetic mean. Thus, the input-oriented *multiplicative* Russell measure is defined as,

$$MRTE(y, x) = \min_{\lambda_1, \ldots, \lambda_N} \left\{ (\prod_{j=1}^N \lambda_j)^{1/N} : (\lambda_1 x_1, \ldots, \lambda_N x_N) \in L(y), \right.$$

$$\left. 0 < \lambda_j \le 1, j = 1, \ldots, N \right\}. \quad (3.2.14)$$

The objective function here is $(\prod_{j=1}^N \lambda_j)^{1/N}$ in contrast to $\sum_{j=1}^N \lambda_j/N$ from the original version in Färe and Lovell (1978). Note that this definition might be somewhat "more natural" than the original one, since the λ_js are "multiplicative" by construction in the Russell-type measures (i.e., we contract the inputs towards the efficient isoquant by multiplying) and so it seems "more natural" to aggregate multiplicative objects with a multiplicative (rather than

---

[5] Also note that if $(\alpha, \beta) = (0, 1)$ or $(\alpha, \beta) = (1, 0)$, then (3.2.6) and (3.2.7) follow immediately from the theorem.

additive) aggregation function. For technical reasons we also assume for this subsection that inputs $x = (x_1, \ldots, x_N)$ are strictly positive, i.e., $x_j > 0$, $j = 1, \ldots, N$. In other words, in this section we assume that for $L(y)$ is a subset of the *interior* of $\mathfrak{R}_+^N$ for any $y \geq \mathbf{0}_M$, $y \neq \mathbf{0}_M$.[6]

Note that the multiplicative Russell measure in (3.2.14) satisfies the following *indication* property

$$MRTE(y, x) = 1 \; if \; and \; only \; if \; x \in eff \; \partial L(y). \tag{3.2.15}$$

Also recall that the input-oriented Farrell measure of technical efficiency is the reciprocal of Shephard's input distance function, i.e.

$$TE_i(y, x) = 1/D_i(y, x), \tag{3.2.16}$$

thus, it is homogeneous of degree (-1) in x and, clearly, satisfies the same *indication* property as $D_i(y, x)$.

Now, assume the technology is *input homothetic*, i.e., satisfies

$$L(y) = H(y)L(\mathbf{1}_M), \; y \in \mathfrak{R}_+^M, \tag{3.2.17}$$

for some appropriate function $H(y)$,[7] then it is equivalent to

$$D_i(y, x) = D_i(\mathbf{1}_M, x)/H(y). \tag{3.2.18}$$

In addition, assume the input aggregation function $D_i(\mathbf{1}_M, x)$ is a *geometric mean*, then the distance function is given by

$$D_i(y, x) = \left(\prod_{j=1}^{N} x_j \right)^{1/N} /H(y). \tag{3.2.19}$$

Furthermore, note that by the definition of the distance function and the complete characterization property (3.2.1), the input distance function takes the form in (3.2.19) *if and only if* the input requirement sets are given by

$$L(y) = H(y) \cdot \left\{ \hat{x} : \left(\prod_{j=1}^{N} \hat{x}_j \right)^{1/N} \geq 1 \right\}, \; \hat{x}_j = \frac{x_j}{H(y)}, \; y \in \mathfrak{R}_+^M. \tag{3.2.20}$$

We are now ready to state the theorem that establishes the relationship between the Farrell and the Russell measures.

Theorem. *Assume that $L(y)$ is interior to $\mathfrak{R}_+^M$ for $y \geq \mathbf{0}_M$ ($y \neq \mathbf{0}_M$), satisfies the main regularity axioms on technology and weak disposability of inputs, then $\forall x \in L(y)$ we have*

---

[6] See Russell (1990) for a related assumption.

[7] For more details on input homotheticity, see Färe and Primont (1995), Zelenyuk (2014b) and references cited therein. Also see Chapter 4.

$$MRTE(y, x) = TE_i(y, x) \Leftrightarrow D_i(y, x) = \left(\prod_{j=1}^{N} x_j\right)^{1/N} /H(y). \quad (3.2.21)$$

Proof. (See Appendix.) □

In words, the theorem says that for the Farrell and Russell efficiency measures to yield identical efficiency scores for any point in the technology set, the technology must satisfy a peculiar case of *input homotheticity* – technology must be of a fairly restricted Cobb–Douglas form for aggregating inputs, and with equal weights in the aggregation. To learn about the cost interpretation of the Russell measure, the reader is invited to visit Färe et al. (2007) and Zelenyuk (2002, 2014b).

3.2.3   Directional Distance Function vs. Additive Measure

This subsection is also based on Färe et al. (2002); Färe et al. (2007) and Zelenyuk (2002). Again, we will focus only on the input-oriented efficiency measures and the output-oriented case is analogous. In particular, we are going to show the relationship between the special case of (1.6.1) – the directional *input* distance function, defined as

$$\vec{D}_i(y, x; -d_x) \equiv \sup\{\beta \; : \; (x - \beta d_x) \in L(y)\}, \quad (3.2.22)$$

where $d_x \in \mathfrak{R}_+^N$ is the directional vector according to which the inefficiency is measured. For the purpose of finding the desired relationship, we choose $d_x = \mathbf{1}_N = (1, 1 \ldots, 1) \in \mathfrak{R}_+^N$. The function $\vec{D}_i(y, x; -\mathbf{1}_N)$ has properties that are similar to those of $D_i(y, x)$ and the ones that we will use are listed in the following theorem.

Theorem. *Given the main regularity axioms on technology and the strong disposability of inputs, we have*

(i) $\vec{D}_i(y, x; -\mathbf{1}_N) \geq 0$ *if and only if* $x \in L(y)$, $(3.2.23)$

(ii) $\vec{D}_i(y, x + \alpha\mathbf{1}_N; -\mathbf{1}_N) = \vec{D}_i(y, x; -\mathbf{1}_N) + \alpha$, $\alpha > 0$,
    $(3.2.24)$

(iii) (a) *if* $\vec{D}_i(y, x; -\mathbf{1}_N) = 0$ *and* $x_j > 0$, $j = 1, \ldots, N$,
    $(3.2.25)$

    then $x \in \partial_d L(y)$,

(iii) (b) $x \in \partial_1 L(y) \Rightarrow \vec{D}_i(y, x; -\mathbf{1}_N) = 0$, $(3.2.26)$

where

$$\partial_1 L(y) \equiv \{x \; : \; x \in L(y), x^o \equiv (x - \lambda\mathbf{1}_N) \notin L(y), \forall \lambda > 0\}.$$

Proof. (See Appendix.) □

Our goal is to derive conditions on the technology, characterized by $L(y)$, $y \in \mathfrak{R}_+^M$, that are necessary and sufficient for the DDF and the additive measure of technical efficiency to yield identical efficiency scores.

The *input*-oriented analogue of the *additive* measure of technical efficiency can be defined as

$$AdTE_i(y, x) = \max_{s_1,\ldots,s_N} \left\{ \frac{1}{N} \sum_{j=1}^N s_j : \right.$$

$$\left. (x_1 - s_1, \ldots, x_N - s_N) \in L(y), s_j \geq 0, \ j = 1, \ldots, N \right\}.$$

$$(3.2.27)$$

Intuitively, this measure of efficiency searches for maximal reduction of "slack" in each input x_n that will still allow the targeted level of output y to be produced. Alternatively, and loosely speaking, one can think of (3.2.27) as a problem of minimizing costs if all input prices are equal to one. Note that the original additive measure introduced by Charnes et al. (1985) simultaneously expanded outputs and contracted inputs, while here we consider a version that contracts only inputs, in the additive form of the original measure, with normalization by the constant N (total number of inputs). Also, we allow for a wide class of technologies – all that satisfy the main regularity axioms and strong disposability of inputs.

The reader might have noticed a remarkable similarity between the additive measure (3.2.27) and the *multiplicative* Russell measure (3.2.14). Since the latter has a relationship to the Farrell measure, which in turn is a multiplicative analog to the DDF – it should be expected that there exists a relationship between (3.2.27) and (3.2.14) that is analogous to the one we have stated in (3.2.21).

To establish such a relationship, consider first a technology that satisfies the property of *translation input homotheticity*, i.e.,

$$L(y) = L(\mathbf{0}_M) + F(y)\mathbf{1}_N, y \in \mathfrak{R}_+^M, \qquad (3.2.28)$$

which in turn is equivalent to

$$\vec{D}_i(y, x; -\mathbf{1}_N) = \vec{D}_i(\mathbf{0}_M, x; -\mathbf{1}_N) - F(y). \qquad (3.2.29)$$

Moreover, if we assume that the aggregator function $\vec{D}_i(\mathbf{0}_M, x; -\mathbf{1}_N)$ is the arithmetic mean, then the DDF may be written as

$$\vec{D}_i(y, x; -\mathbf{1}_N) = \frac{1}{N} \sum_{j=1}^N x_j - F(y). \qquad (3.2.30)$$

From the properties of the DDF listed in (3.2.23)–(3.2.26), it follows that (3.2.30) is true *if and only if* the input requirement sets are of the form given by

$$L(y) = \left\{ \tilde{x} : \frac{1}{N} \sum_{j=1}^{N} \tilde{x}_j \geq 0 \right\} + F(y), \tag{3.2.31}$$

where $\tilde{x} = (x_1 - F(y), \ldots, x_N - F(y))$.

With these building blocks, one should be ready to understand the technology under which the relationship between the DDF and the *additive* measure can be established, as we summarize below.

Theorem. *Given the main regularity axioms on technology and strong disposability of inputs,* $\forall x \in C(L(y)) \equiv \{\hat{x} : \hat{x} = x + \delta \mathbf{1}_N, x \in L(y), \delta \geq 0\}$ *we have*

$$\vec{D}_i(y, x; -\mathbf{1}_N) = AdTE_i(y, x) \tag{3.2.32}$$

if and only if

$$\vec{D}_i(y, x; -\mathbf{1}_N) = \frac{1}{N} \sum_{j=1}^{N} x_j - F(y). \tag{3.2.33}$$

Proof. (See Appendix.)   □

In words, the theorem says that in order to get the equivalence between DDF and the additive measure, technology must be *linear* in inputs, and with equal coefficients. For example, in the two-input case, the isoquants must be straight lines with slopes equal to (-1). The reader might have noticed already a remarkable similarity of the results in this theorem with the result of the theorem for equivalence between the Farrell measure and the Russell measure. The reader is also invited to consult Färe et al. (2002), Färe et al. (2007) and Zelenyuk (2002) to learn about an intuitive cost interpretation of the additive measure.

3.2.4   Hyperbolic vs. Others

First of all, recall that the input and the output distance functions are reciprocals to each other under the CRS, and so, because the hyperbolic efficiency measure is a synthesis of these two, we expect that there might be a one-to-one relationship between the hyperbolic efficiency measure and the input (and output) distance function(s). There is one indeed, as is summarized below.

Theorem. *T exhibits CRS if and only if*

$$HD(x, y) = (D_o(x, y))^{1/2} = (1/D_i(y, x))^{1/2}. \tag{3.2.34}$$

Proof. *T* exhibits CRS means $\delta T = T$, $\forall \delta > 0$, and thus

$$HD(x, y) = \inf_{\lambda} \{\lambda > 0 : (\lambda x, y/\lambda) \in T\}$$

$$= \inf_{\lambda} \left\{ \lambda > 0 \ : \ (x, y/\lambda^2) \in (1/\lambda)T \right\}$$

$$= \inf_{\lambda} \left\{ \lambda > 0 \ : \ (x, y/\lambda^2) \in T \right\} \ \text{(due to CRS)}$$

$$= (\inf_{\theta} \{\theta > 0 \ : \ (x, y/\theta) \in T\})^{1/2} \ \ (\theta = \lambda^2)$$

$$= (D_o(x, y))^{1/2} = (1/D_i(y, x))^{1/2},$$

where we used the rule of monotone transformation in optimization. Using similar logic as was used in Chapter 1, it is easy to show that (3.2.34) implies CRS (see Färe et al., 1994b). □

What about a relationship with the directional distance function? In the light of our discussions above, one might expect there should be some. Indeed, the theorem above can be merged with the results about Shephard's distance functions vs. the directional distance function outlined above (see (3.2.6), (3.2.7), (3.2.8) and (3.2.9)), to relate the latter to the hyperbolic efficiency measure, under CRS. There is also a more general although approximate result which does not require CRS, as described below.

Theorem. *The directional distance function with direction $d = (-x, y)$ gives the first-order approximation (near the frontier) to the hyperbolic efficiency measure. Formally, we have*

$$HD(x, y) \approx 1/(1 + D_d(x, y| - x, y)). \tag{3.2.35}$$

Proof. [8] First, note that $\theta^{-1} \approx 2 - \theta$ in the sense of the first-order Taylor series approximation around $\theta = 1$ (i.e, near the full efficiency). Thus,

$$HD(x, y) = \inf_{\lambda} \{\lambda > 0 \ : \ (\lambda x, y/\lambda) \in T\}$$

$$= 1/\sup_{\theta} \{\theta > 0 \ : \ (x/\theta, y\theta) \in T\} \ \ (\theta = 1/\lambda)$$

$$\approx 1/\sup_{\theta} \{\theta > 0 \ : \ (x(2 - \theta), y\theta) \in T\} \ \ (\theta^{-1} \approx 2 - \theta)$$

$$= 1/\sup_{\theta} \{\theta > 0 \ : \ (2x, 0) + \theta(-x, y) \in T\}$$

$$= 1/\sup_{\theta} \{\theta > 0 \ : \ (x, y) - (-x, y) + \theta(-x, y) \in T\}$$

$$= 1/\sup_{\theta} \{\theta > 0 \ : \ (x, y) + (\theta - 1)(-x, y) \in T\}$$

$$= 1/(1 + \sup_{\theta} \{(\theta - 1) \ : \ (x, y) + (\theta - 1)(-x, y) \in T\})$$

$$= 1/(1 + \sup_{\beta} \{\beta \ : \ (x, y) + \beta(-x, y) \in T\})(\beta = (\theta - 1))$$

$$= 1/(1 + D_d(x, y| - x, y)).$$

□

[8] Chung (1996) used a similar proof in a related context.

3.3 PROPERTIES OF TECHNICAL EFFICIENCY MEASURES

Despite the critiques and the appealing alternatives, the Farrell measure of technical efficiency seems to have successfully "beaten," so far, all of the other alternative measures of technical efficiency, at least by popularity in empirical use. There are a few reasons for this. One reason we have mentioned before is that the Farrell measures give quite simple and intuitive meaning to the efficiency scores they yield. Another is related to the simplicity of computation. Perhaps the most important reason for popularity of the Farrell measures is based on the desirable properties that the Farrell measures possess. Among the most important of which are the relationships to the economic theory concepts of complete (primal) characterization of technology as well as the (dual) relationship to the cost or revenue functions.

In this section, we will follow Färe and Lovell (1978) and Russell (1987, 1990, 1998) to discuss other important properties of an efficiency measure. In our discussion, we focus on the input orientation (results for the output orientation are similar). Throughout the discussion in this section, we assume that technology satisfies the main regularity axioms and *free* (strong) disposability of inputs.

When a number of alternative "measures" are offered for the same purpose, one way to select the best among the alternatives is to define a set of desirable axioms that any measure ought to satisfy. The first attempt of envisioning such axioms was launched by Färe and Lovell (1978). This set of axioms consists of three criteria, which we define below.

Definition (Färe–Lovell Axioms for efficiency measures). Let $E(y, x) \in (0, 1]$ be an input-oriented efficiency measure. We would say that:

(a) $E(y, x)$ is satisfying *Indication Axiom* if and only if $\forall x \in L(y)$, $y \in \mathfrak{R}_+^M$, $y \neq \mathbf{0}_M$ we have

$$E(y, x) = 1 \quad \Leftrightarrow \quad x \in \text{eff } \partial L(y). \tag{3.3.1}$$

(b) $E(y, x)$ is satisfying *Homogeneity Axiom* if and only if $\forall x \in L(y)$, $y \in \mathfrak{R}_+^M$, $y \neq \mathbf{0}_M$ we have

$$E(y, x\lambda) = \lambda^{-1} E(y, x), \quad \forall \lambda > 0. \tag{3.3.2}$$

(c) $E(y, x)$ is satisfying *Monotonicity Axiom* if and only if $\forall x \in L(y)$, $y \in \mathfrak{R}_+^M$, $y \neq \mathbf{0}_M$ we have

$$E(y, x) > E(y, x^o), \quad \forall x^o \geq x. \tag{3.3.3}$$

The first two axioms are already well known to the reader. The indication property says that the measure is always able to indicate whether an observation is on the *efficient* subset of the (input) isoquant or not – clearly a property that a researcher would want to have for any efficiency measure. The next criterion is related to the homogeneity (of degree -1) property of the measure as a function of inputs and outputs. This property is quite useful in technical derivations, as we have seen before, for instance in deriving results in the previous section. Intuitively, this property means that if all inputs were "inflated" by the same positive scalar, the resulting efficiency score must also be inflated by the same scalar to get the original efficiency score. The third property says that the value (score) yielded by the *input*-oriented efficiency measure should decrease if some of the inputs increase. This is quite intuitive: if more inputs are used in the production of the same output with the same technology, the efficiency index should show less efficiency or more inefficiency.

Despite the fact that the Färe–Lovell axioms consist of only three criteria, and very intuitive ones, it turns out that there does not exist an efficiency measure that would satisfy all the three axioms simultaneously, for *all* technologies (that satisfy the main regularity axioms and free disposability of inputs). This was first noted in a short but insightful article of Bol (1986), who provided us with the following theorem.

Theorem. *There does not exist an efficiency measure, $E(y, x)$, that would (simultaneously) satisfy all the Färe–Lovell axioms for all technologies.*

Proof. (See Bol, 1986.) □

Such an impossibility result should not be surprising: too much is required here so that it is simply infeasible. One way to find a "possibility theorem" is to look for a class of technologies under which an efficiency measure satisfying the Färe–Lovell axioms would exist. This route was taken by Dmitruk and Koshevoy (1991), who discovered for us the following encouraging result.

Theorem. *An efficiency measure, $E(y, x) \in (0, 1]$ (defined on $L(y)$) that (simultaneously) satisfies all the Färe–Lovell axioms exists if and only if the technology satisfies the following property:*

$$L(y) \cap \overline{CEF}(y) = eff \partial L(y), \tag{3.3.4}$$

where $\overline{CEF}(y)$ is the closure of the set defined by $CEF(y) = \mathfrak{R}^N_+ - eff \partial L(y)$.

Proof. (See Dmitruk and Koshevoy, 1991.) □

The verbal intuition of this theorem, perhaps, would be more revealing than the statement above. The theorem simply says that there exist efficiency measures that satisfy the Färe–Lovell axioms, not for all, but for a particular (and fairly large) class of technologies. For example, if the *eff* $\partial L(y)$ is a compact set then (3.3.4) is satisfied and such measures would exist. Also, if T is a polyhedral set then (3.3.4) is also satisfied. (Here, it is worth noting, jumping ahead, that the DEA estimator that we will study intensively in this book gives a polyhedral-type estimate of the true technology set.) Dmitruk and Koshevoy (1991) also provide sufficiency conditions for the Farrell efficiency measure (on augmented support) to satisfy the Färe–Lovell axioms.

Another way to reach a possibility result is to *weaken* the set of axioms – this is the route taken first by Russell (1987; 1990). What has motivated Russell to weaken the axioms was perhaps his finding that the monotonicity axiom is incompatible with another useful axiom that Russell has adopted from Eichhorn and Voeller (1976), which we formalize below.

Definition. (Russell Commensurability Axiom). Let $E(y, x) \in (0, 1]$ be an input-oriented efficiency measure. Let $\tilde{y} = \Omega_y \times y$ and $\tilde{x} = \Omega_x \times x$, where Ω_x, Ω_y are diagonal matrices (M by M and N by N, respectively) with diagonal elements being strictly positive constants. Let $\tilde{L}(\tilde{y}) \equiv \{\tilde{x} : \Omega_x^{-1} \times \tilde{x} \in L(y)\}$. We will say $E(y, x)$ satisfies *the Commensurability Axiom* if and only if

$$E(y, x) = E(\tilde{y}, \tilde{x}). \tag{3.3.5}$$

Intuitively, the commensurability axiom or property is about unit (in)dependence of the efficiency measure: it says that if one researcher uses data measured in kilograms, kilometers, etc., and another uses the same data in some other units of measurement (pounds, miles, etc.), this should not matter for using an efficiency measure that satisfies the commensurability property; even the quantitative results would be the same. Often, researchers say that such a measure is independent of the units of measurement. This is, however, strictly speaking not precisely right. With this property, what we can say for sure is that such a measure is independent of the units of measurement *up to a scalar transformation*. Other transformations may or may not influence results (e.g., think of other linear transformations such as from Celsius to Fahrenheit, or a logarithmic transformation, etc.). As a result, the commensurability axiom is a very desirable one, but Russell (1987) shows that it is incompatible with the monotonicity axiom, as is summarized in the next theorem.

Theorem. *There does not exist an efficiency measure, $E(y, x)$, that would (simultaneously) satisfy the monotonicity axiom (3.3.3) and the commensurability axiom (3.3.5), for all technologies.*

Proof. (See Russell, 1987.)   □

Again, one could try to search for a class of technologies that would allow for an efficiency measure to satisfy the monotonicity and commensurability axioms simultaneously. Another way is to realize that demanding strict monotonicity (or maybe also *strict* identification), as stated now, might be "too much" to require. This apparently was a motivation for Russell (1987) to modify the Färe–Lovell axioms into the following set of axioms.

Definition. Let $E(y, x) \in (0, 1]$ be an input-oriented efficiency measure. We will say that an efficiency measure $E(y, x)$ satisfies Färe–Lovell–Russell axioms for efficiency measures if the following is true:

(a) $E(y, x)$ is satisfying the *Weak Indication Axiom* requiring that $\forall x \in L(y)$, $y \in \mathfrak{R}_+^M$, $y \neq \mathbf{0}_M$ we have

$$E(y, x) = 1 \quad \Leftrightarrow \quad x \in weff\ \partial L(y), \tag{3.3.6}$$

where

$$weff\ \partial L(y) \equiv \{x\ :\ x \in L(y), \quad x^o \notin L(y), \forall x^o < x\}. \tag{3.3.7}$$

(b) $E(y, x)$ is satisfying the *Homogeneity Axiom* requiring that $\forall x \in L(y), y \in \mathfrak{R}_+^M$, $y \neq \mathbf{0}_M$ we have

$$E(y, x\lambda) = \lambda^{-1} E(y, x), \quad \forall \lambda > 1. \tag{3.3.8}$$

(c) $E(y, x)$ is satisfying the *Weak Monotonicity Axiom* requiring that $\forall x \in L(y), y \in \mathfrak{R}_+^M$, $y \neq \mathbf{0}_M$ we have

$$E(y, x) \geq E(y, x^o), \quad \forall x^o \geq x. \tag{3.3.9}$$

(d) $E(y, x)$ is satisfying the *Commensurability Axiom* (see definition involving (3.3.5) above).

This set of axioms differs from the Färe–Lovell axioms in three ways. First, the strict indication property is "weakened" by considering not the efficient subset of the isoquant – from which any further decrease in input causes unfeasibility, but only a decrease in *all* inputs. The radial-type contraction of inputs is a special case, and therefore $eff\ \partial L(y)$ and $\partial L(y)$ are equal for the technologies that satisfy free disposability of inputs. Second, the Färe–Lovell (strict) monotonicity axiom is weakened by now requiring the efficiency measure to indicate no less inefficiency if more of any of the inputs are used to produce the same level of outputs with the same technology (while before the measure was required to indicate strictly more inefficiency). Third, the Russell commensurability axiom (3.3.5) is added. The homogeneity axiom is retained as it was in the original Färe–Lovell axioms. With such modification, a quite positive conclusion was reached by Russell, which we summarize in the next theorem.

Theorem. *Assuming technology satisfies the main regularity axioms and free disposability of inputs:*

1. The Farrell input-oriented technical efficiency measure satisfies the Färe–Lovell–Russell axioms.
2. The (original or additive) Russell input-oriented technical efficiency measure satisfies commensurability, (strict) indication and weak monotonicity (but not homogeneity and not strict monotonicity).

    3. The Zieschang input-oriented technical efficiency measure satisfies commensurability, (strict) indication and homogeneity (but not even weak monotonicity).

Proof. (See Russell, 1987.)   □

This theorem clearly favors the Farrell efficiency measure – the only one of the three that satisfies all the Färe–Lovell–Russell axioms. This theorem, however, also shows that the Russell measure beats the Farrell measure in terms of strict identification but loses in terms of homogeneity (as we have noticed before). On the other hand, the Zieschang measure improves upon the Russell measure by restoring homogeneity but, as a result, loses perhaps an even more important property – weak monotonicity.

    The final knockout to the (original or additive) Russell and Zieschang measures was made, ironically, by Russell (1990), who suggested another set of desirable axioms that an efficiency measure ought to satisfy – based on the continuity concept. Intuitively, the continuity, say in x, of an efficiency measure implies that very small changes in x would bring about only very small changes in the value (or score) yielded by such an efficiency measure.[9] Imposition of such axioms has led Russell to derive for us the following conclusion.

Theorem. *Assuming technology satisfies the main regularity axioms and free disposability of inputs:*

    1. There does not exist an efficiency measure that satisfies the strict indication axiom (3.3.1) and the continuity (in x or/and y) axiom of Russell (1990) for all technologies.
    2. The Farrell efficiency measure is jointly continuous in x and y for all $x > \mathbf{0}_N$ (provided that the input requirement correspondence, defining the input sets $L(y)$, is continuous).

Proof. (See Russell, 1990; Russell and Schworm, 2011.)   □

The implication of this theorem is very fundamental. The first statement immediately implies that the Russell and the Zieschang measures do not satisfy the continuity axiom in general, for all technologies – simply because they satisfy the strict indication axiom. In other words, the theorem says that, in general (for all technologies), the price of preserving the strict indication property is losing the continuity property, or the price of having continuity property is losing the strict indication property.[10]

---

[9] The formal definitions of various types of continuity for an efficiency measure are based on the topology of closed convergence – for details see Russell (1990); Russell and Schworm (2011).

[10] Again, note the result is for all technologies and so there still might be a class of technologies that permits these two measures to satisfy these two axioms. Indeed, if for example one considers a class of technologies that do not have the problem of slacks (as those illustrated

Meanwhile, the second statement gives another big favor to the Farrell efficiency measure: it says that the Farrell measure does satisfy the continuity axiom.[11] I.e., intuitively, infinitesimal changes in x and y should cause only infinitesimal changes in the efficiency score yielded by the Farrell efficiency measure. In other words, if any two observations of (x, y) are "close" then the efficiency scores for these observations would also be "close" for the Farrell measure (if the input requirement correspondence is continuous), but not necessarily for the Russell or the Zieschang measures. Finally, it is worth mentioning again that similar developments can be derived for the *output*-oriented Farrell measure of technical efficiency, and we leave this to the readers.

A Brief Summary on Properties of Technical Efficiency Measures. While one might forget many details discussed in this section (and even more details in the provided references), the things not to forget are the following conclusions:

- There does not exist a measure (known or unknown!) that satisfies the Färe–Lovell axioms for all technologies, but some measures do satisfy them for some restricted (still wide) class of technologies.
- The Farrell (same as Russell and Zieschang) technical efficiency measures also do not satisfy the (strict) monotonicity axiom, but this axiom is, in general, incompatible with another, perhaps more desirable axiom – the commensurability property, so its weaker version (compatible with commensurability) might be more practical.
- The Farrell measures may also be unable to identify the efficient subset of an isoquant for some technologies (while the Russell and Zieschang measures do so).
  - However, such a strict indication property is, in general, incompatible with the *continuity* property, also a desirable one, which is satisfied by the Farrell measures, but the Russell and Zieschang measures may not satisfy it in general.
  - If we value the continuity property then the weak indication axiom (compatible with continuity) seems to be more practical.

- Overall, the properties of weak indication, weak monotonicity, homogeneity and commensurability constitute the Färe–Lovell–Russell axioms and the Farrell technical efficiency measures are the only ones from those presented above that satisfy these axioms. Consequently, some preference in the rest of this book will be given to the Farrell efficiency measures, although we will discuss others as well.

The reader is also encouraged to read Russell and Schworm (2011), and Levkoff et al. (2012) for closely related discussion and some generalizations.

---

in Figure 3.1) then the Farrell measure will possess the strict indication property, while the Russell measure will satisfy the continuity property.

[11] Originally, Russell (1990) considered five different continuity properties to show that the Farrell measure outperforms the Russell and the Zieschang technical efficiency measures.

3.4 COST AND REVENUE EFFICIENCY

Recall that the Farrell measures of *technical* efficiency are nothing but the reciprocals of the corresponding Shephard's distance functions. In earlier chapters, we learned that both input and output distance functions have their duals – the cost and revenue functions, respectively. In particular, from the duality theory summarized in Chapter 2 we had

$$C(y, w) \equiv \min_{x} \{wx : D_i(y, x) \geq 1\}, \quad w \in \Re_{++}^{N}, \tag{3.4.1}$$

which can also be written as (for proof, see Färe and Primont, 1995)

$$C(y, w) \equiv \min_{x} \{wx/D_i(y, x)\}, \quad w \in \Re_{++}^{N}, \tag{3.4.2}$$

which immediately implies that

$$C(y, w) \leq w[xTE_i(y, x)], \quad w \in \Re_{++}^{N}. \tag{3.4.3}$$

The statement in (3.4.1) is quite intuitive: the cost of producing output y from some inputs, even technically efficient inputs, is not smaller than the minimal cost of producing this y. In other words, being technically efficient does not ensure cost minimization – proper *allocation* of inputs according to their market prices and their marginal productivities is also needed. So, in some sense, a "superior" measure of efficiency would be the *cost efficiency* measure – defined for an observation (x^o, y) as the ratio of the minimal cost to the actual cost, i.e.,

$$CE(y, w, x^o) \equiv \frac{C(y, w)}{wx^o}, \quad \text{for } wx^o \neq 0. \tag{3.4.4}$$

Using geometric intuition (in Figure 3.3), we can view this measure as a "comparison" (e.g., along the ray r) of two hyperplanes (*isocosts*): one that goes

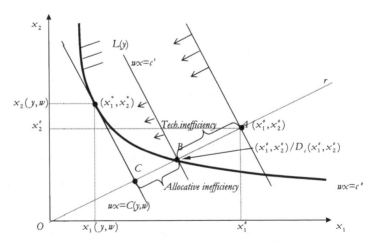

Figure 3.3 Technical, allocative, and cost efficiency measures.

through the cost minimizing allocation of inputs, $wx = C(y, w)$, with the one that goes through the actual allocation, $c^o = wx^o$.

The reader might have noticed that (3.4.3) can be reinterpreted as

$$CE(y, w, x^o) \le TE_i(y, x^o), \quad \forall x^o \in L(y), \; w \in \mathfrak{R}_+^N, \tag{3.4.5}$$

i.e., that the cost efficiency score is always lower than the technical input efficiency score.

Now, let us close the inequality (3.4.5) by introducing the (multiplicative) residual – that would indicate to us about the *allocative (in)efficiency* of any particular observation, $x^o \in L(y)$, after correcting it for technical inefficiency using $TE_i(y, x^o)$. Formally, the input-oriented allocative efficiency is defined as,

$$AE_i(y, w, x^o) \equiv \frac{CE(y, w, x^o)}{TE_i(y, x^o)}. \tag{3.4.6}$$

Using geometric intuition in Figure 3.3, the allocative efficiency can be viewed as a "comparison" (along the ray r) of two hyperplanes: one that goes through the cost minimizing allocation of inputs, $wx = C(y, w)$, with the one that goes through the actual allocation *adjusted for the input technical inefficiency* using $TE_i(y, x^o)$, i.e., the hyperplane defined by $wx = c'$. Also, directly from (3.4.6), we get

$$CE(y, w, x^o) \equiv TE_i(y, x^o) \times AE_i(y, w, x^o). \tag{3.4.7}$$

This is a famous decomposition (which we will be using in future discussions), for which the *cost efficiency* measure is also sometimes called the (Farrell) *input-oriented overall efficiency* measure.

Similar arguments can be made about the *overall* output efficiency, or just the *revenue efficiency* measure, that can be defined as

$$RE(x, p, y^o) \equiv \frac{R(x, p)}{py^o}, \; \text{for } py^o \neq 0. \tag{3.4.8}$$

The analogue of (3.4.5), here, would be

$$RE(x, p, y^o) \ge TE(x, y^o), \quad \forall y^o \in P(x), \; p \in \mathfrak{R}_+^M, \tag{3.4.9}$$

which allows us to define the *output-oriented allocative efficiency* as,

$$AE(x, p, y^o) \equiv \frac{RE(x, p, y^o)}{TE(x, y^o)}, \tag{3.4.10}$$

and thus we will always have the decomposition of the overall efficiency into technical and allocative efficiencies,

$$RE(x, p, y^o) \equiv TE(x, y^o) \times AE(x, p, y^o), \quad \forall y^o \in P(x), \; p \in \mathfrak{R}_+^M. \tag{3.4.11}$$

The geometric intuition of these efficiency measures is presented in Figure 3.4. The allocative efficiency can be understood as a "comparison" (along

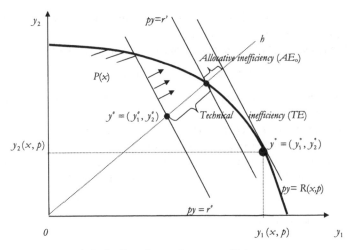

Figure 3.4 Technical, allocative, and revenue efficiency measures.

the ray h from the origin) of two hyperplanes: one that goes through the revenue maximizing allocation of outputs, $py = R(x, p)$, with the one that goes through the actual allocation *adjusted for the output technical inefficiency* using $TE(x, y)$, i.e., the hyperplane defined by $py = r'$. Also, note that (3.4.5) and (3.4.9) are sometimes referred to as Mahler's inequalities.

In a similar fashion, the profit efficiency can be defined and related to the DDF and we leave it for the next section.

3.5 PROFIT EFFICIENCY

Recall from earlier chapters that the DDF is defined as

$$D_d(x, y| - d_x, d_y) \equiv \sup_{\theta} \{\theta \ : \ (x - \theta d_x, y + \theta d_y) \in T\}, \qquad (3.5.1)$$

where $(-d_x, d_y)$ is some nonzero vector in $\mathfrak{R}_-^N \times \mathfrak{R}_+^M$ that stipulates the direction in which the distance between observation (x, y) and the frontier of T is measured. Also recall that the profit function, for given input and output prices (w, p), is defined as

$$\pi(w, p) \equiv \sup_{x,y}\{py - wx : (x, y) \in T\}, \qquad (3.5.2)$$

and the duality between these two functions can be expressed through

$$D_d(x, y|-d_x, d_y) = \inf_{w,p} \left\{ \frac{\pi(w, p) - (py - wx)}{(pd_y + wd_x)} \right\}, \ x \in \mathfrak{R}_+^N, \ y \in \mathfrak{R}_+^M,$$

$$(3.5.3)$$

which implies that for any $(x, y) \in T$ and $p \in \mathfrak{R}^M_{++}$, $w \in \mathfrak{R}^N_{++}$, we have

$$D_d(x, y| - d_x, d_y) \leq \frac{\pi(w, p) - (py - wx)}{(pd_y + wd_x)}. \tag{3.5.4}$$

Clearly, the left-hand side of (3.5.4) can be called the directional-type technical efficiency indicator – because it can measure the distance from a point in the technology set T towards its "upper" boundary or technological frontier, without reference to prices of inputs or outputs. On the other hand, the right-hand side of (3.5.4) can be called a *directional measure of profit efficiency*, i.e.,

$$\Pi E(x, y, p, w| - d_x, d_y) \equiv \frac{\pi(w, p) - (py - wx)}{(pd_y + wd_x)}. \tag{3.5.5}$$

Intuitively, this particular measure of profit efficiency is a difference between the potential and actual profits, normalized by some particular value $(pd_y + wd_x)$ reflecting a monetary value that represents both the objective (such as the market price) and subjective (such as the researcher's choice of direction) importance of all outputs and all inputs relative to each other. In the literature, this measure is sometimes referred to as Nerlovian profit efficiency measure (Chambers et al., 1998; Färe et al., 2008b).

Interestingly, when one chooses such a popular direction as $(-d_x, d_y) = (-x, y)$, then the normalizing value for the profit efficiency measure (3.5.5) becomes $(py + wx)$, which can be understood as the total volume of activities (analogous to the notion of total volume of trade).

Similar to what we have done before, we can close the inequality (3.4.5) by introducing a residual that would indicate to us about the *allocative (in)efficiency* of any particular observation, $(x^o, y^o) \in T$, after correcting it for technical inefficiency using $D_d(x, y| - d_x, d_y)$. Formally, an *additive* profit-based measure of allocative efficiency can be defined as (see Färe et al., 2008b),

$$AE_d(x, y, p, w|-d_x, d_y) \equiv \Pi E(x, y, p, w|-d_x, d_y) - D_d(x, y|-d_x, d_y). \tag{3.5.6}$$

The geometric intuition of the profit-based efficiency measures is presented in Figure 3.5. The profit-based allocative efficiency measure can be understood as a "comparison" (along the vector $(-d_x, d_y)$) of two hyperplanes: the one that goes through the profit maximizing allocation of inputs and outputs, $py - wx = \pi(w, p)$, with the one that goes through the actual allocation *adjusted for technical inefficiency* using $D_d(x, y| - d_x, d_y)$, i.e., the hyperplane defined by $py - wx = \pi^o$. In Section 3.7, we will consider another, more recently introduced and in some respects more advantageous measure of profit efficiency that is coherent with Farrell-type measurement.

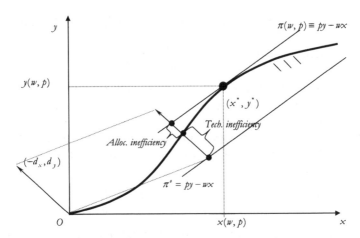

Figure 3.5 Geometric intuition of profit-based efficiency measures.

3.6 SLACK-BASED MEASURES OF EFFICIENCY

The phenomenon of slacks in efficiency measurement have received substantial attention in the literature. We have already mentioned the so-called *additive* technical efficiency measure that was proposed by Charnes et al. (1985). Another efficiency measure, in a similar vein, has been introduced by Tone (2001)

$$TSBE(x, y) = \min_{\substack{s_1^-,...,s_N^- \\ s_1^+,...,s_M^+}} \left\{ \left(1 - \frac{1}{N} \sum_{j=1}^{N} \frac{s_j^-}{x_j} \right) \bigg/ \left(1 + \frac{1}{M} \sum_{m=1}^{M} \frac{s_m^+}{y_m} \right) : \right.$$

$$(x_1 - s_1^-, \ldots, x_N - s_N^-, y_1 + s_1^+, \ldots, y_M + s_M^+) \in T,$$

$$\left. s_j^- \geq 0 \, \forall j = 1, \ldots, N, s_m^+ \geq 0 \, \forall m = 1, \ldots, M \right\}. \qquad (3.6.1)$$

Merging the concept of slack-based measures and the concept of the DDF, Fukuyama and Weber (2009), proposed the so-called directional slack-based (in)efficiency measure, defined as

$$\overrightarrow{FWSBE}(x, y; g_x, g_y) = \max_{\substack{s_1^-,...,s_N^- \\ s_1^+,...,s_M^+}} \left\{ \frac{1}{2} \left(\frac{1}{N} \sum_{j=1}^{N} \frac{s_j^-}{g_{x_j}} + \frac{1}{M} \sum_{m=1}^{M} \frac{s_m^+}{g_{y_m}} \right) : \right.$$

$$(x_1 - s_1^-, \ldots, x_N - s_N^-, y_1 + s_1^+, \ldots, y_M + s_M^+) \in T,$$

$$\left. s_j^- \geq 0 \, \forall j = 1, \ldots, N, \ s_m^+ \geq 0 \, \forall m = 1, \ldots, M \right\}, \qquad (3.6.2)$$

where $g_x = (g_{x_1}, \ldots, g_{x_N})$ and $g_y = (g_{y_1}, \ldots, g_{y_M})$ and so $(-g_x, g_y)$ is a direction in (x, y)-space chosen by the researcher, to reflect the researcher's preferences in orienting the measurement of (in)efficiency. Note that this version of slack-based efficiency measure, given in (3.6.2), is quite general and many special cases can be obtained by specifying various particular directions defined by vector (g_x, g_y).

More recently, Färe and Grosskopf (2010) also merged the concept of slack-based measures and the concept of the DDF, proposing a somewhat different and also very general formulation for efficiency measure, which they dubbed as the slack-based directional technology distance function, and formally defined it as

$$\overrightarrow{SBD_T}(x, y; g) = \max \left\{ \sum_{j=1}^{N} \beta_j + \sum_{m=1}^{M} \gamma_m : \right.$$

$$(x_1 - \beta_1 \cdot g_{x_1}, \ldots, x_N - \beta_N \cdot g_{x_N},$$

$$\left. y_1 + \gamma_1 \cdot g_{y_1}, \ldots, y_M + \gamma_M \cdot g_{y_M}) \in T \right\}, \quad (3.6.3)$$

where the optimization is done over $B = (\beta_1, \ldots, \beta_N) \geq 0$, $\Gamma = (\gamma_1, \ldots, \gamma_M) \geq 0$, while $g = (-g_x, g_y)$ is, again, a direction in (x, y)-space chosen by the researcher, to reflect the researcher's preferences in orienting the measurement of (in)efficiency.

In the rest of this subsection, we will follow Färe et al. (2015), who elaborated on this concept of slack-based DDF by considering one natural choice for the direction – when g_x and g_y are the unit vectors, this measure turns into[12]

$$\overrightarrow{SBD_T}(x, y; 1) = \max \left\{ \sum_{j=1}^{N} \beta_j + \sum_{m=1}^{M} \gamma_m : \right.$$

$$(x_1 - \beta_1 \cdot 1, \ldots, x_N - \beta_N \cdot 1,$$

$$\left. y_1 + \gamma_1 \cdot 1, \ldots, y_M + \gamma_M \cdot 1) \in T \right\}. \quad (3.6.4)$$

Note that if we let $B^* = (\beta_1^*, \ldots, \beta_N^*)$, $\Gamma^* = (\gamma_1^*, \ldots, \gamma_M^*)$ be the optimizers in (3.6.4), then under the main regularity conditions and free disposability of inputs and outputs, $\overrightarrow{SBD_T}(x, y; 1) = 0$ if and only if $(\beta_1^*, \ldots, \beta_N^*, \gamma_1^*, \ldots, \gamma_M^*) = \mathbf{0}$. Thus, if $\overrightarrow{SBD_T}(x, y; 1) = 0$, then we say that each x_n and y_m is fully technically efficient, in the sense that there is no way of increasing any of the outputs or decreasing any of the inputs without decreasing the other outputs or increasing the other inputs or changing the technology.

---

[12] To clarify the notation, note that following Färe et al. (2015) we explicitly write the multiplication by 1 to emphasize that it is multiplication by the unit of measurement corresponding to each input or output, e.g., the first and second elements in $\mathbf{1}$ could stand for 1 gallon of petrol and 1 day of labor, while the last two could stand for 1 pound of apples and 1 kg of carrots, respectively, etc. Also, see Färe et al. (2015) for the proof of independence from units of measurement of this efficiency measure.

In other words, (x, y) is on the efficient subset of the technology frontier of T, i.e. Pareto–Koopmans efficient.

Färe et al. (2015) also noted an interesting relationship with the profit function, by noting that for all $(x, y) \in T$, we have

$$\pi(p, w) \geq \sum_{m=1}^{M} p_m y_m + \sum_{m=1}^{M} p_m \gamma_m^* \cdot 1 \qquad (3.6.5)$$

$$- \sum_{j=1}^{N} w_j x_j + \sum_{j=1}^{N} w_j \beta_n^* \cdot 1.$$

And so, from equation (3.6.5), it follows that for all $(x, y) \in T$, we have

$$\pi(p, w) - (py - wx) \geq \sum_{m=1}^{M} p_m \gamma_m^* \cdot 1 + \sum_{j=1}^{N} w_j \beta_j^* \cdot 1, \qquad (3.6.6)$$

and normalizing with the value of the directional vector, which is $g = 1$ here, i.e., $(\sum_{m=1}^{M} p_m \cdot 1 + \sum_{j=1}^{N} w_j \cdot 1)$, yields $\forall (x, y) \in T$:

$$\frac{\pi(p, w) - (py - wx)}{(\sum_{m=1}^{M} p_m \cdot 1 + \sum_{j=1}^{N} w_j \cdot 1)} \geq \sum_{m=1}^{M} \frac{p_m \gamma_m^* \cdot 1}{\sum_{m=1}^{M} p_m \cdot 1 + \sum_{j=1}^{N} w_j \cdot 1}$$

$$+ \sum_{j=1}^{N} \frac{w_j \beta_j^* \cdot 1}{\sum_{m=1}^{M} p_m \cdot 1 + \sum_{j=1}^{N} w_j \cdot 1}$$

$$(3.6.7)$$

where the l.h.s. is a version of the *Nerlovian profit efficiency* measure when the directional vector is the unit vector. In a sense, a profit efficiency measure is a dual version of the Pareto–Koopmans efficiency defined above – it identifies the Pareto–Koopmans efficiency from the technology point of view and from the market point of view, by considering all the input and output prices and profit maximization with respect to them.

Also note that the measure is now represented as an aggregation of individual "slacks" weighted by the price-share weights

$$S_m = \frac{p_m \cdot 1}{\sum_{m=1}^{M} p_m \cdot 1 + \sum_{j=1}^{N} w_j \cdot 1}, \quad m = 1, \ldots, M$$

and

$$S_j = \frac{w_j \cdot 1}{\sum_{m=1}^{M} p_m \cdot 1 + \sum_{j=1}^{N} w_j \cdot 1}, \quad j = 1, \ldots, N.$$

Note that $S_m \geq 0$ and $S_j \geq 0$ for all $m = 1, \ldots, M$ and $j = 1, \ldots, N$ and $\sum_{m=1}^{M} S_m + \sum_{j=1}^{N} S_j = 1$. So, for all $(x, y) \in T$ we have

$$\frac{\pi(p, w) - (py - wx)}{\left(\sum_{m=1}^{M} P_m \cdot 1 + \sum_{j=1}^{N} w_j \cdot 1\right)} \geq \sum_{m=1}^{M} S_m \gamma_m^* + \sum_{j=1}^{N} S_j \beta_j^*. \quad (3.6.8)$$

Moreover, for the case when $\overrightarrow{SBD_T}(x, y; 1) > 0$ one can also state the following

$$\frac{\pi(p, w) - (py - wx)}{\left(\sum_{m=1}^{M} P_m \cdot 1 + \sum_{j=1}^{N} w_j \cdot 1\right)} \geq \overrightarrow{SBD_T}(x, y; 1) \quad (3.6.9)$$

$$\times \left(\sum_{m=1}^{M} S_m \tilde{\gamma}_m + \sum_{j=1}^{N} S_j \tilde{\beta}_j\right),$$

where

$$\tilde{\gamma}_m = \frac{\gamma_m^*}{\sum_{m=1}^{M} \gamma_m^* + \sum_{j=1}^{N} \beta_j^*}, \quad m = 1, \ldots, M, \quad (3.6.10)$$

and

$$\tilde{\beta}_j = \frac{\beta_j^*}{\sum_{m=1}^{M} \gamma_m^* + \sum_{j=1}^{N} \beta_j^*}, \quad j = 1, \ldots, N. \quad (3.6.11)$$

Intuitively, the left hand side of (3.6.9) is a normalized profit efficiency measure, while the right-hand side is a measure of technical efficiency and so the difference between the two would constitute a type of allocative inefficiency measure that will close the inequality in (3.6.9) and provide a decomposition of the normalized profit efficiency measure. A value added of the representation given in (3.6.9) is that it allows identifying the potential individual contributions of each output and each input as shares of the total technical inefficiency, given by (3.6.10) and (3.6.11), respectively. More of related results and discussions on this type of measurement can also be found in Färe et al. (2015, 2016a) and Pham and Zelenyuk (2018).

Finally, it is worth illustrating with an example the difference between various efficiency measures discussed here and some advantages of the slack based efficiency measures relative to other measures. Figure 3.6 gives one such example, for a technology that is close to Leontief-type technology and is identical to it when the angle α is zero. Clearly, this is a simplification, yet not far from reality: indeed, many real-world production processes often require fixed proportions, such as one person per car or one worker per single machine, or exact proportions of ingredients in a cake or in a concrete of certain type, etc. For our example in Figure 3.6, if $\alpha = 0$, then the efficient subset of the technology is just one point, denoted with C. Suppose α is a very small positive number

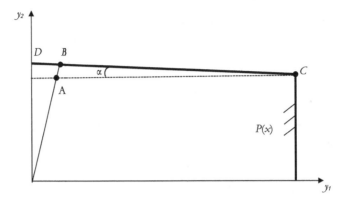

Figure 3.6 Illustration of the advantage of slack-based measures.

($\alpha \to 0$): because $\alpha > 0$ the efficient subset will be the entire segment from C
to D. If a firm were initially at point A and $\alpha > 0$, all efficiency measures will
show some inefficiency: the Farrell (as well as the Zieschang) measure will
show very little inefficiency for very small α, about the same as for allocation
near C, but the slack-based measures will show relatively large inefficiency,
being able to recognize that much more of y_1 can be produced without reducing
y_2, and with the same $P(x)$. This higher discriminatory power of the slack-
based measures seems to be quite appealing in practice, even though some
of their theoretical properties might not be as appealing as in the case of the
Farrell measure.

From our discussions above, one should remember that the Russell-type
measures (as well as slack-based measures or any other that satisfy strict indication axiom) may have problems with continuity. To illustrate this point,
suppose a firm has an allocation at point B in Figure 3.6, then all the
(output-oriented) technical efficiency measures we discussed will indicate full
efficiency of this allocation for any $\alpha > 0$, even if α is very close to zero.
However, when α becomes exactly zero, then the Farrell measure will still
show full efficiency, but the slack-based measures, the additive measure, the
Russell measure and the Zieschang measure will "jump" to show huge inefficiency, all suggesting that the firm should rather choose allocation C. So, a
very small change in α here (from close to zero to exactly zero) is able to cause
a jump, a dramatic change in inefficiency scores of these measures, yet not for
the Farrell measure here.[13] It is worth noting, however, that while this jump is
a continuity problem from a technical standpoint, it might be also viewed as an
advantage from an economic point of view – a much more efficient allocation
is indicated by the slack-based measures here. So, it is the same as in life, some
jumps or discontinuities can actually be beneficial!

---

[13] Although less prone to the discontinuity problem, the Farrell measure is not completely immune
from it, as can be illustrated with a similar example.

3.7 UNIFYING DIFFERENT APPROACHES

Given so many different efficiency measures, a natural question arises: can they all be unified? Such attempts have recently been endeavored by Färe et al. (2018), who proposed a general measure of *profit efficiency*, defined for an observed quantity vector (x^0, y^0) and price vector (w^0, p^0), as

$$\mathscr{E}(x^0, y^0; w^0, p^0|Z) = \sup_{\theta, \lambda, x, y} \{ f(\lambda_1, \ldots, \lambda_N; \theta_1, \ldots, \theta_M) :$$

$$\sum_{m=1}^{M} p_m^0 \theta_m y_m^0 - \sum_{j=1}^{N} w_j^0 \lambda_j x_j^0 \le p^0 y - w^0 x,$$

$$(x, y) \in T \cap Z \}, \tag{3.7.1}$$

where $f(\lambda_1, \ldots, \lambda_N; \theta_1, \ldots, \theta_M)$ is an objective function specified by a researcher and Z is a set of relevant constraints on the analyzed business activities.[14] This general profit efficiency measure is a dual version of the Pareto–Koopmans efficiency defined above, taking into account technology and markets, and in this sense it is a superior criterion than the primal Pareto–Koopmans efficiency that only considers technical efficiency.

Importantly, by choosing different forms of $f(\lambda_1, \ldots, \lambda_N; \theta_1, \ldots, \theta_M)$ many particular efficiency measures can be derived from (3.7.1), including those described above.

An interesting special case of (3.7.1) is obtained by setting $\lambda_1, \ldots, \lambda_N = 1$ and $\theta_1, \ldots, \theta_M = \theta$ so that $f(\lambda_1, \ldots, \lambda_N; \theta_1, \ldots, \theta_M) = \theta$ and so we get

$$\mathscr{E}_o(x^0, y^0; w^0, p^0|Z)$$
$$= \sup_{\theta, x, y} \{ \theta : p^0 \theta y^0 - w^0 x^0 \le p^0 y - w^0 x, (x, y) \in T \cap Z \},$$

$$\tag{3.7.2}$$

which can also be rewritten in terms of the sup-sup (or "maxi-max") approach

$$\mathscr{E}_o(x^0, y^0; w^0, p^0|Z)$$
$$= \sup_{\theta} \left\{ \sup_{x, y} \left\{ \frac{p^0 y - w^0 x + w^0 x^0}{p^0 y^0} : (x, y) \in T \cap Z \right\} \ge \theta \right\},$$

$$\tag{3.7.3}$$

as well as in terms of simple and intuitive notions often used in businesses, e.g.,

$$\mathscr{E}_o(x^0, y^0; w^0, p^0|Z) = \frac{C^0}{R^0} + \frac{\pi(p^0, w^0|Z)}{R^0}, \tag{3.7.4}$$

---

[14] The set of constraints Z (e.g., limits on inputs) may be needed to regularize NDRS cases, where profit maximization may yield profit to be ∞ or 0.

where $C^0 = w^0 x^0$, $R^0 = p^0 y^0$ are the observed total costs and total revenue of the firm at the allocation (x^0, y^0) facing prices (w^0, p^0) and $\pi(p^0, w^0 | Z)$ is the maximal profit feasible at those same prices. That is, intuitively, (3.7.4) says that the profit efficiency measure defined in (3.7.2) or (3.7.3) can be decomposed into two key performance indicators: (i) the realized cost–revenue ratio[15] and (ii) the best possible profit margin for the firm.

Färe et al. (2018) provided many more results and discussion, including a few more of the interesting interpretations of this profit efficiency measure and proof of some important properties of it. Perhaps most importantly, they also showed how to decompose (3.7.2) or (3.7.3) into output-oriented Farrell-type technical, overall (revenue) efficiency measures and another new allocative efficiency measure. Thus, such decomposition embraced the Farrell-type efficiency measures into the profit-maximization behavior framework of neoclassical economics.

3.8 REMARKS ON THE LITERATURE

One of the most prominent contributions to the area of efficiency measurement came from Michel J. Farrell, due to his seminal (Farrell, 1957) work (see Grifell-Tatjé and Lovell, 2005 for a concise narrative about Farrell and his influence). The measures of technical efficiency inspired and named after him are used perhaps more than any other proposed alternatives so far. Somewhat similar ideas, however, appeared earlier – in the works of von Neumann (1945) and of Nobel Laureates Debreu (1951) and Koopmans (1951a,b) and, in the context of consumer theory, in Konüs (1924) and Konüs and Byushgens (1926).

Farrell's work was popularized only about two decades later by the simultaneous appearance of the seminal works of Färe and Lovell (1978) and Charnes et al. (1978), which in turn also in some sense contributed to defining two streams in the literature – one in economics and the other in the fields of operations research/management science/business. Specifically, the former paper had laid out the foundation to axiomatics in the efficiency measurement, suggested an alternative ("Russell") measure and had spurred a series of important papers in the *Journal of Economic Theory* and other outlets – papers by Kopp (1981), Bol (1986), Zieschang (1984), Russell (1990), Dmitruk and Koshevoy (1991), that suggested new measures of efficiency and further developed the axiomatic foundation. Also see Briec (1999) for an alternative measure based on the Hölder distance function, as well as the more recent stream of literature on this topic in the flagship of the field, *Journal of Productivity Analysis*, especially Russell and Schworm (2009, 2011), Levkoff et al. (2012), that give a thorough treatment of axioms for efficiency measurement.

---

[15] This ratio is also a reciprocal of the "return to the dollar" measure of performance proposed by Georgescu-Roegen (1951).

The literature on slack-based measures is more recent and primarily influenced by Charnes et al. (1985) and more recently by Tone (2001), Fukuyama and Weber (2009), Färe and Grosskopf (2010), Cooper et al. (2011a), Färe et al. (2015, 2016a), and Pham and Zelenyuk (2018) to mention just a few. Finally, a unification of different efficiency measures is due to the recent work of Färe et al. (2018).

A key question now is how to empirically *estimate* any of those efficiency scores of a particular observation or DMU. We will focus on this matter in Chapters 7–16.

3.9 EXERCISES

1. Define the (radial-type) input isoquant and its efficient subset.
2. Define the input-oriented Farrell measure of technical efficiency, state its indication property, its intuitive meaning, and its drawback (wrt the efficient subset of the input isoquant).
3. Define the input-oriented Russell, Zieschang and additive measures of technical efficiency.
4. Give an example where the DDF does not (completely) identify the efficient subset of an isoquant. Define an analogue of the Zieschang measure for this case (hint: use the idea of the additive measure and of the DDF).
5. Derive relationships between all the measures defined in the section above and in the exercises above (without looking into the next section).
6. Derive a relationship between the output distance function and the DDF.
7. Derive a relationship between the output-oriented (multiplicative) Russell measure and the Farrell output-oriented technical efficiency measure.
8. Derive a relationship between the output-oriented additive measure and the directional (output) distance function.
9. Prove if the slack-based measures are commensurable (see Färe et al., 2015).
10. Derive a relationship between the input-oriented slack-based directional efficiency measure and the input-oriented Russell measure.[16]
11. Derive an output-oriented framework for the slack-based directional efficiency when some outputs are undesirable.[17]
12. Derive an hyperbolic efficiency measurement framework for the case when some outputs are undesirable.[18]

---

[16] E.g., note that if $g_x = x$ and $g_y = y$ then we have a Russell-type efficiency measure defined on T (see Färe et al., 2016a for a related discussion).

[17] See Pham and Zelenyuk (2018) for a related discussion.

[18] See Pham and Zelenyuk (2018) and Chapter 8 for a related discussion and references.

13. Derive a relationship between the output-oriented slack-based directional efficiency measure and the output-oriented Russell measure.
14. Derive a relationship between the slack-based directional efficiency measure and the Russell measure defined on T.
15. Derive various special cases from the general measure of profit efficiency (3.7.1).[19]

3.10   APPENDIX

The proofs here follow the derivations from Färe et al. (2007) and Zelenyuk (2002) and are included here for completeness and for pedagogical purposes (e.g., some typos found in original sources are corrected).

We start with sketching a proof of the theorem about (3.2.21).

Proof. ($\Leftarrow$) : Assume technology is characterized as in (3.2.19), then

$$
MRTE(y, x) = \min_{\lambda_1, \dots, \lambda_N} \left\{ \left(\prod_{j=1}^{N} \lambda_j \right)^{1/N} : (\lambda_1 x_1, \dots, \lambda_N x_N) \in L(y), \right.
$$
$$
\left. 0 < \lambda_j \leq 1, \ j = 1, \dots, N \right\}
$$
$$
= \min_{\lambda_1, \dots, \lambda_N} \left\{ \left(\prod_{j=1}^{N} \lambda_j \right)^{1/N} : D_i(y, \lambda_1 x_1, \dots, \lambda_N x_N) \geq 1, \right.
$$
$$
\left. 0 < \lambda_j \leq 1, \ j = 1, \dots, N \right\}
$$
$$
= \min_{\lambda_1, \dots, \lambda_N} \left\{ \left(\prod_{j=1}^{N} \lambda_j \right)^{1/N} : \left(\prod_{j=1}^{N} \lambda_j x_j \right)^{1/N} / H(y) \geq 1, \right.
$$
$$
\left. 0 < \lambda_j \leq 1, \ j = 1, \dots, N \right\}
$$
$$
= \min_{\lambda_1, \dots, \lambda_N} \left\{ \left(\prod_{j=1}^{N} \lambda_j \right)^{1/N} : \right.
$$
$$
\left(\prod_{j=1}^{N} \lambda_j \right)^{1/N} \geq H(y) / \left(\prod_{j=1}^{N} x_j \right)^{1/N},
$$
$$
\left. 0 < \lambda_j \leq 1, \ j = 1, \dots, N \right\}
$$
$$
= H(y) / \left(\prod_{j=1}^{N} x_j \right)^{1/N} = 1/D_i(y, x) = TE_i(y, x).
$$

---

[19] See Färe et al. (2018) for a related discussion.

$(\Rightarrow)$: Assume $MRTE(y, x) = TE_i(y, x) \ \forall x \in L(y)$ then

$$MRTE(y, \delta_1 x_1, \ldots, \delta_N x_N)$$

$$= \min_{\lambda_1, \ldots, \lambda_N} \left\{ \left(\prod_{j=1}^N \lambda_j \right)^{1/N} : (\lambda_1 \delta_1 x_1, \ldots, \lambda_N \delta_N x_N) \in L(y), \right.$$

$$\left. 0 < \lambda_j \leq 1, \ 0 < \delta_j \leq 1, \ j = 1, \ldots, N \right\}$$

$$= \left(\prod_{j=1}^N \delta_j \right)^{-1/N} \min_{\lambda_1, \ldots, \lambda_N} \left\{ \left(\prod_{j=1}^N \lambda_j \delta_j \right)^{1/N} : \right.$$

$$(\lambda_1 \delta_1 x_1, \ldots, \lambda_N \delta_N x_N) \in L(y),$$

$$\left. 0 < \lambda_j \leq 1, \ 0 < \delta_j \leq 1, \ j = 1, \ldots, N \right\}$$

$$= \left(\prod_{j=1}^N \delta_j \right)^{-1/N} \min_{\hat{\lambda}_1, \ldots, \hat{\lambda}_N} \left\{ \left(\prod_{j=1}^N \hat{\lambda}_j \right)^{1/N} : \right.$$

$$(\hat{\lambda}_1 x_1, \ldots, \hat{\lambda}_N x_N) \in L(y),$$

$$\left. 0 < \hat{\lambda}_j \leq 1, \ j = 1, \ldots, N \right\} \ (\hat{\lambda}_j = \lambda_j \delta_j)$$

$$= MRTE(y, x) / \left(\prod_{j=1}^N \delta_j \right)^{1/N}.$$

Therefore

$$MRTE(y, \delta_1 x_1, \ldots, \delta_N x_N) = MRTE(y, x) / \left(\prod_{j=1}^N \delta_j \right)^{1/N},$$

$$0 < \delta_j \leq 1, \ j = 1, \ldots, N.$$

Thus, if $MRTE(y, x) = TE_i(y, x) \ \forall x \in L(y)$, then we get

$$MRTE(y, \delta_1 x_1, \ldots, \delta_N x_N) = MRTE(y, x) / \left(\prod_{j=1}^N \delta_j \right)^{1/N}$$

$$= TE_i(y, \delta_1 x_1, \ldots, \delta_N x_N),$$

so we also have

$$MRTE(y, x) = TE_i(y, \delta_1 x_1, \ldots, \delta_N x_N) \left(\prod_{j=1}^N \delta_j \right)^{1/N},$$

and so

$$TE_i(y, x) = TE_i(y, \delta_1 x_1, \ldots, \delta_N x_N) \left(\prod_{j=1}^N \delta_j \right)^{1/N}.$$

Now let $\delta_j = 1/x_j$, $j = 1, \ldots, N$, then we get

$$TE_i(y, x) = TE_i(y, \mathbf{1}_N) \left(\prod_{j=1}^{N} x_j \right)^{-1/N}.$$

Finally, since Farrell measure is *commensurable* (see Russell, 1987) x_j can be scaled so that $x_j \geq 1$, $j = 1, \ldots, N$. So, taking $H(y) = TE_i(y, \mathbf{1}_N)$ and (3.2.16) we conclude that $D_i(y, x) = (\prod_{j=1}^{N} x_j)^{1/N}/H(y)$, as needed for the proof. □

Now, we sketch a proof of (3.2.23)–(3.2.25).

Proof.

(i) The idea of the proof here is similar to the one in Chapter 1 for the theorem of the complete characterization of technology by the output distance function (also see Chambers et al., 1998 for a similar proof).

(ii)

$$\begin{aligned}
\vec{D}_i(y, x + \alpha\mathbf{1}_N; -\mathbf{1}_N) &= \sup\{\beta : (x - \beta\mathbf{1}_N + \alpha\mathbf{1}_N) \in L(y)\} \\
&= \sup\{\beta : (x - (\beta - \alpha)\mathbf{1}_N) \in L(y) \\
&= \alpha + \sup\{\hat{\beta} : (x - \hat{\beta}\mathbf{1}_N \in L(y)\} \\
&\quad (\hat{\beta} = \beta - \alpha) \\
&= \vec{D}_i(y, x; -\mathbf{1}_N) + \alpha.
\end{aligned}$$

(iii) (a) Let $x \in L(y)$ with $x_j > 0$, $j = 1, \ldots, N$ and $x \notin \partial L(y)$. Then, $D_i(y, x) > 1$, and by free disposability, there is an open neighborhood $N_\epsilon(x)$ of x, where ($\varepsilon = \min\{x_1 - D_i(y, x)x_1, \ldots, x_N - D_i(y, x)x_N\}$) such that $N_\varepsilon(x) \in L(y)$. Thus $\vec{D}_i(y, x; -\mathbf{1}_N) > 0$.

(iii) (b) Let $\vec{D}_i(y, x; -\mathbf{1}_N) > 0$ then $x - \vec{D}_i(y, x; -\mathbf{1}_N)\mathbf{1}_N \in L(y)$ and because the directional vector is $\mathbf{1}_N = (1, \ldots, 1)$, each x_j, $j = 1, \ldots, N$ can be reduced when still in $L(y)$. So $D_i(y, x) > 1$ and by the indication property of $D_i(y, x)$, we conclude that $x \notin \partial L(y)$.

□

Proof. Here, we sketch a proof that (3.2.32) $\Leftrightarrow$ (3.2.33).

($\Leftarrow$) : Assume $\forall x \in C(L(y)) = \{\vec{x} : \vec{x} = x + \delta\mathbf{1}_N, x \in L(y), \delta \geq 0\}$ we have

$$\vec{D}_i(y, x; -\mathbf{1}_N) = AdTE_i(y, x). \tag{3.10.1}$$

Also note that on the following translation property of $AdTE_i(y, x)$:

$$AdTE_i(y, x_1 - \delta_1, \ldots, x_N - \delta_N)$$

$$= \max_{s_1,\ldots,s_N} \left\{ \frac{1}{N} \sum_{j=1}^{N} s_j \, : \, (x_1 - \delta_1 - s_1, \ldots, x_N - \delta_N - s_N) \in L(y) \right\},$$

$$= \max_{s_1,\ldots,s_N} \left\{ \frac{1}{N} \sum_{j=1}^{N} (s_j - \delta_j + \delta_j) \, : \right.$$

$$\left. (x_1 - (\delta_1 + s_1), \ldots, x_N - (\delta_N + s_N)) \in L(y) \right\},$$

$$= -\frac{1}{N} \sum_{j=1}^{N} \delta_j + AdTE_i(y, x), \text{ where } s_j \geq 0, \delta_j \geq 0, j = 1, \ldots, N.$$

Therefore, we have

$$AdTE_i(y, x) = AdTE_i(y, x_1 - \delta_1, \ldots, x_N - \delta_N) + \frac{1}{N} \sum_{j=1}^{N} \delta_j.$$

Now let $\delta_j = x_j$ and define $-F(y) = AdTE_i(y, 0)$, then due to (3.10.1) we have,

$$\vec{D}_i(y, x; -\mathbf{1}_N) = AdTE_i(y, x) = \frac{1}{N} \sum_{j=1}^{N} x_j - F(y).$$

$(\Rightarrow)$: Here, assume that $\vec{D}_i(y, x; -\mathbf{1}_N) = \frac{1}{N} \sum_{j=1}^{N} x_j - F(y)$. Take an arbitrary $x \in \mathcal{C}(L(y))$, then there exist some $\hat{x} \in \partial L(y)$, and $\delta \geq 0$, such that

$$\vec{D}_i(y, x; -\mathbf{1}_N) = \vec{D}_i(y, \hat{x} + \delta \mathbf{1}_N; -\mathbf{1}_N) = \vec{D}_i(y, \hat{x}; -\mathbf{1}_N) + \delta.$$

Moreover, since $\hat{x} \in \partial L(y)$, we get $\vec{D}_i(y, \hat{x}; -\mathbf{1}_N) = 0$ and therefore $\vec{D}_i(y, x; -\mathbf{1}_N) = \delta$. Furthermore, note that we also have

$$AdTE_i(y, x) = \max_{s_1,\ldots,s_N} \left\{ \frac{1}{N} \sum_{j=1}^{N} s_j \, : \, \frac{1}{N} \sum_{j=1}^{N} (x_j - s_j) - F(y) \geq 0 \right\}$$

$$= \max_{s_1,\ldots,s_N} \left\{ \frac{1}{N} \sum_{j=1}^{N} s_j : \frac{1}{N} \sum_{j=1}^{N} (x_j - s_j + \delta - \delta) - F(y) \geq 0 \right\}$$

$$= \max_{s_1,\ldots,s_N} \left\{ \frac{1}{N} \sum_{j=1}^{N} s_j \, : \, \delta + \frac{1}{N} \sum_{j=1}^{N} \hat{x}_j - F(y) \geq \frac{1}{N} \sum_{j=1}^{N} s_j \right\}$$

$$= \delta + \frac{1}{N} \sum_{j=1}^{N} \hat{x}_j - F(y) = \delta + \vec{D}_i(y, \hat{x}; -\mathbf{1}_N) = \delta.$$

Since $\hat{x} \in \partial L(y)$, $\vec{D}_i(y, \hat{x}; -\mathbf{1}_N) = 0$ and so we have $\delta = \vec{D}_i(y, x; -\mathbf{1}_N)$ $= AdTE_i(y, x)$, $\forall x \in \mathcal{C}(L(y))$. $\qquad \square$

CHAPTER 4

Productivity Indexes: Part 1

In previous chapters we were focusing on measuring production efficiency in various ways. We now know that one should use the technical efficiency measure if one is concerned with how well the technology potential is used (yet, recall that one still needs to choose an appropriate orientation of measurement – input or output or a mix of these). Furthermore, we learned that one should use cost or revenue (or profit) efficiency if, in addition, one is interested in how well different inputs or outputs (or both) are chosen or allocated with respect to the corresponding prices. The goal of this chapter is to discuss a closely related and, in fact, more general concept – the concept of productivity.

A roadmap for this chapter is useful. We will start by clarifying the differences and relationships between the two main themes of our book: efficiency, which we explored in detail in previous chapters, and productivity, which we will focus on in this chapter. We then consider different approaches to productivity measurement. We will start with the classical growth accounting approach and then move on to the economic approach using index numbers, where we will first consider price indexes, then quantity indexes and then productivity indexes. We also examine some of their decompositions and the relationships among them. After considering a wide range of approaches within the economic approach to index numbers, we will then show that the growth accounting approach can be considered as a restrictive special case. We will finish the chapter with a discussion of transitivity (or circularity) of indexes, what it means in general and for indexes in particular, and how desirable or critical and restrictive this particular property is for an economic index number. We then discuss the sacrifices one must make in order to preserve transitivity and how to mitigate problems with the index number approach when transitivity is not imposed. We conclude with brief remarks on the literature, which will be further discussed in Chapter 7.

4.1 PRODUCTIVITY VS. EFFICIENCY

While a lot has been done on efficiency measurement in production, it is a relatively modern area in economics and long before its academic origins, people already used, and still use, the notion of *productivity*. It is worth noting that there is some confusion between these two notions. To avoid such confusion within this book, let us make these terms more clear here. Whenever we say *production efficiency* we will think of a level of utilization of the potential (maximal capacity) of the production technology. This is also the way Debreu (1951) was thinking of this notion – as a measure of resource utilization. Continuing in this vein, we will think of *production inefficiency* as the notion defining a gap or a "residual" between the actual and the potential performances, where the latter also defines the production frontier.

On the other hand, we will adopt here the most common understanding of *productivity* – as a notion defining the level of (aggregate) output per unit of (aggregate) input. In other words, the concept of efficiency, for example for the context of output orientation, is a concept that relates *two* (aggregate) *output levels*: actual and potential, while the concept of productivity relates the (aggregate) *output level* to the (aggregate) *input level*, regardless of the potential, i.e., regardless of the gap to the frontier. That is, the concept of productivity falls into the category that economists call a "positive" concept, in the sense that it just describes the situation "as is." Meanwhile, the concept of efficiency or inefficiency falls into the category of a "normative" concept, in the sense that it relates "as is" to "as it potentially could be."

In the simplest case, when there is only one input (x) and only one output (y), a natural productivity measure would be the ratio of output to input that produced it, i.e.,

$$SFP = y/x, \tag{4.1.1}$$

which is often referred to as the *single-factor productivity* measure.[1]

Analogously, a *multi-factor productivity* measure, for a single output case, can be defined as

$$MFP = y/Q_i(x), \tag{4.1.2}$$

where $Q_i(x)$ is some function that "appropriately" aggregates the vector of inputs $(x \in \mathfrak{R}_+^N)$ into a positive scalar. Some "appropriate" examples for $Q_i(x)$ will be discussed later in this chapter.

Similarly, a *multi-factor productivity* measure, for a *multi-output* case, can be defined as

$$MFP = Q_o(y)/Q_i(x), \tag{4.1.3}$$

where $Q_o(y)$ is some function that "appropriately" aggregates the vector of outputs $(y \in \mathfrak{R}_+^M)$ into a positive scalar and we will discuss some "appropriate" examples for $Q_o(y)$ later in this chapter.

---

[1] Perhaps the most popular example of this is the labor productivity measure, e.g., often used in macroeconomics when the gross domestic product (GDP) of a country is divided by the amount of labor force of that country.

A natural question one may wonder about is whether the two concepts, efficiency and productivity, are somehow related. The reader must already feel (if not know) that they should be related, and they indeed are. For example, for the single output case, due to homogeneity of degree 1 in outputs of the output-oriented Shephard's distance function, we always have

$$D_o(x, y) = y D_o(x, 1_M) = y/(D_o(x, 1_M))^{-1}. \tag{4.1.4}$$

Since $(D_o(x, 1_M))^{-1}$ depends only on inputs it can be understood as an aggregation of inputs (in fact it would be the production function $f(x)$, as we discussed in Chapter 1). Therefore expression (4.1.4) tells us that the efficiency level obtained from the Shephard–Farrell-type efficiency measure, for the single output case, is in fact also *a* particular measure of productivity, where the aggregate input is obtained via the production function, which is the function that gives the value of maximal output that can be produced from a given level of input. Moreover, if in addition we have a *single input* and CRS technology, we would then have (due to homogeneity of degree –1 in inputs under the CRS)

$$D_o(x, y) = y D_o(x, 1_M) = (y/x) D_o(1_N, 1_M). \tag{4.1.5}$$

That is, the efficiency level obtained from the Shephard–Farrell-type measure for the single-input–single-output case is exactly the single-factor productivity measure (4.1.1), but normalized by the constant $D_o(1_N, 1_M)$. This normalization constant depends on the particular technology involved and, serving as a benchmark relative to which comparison is made, it is what turns the "positive" or "absolute" notion of productivity into a "normative" or "relative" notion of efficiency here.

For a multi-input–multi-output case, we can also show a similar relationship with the help of a particular class of technologies, called the *input homothetic technology*, which can be characterized by

$$D_o(x, y) = H(y)/(D_o(x, 1_M))^{-1}, \ \forall (x, y) \in \mathfrak{R}_+^N \times \mathfrak{R}_+^M, \tag{4.1.6}$$

for some appropriate function $H(y)$.[2] Note that the expression in (4.1.6) is an example of the multi-factor productivity measure (4.1.3), because it is a ratio of aggregated outputs, $H(y)$, to aggregated inputs $(D_o(x, 1_M))^{-1}$.

The discussion above suggests that the concept of *efficiency* and the concept of *productivity* are two different concepts that can explain the same thing, *performance*, from different perspectives and they may coincide in some particular cases. An important context where these two concepts deviate crucially is where one considers *dynamics* – when looking at the *change in productivity*, which turns out to be more general and in fact include the *change in efficiency* as just one of the components. In the next several sections, we will consider

---

[2] E.g., see Zelenyuk (2014b) for more details on homotheticity and references and a related notion of *scale homotheticity*.

some of the most popular approaches to productivity measurement and then show some key relationships among them.

4.2 GROWTH ACCOUNTING APPROACH

One of the classical and most cited works on productivity measurement is that of the Nobel Laureate Robert Solow (Solow, 1957), who originated the so-called growth accounting approach to productivity measurement, which is used by thousands of researchers all over the world.

Theoretically, this method was developed for a single-output case, so in practice, it is usually applied to the case when all outputs are aggregated into a total output, e.g., GDP, or gross value added by an industry or a state, as was also the case in the original application in Solow (1957).

To make our formal discussion more intuitive, let us consider the case of analyzing the productivity of some countries $k = 1, \ldots, n$. Let q_t^k denote GDP and $x_t^k = (x_{1,t}^k, \ldots, x_{N,t}^k)' \in \Re_+^N$ denote the vector of endowed resources for each country k in a period t. For simplicity, we will assume that the technology of a country k in any period t is characterized by the so-called aggregate production function given by

$$q_t^k \equiv \psi_t^k(x_t^k) = a_t^k \psi^k(x_t^k), \; k = 1, \ldots, n, \tag{4.2.1}$$

where ψ^k is the part of k's country aggregate production function that is independent from time, while a_t^k is a function of time. The variable a_t^k is often referred to as *a* measure of *total factor productivity* (TFP), because rearranging (4.2.1) makes it the ratio of the actual output to the aggregate of *all* the inputs for the same period t (aggregated via the time independent part of the production function), i.e., $a_t^k = q_t^k / \psi^k(x_t^k)$.

Note that the technology characterization of this type implies that (i) everyone is fully efficient and (ii) the technology can change over time only via a scaling of the frontier, while the functional form of the input aggregator (including the importance or weights of inputs in the production process) cannot change over time.[3] Both (i) and (ii) are quite restrictive conditions when contrasted with the relative performance and the technological progress one can typically observe in the real world. Thus, when making such simplifying assumptions in modeling, one is risking to misrepresent the reality substantially by missing very important features of the reality, such as heterogeneity in efficiency levels (e.g., improvement of which may help improving the welfare) and non-neutrality of technological change.

Solow's growth accounting method is based on noting that the growth rate of GDP, denoted with $g(q_t^k)$ and given appropriate differentiability of (4.2.1), can be written as[4]

---

[3] Such a peculiar technology has what is often referred to as the Hicks-neutral-type technological change property (we will discuss this type of technology in more detail later in this chapter).

[4] In general, recall that the growth rate of a variable z_t is defined as $g(z_t) := (dz_t/dt)/z_t = d\ln(z_t)/dt \approx (z_{t+\Delta t}/z_t) - 1$.

$$g(q_t^k) \equiv \frac{dq_t^k/dt}{q_t^k} =$$

$$= \frac{1}{q_t^k}\left(\left(\frac{\partial \psi^k(x_t^k)}{\partial x_{1,t}^k}\frac{dx_{1,t}^k}{dt} + \dots + \frac{\partial \psi^k(x_t^k)}{\partial x_{N,t}^k}\frac{dx_{N,t}^k}{dt}\right)a_t^k + \frac{da_t^k}{dt}\psi^k(x_t^k)\right).$$

$$(4.2.2)$$

Now, bringing $(1/q_t^k)$ and (a_t^k) inside the parentheses, noting that $a_t^k/q_t^k = 1/\psi^k(x_t^k)$ or $\psi^k(x_t^k)/q_t^k = 1/a_t^k$ and rearranging terms, will give us

$$g(q_t^k) \equiv \left(\frac{\partial \psi^k(x_t^k)}{\partial x_{1,t}^k}\frac{x_{1,t}^k}{\psi^k(x_t^k) x_{1,t}^k}\frac{1}{dt}\frac{d(x_{1,t}^k)}{dt} + \dots + \frac{\partial \psi^k(x_t^k)}{\partial x_{N,t}^k}\frac{x_{N,t}^k}{\psi^k(x_t^k) x_{N,t}^k}\frac{1}{dt}\frac{dx_{N,t}^k}{dt}\right)$$
$$+ \frac{da_t^k}{dt}\frac{1}{a_t^k}.$$

$$(4.2.3)$$

Furthermore, note that $e_{jt}^k \equiv (\partial \psi_t^k(x_t^k)/\partial x_{j,t}^k) \times (x_{j,t}^k/\psi_j^k)$ is what is known as the *partial scale elasticity* with respect to input j, which, intuitively, tells us about the weight of each input in the production technology. Moreover, notice that $(dx_{j,t}^k/dt)/x_{j,t}^k = (d \ln x_{j,t}^k/dt)$ is just a definition of the *growth rate* of input j, which we denote as $g(x_{j,t}^k)$, while $(da_t^k/dt)/a_t^k = d \ln a_t^k/dt$ is the analogous definition of the growth rate of technology, which we denote as $g(a_t^k)$. Thus, collecting the terms, we get a neat expression for the growth rate of GDP, with its decomposition into various sources,

$$g(q_t^k) = \sum_{j=1}^{N} e_{j,t}\frac{d \ln x_{j,t}^k}{dt} + \frac{d \ln a_t^k}{dt}$$
$$= \sum_{j=1}^{N} e_{j,t}g(x_{j,t}^k) + g(a_t^k), \quad k = 1, \dots, n.$$

$$(4.2.4)$$

In words, expression (4.2.4) says that the growth rate of GDP can be represented as the weighted average of growth rates of each input $x_{j,t}^k$ *weighted* by the partial scale elasticity corresponding to that input, plus the growth rate of technology.

If we, in addition, assume *constant returns to scale* then we could conveniently normalize each variable by one of the input variables, call it $x_{c,t}^k$, and then we get a decomposition of the growth rate of the single factor productivity,

$$g(q_t^k/x_{c,t}^k) \equiv \sum_{\substack{j=1 \\ j \neq c}}^{N} e_{j,t}\frac{d \ln(x_{j,t}^k/x_{c,t}^k)}{dt} + \frac{d \ln a_t^k}{dt}$$
$$= \sum_{j=1, j \neq c}^{N} e_{j,t}g(x_{j,t}^k/x_{c,t}^k) + g(a_t^k), \quad k = 1, \dots, n.$$

$$(4.2.5)$$

The normalizing variable in (4.2.5) is usually chosen to be labor – so that it gives a decomposition of the growth rate of labor productivity into various sources, such as, for example, the growth in capital per worker, human capital per worker, energy per worker, technology, etc.[5]

While this approach was a breakthrough at the time that received a lot of attention from applied researchers all over the world, as any other method it has some limitations that inspired others to look for more powerful methods of productivity growth measurement. First of all, the reader might have noticed that one of the obvious limitations is that the approach presented above is for a single output case. This limitation was addressed in a the seminal work of Jorgenson and Griliches (1967).[6]

As mentioned above, another limitation is the *a priori* imposition that all observations (firms, countries, etc.) $k = 1, \ldots, n$ are efficient, while the reality suggests (and is supported by many studies, besides layman observations) that often there is a variation in efficiency levels (e.g., due to asymmetric information, variation in cognitive abilities or levels of self-discipline by managers and workers, etc.) that places some firms "on the frontier," while others lag behind.

Another major limitation of the growth accounting approach, which we also mentioned above, is the quite restrictive assumption that the technology should have the Hicks-neutral-type technological change property. Geometrically, this assumption requires that the technology shifts the input-isoquant in a "parallel" fashion. Intuitively, it means that from a technological or engineering point of view, the importance of various types of inputs does not change over time. In other words, such technology implies that, if the input prices stay the same over time, the optimal combination of input mix will also stay the same. In practice, obviously, technological changes are likely to be biased towards some inputs, e.g., towards the physical and human capital, as progress goes on. Indeed, most production processes in the old days were very labor-intensive and technological progress was making it less and less intensive, and differently for different industries.[7] In more recent days, technological progress is using much more information and communication technologies (ICT) than before, which is another example of technological bias, etc.[8] Thus, it might be very desirable to have a measure that does not restrict technology to be Hicks-neutral and thus allow a researcher to measure the direction and the size of the bias in the technological change as well as to test for its statistical significance.

Another limitation of Solow's growth accounting method is the need to know the partial scale elasticity for each input in the aggregate production

---

[5] Increase in (physical or human) capital per labor is sometimes referred to as (physical or human) "capital deepening."

[6] Also see Jorgenson (2002) and Zelenyuk (2014c) for various applications of these methods and for references to other works that used this approach for various data sets.

[7] E.g., see related discussions in Greenwood et al. (1997); Acemoglu (2002) and references therein.

[8] For related discussion on ICT impact on productivity see Jorgenson (2002); Zelenyuk (2014c) and references therein.

function. Usually, they are estimated or taken from other studies or models and, often, they are assumed to be the same for all or many k ($k = 1, \ldots, n$) in a sample, which is hardly true in practice, especially when considering countries with different comparative advantages. Finally, a CRS assumption is needed (and so is assumed in most empirical works) to obtain the single-factor-productivity decomposition in equation (4.2.5). These limitations, *inter alia*, served as motivations for developing other approaches and we will consider some of these below.

4.3 ECONOMIC *PRICE* INDEXES

An alternative to the growth accounting approach that is often used in practice is based on the theory of index numbers. To facilitate discussions in this and other subsections, recall that an *index number* is a formula or a statistic (an estimator) designed to measure changes in a set of related variables over time or over space (firms, countries, other characteristics) or both. A collection of different index numbers for different years, space characteristics, etc. is called an *index series*. The theory of index numbers goes back to at least the nineteenth century, and is sometimes referred to as the statistical approach to index numbers, which we will discuss later in the book (in Chapter 7), while here we will focus on the so-called *economic* approach to index numbers.

The economic theory perspective to index numbers is rooted in the works of Konüs (1924); Konüs and Byushgens (1926), Frisch (1936), Malmquist (1953), Moorsteen (1961), Hicks (1961), and the more recent and revolutionary works of Diewert (1976, 1980, 1992b), Diewert and Wales (1992), and the seminal work of Caves et al. (1982a,b) that related the economic approach to the statistical approach to index numbers.

Perhaps the most famous economic indexes are the price indexes, examples of which are the consumer price index (CPI), the GDP price (deflator) index, the producer price index (PPI), etc. Even if one is interested in productivity indexes that measure (output and input) quantity changes, it is still fundamentally important to know about the price indexes. This is because, in general, prices form the quintessence of economics: if there are no prices, there is no economics! And, in particular, the price indexes are also often used to obtain the quantity indexes, as we will discuss in more detail in Chapter 7. The economic approach to index numbers also largely started with developments about the price indexes, e.g., with seminal works of Konüs (1924), Konüs and Byushgens (1926) about the cost of living index. In a sense, the economic approach to quantity indexes (which often serve as building blocks for various productivity indexes) was developed with some analogy to the economic approach to the price indexes. We follow this path here as well.

Specifically, in this section, we will study the theoretical or, as they are sometimes called, the *true price indexes* and then (in Chapter 7) we will discuss how to estimate them from the observed data. Hereafter, we will focus on the so-called *bilateral* indexes, i.e., those that are designed to measure changes between two arbitrary periods (or, more generally, states), which we will typically denote as s and t. At the end of this chapter we will discuss how to use these indexes for multilateral comparisons.

In the scalar case, when there is only one product whose price (w) change is to be measured from period s to period t, a natural price index would be simply,

$$\text{Price Index} \equiv \frac{w_t}{w_s}. \tag{4.3.1}$$

In a multiple product case, one would like to have a similar expression involving an aggregate of prices observed in the period t in the numerator and an aggregate of prices observed in the period s in the denominator. The key question is: "What shall those aggregator functions be?" so that the indexes have some "nice" properties and some economic theory foundation.

As mentioned above, one of the earliest ideas for the construction of price index based on *economic* theory goes back to, at least, Konüs (1924), and Konüs and Byushgens (1926) who used the expenditure functions in consumer theory to introduce what is now called the "cost of living" index. Applied to the context of production analysis, the Konüs-type *input* price index can be defined as a ratio of two cost functions derived for the same output and the same technology, but for input prices observed in different periods. More precisely, let $C^l(y_l, w_\tau)$ be the cost function needed to produce the output observed in the period l ($l = s, t$), with the technology available in the same period l, and given the input prices observed in the period τ, ($\tau = t, s$), i.e.,

$$C^l(y_l, w_\tau) = \min_x \{w_\tau x \ : \ x \in L^l(y_l)\}, \ w_\tau = (w_{1\tau}, \ldots, w_{N\tau}),$$

$$x = (x_1, \ldots, x_N)',$$

where $L^l(y_l)$ is the input requirement set characterizing the lth period possibilities of producing y_l, i.e.,

$$L^l(y_l) = \{x \ : \ x \text{ can produce } y_l \text{ given all possibilities in period } l\}.$$

The following Konüs-type indexes are possible: the input price index with respect to the output level and technology available in the period s would be

$$P_i^s(w_s, w_t, y_s) \equiv \frac{C^s(y_s, w_t)}{C^s(y_s, w_s)}, \tag{4.3.2}$$

and the input price index wrt the output level and technology available in the period t would be

$$P_i^t(w_s, w_t, y_t) \equiv \frac{C^t(y_t, w_t)}{C^t(y_t, w_s)}. \tag{4.3.3}$$

An intuition of the Konüs-type input price indexes is presented in Figure 4.1.

Analogously to the Konüs-type input price indexes, the *output* price indexes can be defined as the ratio of revenue functions for the same input levels and the same technologies, but output price vectors observed in different periods.

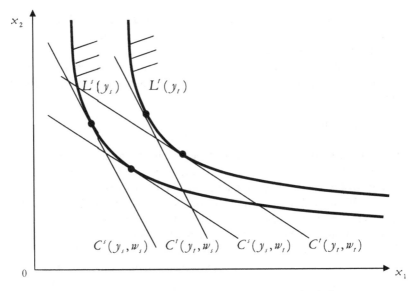

Figure 4.1 Geometric intuition of Konüs-type input price indexes.

These indexes go back to at least Fisher and Shell (1972) and were analyzed by Diewert (1980). In particular, let $R^l(x_l, p_\tau)$ be the revenue function derived for the input level observed in the period l ($l = s, t$), with the technology available in the same period l, and given the output prices observed in the period τ, ($\tau = t, s$), i.e.,

$$R^l(x_l, p_\tau) = \max_y \{p_\tau y : y \in P^l(x_l)\}, \quad p_\tau = (p_{1\tau}, \dots, p_{M\tau}),$$

$$y = (y_1, \dots, y_M)',$$

where $P^l(x_l)$ is the output set characterizing the lth period production possibilities from x_l, i.e.,

$$P^l(x_l) = \{y : x_l \text{ can produce } y \text{ given all possibilities in period } l\}.$$

Then, the following two output price indexes are possible: the output price index with respect to the input level and technology available in the period s would be

$$P_o^s(p_s, p_t, x_s) \equiv \frac{R^s(x_s, p_t)}{R^s(x_s, p_s)}, \tag{4.3.4}$$

and the output price index wrt the input level and technology available in the period t would be

$$P_o^t(p_s, p_t, x_t) \equiv \frac{R^t(x_t, p_t)}{R^t(x_t, p_s)}. \tag{4.3.5}$$

An intuition of the Konüs-type output price indexes can be seen in Figure 4.2.

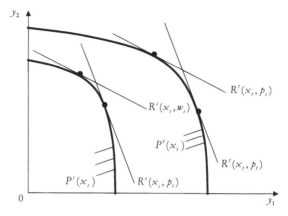

Figure 4.2 Geometric intuition of Konüs-type output price indexes.

These price indexes are often called the *true* price indexes since they are based on functions that are complete characterizations of the *true technology* at certain periods. Clearly, for the real world, they are theoretical concepts, unobserved by a human eye, yet some justified statistical methods can be used to estimate them, as we will discuss in the later chapters.

It is worth noting here that both the input and the output price indexes outlined above depend on the reference technology and reference quantities (i.e., whether it is s or t) of outputs and inputs for the input and output price indexes, respectively. Indeed, in general, for some $y \neq y^o$ and $x \neq x^o$, we have: $P_i^s(w_s, w_t, y) \neq P_i^s(w_s, w_t, y^o)$, $P_o^s(p_s, p_t, x) \neq P_o^s(p_s, p_t, x^o)$, $P_i^s(w_s, w_t, y) \neq P_i^t(w_s, w_t, y^o)$ and $P_o^s(p_s, p_t, x) \neq P_o^t(p_s, p_t, x^o)$. So, an average of the two might be considered as a compromise, as we will discuss in Chapter 7.

Alternatively, some additional restrictions can be placed on technology to make the two equal. For example, it can be shown that the output price indexes would be independent from the reference inputs *if and only if* the technology is *output homothetic*, i.e., $P(x) = G(x)P(1_N)$, for all $x \in \Re_+^N$ for some appropriate function $G(x)$ coherent with the regularity conditions on technology and where $P(x)$ is the output set characterization of technology (as discussed in detail in Chapter 1). Intuitively, this type of technology implies that increases (decreases) in inputs cause radial expansions (contractions) of the output isoquants, all related to the unit-reference output set $P(1_N)$ through the function $G(x)$. This type of technology makes the influence of inputs on the revenue function multiplicatively separable from the output sets and so it will be canceled out in the ratio form of the index. This will result in $P_o^s(p_s, p_t, x_s) = R^s(1_N, p_t)/R^s(1_N, p_s)$ and $P_o^t(p_s, p_t, x_t) = R^t(1_N, p_t)/R^t(1_N, p_s)$, making them different only with respect to the technology. So, if the technology did not change between s and t or if the change is such that $R^t(x, p) = A_o(s, t)R^s(x, p)$, $\forall p$, which is referred to as a type of the Hicks-neutral technological change (in the output space), then we will have $P_o^s(p_s, p_t, x_s) = P_o^t(p_s, p_t, x_t)$. In reality, it is hardly known that these assumptions on technology are satisfied and so it is advised to take the average of the two indexes to reconcile the issue.

Similarly, the input price indexes would be independent from the reference outputs *if and only if* the technology is *input homothetic*, i.e., $L(y) = H(y)L(1_M)$, $\forall y \in \mathfrak{R}_+^M$ for some appropriate function $H(y)$ coherent with the regularity conditions on technology characterized by the input requirement set $L(y)$. Intuitively, this type of technology implies that increases (decreases) in outputs require radial expansions (contractions) of the input isoquants, all related to the unit-reference input set $L(1_M)$ via the function $H(y)$, i.e., the influence of outputs on the cost function is multiplicatively separable from the input requirement sets, and so it will be canceled out in the ratio form of the index (check!). In turn, this will yield $P_i^s(w_s, w_t, y_s) = C^s(1_M, w_t)/C^s(1_M, w_s)$ and $P_i^t(w_s, w_t, y_t) = C^t(1_M, w_t)/C^t(1_M, w_s)$ and so they are different only with respect to the technology. Therefore, if the technology did not change between s and t or if the change is such that $C^t(y, w) = A_i(s, t)C^s(y, w)$, which is a Hicks-neutral technical change (in the input space), then we will have $P_i^s(w_s, w_t, y_s) = P_i^t(w_s, w_t, y_t)$. Clearly, such assumptions on technology may or may not hold in reality and so it is recommended to take the average of the two indexes.

4.4 ECONOMIC *QUANTITY* INDEXES

In our discussion at the beginning of this chapter, we encountered the necessity of aggregating the vector of outputs into a scalar and the vector of inputs into another scalar and then use them in constructing a productivity measure, as the ratio of these two scalars. We also mentioned that one should use an "appropriate" aggregator. An ingenious idea for such an aggregator was proposed by Malmquist (1953), who suggested a quantity index that related two quantity vectors to an indifference curve in a radial fashion – exactly how the Shephard's distance functions compare quantity vectors to the isoquant of input or output sets. Inspired by Malmquist's idea, in their seminal work, Caves et al. (1982a) used the output Shephard's distance functions to construct what they coined the *Malmquist output quantity indexes*. To describe their approach, which became quite popular in productivity measurement, let $D_o^l(x_l, y_\tau)$ be the Shephard's output distance function for the input level observed in the period l ($l = s, t$), with the technology available in the same period l, and given the output level observed in the period τ, ($\tau = t, s$) i.e.,

$$D_o^l(x_l, y_\tau) = \inf\{\theta > 0 : (y_\tau/\theta) \in P^l(x_l)\}, \quad x \in \mathfrak{R}_+^N. \qquad (4.4.1)$$

The Malmquist output quantity index wrt period s as the reference is defined as

$$Q_o^s(y_s, y_t, x_s) \equiv \frac{D_o^s(x_s, y_t)}{D_o^s(x_s, y_s)}, \qquad (4.4.2)$$

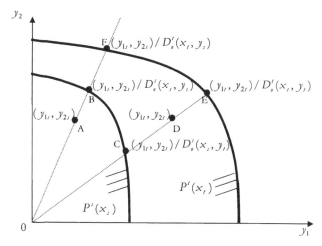

Figure 4.3 Geometric intuition of Malmquist output quantity indexes.

while the Malmquist output quantity index wrt period t as the reference is defined as

$$Q_o^t(y_s, y_t, x_t) \equiv \frac{D_o^t(x_t, y_t)}{D_o^t(x_t, y_s)}. \tag{4.4.3}$$

Figure 4.3 presents a geometric intuition of the Malmquist output quantity indexes. The figure illustrates that the s-period Malmquist output quantity index defined in (4.4.2) measures the distance between the two output allocations, y_s and y_t in two steps. Firstly, it measures the radial distance between points C and D, i.e., between the actual output allocation in the period t and its radial projection onto the output isoquant for x_s for technology in the period s. Secondly, it then adjusts for the output-oriented technical inefficiency that existed in the period s by accounting for the radial distance between points A and B.

On the other hand, the t-period Malmquist output quantity index defined in (4.4.3) measures the distance between the same two output allocations, y_s and y_t, also in two different steps. First, it measures the radial distance between points A and F, i.e., between the actual output allocation in the period s and its radial projection onto the output isoquant for x_t with the technology of period t. Second, it then accounts for the output-oriented technical inefficiency that existed in the period t by discounting the radial distance between points D and E.

In a similar fashion, the Malmquist *input* quantity indexes are defined. For this, let $D_i^l(y_l, x_\tau)$ be the Shephard's input distance function for the output observed in the period l ($l = s, t$), the technology available in this same period l, and the input observed in the period τ, ($\tau = t, s$), i.e.,

$$D_i^l(y_l, x_\tau) = \sup\{\theta > 0 : (x_\tau/\theta) \in L^l(y_l)\}, \ y \in \Re_+^M. \tag{4.4.4}$$

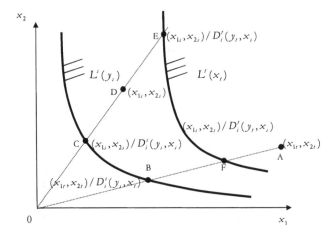

Figure 4.4 Geometric intuition of Malmquist input quantity indexes.

The Malmquist input quantity index wrt period s as the reference is defined as

$$Q_i^s(x_s, x_t, y_s) \equiv \frac{D_i^s(y_s, x_t)}{D_i^s(y_s, x_s)}, \tag{4.4.5}$$

while the Malmquist input quantity index wrt period t as the reference is defined as

$$Q_i^t(x_s, x_t, y_t) \equiv \frac{D_i^t(y_t, x_t)}{D_i^t(y_t, x_s)}. \tag{4.4.6}$$

A geometric insight of these indexes can be obtained from Figure 4.4. Specifically, the s-period Malmquist input quantity index defined in (4.4.5) measures the distance between the two input allocations, x_s and x_t, in the following two steps. Firstly, it measures the radial distance between points A and B, i.e., between the actual input allocation in the period t and its radial projection onto the input isoquant in the period s for y_s. Secondly, it then accounts for the input-oriented technical inefficiency that existed in the period s via the contraction given by the radial distance between points C and D.

In the same vein, the t-period Malmquist input quantity index defined in (4.4.6) measures the distance between the same two input allocations, x_s and x_t, through two different steps. Firstly, it captures the radial distance between points D and E, i.e., between the actual input allocation in the period s and its radial projection onto the input isoquant in the period t for y_t. And, secondly, it then discounts for the input-oriented technical inefficiency that was present in the period t by expanding by the magnitude measured by the radial distance between points A and F.

A natural question is: "When are the quantity indexes wrt different time period equal?" The answer is similar to the one we had in the case of price indexes, i.e., under certain types of homotheticity of technologies. Specifically, the output quantity indexes would be independent from the reference inputs *if and only if* the technology is *output homothetic*, i.e., $P(x) = G(x)P(\mathbf{1}_N)$, for all $x \in \mathfrak{R}_+^N$ for some appropriate function $G(x)$ coherent with the regularity conditions on technology and where $P(x)$ is the output set characterization of technology. As pointed out earlier, this kind of technology implies that increases (decreases) in inputs cause radial expansions (contractions) of the output isoquants relative to the unit-reference output set $P(\mathbf{1}_N)$ via the function $G(x)$. This feature of technology makes the influence of inputs on the output distance function multiplicatively separable from the output sets and so it will be canceled out in the ratio form of the index. This will ensure that $Q_o^s(y_s, y_t, x_s) = D_o^s(\mathbf{1}_N, y_t)/D_o^s(\mathbf{1}_N, y_s)$ and $Q_o^t(y_s, y_t, x_t) \equiv D_o^t(\mathbf{1}_N, y_t)/D_o^t(\mathbf{1}_N, y_s)$, i.e., they would be different only with respect to the technology they are referenced to. Therefore, if the technology did not change between s and t or if the change is such that $D_o^t(x, y) = A_o(s, t)D_o^s(x, y)$, $\forall y$, which is a type of the Hicks-neutral technological change in the output space, then we would have $Q_o^s(y_s, y_t, x_s) = Q_o^t(y_s, y_t, x_t)$. Of course, in reality, it is hardly known that these assumptions on technology are satisfied and so it is a good idea to take the average of the two.

Similarly, the input quantity indexes would be independent from the reference outputs *if and only if* the technology is *input homothetic*, i.e., $L(y) = H(y)L(\mathbf{1}_M)$, $\forall y \in \mathfrak{R}_+^M$ for some appropriate function $H(y)$ coherent with the regularity conditions on technology characterized by the input requirement set $L(y)$. In words, this kind of technology means that increases (decreases) in outputs require radial expansions (contractions) of the input isoquants relative to the unit-reference input set $L(\mathbf{1}_M)$ via the function $H(y)$, i.e., the influence of outputs on the input distance function is multiplicatively separable from the input requirement sets, and so it will be canceled out in the ratio form of the index (check!). In turn, we would have $Q_i^s(x_s, x_t, y_s) = D_i^s(y_s, x_t)/D_i^s(y_s, x_s)$ and $Q_i^t(x_s, x_t, y_t) = i^t(y_t, x_t)/D_i^t(y_t, x_s)$, i.e., different only with respect to the technology to which they are benchmarked. So, if the technology did not change between s and t or if the change is such that $D_i^t(y, x) = A_i(s, t)D_i^s(y, x)$, which is a type of the Hicks-neutral technological change in the input space, then we would have $Q_i^s(x_s, x_t, y_s) = Q_i^t(x_s, x_t, y_t)$. As we pointed out above, these assumptions on technology may or rather may not be satisfied and so it is a good idea to take the average of the two.

Same as with the Konüs-type price indexes defined above, the Malmquist-type quantity indexes can be called the *true* quantity indexes since they are based on functions that are complete characterizations of the true technology. Thus, they are abstract theoretical concepts, unobserved by a human, and some well-justified statistical methods shall be used to estimate them – a topic we will discuss in further chapters, while in the next section we will use these and other concepts to define some of the most popular productivity indexes.

4.5   ECONOMIC *PRODUCTIVITY* INDEXES

One natural way of defining a productivity index would be to take a ratio of two productivity measures. In the simplest, single-input–single-output case, one could take the ratio of the single factor productivity (SFP) measures for different periods, which we discussed at the beginning of this chapter, and thus get what is often referred to as the SFP index,

$$SFP\ Index = \frac{y_t/x_t}{y_s/x_s}. \tag{4.5.1}$$

Note that, this SFP index can be rearranged to possess a different meaning – the ratio of an output index to an input index, i.e.,

$$SFP\ Index = \frac{y_t/y_s}{x_t/x_s}.$$

To generalize this expression for the case of multiple inputs and multiple outputs, one may just replace the scalars in the equation above by some appropriate input and output indexes, respectively. Natural candidates for these would be the Malmquist input and output quantity indexes, discussed in the previous section, which are in a certain sense the true quantity indexes. Some roots of such an approach are found in Hicks (1961) and Moorsteen (1961), Caves et al. (1982a) and were more explicitly pointed out in the seminal work of Diewert (1992a), who briefly mentioned this approach as an alternative, but focused on deriving results for other approaches (which we will also discuss later in this book). Finally, Bjurek (1996) developed this idea more formally, clearly explaining its advantages and defining what he called "Malmquist total factor productivity index," which is probably the most appropriate name for it since it involves the Malmquist quantity indexes as well as generalizing the SFP index to a multi-input–multi-output case. However, at the point when this book was written, a more common name in the literature for this approach appeared to be the Hicks–Moorsteen productivity index approach, and so we follow this most common terminology here.[9]

Formally, the Hicks–Moorsteen productivity index with respect to period s is defined as

$$HMPI^s \equiv HM^s(x_s, x_t, y_s, y_t) \equiv \frac{Q_o^s(y_s, y_t, x_s)}{Q_i^s(x_s, x_t, y_s)}, \tag{4.5.2}$$

---

[9] Other names for this approach we ran across are: "Bjurek index," "Bjurek productivity index," "Bjurek TFP index," Hicks – Moorsteen TFP index or simply Hicks – Moorsteen index. In our opinion, if one were to acknowledge the key scholars who contributed to the conception of this index, then the name of Diewert should definitely be there, e.g., one could call it Malmquist – Hicks – Moorsteen – Diewert – Bjurek productivity or TFP index.

while the Hicks–Moorsteen productivity index wrt period t is defined as

$$HMPI^t \equiv HM^t(x_s, x_t, y_s, y_t) \equiv \frac{Q_o^t(y_s, y_t, x_t)}{Q_i^t(x_s, x_t, y_t)}. \qquad (4.5.3)$$

A natural and practical question here is which period, s or t, to choose as a reference – as in (4.5.2) or as in (4.5.3)? To avoid the arbitrariness of such a choice, researchers often consider the *geometric* mean of the two Hicks–Moorsteen productivity indexes, i.e.,

$$HMPI \equiv HM(x_s, x_t, y_s, y_t) \equiv \left[\frac{Q_o^t(y_s, y_t, x_t)}{Q_i^t(x_s, x_t, y_t)} \times \frac{Q_o^s(y_s, y_t, x_s)}{Q_i^s(x_s, x_t, y_s)} \right]^{\frac{1}{2}}.$$
$$(4.5.4)$$

The reader can find more details on this index in Bjurek (1996), Nemoto and Goto (2004), Färe et al. (2008a), Epure et al. (2011) and the references cited therein. Meanwhile we move on to consider another popular measure of productivity changes – the approach based on the so-called *Malmquist Productivity Indexes* (MPIs), which these days appear to dominate the productivity literature. This alternative and in some sense revolutionary (at that time) view on measuring productivity was proposed in the seminal work of Caves et al. (1982a), and so is sometimes referred to as the CCD-index approach.

The MPIs are constructed as ratios of Shephard's distance functions between the input–output mixes observed in different periods, but relative to the same technology observed in one of the periods. Specifically, in the case of output orientation, and when a researcher wants to measure all the quantities with respect to technology in the period s, Caves et al. (1982a) suggested using the output-oriented period-s MPI, defined as

$$MPI_o^s \equiv M_o^s(x_s, x_t, y_s, y_t) \equiv \frac{D_o^s(x_t, y_t)}{D_o^s(x_s, y_s)}, \qquad (4.5.5)$$

while choosing technology in the period t as the reference, they suggested the output-oriented period-t MPI, defined as

$$MPI_o^t \equiv M_o^t(x_s, x_t, y_s, y_t) \equiv \frac{D_o^t(x_t, y_t)}{D_o^t(x_s, y_s)}. \qquad (4.5.6)$$

Note that the approach to productivity measurement here is conceptually different from a more traditional approach of viewing a productivity indexes as a ratio of aggregate output to aggregate input in general, and different from the Hicks–Moorsteen productivity index in particular. Indeed, comparison over time in the MPI is not done independently for the output allocations between the two periods from the input allocations between the two periods, but jointly. This approach respects the fact that those inputs and outputs are not independent from each other but emerged as "couples" in (x, y)-space, and so it might be desirable to preserve this structure in comparison over time, comparing an observed "couple", (x_s, y_s), to another observed "couple" (x_t, y_t). In this approach, the output-space or the input-space alone, as used in Figure 4.3

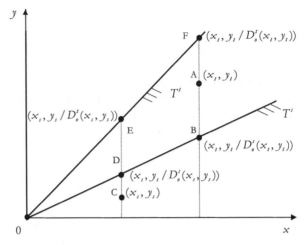

Figure 4.5 Geometric intuition of Malmquist output productivity indexes.

and Figure 4.4, are not very suitable for illustration of the intuition of the MPI, but one can use an input–output space as we do in 4.5.

Figure 4.5 illustrates that the s-period output-oriented Malmquist productivity index defined in (4.5.5) measures the distance between the two input–output allocations, (x_s, y_s) and (x_t, y_t) in the following two steps. Firstly, it accounts for the distance between points A and B, i.e., the actual input–output allocation in the period t and its vertical projection onto the technological frontier in the period s. Secondly, it then accounts for improvements (if any) in the output-oriented technical inefficiency from period s to t, represented by the distance between points C and D.

Alternatively, the t-period output-oriented Malmquist productivity index defined in (4.5.6) measures the distance between the very same two input–output allocations, (x_s, y_s) and (x_t, y_t) through two different steps. Firstly, it accounts for the distance between points C and E, i.e., between the actual input–output allocation in the period s and its vertical projection onto the technological frontier in the period t. Secondly, it then discounts for the output-oriented technical inefficiency that was present in the period t, reflected by the distance between points A and F.

Just as in the case of Hicks–Moorsteen indexes for different periods, and in the spirit of Fisher (see Chapter 7), one may choose to avoid the arbitrariness of the choice between the time periods with respect to which productivity change is measured, by taking the *geometric* mean of the two MPIs, namely, one may use

$$MPI_O \equiv M_o(x_s, x_t, y_s, y_t) \equiv \left[\frac{D_o^s(x_t, y_t)}{D_o^s(x_s, y_s)} \times \frac{D_o^t(x_t, y_t)}{D_o^t(x_s, y_s)} \right]^{\frac{1}{2}}. \quad (4.5.7)$$

Now, recalling that an alternative to the output-oriented Shephard's distance function is the input-oriented Shephard's distance function, one can, in a similar fashion, define the input-oriented s-period MPI as

$$MPI_i^s \equiv M_i^s(y_s, y_t, x_s, x_t) \equiv \frac{D_i^s(y_t, x_t)}{D_i^s(y_s, x_s)}, \tag{4.5.8}$$

and, alternatively, define the input-oriented t-period MPI as

$$MPI_i^t \equiv M_i^t(y_s, y_t, x_s, x_t) \equiv \frac{D_i^t(y_t, x_t)}{D_i^t(y_s, x_s)}. \tag{4.5.9}$$

Again, to avoid the arbitrariness of the choice between the time period with respect to which productivity is measured, researchers usually follow the Fisher approach (see Chapter 7) to consider the geometric mean of the two input-oriented MPIs, i.e.,

$$MPI_i \equiv M_i(y_s, y_t, x_s, x_t) \equiv \left[\frac{D_i^s(y_t, x_t)}{D_i^s(y_s, x_s)} \times \frac{D_i^t(y_t, x_t)}{D_i^t(y_s, x_s)} \right]^{\frac{1}{2}}. \tag{4.5.10}$$

The geometric intuition of these measures is similar to that we outlined for the output orientation and thus is left for the imagination of the reader. There is an important difference, however: the measurement scale of the input-oriented MPI defined in (4.5.10) is the reciprocal to that of the output-oriented MPI, in the same fashion as the measurement scale of the input-oriented Shephard's distance function is reciprocal to that of the output-oriented Shephard's distance function. Thus, values lower than 1 would indicate an increase (rather than a decrease) for the case of input-oriented MPI defined in (4.5.10). In this respect, to avoid confusion in interpretations, one could (and some do) use the reciprocal of the input-oriented MPI, i.e., $[M_i(y_s, y_t, x_s, x_t)]^{-1}$, to operate with the traditional measurement scale used for the indexes.

A few remarks on the advantages and disadvantages of MPI vs. HMPI are in order. So far, MPI appears to be the most popular theoretical productivity index in practice, although later some limitations of this approach were noted. One of the reasons for MPI's popularity appears to be an existence of very intuitive decompositions, some of which we will discuss in the next section.[10]

A major issue with MPI, as was noted by Grifell-Tatjé and Lovell (1995), is that under non-constant returns to scale, the MPI may inaccurately measure what one usually understands to be the productivity changes. Moreover, for some observations, under non-CRS technology, the MPI might be undefined (i.e., may have no feasible solutions).[11] This is also one of the reasons why MPI is usually used with the assumption of CRS technology – an assumption that is also fairly common in economic theory models – and so this is how we recommend it to be used as well.

---

[10] Another natural (and perhaps very important) reason for the high popularity of MPI is that early papers on MPI were published in the very top journals (*Econometrica* and *American Economic Review*), and for good reasons, which implicitly gave very strong endorsement and a relatively wide audience for this approach to date.

[11] Both of these problems can be seen if one changes Figure 4.5 such that technology is non-CRS and we leave it as an exercise for the readers.

An advantage of HMPI is that it has a "TFP interpretation" in the sense that it is an aggregate output divided by aggregate input.[12] This is a desirable, though not a necessary property for a productivity index in a general sense. HMPI is also more immune to the problem of infeasible solutions, whether technology is CRS or not.[13]

An issue with the HMPI, on the other hand, is that it involves "unreal" allocations in the comparisons, such as (x_s, y_t) and (x_t, y_s), in the sense that they were not observed in reality, and so it may effectively ignore the nature of the production process where inputs and outputs go together as a "pair," which is what MPI tries to respect. This issue may be hard to notice as a problem in practice when the changes in inputs and outputs are relatively small, yet it may be problematic (e.g., indexes may yield strange results) when the changes are large, making x_s an inadequate reference for y_t or making x_t an inadequate reference for y_s.[14]

All in all, as in many other contexts, these two (and other) approaches to productivity measurement have some advantages, yet also have disadvantages and it is important to know and acknowledge them, as well as consider them carefully when applying in practice.

What is also worth underlining is that similarly to the price and quantity indexes defined above, the productivity indexes defined in this section are often referred to as the "true productivity indexes," in the sense that they are based on functions that are complete characterizations of the *true* technology. Of course, being abstract theoretical concepts, they are not observable in the real world and so some well-justified statistical methods shall be used to estimate them, which we will discuss in further chapters. We also note that MPI and HMPI are just two of the many proposed candidates for the true productivity indexes, yet they appear to be the most popular in practice and so we mainly focus on them and on some of their variations and extensions.

4.6 DECOMPOSITION OF PRODUCTIVITY INDEXES

One particular reason for the high popularity of the MPIs is the possibility of decomposing the (total) productivity change into several quite intuitive components representing conceptually different sources of the entire productivity change. At least since the work of Nishimizu and Page (1982), many decompositions of the MPIs have appeared in the productivity literature, but perhaps the most popular in practical use is the version suggested by Färe et al. (1989a,

---

[12] Although, one may also view this as an imposition of multiplicative separability constraint requiring that the aggregate output can be decomposed into a productivity measure and aggregate input, which may be viewed as undesirable or too restrictive.

[13] See related discussions in Bjurek (1996), Briec and Kerstens (2011), Epure et al. (2011), Peyrache (2013a) and references cited therein.

[14] This is a similar (although perhaps less dramatic) reason for why indexes with fixed weights are often viewed as potentially problematic or inadequate.

1992b), although often cited to originate from the more famous work of Färe et al. (1994c). This decomposition states that

$$
\begin{aligned}
M_o(x_s, x_t, y_s, y_t) &\equiv \left(M_o^s(x_s, x_t, y_s, y_t) \times M_o^t(x_s, x_t, y_s, y_t) \right)^{1/2} \\
&= \left[\frac{D_o^s(x_t, y_t)}{D_o^s(x_s, y_s)} \times \frac{D_o^t(x_t, y_t)}{D_o^t(x_s, y_s)} \right]^{1/2} \\
&= \frac{D_o^t(x_t, y_t)}{D_o^s(x_s, y_s)} \times \left[\frac{D_o^s(x_s, y_s)}{D_o^t(x_s, y_s)} \times \frac{D_o^s(x_t, y_t)}{D_o^t(x_t, y_t)} \right]^{1/2} \\
&\qquad\qquad\qquad\qquad\qquad\qquad\qquad\qquad\qquad (4.6.1) \\
&= Eff\Delta \quad \times \quad [Tech\Delta_s \quad \times \quad Tech\Delta_t]^{1/2} \\
&= Eff\Delta \quad \times \quad Tech\Delta.
\end{aligned}
$$

In words, expression (4.6.1) says that the Malmquist productivity index can be decomposed into (at least) *two sources of productivity change: (i) efficiency change and (ii) technology change.* Indeed, the first component is the ratio of the efficiency measure in the period t to the efficiency measure in the period s, i.e., an efficiency index. If the resulting score of this component is larger than unity then there is an "improvement in efficiency" over time or what is often called the "catching up" to the frontier effect; and $(Eff\Delta - 1)\%$ gives a percentage measure of such an improvement. If the score is less than unity, then there is "deterioration in efficiency" or "lagging behind," and the percentage measure of such deterioration is given by $(1 - Eff\Delta)\%$. Clearly, if the score is equal to unity, then there is no catching up or lagging behind for the particular observation, meaning that the efficiency level (relative to frontiers) in both periods remained the same, whether low or high, and whether the frontier shifted or not.

The second component of (4.6.1) consists of two parts, both of which compare technologies (characterized by distance functions) between the two periods, s and t, but one part keeps the observations fixed at period s, while the other part keeps them fixed at period t. The geometric average of these two measures of technological change helps circumvent an arbitrary choice of the reference period (s or t) with respect to which the technology shift is measured.[15] The quantity given by $(Tech\Delta - 1)\%$ would then represent the percentage change in the technological frontier – positive in the case of technological improvement and negative in the case of technological deterioration.

An interesting extension to the decomposition above was also offered by Färe et al. (1994c), who in addition also decomposed the efficiency change into two components: the *scale efficiency change* and the *pure technical efficiency* change. Specifically, assuming that all distance functions in (4.6.1) are defined

---

[15] These two parts measuring technological change in both periods would be equivalent under (and only under) a particular type of technology – the Hicks output-neutral technology, as we discuss later in this chapter.

wrt a CRS technology (which is not a necessary, yet often a natural assumption in economic growth theory and measurement, e.g., on country-level analysis), one can additionally define the measure of distance to the non-CRS frontier by $D_o^\tau(x_\tau, y_\tau | V)$, $\tau = s, t$, and then have the following decomposition:

$$
M_o(x_s, x_t, y_s, y_t) \equiv \left[\frac{D_o^s(x_s, y_s)}{D_o^t(x_s, y_s)} \times \frac{D_o^s(x_t, y_t)}{D_o^t(x_t, y_t)} \right]^{\frac{1}{2}} \tag{4.6.2}
$$

$$
\times \frac{D_o^t(x_t, y_t | V)}{D_o^s(x_s, y_s | V)} \times \frac{SE_o^s(x_s, y_s)}{SE_o^t(x_t, y_t)}
$$

$$
= Tech\Delta \quad \times \quad PEff \,\Delta \quad \times \quad ScEff \,\Delta,
$$

where

$$
SE_o^\tau(x_\tau, y_\tau) \equiv \frac{D_o^\tau(x_\tau, y_\tau | V)}{D_o^\tau(x_\tau, y_\tau)}, \quad \tau = s, t, \tag{4.6.3}
$$

is the output-oriented Farrell-type scale efficiency measure for observation (x_τ, y_τ) with respect to technology in the period τ, $(\tau = s, t)$. Incidentally, note that the quantity $(ScEff \,\Delta - 1)\%$ would thus represent the percentage change in scale efficiency – positive in the case of improvement in scale efficiency and negative in the case of deterioration in scale efficiency. One has to remember, however, that the scale efficiency measure (4.6.3) does not indicate the source of scale inefficiency, and while it can be identified in an additional step, note that this source may be different for different periods and so one has to be careful in the interpretation. Moreover, note that both the level of scale inefficiency and the source might be totally different for different orientations of measurement. This is one of the reasons why this scale component of the decomposition has to be used and interpreted with special care and with attention to the sensitivity of results with respect to chosen orientation.

As we mentioned already, the decomposition we have just outlined is one of many that appeared in the stream of productivity research on MPI and on other productivity indexes. Yet this particular decomposition appears to be the most popular in practice. For other variants of decomposing the productivity indexes, the reader is invited to explore the works and learn about somewhat different perspectives of Grifell-Tatjé and Lovell (1995, 1999), Färe et al. (1997b), Førsund (1997), Balk (1998, 2008), O'Donnell (2010, 2012a,b), to mention just a few. Also, see Färe et al. (1997a) for a formal discussion of biased technological change and Färe et al. (2008a) for a nice, general overview.[16]

Meanwhile, we will present here just one more, and quite interesting, decomposition that was suggested by Kumar and Russell (2002). To

---

[16] In the later chapters, we will discuss methods to estimate MPIs and their components such as the "catching up" to the frontier effect, but an anxious reader may jump ahead to read a recent review of many applications of such methods in Badunenko et al. (2017).

make our discussion more intuitive, let us consider the case of two inputs, labor (L) and capital (K) used to produce a single or aggregate output Y (such as GDP) of a country. Let the technology for this country be characterized by the aggregate production function, $f^\tau(K_\tau, L_\tau)$, $\tau = s, t$. Note that in this case, the output-oriented distance function would be $D_o^\tau(K_\tau, L_\tau, Y_\tau) = Y_\tau/f^\tau(K_\tau, L_\tau)$. Now, assuming CRS for the technology, we get $Y_\tau/L_\tau = D_o^\tau(K_\tau, L_\tau, Y_\tau)f^\tau(K_\tau/L_\tau)$ and therefore, the change in the labor-productivity index can be presented as

$$\frac{Y_t/L_t}{Y_s/L_s} = \frac{D_o^t(K_t, L_t, Y_t)f^t(K_t/L_t)}{D_o^s(K_s, L_s, Y_s)f^s(K_s/L_s)}. \tag{4.6.4}$$

Furthermore, Kumar and Russell (2002) note one simple, yet very interesting decomposition variant, namely

$$\frac{Y_t/L_t}{Y_s/L_s} = \frac{D_o^t(K_t, L_t, Y_t)}{D_o^s(K_s, L_s, Y_s)} \times \left[\frac{f^t(K_s/L_s)}{f^s(K_s/L_s)} \frac{f^t(K_t/L_t)}{f^s(K_t/L_t)}\right]^{1/2} \tag{4.6.5}$$
$$\times \left[\frac{f^s(K_t/L_t)}{f^s(K_s/L_s)} \times \frac{f^t(K_t/L_t)}{f^t(K_s/L_s)}\right]^{1/2}$$
$$= Eff\Delta \times Tech\Delta \times KLACC\Delta.$$

That is, the labor productivity change is decomposed into three components or contributions: (i) (technical) efficiency change $(Eff\Delta)$, (ii) technological change $(Tech\Delta)$ and (iii) capital (per labor) accumulation change $(KLACC\Delta)$. The latter component is also known in the literature as the contribution to the change in labor productivity due to the change in "capital deepness" (i.e., change in K/L also known as capital per labor intensity).

Although this decomposition (4.6.5) is done for a special case of single-output CRS technology, it is very interesting and useful because, in some sense, it is an extension to the discrete version of the Solow (1957) decomposition and is also a twist of the Färe et al. (1989a) decomposition. Indeed, it allows for decomposing labor productivity change into contributions from technological change and from change in capital per labor (the last component in the equation above), as in the Solow approach, but also shows the contribution from the efficiency change or the "catching up to the frontier" effect as in the Färe et al. (1989a) approach. The reader is also encouraged to check out other interesting uses of this index in testing various hypotheses and with the use of various statistical methods in Kumar and Russell (2002) and its various follow-ups, e.g., Henderson and Russell (2005), Badunenko et al. (2008), Zelenyuk (2014c), Trinh and Zelenyuk (2015) and a recent review by Badunenko et al. (2017), to mention a few.

4.7 DIRECTIONAL PRODUCTIVITY INDEXES

The appearance of the directional distance function (which we considered in Chapter 1) as a measure of efficiency or, more generally, as a complete characterization of technology, made it possible to introduce directional productivity indexes and indicators and we will consider some of these in this and the next sections. One of the first examples of such an index was proposed by Chung et al. (1997a) who called them the Malmquist–Luenberger Productivity Indexes.

Let us first describe the idea of Chung et al. (1997a), but with somewhat greater generality. Let $D_d^\tau(x^l, y^l; -d_x^r, d_y^r)$ be the directional distance function defined for the input–output mix observed in the period l $(l = s, t)$, for technology used in the period τ, $(\tau = s, t)$, and with the directional vectors chosen by the researcher as the measurement orientation be $(-d_x^r, d_y^r)$, for $r = s, t$. Formally, this function would be given by

$$D_d^\tau(x_l, y_l; -d_x^r, d_y^r) = \sup\{\theta : (x_l - \theta\, d_x^r, y_l + \theta\, d_y^r) \in T^\tau\},$$

where T^τ is the technology set characterizing production possibilities for period τ, $(\tau = s, t)$, i.e.,

$$T^\tau = \{(x, y) : \ x\ can\ produce\ y\ given\ possibilities\ in\ period\ \tau\}.$$

Now, we define two types of Malmquist–Luenberger Productivity Indexes: [17]

$$MLPI_o = \left[\frac{\left(1 + D_d^s(x_s, y_s; -d_x^s, d_y^s)\right)\left(1 + D_d^t(x_s, y_s; -d_x^s, d_y^s)\right)}{\left(1 + D_d^s(x_t, y_t; -d_x^t, d_y^t)\right)\left(1 + D_d^t(x_t, y_t; -d_x^t, d_y^t)\right)} \right]^{1/2},$$

$$(4.7.1)$$

and

$$MLPI_i = \left[\frac{\left(1 - D_d^s(x_s, y_s; -d_x^s, d_y^s)\right)\left(1 - D_d^t(x_s, y_s; -d_x^s, d_y^s)\right)}{\left(1 - D_d^s(x_t, y_t; -d_x^t, d_y^t)\right)\left(1 - D_d^t(x_t, y_t; -d_x^t, d_y^t)\right)} \right]^{1/2}.$$

$$(4.7.2)$$

Note that these are not exactly the input-oriented and output-oriented indexes, respectively. Indeed, both of them may have any orientation of the input–output mix defined by the chosen direction $(-d_x^r, d_y^r)$. Yet, they differ from each other in the style they are defined – whether to focus more on the expansion of outputs (output-focused), as in (4.7.1) or more on the contraction of inputs (input-focused), as in (4.7.2). Presentation of the geometric intuition of the two indexes is similar to the cases we presented above and so is left as a drawing exercise for the reader.

Note that to avoid the ambiguity of choice between (4.7.1) and (4.7.2), researchers may follow the example of Moorsteen (1961) and Hicks (1961), who defined their indexes as ratios of an "output quantity index" to an "input

---

[17] These indexes are slightly generalized versions of those proposed by Zelenyuk (2002).

quantity index." Specifically, Zelenyuk (2002) suggested using what he called the *Total Malmquist–Luenberger Productivity Index,* defined as

$$TMLPI \equiv MLPI_o / MLPI_i. \tag{4.7.3}$$

We will show later in this chapter that under certain restrictions on the directions, this index is equivalent to the MPI if and only if technology exhibits CRS, meaning that TMLPI is a generalization of the MPI.

4.8 DIRECTIONAL PRODUCTIVITY CHANGE INDICATORS

At the end of the previous section, we witnessed that, to be used in construction of a productivity index, the directional distance functions had to go through transformations, made via appropriate choice of the directional vector and a unit shift, as is done in (4.7.1) and (4.7.2). This is because the directional distance function, in its original form, does not have a multiplicative nature that is compatible with an index number, because it has an additive element. More precisely, the directional distance function has an additively multiplicative nature, in the sense that it gives a number that needs to be *multiplied* by the prespecified vector to be *added* to the point in the set to move this point onto the frontier of this set. This suggests that there might be an alternative, an additive, a way of defining a measure of productivity change based on the directional distance functions. Indeed, this route was taken by Chambers (1996), who defined what are now known as the Luenberger productivity change *indicators*. To outline this approach, we use the notation adopted in the previous section, and define the s-period Luenberger productivity change indicator as

$$LPI_s := LPI(x_s, y_s; x_t, y_t | d_x^t, d_y^t; d_x^s, d_y^s, T^s)$$
$$= D_d^s(x_s, y_s; -d_x^s, d_y^s) - D_d^s(x_t, y_t; -d_x^t, d_y^t), \tag{4.8.1}$$

while the t-period Luenberger productivity change indicator is defined as

$$LPI_t := LPI(x_s, y_s; x_t, y_t | d_x^t, d_y^t; d_x^s, d_y^s, T^t)$$
$$= D_d^t(x_s, y_s; -d_x^s, d_y^s) - D_d^t(x_t, y_t; -d_x^t, d_y^t). \tag{4.8.2}$$

Similarly as for the productivity indexes, to avoid the ambiguity in the choice between the period with respect to which productivity is to be measured, researchers can take an average between the two. Because the nature of this indicator is additive (the difference of two functions), an adequate average would certainly be the arithmetic average, unlike for the indexes where the geometric average was taken because of their multiplicative nature. Thus, the Luenberger indicator of productivity change from s to t would be

$$LPI_{st} := LPI(x_s, y_s; x_t, y_t | d_x^t, d_y^t; d_x^s, d_y^s, T^s, T^t)$$
$$= \frac{1}{2}(LPI_s + LPI_t). \tag{4.8.3}$$

Similarly, as the Malmquist productivity index, the Luenberger productivity change indicator can be easily decomposed to show the sources of productivity change from s to t, e.g.

$$LPI_{st} = LEff\,\Delta + LTech\,\Delta, \tag{4.8.4}$$

where

$$LEff\,\Delta = D_d^s(x_s, y_s; -d_x^s, d_y^s) - D_d^t(x_t, y_t; -d_x^t, d_y^t) \tag{4.8.5}$$

and

$$LTech\,\Delta = \frac{1}{2}\big(D_d^t(x_s, y_s; -d_x^s, d_y^s) - D_d^s(x_s, y_s; -d_x^s, d_y^s)$$
$$+ D_d^t(x_t, y_t; -d_x^t, d_y^t) - D_d^s(x_t, y_t; -d_x^t, d_y^t)\big). \tag{4.8.6}$$

We shall also note that, as for the MPI, this is just one of various possible decompositions (originally suggested by Chambers et al., 1996a), and one can easily define others, analogous to various decompositions of the MPI. As a matter of fact, one can easily notice that decompositions (4.8.5)–(4.8.6) are just the additive analogues to multiplicative decompositions that we presented for the MPI in previous sections.

Finally, the reader must have realized by now that one can also define the Hicks–Moorsteen-type indexes based on the directional distance functions – this was done in Briec and Kerstens (2004), who named them Luenberger–Hicks–Moorsteen Productivity indicators and showed their relationships with other indexes.

4.9   RELATIONSHIPS AMONG PRODUCTIVITY INDEXES

A natural question that must have already entered the reader's mind is: "How are all these different measures of productivity changes related to each other?" Some of the answers to this question were given in the productivity literature and we outline some of the most important results here in this section. The simplest, but important to know, result is obtained for a single-input–single-output case, which we state in the next theorem.

Theorem. *In the single-input–single-output case (i.e., $N = 1, M = 1$), we have*

$$M_o^\tau(x_s, x_t, y_s, y_t) = 1/M_i^\tau(y_s, y_t, x_s, x_t) = \frac{y_t/y_s}{x_t/x_s} = SFP\ Index, \tag{4.9.1}$$

$\forall(x_\tau, y_\tau) \in \mathfrak{R}_+ \times \mathfrak{R}_+$, $(\tau = s, t)$ *if and only if technologies in both periods s and t exhibit (global) CRS (i.e., $\lambda T^\tau = T^\tau$, $\forall \lambda > 0$).*

The proof of this theorem is simple (and is based on the homogeneity properties of the distance functions in inputs and outputs) and we leave it to the reader.[18] Intuitively, this theorem says that the Malmquist productivity index is a generalization of the SFP Index, and is identical to it in the single-input–single-output case.

How about the *input- vs. output-oriented* MPIs? The reader might have guessed already that there must be a relationship between them under any (global) CRS technology – since then we have the reciprocal relationship between the input and output distance functions. We formalize this relationship in the next theorem, and because the proof is similar to those we made in previous chapters, we also leave it to the reader.

Theorem. *In a multi-input–multi-output case, we have*

$$M_o^\tau(x_s, x_t, y_s, y_t) = 1/M_i^\tau(y_s, y_t, x_s, x_t), \quad (4.9.2)$$

$\forall (x_\tau, y_\tau) \in \mathfrak{R}_+^N \times \mathfrak{R}_+^M$, $\tau = s, t$ *if and only if technologies in both periods s and t exhibits (global) CRS.*

The next question deals with the equivalence of the MPIs defined with respect to different time periods. From the related discussion above, the reader might expect these indexes are not equivalent in general, yet they may be so if technology change satisfies some types of Hicks neutrality – this being the notion we mentioned above and now restate more formally.

Definition. Technology change between some periods s and t is Hicks output-neutral if and only if the output set characterization of technology in the period t (denoted as $P^t(x)$) can be multiplicatively decomposed into output set characterization of technology in the period s and a scaling factor, i.e.,

$$P^t(x) = A_o(x, s, t) P^s(x), \ \forall x \in \mathfrak{R}_+^N \quad (4.9.3)$$

and it is Hicks input-neutral if and only if the input set characterization of technology in the period t ($L^t(y)$) can be multiplicatively decomposed into input set characterization of technology in the period s and a scaling factor, i.e.,

$$L^t(y) = A_i(y, s, t) L^s(y), \ \forall y \in \mathfrak{R}_+^M. \quad (4.9.4)$$

Intuitively, this means that in the case of Hicks output-neutral technology, the output sets expand or contract radially (between s and t) in a "parallel" manner, different by a scalar factor $A_o(x, s, t)$, which is the same constant for a fixed (x, s, t), yet it is allowed to vary with x, and depend on s and t. Similarly, in the case of Hicks input-neutral technology, the input sets expand (or contract) radially (between s and t) also in a "parallel" manner by a scalar factor $A_i(y, s, t)$ which is the same constant for a fixed (x, s, t), yet it is allowed

---

[18] To our knowledge, this result goes back to Berg et al. (1992), Grifell-Tatjé and Lovell (1995) and formally proven by Färe and Grosskopf (1996).

to vary with x, and depend on s and t. It is also common to assume a more restrictive form of Hicks neutrality, where the scaling factors are independent from x and y, i.e., $A_o(s, t)$ and $A_i(s, t)$ instead of $A_o(x, s, t)$ and $A_i(y, s, t)$.[19]

It is also possible to have an even stricter case, when technology is both Hicks output-neutral and Hicks input-neutral, which is usually referred to as the *joint output and input Hicks neutrality*. We shall note that this is just one of the various versions defining the notion of neutrality of technological change – the notion that goes back at least to Hicks (1932).[20]

Importantly, note that this definition is *local*, in the sense that we do not restrict the neutrality to hold globally for all the periods (which is too restrictive). It imposes the Hicks neutrality to hold for some periods, s and t, and allow for potentially different types of technology change in other periods. As a result, this definition appears to be more practical than commonly used global versions.[21] Indeed, such a neutrality assumption about the technology change might be considered as a suitable simplification for changes in very short periods, yet it looks overly restrictive for longer (and certainly so for all) periods.

The next lemma helps clarifying the implications of the Hicks output-neutral technology change for the revenue and the Shephard's output distance functions.

Lemma. *In a multi-input–multi-output case, we have*

$$D_o^t(x, y) = D_o^s(x, y)/A_o(x, s, t), \; \forall (x, y) \in \Re_+^N \times \Re_+^M, \qquad (4.9.5)$$

and

$$R^t(x, p) = R^s(x, p)A_o(t), \; \forall x \in \Re_+^N, \; p \in \Re_{++}^M, \qquad (4.9.6)$$

if and only if technology change between s and t is Hicks output-neutral, i.e., satisfies (4.9.3).

Proof. Suppose (4.9.3) is true, then

$$D_o^t(x, y) = \inf_\theta \{\theta > 0 \; : \; y/\theta \in P^t(x)\} = \inf_\theta \{\theta > 0 \; : \\ y/\theta \in A_o(x, s, t)P^s(x)\} = \inf_\theta \{(\theta A_o(x, s, t)) > 0 \; : \; y/(\theta A_o(x, s, t)) \in$$

---

[19] Sometimes definitions also have the scaling factor depending only on s or on t, which might be misleading because the difference between technologies typically depends also on the distance in time, i.e., the further t is from s the bigger the scaling factor can be in the case of continuing technology progress.

[20] Other versions and relationships between them can be found in Blackorby et al. (1976) and Chambers and Färe (1994).

[21] The special case of *global* Hicks output-neutral technology change is usually defined as a situation when $P^\tau(x) = A(\tau, x)\tilde{P}(x)$, $\forall x \in \Re_+^N$ and for all τ, i.e., the output set at any τ can be multiplicatively decomposed into some other output set characterization of technology that *does not depend on time* (denoted as $\tilde{P}(x)$), and a scaling factor $A(\tau, x)$ or even more restrictively on $A(\tau)$. This structure, however, appears to be too restrictive.

$P^s(x)\}/A_o(x, s, t) = \inf_{\tilde{\theta}}\{\tilde{\theta} > 0 \;\; : \;\; y/\tilde{\theta} \in P^s(x)\}/A_o(x, s, t) = D_o^s(x, y)/A_o(x, s, t).$

Suppose (4.9.5) is true, then

$P^t(x) = \{y \;\; : \;\; 0 \le D_o^t(x, y) \le 1\} = \{y \;\; : \;\; 0 \le D_o^s(x, y)/A_o(x, s, t) \le 1\} = A_o(x, s, t)\{y/A_o(x, s, t) \;\; : \;\; 0 \le D_o^s(x, y/A_o(x, s, t)) \le 1\} = A_o(x, s, t)\{\tilde{y} \;\; : \;\; 0 \le D_o^s(x, \tilde{y}) \le 1\} = A_o(x, s, t)P^s(x).$

A proof for the revenue function is similar and is left as an exercise. $\square$

This lemma helps establishing the following key theorem.

Theorem. *In a multi-input–multi-output case, we have*

$$M_o^s(x_s, x_t, y_s, y_t) = M_o^t(x_s, x_t, y_s, y_t), \tag{4.9.7}$$

$\forall(x_s, y_s),\ (x_t, y_t) \in \Re_+^N \times \Re_+^M$ *if and only if technology change between s and t is Hicks output-neutral and independently from x, i.e., satisfies (4.9.3) with $A_o(x, s, t) = A_o(s, t)$.*

The proof of this result is almost immediate and is left as an exercise (also see Färe et al., 2008a). Intuitively, this theorem says that the output-oriented MPIs are invariant wrt the time relative to which they are measured, s or t, *if and only if* the output set in the period t is a radial expansion or contraction of the output set in the period s. Roughly speaking, such technology means that, with time, the output sets (for the same level of inputs) change in an equiproportional or "radial" way *in all outputs*, i.e., without a "productivity bias" for any of the outputs relative to the other outputs. One can establish a similar result for the input-oriented MPI, in which case the notion of the (local and global) Hicks input-neutral technology change must be involved together with the following lemma.

Lemma. *In a multi-input–multi-output case, we have*

$$D_i^t(y, x) = D_i^s(y, x)/A_i(y, s, t), \quad \forall(x, y) \in \Re_+^N \times \Re_+^M, \tag{4.9.8}$$

and

$$C^t(y, w) = C^s(y, w)A_i(y, s, t), \quad \forall w \in \Re_{++}^N,\ y \in \Re_+^M, \tag{4.9.9}$$

if and only if technology change between s and t is Hicks input-neutral, i.e., satisfies (4.9.4).

Proof. Suppose (4.9.4) is true, then

$D_i^t(y, x) = \sup_{\theta}\{\theta > 0 \;\; : \;\; x/\theta \in L^t(y)\} = \sup_{\theta}\{\theta > 0 \;\; : \;\; y/\theta \in A_i(y, s, t)L^s(y)\} = \sup_{\theta}\{(\theta A_i(y, s, t)) > 0 \;\; : \;\; x/(\theta A_i(y, s, t)) \in L^s(y)\}/A_i(y, s, t) = \sup_{\tilde{\theta}}\{\tilde{\theta} > 0 \;\; : \;\; y/\tilde{\theta} \in L^s(y)\}/A_i(y, s, t) = D_i^s(y, x)/A_i(y, s, t).$

Suppose (4.9.8) is true, then

$L^t(y) = \{x \ : \ D_i^t(y, x) \geq 1\} = \{y \ : \ D_i^s(y, x)/A_i(y, s, t) \geq 1\} = A_i(y, s, t)\{x/A_i(y, s, t) \ : \ D_i^s(y, x/A_i(y, s, t)) \geq 1\} = A_i(y, s, t)\{\tilde{x} \ : \ D_i^s(y, \tilde{x}) \geq 1\} = A_i(y, s, t)L^s(y).$

A proof for the cost functions is similar and is left as an exercise.   □

The reader might also wonder about a relationship between the Hicks–Moorsteen and the Malmquist productivity indexes. To answer this question, we first need to use the concept of *inverse homotheticity*, attributed to Shephard (1970) and outlined in the next definition.

Definition. Technology in the period l is *inverse homothetic* if and only if

$$D_o^\tau(x_l, y_l) = D_o^\tau(x_*, y_l)/F(D_i^\tau(y_*, x_l)), \tag{4.9.10}$$

$\forall(x_l, y_l) \in \Re_+^N \times \Re_+^M$, $l, \tau = s, t$ where F is a strictly positive, continuous, increasing function, and x_* and y_* are arbitrary input and output vectors, respectively (e.g., can be unit vectors, as in Färe and Primont, 1995).

Inverse homotheticity is a property that is more restrictive than the input homotheticity alone or the output homotheticity alone, which we used earlier. In fact, another and easier way to understand the *inverse homothetic* technology is to think of it as a technology that is *both* (or jointly) input homothetic and output homothetic at the same time (Färe and Primont, 1995). The next theorem describes what this property implies for the productivity indexes.

Theorem. *In a multi-input–multi-output case, we have*

$$M_o^\tau(x_s, x_t, y_s, y_t) = HM^\tau(x_s, x_t, y_s, y_t), \tag{4.9.11}$$

$\forall(x_s, y_s), (x_t, y_t) \in \Re_+^N \times \Re_+^M$ *if and only if technology in both periods ($\tau = s, t$) is inverse homothetic and exhibits CRS.*

The proof of this theorem is relatively straightforward and we leave it to the reader (the original proof can be found in Färe et al., 1996).[22] What is important to highlight is the intuition behind this theorem: it says that the two productivity indexes are equivalent if and only if the input and output distance functions are multiplicatively separable in outputs and inputs, respectively, and, in addition, the technology set in each period must exhibit CRS. This is quite a restrictive condition, yet note that it is not only sufficient but also the necessary condition for the two indexes to be equivalent.

Now, let us turn to showing some equivalences for the directional productivity indexes and indicators. For this, recall from Chapter 3 that, $\forall(x_\tau, y_\tau) \in \Re_+^N \times \Re_+^M$, $\tau, l = s, t$, we have

$$D_d^\tau(x_l, y_l; 0, y_l) = \frac{1}{D_o^\tau(x_l, y_l)} - 1, \tag{4.9.12a}$$

---

[22] Also see Peyrache (2013c,a) and Mizobuchi (2017a,b) for more recent related discussions.

and

$$D_d^\tau(x_l, y_l; -x_l, 0) = 1 - \frac{1}{D_i^\tau(x_l, y_l)}. \qquad (4.9.12b)$$

This implies that for the special cases of directions $(0, y_l)$ and $(-x_l, 0)$, and $\forall(x_l, y_l) \in \Re_+^N \times \Re_+^M$, $l, \tau = s, t$ we have,

$$MLPI_o = \left[\frac{\left(1 + D_d^s(x_s, y_s; 0, y_s)\right)}{\left(1 + D_d^s(x_t, y_t; 0, y_t)\right)} \frac{\left(1 + D_d^t(x_s, y_s; 0, y_s)\right)}{\left(1 + D_d^t(x_t, y_t; 0, y_t)\right)} \right]^{1/2}$$
$$= MPI_o, \qquad (4.9.13a)$$

and

$$MLPI_i = \left[\frac{\left(1 - D_d^s(x_s, y_s; -x_s, 0)\right)}{\left(1 - D_d^s(x_t, y_t; -x_t, 0)\right)} \frac{\left(1 - D_d^t(x_s, y_s; -x_s, 0)\right)}{\left(1 - D_d^t(x_t, y_t; -x_t, 0)\right)} \right]^{1/2}$$
$$= MPI_i. \qquad (4.9.13b)$$

Moreover, we can also establish a relationship between MLPI and MPI for a more general directional vector, taking into account both input and output directions, under a CRS assumption. In particular, following Zelenyuk (2002) and Zelenyuk (2014a), note that for any pair of scalars $(\alpha, \beta) \geq 0$, we have

$$D_d^\tau(x_l, y_l; -\alpha x_l, \beta y_l) = (D_i^\tau(x_l, y_l) - 1)/(\alpha D_i^\tau(x_l, y_l) + \beta), \quad (4.9.14a)$$

and

$$D_d^\tau(x_l, y_l; -\alpha x_l, \beta y_l) = (1 - D_o^\tau(x_l, y_l))/(\beta D_o^\tau(x_l, y_l) + \alpha). \quad (4.9.14b)$$

$\forall(x_l, y_l) \in \Re_+^N \times \Re_+^M$, $l, \tau = s, t$ *if and only* if technology exhibits constant returns to scale, i.e., $\lambda T = T, \forall \lambda > 0$.

Rearranging these expressions and plugging them into (4.6.3), we can see, after collecting the terms, that under (global) CRS, we have

$$TMLPI = MPI_o, \quad \forall(x_l, y_l) \in \Re_+^N \times \Re_+^M, \ l = s, t. \qquad (4.9.15)$$

This means that TMLPI is a generalization of MPI_o (and of MPI_i). Recalling that MPI_o is a generalization of SFP and, as we will see in Chapter 7, of such TFP indexes as the Fisher and Törnqvist productivity indexes, the result in (4.9.15) also tells us that so is the TMLPI.

We can also decompose TMLPI, similarly as for MPI, to get

$$TMLPI = Eff\Delta \times Tech\Delta, \qquad (4.9.16)$$

i.e., under CRS, the decomposition of the directional productivity index, $TMLPI$, is equivalent to the popular decomposition of the MPI_o.

An important question now is whether *TMLPI* can give some added value that cannot be obtained from either MPI_o or MPI_i? It can. *TMLPI* can account for the *weight* of the output orientation relative to the input orientation, described by the directional vector $(-\alpha x, \beta y)$, $(\alpha, \beta) \geq 0$. Results

(4.9.14a) and (4.9.14b) imply that *TMLPI* is invariant to this weight under the (global) *CRS*. But what if the technology does not exhibit CRS? Also, what if the productivity index is decomposed and some parts are based on a non-CRS assumption?[23] In such cases, the measurement based *only on the input* orientation might yield potentially very different conclusions from those derived based on *only the output* orientation. If the context of the study implies that *both* orientations are important, then *TMLPI* might be a preferred way to follow.

We now consider the relationship between the Luenberger productivity change indicator and the MPIs. Again using (4.9.12a) we get,

$$LPI_s = \frac{1}{D_o^s(x_s, y_s)} - \frac{1}{D_o^s(x_t, y_t)}. \tag{4.9.17}$$

On the other hand, let us take the logarithm of an s-period MPI, and we get

$$\ln\left(MPI_o^s\right) = \ln\left(\frac{1}{D_o^s(x_s, y_s)}\right) - \ln\left(\frac{1}{D_o^s(x_t, y_t)}\right). \tag{4.9.18}$$

Expressions (4.9.17) and (4.9.18) look very similar, with the difference being the logs in (4.9.18). A closer look reveals that they are not only similar looking, but they are also similar numerically. This can be seen by taking the first-order Taylor series approximation, for the case when the denominator is close to unity (which is a natural point of approximation of this function from the economic point of view, because firms strive to be efficient).[24]

Curiously enough, division of (4.9.17) by (4.9.18) would give what is referred to as the logarithmic mean, which indeed, for any two real positive numbers a_1 and a_2, is defined as

$$M_{\ln}(a_1, a_2) \equiv \lim_{(\xi_1, \xi_2) \to (a_1, a_2)} \frac{\xi_1 - \xi_2}{\ln(\xi_1) - \ln(\xi_2)}$$

$$= \begin{cases} a, & a_1 = a_2 = a \\ \frac{a_1 - a_2}{\ln(a_1) - \ln(a_2)}, & a_1 \neq a_2 \end{cases}. \tag{4.9.19}$$

Rearranging (4.9.19) for the case when $a_1 \neq a_2$, we get

$$\ln(a_1) - \ln(a_2) = \frac{a_1 - a_2}{M_{\ln}(a_1, a_2)}. \tag{4.9.20}$$

Expression (4.9.20) helps in relating (4.9.17) and (4.9.18), as was noted by Balk et al. (2005). Specifically, one can immediately get

$$MPI_o^s = \exp\left\{ LPI^s / M_{\ln}\left(\frac{1}{D_o^s(x_s, y_s)}, \frac{1}{D_o^s(x_t, y_t)}\right) \right\}. \tag{4.9.21}$$

---

[23] For a review of measuring productivity changes with MPI under a non-CRS assumption and of decomposition issues, see Grifell-Tatjé and Lovell (1999) and Färe et al. (1997b). Also see Balk (1998, 2008) for related discussions.

[24] See Boussemart et al. (2003).

Similarly, for the t-period MPI one can also get

$$MPI_o^t = \exp\left\{LPI_{\ln}^t / M_{\ln}\left(\frac{1}{D_o^t(x_s, y_s)}, \frac{1}{D_o^t(x_t, y_t)}\right)\right\}, \quad (4.9.22)$$

and thus, for the average of the two periods MPIs, one would get

$$MPI_o \equiv \left(MPI_o^s \times MPI_o^t\right)^{1/2}$$

$$= \exp\left\{\frac{1}{2}\left(\frac{LPI^s}{M_{\ln}\left(\frac{1}{D_o^s(x_s,y_s)}, \frac{1}{D_o^s(x_t,y_t)}\right)}\right.\right.$$

$$\left.\left. + \frac{LPI^t}{M_{\ln}\left(\frac{1}{D_o^t(x_s,y_s)}, \frac{1}{D_o^t(x_t,y_t)}\right)}\right)\right\}. \quad (4.9.23)$$

It is important to note that this relationship is shown for a specific directional vector $(0, y)$ that gave the relationship (4.9.16) and one can also derive a similar relationship for the direction $(-x, 0)$ with the input-oriented MPI, and we leave it to the reader as an exercise.[25] Moreover, one could also use the relationships derived by Zelenyuk (2002, 2014a), listed in (4.9.12a–4.9.12b) and (4.9.13a–4.9.13b), to obtain relationships analogous to (4.9.21)–(4.9.23) for a more general direction $(-\alpha x, \beta y)$, $(\alpha, \beta) \geq 0$, and to the TMLPI, for the case of CRS technology, which we also leave to the reader as an interesting exercise.

Finally, it is worth noting that one can also impose a version of Hicks-neutrality on technology via the directional distance function, e.g., by assuming that the technology effect is separable from the input–output aggregating function, i.e., technological impact comes as a shift in the technology frontier without augmenting the relative importance of each input in producing any of the outputs. In particular, one could use the same Hicks-neutrality definition as we used for the Shephard's distance function when using MLPIs or TMLPI, while for the context of LPIs one may define an additive analogue to it, e.g.,

$$D_d^t(x, y; -d_x, d_y) = \mathcal{A}_d(t) + D_d^s(x, y; -d_x, d_y), \ \forall(x, y) \in \mathfrak{R}_+^N \times \mathfrak{R}_+^M.$$

With this type of structure on technology, sometimes referred to as *parallel neutrality,* one can then obtain equality of (4.9.21) and (4.9.22) or of the elements in (4.6.1) and (4.6.2), which is left as an exercise (see Briec et al., 2006 and Färe et al., 2008a for a related discussion and more details).

---

[25] Note, however, that this relationship is not giving a "closed form," in the sense that the right-hand side involves the left-hand side. Indeed, looking closer at (4.9.21) and (4.9.22) reveals their denominators involve expressions whose denominator is exactly the log of the left-hand side. So, in some sense, this relationship is tautological.

4.10 INDEXES VS. GROWTH ACCOUNTING

Let us now look at a relationship between the productivity indexes and the productivity change measures from the growth accounting approach of Solow (1957) that we considered at the beginning of the chapter.

First of all, recall that Solow's approach is more restrictive, in the sense that it was derived for the single-output case with the technology characterized by the aggregate production function with a restriction that technological change is Hicks-neutral, i.e. when technology is characterized by some aggregate production function of the following form

$$q_t^k \equiv \psi_t(x_t^k) = a_t^k \psi(x_t^k), \qquad k = 1, \ldots, n. \tag{4.10.1}$$

The Malmquist productivity index approach does not make such restrictive assumptions in its definition. An important question, then, is: what if the technology is indeed like that given by (4.10.1) – would MPI give the same answer as Solow's approach?

To answer this question, note that there is another important difference: the MPI approach does not require full efficiency, while the Solow approach does. Instead, we know that MPI allows for the existence of inefficiency and allows measuring changes in inefficiency as one of the sources of the productivity change along with the technological change. This is one of the key advantages of the MPI over Solow's approach. In fact, because of this, Solow's approach can be viewed as a special case of the MPI approach. This can be seen if we incorporate the technology assumption (4.10.1) into the MPI component of technological change, and noting that the output distance function would be $D_o^\tau(x_l, q_l) = q_l/(a_\tau^k \psi(x_l^k))$ where $l, \tau = s, t$, and therefore

$$
\begin{aligned}
Tech\, \Delta &\equiv \left[\frac{D_o^s(x_s, y_s)}{D_o^t(x_s, y_s)} \times \frac{D_o^s(x_t, y_t)}{D_o^t(x_t, y_t)} \right]^{1/2} \\
&= \left[\frac{q_s/(a_s \psi(x_s))}{q_s/(a_t \psi(x_s))} \times \frac{q_t/(a_s \psi(x_t))}{q_t/(a_t \psi(x_t))} \right]^{1/2} \\
&= \left[\frac{a_t}{a_s} \times \frac{a_t}{a_s} \right]^{1/2} = \frac{a_t}{a_s}.
\end{aligned}
$$

Thus, the technology change component of MPI gives a ratio of Solow's growth accounting TFP-measure in the period t to that in the period s, i.e., an index for Solow's TFP. Thus, the natural logarithm of the technological change component of the MPI gives a discrete approximation to the theoretical (continuous) version of Solow's growth accounting, since we have

$$
\begin{aligned}
\ln(Tech\, \Delta) &= \ln(a_t/a_s) \\
&\approx a_t/a_s - 1 \\
&\approx g(a_t) \equiv d\ln a_t/dt.
\end{aligned}
$$

Finally, it must be also clear that similar relationships can be shown for other productivity indexes – directly or indirectly (e.g., via a relationship to the MPI).

One can also establish relationships for the measures of productivity change based on directional distance functions, such as the MLPIs, TMLPI, and LPIs, and we leave these tasks as exercises for the readers.

4.11 MULTILATERAL COMPARISONS, TRANSITIVITY, AND CIRCULARITY

As we emphasized above, the indexes we have been considering in this chapter are *bilateral* indexes, i.e., they are designed to measure changes between two periods (or, more generally, states), some s and t. Thus, one should be careful in using and especially in interpreting them for multilateral comparisons. Indeed, if one has to compare across more than two periods or states then a question of internal coherence for the indexes across all periods or states arises. One of the properties that characterizes such coherence is the *transitivity* property and a closely related *circularity* property.

4.11.1 General Remarks on Transitivity

In general, in formal logic, a relation (whatever logical rule it is based on) is called transitive if and only if, when suggesting that a is related to b and that b is related to c, this same relation (based on the same rule) must also guarantee that a is related to c.[26]

In layman terms, and in the productivity context, the general notion of transitivity can be seen as a requirement that ensures that if a measure suggests that firm A is more productive than firm B and if according to the same measure the firm B is also more productive than firm C, then the same measure should also conclude that firm A is more productive than firm C. Such notion of transitivity seems intuitive and hard to argue with, at least on a layman level, and so this seems like a natural property that one may expect to hold when comparing various phenomena. This "natural" perception is often misconceived due to thinking of a univariate context, where transitivity is trivially satisfied when comparing numbers on a real line: indeed, $\forall a, b, c \in \mathfrak{R}$ we obviously have $a > b$ and $b > c$ implies $a > c$. Things get more tricky, however, when comparing points (vectors) in a multidimensional space – because some elements of one vector may be larger than corresponding elements of another vector while the opposite could be for other elements – what's the best way to compare then? In general, to be able to rank vectors in multidimensional space one often needs to aggregate each vector into a scalar and then rank the scalars. This sounds easy, yet the problem is that the result may depend on how one aggregates – and that there are infinitely many possibilities to do so! One might be tempted to use the Euclidean norm for the aggregation and comparison of vectors (as it has very nice mathematical properties), yet this would only measure the *length* of the vector, ignoring the *direction*, which is usually very

---

[26] Formally, a relation $\mathcal{R}$ is transitive on a set $\mathcal{A}$ means $\forall a, b, c \in \mathcal{A} \; : \; a\mathcal{R}b \wedge b\mathcal{R}c \Rightarrow a\mathcal{R}c$.

important from the economic point of view. Indeed, taking a glance at the output and input sets we were drawing above (Figure 4.3 and 4.4), one should immediately realize that vectors of very different lengths can be on the same output (or input) isoquants and thus, according to economic theory, must be treated as equivalent bundles from a technological point of view.

Note that by adopting the notions from economic theory, such as isoquants, isorevenue, isocosts, isoprofits, one imposes particular "norms" of equivalence relations, which are transitive (as well as reflexive and symmetric), as any equivalence relations must be. This, in turn, imposes the "norms" on how the bundles need to be aggregated to be relevant to what is being aggregated, to adequately and coherently represent an economic phenomenon.[27] As a result, this also imposes particular structure on how the changes in those "norms" (e.g., isoquants) should occur to preserve the transitivity both due to those equivalence relations in the multidimensional space and for the scalar-indexes (obtained due to aggregation from the multidimensional space). We will see how this intuitive explanation is reflected formally in the next subsection.

Thus, in a nutshell, the crux of the problem is that we try to use one dimension to compare phenomena characterized by multidimensional aspects. Indeed, in the case of comparing the productivity of firms one (perhaps naively) wants to use a unidimensional productivity measure to compare many firms that use many outputs, produced from many inputs, potentially facing many different prices for those inputs and outputs, possibly using many different technologies, possibly in many different periods. This is clearly a much more challenging task than when we compare numbers on the real line. When there are many aspects then one needs to collapse or aggregate them into a single number and by doing so, some information will inevitably be lost (except for peculiar cases), possibly a lot of information, possibly in different degrees for each analyzed unit (e.g., firm) will be lost and this may impact dramatically on how a unit will compare to other units, potentially changing their rankings.

Another way to see the problem is to note that such aggregation of many dimensions involves weights of aggregation and the results may differ, perhaps radically, depending on the choice of weights. That is, those aggregations may produce different values which after lining up on the real line, will produce potentially different rankings from different weights. Is it possible to find some objective weights for the aggregation? The answer is "In general, no!" yet it might be possible in some specific (and quite restrictive) cases and we will see this in the next subsection.

4.11.2 Transitivity and Productivity Indexes

While there are many versions of transitivity adopted in various particular contexts, the most commonly adopted definition specifically for index numbers

---

[27] When also considering prices, different (and perhaps superior) norms are imposed through the notions of isorevenue or isocosts or isoprofit.

seems to be the following. Below we let $\mathcal{I}$ be a set of indexes of periods or states of interest and $r, s, t \in \mathcal{I}$.

Definition. An index comparing two periods (or states) s and t, denoted as I_{st}, is *transitive* if and only if

$$I_{st} = I_{sr} \times I_{rt}, \quad s, r, t \in \mathcal{I}. \tag{4.11.1}$$

That is, transitivity requires that the index comparing s and t can be also obtained indirectly via another period (or state) r, i.e., be decomposed in a multiplicative way exactly into two indexes using the same formula but representing the comparison between s and r and r and t. Note that because it is for any $r, s, t \in \mathcal{I}$, by induction, (4.11.1) will require the index to be "decomposable" into any finite number of indexes that use the same formula but bilaterally between different periods or states, connecting s to t, and regardless of the path taken. A reader must sense that such a property requires some type of multiplicative separability between time periods, i.e., to be of the form $I_{st} = a_s / a_t$ for some aggregating function a_τ that depends only on one of the periods s or t rather than both. Clearly, while very convenient, this is a very restrictive structure and we will see below what it implies for the technology if we want a productivity index to satisfy it *exactly*. Incidentally, note that this transitivity implies the so-called *identity* property, stated next.

Definition. An index comparing two periods (or states) s and t, denoted as I_{st} satisfies the identity property if and only if

$$I_{st} = 1, \text{ for } s = t \in \mathcal{I}. \tag{4.11.2}$$

To see this, let $r = s$ in (4.11.1) to get $I_{st} = I_{ss} \times I_{st}$, implying $I_{ss} = 1$. Transitivity also implies another useful property – the so-called *time-reversal* property, defined next.

Definition. An index comparing two periods (or states) s and t, denoted as I_{st} satisfies the time-reversal property if and only if

$$I_{st} = 1/I_{ts}, \quad s, t \in \mathcal{I}. \tag{4.11.3}$$

Note that from (4.11.1) we get $I_{st} = I_{sr} \times I_{rk} \times I_{kt}$ and selecting $r = t$ and $k = s$ we get $I_{st} = I_{st} \times I_{ts} \times I_{st}$ implying (4.11.3). Another implication of transitivity is the so-called *circularity* property, sometimes referred to as the generalized time-reversal property, defined below.

Definition. An index comparing two periods (or states) s and t, denoted as I_{st} is *circular* with respect to another period (or state) r if and only if

$$I_{sr} \times I_{rt} \times I_{ts} = 1, \forall r, s, t \in \mathcal{I}. \tag{4.11.4}$$

That is, circularity means that one can always "circle back" to the starting point for an index, the unity, by simply measuring in reverse with just one step, from t to s, to perfectly cancel out what was measured and compounded from the two steps, from s to r and then from r to t.

It should be clear that transitivity implies circularity (and identity and time reversal properties), while circularity and identity (or circularity and time reversal) imply transitivity. For these reasons, transitivity and circularity are often viewed as equivalent properties.

In general, MPI and HMPI satisfy the identity property and the time reversal property, yet not the transitivity (or circularity) property.

Note however that the efficiency change component of the MPI satisfies transitivity, and it is the technical change component that prevents the MPI from satisfying transitivity in general – because it consists of two terms that use different technologies as references. This immediately hints that, for MPI to satisfy transitivity, the technology either must not change at all or must change in a very peculiar way. For the HMPI, the story is less clear, although similar: not only must the technology change in a peculiar way, but also the aggregating (distance) functions should have a peculiar structure with respect to the reference points (i.e., inputs for the output distance functions and outputs for the input distance functions), i.e., some type of homotheticity imposed.

Importantly, also note that this definition of transitivity (4.11.1) is much more restrictive than the more general one we discussed intuitively in the previous subsection (where we only required ordinal relations, i.e., consistency in ordering), because here we also require the ability to decompose the index *exactly and in particular (multiplicative) fashion* into sub-periods.

The reader must already sense that this form of transitivity, (4.11.1), is quite a restrictive property, and to hold it must require strong restrictions on the aggregating functions. On the other hand, if one wants to preserve relationships of (or relevance and adequacy of) the indexes to economic phenomena under analysis then those aggregating functions must be related to the concepts characterizing those phenomena (e.g., cost or revenue or distance functions) in those periods or states, where transitivity is inherent and in fact is even more important to preserve. Thus, imposing additional and more restrictive transitivity on productivity indexes would be, effectively, imposing certain separability structures onto technologies behind the units whose productivity is analyzed, for such productivity indexes to be coherent with economic theory.

The first formal answer to what conditions need to be imposed appears to go back to Färe and Grosskopf (1996), and we summarize their result (with modification to the "local" case[28]) below.

Theorem. *In a multi-input–multi-output case and for CRS technologies, the output-oriented Malmquist productivity index satisfies transitivity wrt s, r, t if the difference between technologies in periods (or states) s, r, t is Hicks*

---

[28] See Pastor and Lovell (2007) for similar ideas on "local" notion of Hicks neutrality.

output-neutral such that the scaling of output sets is independent from x, i.e.,
$A_o(x, s, t) = A_o(s, t)$.

The proof of this result is simple and is left as an exercise. As a hint, note that CRS will ensure $A_o(x, s, t) = A_o(s, t) = 1/A_i(y, s, t) = 1/A_i(s, t)$.[29]

Importantly, note that this theorem only gives a sufficient condition, not a necessary one. It turns out that the necessary and sufficient condition is quite nearby, with no need to assume CRS (although note that the assumption of CRS is usually advised for MPI for other reasons). We summarize this in the next theorem.[30]

Theorem. *In a multi-input–multi-output case, the output-oriented Malmquist productivity index satisfies transitivity wrt s, r, t if and only if the difference between technologies in periods (or states) s, r, t is Hicks output-neutral such that the scaling of output sets is independent from x, i.e., $A_o(x, s, t) = A_o(s, t)$.*

Proof. To sketch a proof, note that the difference between technologies in periods (or states) s, r, t is Hicks output-neutral with $A_o(x, s, t) = A_o(s, t)$, implies that $D_o^t(x, y) = D_o^s(x, y)/A(s, t)$ and $D_o^r(x, y) = D_o^s(x, y)/A(s, r)$ and so

$$M_o(x_s, x_t, y_s, y_t) \equiv \left[\frac{D_o^s(x_t, y_t)}{D_o^s(x_s, y_s)} \times \frac{D_o^t(x_t, y_t)}{D_o^t(x_s, y_s)} \right]^{\frac{1}{2}}$$

$$= \left[\frac{D_o^s(x_t, y_t)}{D_o^s(x_s, y_s)} \times \frac{D_o^s(x_t, y_t)/A(s, t)}{D_o^s(x_s, y_s)/A(s, t)} \right]^{\frac{1}{2}}$$

$$= \left[\frac{D_o^s(x_t, y_t)}{D_o^s(x_s, y_s)} \times \frac{D_o^s(x_t, y_t)}{D_o^s(x_s, y_s)} \right]^{\frac{1}{2}}, \qquad (4.11.5)$$

and similarly,

$$M_o(x_s, x_r, y_s, y_r) = \left[\frac{D_o^s(x_r, y_r)}{D_o^s(x_s, y_s)} \times \frac{D_o^s(x_r, y_r)}{D_o^s(x_s, y_s)} \right]^{\frac{1}{2}}, \qquad (4.11.6)$$

and

$$M_o(x_r, x_t, y_r, y_t) = \left[\frac{D_o^s(x_t, y_t)}{D_o^s(x_r, y_r)} \times \frac{D_o^s(x_t, y_t)}{D_o^s(x_r, y_r)} \right]^{\frac{1}{2}}. \qquad (4.11.7)$$

Multiplying (4.11.6) and (4.11.7) and canceling terms gives (4.11.5), thus implying the transitivity statement for the MPI, i.e.,

---

[29] Färe and Grosskopf (1996) give a sketch of a proof.

[30] This formulation of the theorem appears to be new, though the "if" part of it was mentioned in passing in footnote 17 of Mizobuchi (2017a), and perhaps by others, and is clearly inspired by the above-mentioned result of Färe and Grosskopf (1996).

$$M_o(x_s, x_r, y_s, y_r) \times M_o(x_r, x_t, y_r, y_t) = M_o(x_s, x_t, y_s, y_t).$$
(4.11.8)

To prove the necessity, assume (4.11.8), then we have

$$\left[\frac{D_o^s(x_r, y_r)}{D_o^s(x_s, y_s)} \times \frac{D_o^r(x_r, y_r)}{D_o^r(x_s, y_s)} \times \frac{D_o^r(x_t, y_t)}{D_o^r(x_r, y_r)} \times \frac{D_o^t(x_t, y_t)}{D_o^t(x_r, y_r)} \right]^{\frac{1}{2}}$$

$$= \left[\frac{D_o^s(x_t, y_t)}{D_o^s(x_s, y_s)} \times \frac{D_o^t(x_t, y_t)}{D_o^t(x_s, y_s)} \right]^{\frac{1}{2}},$$

and after canceling terms, we get

$$\frac{D_o^s(x_r, y_r)}{D_o^t(x_r, y_r)} = \frac{D_o^s(x_t, y_t)}{D_o^r(x_t, y_t)} \times \frac{D_o^r(x_s, y_s)}{D_o^t(x_s, y_s)},$$

while after rearranging, we get

$$D_o^t(x_r, y_r) \left(\frac{D_o^s(x_t, y_t)}{D_o^r(x_t, y_t)} \times \frac{D_o^r(x_s, y_s)}{D_o^t(x_s, y_s)} \right) = D_o^s(x_r, y_r).$$

Note that the last equation should hold for all $(x_r, y_r), (x_s, y_s), (x_t, y_t) \in \mathfrak{R}_+^N \times \mathfrak{R}_+^M$ (except for singularity points), but the r.h.s. actually does not depend on (x_t, y_t) and (x_s, y_s), i.e., (x_t, y_t) and (x_s, y_s) do not matter for the equality and can be considered fixed, meaning that the expression in parentheses is only a function of time periods, s and t, call it $A_o(s, t)$ and so we have

$$D_o^t(x_r, y_r) = D_o^s(x_r, y_r)/A(s, t),$$

which should hold for all $(x_r, y_r) \in \mathfrak{R}_+^N \times \mathfrak{R}_+^M$, implying the Hicks output-neutrality with $A(x, s, t) = A(s, t)$. □

Note that the statement and the proof of this important result are made with respect to some periods or states s, r, t so that it can be adapted both for time series and for cross-section (or eventually extended to panel context). By induction it also generalizes to any number of periods or states. Also note that this formulation emphasizes the possibility of local neutrality (and therefore local transitivity), e.g., for a short period between s and t or for a sub-set of a cross-section. Meanwhile, if technology is output Hicks neutral *globally* then all the expressions can be simplified further. In particular, all the differences between technologies can be related to one common technology (and so only one time subscript can be kept), e.g., characterized by some fixed output set $\tilde{P}(x)$ independent of the time subscript and a scaling factor $A_o(x, \tau)$, i.e.,

$$P^\tau(x) = A_o(x, \tau) \tilde{P}(x), \forall \tau, x \in \mathfrak{R}_+^N,$$

which is equivalent to

$$D_o^\tau(x, y) = \tilde{D}_o(x, y)/A_o(x, \tau), \quad \forall(x, y) \in \mathfrak{R}_+^N \times \mathfrak{R}_+^M,$$
(4.11.9)

as well as

$$R^\tau(x, p) = \tilde{R}(x, p) A_o(x, \tau), \quad \forall x \in \mathfrak{R}_+^N, \; p \in \mathfrak{R}_{++}^M,$$
(4.11.10)

where $\tilde{D}_o(x, y)$ and $\tilde{R}(x, p)$ are the distance function and the revenue function defined wrt $\tilde{P}(x)$.

So, for the case when $A_o(x, \tau) = A_o(\tau)$, plugging (4.11.9) into MPI will give global transitivity for all τ and all $(x, y) \in \mathfrak{R}_+^N \times \mathfrak{R}_+^M$ as is summarized below.

Theorem. *In a multi-input–multi-output case, the output-oriented Malmquist productivity index satisfies transitivity globally (i.e., $\forall \tau$) if and only if the difference is Hicks output-neutral globally, i.e., (4.11.9) holds, and such that the scaling of output sets is independent from x, i.e., $A_o(x, \tau) = A_o(\tau)$, $\forall \tau$.*

Similar results can be derived for the Hicks–Moorsteen index(es) and there are at least two ways to get transitivity there. The first way is to impose conditions that make the Hicks–Moorsteen and Malmquist productivity indexes equivalent in addition to the condition when the latter is transitive, i.e., impose inverse homotheticity and CRS in addition to the Hicks output-neutrality. The second and alternative way is to require inverse homotheticity and the Hicks joint input and output neutrality where the scaling factors do not depend on x or y, as was discovered by Peyrache (2013c), and we summarize (with slight modification to the local context) in the next theorem.

Theorem. *In a multi-input–multi-output case, the Hicks–Moorsteen productivity index satisfies transitivity wrt s, r, t if and only if the technologies are inverse homothetic and the difference between technologies in these periods (or states) s, r, t is Hicks joint output and input neutral such that the scaling is independent from x or y, i.e., $A_o(x, s, t) = A_o(s, t)$ and $A_i(y, s, t) = A_i(s, t)$.*

Proof. To sketch a proof, we first apply the definitions of Hicks input and output neutrality and then the definitions of input and output homotheticity onto the definition of HMPI, i.e.,

$$
\begin{aligned}
HM(x_s, x_t, y_s, y_t) &\equiv \left[\frac{\frac{D_o^t(x_t, y_t)}{D_o^t(x_t, y_s)}}{\frac{D_i^t(y_t, x_t)}{D_i^t(y_t, x_s)}} \times \frac{\frac{D_o^s(x_s, y_t)}{D_o^s(x_s, y_s)}}{\frac{D_i^s(y_s, x_t)}{D_i^s(y_s, x_s)}} \right]^{\frac{1}{2}} \\[2ex]
&= \left[\frac{\frac{D_o^s(x_t, y_t)/A_o(s,t)}{D_o^s(x_t, y_s)/A_o(s,t)}}{\frac{D_i^s(y_t, x_t)/A_i(s,t)}{D_i^s(y_t, x_s)/A_i(s,t)}} \times \frac{\frac{D_o^s(x_s, y_t)}{D_o^s(x_s, y_s)}}{\frac{D_i^s(y_s, x_t)}{D_i^s(y_s, x_s)}} \right]^{\frac{1}{2}} = \left[\frac{\frac{D_o^s(x_t, y_t)}{D_o^s(x_t, y_s)}}{\frac{D_i^s(y_t, x_t)}{D_i^s(y_t, x_s)}} \times \frac{\frac{D_o^s(x_s, y_t)}{D_o^s(x_s, y_s)}}{\frac{D_i^s(y_s, x_t)}{D_i^s(y_s, x_s)}} \right]^{\frac{1}{2}} \\[2ex]
&= \left[\frac{\frac{G^s(x_t) D_o^s(1, y_t)}{G^s(x_t) D_o^s(1, y_s)}}{\frac{H^s(y_t) D_i^s(1, x_t)}{H^s(y_t) D_i^s(1, x_s)}} \times \frac{\frac{G^s(x_s) D_o^s(1, y_t)}{G^s(x_s) D_o^s(1, y_s)}}{\frac{H^s(y_s) D_i^s(1, x_t)}{H^s(y_s) D_i^s(1, x_s)}} \right]^{\frac{1}{2}} \\[2ex]
&= \left[\frac{\frac{D_o^s(1, y_t)}{D_o^s(1, y_s)}}{\frac{D_i^s(1, x_t)}{D_i^s(1, x_s)}} \times \frac{\frac{D_o^s(1, y_t)}{D_o^s(1, y_s)}}{\frac{D_i^s(1, x_t)}{D_i^s(1, x_s)}} \right]^{\frac{1}{2}} = \frac{\frac{D_o^s(1, y_t)}{D_o^s(1, y_s)}}{\frac{D_i^s(1, x_t)}{D_i^s(1, x_s)}},
\end{aligned}
\tag{4.11.11}
$$

i.e., the index becomes independent of the reference technology and the reference-inputs for the numerator and reference-outputs for the denominator and so

$$HM(x_s, x_r, y_s, y_r) = \frac{D_o^s(1, y_r)}{D_o^s(1, y_s)} \bigg/ \frac{D_i^s(1, x_r)}{D_i^s(1, x_s)}, \tag{4.11.12}$$

and

$$HM(x_r, x_t, y_r, y_t) = \frac{D_o^s(1, y_t)}{D_o^s(1, y_r)} \bigg/ \frac{D_i^s(1, x_t)}{D_i^s(1, x_r)}. \tag{4.11.13}$$

Multiplying (4.11.12) and (4.11.13) and canceling terms gives (4.11.5)

$$\frac{\frac{D_o^s(1,y_r)}{D_o^s(1,y_s)}}{\frac{D_i^s(1,x_r)}{D_i^s(1,x_s)}} \times \frac{\frac{D_o^s(1,y_t)}{D_o^s(1,y_r)}}{\frac{D_i^s(1,x_t)}{D_i^s(1,x_r)}} = \frac{\frac{D_o^s(1,y_t)}{D_o^s(1,y_s)}}{\frac{D_i^s(1,x_t)}{D_i^s(1,x_s)}},$$

i.e.,

$$HM(x_s, x_r, y_s, y_r) \times HM(x_r, x_t, y_r, y_t) = HM(x_s, x_t, y_s, y_t), \tag{4.11.14}$$

implying that transitivity statement for the HMPI is satisfied.

The proof of necessity is similar (yet lengthier) to the one we gave above and so is left as an exercise (see Peyrache, 2013c for details). $\quad\square$

The "global" version of this theorem is stated next.

Theorem. *In a multi-input–multi-output case, the Hicks–Moorsteen productivity index satisfies transitivity globally if and only if the technologies are globally inverse homothetic and the difference between technologies in all periods (or states) τ is Hicks joint output and input neutral such that the scaling is independent from x or y, i.e., $A_o(x, \tau) = A_o(\tau)$ and $A_i(y, \tau) = A_i(\tau)$.*

A key question is therefore: how restrictive are these conditions needed for MPI and HMPI to be transitive? It should be clear that the Hicks neutrality (especially its global version) is an extremely restrictive structure, even without the input and output homotheticity and especially with it. Indeed, even the very recent history clearly teaches us that technology change may, and often does, happen with a bias: at different times different inputs become relatively more productive than others or some of the outputs become relatively easier to produce than others with the same sets of inputs.

We conclude this subsection with a concise yet quite precise statement from Färe and Grosskopf (1996) on this matter:

> Since satisfaction of the circular test is in effect asking that productivity and technical change be path independent, one would expect that this would require imposing a lot of structure on the problem. Requiring that technology

be ...Hicks neutral is, we believe, extremely restrictive. As a consequence, we find ourselves in agreement with Fisher (1922). We would rather abandon the circular test and allow for the possibility of nonneutral technical change. We find the march of time to be a natural "path" upon which technical change should be allowed to be dependent. (Färe and Grosskopf, 1996, p. 91.)

4.11.3   Dealing with Non-Transitivity

While in the context of time series the circularity property is usually viewed as not critical (because it is too restrictive),[31] it is usually considered more important or sometimes even critical for cross-sectional comparisons (i.e., across different firms). The theoretical answers outlined in the previous subsection remain true for such cases as well – Hicks neutrality (at least) is needed for the bilateral indexes to satisfy the transitivity (circularity) property. However, it is also often possible to "cure" the non-transitivity or to "transitivise" the indexes and here we briefly discuss some of the main approaches for this.

One common way to "cure" the non-transitivity (or rather impose transitivity), is to fix the weights of aggregation and use them throughout all the comparisons, e.g., compare relative to one period (or state) – such indexes are called *fixed-base indexes*. To implement this strategy for MPI, one would need to fix the technology against which all observations will be compared, while for HMPI one would also need to fix the reference inputs for the output distance functions and fix reference outputs for the input distance functions in the definition of HMPI.[32]

While easy to implement, one problem with the fixed-base approach is that the choice of what is to be used as the base is hardly ever objective and, as discussed above, different choices may yield different conclusions. In fact, there are infinitely many options for the base and some of them can yield radically different conclusions.

Moreover, even if all people happen to agree on a certain period (or state) as the base, another and more subtle yet as important problem with fixed-base indexes is that, except for special cases, the agreed fixed base (which defines the fixed weights of aggregation) may happen to be quite inadequate or even totally irrelevant for measuring and comparing the productivity of some or even most of the units. Indeed, the further a studied period or state is from the selected base, the less relevant that base could be in terms of weights it implies for valuing the bundles the weights are supposed to meaningfully aggregate.[33] For example, the prices or technology could change dramatically over time such that the "old prices" or the "old inputs" could become

---

[31] An exception is the context of forecasting, where the transitivity (circularity) can be a very useful property for the index whose values need to be forecasted from historical values (e.g., see Daskovska et al., 2010).

[32] E.g., see O'Donnell (2014), who refers to it as Färe-Primont productivity index.

[33] With similar reasoning, Frisch (1936) referred to indexes with fixed weights as 'absurd'. Also, see Fisher (1922) and Diewert and Fox (2017) for more discussion.

completely inadequate (or even completely obsolete) for weighting the outputs in later periods.[34]

It might be tempting to "cure" the potential inadequacy of the fixed-base approach by updating the base on some regular basis. Such practice has been used widely by various researchers and statistical agencies, yet was proven to introduce serious problems of confusion and the misrepresenting of economic phenomena. For example, the Bureau of Economic Analysis (BEA), which is a key statistical information authority in the USA, has clearly admitted in its 2009 manual that such practice introduces "inconvenience and confusion associated with BEA's previous practice of updating weights and years—and thereby rewriting economic history—about every 5 years."[35]

All in all, the fix-base indexes may be inadequate, i.e., inadequately representing the phenomena of interest and therefore we discourage from relying on such indexes alone (although they can be useful to present along with other indexes, and interpreted carefully).

Another way to deal with (yet not resolve!) the non-transitivity in the time-series context is to construct a new series of index numbers by compounding the bilateral indexes – usually referred to as *chained indexes*. To be precise, a chained index between period s and t, constructed with a help of another period r, is defined as

$$I_{st}^* = I_{sr} \times I_{rt}, \ \forall r \in [s, t]. \tag{4.11.15}$$

So, comparing (4.11.15) to (4.11.1), one may get an impression that I_{st}^* is transitive by construction, yet it is generally not (unless I_{st} is transitive), and there is usually some difference, often referred to as "chaining drift." To see this, suppose we have four periods: 0,1,2,3 and so applying (4.11.15) we get: $I_{0,1}^* = I_{0,1}$, $I_{0,2}^* = I_{0,1} \times I_{1,2}$ and $I_{0,3}^* = I_{0,1} \times I_{1,2} \times I_{2,3}$ and so we have transitivity statement holding for $I_{0,2}^* = I_{0,1}^* \times I_{1,2}$ and $I_{0,3}^* = I_{0,2}^* \times I_{2,3}$, but in general it can be that $I_{0,3}^* \neq I_{0,1}^* \times I_{1,3}$ (because $I_{0,3} \neq I_{0,3}^*$) although we do have $I_{0,3}^* = I_{0,1}^* \times I_{1,3}^*$ (where $I_{1,3}^* = I_{1,2} \times I_{2,3}$), i.e., there is "some transitivity," on a particular path. Yet, note that there is potential dependency of I_{st}^* on the path (and also on the starting point), e.g., the end value of the index I_{st}^* may differ if one were to take shorter or longer intervals for chaining

---

[34] E.g., think of prices and labor costs for computing services for the 1970s and for these days—would those prices be adequately weighting the computing services these days?! Certainly not! Back in the 1970s one would need to work a lot to carefully program even relatively simple econometric estimations and use many hours of gigantic and very expensive computing facilities for what now takes (when we write this in 2017 just a few seconds after a push of a few buttons with freeware and a much cheaper computer than in the 1970s! Some scholars proposed using averages (of prices, inputs, etc.) over the whole time span. First of all, once additional period or firm is added, everything may need to be recomputed because, in principle, the average may change due to additional data. More importantly, would such average weights be adequately weighting the computer services in the 1970s or these days? Indeed, they could be way off anything adequate both for the 1970s and for these days and possibly for many other periods in the comparison! So, what is the meaning of such aggregation?!

[35] www.bea.gov/national/pdf/NIPAhandbookch1-4.pdf (accessed 10/09/2017.)

between s and t. We will refer to such seeming transitivity due to chaining as *path-dependent quasi-transitivity* to emphasize that while chaining of bilateral indexes may (and often do) serve well for comparing of a time series of non-transitive index numbers, it does not resolve the non-transitivity problem or resolve it on a selected path.[36]

Finally, another – and perhaps the biggest – problem with chained indexes is that an error or abnormal behavior (e.g., sudden dramatic changes in output due to natural disasters, etc.) observed at one of the periods will penetrate into further periods, potentially compounded with other errors and erratic changes. For this reason, chaining of indexes is usually not recommended for cases where large changes occurred or (especially and) with high frequency.

All in all, the chained indexes are also not without limitations and the *caveats* we mentioned shall be considered carefully when applying them in practice. An important question is: how different are the results from the fixed-base indexes vs. the chained indexes? Or, which one should be preferred? There is no one answer to these questions because it may differ for different indexes and for different data sets or contexts, but we give some practical guidance in the next subsection.

The last "cure" for the non-transitivity that we briefly discuss here is the so-called GEKS (EKS) procedure – abbreviated from the authors who contributed to its development: Gini (1931); Elteto and Köves (1964); Szulc (1964). The idea of the method is to produce an optimal (in the sense of minimizing squared difference) set of values that satisfy transitivity for any given set of values from non-transitive bilateral indexes.[37] As a consequence of such a procedure, the resulting index numbers use the economic theory justified way of aggregating information from the bilateral indexes and obey transitivity within the sample.

Importantly, the GEKS procedure is general and, at least in principle, can be applied to any method of estimation of non-transitive bilateral indexes. This approach is one of the most popular in practice for "transitivizing" the non-transitive bilateral indexes in cross-sectional (or panel data) contexts and, in fact, adopted by many researchers and organizations (World Bank, OECD, etc.).

To the context of productivity, the application of the GEKS procedure goes back (at least) to the seminal work of Caves et al. (1982b). Their ideas

---

[36] A special case of this dependency, it is possible that I_{st}^* does not satisfy the identity test. To see this, consider a case when the measured phenomenon, after several periods starting from s returns to its original value at the time τ – the fixed-base index between base s and period τ will be unity, but since without transitivity one cannot guarantee general equality of $I_{s\tau}$ and $I_{s\tau}^*$, the latter might, therefore, be different from unity (and the difference may be path-dependent). This type of comparison was first suggested by Walsh, and is sometimes referred to as the Walsh test. For this and other related formal and historical details, see 'The Lectures of Diewert' (http://economics.ubc.ca/faculty-and-staff/w-erwin-diewert/).

[37] The standard approach uses ordinary (or equally weighted) least squares criterion. In principle, one may also use a weighted least squares criterion, e.g., by adapting the ideas discussed in Chapter 5 or kernel-based weighting.

were then extended in Balk and Althin (1996) for the context of MPI and by Peyrache (2013c) for HMPI.[38] An important insight from Peyrache (2013c) is that applying GEKS procedure to data is, in essence, implicitly imposing the "closest" (in the ordinary least-squares sense) homothetic and Hicks neutral (both for input and output sets) structure on the data to produce transitive index numbers from the bilateral HMPI. Similarly, an adaptation of GEKS to MPI is, in essence, implicitly imposing the closest Hicks neutral structure on the data to produce transitive index numbers from the bilateral MPI.

Like other methods, GEKS is not without limitations or *caveats*. Besides the increased complexity of computations, everything needs to be re-estimated if an observation (in a cross-section or in time-series or both) is added to, removed from or corrected in the data, i.e., all the index numbers from this procedure are always conditional on a particular sample (and this needs to be acknowledged when presenting the results). Typically, small changes to a relatively large sample do not lead to dramatic changes, although one may sometimes come up with some extreme examples that will exaggerate the problem and for this reason, a sensitivity analysis is useful when GEKS is applied in practice.[39]

4.11.4   What to Do in Practice?

While there are ways to deal with non-transitivity of indexes, one should not assume that transitivising should necessarily provide a better description of a phenomenon. Indeed, as is often in life in general, with any cure there is usually a side effect, and sometimes it's even more severe than the problem one may want to cure. Thus, some general advice to carefully consider whether the cure is worth the side effect is well-warranted here as well! Sometimes transitivity is just not a natural property for a measure that simplifies a multivariate phenomenon (where transitivity may hold) into a scalar measure and while there is a way to transitivise, it may or may not be the best and only way to go. So, what to do? Below we give some practical guidance, which should not be taken as a panacea, rather as a rule-of-thumb for practice.

When using the indexes in practice, considering the fact that I_{st}^* and I_{st} are generally different, we recommend to give readers a more complete picture of the analyzed phenomena by presenting several sets of indexes portraying the phenomenon from different angles. For example, for a time series from say 0 to T the following three series of indexes can be presented:

---

[38] Also see Fox (2003) for related discussion.

[39] E.g., one may try to randomly remove a small percentage (e.g., 1% or 5%) of the data or add a small noise to some or all observations (e.g., 1% or 5% of a standard deviation of each variable) and see if the general conclusions change. Alternatively, one can try to adapt more formal approaches, such as bootstrap or bagging, to check the sensitivity of results. Similar sensitivity analysis can also be useful for checking the robustness of the other methods we discussed.

(i) $I_{0,1}$, $I_{1,2}$, $I_{2,3}$, ..., $I_{T-1,T}$, which are the bilateral indexes between two adjacent periods;

(ii) $I_{0,1}^*$, $I_{0,2}^*$, $I_{0,3}^*$, ..., $I_{0,T}^*$, which are the chained indexes, constructed by compounding the bilateral indexes from (i) via (4.11.15), starting from a selected base 0, i.e., $I_{0,t}^* = I_{0,1} \times I_{1,2} \times ... \times I_{t-1,t}$, for any $t = 1, ..., T$;

(iii) $I_{0,1}$, $I_{0,2}$, $I_{0,3}$, ..., $I_{0,T}$, which are the bilateral indexes between a selected base 0 and the other periods.

To avoid confusion, while presenting such results it is also useful to remind general readers that the indexes in (ii) and (iii) shall not be expected to be identical, for the reasons we explained above. Moreover, researchers are encouraged to explore the difference between I_{st}^* and I_{st} and check the sensitivity of both approaches to general conclusions to small data perturbations, to changes of the base and, for chained indexes, to change of the path.

One is also encouraged to use the GEKS method, especially for cross-section and panel data, yet also check the sensitivity of general conclusions to small data perturbations.

4.12 CONCLUDING REMARKS

We conclude this section by noting again that the indexes we outlined above are theoretical, abstract concepts, unobserved by a human eye, and with no particular functional form imposed on the technologies. To be used in practice they need to be estimated and some additional assumptions need to be made. The importance of this and previous chapters, however, should not be under-valued – they give the ideas and the foundations for what to measure, while the estimation issue, in a sense, is a detail, though a very important one, and we will consider it in the chapters that follow.

Finally, as already noted, here we presented just a few of the many candidates for the true (theoretical) productivity indexes and focused mainly on MPI and HMPI (as well as on some of their variations and extensions) because they appear to be the most popular in practice so far and are likely to be so in the near future. The literature on the indexes in general is enormous and in this chapter we just cited a few works closely related to the origins of the concepts we discussed, although probably missed some other great works. A reader can find more details and references in the classical books of Diewert (1981), Diewert and Nakamura (1993) and Balk (1998) and more recent work of Balk (2008) and from what we refer to as "The Lectures of Diewert."[40] We will note more on this literature in the context of Chapter 7.

4.13 EXERCISES

1. Prove that (4.9.1) holds if and only if it is the one-input–one-output CRS technology case.

---

[40] http://economics.ubc.ca/faculty-and-staff/w-erwin-diewert/ (accessed on 15/9/2017).

2. Prove that (4.9.2) holds if and only if technology exhibits CRS.
3. Show that (4.9.10) holds if and only if the technology is both input homothetic and output homothetic.
4. Show that (4.9.11) holds if and only if (4.9.10) holds.
5. Show that (4.9.14a and 4.9.14b) holds under CRS.
6. Derive relationships similar to (4.9.21)–(4.9.23) for the input-oriented MPI.
7. Derive a relationship similar to (4.9.23) for a general direction, under CRS.
8. Confirm that the efficiency change component of MPI is transitive.
9. Complete the proof about transitivity of HMPI (see Peyrache, 2013a).

CHAPTER 5

Aggregation

So far, we have focused on measuring the efficiency of an *individual* production or decision-making unit (firm, country, etc.) relative to a frontier consistent with a behavior of this unit. In practice, researchers are often also interested in measuring the efficiency of a *group* of similar units (entire industry of firms, region of countries) or particular types of these units (e.g., public firms vs. private firms, etc.) within such groups. Even when the focus is on the efficiency of individual units, at the end of the day, researchers might want to have just one or several aggregate numbers that summarize the results. This is especially important when the number of individual units is large and each of them cannot be published or easily comprehended. But, how can we aggregate? Can we just take an average? Which one: arithmetic, geometric, harmonic? Shall it be a weighted or a non-weighted average? The goal of this chapter is to outline the recently obtained and practically useful results of previous studies to answer these imperative questions.

5.1 THE AGGREGATION PROBLEM

The problem of constructing a group measure or a group score from individual analogues is an aggregation question, which has been recently studied in a number of works.[1] The most important question here is the choice of aggregation *weights*. To illustrate the point, consider a hypothetical example (adapted from Simar and Zelenyuk, 2007) of an industry consisting of four firms, two firms in each of two types, whose efficiency and "an economic weight" (whatever that might be) are summarized in Table 5.1. Here, if a researcher were to use the simple (equally weighted) arithmetic average then group A and group Z are, on average, equally efficient. Note however that the efficiency scores are "standardized" so that they are between 0 and 1 and so they disregard the

---

[1] See Li and Ng (1995), Blackorby and Russell (1999), Ylvinger (2000), Färe and Zelenyuk, (2002, 2003, 2007), Färe et al. (2004), Simar and Zelenyuk (2007), Nesterenko and Zelenyuk (2007), Mayer and Zelenyuk (2014a,b), and references cited therein.

Table 5.1 *A hypothetical example of the aggregation problem.*

Firms	Weight in A	Efficiency	Firms	Weight in Z	Efficiency
A1	90%	100%	Z1	10%	100%
A2	10%	50%	Z2	90%	50%
Simple Average		**75%**	Simple Average		**75%**
Weighted Average		**95%**	Weighted Average		**55%**

relative weights of the firms that attained these scores. If another researcher wanted to use a *weighted* arithmetic average, then a dramatically different conclusion might be reached – depending on the weighting scheme. For the example, in Table 5.1, group A has a higher-weighted average efficiency than that of group Z, yet the industry average could still be closer to the score of group Z if its group weight dominates the weight of group A (e.g., if their weight in the industry is 90 percent as in the table). Clearly one can find other weights that may imply completely different conclusions. Differences in conclusions could lead to differences in policy implications and thus good justification for the choice of weights is needed.

From this simple example, it should be clear that the choice of weights is the critical part here in the aggregation of efficiency and productivity measures. In fact, the selection of weights is one of the most fundamental questions in index number theory and economic measurement in general – because by choosing the weights one effectively chooses conclusions! Intuitively, it is like selecting the judges or the social norms – the verdicts will depend on who is chosen. Therefore, as is in general, the key here is to select the weights as objectively and as transparently as possible, based on some axioms or principles or clear assumptions and, most importantly, such that the resulting weights are relevant (in terms of the information they contain) to the phenomena that are being measured and aggregated. If someone does not agree with some of those axioms or assumptions, they can try to replace them with better ones and possibly derive better weights.

Fundamental ideas for measuring group efficiency were laid out by, not surprisingly, Farrell (1957), in his seminal paper where he also introduced the concept of the "Structural Efficiency of an Industry." Considering a single output case, his idea was to take the *arithmetic* average of efficiency scores of individual firms and *weight* them by the observed output shares of these firms within the group. At that time, Farrell did not provide any formal justifications for such an aggregation scheme. Moreover, the idea was applicable only for the single output case. As a result, this approach was rarely used and many researchers tended to use simple (equally weighted) averages to report the efficiency of industries or groups within it.

Färe and Zelenyuk (2003) used an economic optimization principle and gave theoretical justifications for the Farrell weighting scheme, while also generalizing it to the multiple output case. The goal of this chapter is to outline this aggregation approach, where we will mainly follow Färe and Zelenyuk (2003, 2005, 2007), Simar and Zelenyuk (2007), Färe et al. (2004) and Zelenyuk (2006).

A typical application of the methodology described here is a study of efficiency or productivity levels or their changes in an economic system as a whole (e.g., an industry), or *distinct groups* within such a system (e.g., non-regulated vs. regulated, foreign vs. local, public vs. private firms). The results outlined in this chapter provide applied researchers with a way to measure group efficiency, group scale elasticity and changes in group productivity, with intuitive weights derived based on the neoclassical economic theory reasoning.

5.2 AGGREGATION IN OUTPUT-ORIENTED FRAMEWORK

5.2.1 Individual Revenue and Farrell-Type Efficiency

The methodology outlined here is general and can be used to analyze various economic systems that can be considered as a composition of distinct units that use some inputs to produce some outputs. We consider an example of a group (e.g., industry, sector, etc.) with n firms. To make our discussion smooth and self-contained, we will refresh the definitions previously used. In particular, for each firm k $(k = 1, 2, \ldots, n)$ we will use the vector $x^k = (x_1^k, \ldots, x_N^k)' \in \mathfrak{R}_+^N$ to denote the N *inputs* that firm k employs to produce a vector of M *outputs*, $y^k = (y_1^k, \ldots, y_M^k)' \in \mathfrak{R}_+^M$. For generality of the aggregation result, we allow for each firm k to use a different technology that can be characterized by the set T^k,

$$T^k \equiv \{(x^k, y^k) : x^k \ can \ produce \ y^k\}, \tag{5.2.1}$$

with an equivalent characterization given via the *output sets*

$$P^k(x^k) \equiv \{y^k : x^k \ can \ produce \ y^k\}, \ x^k \in \mathfrak{R}_+^N. \tag{5.2.2}$$

We assume the technology satisfies the main regularity axioms of production theory and free disposability (see Chapter 1), so that the *output-oriented* (Shephard, 1970) distance function $D_o^k : \mathfrak{R}_+^N \times \mathfrak{R}_+^M \rightarrow \mathfrak{R}_+^1 \cup \{+\infty\}$, defined as

$$D_o^k(x^k, y^k) \equiv \inf\{\theta : y^k/\theta \in P^k(x^k)\}, \tag{5.2.3}$$

gives a complete characterization of the technology of firm k, i.e.,

$$D_o^k(x^k, y^k) \leq 1 \quad \Leftrightarrow \quad y^k \in P^k(x^k). \tag{5.2.4}$$

The *Farrell* output-oriented measure of *technical efficiency* is defined as

$$TE^k(x^k, y^k) \equiv \max\{\theta : \theta \, y^k \in P^k(x^k)\} = (D_o^k(x^k, y^k))^{-1}, \ (x^k, y^k) \in T^k, \tag{5.2.5}$$

while the *dual* characterization of $P^k(x^k)$ is given via the *revenue* function

$$R^k(x^k, p) \equiv \max_y \{py : y \in P^k(x^k)\}, \tag{5.2.6}$$

where $p = (p_1, \ldots, p_M) \in \Re_{++}^M$ denotes the vector of output prices.[2] Naturally, the efficiency criterion for a firm in the *dual* framework is the *revenue* (or overall output) efficiency, defined as

$$RE^k(x^k, y^k, p) \equiv R^k(x^k, p)/py^k. \tag{5.2.7}$$

Also recall that

$$R^k(x^k, p) \geq py^k/D_o^k(x^k, y^k), \tag{5.2.8}$$

giving a rise to the *allocative* (in)efficiency measure of firm k, defined as

$$AE^k(x^k, y^k, p) \equiv RE^k(x^k, y^k, p)/TE^k(x^k, y^k). \tag{5.2.9}$$

This decomposition (5.2.9) will be used to derive aggregation results.

5.2.2   Group Farrell-Type Efficiency

We start by focusing on a *subgroup*, and call it (sub)group l ($l = 1, \ldots, \mathscr{L}$), of n_l firms out of the original group of n firms. In practice, the grouping can be based on various criteria such as ownership structure, geographic region, regulation regimes, etc. For each group l ($l = 1, \ldots, \mathscr{L}$), let the input allocation across firms *within* group l be $X^l = (x^{l,1}, \ldots, x^{l,n_l})$, while the *sum* of output vectors over all the firms in the lth group be $\bar{Y}^l = \sum_{k=1}^{n_l} y^k$.

A key step in the derivation is the assumption about *group technology*, i.e., the *aggregate* technology of *all* firms within a (sub)group. A natural way to proceed in our context (of output orientation) is to assume a linear aggregation structure of the output sets (Färe and Zelenyuk, 2003), i.e., for each group l ($l = 1, \ldots, \mathscr{L}$), assume

$$\bar{P}^l(X^l) \equiv \sum_{\oplus k=1}^{n_l} P^{l,k}(x^{l,k}), \tag{5.2.10}$$

which is the Minkowski sum[3] of the individual output sets across all DMUs k ($k = 1, \ldots, n_l$) within group l. As a result, $\bar{P}^l(X^l)$ will inherit the regularity conditions imposed on the individual output sets. In particular, a well-known result from mathematics is that the Minkowski sum of convex sets is also a

---

[2] Note that for the purpose of obtaining the desired aggregation results, a necessary assumption is that all firms face the same output prices.

[3] The symbol $\oplus$ is used following a common notation in mathematics to distinguish the summation of sets (or Minkowski summation) from the standard summation, e.g., see Oks and Sharir (2006).

convex set. So, if the individual output sets are convex this ensures that $\bar{P}^l(X^l)$ is also convex.[4]

Further, using the lth subgroup technology (5.2.10), we can define the *subgroup revenue* function as

$$\bar{R}^l(X^l, p) \equiv \max_y \{py \ : \ y \in \bar{P}^l(X^l)\}, \tag{5.2.11}$$

which in turn can be used, analogously to (5.2.8), to define the lth subgroup *revenue efficiency*, as

$$\overline{RE}^l(X^l, \bar{Y}^l, p) \equiv \bar{R}^l(X^l, p)/p\bar{Y}^l. \tag{5.2.12}$$

The key results are summarized in the theorem and corollaries below.

Theorem. *For each subgroup $l \in \{1, \ldots, \mathscr{L}\}$, the maximal revenue of the subgroup of firms is identical to the sum of the maximal revenues of all firms in this subgroup, if these maximizations are done under the same prices p. Formally,*

$$\bar{R}^l(X^l, p) = \sum_{k=1}^{n_l} R^{l,k}(x^{l,k}, p). \tag{5.2.13}$$

This theorem is an extension of the result from Färe and Zelenyuk (2003) and its original statement and proof can be found in Simar and Zelenyuk (2007). Importantly, note that this theorem is a revenue-analog to the aggregation theorem for the profit functions found in Koopmans (1957), while the cost-analog can be found in Färe et al. (2004)).

This theorem gives us a key to the aggregation problem and so it is vital to understand the economic intuition behind it. The theorem says that the summation of the revenues of individual (and independent) firms in a (sub)group (all with revenue-maximizing behavior) would be the same as the revenue optimized (e.g., by a social planner) over the aggregate technology for this (sub)group defined in (5.2.10), assuming the output prices are the same for all firms in this (sub)group. In the next corollaries (adapted from Färe and Zelenyuk (2003) and Simar and Zelenyuk (2007)), we use this theorem to obtain key results for the aggregation of efficiency scores.

Corollary. *For each subgroup $l \in \{1, \ldots, \mathscr{L}\}$, the aggregate revenue efficiency of the lth subgroup of firms is identical to the weighted sum of revenue efficiencies of all firms in this subgroup, where the aggregation weights are the actual revenue shares of the firms in the subgroup (when all are optimized under the same prices p), i.e.*

---

[4] For these and more properties and details regarding Minkowski summation, see for example a classical work of Krein and Smulian (1940), or a more extensive recent review in Schneider (1993), and a more recent work of Oks and Sharir (2006), as well as references therein. For a classical example of using Minkowski summation in economics, see Shapley–Folkman–Starr theorem and related results (e.g., see Starr, 2008 and references therein).

$$\overline{RE}^l(X^l, \bar{Y}^l, p) = \sum_{k=1}^{n_l} RE^{l,k}(x^{l,k}, y^{l,k}, p) \times S^{l,k}, \tag{5.2.14}$$

where

$$S^{l,k} = py^{l,k}/p\bar{Y}^l, \quad k = 1, \dots, n_l. \tag{5.2.15}$$

Corollary. *For each subgroup* $l \in \{1, \dots, \mathscr{L}\}$*, one can decompose the aggregate revenue efficiency into the aggregate technical efficiency and the aggregate allocative efficiencies as follows:*

$$\overline{RE}^l(X^l, \bar{Y}^l, p) = \overline{TE}^l \times \overline{AE}^l, \tag{5.2.16}$$

where

$$\overline{TE}^l \equiv \sum_{k=1}^{n_l} TE^{l,k}(x^{l,k}, y^{l,k}) \times S^{l,k}, \tag{5.2.17}$$

and

$$\overline{AE}^l \equiv \sum_{k=1}^{n_l} AE^{l,k}(x^{l,k}, y^{l,k}, p) \times S_{ae}^{l,k}, \tag{5.2.18}$$

where,

$$S^{l,k} \equiv \frac{py^{l,k}}{p\bar{Y}^l}, \; S_{ae}^{l,k} \equiv \frac{p(y^{l,k}TE^{l,k}(x^{l,k}, y^{l,k}))}{p\sum_{k=1}^{n_l}(y^{l,k}TE^{l,k}(x^{l,k}, y^{l,k}))}, \; k = 1, \dots, n_l. \tag{5.2.19}$$

In words, note that the role of the aggregate technical efficiency is played here by the weighted sum of the technical efficiencies, where the aggregation weights are the actual revenue shares. Meanwhile, the role of the aggregate allocative efficiency is played by the weighted sum of the allocative efficiencies, where the aggregation weights are also the revenue shares, but corrected for technical inefficiency.

The theorem above is perhaps best understood through geometry, as we illustrate in Figure 5.1.

Let us now clarify a few important aspects about the aggregation results outlined so far.

***Remark* 5.1.** Clearly, for $\mathscr{L} = 1$, the aggregate measures above are measures for the entire group, e.g., industry efficiency.

***Remark* 5.2.** The measure (5.2.17) is a *multi-output* generalization of Farrell's measure of "*structural efficiency of an industry,*" (Farrell, 1957, pp. 261–262). In the productivity analysis of countries, for example, researchers typically use a single aggregate output as a proxy for all outputs, e.g., GDP (e.g., see Färe et al., 1994c; Kumar and Russell, 2002; Zelenyuk and Henderson, 2007, etc.) in this case the GDP-shares would be the weights.

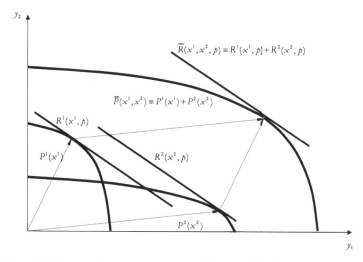

Figure 5.1 Aggregation over output sets and revenue functions.

***Remark* 5.3.** In the context of aggregation over industries, Domar (1961) proposed a similar weighting scheme, although using a different derivation method than outlined here (also imposed more restrictive assumptions). The same weighting scheme and decomposition of aggregate revenue into aggregate technical efficiency and aggregate allocative efficiency was also proposed in the inspiring paper of Li and Ng (1995), who used a similar framework, but without an explicit relationship to the revenue defined on the sum of the output sets and without an analogue of the Koopmans (1957) theorem, which underpins the theoretical foundation for this aggregation.

***Remark* 5.4.** While typically the *technical* efficiency is presumed to be a price independent measure of efficiency, the aggregation weights for computing the (sub)group *technical* efficiency obtained above *depend* on prices. This might be viewed as undesirable. On the other hand, note that these weights were *not* chosen arbitrarily but were derived from an economic criterion of certain optimizing behavior, which researchers also often consider when making their choice of orientation in measuring efficiency. Intuitively, if one aims to account for the *economic* importance of a firm in gaining the particular "standardized" efficiency score then, since prices contain valuable economic information, it is not surprising that the weights derived using the *economic* optimization principle are price-dependent. Another consideration is more practical: in some cases, price information may be unavailable (or unreliable). To circumvent this problem, one may use the shadow prices (e.g., see Li and Ng, 1995). Alternatively, one may impose an extra assumption to make the derived weights price-independent (as we outline in a subsection below).

Remark 5.5. A type of "Law of One Price" assumption is imposed to obtain the aggregation results: indeed, prices are assumed to be the same for all DMUs within a group to be aggregated. Although quite common in theory, this simplifying assumption is hardly true in reality (e.g., see Kuosmanen et al., 2006 for related discussion and for references therein). On the other hand, such an assumption is coherent with conclusions from many models of economic theory (e.g., perfect competition, Cournot-type oligopoly, etc.) and such "common prices" can be viewed as a theoretical benchmark needed to derive the results.

Remark 5.6. It is not unusual that *positive* aggregation results in economics require extra and relatively strong assumptions (e.g., recall the very strict assumptions required for solutions to aggregation of demands over goods or consumers!). As a matter of fact, Blackorby and Russell (1999) derived several *impossibility* results for a more general context of aggregating efficiency scores (without optimization criterion), concluding that very strong assumptions on the technology are needed for establishing positive aggregation results.

5.2.3 Aggregation over Groups

Here we consider the case when a researcher is interested in comparing aggregate efficiency scores across (sub)groups *within* a larger group. E.g., suppose again we have some partitioning of the entire group into $\mathscr{L}$ non-intersecting and exhaustive subgroups $l = 1, \ldots, \mathscr{L}$, and let $\bar{Y} \equiv \sum_{k=1}^{n} y^k$ and the input allocation among firms *within* all the groups by $X = (X^1, \ldots, X^{\mathscr{L}})$.

One immediate implication from the discussions above is that

$$\bar{P}(X) = \sum_{\oplus k=1}^{n} P^k(x^k) = \sum_{\oplus l=1}^{\mathscr{L}} P^l(X^l) = \sum_{\oplus l=1}^{\mathscr{L}} \sum_{\oplus k=1}^{n_l} P^{l,k}(x^{l,k}). \quad (5.2.20)$$

i.e., the aggregate technology of all groups together is the Minkowski sum of the group output sets across $l = 1, \ldots, \mathscr{L}$ and so $\bar{P}(X)$ would inherit its properties from the properties of (sub)group technologies and, ultimately, from the regularity conditions imposed on the individual output sets.

Several important implications of the previous theorem can be summarized in the following corollaries (also adapted from Simar and Zelenyuk, 2007).

Corollary. *The optimal revenue of a group of subgroups of firms is identical to the sum of optimal revenues of all its (non-intersecting) subgroups of firms (when all are optimized under the same prices p), i.e.,*

$$\bar{R}(X, p) = \sum_{l=1}^{\mathscr{L}} \bar{R}^l(X^l, p) = \sum_{l=1}^{\mathscr{L}} \sum_{k=1}^{n_l} R^{l,k}(x^{l,k}, p), \quad (5.2.21)$$

where

$$\bar{R}(X, p) \equiv \max_{y}\{py : y \in \bar{P}(X)\}. \quad (5.2.22)$$

This is an analogue of (5.2.13) (extended to aggregation between the subgroups) and the next corollary is a corresponding analogue of (5.2.14)–(5.2.15).

Corollary. *The revenue efficiency of a group of subgroups of firms is identical to the weighted sum of revenue efficiencies of all its (non-intersecting) subgroups of firms (when all are optimized under the same prices p), i.e.,*

$$\overline{RE}(X, \bar{Y}, p) = \sum_{l=1}^{\mathscr{L}} \overline{RE}^l(X^l, \bar{Y}^l, p) \times S^l, \tag{5.2.23}$$

where the aggregation weights are the actual revenue shares of these subgroups in the group

$$S^l = p\bar{Y}^l / \left(p \sum_{l=1}^{\mathscr{L}} \bar{Y}^l \right), \quad l = 1, \ldots, \mathscr{L}. \tag{5.2.24}$$

Now we give the "between-the-group aggregation" analog of (5.2.16)–(5.2.17).

Corollary. *One can decompose the revenue efficiency of the group of subgroups into the aggregate (over the subgroups) technical efficiencies and the aggregate (over the subgroups) allocative efficiencies as following*

$$\overline{RE}(X, \bar{Y}, p) = \overline{TE} \times \overline{AE}, \tag{5.2.25}$$

where

$$\overline{TE} = \sum_{l=1}^{\mathscr{L}} \overline{TE}^l \times S^l, \tag{5.2.26}$$

and

$$\overline{AE} = \sum_{l=1}^{\mathscr{L}} \overline{AE}^l \times S^l_{ae}, \tag{5.2.27}$$

where

$$S^l = p\bar{Y}^l / \left(p \sum_{l=1}^{\mathscr{L}} \bar{Y}^l \right), \quad l = 1, \ldots, \mathscr{L}, \tag{5.2.28}$$

and

$$S^l_{ae} = \left(p\bar{Y}^l \times \overline{TE}^l \right) / \left(p \sum_{l=1}^{\mathscr{L}} \bar{Y}^l \times \overline{TE}^l \right), \quad l = 1, \ldots, \mathscr{L}. \tag{5.2.29}$$

In words, note that the aggregate (over subgroups) technical efficiency here is the weighted sum of the subgroup technical efficiencies of all the non-intersecting subgroups, and such that the aggregation weights are the actual revenue shares of these subgroups. Meanwhile, the role of the aggregate (over subgroups) allocative efficiency is played here by the weighted sum of the subgroup allocative efficiencies of all the non-intersecting subgroups and such that the aggregation weights are also using the actual revenue shares but after correcting them for the subgroup technical inefficiency.

Thus, the efficiency scores of the subgroups of firms can also be aggregated into efficiency scores of the entire group in the same fashion as the efficiency scores of individual members of the subgroup are aggregated into the efficiency score of this subgroup. Therefore, there is "internal consistency" in this type of aggregation *within* and *between* the subgroups.

5.3 PRICE-INDEPENDENT WEIGHTS

In this section, we follow and adopt the standardization proposed by Färe and Zelenyuk (2003, 2007) and Simar and Zelenyuk (2007) for turning the derived price-dependent weights into price independent weights, while still preserving the same aggregation structure derived from the economic optimization. We first show this for the context of aggregation of efficiency scores within the *entire* group. The key here is an extra assumption:

$$p_m \bar{Y}_m / \left(\sum_{m=1}^{M} p_m \bar{Y}_m \right) = a_m, \ m = 1, \ldots, M, \tag{5.3.1}$$

where $\bar{Y}_m \equiv \sum_{k=1}^{n} y_m^k$ and $a_m \in (0, 1)$ is a constant (known or estimated). In words, (5.3.1) says that the weight of the *industry* revenue from an output m relative to the industry total revenue equals a_m and, by construction, $\sum_{m=1}^{M} a_m = 1$. Now, let $\varpi_m^k = y_m^k / \bar{Y}_m$ be the weight of the kth firm in the group in terms of the mth output, and let us impose (5.3.1) on the weights for the aggregation of the revenue and technical efficiency scores. As a result, we get

$$S^k = \sum_{m=1}^{M} a_m \varpi_m^k, \ k = 1, \ldots, n. \tag{5.3.2}$$

Intuitively, (5.3.2) says the weight of a firm is itself the weighted average over all of its output-shares in its group, weighted by a_m ($m = 1, \ldots, M$), which are the firm's shares of revenue from output m in the industry total revenue.

Now, combine (5.3.1) and (5.2.28) to get the "*between* the subgroups" weights

$$\mathcal{S}^l = \sum_{m=1}^{M} a_m W_m^l, \ l = 1, \ldots, \mathcal{L}, \tag{5.3.3}$$

where $W_m^l = \bar{Y}_m^l / \bar{Y}_m$ is the lth *subgroup's* share in the entire group in terms of the mth-output. In turn, we can also obtain the *weight* for an individual efficiency of firm k "*within* a subgroup l," by simply noticing that

$$S^{l,k} = S^k / S^l, \quad k = 1, \ldots, n_l; \ l = 1, \ldots, \mathscr{L}. \tag{5.3.4}$$

Intuitively, we get what we had for the individual weights in (5.3.2) but we now account for the weight of each particular (sub)group in the entire group.

The price-independent weights for aggregation of *allocative* efficiencies are obtained in a similar manner to the weights for aggregating technical efficiencies, yet here the actual outputs are replaced with their *technically efficient* analogues, i.e.,

$$S_{ae}^k = \frac{S^k \times TE^k(x^k, y^k)}{\sum_{k=1}^n S^k \times TE^k(x^k, y^k)}, \quad k = 1, \ldots, n, \tag{5.3.5}$$

where S^k is given in (5.3.2).

Now we can use the standardization (5.3.1), combining it with (10.1.4), to obtain the "*between* the subgroups" weights

$$S_{ae}^l = \frac{\sum_{m=1}^M a_m W_m^l \overline{TE}^l}{\sum_{l=1}^L \sum_{m=1}^M a_m W_m^l \overline{TE}^l} = \frac{\overline{TE}^l \times S^l}{\sum_{l=1}^L \overline{TE}^l \times S^l}, \quad l = 1, \ldots, \mathscr{L}, \tag{5.3.6}$$

where $W_m^l = \bar{Y}_m^l / \bar{Y}_m$ is the lth *subgroup's* weight in the entire group in terms of the mth-output. Note the analogy with what we had for the individual firms. In turn, expression (5.3.6) helps in getting the weight of an individual efficiency of firm k "*within* a subgroup l"

$$S_{ae}^{l,k} = S_{ae}^k / S_{ae}^l, \quad k = 1, \ldots, n_l; \ l = 1, \ldots, \mathscr{L}.$$

Remark 5.7. Clearly, while all the derivations here were obtained for the output orientation case, similar developments can be extended to the input orientation case. We leave this task as an exercise for the readers (also see Färe et al., 2004 and Mayer and Zelenyuk, 2014a,b). In the next section we will consider another application of the Koopmans-type aggregation theorem.

5.4 GROUP-SCALE ELASTICITY MEASURES

Researchers are frequently interested in measuring the economies of scale pertinent to a firm or to an industry, and often resort to estimating such measures as scale elasticity. To analyze the economies of scale for the industry as a whole, researchers typically estimate the elasticity *at* the non-weighted mean (or, alternatively at the median) of the data or take the (non-weighted) mean of the *individual* estimates of scale elasticities. These measures are not equal to each other, in general, and both have their own theoretical or practical appeals.

However, both of these measures overlook the issue of economic weights in averaging and thus may misrepresent reality for the same reasons as we discussed in the previous sections for the contexts of aggregation of efficiency measure or productivity indexes.

In this section, we consider another theoretical measure of the scale elasticity of a *group*, which is based on similar derivations of the aggregation weights as those considered above, first developed by Färe and Zelenyuk (2012), whom we closely follow here.

In the previous section we considered the output-oriented framework. Now let us consider the input orientation – because researchers often focus on the elasticity of the cost function. (Of course, similar developments can be made for the output orientation using the revenue function.) So, suppose the technology of firm k can be characterized by the input requirement set,

$$L^k(y^k) \equiv \{x \ : \ x \ can \ produce \ y^k\}, \ y \in \mathfrak{R}^M_+, \tag{5.4.1}$$

which we assume satisfies the main regularity axioms of production theory and free disposability (see Chapter 1), so that this technology can be equivalently characterized via the *cost* function,

$$C^k(y^k, w) \equiv \min_x \{wx \ : \ x \in L^k(y^k)\}, \tag{5.4.2}$$

where $w \equiv (w_1, \ldots, w_N) \in \mathfrak{R}^N_{++}$ is the vector of input prices. The *input-oriented* Shephard (1953) distance function $D^k_i : \mathfrak{R}^M_+ \times \mathfrak{R}^N_+ \to \mathfrak{R}^1_+ \cup \{\infty\}$, defined as

$$D^k_i(y^k, x^k) \equiv \sup_\delta \{\delta > 0 \ : \ (x^k/\delta) \in L^k(y^k)\}, \tag{5.4.3}$$

also gives a complete characterization of the technology of firm k, i.e.,

$$D^k_i(y^k, x^k) \geq 1 \quad \Leftrightarrow \quad x^k \in L^k(y^k). \tag{5.4.4}$$

Both the dual and the primal characterizations can be used to measure *economies of scale* via the *scale elasticity*, which for the *dual* framework is defined as:

$$e_c(y^k, w) \equiv \left. \frac{\partial \ln C^k(y^k\theta, w)}{\partial \ln \theta} \right|_{\theta=1} = \frac{\nabla^T_{y^k} C^k(y^k, w) y^k}{C^k(y^k, w)}, \tag{5.4.5}$$

while for the *primal* framework it is defined as

$$e_i(y^k, x^k) \equiv \left. \frac{\partial \ln \lambda}{\partial \ln \theta} \right|_{\substack{D^k_i(y^k\theta, x^k\lambda)=1, \\ \theta=1, \lambda=1}} = -\nabla^T_{y^k} D^k_i(y^k, x^k) y^k. \tag{5.4.6}$$

Let x^{*k} be a solution to (5.4.2), i.e.,

$$x^{*k} \equiv \arg\min_x \{wx : x \in L^k(y^k)\},$$

then as we have seen in earlier chapters, we can obtain equality between the dual and the primal measures, i.e.,

$$e_c(y^k, w) = e_i(y^k, x^{*k}).$$ (5.4.7)

In words, this result says that the same information on the scale elasticity of an *individual* firm k can be derived from the primal and dual approaches. Next, we outline analogous results for the aggregate or group measures of scale elasticity and, most importantly, its relationship to the individual elasticity measures.

To consider the aggregate level, and similar to what we have done for the aggregation of efficiency in previous sections, let the *group* input requirement set be defined as

$$\bar{L}(y^1, \ldots, y^n) = \sum_{\oplus k=1}^{n} L^k(y^k),$$ (5.4.8)

which is the Minkowski sum of the individual input requirement sets across all DMUs $k \in \{1, \ldots, n\}$. Thus, $\bar{L}(y^1, \ldots, y^n)$ inherits the regularity conditions imposed on the individual input requirement sets. E.g., the convexity of the individual input requirement will ensure convexity of $\bar{L}(y^1, \ldots, y^n)$.

Furthermore, the *group* cost function, which is an *aggregate* analogue of (5.4.2), can be defined as

$$\bar{C}(y^1, \ldots, y^n, w) \equiv \min_x \{wx \,:\, x \in \bar{L}(y^1, \ldots, y^n)\},$$ (5.4.9)

and the *group* input-oriented distance function, i.e., the *aggregate* analogue of (5.4.3), can be defined as

$$\bar{D}_i\left(y^1, \ldots, y^n, \sum_{k=1}^{n} x^k\right) \equiv \sup_\delta \{\delta > 0 \,:\, \left(\sum_{k=1}^{n} x^k/\delta\right) \in \bar{L}(y^1, \ldots, y^n)\}.$$ (5.4.10)

Now, the *economies of scale* for the *group* can be obtained from the measures of scale elasticity defined for the aggregate technology – in a similar fashion as we did for the individual technologies. In particular, we have

$$
\begin{aligned}
\bar{E}_c(y^1, \ldots, y^n, w) &\equiv \left. \frac{\partial \ln \bar{C}^k(y^1\theta, \ldots, y^n\theta, w)}{\partial \ln \theta} \right|_{\theta=1} \\
&= \frac{\nabla_Y' \bar{C}(y^1, \ldots, y^n, w)Y}{\bar{C}(y^1, \ldots, y^n, w)},
\end{aligned}
$$ (5.4.11)

where $\nabla_Y' \bar{C}(y^1, \ldots, y^n, w) \equiv (\partial \bar{C}(y^1, \ldots, y^n, w)/\partial y^1, \ldots, \partial \bar{C}(y^1, \ldots, y^n, w)/\partial y^n)$ and $Y \equiv (y^1, \ldots, y^n)'$. On the other hand, for the primal framework, we get

$$\overline{E}_i\left(y^1,\ldots,y^n,\sum_{k=1}^n x^k\right) \equiv \left.\frac{\partial \ln \lambda}{\partial \ln \theta}\right|_{\overline{D}_i\left(y^1\theta,\ldots,y^n\theta,\sum_{k=1}^n x^k\lambda\right)=1,\,\theta=1,\,\lambda=1}$$

$$= -\nabla_Y' \overline{D}_i\left(y^1,\ldots,y^n,\sum_{k=1}^n x^k\right)Y.$$

$$(5.4.12)$$

Now, let x^* be a solution to (5.4.9), i.e.,

$$x^* \equiv \arg\min_x\{wx \ : \ x \in \overline{L}(y^1,\ldots,y^n)\},$$

then the dual and the primal measures of *group* scale elasticity are equal, i.e.,

$$\overline{E}_c(y^1,\ldots,y^n,w) = \overline{E}_i(y^1,\ldots,y^n,x^*). \qquad (5.4.13)$$

Clearly, (5.4.13) is an aggregate analog to (5.4.7). Now, our goal is to find a relationship between the aggregate and the individual measures of scale elasticity – so that we can obtain the group measures from the individual ones. As before, the key step for reaching this objective is the following theorem.

Theorem. *Given definitions (5.4.1), (5.4.2), (5.4.8), and (5.4.9), we have*

$$\overline{C}(y^1,\ldots,y^n,w) = \sum_{k=1}^n C^k(y^k,w). \qquad (5.4.14)$$

The theorem is adapted from Färe et al. (2004) (where its proof can be found) and it says that the cost function of the group is the sum of individual cost functions of all firms in this group. This is the cost analog of the aggregation theorem of Koopmans (1957) for profit functions.

Now, while treating expression (5.4.14) as an identity, we differentiate both of its sides *along* the ray from the origin through the point $Y \equiv (y^1,\ldots,y^n)'$ to measure the change in costs due to an infinitesimal and *equiproportional* change of *all* outputs. Such "radial" differentiation of the l.h.s. of (5.4.14) gives

$$\left.\frac{\partial \overline{C}(y^1\theta,\ldots,y^n\theta,w)}{\partial \theta}\right|_{\theta=1} = \nabla_Y' \overline{C}(y^1,\ldots,y^n,w)Y. \qquad (5.4.15)$$

Furthermore, differentiating the r.h.s. along the same ray gives

$$\left.\partial\left(\sum_{k=1}^n C^k(y^k\theta,w)\right)\Big/\partial\theta\right|_{\theta=1} = \sum_{k=1}^n \nabla_{y^k}' C^k(y^k,w)y^k. \qquad (5.4.16)$$

Putting the two sides together yields the desired result:

$$\overline{E}_c(y^1,\ldots,y^n,w) = \sum_{k=1}^n e_c(y^k,w)\cdot S^k, \qquad (5.4.17)$$

where

$$S^k \equiv C^k(y^k, w) / \sum_{k=1}^{n} C^k(y^k, w).$$

The obtained mathematical result is fairly intuitive: The dual scale elasticity of a group can be derived as the *weighted* sum of the *individual* dual scale elasticity scores of all firms in this group, where the weights are the cost shares. As before, an advantage of this result is that the weights here are derived from economic principles (i.e., optimization behavior) rather than being *ad hoc*.

One can also obtain a similar aggregation result for the *primal* measures of scale elasticity. Specifically, using (5.4.7) and (5.4.13), we immediately attain

$$\overline{E}_i(y^1, \ldots, y^n, x^*) = \sum_{k=1}^{n} e_i(y^k, x^{*k}) S^k, \tag{5.4.18}$$

where

$$S^k \equiv C^k(y^k, w) / \sum_{k=1}^{n} C^k(y^k, w). \tag{5.4.19}$$

These results give a practical way of obtaining the *group* scale elasticity measure from the *individual* scale elasticity measures. In particular, (5.4.18) states that one can get the primal group (aggregate) scale elasticity measure from the *weighted* arithmetic average of the individual scale elasticity scores of all firms in this group, where the weights are the individual cost shares. Again, an advantage of such weights is that they are not *ad hoc* weights, but derived from economic principles.

A *caveat* here is that a researcher might lack the price information needed to obtain the cost functions for computing the weights. In such a case, one may try the shadow prices, if they can be obtained via estimation using the primal information. Alternatively, in a similar way as we presented for the case of efficiency aggregation, one can derive the price independent weights in a manner similar to Färe and Zelenyuk (2003, 2007), by imposing the extra assumption,

$$w_j \sum_{k=1}^{n} x_j^{*k} / \left(\sum_{j=1}^{N} w_j \sum_{k=1}^{n} x_j^{*k} \right) = b_j, \quad j = 1, \ldots, N, \tag{5.4.20}$$

where $b_j \in (0, 1)$ is a known (or estimated) constant so that $\sum_{j=1}^{N} b_j = 1$. Intuitively, (5.4.20) says that the share of the group expenditures on input j in the group total cost equals b_j. Let $\varpi_j^k = x_j^k / \sum_{k=1}^{n} x_j^k$ be the share of the kth firm in the group in terms of the jth-input, then using (5.4.20) we get the price-independent weights possessing intuitive economic meaning

$$S^k = \sum_{j=1}^{N} \varpi_j^k b_j, \quad k = 1, \ldots, n. \tag{5.4.21}$$

Intuitively, (5.4.21) says that each firm's weight is constructed as the weighted average across all input-shares of this firm relative to the group, where the latter weights are the shares of the total industry expenditures on the input j relative to the total cost in the industry.

A similar analysis can also be carried out for other measures based on the cost, revenue and profit functions to get aggregation solutions for the demand and supply functions (involving Shephard's/Hotelling lemmas), and we leave this to the readers. Moreover, all such aggregation results can also be generalized to the context of aggregation *within subgroups* (e.g., private vs. public, non-regulated vs. regulated firms, etc.) and then aggregation *between* these subgroups into a larger group – as we have done above for the aggregation of efficiency scores in the output orientation case. Finally, similar developments can be derived for the case of aggregation of scale efficiency scores (see Zelenyuk, 2002, 2015).

All in all, the aggregate measures considered here, which account for the importance of each DMU via weights derived from economic principles shall serve as useful measures in practice, for analyzing and summarizing results.

5.5 AGGREGATION OF PRODUCTIVITY INDEXES

Empirical studies using productivity indexes typically report some aggregates of the productivity indexes that they estimate – to indicate about the overall tendencies, make an inference, etc. Usually, the *equally weighted geometric mean* is used for such a purpose. The discussion of the aggregation problem and possible solutions in a closely related field we covered in previous sections – efficiency analysis – hints at the importance of using *justified weights* in the aggregation of *productivity indexes* as well. These weights are needed to account for the relative importance of each observation whose index is entering into the average. One such aggregation scheme was proposed by Zelenyuk (2006), who derived similar results for the Malmquist productivity index (MPI), and we summarize it in the next subsections.[5]

5.5.1 Individual Malmquist Productivity Indexes

Let us first adapt all the definitions stated above to the inter-temporal framework – by adding the subscript τ ($\tau \in \{s, t\}$) whenever appropriate. We will be focusing on measuring productivity changes between two periods, s and t (with a conventions that $s < t$), which may or may not be adjacent periods. Recall, from Chapter 4, that the MPI can be defined as

$$M^k(y_s^k, y_t^k, x_s^k, x_t^k) \equiv \left[\frac{D_s^k(x_t^k, y_t^k)}{D_s^k(x_s^k, y_s^k)} \times \frac{D_t^k(x_t^k, y_t^k)}{D_t^k(x_s^k, y_s^k)} \right]^{1/2}, \qquad (5.5.1)$$

---

[5] Also see Mayer and Zelenyuk (2014a,b) for further extensions of this approach.

where $D_s^k(x_t^k, y_t^k)$ is the Shephard's output-oriented distance function characterizing the technology of DMU k in period s and evaluated at points (x_t^k, y_t^k)
that was defined and discussed in detail in Chapter 1 and Chapter 4 (but we
dropped the subscript "o" to simplify notation).

Now, take the revenue efficiency measure and, recalling its dual relationship
to the distance function, define the *revenue* (or dual) analogue of the *MPI*

$$RM^k(\cdot) \equiv RM^k(p_s, p_t, y_s^k, y_t^k, x_s^k, x_t^k)$$

$$\equiv \left[\left(\frac{RE_s^k(x_t^k, y_t^k, p_t)}{RE_s^k(x_s^k, y_s^k, p_s)} \times \frac{RE_t^k(x_t^k, y_t^k, p_t)}{RE_t^k(x_s^k, y_s^k, p_s)} \right)^{-1} \right]^{1/2},$$

$$(5.5.2)$$

which can also be decomposed as

$$RM^k(\cdot) \equiv M^k(\cdot) \times AM^k(\cdot), \tag{5.5.3}$$

where $M^k(\cdot)$ is from (5.5.1), and $AM^k(\cdot)$ is the allocative analogue, defined as

$$AM^k(\cdot) \equiv AM^k(p_s, p_t, y_s^k, y_t^k, x_s^k, x_t^k)$$

$$\equiv \left[\left(\frac{AE_s^k(x_t^k, y_t^k, p_t)}{AE_s^k(x_s^k, y_s^k, p_s)} \times \frac{AE_t^k(x_t^k, y_t^k, p_t)}{AE_t^k(x_s^k, y_s^k, p_s)} \right)^{-1} \right]^{1/2}.$$

$$(5.5.4)$$

The next subsection defines the *group* analogs of these *individual* indexes.

5.5.2 Group Productivity Measures

The definitions and results shown above can now be adapted to the intertemporal framework. As it was for the efficiency aggregation case, a key
step for obtaining our aggregation result for productivity indexes is to define
a *group technology* and, as before, we assume the *additive structure of
aggregation of the output sets*, i.e.,

$$\bar{P}_\tau(X) \equiv \sum_{\oplus k=1}^{n} P_\tau^k(x^k), \forall \tau, \tag{5.5.5}$$

and we define the *group revenue* function at the time τ as

$$\bar{R}_\tau(X, p) \equiv \max_y \{py : y \in \bar{P}_\tau(X)\}, \tag{5.5.6}$$

and the revenue efficiency at the time τ as

$$\overline{RE}_\tau(X, \bar{Y}, p) \equiv \bar{R}_\tau(X, p)/p\bar{Y}. \tag{5.5.7}$$

Now, for measuring productivity changes between period s and t, let us define
the *group* (aggregate) analog of (5.5.2) as

$$\overline{RM}(p_s, p_t, \bar{Y}_s, \bar{Y}_t, X_s, X_t) \equiv \left[\left(\frac{\overline{RE}_s(X_t, \bar{Y}_t, p_t)}{\overline{RE}_s(X_s, \bar{Y}_s, p_s)} \times \frac{\overline{RE}_t(X_t, \bar{Y}_t, p_t)}{\overline{RE}_t(X_s, \bar{Y}_s, p_s)} \right)^{-1} \right]^{\frac{1}{2}}$$

(5.5.8)

where we note that the time subscripts indicate the specific values of efficiency measures for particular periods $\tau \in \{s, t\}$.

The aim now is to find an aggregation function $f_R(\cdot)$ that can relate (5.5.8) to the information from the individual measures (5.5.2) or their components, for all k, i.e., find

$$\overline{RM}(p_s, p_t, \bar{Y}_s, \bar{Y}_t, X_s, X_t) = f_R(RE_\tau^1(\cdot), \dots, RE_\tau^n(\cdot)), \ \tau \in \{s, t\},$$

(5.5.9)

such that, ideally, the decomposition (5.5.3) is also maintained at the *aggregate* level. That is, we want

$$\overline{RM}(p_s, p_t, \bar{Y}_s, \bar{Y}_t, X_s, X_t) = \overline{M}(\cdot) \times \overline{AM}(\cdot),$$

(5.5.10)

thus implying another need to find some aggregation functions $f_D(\cdot)$, $f_A(\cdot)$, so that the aggregate *primal* MPI is related to the information from all k individual analogues (5.5.1) or from their components, i.e.,

$$\overline{M}(\cdot) \equiv \overline{M}(\bar{Y}_s, \bar{Y}_t, X_s, X_t) \equiv f_D(D_\tau^1(\cdot), \dots, D_\tau^n(\cdot)), \ \tau \in \{s, t\}, \quad (5.5.11)$$

while the aggregate *allocative* MPI is related to the information from (5.5.4) or from their components, for all k, i.e.,

$$\overline{AM}(\cdot) \equiv \overline{AM}(\bar{Y}_s, \bar{Y}_t, X_s, X_t) \equiv f_A(AE_\tau^1(\cdot), \dots, AE_\tau^n(\cdot)), \ \tau \in \{s, t\}.$$

(5.5.12)

We will see how to find such functions in the next subsection.

5.5.3   Aggregation of the MPI

As in the context of aggregation of efficiency, the fundamental result here is an inter-temporal extension of the aggregation result from Färe and Zelenyuk (2003) (and inspired by Koopmans, 1957), which we now restate with the time subscript $\tau \in \{s, t\}$,

$$\bar{R}_\tau(X, p) = \sum_{k=1}^n R_\tau^k(x^k, p),$$

(5.5.13)

for any $x^k \in \mathfrak{R}_+^N$, $\forall k = 1, \dots, n$, $p \in \mathfrak{R}_+^M$, and so

$$\overline{RE}_\tau(X_j, \bar{Y}_j, p_j) = \sum_{k=1}^n RE_\tau^k(x_j^k, y_j^k, p_j) \times S_j^k, \ j, \tau \in \{s, t\},$$

(5.5.14)

where

$$S_j^k \equiv \frac{p_j y_j^k}{p_j \bar{Y}_j}, \quad k = 1, \dots, n; \; j \in \{s, t\}, \tag{5.5.15}$$

and the desired decomposition on the aggregate level is

$$\overline{RE_\tau}(X_j, \bar{Y}_j, p_j) = \overline{TE_\tau}(j) \times \overline{AE_\tau}(j), \quad j, \tau \in \{s, t\}, \tag{5.5.16}$$

where

$$\overline{TE_\tau}(j) \equiv \sum_{k=1}^n [D_\tau^k(x_j^k, y_j^k)]^{-1} \times S_j^k, \quad j, \tau \in \{s, t\}, \tag{5.5.17}$$

$$\overline{AE_\tau}(j) \equiv \sum_{k=1}^n AE_\tau^k(x_j^k, y_j^k, p_j) \times S_{ae,j}^k, \quad j, \tau \in \{s, t\}, \tag{5.5.18}$$

and

$$S_{ae,j}^k \equiv \frac{p_j \left(y_j^k / D_\tau^k(x_j^k, y_j^k) \right)}{p_j \sum_{k=1}^n \left(y_j^k / D_\tau^k(x_j^k, y_j^k) \right)}, \quad k = 1, \dots, n; \; j, \tau \in \{s, t\}. \tag{5.5.19}$$

Now, we can apply (5.5.8), (5.5.14), and (5.5.15) and get a desired aggregation result, a solution to (5.5.9), for the MPI, which is

$$\overline{RM}(p_s, p_t, \bar{Y}_s, \bar{Y}_t, X_s, X_t)$$
$$= \left[\left(\frac{\sum_{k=1}^n RE_s^k(x_t^k, y_t^k, p_t) \times S_t^k}{\sum_{k=1}^n RE_s^k(x_s^k, y_s^k, p_s) \times S_s^k} \right. \right.$$
$$\left. \left. \times \frac{\sum_{k=1}^n RE_t^k(x_t^k, y_t^k, p_t) \times S_t^k}{\sum_{k=1}^n RE_t^k(x_s^k, y_s^k, p_s) \times S_s^k} \right)^{-1} \right]^{1/2}. \tag{5.5.20}$$

Note that the desired decomposition for the *aggregate* level is

$$\overline{RM}(p_s, p_t, \bar{Y}_s, \bar{Y}_t, X_s, X_t) = \overline{M}(\cdot) \times \overline{AM}(\cdot), \tag{5.5.21}$$

with the solutions to (5.5.11) and (5.5.12) given, respectively, by

$$\overline{M}(\bar{Y}_s, \bar{Y}_t, X_s, X_t) = \left[\left(\frac{\overline{TE_s}(t)}{\overline{TE_s}(s)} \times \frac{\overline{TE_t}(t)}{\overline{TE_t}(s)} \right)^{-1} \right]^{1/2}, \tag{5.5.22}$$

with the four components inside (5.5.22) given in (5.5.17), and

$$\overline{AM}(p_s, p_t, \bar{Y}_s, \bar{Y}_t, X_s, X_t) = \left[\left(\frac{\overline{AE_s}(t)}{\overline{AE_s}(s)} \times \frac{\overline{AE_t}(t)}{\overline{AE_t}(s)} \right)^{-1} \right]^{1/2}, \tag{5.5.23}$$

where the four components inside (5.5.23) are given in (5.5.18).

As for the case of efficiency and elasticity measurement, the theoretical and practical importance of the results presented here is that they give a way of aggregating the MPIs. Specifically, they suggest how one can get a *group* productivity score from the *individual* analogues. Importantly, the aggregation function and the weights of aggregation that are suggested are *not* selected in an *ad hoc* way, but rather derived from economic principles so the decomposition defined on the individual level is maintained at the group level.

Also note that while the derivations were performed for the output orientation case, similar developments can be done for the input orientation as well, where the cost minimization can be used as the criterion for deriving the weights for the input-oriented indexes.

5.5.4   Geometric vs. Harmonic Averaging of MPI

While summarizing a large number of point-estimates of MPIs, researchers often resort to the (equally weighted) *geometric* mean of the *individual* estimates (e.g., see Färe et al., 1994a). This practice appears to be inspired by the multiplicative nature of the MPI. In the previous subsection, the derivations yielded both the aggregation function and, more importantly, the system of weights. As we discussed earlier, the weights can be dramatically influential for drawing conclusions, both quantitative and qualitative. And, what about the functional form of aggregation?

Following Zelenyuk (2006), note that (5.5.22) can be rewritten in terms of the four components of *the harmonic* aggregations of the individual distance functions

$$\overline{M}(\cdot) = \left[\left(\frac{\left(\sum_{k=1}^{n}[D_s^k(x_t^k, y_t^k)]^{-1} \times S_t^k\right)^{-1}}{\left(\sum_{k=1}^{n}[D_s^k(x_s^k, y_s^k)]^{-1} \times S_s^k\right)^{-1}} \right. \right.$$
$$\left. \left. \times \frac{\left(\sum_{k=1}^{n}[D_t^k(x_t^k, y_t^k)]^{-1} \times S_t^k\right)^{-1}}{\left(\sum_{k=1}^{n}[D_t^k(x_s^k, y_s^k)]^{-1} \times S_s^k\right)^{-1}} \right)^{\frac{1}{2}} \right]. \tag{5.5.24}$$

The geometric analogue of (5.5.24) is defined as

$$\overline{M}^G(\cdot) \equiv \left[\frac{\prod_{k=1}^{n} D_s^k(x_t^k, y_t^k)^{W_t^k}}{\prod_{k=1}^{n} D_s^k(x_s^k, y_s^k)^{W_s^k}} \times \frac{\prod_{k=1}^{n} D_t^k(x_t^k, y_t^k)^{W_t^k}}{\prod_{k=1}^{n} D_t^k(x_s^k, y_s^k)^{W_s^k}} \right]^{1/2}, \tag{5.5.25}$$

for some weights W_t^k, W_s^k. The aggregation that is frequently used in practice is a special case of (5.5.25), which assumes equal weights across all k. Clearly, (5.5.24) gives, in general, different values from (5.5.25), and there is no *exact* general relationship between the two. Yet, if one takes the first-order approximation of $\prod_{k=1}^{n} D_s^k(x_t^k, y_t^k)^{S_t^k}$ and of $\left(\sum_{k=1}^{n}[D_s^k(x_t^k, y_t^k)]^{-1} \times S_t^k\right)^{-1}$ around *unity* (a natural point around which an approximation of productivity and efficiency indexes can be done), then they are both equal to $\sum_{k=1}^{n} D_s^k(x_t^k, y_t^k) \times S_t^k$. As a result, we can say that for $(W_t^k, W_s^k) = (S_t^k, S_s^k)$, we have

$$\overline{M}(\bar{Y}_s, \bar{Y}_t, X_s, X_t) \cong \overline{M}^G(\bar{Y}_s, \bar{Y}_t, X_s, X_t). \tag{5.5.26}$$

Intuitively, (5.5.26) is the *first-order-approximation* relationship between the *harmonic* aggregate MPI derived above and the *geometric* aggregate of individual MPIs, provided both use the same set of weights. In turn, this means that, for anyone who prefers the geometric aggregation (e.g., to preserve "multiplicativity") this relationship gives a justification for the choice of aggregation weights – to be those derived from economic principles – for accounting economic weights rather than equal weights.

A natural question one may ask here is regarding a typical difference between the results of the harmonic and geometric aggregations in practice. The simulation results of Zelenyuk (2006) suggest that (as one would expect theoretically) the geometric aggregation always yields a larger aggregate productivity score when compared to the harmonic aggregation (with the same weighting scheme in both aggregations), yet the difference is fairly small.[6] So, a practical implication one can draw from this subsection is that the geometric-type and the harmonic-type aggregations of the productivity indexes, with the same weights, give very similar aggregate scores for distributions with a fairly wide range of individual scores.[7] In turn, this may justify a use of geometric aggregation for the productivity indexes with the theoretically justified weighting scheme as discussed above, which may yield very different results relative to the naive (equally weighted) aggregation, whether arithmetic, geometric or harmonic.

5.5.5 Decomposition into Aggregate Changes

The aggregation results discussed in the previous subsections can be extended to the context of aggregation of components of various types of decompositions of MPIs. Here, for the sake of brevity, and again following Zelenyuk (2006), we limit discussion to only one, yet apparently the most popular, decomposition (Färe et al., 1994a), saying that

$$M^k(\cdot) \equiv Eff \, \Delta^k(\cdot) \times Tech \, \Delta^k(\cdot), \tag{5.5.27}$$

where the *change in efficiency* is measured for by

$$Eff \, \Delta^k(\cdot) \equiv \frac{D_t^k(x_t^k, y_t^k)}{D_s^k(x_s^k, y_s^k)}, \tag{5.5.28}$$

---

[6] E.g., when the range of productivity changes (on uniform distribution around unity) is 50 percentage points, then roughly 1 percentage point of the square-root of mean squared difference is observed.

[7] An important *caveat* with the geometric aggregation, however, is that it does not tolerate well the zero values in the aggregation (unless their weights are set to zero with the convention that $0^0 = 1$). They are also much more sensitive to very low values (those close to zero), which may drive the entire average to be unreasonably low despite the majority of the other values being relatively high. E.g., if out of ten observations, one has a score of 0.001 while nine have scores equal to 1, then the aggregate scores from the equally weighted arithmetic average will be 0.9 while the equally weighted geometric average will give 0.5. The economically justified aggregation weights may correct this discrepancy by assigning very low weight to very inefficient or very unproductive units.

and the *technological change* is measured by

$$Tech \, \Delta^k(\cdot) \equiv \left[\frac{D_s^k(x_t^k, y_t^k)}{D_t^k(x_t^k, y_t^k)} \times \frac{D_s^k(x_s^k, y_s^k)}{D_t^k(x_s^k, y_s^k)} \right]^{1/2}. \tag{5.5.29}$$

The goal is to have *group* analogues related to the corresponding individual measures (5.5.28) and (5.5.29) or its components, via some function $f_E(\cdot)$, and $f_{TC}(\cdot)$. Similarly to the above, a natural choice is to set

$$\overline{Eff \, \Delta}(\cdot) = \left(\frac{\overline{TE_t}(t)}{\overline{TE_s}(s)} \right)^{-1} = \frac{\left(\sum_{k=1}^n [D_t^k(x_t^k, y_t^k)]^{-1} \times S_t^k \right)^{-1}}{\left(\sum_{k=1}^n [D_s^k(x_s^k, y_s^k)]^{-1} \times S_s^k \right)^{-1}}, \tag{5.5.30}$$

and

$$\overline{Tech \, \Delta}(\cdot) = \left[\left(\frac{\overline{TE_s}(t)}{\overline{TE_t}(t)} \times \frac{\overline{TE_s}(s)}{\overline{TE_t}(s)} \right)^{-1} \right]^{1/2}$$

$$= \left[\frac{\left(\sum_{k=1}^n [D_s^k(x_t^k, y_t^k)]^{-1} \times S_t^k \right)^{-1}}{\left(\sum_{k=1}^n [D_t^k(x_t^k, y_t^k)]^{-1} \times S_t^k \right)^{-1}} \frac{\left(\sum_{k=1}^n [D_s^k(x_s^k, y_s^k)]^{-1} \times S_s^k \right)^{-1}}{\left(\sum_{k=1}^n [D_t^k(x_s^k, y_s^k)]^{-1} \times S_s^k \right)^{-1}} \right]^{1/2}. \tag{5.5.31}$$

Again, the first-order-approximation relationship exists between the harmonic-type aggregations (5.5.30) and (5.5.31) and their geometric analogues. Finally, these aggregation results can also be extended to aggregation across or over larger groups, in a similar fashion to that described for aggregation of efficiency scores, i.e., extending Simar and Zelenyuk (2007).

5.6 CONCLUDING REMARKS

For the sake of brevity, in this chapter, we presented only some of the main results on aggregation in efficiency and productivity analysis. These results can be readily used by *practitioners* to summarize their results of estimation of individual scores when measuring efficiency, elasticity and productivity indexes into the corresponding *group* (or aggregate) measures, so that these group measures account for the economic importance of each observation (e.g., firm) in the group (e.g., industry) via a theoretically grounded weighting scheme.

Many of the presented results can be extended to obtain analogous results in many other contexts. In particular, the reader must have noticed that a natural extension would be to derive similar results for other orientations as well as for other efficiency and productivity measures, indexes and indicators, e.g., those defined in terms of the directional distance functions. We leave these to the readers to explore and try as exercises and, potentially, for new research papers. In the remaining part of this chapter we will mention just a few interesting extensions and applications of the aggregation ideas presented above.

First of all, note that some (but not all) results for the input orientation were presented in Färe et al. (2004). Furthermore, an important theoretical extension that allows for the reallocation of inputs among firms being aggregated was proposed by Nesterenko and Zelenyuk (2007), and was further developed by Mayer and Zelenyuk (2014a,b), who extended the theory for aggregating MPI (to allow for reallocation) as well as developed a theoretical framework for aggregating HMPI. Early aggregation results for directional distance functions were developed by Färe et al. (2008b) (also see Zelenyuk, 2002). A theoretical framework for aggregation of growth rates in the Solow's growth accounting framework was developed by Zelenyuk (2013a), while the theory for aggregation of scale efficiency was developed by Zelenyuk (2015).

Some related discussions and interesting interpretations in the terms of industrial organization context is given by Raa (2011) (also see Pachkova, 2009). Further interesting results and various extensions were also unveiled by Mussard and Peypoch (2006), Cooper et al. (2007a), Li and Cheng (2007), Kuosmanen et al. (2010), Peyrache (2013b, 2015), Färe and Karagiannis (2014), Karagiannis (2015), and Karagiannis and Lovell (2015).

This paradigm to aggregating efficiency or productivity indexes has also been used for various interesting applications, to analyze real-world phenomena: e.g., see Henderson and Zelenyuk (2007), Henderson et al. (2007), Pilyavsky and Staat (2008), Weill (2008), Ferrier et al. (2009), Badunenko (2010), Badunenko and Tochkov (2010), Suárez and de Jorge (2010), Hall et al. (2012), and Mugera and Ojede (2014), to mention just a few.

Last, yet never least, the readers are also recommended to study the early works on this subject that inspired many of the results presented in this section, in particular the works of Førsund and Hjalmarsson (1979), Färe et al. (1992a), Li and Ng (1995), Blackorby and Russell (1999), Ylvinger (2000), and, most importantly, the classical works of Farrell (1957) and Koopmans (1957).

5.7 EXERCISES

1. Allow for reallocation of inputs in the output oriented framework and derive the relevant aggregation theory (see Nesterenko and Zelenyuk (2007) and Mayer and Zelenyuk (2014, 2017) for some results).
2. Derive the input-oriented versions of the output-oriented results outlined above.
3. In the input-oriented framework, allow for reallocation of outputs and derive the relevant aggregation theory (see Mayer and Zelenyuk (2014, 2017) for some results).
4. Derive the aggregation theory for the directional distance function (see Färe, Grosskopf and Zelenyuk (2008) and Zelenyuk (2002) for some results).
5. Derive the aggregation theory for the scale efficiency (see Zelenyuk (2015)).

CHAPTER 6

Functional Forms: Primal and Dual Functions

Implementing the theoretical constructs of production and its efficient application, a subject discussed in previous chapters, requires that we specify estimable and parsimonious parametric or nonparametric relationships. This allows the practitioner to utilize standard regression, linear programming, or formal kernel-based or other nonparametric techniques to estimate the relative contributions of different factors of production to single or multiple outputs produced under the control of a firm. It also allows one to model substitution possibilities, returns to scale, returns to scope, productivity change, and many other production-related summary measures of a technology. In this chapter and in Chapters 11–16, we will focus primarily on the econometric estimation of production relationships and we will need to distinguish between linear programming methods, which are often referred to as nonparametric, and kernel-based methods or methods that are based on series expansions, which are typically referred to as nonparametric in the econometrics and in much of the classical statistics literature. In order to maintain this distinction, we will use the term "nonparametric econometric" approaches when referring to kernel-based methods and methods based on series expansions when appropriate.

Duality among production, cost, revenue, and profit functions places restrictions on the functional relationships. These restrictions, such as linear homogeneity, concavity or convexity, and symmetry, need to be imposed in a natural and relatively transparent way. Also, to the extent that random errors are introduced into the optimization process, the stochastic portion of the production models needs to be consistent with the optimization assumptions used to generate side conditions based on assumptions of cost minimization, output maximization, and/or profit or expected profit maximization. These side conditions provide the researcher additional degrees of freedom. The additional degrees of freedom allow one to estimate meaningful relationships that exploit second-order (and higher) terms and allow for flexibility in modeling a technology.

The additional information contained in the optimizing assumptions comes at a cost, however. If the assumptions are not valid or the side conditions cannot be properly embedded within a parametric or a nonparametric econometric specification of technology or its dual forms, then biased estimates of the technology may be generated. Moreover, nonparametric econometric specifications may not be consistent with the regularity conditions needed to ensure that a dual representation of the technology has in fact been estimated. This latter issue is quite a relevant one if, for example, the nonparametric functional approach to estimate primal or dual relationships currently lacks a well-developed testing framework for monotonicity or curvature to be carried out (locally or globally), as one might carry out with flexible parametric functional forms such as the translog or generalized Leontief.

In this chapter, we explore a number of these issues. We first discuss many well-known and well-used empirical vehicles for modeling and estimating the primal production function, or its multi-output counterpart, the distance function, following on the classic work by Chambers (1988). We present a variety of dual functions as well, including the cost, revenue, and profit functions. We also discuss how the different functional forms admit to restrictions required by duality in order for the analyst to properly interpret the estimated relationships as representations of the underlying technology.

6.1 FUNCTIONAL FORMS FOR PRIMAL PRODUCTION ANALYSIS

Functional forms, which represent the algebraic relationships between dependent variables and regressors, are of great importance when specifying a production relationship. In this section various commonly used functional forms to estimate the direct production function (or distance function) will be discussed along with various measures of scale, scope, substitution, and transformation possibilities. It should be noted that such specifications of technology are largely fictions that economists and productivity modelers utilize to parsimoniously summarize the very real engineering black box of a production process. As such production processes are increasingly developed within a supply chain, or within a network of linked production processes, the fictions commonly utilized by economist and productivity modelers may become difficult to square with reality. However, in such settings, a perspective can be adopted wherein the functional relationships between inputs and outputs can be viewed simply as an aggregator that summarizes, often in a rather flexible manner, the contribution of inputs to the generation of output(s), and nothing more or nothing less.

Of course, engineering production processes are quite relevant when detailed production information is available to the econometrician. Situations in which such detailed engineering data is available were the source of the early work by Griffin (1977, 1978) who constructed approximations to static technologies in the oil refining industry, utilizing pseudo-data generated by a series of detailed linear programming models that related the many optimizations and binding constraints in the refining of petroleum. Work by Sickles and Streitwieser (1992, 1998) focused on regulatory distortions in the pipeline transmission of natural gas, wherein the physical dimensions of the pipeline and the fluid flow pressures were considered in the description of the technology and the physical scale returns to larger dimensioned pipelines. In their study of efficient optimal dynamic production policy in Saudi Arabia, Gao et al. (2009) considered a production process based on an engineering computer model of dynamic fluid flow. Using this model they simulated the effects of water injection rates, the cumulative production of the field, and the number of oil wells on the cost of production and short-run production capacity in a large oil field in Saudi Arabia. The particular black oil simulator they used solved a system of homogeneous difference equations that modeled the fluid dynamics within and among a set of three-dimensional grids that partitioned the vast Ghawar oil field in Saudi Arabia. These are but a few examples of alternatives to the functional approximations we discuss below. We will not pursue them in our discussions as they are outside the scope of this book. Those interested in such approaches can find them in the engineering literature. Several survey chapters that speak to interface between engineering and economics with a focus on productive efficiency can be found in the excellent contributions by Triantis (2011, 2014, 2016). Depending on the particular production process under consideration, the engineering models may provide substantial insight and instruction to the applied researcher on the form of the estimation equation for production and for its dual representations.

Before we move further into our discussion of functional forms, we will provide a short review of how substitution possibilities between inputs, a crucial technical property of the production technology, can be characterized by a measure labeled the elasticity of substitution (σ).

6.1.1   The Elasticity of Substitution: A Review of the Allen, Hicks, Morishima, and Uzawa Characterizations of Substitution Possibilities

The elasticity of substitution (σ) is defined as the percentage change in factor proportions due to a change in marginal rate of technical substitution (MRTS). For a simple one-output–two-input production process $y = f(L, K)$, where L is labor and K is capital whose marginal products are f_L and f_K, its mathematical form is

$$\sigma_{LK} = \frac{d \ln(L/K)}{d \ln(f_K/f_L)} \tag{6.1.1}$$

$$= \frac{d(L/K)}{d(f_K/f_L)} \times \frac{f_K/f_L}{L/K}.$$

Geometrically, σ_{LK}, or simply σ, as we will refer to it in much of our brief discussion below, is a measure of the curvature of an isoquant. Intuitively, the more curved or convex the isoquant is, the smaller is σ. In the extreme case where there is no substitution, as in a Leontief technology, any change in the MRTS will not lead to any change in the factor proportions. In the other extreme case where there is perfect substitution (linear production technology), $\sigma = \infty$ since the MRTS does not change at all. Diminishing marginal productivity guarantees that $\sigma < \infty$.

An alternative expression for σ can be derived by first totally differentiating f_K/f_L with respect to K and L and then by applying the definition of the isoquant $f_K/f_L = -dL/dK$ to obtain

$$d(f_K/f_L) = \left\{ f_K \frac{\partial(f_K/f_L)}{\partial L} - f_L \frac{\partial(f_K/f_L)}{\partial K} \right\} dL/f_K. \qquad (6.1.2)$$

Next totally differentiate L/K and substitute $dK = -(f_L/f_K)dL$ to obtain

$$d(L/K) = (f_K K + f_L L)dL/f_K K^2. \qquad (6.1.3)$$

With a bit more algebraic manipulation the expression for σ then becomes

$$\sigma = \frac{f_K(f_K K + f_L L)}{f_L K L \left(f_K \frac{\partial(f_K/f_L)}{\partial L} - f_L \frac{\partial(f_K/f_L)}{\partial K} \right)}. \qquad (6.1.4)$$

It is straightforward to evaluate the terms $\frac{\partial(f_K/f_L)}{\partial L}$ and $\frac{\partial(f_K/f_L)}{\partial K}$. We combine them to get

$$f_K \left(\frac{\partial(f_K/f_L)}{\partial L} \right) - f_L \left(\frac{\partial(f_K/f_L)}{\partial K} \right) = \frac{2 f_{KL} f_L f_K - f_{LL} f_K^2 - f_{KK} f_L^2}{f_L^2}, \qquad (6.1.5)$$

where f_{KK}, f_{KL}, and f_{LL} are second partial derivatives of f. Substituting this into the formulation of σ in the previous equation and applying Young's theorem ($f_{KL} = f_{LK}$), we have the alternative expression for σ

$$\sigma = \frac{f_L f_K(f_K K + f_L L)}{K L(2 f_{KL} f_L f_K - f_{LL} f_K^2 - f_{KK} f_L^2)}. \qquad (6.1.6)$$

Here the term in parentheses in the denominator is the determinant of the bordered Hessian of the production function denoted as $|B|$, and $f_L f_K$ is the cofactor of the LKth term denoted as $|B_{LK}|$. With a bit more algebra, this leads to the following expression for σ

$$\sigma = \frac{f_K K + f_L L}{K L} \frac{|B_{LK}|}{|B|}. \qquad (6.1.7)$$

6.1.1.1 The Elasticity of Substitution Under Constant Returns to Scale

Under constant returns to scale (CRS), Euler's theorem implies that $f_K K + f_L L = y$. In addition, CRS implies that the total marginal product is homogeneous of degree 0 in the factors. By Euler's theorem we have again that

$$f_{KK}K + f_{KL}L = 0, \tag{6.1.8}$$

$$f_{LK}K + f_{LL}L = 0. \tag{6.1.9}$$

Substituting these into the expression for σ, we have

$$\sigma = \frac{f_L f_K}{f_{KL}} Y, \tag{6.1.10}$$

which is the expression introduced by Hicks (1932) and independently developed by Robinson (1933). This gives the intuitive interpretation that the less an increase in labor raises the marginal product of capital (f_{KL} decreases), the more is the elasticity of substitution. In the case of a CRS technology with one output and two inputs we can also express σ as the elasticity of output per capita with respect to the marginal product of labor.

6.1.1.2   Elasticities of Substitution in Multi-Input Cases

When more than two inputs are involved in production, substitution between inputs cannot be examined without controlling for possible cross effects from other inputs. Three measures for multi-input technologies have been proposed and we discuss each in turn.

The first is the simplest and is the direct elasticity of substitution between two factors x_i and x_j, denoted as

$$\sigma_{ij}^D = [(f_i x_i + f_j x_j)/x_i x_j](|B_{ij}|/|B|), \tag{6.1.11}$$

where $|B_{ij}|$ is, defined as before, the cofactor of ijth term in the determinant of the bordered Hessian matrix of a production function denoted as $|B|$. The direct elasticity clearly assumes that other factors are held constant and thus ignores the possible cross effects from other inputs.

The second measure is the Allen–Uzawa (Allen, 1938; Uzawa, 1962) elasticity of substitution (AES), also known as the partial elasticity of substitution, defined as

$$\sigma_{ij}^A = \left(\left(\sum_k f_k x_k \right) / x_i x_j \right)(|B_{ij}|/|B|). \tag{6.1.12}$$

It is the same as the direct elasticity where there are only two inputs. An alternative expression for the AES can be derived from a cost-minimizing firm, and it turns out to be

$$\sigma_{ij}^A = e_{ij}/s_j, \tag{6.1.13}$$

where $e_{ij} = \partial \ln x_i / \partial \ln w_j$, the elasticity of the demand for the ith factor with respect to the price of jth factor. The denominator $s_j = w_j x_j / \sum_i w_i x_i$ is the jth factor's share of total expenditures. This alternative expression will be useful in our brief discussion of the third measure.

The third measure is the Morishima elasticity of substitution (MES), defined as

$$\sigma_{ij}^M = (f_j/x_i)(|B_{ij}|/|B|) - (f_j/x_j)(|B_{ij}|/|B|).$$ (6.1.14)

The Morishima measure can be rewritten in terms of the Allen-Uzawa measure

$$\sigma_{ij}^M = (f_j x_j / f_i x_i)(\sigma_{ij}^A - \sigma_{jj}^A).$$ (6.1.15)

An implication from this last expression is that when $\sigma_{ij}^M > 0$, which means the inputs are substitutes by the Morishima measure, it is quite possible that the Allen-Uzawa measure is $\sigma_{ij}^A < 0$, which indicates that the inputs are complements. Although the AES is a standard measure of substitution possibilities in production reported in many empirical studies, it has been noted by Blackorby and Russell (1989) that the AES has some problems. In fact, Blackorby and Russell refer to the AES as "(incrementally) completely uninformative." As noted by Christev and Featherstone (2009, p. 1166), Blackorby and Russell "provide counterfactual examples and conclude that these elasticities are not a measure of the "ease of change" or substitution, reveal no information about relative factor shares, and cannot be interpreted as a logarithmic derivative of quantity ratios to marginal rates of substitution (Blackorby and Russell, 1989, p. 883). They reason that the Morishima elasticity of substitution is the natural generalization of the original Hicksian concept.

6.1.2 Linear, Leontief, Cobb–Douglas, CES, and CRESH Production Functions

The concept of an output set was discussed in Chapter 1. Its functional representation was also provided. Specifically, the *output set* is

$$P(x) \equiv \{y \in \Re_+^M : y \text{ is producible from } x, x \in \Re_+^N\},$$

while the *production function* $f : \Re_+^N \to \Re_+^1$ can be defined in its general form as

$$f(x) \equiv \max\{y: (x, y) \in T\}$$
$$= \max\{y: y \in P(x)\}.$$ (6.1.16)

Thus the production function is just the maximal value of output (y) that can be produced for each particular level of input (x). As $P(x)$ is a compact set, we are sure that the maximum exists (and is clearly unique).

The simplest functional form for production relates the level of the single output to a linear combination of the multiple factor inputs. It is referred to as the *linear production function* and is given by

$$y = \beta_0 + \sum_{j=1}^N \beta_j x_j.$$ (6.1.17)

Marginal products are

$$MP_j = \frac{\partial y}{\partial x_j} = \beta_j, \ j = 1, \ldots, N. \tag{6.1.18}$$

The function is linear homogeneous and thus returns to scale (RTS) are constant when $\beta_0 = 0$. For the linear production function the production isoquants are linear. Thus the ratio of marginal products, or the MRTS is constant. Since the elasticity of substitution (Allen–Uzawa) is defined as the percentage change in factor proportions divided by the change in the MRTS, the inputs are perfect substitutes since the elasticity of substitution is given by

$$\sigma_{jk} = \frac{d(x_j/x_k)/(x_j/x_k)}{d(MP_k/MP_j)/(MP_k/MP_j)} = \infty, \ j \neq k. \tag{6.1.19}$$

Since $\frac{MP_j}{MP_k} = \frac{\beta_j}{\beta_k}$ is constant, the denominator is 0 and thus the elasticity of substitution is unbounded. Any relative price change would induce a complete substitution away from the relatively more expensive input and towards the alternative input whose relative price had fallen.

The *fixed coefficient (Leontief) production function* is the polar case of the linear production function in regard to the elasticity of substitution, which for the Leontief production function is 0. Such a technology in which the factor inputs are used in fixed proportions, usually established by some engineering blueprint that is not changeable, was named after the Nobel laureate Wassily Leontief. Leontief introduced the input–output model of an economy in 1925 (Leontief, 1925), the year he emigrated from the USSR. Leontief developed and calculated an input–output table for the US economy in 1941 using the new computing resources at Harvard University. This and subsequent uses to which the fixed proportions technology was put led to his Nobel Memorial Prize in Economic Sciences in 1973. For an excellent summary of his life and contributions see Baumol and ten Raa (2009). The Leontief production function is a special limiting case of the constant elasticity of substitution production function that we will discuss below. For the fixed proportions production function, output will not be affected by one input change without a corresponding change in the other inputs. If one simply takes the amount (in units) of each input required to produce one unit of output, divides the amount of each available input by the input needed to produce one output unit, and then finds the smallest of the possible output quantities per unit of input use, we have a production function that can be represented as

$$y = f(x_1, \ldots, x_N) = \min\{\beta_1 x_1, \ldots, \beta_N x_N\}, \ \beta_j > 0, \ j = 1, \ldots, N, \tag{6.1.20}$$

where the $\beta_i's$ are activity coefficients that indicate the activity necessary for a particular factor input. The function is linear homogeneous and thus the fixed coefficient production function also exhibits CRS by construction.

It has a rectangular input requirement set given by $L(y) \equiv \{x \in \Re_+^N :$ $\min\{\beta_1 x_1, \ldots, \beta_N x_N\} \geq y \in \Re_+^1$ is producible from $x \in \Re_+^N\}$.

The next relatively simple production function we discuss provides an estimating equation that relates inputs to output and allows for substitution possibilities between the polar cases of 0 and ∞. Charles Cobb and Paul Douglas established as their *nom de guerre* the *Cobb–Douglas production function* (Cobb and Douglas, 1928). The function relates output levels to a linear combination of exponentiated levels of the of inputs and takes the form

$$y = \beta_0 \prod_{j=1}^N x_j^{\beta_j}, \tag{6.1.21}$$

with marginal products given by

$$MP_j = \frac{\partial y}{\partial x_j} = \beta_0 \beta_j x_j^{-1} \prod_{k=1}^N x_k^{\beta_k}, \quad j = 1, \ldots, N, \tag{6.1.22}$$

and returns to scale

$$RTS = \sum_{k=1}^N \beta_k. \tag{6.1.23}$$

Also,

$$\sigma_{jk} = \frac{d \ln(x_j/x_k)/(x_j/x_k)}{d \ln(\partial y/\partial x_k)/(\partial y/\partial x_j)} = \frac{\beta_j}{\beta_k} \frac{\beta_k}{\beta_j} = 1, \tag{6.1.24}$$

and thus the elasticity of substitution is unitary for any set of marginal products and input factor combinations. The Cobb–Douglas production function is typically transformed into the log-linear form

$$\ln y = \ln \beta_0 + \sum_{j=1}^N \beta_j \ln x_j, \tag{6.1.25}$$

and the parameters thus can be estimated effortlessly using linear regression if additive errors are appended to the right-hand side of the expression. If instead the additive errors are appended to the multiplicative form of the Cobb–Douglas then it is well known that standard linear regression techniques will not be appropriate. The Cobb–Douglas production function is the workhorse of applied production economists, especially those involved in economic growth. Its ubiquitous use is based in part on its parsimony and in part on its transparent empirical insight. One can readily identify output elasticities and scale economies from the parameter estimates of a simple linear regression of $\ln y$ on $\ln x$.

Although the Cobb–Douglas is the iconic functional form for production (or cost) estimation, it does have its limitations, none more obvious than the constant and unitary elasticity of substitution implied by its functional specification. Although this assumption appeared to be consistent with the relatively stable factor shares for labor and capital in US manufacturing (1889–1922), which Cobb and Douglas used to motivate this particular functional form, the assumptions are nonetheless quite strong and may not be consistent with many empirical settings, aside from manufacturing during a rather early part of America's industrial history. To address these shortcomings in part, Solow (1956) and Arrow et al. (1961) introduced a *constant elasticity of substitution (CES) function* with a non-unitary elasticity of substitution, allowing for factor shares to have constant changes (as opposed to levels, as with the Cobb–Douglas) when marginal rates of technical substitution change. Although much early attention was devoted to the two-input form of the CES, the general CES with CRS (Blackorby and Russell, 1981, 1989) can be written as

$$y = \beta_0 \left[\sum_{j=1}^{N} \beta_j x_j^{\rho} \right]^{1/\rho}, \tag{6.1.26}$$

where $\beta_0, \beta_j > 0$, and $\rho \leq 1$. The CES nests the Cobb–Douglas. When $\rho \to 0$ the expression can be shown to have the limiting Cobb–Douglas form

$$y = \beta_0 \prod_{j=1}^{N} x_j^{\beta_j}. \tag{6.1.27}$$

The CES also nests the Leontief. Since the Leontief production function exhibits constant returns to scale and has zero elasticity of substitution one can explore the limiting behavior of a re-parameterized version of the CES as $\rho \to -\infty$ using L'Hospital's rule. This was the relatively transparent approach taken by Csontos and Ray (1992) in revisiting the original proof of Arrow et al. (1961), which was based on a general result for functions of mean order $-\infty$.

When not constrained to take on either of these limiting cases for ρ the CES has an elasticity of substitution that is constant and given by

$$\sigma = 1/(1 - \rho), \tag{6.1.28}$$

and corresponds to the percentage change in the input ratio given a percentage change in relative factor prices for the two-input case addressed by Hicks (1932) and Hicks and Allen (1934). The extension of the original two-factor CES of Arrow et al. (1961) to a multi-input setting is not without its limitations. Such a generalization does not allow for different constant elasticities of substitution between input pairs without suffering from other shortcomings, which has restricted the use of the CES in general treatments of multi-input technologies ($N > 2$) (Uzawa, 1962). Moreover, Blackorby and Russell (1981, 1989) have pointed out that for more than two inputs, the Morishima elasticity of substitution, which is the proper elasticity concept to use in such settings, and the Hicks elasticity of substitution are not equivalent for the CES. A recent survey by Klump et al. (2012) provides much more detail on this classic functional form.

The last functional form we consider before moving to the so-called "flexible functional forms" is the *CRESH production function* of Hanoch (1971). The functional form is homothetic: that is, it is a monotonically increasing function of a positive linear homogeneous function and has elasticities of substitution that can change along isoquants and between factor pairs, but has elasticities of substitution whose ratios are fixed. The production technology is parameterized as

$$ye^{\theta y} = \left[\sum_{j=1}^{N} \beta_j x_j^{-\rho_j} \right]^{-\gamma/\rho}, \tag{6.1.29}$$

where monotonicity and quasi-concavity impose the restrictions $\theta \geq 0$, $\gamma > 0$, $\beta_j > 0$, $j = 1, \ldots, N$, and $\sum_{j=1}^{N} \beta_j = 1$. Additional sign restriction on ρ and the $\rho_j's$ are needed in order to assure global or local regularity of the technology and can be found in Hanoch (1971). The function nests the homogeneous CES when $\theta = 0$, and $\rho_1 = \ldots = \rho_N$ and the Cobb–Douglas when $(\rho_1 = \ldots = \rho_N) \to 0$, among others. Returns to scale and Allen–Uzawa elasticities (alternative Morishima elasticities can be calculated according to the Blackorby and Russell, 1989 formulations) are given by

$$RTS = \frac{\gamma}{1 + \theta y} \frac{\sum_{j=1}^{N} \rho_j \beta_j x_j^{-\rho_j}}{\sum_{j=1}^{N} \rho \beta_j x_j^{-\rho_j}}, \tag{6.1.30}$$

and

$$\sigma_{jk} = \frac{1}{(1 + \rho_j)(1 + \rho_k)} \frac{\sum_{l=1}^{N} \rho_l \beta_l x_l^{-\rho_l}}{\sum_{l=1}^{N} \left(\frac{\rho_l \beta_l}{1 + \rho_l} \right) x_l^{-\rho_l}}, \quad j \neq k. \tag{6.1.31}$$

Guilkey et al. (1983) utilized this functional form in their simulation study of flexible functional forms in order to specify various technologies that were identified by three popular generalizations of the cost functions we have just considered. These are the generalized Leontief, the generalized Cobb–Douglas, and the transcendental (translog) cost functions. We turn to these flexible functional forms next.

6.1.3 Flexible-Functional Forms and Second-Order Series Approximations of the Production Function

The production functions we have outlined in the previous section do not, in general, allow for substitution possibilities to vary across a wide space of inputs. Their multiple output technology distance function generalizations also do not, in general, allow for substitution and transformation possibilities to vary across a wide space of inputs and outputs. However, due to their parametric forms, the functional forms do often satisfy the regularity conditions, that we saw in Chapter 1, needed in order to develop a theory of production and other dual forms, such as the cost, revenue, and profit functions. There are exceptions, such as when we consider extensions of these forms to a multi-output distance function, which may not satisfy such conditions. For example, the multiple output Cobb–Douglas distance function has a production possibility frontier that is convex instead of concave. However, many of the production functions that we have outlined above, under reasonable parametric restrictions, are consistent with the three equivalent characterizations of technology in terms of the technology set, the output set, and the input requirement set, given by $(x, y) \in T \Leftrightarrow y \in P(x) \Leftrightarrow x \in L(y)$.

It is important at this stage to further consider the regularity conditions that are imposed on the multi-output generalization of the single-output production function, whose functional representations we have just examined. We consider such multi-output generalizations at this juncture in part because we wish to discuss more generalized and flexible parametric functional representations of production. However, we also consider such multi-output technologies since the regularity conditions needed to specify such forms naturally convey an additional regularity condition on the functional representation of production, and this is the requirement that it be (quasi-)concave, which ensures (non-increasing) diminishing marginal rates of substitution. This is a direct result of the main axioms used in defining the input requirement set in Chapter 2 and is discussed at length in Diewert (1971). Thus, monotonicity and quasi-concavity are properties that **all** well-defined production functions (and their distance function extensions) possess if they are to be considered production functions. This is not always appreciated in empirical work, especially in estimating nonparametric or semiparametric econometric models of production, wherein such tests are often not carried out, the imposition of monotonicity and curvature are not feasible or are computationally cumbersome, or the imposition of such restrictions is done in such a way that the function space over which the nonparametric production function can be specified is severely limited (Pya and Wood, 2015; Du et al., 2013; Wu and Sickles, 2018).

It should be of no surprise that firms that produced only one output are rather rare and that firms that produce more than one output from a set of equivalent or different inputs are the rule. Although it seems in theory possible to model a separate production function for each output, such a course of action is both empirically infeasible and theoretically suspect, as each production process for each output would need to be considered as independent. However, as we discussed in Chapter 1, we can adopt a particularly popular *implicit* function characterization of technology – Shephard's distance functions – to functionally represent such multi-output production processes.

Such an approach is utilized in advanced production theory and in the modern analysis of productivity and efficiency.

The analogue to the production function we studied in the last section is the *output-oriented* Shephard (1970) distance function (D_o) introduced in Chapter 1. The output distance function $D_o : \Re_+^N \times \Re_+^M \to \Re_+^1 \cup \{+\infty\}$ is defined as $D_o(x, y) \equiv \inf\{\theta > 0 : (x, y/\theta) \in T\} = \inf\{\theta > 0 : y/\theta \in P(x)\}$ and provides, for any particular combination (x^0, y^0), the smallest scalar needed to divide actual output, y^0, so that it expands up to the level at which it just reaches the frontier of T, without changing the input vector x^0. The output distance function (and its special case, the single-output production function) is linearly homogeneous in outputs, monotonic, and quasi-concave, properties it inherits from the very reasonable assumptions that are discussed in Chapter 2 relating to the input requirement set (recall that the input requirement set and the output set are equivalent under the four main axioms of Chapter 1). Its quasi-concavity is motivated by the nonincreasing marginal rate of technical substitution between any two inputs and is utilized in the duality theory between cost and production.

When we consider a single output technology, D_o is the ratio of actual output to the potential (maximal) output that can be produced with the same level of input and thus $f(x^o) = y^o/D_o(x^o, y^o)$. Shephard's distance function is a very convenient *generalization* of the production function. Moreover, in the multiple-output case, Shephard's output distance function provides the smallest scalar necessary to radially expand *all* the outputs until they reach the frontier of the output set, while keeping the input at its original level (see Figure 1.11, Chapter 1). Such a scalar measure will allow us to ultimately identify the frontier of the set (Chapter 11) as well as the distances from a position inside the set to the frontier, and so allow us to operationalize and estimate the level of productivity (technical) efficiency for a multi-output (or single-output) firm.

Before we examine the flexible functional forms that have been used to specify and estimate multi-output–multi-input distance functions, we note that they can be motivated in at least two important and very different ways. Many are flexible in the sense of Diewert (1974a,b) in that they impose no prior restrictions on the Allen–Uzawa (or Morishima) elasticities of substitution and can provide an approximation with no approximation error for an arbitrary function and its first two derivatives at a particular point (Diewert, 1971; Wales, 1977; Fuss et al., 1978; Caves and Christensen, 1980). However, these flexible functional forms are also parametric generalizations of many of the functional forms we have already considered accomplished by adding second-order terms. Given this latter interpretation, they can be considered as series approximations (typically truncated at the second-order terms) to such forms as the linear, Leontief, Cobb–Douglas, and CES functional forms, and thus particular nonparametric econometric alternatives to these earlier and less complicated production functions. The function space for nonparametric alternatives is quite dense and these series approximations are formed by assuming a rather limited set of basis functions. We will discuss nonparametric kernel-based alternatives at the end of this chapter.

Additional considerations should also be made in assessing the appropriateness of all of these parametric/nonparametric econometrically based functional representations of technology or their dual counterparts based on the sage advice of some of the pioneers of modern applied production theory. In their chapter in the seminal monograph by Fuss and McFadden (1978) and Fuss et al. (1978) laid out a set of criteria for selecting functional forms. As more computational power provides empirical researchers added leverage to exploit the relatively free and uncomplaining use of electrons to replace the labors of their graduate students, it seems appropriate to reconsider the advice of Professors Fuss, McFadden, and Mundlak. Among their listed criteria, which have passed the test of time, are the following (slightly edited from the original, pp. 224–225)

(1) Parsimony in parameters: The functional form should contain no more parameters than are necessary for consistency with the maintained hypothesis;

(2) Ease of interpretation: Excessively complex or parameter-rich functional forms may contain implausible implications, which are hidden from easy detection;

(3) Computational ease: The trade-off between the computational requirements of a functional form and the thoroughness of empirical analysis should be weighted carefully in the choice of a model;

(4) Interpolative robustness: Within the range of observed data, the chosen functional form should be well-behaved, displaying consistency with the maintained hypotheses, such as positive marginal products or convexity. If these properties must be checked numerically, then the form should admit convenient computational procedures for this purpose;

(5) Extrapolative robustness: The functional form should be compatible with the maintained hypotheses outside the range of observed data. This is a particularly important criterion for forecasting applications.

Keeping in mind the criteria of Fuss, McFadden, and Mundlak, we now extend our discussion of production and multi-output distance functions, and their dual cost, revenue, and profit functions, to a more general parametric set of representations. We first discuss the single-output generalizations and refinements, and then move to the multi-output distance function specifications. After we have discussed these functional representations, we will endeavor to discuss several of the common dual forms, whose specifications in many cases can be introduced as a reparameterization of the underlying representations given for the primal technology.

For a detailed discussion of an array of additional functional forms see the excellent survey by Griffin et al. (1987) and Thompson (1988). In their discussion of flexible production functions, they point to the work of Barnett (1983) and Barnett and Lee (1985) who noted that although second-order Taylor series in general (and the translog in particular) have tended to be the default functional forms utilized by empirical researchers, there are other forms that also provide local flexibility. They go on to note that locally flexible forms often do quite poorly in approximating an underlying technology and its curvature properties when one strays too far from the point of expansion (or perfect approximation) and offer up their own new form based on Laurent expansions. Despotakis (1986) made a similar point confirmed earlier in the simulation studies carried out by Guilkey et al. (1983). Gallant (1981, 1982) pointed out that global flexibility in the curvature properties of the underlying technology (Sobolev flexibility) is in general preferred over local flexibility. The Sobolev distance measure is less tractable in applied econometric analysis than standard distance metrics such as ℓ^2- norms usually adopted in fitting regression-based functions. In Diewert and Wales (1992) criteria under which a functional form will be flexible in terms of its ability to characterize an arbitrary degree of (biased) technological progress (TP) for each variable input are established. Thus flexibility, which requires that the function can provide a second-order approximation to an arbitrary twice continuously differentiable true function that satisfies the required properties at an arbitrary point, is extended to deal with technical progress, typically a major component of productivity growth. They point out that their normalized quadratic functional form can be made TP flexible by a relatively straightforward parameterization. Such transparency in the parameterization of a TP flexible functional form using the normalized quadratic is lost when forms such as the Laurent and Fourier expansions introduced by Barnett and by Gallant are considered.

The issue of flexibility is also of concern for another reason. Since the estimates from the Diewert flexible functions we consider below are based on a fit of the data that is presumably generated by the "true" functional form, instead of a series expansion of the "true" functional form, there may be no point in the data wherein the "true" function and its curvature are approximated with no error, which is inconsistent with the notion of Diewert flexibility. White (1980) made a similar point in analyzing least squares estimates of linearized series expansions, which he found to be quite misleading when used to estimate the parameters of the underlying "true" function.

6.1.3.1 Quadratic Function

We now move to briefly summarize various flexible functional forms that have been the workhorses for empirical work in productivity. Berndt (1991) also has an excellent discussion of a subset of the functions we discuss below as well as standard empirical methods for estimating them in the absence of inefficiency. We first consider a relatively straightforward generalization of the linear production function, the *quadratic production function,* expressed as

$$y = \beta_0 + \sum_{j=1}^{N} \beta_j x_j + \sum_{j=1}^{N} \sum_{k=1}^{N} \beta_{jk} x_j x_k, \beta_{jk} = \beta_{kj}, \forall j \neq k. \quad (6.1.32)$$

Marginal products are given by

$$MP_j = \frac{\partial y}{\partial x_j} = \beta_j + \sum_{k=1}^{N} 2\beta_{jk} x_k, \quad j = 1, \ldots, N. \quad (6.1.33)$$

Returns to scale are driven by β_0 and the β_{ij}. When $\beta_0 = 0$ and $\beta_{jk} = 0$, $i \neq j$, returns to scale are constant, while in general decreasing and increasing returns to scale depend on the sign of β_0 and the β_{jk}. The function is monotone for $\beta_j \geq 0$ and for positive semi-definite $[\beta]_{jk}$, however, these are only sufficient conditions and other configurations and sample values for the input levels will give a positive marginal product. The quadratic production function is often used when input usage is zero for selected inputs, for example, new inputs that are introduced during the period under study, a situation that is also handled rather easily by another flexible functional form, the generalized Leontief that we consider next. Generalizations of the quadratic were considered by Denny (1974).

6.1.3.2   Generalized Leontief

The next flexible functional form we consider is a restricted form of the *generalized Leontief production function* (Diewert, 1971). It is a second-order expansion in square-roots of the inputs and can be written as

$$y = \sum_{j=1}^{N} \sum_{k=1}^{N} \beta_{jk} x_j^{1/2} x_k^{1/2}, \beta_{jk} = \beta_{jk}, \forall j, k, \quad (6.1.34)$$

with marginal products

$$MP_j = \frac{\partial y}{\partial x_j} = \sum_{k=1}^{N} \beta_{jk} x_k^{1/2} x_j^{-1/2}. \quad (6.1.35)$$

Returns to scale are constant, while monotonicity may hold locally for particular values of the parameters and levels of inputs. Concavity is guaranteed if all of the $\beta_{ij} \geq 0 \; \forall \; i \neq j$, in which case all inputs are substitutes or unrelated.[1]

---

[1] The Cobb–Douglas production function also can be generalized by adding second-order terms to give the *generalized Cobb–Douglas production function* of Fuss et al. (1978) based on the functional form introduced by Diewert (1973). However, in its original form it lacks invariance and in its modified form the parameters appear not to be invariant with respect to a normalization required to identify them. We do not discuss the generalized Cobb–Douglas production here but do explore such a generalization when we discuss flexible cost functions later in the chapter. Interested readers can seek out the cited references above.

6.1.3.3 Translog Production Function

Another generalized form of the Cobb–Douglas function with quadratic and cross-product terms, introduced by Christensen et al. (1971), is the ubiquitous *translog production function*

$$\ln y = \beta_0 + \sum_{j=1}^{N} \beta_j \ln x_j + \sum_{j=1}^{N} \sum_{k=1}^{N} \beta_{jk} (\ln x_j)(\ln x_k), \ \beta_{jk} = \beta_{kj}, \forall j, k.$$

$$(6.1.36)$$

Marginal products are given by

$$MP_j = \frac{\partial y}{\partial x_j} = y \left[\beta_j + 2 \sum_{k=1}^{N} \beta_{jk} \ln(x_k) \right] / x_j, \ j = 1, \dots, N; \ x_j > 0.$$

$$(6.1.37)$$

The production function is homogeneous of degree $\theta = \sum_{j=1}^{N} \beta_j$, when $\sum_{k=1}^{N} \beta_{jk} = 0, \forall j$. Monotonicity and concavity are met when $\beta_j > 0, j = 1, \dots, N$ and all of the $\beta_{jk} > 0$, when $x_k \geq 1$. The translog reduces to a Cobb–Douglas technology when $\beta_{jk} = 0, \forall j, k$.

6.1.3.4 The Generalized Box–Cox

The *generalized Box–Cox production function* was introduced by Appelbaum (1979) and Berndt and Khaled (1979) to circumvent the problem of zero outputs and inputs and to allow for a more general treatment of functional form by nesting within the output and input specifications both a natural log and a level formulation. As such it nests both the translog and the quadratic. The generalized Box–Cox is given by

$$y(\theta) = \beta_0 + \sum_{j=1}^{N} \beta_j x_j(\lambda) + \sum_{j=1}^{N} \sum_{k=1}^{N} \beta_{jk} x_j(\lambda) x_k(\lambda), \beta_{jk} = \beta_{kj}, \forall j, k,$$

$$(6.1.38)$$

where $y(\theta) = (y^{2\theta} - 1)/(2\theta)$ and $x_j(\lambda) = (x_j^{\lambda} - 1)/\lambda, \lambda > 0$. Marginal products, for $x_j > 0$, are

$$MP_j = \frac{\partial y}{\partial x_j} = x_j^{\lambda-1} y^{1-2\theta} \left[\lambda \beta_j + 2 \sum_{k=1}^{N} \beta_{jk} (x_k^{\lambda} - 1) \right] / \lambda. \quad (6.1.39)$$

Conditions under which the function is linearly homogeneous are rather cumbersome and come with little intuition. Moreover, monotonicity, and concavity are not generally met by any obvious set of parametric restrictions. As with many flexible functional forms, this necessitates the calculation of estimated marginal products as well as estimates of the second-order derivatives needed to check for local and global concavity.

6.1.3.5   The Augmented Fourier Functional Form

The next flexible functional form we consider augments the quadratic production function with higher-order terms based on a Fourier expansion. This is referred to as the *augmented Fourier production function* (Gallant, 1984) and can be written as

$$y = \sum_{j=1}^{N} \beta_j x_j + \sum_{j=1}^{N}\sum_{k=1}^{N} \beta_{jk} x_j x_k + \sum_{|h|^* \leq H} \beta_h \exp\left(i \sum_{j=1}^{N} h_j x_j\right), \quad (6.1.40)$$

where $\beta_{jk} = \beta_{kj}, \forall j, k$, and where all $x_i \in [0, 2\pi]$, $\beta_h = \beta_h' + i\beta_h$, $i^2 = -1$.
Marginal products are

$$MP_j = \frac{\partial y}{\partial x_j} = \beta_j + \sum_{k=1}^{N} 2\beta_{jk} x_k + i \sum_{|h|^* \leq H} h_j \beta_h \exp\left(i \sum_{j=1}^{N} h_j x_j\right).$$
$$(6.1.41)$$

The function has no natural parameterization to allow for homogeneity, homotheticity, monotonicity, or concavity but these conditions can be checked in the sample observations. For example, marginal products can be calculated to check for monotonicity and the eigenvalues of the Hessian can be calculated to check sample observations for local (global) concavity. The function tends to be over-parameterized and is rather cumbersome to utilize in applied work. Moreover, there are no particularly transparent special cases nested within this functional form that are well-behaved.

6.1.4   Choice of Functional Form Based on Solutions to Functional Equations

Chambers et al. (2013) discuss the issue of how to choose a flexible functional form based on solutions to functional equations that satisfy the conditions of homogeneity and translation invariance, two quite reasonable properties that a flexible functional form may possess. They point out that the generalized quadratic function, a flexible functional form, satisfies this property. The authors show that if for some finite J a function satisfies the following form and conditions

$$\zeta^{-1}(F(q)) = a_0 + \sum_{j=1}^{J} \beta_j h(q_j) + \sum_{j=1}^{J}\sum_{k=1}^{J} \beta_{jk} h(q_j) h(q_k), \quad (6.1.42)$$

where $F : \Re^J \to \Re$, $h : \Re \to \Re$, and $\zeta : \Re \to \Re$ with an inverse ζ^{-1}, β_j, β_{jk} are constants, and $q_j \in \Re_+$, then F is referred to as the generalized quadratic function (see Chambers, 1988), the transformed quadratic function (see Diewert, 2002), or is said to have a second-order Taylor series approximation interpretation of Färe and Sung (1986). Moreover, if $\beta_j = 0$, $j = 1, \ldots, J$, $\beta_{jk} \neq 0$, $j = 1, \ldots, J$, then it is a generalized quasi-quadratic function as in Färe and Sung (1986). $F(q)$ is homogeneous of degree 1 if $F(\lambda q) = \lambda F(q)$ and it satisfies the translation property if $F(q + ag) = F(q) + a$, $a \in \Re$, where $g \in \Re^J$ and $g \neq 0$ is a directional vector.

The generalized quasi-quadratic functional form specification and constraints required in order for the function to satisfy the conditions of homogeneity and translation invariance yield functional equations for which there are only two sets of global solutions (functional forms). When the functional form has the generalized quasi-quadratic functional form and the homogeneity condition is imposed, one solution is the *translog* function of Christensen et al. (1971),

$$F(q) = \beta_0 + \sum_{j=1}^{J} \beta_j \ln(q_j) + \sum_{j=1}^{J}\sum_{k=1}^{J} \beta_{jk} \ln(q_j) \ln(q_k), \qquad (6.1.43)$$

while the other is the *quadratic mean of order-r* function of Denny (1974) and Diewert (1976), which for nonzero r is

$$F(q) = \left(\beta_0 + \sum_{j=1}^{J}\sum_{k=1}^{J} \beta_{jk} q_j^{r/2} q_k^{r/2} \right)^{1/r}. \qquad (6.1.44)$$

When the functional form has the generalized quasi-quadratic functional form and the homogeneity and translation invariance condition are imposed, the solutions to the functional equations also have two functional forms, one of which is the *quadratic* function

$$F(q) = \beta_0 + \sum_{j=1}^{J} \beta_j q_j + \sum_{j=1}^{J}\sum_{k=1}^{J} \beta_{jk} q_j q_k, \qquad (6.1.45)$$

while the other takes the form

$$F(q) = \frac{1}{2\lambda} \ln \sum_{j=1}^{J}\sum_{k=1}^{J} \beta_{jk} \exp(\lambda q_j) \exp(\lambda q_k), \quad \lambda \neq 0. \qquad (6.1.46)$$

Kolm (1976) noted that this function is the *exponential mean of order-λ*. Diewert (1993) discusses a special case of this function, the Nagumo mean of order lambda (Diewert uses s instead of λ), which is defined as[2]

---

[2] We thank Professor Diewert for pointing this out to us.

$$F(q) \equiv (1/\lambda) \ln \left[\sum_{j=1}^{J} (1/J) \exp(\lambda q_j) \right]; \lambda \neq 0; \qquad (6.1.47)$$

$$F(q) \equiv \sum_{j=1}^{J} (1/J) q_j; \lambda = 0. \qquad (6.1.48)$$

Denny (1974) and Diewert (1976) used an analogous quadratic generalization of the Hardy et al. (1934) ordinary mean of order r in their work on the quadratic mean of order r.

The normalized quadratic functional form has its drawbacks, of course. As the number of inputs (and outputs) increases, the parameterization becomes quite unwieldy and empirically problematic. One can deal with this problem by limiting the flexibility of the normalized quadratic (see, for example, Diewert and Wales, 1988). The multicollinearity that often renders point estimates of second-order parameters quite unstable has motivated many to simplify flexible forms via parameter restrictions or conversely add information in the form of side-conditions implied by optimizing assumptions. Absent the use of such side conditions semi-flexible functional forms have been utilized. For example, when using distance functions, wherein only quantities are relevant, flexibility often means that regularity conditions are violated. This motivated Sickles et al. (2002) to assume separability between airline outputs and inputs while allowing for proper curvature in a translog distance function describing airline outputs and inputs.

The trade-offs between axiomatic purity and empirical practicality are cogently analyzed by Neary (2004) and by Diewert and Wales (1988), who focused their techniques on modeling issues in consumer theory, using semi-flexible specifications of the normalized quadratic functions. For their normalized quadratic expenditure function to be concave in the N-goods' prices the parameter matrix specifying the quadratic terms must be negative semi-definite. Diewert and Wales (1988) reparameterize the second-order terms using Cholesky decompositions with at most $K \leq N - 1$ nonzero columns and describe such a function as having the property of being flexible up to degree K. Choice of K between 1 and $N - 1$ then becomes not only a theoretical issue but also a practical one by taking into consideration computational feasibility and degrees of freedom. The generalization of their semi-flexible normalized quadratic functional form in the producer context can be found in Diewert and Lawrence (2002), wherein they allow for an arbitrary substitution matrix at two sample points (instead of the usual one sample point) in order to avoid trends in the elasticities that appears to be a recurring shortcoming of the normalized quadratic functional form. Again, we can see in these papers and many like them, the very real tensions between specifying functional forms that meet regularity conditions, are flexible, and are empirically feasible.

6.2 FUNCTIONAL FORMS FOR DISTANCE FUNCTION ANALYSIS

In order to move from a single to a multi-output technology, we first consider how one can specify the multi-output Cobb–Douglas distance function (Klein, 1953). The M-output, N-input deterministic distance function $D_o(x, y)$ can be written as a Young-like Lowe index, described in Balk (2008)

$$D_o(x, y) = \frac{\prod_{j=1}^{M} y_j^{\theta_j}}{\prod_{k=1}^{N} x_k^{\beta_k}}, \tag{6.2.1}$$

where $y_j, x_k > 0$. The output-distance function $D_o(x, y)$ is nondecreasing, linearly homogeneous and concave in y, and nonincreasing and quasi-concave in x. The econometrician adds the condition that $D_o(x, y) \leq 1$ in order to utilize this function to estimate inefficiency by $1 - D_o(x, y)$, since the output-distance function defined above can hypothetically take on values greater than one. After taking natural logs and rearranging terms by normalizing with respect to the first output (since an implication of linear homogeneity in outputs is that $\sum_{j=1}^{M} \theta_j = 1$), we can write the distance function as

$$-\ln y_1 = \sum_{j=2}^{M} \theta_j \ln(y_j/y_1) - \sum_{k=1}^{N} \beta_k \ln(x_k) + u, \ u \geq 0. \tag{6.2.2}$$

The term u is non-negative, owing to the inequality in the definition of the distance function that allows for technical inefficiency, which we will explicitly model in Chapter 11. Here we have approximated the non-negative difference $1 - D_o(x, y)$ by $u \approx 1 - \exp(-u)$ and labeled it inefficiency. This is the convention used by Aigner et al. (1977) when they introduced the stochastic version of this function by appending to the relationship a disturbance term to account for standard measurement errors represented by the usual disturbance term in the regression model. Schmidt and Sickles (1984) also used this convention when they introduced the fixed effects panel stochastic frontier to address potential issues of endogeneity between the inefficiencies and the input choices by firms without making formal parametric assumptions utilized by the error components model of Pitt and Lee (1981) that did not allow for such correlations.

The Cobb–Douglas specification of the distance function used in Klein (1953) has been criticized for its assumption of separability of outputs and inputs and for incorrect curvature as the production possibility frontier is convex instead of concave. However, as pointed out by Coelli (2000), the Cobb–Douglas at least remains a parsimonious first-order local approximation to the true function that can approximate the true distance function to the first order at any interior point. However, given this Cobb–Douglas technology, revenue maximization would always force the producer to be at the boundary of the production possibilities set and always produce a single output. Thus the appeal of the Cobb–Douglas distance function on the basis of its ability to provide a first-order approximation property is rather questionable.

If one considers the translog output distance function (Caves et al., 1982a; Lovell et al., 1994; Coelli and Perelman, 1999), where the second-order terms allow for greater flexibility, proper local curvature, and lift the assumed separability of outputs and inputs, then the distance function (for $u \geq 0$) takes the form

$$- \ln y_1 = \sum_{j=2}^{M} \theta_j \ln(y_j/y_1) + 1/2 \sum_{j=2}^{M} \sum_{l=2}^{M} \theta_{jl} \ln(y_j/y_1) \ln(y_l/y_1) + \sum_{k=1}^{N} \beta_k \ln x_k$$

$$+ 1/2 \sum_{k=1}^{N} \sum_{p=1}^{N} \beta_{kp} \ln x_k \ln x_p + \sum_{j=2}^{M} \sum_{k=1}^{N} \delta_{jk} \ln(y_j/y_1) \ln x_k + u.$$

(6.2.3)

In the translog output distance function specification, the input and output elasticities are

$$s_p = \beta_p + \sum_{k=1}^{N} \beta_{kp} \ln x_k + \sum_{j=2}^{M} \delta_{pj} \ln(y_j/y_1), \; p = 1, 2, \ldots, N,$$

(6.2.4)

$$r_j = \theta_j + \sum_{l=2}^{M} \theta_{jl} \ln(y_j/y_1) + \sum_{k=1}^{N} \delta_{kj} x_k, \; j = 2, \ldots, M. \qquad (6.2.5)$$

Economies of scope can be constructed following Hajargasht et al. (2008), who derive the expressions for economies of scope in terms of the derivative of the distance function utilizing the duality between the cost function, which we consider in the next section, and the input distance function. Imposition of curvature properties for the translog distance function is much more of a challenge than it was for the translog production function (or cost function we discuss below) and of course the imposition of such conditions compromises the flexibility of the translog. The quadratic and generalized-Leontief output distance functions have similar generalizations. They both suffer from the problem that imposition of proper curvature restrictions tends to also compromise the flexibility of the functions. For more specifics on these alternatives see Diewert (1971, 2002), Serletis and Shahmoradi (2007), and Serletis and Feng (2015).

There are a number of practical problems with estimating the distance function. One has to do with the substantial multicollinearity due to the large number of parameters when one considers technologies with many outputs and many inputs. Another problem is in finding proper instruments for the right-hand-side endogenous outputs. A coherent error structure to address such endogeneity along with the errors appended to additional equations that relate the parameters in the distance function to derived output supply and input demand relationships based on profit maximization is fraught with difficulties. We take up the problem of endogeneity in Chapter 14. Not the least of these difficulties is in relating how allocation errors in the output supply and input demand equations impact the inefficiency specified in the distance function. O'Donnell (2016) and Diewert and Fox (2017) have recently approached the construction of the distance function in very different manners. O'Donnell bases his econometric and index number approach on a multi-factor decomposition involving various measures of distorted scale and scope inefficiencies and constraints on productivity due to environmental variables in order to calculate the contribution of these in efficiency factors to a fixed-weighted Lowe productivity index,[3] while Diewert and Fox focus on minimal regularity conditions on the technology that ensure the existence of the output distance function (see equation (A2) in the Appendix of Diewert and Fox, 2017). They provide a theoretical justification for the geometric average form of the Bjurek productivity index based in part on the free disposability assumptions of Tulkens (1993).

6.3 FUNCTIONAL FORMS FOR COST ANALYSIS

Chapter 2 discussed production theory via the dual approach and specifically detailed how the cost function and factor demand equations can be linked back to the properties of the technology. We considered a firm producing outputs, $y \in \Re_+^M$, using inputs, $x \in \Re_+^N$ with corresponding prices $w = (w_1, \ldots, w_N) \in \Re_{++}^N$, and using the available technology characterized by the input requirement set $L(y)$, $y \in \Re_+^M$. The input requirement set can also be completely characterized by the Shephard's input distance function as $x \in L(y) \Leftrightarrow D_i(y, x) \geq 1$ where $D_i(y, x) \equiv \sup\{\theta > 0 : x/\theta \in L(y)\}$.

Assuming that the prices of inputs are strictly positive and fixed, the decision of how much of each input the firm should employ to achieve its production plan y and a determination of the resulting total cost that such production would incur can be formulated by defining the long run (total) cost function, as $C(y, w) \equiv \min_x \{wx : x \in L(y)\}$. Moreover, the solution to the optimization problem $x(y, w) \equiv \arg\min_x \{wx : x \in L(y)\}$ is called the conditional (on output) demand functions for inputs.

Estimating the direct production function or multi-output distance function may be rendered infeasible for a series of reasons. The most obvious is that the factor inputs are under the control of the firm, and firms may reallocate their use based on profit-maximizing or cost-minimizing allocations.

---

[3] See Balk and Diewert (2010) for a critique on the substitution bias induced by the Lowe index in a consumer price setting.

As such, it may be difficult to argue that they are exogenous in a regression-based or likelihood-based estimating procedure. However, if the production function is stochastic and the firm is assumed to base its allocation decisions on expected profit maximization as in Zellner et al. (1966), then the inputs can be treated as weakly exogenous and standard regression-based or likelihood-based estimations can yield consistent estimates.

Zellner et al. (1966) viewed the stochastic shocks to the deterministic production function as representing idiosyncratic disturbances due to weather, machine breakdowns, and labor performance, among many other uncontrollable random factors. If the firm does not see the shocks when it makes its input allocations and if production is not instantaneous, then the disturbance cannot affect output levels until after the inputs have been selected. Since the firm cannot maximize a function that it cannot observe, as it is stochastic, the firm is assumed to maximize what it expects the function to be, that is it is assumed to maximize expected profit. Under a seemingly innocuous assumption that the idiosyncratic error is not correlated with the errors in allocating inputs, consistent estimates of the production function parameters can be obtained by standard least squares regressions. In regard to the errors in input allocations, Hoch (1958) pointed out that inefficiency in such a setting may be due to the "possibility that the firm may exhibit systematic errors, perhaps as a result of institutional or other constraints, with respect to satisfying the first order conditions" (in this case of profit maximization) (Zellner et al., 1966).

If one is unwilling to adopt the expected profit-maximizing assumptions of Zellner et al. (1966), then instruments may be found, such as lagged input levels or factor prices if the input markets are competitive and thus exogenous to the firm. Often times alternative instruments may be hard to find, and of course the use of weak instruments may cause more problems than the potential endogeneity of the inputs may have caused in the first place (see, for example, Wooldridge, 2013). We provide a discussion of endogeneity in production function estimation in Chapter 14.

As firms tend to be price takers, it is thought that alternatives to specifying and estimating the primal production or distance function, such as specifying and estimating the cost dual, may be more defensible on statistical grounds, especially when the firm is thought to be a cost minimizer with production targets given. This argument has particular resonance for regulated firms whose output levels are viewed as determined by the regulating authority. We will focus, in this next section, on a somewhat briefer set of cost functions (than production or distance functions) that have dominated the empirical productivity literature: the translog, the generalized Leontief, and, to a lesser extent, the generalized Cobb–Douglas. We also discuss specifications that nest flexible and non-flexible forms via single parameter power transformations, the CES-translog and CES-generalized Leontief cost functions. Although the cost function dual has been developed in part to allow for a relatively easy empirical description of multi-output technologies, we will focus on single-output–multi-input technologies in our presentation of functional forms. Extensions to multiple outputs are relatively straightforward as we point out in our discussion of variable cost functions later in this chapter where we consider multi-output technologies. We also consider such multi-output cost functions as special cases of multi-output restricted profit functions that are considered in the last several sections of this chapter. Our previous discussion of functional forms for distance functions specifically addressed how multi-output technologies can be represented via a parametric (or nonparametric) functional relationship used in standard econometric modeling exercises.

6.3.1 Generalized Leontief

The first flexible cost function we consider is the *generalized Leontief (GL) cost function*, which we write in a somewhat more general form than Diewert (1971) as

$$C(y, w) = y \sum_{j=1}^{N} \sum_{k=1}^{N} \beta_{jk} w_j^{1/2} w_k^{1/2} + y^2 \sum_{j=1}^{N} \beta_{yj} w_j + \sum_{j=1}^{N} \beta_j w_j. \quad (6.3.1)$$

The function is, by construction, linearly homogeneous in input prices and symmetric if $\beta_{jk} = \beta_{kj}, \forall j \neq k$. Input demand equations are linear in parameters and are given by

$$x_j(y, w) = y \sum_{k=1}^{N} \beta_{jk} (w_k/w_j)^{1/2} + y^2 \beta_{yj} + \beta_j, \quad j = 1, \dots, N. \quad (6.3.2)$$

Returns to scale and Allen–Uzawa partial elasticities of substitution are given by

$$RTS(y, w) = \left(\sum_{j=1}^{N} \sum_{k=1}^{N} \beta_{jk} w_j^{1/2} w_k^{1/2} + 2y \sum_{j=1}^{N} \beta_{yj} w_j \right)^{-1} (C(y, w)/y),$$

$$(6.3.3)$$

$$\sigma_{jk}(y, w) = \left(\frac{1}{2} \beta_{jk} y w_j^{-1/2} w_k^{1/2} \right) (C(y, w)/x_j(y, w) x_k(y, w)), \quad j \neq k.$$

$$(6.3.4)$$

The GL approximation is non-homothetic unless $\beta_{yi} = \beta_i = 0, \forall i$, in which case it is linearly homogeneous. Thus the GL approximation is incapable of distinguishing among homotheticity, homogeneity, and linear homogeneity. It nests the Leontief fixed proportions cost function and collapses to it when $\beta_{ij} = 0, \forall i \neq j$. The GL functional form has been used widely in empirical work, especially in its multi-output extension as it (like the quadratic) accommodates zero levels of outputs in a very natural way as functional forms such as the translog do not. The generalized-Leontief multiproduct cost function for physician private services was used by Gunning and Sickles (2011, 2013) in their analysis of non-competitive pricing behavior and market power in the physician services market.

6.3.2   Generalized Cobb–Douglas

The next approximation we consider is the *extended generalized Cobb–Douglas (EGCD) cost function* of Magnus (1979). It is based on the generalized Cobb–Douglas cost function of Diewert (1973) and is given by

$$\ln C(y, w) = \beta_0 + \beta_y \ln y + \frac{1}{2}\beta_{yy}(\ln y)^2$$

$$+ \sum_{j=1}^{N} \sum_{k=1}^{N} \beta_{jk} \ln(\beta_j w_j + \beta_k w_k) + \sum_{j=1}^{N} \beta_{yj} \ln y \ln w_j,$$

$$(6.3.5)$$

where symmetry and linear homogeneity in input prices are satisfied if $\beta_k > 0$, $\forall k$, $\beta_{jk} = \beta_{kj}$, $\forall j \neq k$, $\sum_{j=1}^{N} \sum_{k=1}^{N} \beta_{jk} = 1$, and $\sum_{j=1}^{N} \beta_{yj} = 0$. Input demand share equations are nonlinear in parameters and are given by

$$m_j(y, w) = 2\sum_{k=1}^{N} \beta_{jk}\beta_j w_j(\beta_j w_j + \beta_k w_k)^{-1} + \beta_{yj} \ln y, \quad j = 1, \ldots, N,$$

$$(6.3.6)$$

while returns to scale and Allen–Uzawa partial elasticities of substitution are given by

$$RTS(y, w) = \left(\beta_y + \beta_{yy} \ln y + \sum_{j=1}^{N} \beta_{yj} \ln w_j \right)^{-1}, \quad (6.3.7)$$

$$\sigma_{jk}(y, w) = 1 - \frac{2\beta_{jk}\beta_j\beta_k w_j w_k}{(\beta_j w_j + \beta_k w_k)^2 m_j(y, w)m_k(y, w)}, \quad j \neq k. \quad (6.3.8)$$

The EGCD form is homothetic if $\beta_{yj} = 0$, $\forall j$, homogeneous if $\beta_{yy} = \beta_{yj} = 0$, $\forall i$, and linearly homogeneous if $(\beta_y - 1) = \beta_{yy} = \beta_{yj} = 0$, $\forall j$. It collapses to the Cobb–Douglas if $\beta_{jk} = 0$, $\forall j \neq k$.

6.3.3   Translog

One of the most widely used of all cost functions in empirical applications is the *translog (TL) cost function*, which we write as

$$\ln C(y, w) = \beta_0 + \beta_y \ln y + \frac{1}{2}\beta_{yy}(\ln y)^2 + \sum_{j=1}^{N} \beta_j \ln w_j$$

$$+ \frac{1}{2}\sum_{j=1}^{N} \sum_{k=1}^{N} \beta_{jk} \ln w_j \ln w_k + \sum_{j=1}^{N} \beta_{yj} \ln y \ln w_j.$$

$$(6.3.9)$$

Symmetry and linear homogeneity in the (N) factor input prices (w_j)
require that $\beta_{jk} = \beta_{kj}, \forall j \neq k$, and that $\sum_{j=1}^{N} \beta_j = 1$, $\sum_{k=1}^{N} \beta_{jk} = \sum_{j=1}^{N} \beta_{yj} = 0$.
Cost-minimizing input demand shares are linear in parameters and are given by

$$m_j(y, w) = \beta_j + \sum_{k=1}^{N} \beta_{jk} \ln w_k + \beta_{yj} \ln y, \quad j = 1, \ldots, N, \quad (6.3.10)$$

while returns to scale and Allen–Uzawa partial elasticities of substitution are given by

$$RTS(y, w) = \left(\beta_y \beta_{yy} \ln y + \sum_{j=1}^{N} \beta_{yj} \ln w_j \right), \quad (6.3.11)$$

$$\sigma_{jk}(y, w) = \left[\beta_{jk} + m_j(y, w) m_k(y, w)) / m_j(y, w) m_k(y, w) \right]^{-1}, \quad j \neq k. \quad (6.3.12)$$

As Blackorby and Russell (1989) have noted, the Morishima elasticity of substitution is the more appropriate and informative measure of substitution possibilities and for the translog it is given by

$$\sigma_{jk}^{M}(y, w) = \eta_{ij} - \eta_{jj}, \quad (6.3.13)$$

where η is the price elasticity of demand.

The TL cost function is homothetic if $\beta_{yj} = 0$, $\forall j$, homogeneous if $\beta_{yy} = \beta_{yj} = 0$, $\forall j$, and linearly homogeneous if $(\beta_y - 1) = \beta_{yy} = \beta_{yj} = 0$, $\forall j$. The translog cost function nests the Cobb–Douglas cost function and collapses to it when $\beta_{yy} = \beta_{yi} = \beta_{jk} = 0$, $\forall j, k$. Christensen and Greene (1976) estimated the average cost function specified as translog in their classic study of scale economies in stream powered electricity generation. The translog cost function has been the workhorse of empirical cost studies for almost fifty years. Economies of scale and scope have been addressed in a variety of contexts using the translog cost function. For example, Evans and Heckman (1984) used the translog functional form to test the subadditivity of the cost function based on multiple outputs local and toll (long distance) service and found that pre-divestiture Bell data was inconsistent with a natural monopoly. Röller (1990a,b) modified this test by constraining the cost function to be "proper," a term requiring not only standard regularity conditions on the cost function but also requiring positive marginal cost schedules. This last property is argued by Röller to be the most important as it ensures that the degenerate translog behavior when outputs are close to zero (hence the cost function is sub-additive) is not too excessive. He estimated a CES-Quadratic cost function and found that pre-divestiture Bell data was actually fully consistent with a natural monopoly. This points out not only the crucial role the properties of a flexible function form possesses but also the importance of how outputs are aggregated in productivity studies. Evans and Heckman (1984) considered a two-output technology (local and toll service) while Röller (1990a) considered a three-output technology (local, interstate, and intrastate). Lovell and Sickles (1999) considered a similar output partition using the translog cost function and local subadditivity tests and had similar conclusions regarding the rejection of AT&T's natural monopoly position that led to the breakup and divestiture of the Bell System.

6.3.4   CES-Translog and CES-Generalized Leontief

The *CES-translog cost function* of Pollak et al. (1984) was developed to combine the CES and the translog cost functions in a way that took advantage of both. The CES can satisfy global concavity under relatively easy to impose parametric restrictions, while the translog, although flexible, cannot. The CES-translog provides a wider set of substitution possibilities than either the CES or the translog, while imposing more curvature structure. This is because the first-order terms on which the power series expansions pivot are globally convex under easy to implement parametric restrictions. Moreover, the CES-translog contains only one more parameter than the translog and thus provides an empirically tractable alternative specification for cost function estimation.

The N-factor CES-translog cost function can be written as follows,

$$
\ln C(y, w) = \beta_0 + \beta_y \ln y + \ln \left[\sum_{j=1}^{N} \beta_j w_j^{1-\varepsilon} \right]^{1/(1-\varepsilon)}
$$

$$
+ \frac{1}{2} \sum_{j=1}^{N} \sum_{k=1}^{N} \beta_{jk} \ln w_j \ln w_k + \sum_{j=1}^{N} \beta_{yj} \ln y \ln w_j,
$$

$$(6.3.14)$$

where $\beta_{jk} = \beta_{kj}, \forall j, k; \sum_{j=1}^{N} \beta_j = 1; \sum_{j=1}^{N} \beta_{jk} = 0, \forall k; \sum_{j=1}^{N} \beta_{yj} = 0.$ By Shephard's lemma, the cost-minimizing input demand shares are given by

$$
m_j = \frac{\beta_j w_j^{(1-\varepsilon)}}{\sum_{k=1}^{N} \beta_k w_k^{1-\varepsilon}} + \sum_{k=1}^{N} \beta_{jk} \ln w_k + \beta_{yj} \ln y. \qquad (6.3.15)
$$

The Allen–Uzawa partial elasticities of substitution are given by

$$
\sigma_{jk}(y, w) = \left\{ (\varepsilon - 1) \left[\frac{\beta_j w_j^{(1-\varepsilon)}}{\sum_{l=1}^{N} \beta_l w_l^{1-\varepsilon}} \right] \right.
$$

$$
\left. \times \left[\frac{\beta_k w_k^{(1-\varepsilon)}}{\sum_{l=1}^{N} \beta_l w_l^{1-\varepsilon}} \right] + \beta_{jk} + m_j m_k \right\} \Big/ m_j m_k, \forall j \neq k.
$$

When all of the β_{jk} and β_{yl} terms are zero, the CES-translog factor demand system and cost function reduce to those of the CES. When $\varepsilon \to 1$, the CES-translog factor demand system reduces to that of the translog and its cost function approaches the translog. Regularity conditions are difficult to establish parametrically, but the CES-translog is clearly well-behaved around its well-behaved translog and CES special cases.

The procedure Pollak et al. (1984) used to generalize the translog to the CES-translog can also be applied to other flexible functional forms. For example, replacing the first-order terms of the generalized Leontief cost function with the more general CES first-order terms yields the *CES-generalized Leontief cost function*

$$C(y, w) = y \left(\sum_{j=1}^{N} \beta_j w_j^{(1-\varepsilon)} \right)^{1/(1-\varepsilon)} + y \sum_{j=1}^{N} \sum_{k \neq j}^{N} \beta_{jk} w_j^{1/2} w_k^{1/2}, \qquad (6.3.16)$$

where $\beta_{jk} = \beta_{kj}, \forall j \neq k$. By Shephard's lemma, the cost-minimizing input demand functions in input–output form are given by

$$\frac{x_j}{y} = \frac{\beta_j}{w_j^{\varepsilon}} \left[\sum_{k=1}^{N} \beta_k w_k^{1-\varepsilon} \right]^{\varepsilon/(1-\varepsilon)} + \sum_{k \neq j}^{N} \beta_{jk} w_j^{-1/2} w_k^{1/2}, \quad j = 1, \ldots, N.$$

$$(6.3.17)$$

The parameter ε serves the same role as before. When $\varepsilon = 0$ the CES-generalized Leontief cost function and factor demand system collapses to a re-parameterized form of the generalized Leontief, while when all of the $\beta_{jk} = 0$ the CES-generalized Leontief cost function and factor demand system reduce to those of the CES. As with the CES-translog, the CES-generalized Leontief pivots off the CES in a transparent and parsimonious fashion.

6.3.5   The Symmetric Generalized McFadden

One of the most common problems faced when using flexible functional forms to estimate the technology via the primal or its dual functional representations is a violation of the regularity conditions. For the cost function, these often hinge on its required curvature properties. This is because linear homogeneity in prices is often relatively easy to impose, while monotonicity is often not an issue as estimated factor demands (or factor shares, or input–output ratios, depending on the functional form utilized) based on the use of Shephard's lemma are most often positive with no parametric restrictions. However, that is not the case for concavity. This poses a problem in estimating flexible functional forms and is even more relevant when one utilizes nonparametric econometric methods.

Curvature restrictions, as well as monotonicity, may prove quite difficult to impose. Often researchers simply avoid testing for the regularity conditions.

This is particularly prevalent when estimating nonparametric specification, such as local linear estimators. In these cases, the functions tend to substantially overfit and it may not be feasible to test global or even local properties over a reasonable range of sample observations. As the cost function is concave in factor prices when the Hessian is negative semi-definite, its eigenvalues should always be checked to see if one is, in fact, estimating a cost function and not some other relationship whose interpretation is rendered meaningless if linear homogeneity in prices, monotonicity, and concavity are not met, at least within a relatively large portion of the price space.[4]

We mention these issues in part to provide a segue to a flexible functional form that does possess proper curvature, the *modified symmetric generalized McFadden (SGM) cost function* proposed by Diewert and Wales (1987), which can impose global concavity without a loss of flexibility. Many attempts have been made to impose curvature properties locally or globally for flexible functional forms prior to Diewert and Wales (1987). These include Jorgenson and Lau (1979) and Jovanovic (1982), who utilized Cholesky decompositions to test and impose curvature in the translog model, and Gallant and Golub (1984) who developed alternative approaches to impose curvature locally. More recently Wolff et al. (2010) have adopted simulation methods based on the Metropolis–Hastings algorithm to impose nonlinear inequality constraints in regions of the price/quantity space. These earlier and more recent approaches either do not impose global curvature or, when they do, sacrifice the flexibility of the flexible form. The SGM does not.

The SGM cost function is given by

$$C(y, w) = g(w)y + \sum_{j=1}^{N} \beta_j w_j + y \sum_{j=1}^{N} \beta_{jj} w_j. \qquad (6.3.18)$$

The function $g(w)$ is defined as

$$g(w) \equiv \frac{1}{2}\left(\frac{w'Sw}{\theta'w}\right) = \frac{1}{2} \frac{(w_1, w_2, \ldots, w_N)\begin{pmatrix} s_{11} & s_{12} & \cdots & s_{1N} \\ s_{21} & s_{22} & \cdots & s_{2N} \\ \vdots & \vdots & & \vdots \\ s_{N1} & s_{N2} & \cdots & s_{NN} \end{pmatrix}\begin{pmatrix} w_1 \\ w_2 \\ \vdots \\ w_N \end{pmatrix}}{(\theta_1, \theta_2, \ldots, \theta_N)\begin{pmatrix} w_1 \\ w_2 \\ \vdots \\ w_N \end{pmatrix}},$$

$$(6.3.19)$$

where S is a symmetric negative semi-definite matrix and θ is a vector of nonnegative parameters (not all zero). Here $w \equiv (w_1, w_2, \ldots, w_N)'$ is the vector

---

[4] Matzkin (1994) provides an excellent treatment of how to impose curvature restrictions using nonparametric methods.

of variable factor input prices. $C(y, w)$ is linear homogeneous in w. Use of Shepherd's lemma yields the following vector of factor-demand equations

$$x_j(y, x) = \left[\frac{\partial g(w)}{\partial w_j} \right] y + \beta_j + y\beta_{jj}, \; j = 1, \ldots, N, \qquad (6.3.20)$$

where

$$\frac{\partial g(w)}{\partial w} = \frac{Sw}{\theta' w} - \frac{1}{2}\theta \frac{w'Sw}{(\theta' w)^2}. \qquad (6.3.21)$$

See Kumbhakar (1994) for a generalization to the multi-output case. Both Diewert and Wales (1987) and Kumbhakar (1994) also discuss particular parametric restrictions on S. The advantages of the SGM are that the researcher has the freedom to impose concavity in factor prices without loss of flexibility in its ability to model curvature. If concavity needs to be imposed then the Cholesky decomposition method due to Rissanen (1973) can be utilized wherein S is replaced by the (negative of the) product of an $(n \times n)$ lower triangular matrix B with its transpose, i.e., $S = -BB'$ (Diewert and Wales, 1987).

6.4 TECHNICAL CHANGE, PRODUCTION DYNAMICS, AND QUASI-FIXED FACTORS

The translog and generalized Leontief cost functions are by far the most widely used cost functions in productivity analysis. Although the way in which productivity change is introduced into each of these functional representations of technology may differ depending on the functional form, the measurement of productivity change is in most cases accommodated in one of two ways. The first is by directly modeling the determinants of technical change (innovation) and including them as additional regressors, often times included in the functional representations of technology as additive conditioning variables (Arrow, 1962; Romer, 1986; Coe and Helpman, 1995; Coe et al., 1997; Diao et al., 2005; Blazek and Sickles, 2010; and many others).

A second way in which productivity change is often measured is to proxy the impacts of diffused technical innovation using an assumed deterministic time trend or a series of time dummies. Non-neutral productivity change can be specified by allowing the time variables or dummies to interact with selected factor prices. Sickles (1985) specified such biasing technical change using a deterministic trend while Baltagi and Griffin (1988) used time dummy variables. As productivity is measured by the relationship between observed output levels and their predictions based on the levels of utilized inputs, proper measurement of the primal or dual functional representations of technology is essential in developing measurement methods for identifying and estimating productive efficiency and technical change. It should always be kept clear in any analysis of productivity and efficiency that the functional representations used in empirical work adhere to the principles espoused by Fuss, McFadden, and Mundlak, which we repeat at this juncture, in part because much of the criticisms of semiparametric and nonparametric econometric functional representations of technology are based on a failure to adhere to these crucial and time-tested principles. These principles are *parsimony in parameters, ease of interpretation, computational ease, interpolative robustness, and extrapolative robustness.*

Quasi-fixed factors can be addressed quite naturally and in a way that offers an unstructured approach to model short run and long run production dynamics without resorting to an alternative formal structural dynamic model in the spirit of Jovanovic (1982) and its many empirical extensions, none more impactful than Olley and Pakes (1996) and subsequent work by Levinsohn and Petrin (2003) and Ackerberg et al. (2015). Recent extensions of the Olley and Pakes model that provide a new productivity decomposition have been proposed by Melitz and Polanec (2015). This class of models utilizes optimal control approaches that usually rely on either explicit or implicit solutions to the Euler equations, consistent with the maximization of discounted valuations of profits over the firm's life. For a very accessible survey of the empirical methods utilized in such structural models as they are used to estimate establishment-level data see Van Beveren (2012). We do not pursue such a structural approach below. The class of structural dynamic models introduced by Olley and Pakes (1996) is discussed in a later chapter addressing issues of endogeneity in dynamic models with inefficiency. Captain et al. (2007) introduced a calibrated dynamic model with intertemporal nonseparability while Chang and Stefanou (1988), Stefanou (2009), and Serra et al. (2011) discuss more classical steady-state dynamic models of efficiency. Stefanou and his colleagues' work is particularly enlightening in regard to pointing out conceptual and methodological issues that researchers must face up to when distinguishing between dynamic efficiencies and the concept of a steady-state in endogenous growth models. Stefanou and colleagues also point out that other distinctions, such as the proper characterization of adjustment costs and inefficiency, as well as whether or not dynamic efficiency provides scope for a different trajectory of growth or simply temporal deviations in a common growth trajectory, need to be carefully considered in specifying a dynamic model in which efficiency can exist. This latter issue is quite related to the notion of variable and long-run costs that we discuss below based on variable and quasi-fixed input choices. Many other scholars have provided formal structural dynamic models of optimal and suboptimal input allocations, levels of operations (scale), and output mix, but we leave the interested reader to explore these referenced papers and the papers referenced therein. We present below a relatively brief coverage of how short-run and long-run allocations can be modeled without relying on such dynamic structural approaches by adopting relatively parsimonious and transparent modification of the models and methods presented in this chapter. The vehicle for presenting a dynamic model of short-run/long-run allocations is the approach taken by Sickles and Streitwieser (1998) in their study of productivity and efficiency in the US interstate natural gas transmission industry after the Natural Gas Policy Act of 1978.

We begin with the same assumptions made in Chapter 2 when we discussed the duality between cost and production. We maintain the assumption that input prices are given, strictly positive, and fixed. Input allocations are based on the levels needed for the firm to employ its factors of production in order to meet its production target, given by y. The level of total cost that such production would incur is, however, split into two components. These are short-run variable (or restricted) costs and long-run total costs, the latter of which can be constructed using the expression $C(y, w) \equiv \min_x \{ wx : x \in L(y) \}$ with corresponding conditional (on output) input demand functions $x(y, w) \equiv \arg\min_x \{ wx : x \in L(y) \}$. The short-run variable cost function is given by $C^V(y, w^V, x^F) \equiv \min_{x^V} \{ w^V x^V : x^V \in L(y|x^F) \}$ where the superscripts differentiate the variable and the fixed factors.[5]

The Sickles and Streitwieser (1998) cost function study began with the assumption that during the study period levels of output by firms in the heavily regulated environment of the US interstate natural gas transmission industry could safely be assumed to be given to the firm by the regulators. The solution to the short-run cost-minimizing problem for the firm operating at full capacity is the short-run variable cost function

$$C^V = G(y, w^V, x^F). \tag{6.4.1}$$

G is linear homogeneous in prices, nondecreasing, and concave in the variable factor prices w^V, nonincreasing and convex in the levels of quasi-fixed factors x^F, and nonnegative and nondecreasing in output y. Sickles and Streitwieser approximated G with a non-homothetic translog function that included additional treatments for technical change and regulatory controls (omitted below). Their multi-output/multi-input translog cost function with quasi-fixed factors is written as

$$\ln C^V = \beta_0 + \beta_y \ln y + \tfrac{1}{2}\beta_{yy}(\ln y)^2 + \sum_{j=1}^{N_V} \beta_{j,V} \ln w_j^V + \sum_{j=1}^{N_F} \beta_{j,F} \ln x_j^F$$

$$+ \tfrac{1}{2}\sum_{j=1}^{N_V}\sum_{k=1}^{N_V} \beta_{jk,V} \ln w_j^V \ln w_k^V + \tfrac{1}{2}\sum_{j=1}^{N_V}\sum_{k=1}^{N_V} \beta_{jk,F} \ln x_j^F \ln x_k^F$$

$$+ \tfrac{1}{2}\sum_{j=1}^{N_V}\sum_{k=1}^{N_F} \beta_{jk,V,F} \ln w_j^V \ln x_k^F + \sum_{j=1}^{N_V} \beta_{j,y} \ln y \ln w_j^V$$

$$+ \sum_{j=1}^{N_F} \beta_{j,F} \ln y \ln x_j^F. \tag{6.4.2}$$

Conditions for linear homogeneity and symmetry are easily imposed linear restrictions. Monotonicity and concavity conditions can be checked after

---

[5] Much of this discussion is based on Diewert (1974a,b).

estimation. Given exogenous input prices and utilizing Shephard's Lemma, the first-order conditions in share form for the cost-minimizing levels of variable inputs used in the short-run production of y can be written as

$$m_{j,V} = \beta_{j,V} + \sum_{k=1}^{N_V} \beta_{jk,V} \ln w_k^V + \beta_{j,y} \ln y + \sum_{k=1}^{N_F} \beta_{jk,V,F} \ln x_k^F, \quad j=1,\ldots,N_V.$$

(6.4.3)

The "shadow share" equation for the quasi-fixed inputs is $-\partial \ln G/\partial \ln x_k^F = Z_k x_k^F/C^V$ and can either be added explicitly to the model or constructed after the model parameters are estimated as in Morrison (1987). The shadow price, Z_k, is interpreted as the *ex post* value of the quasi-fixed input x_k^F. As Berndt and Hesse (1986, p. 967) have pointed out, Z_k is "the best firms can do for their shareholders in the short run given exogenous input prices, output demand, and" the quasi-fixed factor (s).

The shadow value equations for the translog variable cost function are given by

$$m_{k,F} = - \left[\beta_{k,F} + \sum_{l=1}^{N_V} \beta_{kl,V,F} \ln w_l^V + \sum_{l=1}^{N_F} \beta_{kl,F} \ln x_l^F + \beta_{k,F} \ln y \right],$$

$$k = 1,\ldots,N_F,$$

(6.4.4)

where regularity conditions require the shadow share equations to be positive. Caves et al. (1981) note that the total, or long-run cost function $C^T = C^V + \sum_{k=1}^{N_F} w_k^F x_k^F$ can then be derived by establishing a market price of the quasi-fixed factor (w_k^F). Using the envelope condition $-\partial G/\partial x_k^F = Z_k^*$ to solve for the optimal level of the quasi-fixed factor, the optimal use of the fixed factor in total (long-run) costs is then expressed as

$$x_k^* = g(w, y, Z^*),$$

(6.4.5)

and thus the long-run total cost function can be expressed in terms of these estimated relationships as

$$C^T = H(w, y, Z^*).$$

(6.4.6)

Modeling economies of scope and scale in regulated public utilities has been the focus of a series of papers by Saal and Parker (2001) and Saal et al. (2007, 2013) that examine the regulation of public utilities utilizing many of the approaches we have just outlined for average cost functions as well as frontier functions we discuss throughout our book. Many of these studies involve the supply of water resources and the proper disposal and treatment of sewage waste. The issues they explore are becoming increasingly important; safe and reliable drinking water has become a major public health risk, even in highly developed countries such as the USA.

6.5 FUNCTIONAL FORMS FOR REVENUE ANALYSIS

In Section 6 of Chapter 2, we discussed the revenue function and showed how it could be viewed as the solution to the maximizing behavior of firms. For fixed output prices and production technology, the behavior yields a correspondence between maximizing levels of revenue and input use.

Recall that we began with a given level of input use and fixed output prices listed in the *row* vector $p = (p_1, \ldots, p_M) \in \Re_+^M$ (ordered in the same way as the output vector) and the output set $P(x)$. How much of each output should the revenue-maximizing firm produce? What will be the corresponding level of maximum revenue? Recall that the *revenue function* is defined for $R : \Re_+^N \times \Re_{++}^M \to \Re_+^1 \cup \{+\infty\}$ as $R(x, p) \equiv \max_y \{ p\,y : y \in P(x) \}$, and the solution to the optimization problem is the vector of supply functions (conditional on the level of the inputs) given by

$$y(x, p) \equiv \arg\max_y \{ p\,y : y \in P(x) \}.$$

The functional form for the revenue function will then determine the functional form for the supply equations consistent with it and with the assumption of revenue maximization. In order for the duality of revenue and production to hold, the revenue function is restricted to have a set of properties or regularity conditions. These are detailed in Chapter 2.6. The main properties of the revenue function are that it is nonnegative, nondecreasing in output prices, linearly homogeneous and symmetric in output prices, and convex in prices. The corresponding properties for the output supply equations are that they are non-negative, homogeneous of degree zero in prices, and that $\nabla_p y(x, p)$ is a revenue-maximizing semi-definite matrix, $p \in \Re_+^M$, and $x \in \Re_+^N$.

Functional forms similar to those used in production and cost analysis are usually specified for the revenue function. We begin with the translog revenue function of Diewert (1974c) with M outputs and N inputs,

$$
\ln R(x, p) = \beta_0 + \sum_{j=1}^{N} \beta_{j,x} \ln x_j + \frac{1}{2} \sum_{j=1}^{N} \sum_{k=1}^{N} \beta_{jk,x} \ln x_j \ln x_k
$$

$$
+ \sum_{j=1}^{M} \beta_{j,p} \ln p_j + \frac{1}{2} \sum_{j=1}^{M} \sum_{k=1}^{M} \beta_{jk,p} \ln p_j \ln p_k
$$

$$
+ \sum_{j=1}^{N} \sum_{k=1}^{M} \beta_{jk,xp} \ln x_j \ln p_k. \tag{6.5.1}
$$

Homogeneity of degree 1 in output prices requires that

$$
\sum_{j=1}^{M} \beta_{j,p} = 1, \sum_{j=1}^{M} \beta_{jk,p} = 0, \forall k, \sum_{j=1}^{N} \beta_{jk,xp} = 0, \; k = 1, \ldots, M.
$$

Instead of expressing the output supply equations $y(x, p)$ in level form, we can write the conditional output supply equations in terms of revenue shares since those equations are linear in parameters for the translog revenue function and thus facilitate the use of standard linear regression techniques. The output share equations are

$$s_j^y = \beta_{j,p} + \sum_{k=1}^{M} \beta_{jk,p} \ln p_k + \sum_{k=1}^{N} \beta_{kj,xp} \ln x_k, \quad j = 1, \ldots, M. \quad (6.5.2)$$

An alternative functional form for the revenue function, that is similar in spirit to the generalized-Leontief and quadratic forms used in production and cost estimation, was introduced by Diewert (1974c, 1982). However, under relatively straightforward parameter constraints the revenue function satisfies also properties (i)–(v) in Chapter 2.6. The family of functional forms from which this particular parameterization is referred to as the *mean of order two revenue function* as in Diewert (1974b). Diewert considers the case of one input (x_1) and M outputs, which we consider here. The form can be easily extended to N inputs but the notation gets a bit clumsy. The revenue function is

$$\ln R(x_1, p) = \sum_{j=1}^{M} \sum_{k=1}^{M} \beta_{jk} \left(\frac{1}{2} p_j^2 + \frac{1}{2} p_k^2 \right)^{1/2} x_1. \quad (6.5.3)$$

If all the parameters are non-negative, it is easy to verify that the mean of two revenue function satisfies the properties (i)–(v) in Section 2.6.

Applying Shephard's lemma to the revenue function above, the conditional supply functions in level form are

$$y_j(x_1; p) = \sum_{k=1}^{M} \beta_{jk} \left(\frac{1}{2} p_j^2 + \frac{1}{2} p_k^2 \right)^{-1/2} p_j x_1, \quad j = 1, \ldots, M. \quad (6.5.4)$$

If constant returns to scale are satisfied, then the revenue function $R(x_1, p)$ can be expressed as $R(p)x_1$, in which case revenue is a function of price alone, or alternatively the revenue function can be viewed as the unit input revenue function. In this the case any given functional form for the revenue function under constant returns to scale will have the flexible elasticity of substitution property if it can approximate to the second order the function $R(p)x_1$.

It is well-known that the revenue function is a Shephard (1970) type output distance function in price space. Chambers et al. (2013) considered both quadratic and translog revenue functions in their dual price space representations of the Shephard output distance and the directional output distance function that we discussed in Chapter 1 (Luenberger, 1992; Chambers et al., 1996b). Chambers et al. (2013) point out that the quadratic satisfies homogeneity, while the translog satisfies the property of translation. They are able to show that within the family of generalized quadratic functions the Shephard distance function yields the translog revenue function in the dual price space and the directional output distance function yields the quadratic. They go on to show in a series of Monte Carlo experiments that the quadratic is preferred over the translog when there is substantial curvature in the underlying technology.

6.6 FUNCTIONAL FORMS FOR PROFIT ANALYSIS

In Section 7 of Chapter 2, we discussed the technical properties and duality relationship between the underlying technology set T and the profit function π. Recall that the technology set T is defined as

$$T \equiv \{(x, y) \in \Re_+^N \times \Re_+^M : y \in \Re_+^M \text{ is producible from } x \in \Re_+^N\}.$$

The firm's optimal output and input allocations based on maximizing profits, which are given by the function $\pi : \Re_{++}^N \times \Re_{++}^M \to \Re_+^1 \cup \{+\infty\}$, and that are attainable using the technology set T, are based on the solution to the optimization problem

$$\pi(p, w) \equiv \max_{x, y} \{ p\,y - wx : (x, y) \in T \}. \tag{6.6.1}$$

The solution to this optimization problem provides us with the (unconditional) demand and supply functions for each input and output, given output and input prices w, p

$$(x(p, w), y(p, w)) \equiv \arg\max_{x, y} \{ p\,y - wx : (x, y) \in T \}. \tag{6.6.2}$$

The Theorem of Section 7, Chapter 2 made explicit the properties of the profit function and the corresponding input demand and output supply functions that are derived from the maximization of profits. The main properties of the profit function are that it is nonnegative, nondecreasing in output prices, nonincreasing in input prices, linearly homogeneous in input and output prices, and convex in input and output prices. The output supply functions are nonnegative, homogeneous of degree zero in output prices, and possess curvature properties that essentially require supply functions not to be downward sloping in output price, that is $\nabla_p y(w, p)$ is a *symmetric positive* semi-definite matrix. Input demand functions have a similar and intuitive set of properties in that they are nonnegative, homogeneous of degree zero in factor prices and have a curvature such that $\nabla_w x(w, p)$ is *symmetric positive* semi-definite matrix, ensuring that demand curves do not slope upwards.

Diewert (1974c) also pointed out that a functional form for a profit function satisfying the properties we have discussed in Chapter 2, and which could provide a second-order (local) approximation to such a function that was twice differentiable, could be based on a quadratic form, such as we have considered in our discussion of distance, cost, and revenue functions. Diewert noted, however, that for such a quadratic function, there is a fundamental problem: one would like to have a second-order approximation to a function that is linearly homogeneous, in which case the second-order approximation reduces to a first-order approximation. It is this point that in part appeared to lead him to explore alternatives, such as the generalized quadratic in square roots, and its closely related special case, the generalized Leontief profit function as well as other functional forms that did not have such a reductionist property. Such a short-coming of the first-order terms on which the second-order expansions pivot also motivated Pollak et al. (1984) in their work on cost functions and Behrman et al. (1992) in their extended work on profit functions, and Ballivian and Sickles (1994) in their work on restricted profit functions. The extended profit functions developed by Behrman et al. (1992) added second-order terms in square roots but utilized first-order terms that nested technologies that satisfied, under relatively straightforward restrictions, the properties of a well-defined profit function.

We discuss these extended flexible profit functions next. We begin with a production unit using variable inputs x available at given prices w, together with quasi-fixed input H to produce outputs y for sale at given prices p. Define the $(M+N) \times 1$ price vector $q = \begin{pmatrix} p \\ w \end{pmatrix}$ and the corresponding variable quantity vector $u = \begin{pmatrix} y \\ -x \end{pmatrix}$. The generalized Leontief (GL) variable profit function can be written as

$$\pi(q, H) = \sum_{j=1}^{M+N} \sum_{k=1}^{M+N} \beta_{jk} q_j^{1/2} q_k^{1/2} + \sum_{j=1}^{M+N} \beta_{jH} q_j H^{1/2}, \ \beta_{jk} = \beta_{kj}, \forall j, k$$

(6.6.3)

or

$$\pi(q, H) = \sum_{j=1}^{M+N} \beta_{jj} q_j + \sum_{j=1}^{M+N} \sum_{k \neq j}^{M+N} \beta_{jk} q_j^{1/2} q_k^{1/2}$$
$$+ \sum_{j=1}^{M+N} \beta_{jH} q_j H^{1/2}, \ \beta_{jk} = \beta_{kj}, \forall j, k.$$

(6.6.4)

We can allow the generalized Leontief second-order terms to pivot off a well-defined constant elasticity of transformation, constant elasticity of substitution technology represented by the *CET-CES-GL variable profit function*

$$\pi(q, H) = \left(\sum_{j=1}^{M+N} \beta_{jj} q_j^{\varepsilon} \right)^{1/\varepsilon} + \sum_{j=1}^{M+N} \sum_{k \neq j}^{M+N} \beta_{jk} q_j^{1/2} q_k^{1/2}$$
$$+ \sum_{j=1}^{M+N} \beta_{jH} q_j H^{1/2}, \beta_{jk} = \beta_{kj}, \forall j, k.$$

(6.6.5)

The CET-CES-GL system of variable profit maximizing output supply and variable input demand equations are thus

$$u_j(q, H) = \gamma_{jj} q_j^{\varepsilon-1} \left(\sum_{k=1}^{M+N} \beta_{kk} q_k^{\varepsilon} \right)^{(1-\varepsilon)/\varepsilon}$$

$$+ \sum_{\substack{k \neq j}}^{M+N} \beta_{jk} q_j^{-1/2} q_k^{1/2} + \beta_{jH} H^{1/2}, j = 1, \ldots, M, \ldots, M+N.$$

$$(6.6.6)$$

In fact, the cost, revenue, and profit functions can all be generalized to a broader case: the restricted profit function of McFadden (1978). We can consider the environment wherein $M + N$ commodities are traded in competitive markets with prices given by the vector q. All of them are chosen by the firm to be an input or an output. A production plan represented by the vector u is an $M + N$-dimensional vector, in which an element of u is positive when it is the net product output and negative when it is utilized as an input. The profit $\pi = q \cdot u$ is the inner product of the two vectors. The restricted profit function also can be reduced to some specific function such as the cost function. If y is an output bundle, and all commodities in the net output bundle are inputs, then π is the negative of cost.

Coelli et al. (2005) make this point rather succinctly in their discussion of the restricted profit function of Lau (1976). Jorgenson and Lau (1974), Lau (1976) and others pointed out, with varying degrees of generality, that the special cases of the long-run profit function are linked via duality with the cost and revenue functions we have detailed above. For example, if outputs are fixed, then the cost function is simply the negative of the corresponding restricted profit function, while if the inputs are fixed then the restricted profit function is equivalent to the revenue function.

6.7 NONPARAMETRIC ECONOMETRIC APPROACHES TO MODEL THE DISTANCE, COST, REVENUE, AND PROFIT FUNCTIONS

This chapter has given considerable attention to developing the links between theoretical properties of the various dual representations of technology and their empirical counterparts. We have tried to be clear that in order for the empirical representations of technology or its cost, revenue, or profit function duals to be meaningful, the properties needed in order to derive the duality relationships cannot be ignored. The main properties involve nonnegativity, monotonicity, homogeneity, and convexity (concavity). For particular dual relationships, such properties **must** either be satisfied by linear or inequality restrictions or be checked after the functional representations have been estimated, in order to see if the properties are consistent with the unrestricted functional representations.

The upshot of this is that empirical researchers must ask and be able to answer the question, "Is what I have just estimated really a cost function, or it is just a function?" If the answer is the latter, then that is well and good and a *relationship* between the particular variables in the relationship has been established. However, there can be no interpretation of the resulting empirical relationship as a dual representation of the underlying technology that presumably one has undertaken the empirical exercise in order to better understand. Such questions as: "What are the scale properties of technology?"; "Are there economies of scope?"; "What are the substitution possibilities?"; "What are marginal products of the factor inputs?"; "Are particular input pairs substitutes in production or complements?"; and "What is the level and what is the growth rate of productivity, efficiency, innovation?" are not well defined since the underlying theoretical structure under which the questions are posed is itself not well defined.

Nonparametric econometric modeling has been the focus of much research over the last several decades and is fairly well developed. There are a number of useful papers on the topic. A brief list of those that relate specifically to the imposition of shape restrictions includes Matzkin (1991, 1994), Ruud (1997), Mammen and Thomas-Agnan (1999), Hall and Huang (2001), Aït-Sahalia and Duarte (2003), Lewbel (2010), Shively et al. (2011), Du et al. (2013), and Wu and Sickles (2018). Fox (1998) also has a very nice treatment of nonparametric specifications for technical change. Semiparametric approximations of technical progress based on linear or quadratic splines (Diewert and Wales, 1992) have proven to be quite useful in practice to address different epochs of technical change. Such approximations are used in the Kneip et al. (2012) time-varying productivity model discussed in Chapter 12. Henderson et al. (2015) have developed flexible, semiparametric methods for estimating systems of equations that use smooth coefficients. For students familiar with parametric regression models with either quadratics or interactions, these smooth coefficient models offer a further generalization. Henderson et al. (2015) find in their banking application that the largest banks, as measured by assets, have decreasing returns to scale, something that is at odds with the common notion that even the largest banks could be bigger to achieve economies of scale. Inanoglu et al. (2016) found similar results. Other semi-nonparametric approaches to production function estimation are also discussed in Chapter 15.

6.8   CONCLUDING REMARKS

We have endeavored in this chapter to provide the interested reader with an overview of how specific functional representations of technology can be specified and how various optimizing frameworks provide applied productivity modelers with a coherent program for specifying primal or dual relationships in their productivity analyses. We have pointed out how flexibility and parsimony may be in conflict and have stressed the necessity of ensuring that interpretations of results from any productivity study must adhere to the professional standards that are no less current and important now than they were forty years ago when first enunciated by Fuss et al. (1978).

6.9 EXERCISES

1. Derive the limiting conditions under which the CES production function collapses to the Leontief and to the Cobb–Douglas.
2. What are the assumptions made in the Zellner et al. (1966) study of the expected profit maximization hypothesis? Can you formulate conditions in three empirical settings in which these assumptions would be valid, based on the institutional setting of the industry or sector under consideration?
3. Assume that you have a Cobb–Douglas technology with one output (y) and two inputs, capital (K) and labor (L). The econometric model is

$$\ln y = \beta_1 + \beta_2 \ln K + \beta_3 \ln L + \epsilon - u,$$

where u is a random variable with positive support and ϵ is the usual idiosyncratic disturbance term with $E(\epsilon) = 0$. The errors are independent of each other and of the explanatory variables. In this problem, the term represents radial technical inefficiency.

   (a) Assuming that the firm is a cost minimizer, derive the cost function that is dual to this production function.
   (b) Interpret the role of the inefficiency term in the cost function.
   (c) How is this term impacted by increasing (decreasing) returns to scale?
   (d) Consider an alternative model in which an additional variable t is added to account for the neutral technical change. Here t is a time trend (think of the data here as a time series of observations on a firm, industry, or economy). How are your answers to (a)–(c) modified when considering productivity growth?

4. Regularity conditions are necessary in order to be able to interpret dual relationships such as a cost or revenue function in terms of the underlying technology. Conditions such as monotonicity, convexity, and homogeneity are often necessary and sufficient conditions for such duality relationships to exist.

   (a) Examine how such conditions can be imposed (locally) for the translog cost function based on a two-output/two-input technology.
   (b) Develop the statistical tests and assumptions needed to establish whether or not such conditions are borne out by the data.
   (c) Tests for natural monopoly in a multiproduct firm are often based on tests for the presence of declining ray average long-run costs and of local "subadditivity" or cost complementarities (Evans and

Heckman, 1984). Detail how such a test can be constructed and the difficulties inherent in developing global alternatives to such local tests.

(d) Can you modify the translog functional form to address the issues alluded to in question (c)? (Hint: see Röller, 1990b.)

5. Imposition of curvature conditions for semi-nonparametric models may be rather difficult. Provide two methods for imposing homogeneity in a nonparametric econometric model of production.

CHAPTER 7

Productivity Indexes: Part 2

In Chapter 4 we considered the economic approach to indexes – the so-called true indexes for measuring changes in prices, in quantities and in productivity. We stated that those true indexes are abstract, theoretical concepts, unobserved in reality, and so in practice they need to be estimated. In this chapter, we will consider what is often referred to as the "statistical approach" to index numbers, with the aim to summarize the key results, mostly following the seminal works of Erwin Diewert, besides the classical works of Laspeyres, Paasche, Fisher, and Törnqvist (see the last section for a historical narrative).[1]

7.1 DECOMPOSITION OF THE VALUE CHANGE INDEX

As with the economic approach that we considered in Chapter 4, the most popular framework for the application of index numbers is constructing indexes to represent price and quantity changes. Among examples of indexes known to a wide audience, one could certainly mention the consumer price index (CPI), used for computing inflation, the GDP deflator, as well as the nominal and the real GDP indexes, used to compute the nominal and real economic growth rates of countries. These indexes were first computed long before the origination of the economic approach to index numbers. What was the logic behind their construction? More importantly, how are they related to the so-called "true economic indexes" that are justified by economic theory?

To facilitate our answers to these questions, we will slightly change our notation to a more common one in the statistical approach to index numbers. Namely, we let $q_\tau = (q_{1\tau}, \ldots, q_{M\tau})' \in \mathfrak{R}_{++}^M$ be the (column) vector of certain goods and services (inputs, outputs, etc.) and $p_\tau = (p_{1\tau}, \ldots, p_{M\tau}) \in \mathfrak{R}_{++}^M$ be the (row) vector of their corresponding

---

[1] As mentioned before, we recall that we maintain the common assumption that the main regularity conditions of production theory hold (see Chapter 1 for details), although some of these results may require weaker conditions.

prices, observed in period $\tau = s, t$.[2] We will start with an instructive (and classical) way of looking at the price and quantity indexes, which goes via the so-called *Value Change Index*, defined as

$$V(p_s, p_t, q_s, q_t) \equiv \frac{\sum_{m=1}^{M} p_{mt} q_{mt}}{\sum_{m=1}^{M} p_{ms} q_{ms}} = \frac{p_t q_t}{p_s q_s}. \tag{7.1.1}$$

What is now of interest is to decompose the value change index into a price change, represented by some price index P_{st}, and a quantity change, represented by some quantity index Q_{st}. In the simplest, one-commodity, case it would be straightforward to do so,

$$V(p_s, p_t, q_s, q_t) = \frac{p_t q_t}{p_s q_s} = \frac{p_t}{p_s} \times \frac{q_t}{q_s} \tag{7.1.2}$$
$$= Price\ Change \times Quantity\ Change = \mathcal{P}_{st} \times Q_{st}.$$

In the multi-product case, the decomposition is not as straightforward. The difficulty comes from the fact that it is not unique: different variants for the price index yield different quantity indexes, and no variant is absolutely superior to the others. The issues of desirable properties and relative superiority are exactly the issues around which the essence of the statistical (or mathematical) theory of index numbers (for prices, quantities, productivity, etc.) are based upon.

7.2   THE STATISTICAL APPROACH TO PRICE INDEXES

In a sense, the quintessence of economics is about prices – if there are no prices there is no need for economics. So, we first consider price indexes. The main purpose of these indexes is to provide a proper measurement of *aggregate* changes in prices, which in turn would enable one to obtain real quantities (of outputs, inputs, GDP, etc.) and their growth from the nominal counterparts, which then can be used for the productivity indexes.

A simple, yet fundamental idea in index theory, is attributed to Laspeyres, who suggested what is now called the *Laspeyres Price Index*, defined as

$$\mathcal{P}_{st}^{L} \equiv \frac{\sum_{m=1}^{M} p_{mt} q_{ms}}{\sum_{m=1}^{M} p_{ms} q_{ms}} = \frac{p_t q_s}{p_s q_s}. \tag{7.2.1}$$

Intuitively, the Laspeyres price index measures the change in value of N goods keeping the quantity of these goods fixed at period s ($s < t$), sometimes

---

[2] Some of the results can be extended to cases where some prices or quantities are zero, though for some definitions (e.g., those involving logs) and some properties, the strict positivity is critical and therefore, without much practical loss of generality, we assume it throughout this chapter.

referred to as the *base-period*. Another useful interpretation of the Laspeyres price index can be seen after rearranging (7.2.1) as

$$\mathcal{P}_{st}^{L} = \sum_{m=1}^{M} \left(\frac{p_{mt}}{p_{ms}} \right) \varpi_{ms}, \qquad \varpi_{ms} = \frac{p_{ms}q_{ms}}{\sum\limits_{m=1}^{M} p_{ms}q_{ms}}, \qquad (7.2.2)$$

i.e., the Laspeyres price index is simply the *weighted* average of the individual price indexes for each good m ($m = 1, \ldots, M$) with the weights being the value shares of each good m in the total value of all M goods observed in period s, which we would refer to as the Laspeyres weights.

An alternative, yet very similar, idea is attributed to Paasche, who suggested what is now referred to as the *Paasche Price Indexes*, defined as

$$\mathcal{P}_{st}^{P} \equiv \frac{\sum\limits_{m=1}^{M} p_{mt}q_{mt}}{\sum\limits_{m=1}^{M} p_{ms}q_{mt}} = \frac{p_t q_t}{p_s q_t}. \qquad (7.2.3)$$

Intuitively, the Paasche price index measures the change in value of M goods keeping the quantity of these goods fixed or measured at period t ($t > s$), which is sometimes referred to as the *current-period*.[3]

Similar to the Laspeyres index, the Paasche price index has another interpretation. It is a weighted average of the individual price indexes with weights being the value shares of each good in the total value of all goods but valued at the prices of period t rather than s, which we will refer to as the Paasche weights. Moreover, it is not an arithmetic but rather a harmonic averaging. Indeed, rearranging (7.2.3), we get

$$\mathcal{P}_{st}^{P} = \left(\sum_{m=1}^{M} \left(\frac{p_{mt}}{p_{ms}} \right)^{-1} \varpi_{mt} \right)^{-1}, \qquad \varpi_{mt} = \frac{p_{mt}q_{mt}}{\sum\limits_{m=1}^{M} p_{mt}q_{mt}}. \qquad (7.2.4)$$

One shall easily see that, in general, the *Laspeyres*-type and *Paasche*-type indexes are not equal, except for very special cases.[4] These two quite similar yet different ideas started a dispute about which of the indexes are "better" in theory or in practice. In some respects a simple, yet also genius, attempt to reconcile this argument was proposed by Fisher (1922), who suggested what

---

[3] The meaning of "base" and "current" should be understood in the relative and local (rather than global) sense here, when comparing s to t where $s < t$.

[4] E.g., the two will be equal if the basket of goods change equi-proportionately, i.e., $q_{mt}/q_{ms} = a$, where a is a constant for all m, or when prices change equi-proportionately, i.e., $p_{mt}/p_{ms} = b$ where b is a constant for all m. In general, the larger the variation in these ratios across m the larger might be the gap between the two indexes (see von Bortkiewicz (1924) for one of the early studies of the gap).

is now called the *Fisher (Ideal) Price Index* – it is merely the simple geometric mean of the *Laspeyres*-type and *the Paasche*-type indexes,[5] i.e.,

$$\mathcal{P}_{st}^{F} \equiv \left(\mathcal{P}_{st}^{L} \times \mathcal{P}_{st}^{P}\right)^{1/2}. \tag{7.2.5}$$

We will see later in the chapter that despite its "simplicity," Fisher's idea – just averaging the two existing indexes – had fundamental consequences that made his index deserve the name "ideal" in some respects.

The last, yet not the least, idea that needs to be mentioned here is attributed to Törnqvist (1936), who suggested what is now, not surprisingly, called the *Törnqvist Price Index*, defined as

$$\mathcal{P}_{st}^{T} \equiv \prod_{m=1}^{M} \left(\frac{p_{mt}}{p_{ms}}\right)^{\frac{\varpi_{mt}+\varpi_{ms}}{2}}. \tag{7.2.6}$$

A formula that seems to be more popular in practice for the Törnqvist Price Index is its logarithmic form, also known under a different name (due to Jorgenson and Nishimizu, 1978 and Diewert, 1992a) as the *translog price index*, given by

$$\ln(\mathcal{P}_{st}^{T}) = \sum_{m=1}^{M} \frac{\varpi_{mt} + \varpi_{ms}}{2} \left[\ln(p_{mt}) - \ln(p_{ms})\right]. \tag{7.2.7}$$

Here, note that for a small change in prices between s and t, one may rely on the first-order approximation: $\ln(p_{it}) - \ln(p_{is}) = \ln(p_{it}/p_{is}) \approx (p_{it}/p_{is}) - 1$. This gives a nice intuitive interpretation of the logarithmic version of the Törnqvist index as, approximately, a weighted arithmetic average of the percentage growth in prices, with weights being the simple average of the Laspeyres weights and Paasche weights, and so in some sense, this index also tries to reconcile the Laspeyres–Paasche dispute about which weights must be used.

7.3   QUANTITY INDEXES: THE DIRECT APPROACH

As for the price indexes, one can define the indexes to measure the aggregate changes in quantities. Specifically, the *Laspeyres Quantity Index* is given by

$$Q_{st}^{L} \equiv \frac{p_s q_t}{p_s q_s} = \frac{\sum_{m=1}^{M} q_{mt} p_{ms}}{\sum_{m=1}^{M} q_{ms} p_{ms}} \tag{7.3.1}$$

$$= \sum_{m=1}^{M} \left(\frac{q_{mt}}{q_{ms}}\right) \varpi_{ms}, \quad \varpi_{ms} = \frac{p_{ms} q_{ms}}{\sum_{i=1}^{M} p_{ms} q_{ms}},$$

---

[5] Another alternative is to use the same formula as Laspeyres and Paasche but with average quantities (i.e., $\frac{1}{2}(q_{mt} + q_{ms})$ instead of only q_{mt} (as in *Paasche*) or only q_{ms} (as in Laspeyres)), which is usually referred to as Marshall–Edgeworth price index.

while the *Paasche Quantity Index* is given by

$$Q_{st}^P \equiv \frac{p_t q_t}{p_t q_s} = \frac{\sum_{m=1}^{M} q_{mt} p_{mt}}{\sum_{m=1}^{M} q_{ms} p_{mt}} \tag{7.3.2}$$

$$= \left(\sum_{m=1}^{M} \left(\frac{q_{mt}}{q_{ms}} \right)^{-1} \varpi_{mt} \right)^{-1}, \quad \varpi_{mt} = \frac{p_{mt} q_{mt}}{\sum_{m=1}^{M} p_{mt} q_{mt}}$$

and the geometric average of these two is the *Fisher Ideal Quantity Index:*

$$Q_{st}^F \equiv \left(Q_{st}^L \times Q_{st}^P \right)^{1/2}. \tag{7.3.3}$$

Finally, the *Törnqvist Quantity Index* is defined as

$$Q_{st}^T \equiv \prod_{m=1}^{M} \left(\frac{q_{mt}}{q_{ms}} \right)^{\frac{\varpi_{mt} + \varpi_{ms}}{2}}, \tag{7.3.4}$$

or, in the logarithmic form, the *translog quantity index* is given by

$$\ln(Q_{st}^T) = \sum_{m=1}^{M} \frac{\varpi_{mt} + \varpi_{ms}}{2} \left[\ln(q_{mt}) - \ln(q_{ms}) \right]. \tag{7.3.5}$$

7.4 QUANTITY INDEXES: THE INDIRECT APPROACH

The approach we outlined in the previous section is often called the direct approach to measuring quantities – since the quantity indexes are defined directly, using the same formulas as the corresponding indexes used for measuring prices. In this section, we consider another alternative approach to defining statistical quantity indexes, which is usually called, not surprisingly, the *indirect* (or *implicit*) approach. It is based on the desire (postulated in a property, axiom or test) to have indexes that decompose the index of *Value Change* into an index representing the price changes and an index representing the quantity changes, i.e.,

$$Value \; Change := \frac{\sum_{m=1}^{M} p_{mt} q_{mt}}{\sum_{m=1}^{M} p_{ms} q_{ms}} \tag{7.4.1}$$

$$= Price \; Change \times Quantity \; Change =: \mathcal{P}_{st} \times \mathcal{Q}_{st}.$$

This property is often referred to as the *product test* for index numbers (Fisher, 1911, Frisch, 1930). If one believes or accepts (7.4.1) then one would expect that by dividing the value change index by the price change index, the result must be what is usually called the "indirect quantity index" (or "implicit quantity index"), i.e.,

$$Q_{st}^{indirect} = Value\ Change/Price\ Change \tag{7.4.2}$$

$$= \frac{\sum_{m=1}^{M} P_{mt}q_{mt}}{\sum_{m=1}^{M} P_{ms}q_{ms}} / \mathcal{P}_{st}.$$

Examples of such quantity indexes are very well known – the *real* GDP index, the *real* industrial output index, the indexes of *real* exports and of *real* imports and many other quantity indexes that describe the evolution of an economy. Most such indexes are indeed obtained indirectly, by deflating the *nominal* value change index by an appropriate price index (e.g., the GDP deflator for the case of GDP, or the PPI for the case of industrial output, etc.). Equivalently, as (7.4.2) suggests, one can deflate the nominal values by an appropriate price index, to get real values, and then divide it by the base-period value to obtain the indirect quantity index.

Which price index should be used to get an indirect output quantity index? In principle, any "appropriate" index can be used, including (but not limited to) those discussed above. For example, the *indirect Laspeyres quantity index* is obtained by dividing the (nominal) value change by the *Laspeyres price index*, i.e.,

$$Q_{st}^{L\ indirect} = \left(\sum_{m=1}^{M} P_{mt}q_{mt} / \sum_{m=1}^{M} P_{ms}q_{ms} \right) / \mathcal{P}_{st}^{L}, \tag{7.4.3}$$

while the *indirect Paasche quantity index* is obtained by deflating with the *Paasche price index*, i.e.,

$$Q_{st}^{P\ indirect} = \left(\sum_{m=1}^{M} P_{mt}q_{mt} / \sum_{m=1}^{M} P_{ms}q_{ms} \right) / \mathcal{P}_{st}^{P}. \tag{7.4.4}$$

Furthermore, the *indirect Fisher quantity index* is obtained by deflating with the *Fisher price index*,

$$Q_{st}^{F\ indirect} = \left(\sum_{m=1}^{M} P_{mt}q_{mt} / \sum_{m=1}^{M} P_{ms}q_{ms} \right) / \mathcal{P}_{st}^{F}, \tag{7.4.5}$$

while the *indirect Törnqvist quantity index* is obtained by deflating with the *Törnqvist price index*,

$$Q_{st}^{T\ indirect} = \left(\sum_{m=1}^{M} P_{mt}q_{mt} / \sum_{m=1}^{M} P_{ms}q_{ms} \right) / \mathcal{P}_{st}^{T}. \tag{7.4.6}$$

A natural question now is: how are the direct and indirect quantity indexes related? In some sense, an ideal situation is when the two are equivalent. However, it turns out that only the Fisher approach possesses this property of yielding the same index whether obtained directly or indirectly (which is also known as the self-duality or factor-reversal property), i.e.,

$$Q_{st}^{F\ indirect} = Q_{st}^{F}, \tag{7.4.7}$$

and so this is probably why it is often referred to as the Fisher *ideal* index.

Other known indexes are not self-dual, but still might have a "dual counterpart" that happens to be another famous index. Indeed, a very important fact to know is that if one uses the *Laspeyres price index* to obtain the *indirect quantity index* via formula (7.4.2), then this quantity index will be exactly the *Paasche quantity index*, i.e.,

$$Q_{st}^{L\ indirect} = Q_{st}^{P}. \qquad (7.4.8)$$

On the other hand, if the *Paasche price index* is used to get the *indirect quantity index*, then the quantity index will be the *Laspeyres quantity index*, i.e.,

$$Q_{st}^{P\ indirect} = Q_{st}^{L}. \qquad (7.4.9)$$

What about the Törnqvist index? Well, it turns out that from the cohort of popular indexes mentioned above, this index is not endowed with a dual counterpart, meaning that the indirect quantity index obtained with the help of the Törnqvist price index and equation (7.4.2) is not guaranteed to be equal to the *direct* Törnqvist quantity index or any other known direct index, i.e.,

$$Q_{st}^{T\ indirect} \neq Q_{st}^{T}. \qquad (7.4.10)$$

The proofs of these results are simple and are left as an exercise.

7.5 PRODUCTIVITY INDEXES: STATISTICAL APPROACH

Recall from Chapter 4 that one natural way of defining productivity indexes is based on a simple principle that productivity is a measure of (aggregate) output per unit of (aggregate) input. Thus, using statistical quantity indexes as aggregators of outputs and inputs, as described above, one can define the statistical *productivity* indexes in the spirit of Laspeyres, Paasche, Fisher, Törnqvist or, perhaps, a mixture of some of them.

Note, however, that because of the nature of the quantity indexes, there will also be several approaches to statistical productivity indexes: direct, indirect and mixed. In principle, one could take different formulas (or resulting numbers computed by others) for the output and input quantity indexes. For example, to aggregate the outputs, one could have the direct Laspeyres quantity index, while for aggregation of inputs one might happen to have only the indirect Laspeyres quantity index (which is equal to Paasche quantity index) or some other quantity index that is available. Of course, it seems to be logically "consistent" or sensible to choose the same formula whenever possible, yet often such a choice is restricted or even dictated not by researchers, but by data availability. In any case, it is useful to check (and clearly cite) the nature of the index numbers used in a research work and, whenever possible, understand and state what that implies for the properties of the index numbers that are used.

One of the popular productivity indexes in the statistical approach, both in theory and practice, is the Fisher Productivity index, defined as

$$FPI_{st} := \frac{Q^F_{st,output}}{Q^F_{st,input}}, \tag{7.5.1}$$

which is the same whether one uses direct or indirect quantity indexes – due to the self-duality property described in the previous section.

Another popular index is the Törnqvist Productivity index, defined as

$$TPI_{st} := \frac{Q^T_{st,output}}{Q^T_{st,input}}, \tag{7.5.2}$$

which gives different values for whether it uses direct or indirect quantity indexes in the numerator and/or denominator.

Sometimes, due to data availability, researchers might be restricted to use the Laspeyres or Paasche productivity indexes, defined respectively as

$$LPI_{st} := \frac{Q^L_{st,output}}{Q^L_{st,input}}, \tag{7.5.3}$$

and

$$PPI^P_{st} := \frac{Q^P_{st,output}}{Q^P_{st,input}}. \tag{7.5.4}$$

As seen in the previous section, we also have the following relationships

$$LPI^{indirect}_{st} := \frac{Q^{L\ indirect}_{st,output}}{Q^{L\ indirect}_{st,input}} = \frac{Q^P_{st,output}}{Q^P_{st,input}} =: PPI^{direct}_{st}, \tag{7.5.5}$$

and

$$PPI^{indirect}_{st} := \frac{Q^{P\ indirect}_{st,output}}{Q^{P\ indirect}_{st,input}} = \frac{Q^L_{st,output}}{Q^L_{st,input}} =: LPI^{direct}_{st}. \tag{7.5.6}$$

In the next section, we continue the discussion of various properties of index numbers that might help us choose which one to use in theory or in practice.

7.6 PROPERTIES OF INDEX NUMBERS

Having several competing indexes aiming to measure the same phenomena, each with its own perspective or twist, a researcher might wonder which one is better, in general or in specific cases. One common way to approach this question is first decide on a set of desirable criteria – properties or axioms (also referred to here as "tests") – for an index number and then analyze which of the proposed indexes satisfy most or all of them. In the theory of statistical index numbers this approach is often referred to as the "test approach" (or "axiomatic approach") and is usually attributed to Irving Fisher (e.g., see

Fisher, 1911, 1921, 1922). We touched on this approach in Chapter 4 (and a similar approach was discussed in Chapter 3 for efficiency measures), and here we will consider it in more detail.

It is worthwhile noting that there is no absolute agreement between scientists on which of these axioms or tests are the most or least important. Here, we list and discuss a few properties that we think are among the most important to know. By and large, we will follow here the work of Erwin Diewert.[6]

In the definitions below we denote with I_{st} an index number formula of interest and let P_{st} and Q_{st} denote price and quantity indexes of interest, all measuring the change between periods s and t, where $s < t$. Let us first consider the types of properties that are usually considered to be more or less indisputable – these are: positivity, continuity, identity, proportionality, invariance, commensurability, and mean-value properties.

Positivity property: This property requires that an index I_{st} be strictly positive everywhere. In particular, for the price and quantity indexes it would require, respectively, that

$$\mathcal{P}_{st}(p_s, p_t, q_s, q_t) > 0, \tag{7.6.1a}$$

$$\mathcal{Q}_{st}(p_s, p_t, q_s, q_t) > 0. \tag{7.6.1b}$$

Continuity property: This property requires that an index I_{st} must be a continuous function in all of its arguments (prices and/or quantities). In particular, for the price and quantity indexes,

$$\mathcal{P}_{st}(p_s, p_t, q_s, q_t) \text{ is a continuous function in all its arguments,} \tag{7.6.2a}$$

and

$$\mathcal{Q}_{st}(p_s, p_t, q_s, q_t) \text{ is a continuous function in all its arguments.} \tag{7.6.2b}$$

Identity property: This property (also discussed in Chapter 4) requires that an index I_{st} yields the value of 1 (meaning no change) if the variable of interest has not changed over time, even if the variable representing the weights has changed. For price indexes, this property is often called the *constant price test* and is defined as

$$\mathcal{P}_{st}(p, p, q_s, q_t) = 1. \tag{7.6.3a}$$

The identity property for the quantity index is defined analogously, as

$$\mathcal{Q}_{st}(p_s, p_t, q, q) = 1. \tag{7.6.3b}$$

Note that (7.6.3a) or (7.6.3b) should not be confused with the *constant quantity test for price indexes* – the property saying that if the measuring basket

---

[6] E.g., see Diewert (1992a,b) and references cited therein. This approach was also adopted and further extended by Diewert in the International Labor Office for their CPI manual (International Labour Office, Internatonal Monetary Fund, Organisation for Economic Co-operation and Development, Statistical Office of the European Communities (Eurostat), United Nations, World Bank, 2004).

of goods stays the same in any two periods, then the price index must be the ratio of the expenditures for this basket in the two periods, i.e., formally

$$\mathcal{P}_{st}(p_s, p_t, q, q) = \frac{\sum_{m=1}^{M} p_{mt} q_m}{\sum_{m=1}^{M} p_{ms} q_m}. \tag{7.6.4a}$$

One can also define the quantity index analogue of (7.6.4a), call it the *constant price test for quantity indexes* – the property that requires the quantity index to be the ratio of expenditures for the two periods at the same price,

$$Q_{st}(p, p, q_s, q_t) = \frac{\sum_{m=1}^{M} p_m q_{mt}}{\sum_{m=1}^{M} p_m q_{ms}}. \tag{7.6.4b}$$

Proportionality or *Homogeneity properties*: There are several related properties in this context:

(i) *Homogeneity of degree 1 in the variable of interest in period t*: If the variables of interest (e.g., prices for the price index, quantity for the quantity indexes) for period t increase (decrease) by the same proportion, the index representing them should also increase (decrease) by that same proportion. Specifically for the price and quantity indexes, respectively, this formally means

$$\mathcal{P}_{st}(p_s, \lambda p_t, q_s, q_t) = \lambda \mathcal{P}_{st}(p_s, p_t, q_s, q_t), \ \forall \lambda > 0, \tag{7.6.5a}$$

and

$$Q_{st}(p_s, p_t, q_s, \lambda q_t) = \lambda Q_{st}(p_s, p_t, q_s, q_t), \ \forall \lambda > 0. \tag{7.6.5b}$$

(ii) *Homogeneity of degree −1 in the variable of interest in period s*: If the variables of interest (e.g., prices for the price index or quantity for the quantity indexes) for period s increase (decrease) by the same proportion, the index I_{st} should also decrease (increase) by that same proportion. Specifically for the price and quantity indexes, respectively, this means

$$\mathcal{P}_{st}(\lambda p_s, p_t, q_s, q_t) = \mathcal{P}_{st}(p_s, p_t, q_s, q_t)/\lambda, \ \forall \lambda > 0, \tag{7.6.6a}$$

and

$$Q_{st}(p_s, p_t, \lambda q_s, q_t) = Q_{st}(p_s, p_t, q_s, q_t)/\lambda, \ \forall \lambda > 0. \tag{7.6.6b}$$

Invariance Properties:

(i) *Homogeneity of degree 0 in quantities for the price index*: The price index should not change if the quantities, which are used as weights (whether period s or t), change proportionally. Another name for this property is *invariance to proportional changes* in quantities for the price index, and it is formally defined as,

$$\mathcal{P}_{st}(p_s, p_t, q_s, \lambda q_t) = \mathcal{P}_{st}(p_s, p_t, q_s, q_t), \ \forall \lambda > 0, \tag{7.6.7a}$$

and

$$P_{st}(p_s, p_t, \lambda q_s, q_t) = P_{st}(p_s, p_t, q_s, q_t), \ \forall \lambda > 0. \qquad (7.6.7b)$$

(ii) *Homogeneity of degree 0 in prices for quantity index*: The quantity index should not change if the prices, which are used as weights (in period s or t), change proportionally. Another name for this property is *invariance to proportional changes* in prices for the quantity index. Formally,

$$Q_{st}(p_s, \lambda p_t, q_s, q_t) = Q_{st}(p_s, p_t, q_s, q_t), \ \forall \lambda > 0, \qquad (7.6.8a)$$

and

$$Q_{st}(\lambda p_s, p_t, q_s, q_t) = Q_{st}(p_s, p_t, q_s, q_t), \ \forall \lambda > 0. \qquad (7.6.8b)$$

These invariance properties, if imposed, mean that the absolute magnitude of the vectors that represent the weights in the index does not matter. This feature is quite natural as one would expect that the weights in the index must sum to unity. So, what should matter is not the absolute magnitude of the vector representing the weights but its direction, defining the relative magnitudes or importance of each element of the vector.

(iii) *Order invariance:* This property requires that the index I_{st}, measuring the change from s to t, does not depend on the *ordering* of commodities (with the corresponding ordering of their prices). This property is also called the *Commodity Reversal Property,* but it should not be confused with other reversal properties we consider below. In particular, for the price and quantity indexes, respectively, the order invariance test states that

$$P_{st}(p_s, p_t, q_s, q_t) = P_{st}(\tilde{p}_s, \tilde{p}_t, \tilde{q}_s, \tilde{q}_t), \qquad (7.6.9a)$$

and

$$Q_{st}(p_s, p_t, q_s, q_t) = Q_{st}(\tilde{p}_s, \tilde{p}_t, \tilde{q}_s, \tilde{q}_t), \qquad (7.6.9b)$$

where $\tilde{q}$ is denoting here a permutation of the elements of the vector q while $\tilde{p}$ denotes the same permutation of the corresponding prices in vector p.

Commensurability properties: These properties also belong to the type of invariance properties, but often carry their own name – commensurability – apparently first given by Fisher (1921). They require that the index I_{st} be independent of whether its arguments are measured, for example, in Australian or in US dollars or any other currency, in meters or in miles, in kg. or in lb., etc. Often, this property is called *the independence of units of measurement*, which is not quite correct – a more appropriate name for it would be the "independence of *multiplicative changes*" (or up to scaling transformation) in units of measurement. Indeed, logarithmic or general linear (e.g., such as conversion of Fahrenheit into Celsius, etc.) and other more general transformations are not considered in this definition. Another name for this property often used in the literature is *dimensional invariance property*. Let us be precise in our meaning of this property, by considering several types of it:

(i) *Commensurability of the price index to different currencies* follows from (7.6.5a) and (7.6.6a), i.e.,

$$\mathcal{P}_{st}(\lambda p_s, \delta p_t, q_s, q_t) = (\delta/\lambda)\mathcal{P}_{st}(p_s, p_t, q_s, q_t), \ \forall \lambda, \delta > 0.$$
(7.6.10a)

(ii) *Commensurability of the quantity index to different currencies* follows from the invariance properties of the quantity indexes (7.6.7b) and (7.6.8b), i.e., we have

$$Q_{st}(\lambda p_s, \delta p_t, q_s, q_t) = Q_{st}(p_s, p_t, q_s, q_t), \ \forall \lambda, \delta > 0. \qquad (7.6.10b)$$

(iii) *Commensurability in quantities for price and quantity indexes.* This is the main definition of the commensurability property commonly used. For this definition, let Ω be a strictly positive *diagonal* matrix of dimension M by M (where M is the number of elements in commodity vector q). Matrix Ω transforms the units of measurement for quantities in q. Commensurability in quantities for price and quantity indexes is then defined, respectively, as

$$\mathcal{P}_{st}(\Omega^{-1} p_s, \Omega^{-1} p_t, \Omega q_s, \Omega q_t) = \mathcal{P}_{st}(p_s, p_t, q_s, q_t), \qquad (7.6.11a)$$

and

$$Q_{st}(\Omega^{-1} p_s, \Omega^{-1} p_t, \Omega q_s, \Omega q_t) = Q_{st}(p_s, p_t, q_s, q_t). \qquad (7.6.11b)$$

In words, this property requires that the index values shall not be changed by any scalar transformation of units of measurement of any quantity, as long as an appropriate transformation is also made for the corresponding prices.

Mean Value Properties: This set of properties requires that the index must essentially be some type of an average of the observed data. Thus, the index shall always give values between the minimal and the maximal values in the data it aggregates. Specifically, it requires that the price index satisfies

$$\min_{m}(p_{mt}/p_{ms}) \leq \mathcal{P}_{st} \leq \max_{m}(p_{mt}/p_{ms}), \qquad (7.6.12a)$$

while for the quantity index it requires

$$\min_{m}(q_{mt}/q_{ms}) \leq Q_{st} \leq \max_{m}(q_{mt}/q_{ms}). \qquad (7.6.12b)$$

Laspeyres–Paasche Bounding Property: This property requires an index to be bounded by the Paasche and Laspeyres indexes. In the case of the price index, the property requires at least one of the following statements to be satisfied:

$$\mathcal{P}_{st}^{L} \leq \mathcal{P}_{st} \leq \mathcal{P}_{st}^{P} \quad \text{or} \quad \mathcal{P}_{st}^{P} \leq \mathcal{P}_{st} \leq \mathcal{P}_{st}^{L}. \qquad (7.6.13a)$$

Similarly, for the case of the quantity index, the property requires at least one of the following statements to be satisfied,

$$Q_{st}^L \leq Q_{st} \leq Q_{st}^P \quad \text{or} \quad Q_{st}^P \leq Q_{st} \leq Q_{st}^L. \tag{7.6.13b}$$

The logic behind this property is better understood after the reader learns about the relationship between the economic and statistical indexes, discussed in later sections. In particular, we note that the economic price and quantity indexes discussed in Chapter 4, are indeed bounded between the Paasche and Laspeyres indexes.

Reversal Properties: There are several types of reversal properties and they also can be viewed as types of invariance properties.

(i) *Time Reversal Property:* This property (as also discussed in Chapter 4) requires that the index aiming to measure the change from s to t, be equal to its reciprocal if the same formula is applied to the same data, but the direction of measuring the change is reversed to be from t to s rather than from s to t. In particular for the price and quantity indexes, this implies

$$\mathcal{P}_{st}(p_s, p_t, q_s, q_t) = 1/\mathcal{P}_{st}(p_t, p_s, q_t, q_s), \tag{7.6.14a}$$

and

$$Q_{st}(p_s, p_t, q_s, q_t) = 1/Q_{st}(p_t, p_s, q_t, q_s). \tag{7.6.14b}$$

(ii) *Weights Reversal/Symmetry Property:* This property requires the index to be invariant to the switching of weights between the periods. In particular, for the price indexes, it would be the *Quantity Reversal Property for a Price Index*, requiring that

$$\mathcal{P}_{st}(p_s, p_t, q_s, q_t) = \mathcal{P}_{st}(p_s, p_t, q_t, q_s), \tag{7.6.15a}$$

and for the quantity indexes it would be the *Price Reversal Property for a Quantity Index,* requiring that

$$Q_{st}(p_s, p_t, q_s, q_t) = Q_{st}(p_t, p_s, q_s, q_t). \tag{7.6.15b}$$

This last property, (7.6.15b), shall not be confused with another reversal test that Diewert (1992a) called the *Price Reversal Property for a Price Index,* which requires that

$$\frac{\sum_{m=1}^M p_{mt} q_{mt} / \sum_{m=1}^M p_{ms} q_{ms}}{\mathcal{P}_{st}(p_s, p_t, q_s, q_t)} = \frac{\sum_{m=1}^M p_{ms} q_{mt} / \sum_{m=1}^M p_{mt} q_{ms}}{\mathcal{P}_{st}(p_t, p_s, q_s, q_t)}. \tag{7.6.16}$$

Note that the numerator of the l.h.s. of (7.6.16) is the index value change between s and t, and so dividing it by the price index measuring the price change between s and t makes the entire l.h.s. be the indirect quantity index $Q_{st}^{indirect}(p_s, p_t, q_s, q_t)$. Similarly, the r.h.s. can be interpreted as the *indirect* quantity index with prices (here representing weights for aggregating quantities) interchanged between the two periods – as in the r.h.s. of (7.6.15b). In this sense, property (7.6.16) can be understood as a special case of property (7.6.15b), where quantity indexes are obtained indirectly, via (7.4.2).

(iii) *Factor Reversal Property:* This property requires that if one interchanges prices with quantities in the price (quantity) index, then one should get the quantity (price) index that would decompose the value change index, i.e.,

$$\mathcal{P}_{st}(p_s, p_t, q_s, q_t) \times \mathcal{P}_{st}(q_s, q_t, p_s, p_t)$$
$$= V_{st}(p_s, p_t, q_s, q_t) := \frac{\sum_{m=1}^{M} p_{mt} q_{mt}}{\sum_{m=1}^{M} p_{ms} q_{ms}}, \qquad (7.6.17a)$$

and

$$Q_{st}(p_s, p_t, q_s, q_t) \times Q_{st}(q_s, q_t, p_s, p_t)$$
$$= V_{st}(p_s, p_t, q_s, q_t) := \frac{\sum_{m=1}^{M} p_{mt} q_{mt}}{\sum_{m=1}^{M} p_{ms} q_{ms}}. \qquad (7.6.17b)$$

This property is sometimes called the *functional form symmetry,* or, as mentioned above, the *self-duality* property of an index.

A more general property that requires a decomposition of the value change into a price index and a quantity index, not necessarily with the same formula for the two, is known as the *product test*, which was already formally stated in (7.1.2) and in (7.4.1).

Monotonicity Properties: These properties require that the index, as a function, should be monotonic in the variables of interest (prices for the price indexes, quantities for the quantity indexes). In particular, there are four types of monotonicity properties considered in the literature:

(i) *Monotonicity of Price Index in period-t prices,* requiring that

$$\mathcal{P}_{st}(p_s, p_t, q_s, q_t) < \mathcal{P}_{st}(p_s, p, q_s, q_t), \ p > p_t. \qquad (7.6.18a)$$

(ii) *Monotonicity of Price Index in period-s prices,* requiring that

$$\mathcal{P}_{st}(p_s, p_t, q_s, q_t) > \mathcal{P}_{st}(p, p_t, q_s, q_t), \ p > p_s. \qquad (7.6.18b)$$

(iii) *Monotonicity of Quantity Index in period-t quantities,* requiring that

$$Q_{st}(p_s, p_t, q_s, q_t) < Q_{st}(p_s, p_t, q_s, q), \ q > q_t. \qquad (7.6.19a)$$

(iv) *Monotonicity of Quantity Index in period-s quantities,* requiring that

$$Q_{st}(p_s, p_t, q_s, q_t) > Q_{st}(p_s, p_t, q, q_t), \ q > q_s. \qquad (7.6.19b)$$

Transitivity Property: This (and closely related *circularity*) property was discussed in detail in Chapter 4. For the price and quantity indexes, respectively, this property would require that for any periods r, s, t we have

$$\mathcal{P}_{st}(p_s, p_t, q_s, q_t) = \mathcal{P}_{sr}(p_s, p_r, q_s, q_r) \times \mathcal{P}_{rt}(p_r, p_t, q_r, q_t), \quad (7.6.20a)$$

and

$$Q_{st}(p_s, p_t, q_s, q_t) = Q_{sr}(p_s, p_r, q_s, q_r) \times Q_{rt}(p_r, p_t, q_r, q_t). \quad (7.6.20b)$$

7.7 SOME KEY RESULTS IN THE STATISTICAL APPROACH TO INDEX NUMBERS

Besides a mechanical check for whether a particular index satisfies a particular test, axiom or property or a set of them, one could also derive general theorems describing possibilities of satisfying certain properties. One could, for example, show conditions of existence of an index that satisfies a set of properties, or even derive a functional form (equation) that an index must have, or prove which functional forms of indexes constitute necessary and/or sufficient conditions for satisfying certain sets of properties. Sometimes such an approach may also yield "negative" or impossibility theorems and this is also beneficial as it gives the clear conclusion that there are no indexes that satisfy a certain set of properties, and this, in turn, helps researchers avoid wasting time and efforts on searching for nonexistent indexes. Such impossibility theorems also help in understanding which particular properties are critical, redundant, contradictory, etc.

Various theorems have been proven in the index numbers literature, clarifying the implications of each of the properties mentioned above (and others) and of their combinations. Here, we only provide a few fundamental results, while more details can be found in Eichhorn (1976), Eichhorn and Voeller (1976), Funke and Voeller (1978), Vogt (1980), and Aczél and Dhombres (1989).

Theorem. *The only price index that satisfies the positivity (7.6.1a), quantity reversal (7.6.15a), time reversal (7.6.14a), and factor reversal (7.6.17a) properties is the Fisher ideal price index defined in (7.2.5).*

This theorem is from Funke and Voeller (1978) and a somewhat alternative theorem was later provided by Diewert (1992a), who instead of imposing the factor reversal test directly, imposed the price reversal property for a price index, (7.6.16). Importantly, note that assumption (7.6.16) is not a weaker requirement than (7.6.17a), but in a certain sense (7.6.16) is an implication of property (7.6.15b). We skip the proof of this theorem, because our main concern is productivity indexes, which are based on quantity indexes, and instead we state and prove its quantity analogue – the next theorem.

Theorem. *The only quantity index that satisfies the positivity (7.6.1b), price reversal (7.6.15b), time reversal (7.6.14b), and factor reversal (7.6.17b) properties is the Fisher ideal quantity index defined in (7.3.3).*

Proof. [7] First of all, note that due to the factor reversal test, (7.6.17b), we have

$$Q_{st}(p_s, p_t, q_s, q_t) \times Q_{st}(q_s, q_t, p_s, p_t) = V_{st}(p_s, p_t, q_s, q_t) := \frac{\sum_{m=1}^{M} p_{mt}q_{mt}}{\sum_{m=1}^{M} p_{ms}q_{ms}},$$

which in turn implies that

$$Q_{st}(q_s, q_t, p_s, p_t) = \frac{\sum_{m=1}^{M} p_{mt}q_{mt} / \sum_{m=1}^{M} p_{ms}q_{ms}}{Q_{st}(p_s, p_t, q_s, q_t)}.$$

Analogously, from the factor reversal test, we can also conclude that

$$Q_{st}(p_s, p_t, q_t, q_s) \times Q_{st}(q_t, q_s, p_s, p_t) = V_{st}(p_s, p_t, q_t, q_s) := \frac{\sum_{m=1}^{M} p_{mt}q_{ms}}{\sum_{m=1}^{M} p_{ms}q_{mt}},$$

which in turn implies that

$$Q_{st}(q_t, q_s, p_s, p_t) = \frac{\sum_{m=1}^{M} p_{mt}q_{ms} / \sum_{m=1}^{M} p_{ms}q_{mt}}{Q_{st}(p_s, p_t, q_t, q_s)}.$$

Note that (7.6.15b) implies $Q_{st}(q_s, q_t, p_s, p_t) = Q_{st}(q_t, q_s, p_s, p_t)$, and so

$$\frac{\sum_{m=1}^{M} p_{mt}q_{mt}}{\sum_{m=1}^{M} p_{ms}q_{ms}} / Q_{st}(p_s, p_t, q_s, q_t) = \frac{\sum_{m=1}^{M} p_{mt}q_{ms}}{\sum_{m=1}^{M} p_{ms}q_{mt}} / Q_{st}(p_s, p_t, q_t, q_s).$$

Furthermore, after rearranging the terms we can get

$$\frac{\sum_{m=1}^{M} p_{mt}q_{mt}}{\sum_{m=1}^{M} p_{mt}q_{ms}} \frac{\sum_{m=1}^{M} p_{ms}q_{mt}}{\sum_{m=1}^{M} p_{ms}q_{ms}} = \frac{Q_{st}(p_s, p_t, q_s, q_t)}{Q_{st}(p_s, p_t, q_t, q_s)}$$

$$= \frac{Q_{st}(p_s, p_t, q_s, q_t)}{Q_{st}(p_t, p_s, q_t, q_s)} \qquad \text{(using (7.6.15b))}$$

$$= Q_{st}(p_s, p_t, q_s, q_t)Q_{st}(p_s, p_t, q_s, q_t) \qquad \text{(using (7.6.14b))}$$

$$= (Q_{st}(p_s, p_t, q_s, q_t))^2.$$

Finally, relying on positivity property (7.6.1b), we can state that

$$Q(p_s, p_t, q_s, q_t) = \left(\frac{\sum_{m=1}^{M} p_{mt}q_{mt}}{\sum_{m=1}^{M} p_{mt}q_{ms}} \frac{\sum_{m=1}^{M} p_{ms}q_{mt}}{\sum_{m=1}^{M} p_{ms}q_{ms}} \right)^{1/2} =: (Q_{st}^P Q_{st}^L)^{\frac{1}{2}} =: Q_{st}^F,$$

which is exactly what we had to prove.   □

---

[7] This proof is similar to proofs found in Diewert (1992a) for the price indexes.

It is straightforward to check, one by one, that the Fisher price and quantity indexes also satisfy all the other properties listed above, *except* for the transitivity property. The situation with the other indexes is not so "ideal." Clearly, as the theorems above suggest, no other index satisfies the factor reversal test! We summarize some of the important known facts in the following theorems.

Theorem. *The Laspeyres and Paasche price and quantity indexes do not satisfy the reversal properties (7.6.14a), (7.6.17a) and (7.6.14b), (7.6.17b), and transitivity property (7.6.20a) and (7.6.20b).*

The proof of this theorem is simple, and is done by substituting the definition of the indexes into the definition of the properties. It is also easy to check that other tests/properties listed in the previous section are satisfied by the Laspeyres and Paasche price and quantity indexes.

Many scholars believe the factor reversal test and the quantity reversal tests are irrelevant or not crucial, yet the time reversal test is important. On this basis, some consider the failure of the Laspeyres and Paasche indexes to satisfy the time reversal test as "a fatal flaw" (e.g., see Diewert, 1992a). Yet, many statistical offices use the Laspeyres price indexes. Are they wrong in using it? If one believes in the critical importance of the time reversal test then the answer is "yes." However, if one is comfortable with the fact that the counterpart in the reversal tests is not the "identical twin," in terms of the functional form, but some other meaningful index, e.g., one that is "dual" to it, as is stated in the corollary above, then the use of the Laspeyres and the Paasche indexes can be justified. In this respect, a nice metaphoric argument was articulated by Samuelson and Swamy (1974), stating that "A man and wife should be properly matched: but this does not mean I should marry my identical twin." What about the Törnqvist index? The next theorem gives clarifications.

Theorem. *The Törnqvist (or translog) price and quantity indexes do not satisfy the constant weight tests (7.6.4a), (7.6.4b), the Paasche and Laspeyres bounding property (7.6.13a), the reversal properties (7.6.15a), (7.6.17a), and (7.6.15b), (7.6.17b), all the monotonicity properties (7.6.18a), (7.6.19a), and (7.6.18b), (7.6.19b), the transitivity property (7.6.20a), (7.6.20b), and the product test (7.4.1). Moreover, the indirect Törnqvist price and quantity indexes also fail the identity property (7.6.3a)–(7.6.3b) and the mean value properties (7.6.12a), (7.6.13a), and (7.6.12b), (7.6.13b).*

It is straightforward to check, one by one, that the few remaining properties listed in the previous section are satisfied by the Törnqvist price and quantity indexes. Thus, we see that the Törnqvist index, despite its nice intuitive meaning in the logarithmic form, is not so robust, failing quite a few reasonable properties. Perhaps the most upsetting fact is the failure to satisfy the identity test for the indirect Törnqvist price (quantity) index. This is due to the fact that the direct Törnqvist quantity (price) index might not be identical to the value change index (as the Fisher, Laspeyres, and Paasche indexes are) when the weights are held constant over time, thus making the indirect counterpart not equal to unity. On the other hand, other important properties were discovered for the Törnqvist index, e.g., see Diewert (1976, 1981), Caves et al. (1982a) and Diewert and Morrison (1986), giving it an economic theory justification, and so it has been fairly popular in practice and will probably continue to be so in the future, despite its many pitfalls.

Again, note that none of the indexes is immune from pitfalls and limitations. In particular, note that none of the indexes above satisfies the transitivity property. Is this fact upsetting? As we discussed in Chapter 4, this property, though sometimes viewed as desirable, is often viewed as not critical or too restrictive for the context where s and t are time periods.[8] As discussed in Chapter 4, sometimes an index can be modified by fixing the weights to be the same in all periods to make it transitive. This tempting "trick" may seem like an innocent step, yet it is often not, because it may also imply dramatic restrictions if one wants to preserve relevancy of the index for measuring phenomena of interest. Indeed, as argued since at least Laspeyres and Paasche, the aggregation weights in the construction of an index must be relevant benchmarks. Laspeyres viewed the base-period weights as the relevant benchmark, which is quite natural – after all this is how one computes a growth forward. Paasche took a "modernistic" or "in hindsight" view and argued that the current-period weights can serve as a more relevant benchmark – after all, the present matters more than the past. In general, and as recognized by Fisher, both perspectives give useful and relevant benchmarks from different (and potentially radically different) perspectives. A natural way to utilize both perspectives is to take an appropriate average of indexes based on those perspectives, i.e., use the Fisher index. It might seem tempting though, to take an average of the two weights (i.e., use the Törnqvist weights), which will make Laspeyres, Paasche, and Fisher indexes identical, but then one will also be risking to weight or associate the quantities (prices) with completely irrelevant prices (quantities), in both periods. That is, by choosing to use some other p^* different from p^s and p^t, one is risking to use allocations or baskets p^*q_s and p^*q_t that have never been observed in any periods, and perhaps even represent impossible or irrational allocations (e.g., those that may violate the revealed preferences or other axioms in economics, etc.) or allocations that are relevant only under very strict assumptions. In his seminal article in *Econometrica* about the index numbers, Frisch (1936) used similar logic to conclude that indexes with fixed weights are "absurd."[9] While this may sound too extreme, it delivers the important message that one must be very careful using fixed-weights indexes. See Chapter 4 for more discussion, references and practical recommendations.

---

[8] In the context of cross-sectional analysis (i.e., where s and t are subscripts for firms, countries, etc.) and for panel data, preserving transitivity is more important and there are various ways to modify the indexes (or data) to make them compatible with the transitivity property – see Chapter 4 for more detailed discussion and references.

[9] Also see Diewert and Fox (2017) for related discussion.

Overall, we conclude that the price index that satisfies the majority of properties for the index numbers is the Fisher ideal price index. Similar results can be stated for the quantity index, both direct and indirect, since it is the same for the Fisher index. Because a productivity index in the statistical approach is often defined as the ratio of an output quantity index to an input quantity index, this "superiority" of the Fisher quantity index is then inherited, to some extent, by the Fisher Productivity Index, which can also be called the "Fisher ideal productivity index," to remind us that it is the same whether obtained directly or indirectly. In the next section we present more of the interesting results about the statistical indexes – about their relationship with the economic indexes we discussed in Chapter 4.

7.8 RELATIONSHIP BETWEEN ECONOMIC AND STATISTICAL APPROACHES TO INDEX NUMBERS

Is there a relationship between the economic and the statistical approaches? These approaches are clearly different. For example, the *quantity* indexes in the statistical approach involve prices (as weights) but in the economic approach, the quantity indexes, such as the Malmquist quantity indexes, involve only quantity data. Still, those indexes are aiming to measure the same things. Are there any conditions under which they are equivalent? Some of these questions have been tackled since the origin of the economic approach. It was the period of the late 1970s and all of the 1980s that brought revolutionary discoveries in index number theory by deriving new relationships between the statistical and economic approaches to index numbers. Such discoveries also brought empirical tools for estimating the true economic indexes as well as giving an economic theory justification for what statisticians had been using for a long time, and in this section we will outline several such relationships.[10]

7.8.1   Flexible Functional Forms

Naturally, the relationship between the economic and statistical approaches to index numbers is established through making certain assumptions on the technology underlying the production process. The key assumption here is that the primal or dual characterizations of technology (i.e., distance functions or revenue or cost or profit functions) have particular functional forms. The aspect that made such results influential and popular is that the assumed functional forms are fairly general – they are the *flexible* functional forms that we considered in Chapter 6. Here we employ some of those ideas. In particular, recall that the *Quadratic* function for some arbitrary variables $\tilde{x}$ and $\tilde{y}$, is defined as[11]

---

[10] Here, we follow Diewert (1983a), Caves et al. (1982a), and Diewert (1992a).

[11] Note, to stay general, in this subsection we use "~" in $\tilde{x}$ and $\tilde{y}$ to distinguish them from x and y that are reserved for inputs and outputs; so if for example $\tilde{x} = x$ and $\tilde{y} = p$, then the functions

$$f(\tilde{x}_1, \ldots, \tilde{x}_N, \tilde{y}_1, \ldots, \tilde{y}_M) = a_o + \sum_{m=1}^{M} a_m \tilde{y}_m + \sum_{j=1}^{N} b_j \tilde{x}_j + \frac{1}{2} \sum_{m=1}^{M} \sum_{r=1}^{M} a_{mr} \tilde{y}_m \tilde{y}_r$$

$$+ \frac{1}{2} \sum_{l=1}^{N} \sum_{j=1}^{N} b_{lj} \tilde{x}_l \tilde{x}_j + \frac{1}{2} \sum_{m=1}^{M} \sum_{j=1}^{N} c_{mj} \tilde{y}_m \tilde{x}_j,$$

$$(7.8.1)$$

while the *Translog* function of some arbitrary variables $\tilde{x}$ and $\tilde{y}$, is given by

$$\ln \psi(\tilde{x}_1, \ldots, \tilde{x}_N, \tilde{y}_1, \ldots, \tilde{y}_M)$$

$$= a_o + \sum_{m=1}^{M} \alpha_m \ln \tilde{y}_m + \sum_{j=1}^{N} \beta_j \ln \tilde{x}_j$$

$$+ \frac{1}{2} \sum_{m=1}^{M} \sum_{r=1}^{M} \alpha_{mr} \ln \tilde{y}_m \ln \tilde{y}_r + \frac{1}{2} \sum_{l=1}^{N} \sum_{j=1}^{N} \beta_{lj} \ln \tilde{x}_l \ln \tilde{x}_j$$

$$+ \frac{1}{2} \sum_{m=1}^{M} \sum_{j=1}^{N} \gamma_{mj} \ln \tilde{y}_m \ln \tilde{x}_j. \qquad (7.8.2)$$

Also recall that certain restrictions must be made on the parameters to satisfy the properties suggested by calculus as well as economic theory. Such restrictions also help improve on estimation, since the number of parameters can be reduced substantially. An obvious restriction, for example, is the *symmetry* condition, stating that, say for the translog form, we must have $\beta_{lj} = \beta_{jl}$, $\gamma_{lj} = \gamma_{jl}$, due to Young's theorem in calculus. Other restrictions can be function specific. For example, for the cost function, restrictions must conform to the economic theory of the cost function, i.e., they must satisfy such properties as homogeneity of degree 1 in prices, monotonicity and concavity in prices (see Chapter 2).

Another very useful functional form was suggested by Diewert (1992a), and so we will call it the Diewert function, which in matrix form for arbitrary $\tilde{x}$ and $\tilde{y}$ is given by

$$f(\tilde{x}, \tilde{y}) = \theta[(\tilde{x}'A\tilde{x})(\tilde{y}'C\tilde{y})^{\gamma} + (\alpha'\tilde{x})(\beta'\tilde{y}^{\gamma})(\tilde{x}'B\tilde{y}^{\gamma})]^{\frac{1}{2}}, \qquad (7.8.3)$$

where $A = A'$, $C = C'$, and B are the parameter matrices and α, β are (column) parameter vectors, all conformable with (column) vectors $\tilde{x}$ and $\tilde{y}$ and γ is either 1 or -1 depending on the context, with convention that $\tilde{y}^{-1} = (1/\tilde{y}_1, 1/\tilde{y}_2, \ldots)$.[12] Using this function, Diewert (1992a) formally proved that (7.8.3) belongs to the class of flexible functional forms and, more importantly,

---

can be used to model the revenue function and when $\tilde{x} = y$ and $\tilde{y} = w$, then they can be used to model the cost function.

[12] Clearly, the round parentheses in (7.8.3) can be dropped and are merely used for convenience of reading this formula.

showed how it can be used to establish some important relationships between the true indexes and the Fisher indexes.

The following subsections will outline some of the most important results that relate the true economic indexes to the indexes from the statistical approach, using these functions.

7.8.2 Relationships for the Price Indexes

First of all, from the duality theory discussed in Chapter 2, it should be clear that, assuming optimal economic behavior with respect to maximizing revenues (thus, no allocative or technical inefficiency) and given the standard regularity conditions of production theory (see Chapter 1), the Laspeyres and Paasche output price indexes provide the lower and upper bounds for the true economic output price indexes, respectively. Formally, we have

$$\mathcal{P}_o^s(p_s, p_t, x_s) := \frac{R^s(x_s, p_t)}{R^s(x_s, p_s)} \geq \frac{\sum_{m=1}^M p_{mt} y_{ms}}{\sum_{m=1}^M p_{ms} y_{ms}} =: \mathcal{P}_{st}^L, \qquad (7.8.4)$$

and

$$\mathcal{P}_o^t(p_s, p_t, x_t) := \frac{R^t(x_t, p_t)}{R^t(x_t, p_s)} \leq \frac{\sum_{m=1}^M p_{mt} y_{mt}}{\sum_{m=1}^M p_{ms} y_{mt}} =: \mathcal{P}_{st}^P. \qquad (7.8.5)$$

A natural question is: do the inequalities above ever become equalities? If so, then under what conditions? It turns out that if, in addition to the standard regularity conditions of production theory, one assumes revenue maximizing behavior and that the revenue functions for both periods s and t are characterized by the translog functions with proper restrictions on coefficients, then the geometric mean of the two true price indexes is exactly equal to the Törnqvist output price index, i.e.,

$$\left(\mathcal{P}_o^s(p_s, p_t, x_s) \times \mathcal{P}_o^t(p_s, p_t, x_t)\right)^{1/2} = \prod_{m=1}^M \left(\frac{p_{mt}}{p_{ms}}\right)^{\frac{v_{mt} + v_{ms}}{2}} \equiv \mathcal{P}_{st}^T. \quad (7.8.6)$$

This important result is from Diewert (1983b), where its elegant proof can be found. In words, this result says that when the revenue functions are of the translog functional forms (with certain restrictions) then the unknown *true* price indexes can be estimated *exactly* via the statistical approach to index numbers through the Törnqvist price indexes. This result is particularly important since it implies that there is no need to know (or estimate) the coefficients of the revenue function. What is needed is just a belief or assumption that has translog form (with unknown parameters, as long as they satisfy the mentioned restrictions) – and then the true, but unknown in practice, price indexes can be computed by applying the simple formula of the Törnqvist price indexes.

A natural question is how strict is the assumption that the revenue functions are translog? To understand this, recall that the translog functional form is the second-order approximation to virtually any unknown (twice differentiable) functional form where the original input and output variables can be taken in logarithms (i.e., are strictly positive). Therefore, this result essentially says that the Törnqvist price indexes are the (second-order) approximations to the geometric mean of the *true* (but unknown) price indexes, for virtually any underlying technology (as long as it can be approximated via the second-order Taylor's series). We can summarize this intuitive conclusion as follows:

$$\mathcal{P}_{o,st}^T \approx \left(\mathcal{P}_o^s(p_s, p_t, x_s) \times \mathcal{P}_o^t(p_s, p_t, x_t)\right)^{1/2}. \tag{7.8.7}$$

By now it should also be clear that similar results can be derived for the *Input Price* Indexes, where the cost functions are used as (dual) characterizations of technology. To see this, note that assuming optimal economic behavior wrt minimizing the cost function (thus, no allocative or technical inefficiency) and given the standard regularity conditions of production theory, we have

$$\mathcal{P}_i^s(w_s, w_t, y_s) \equiv \frac{C^s(y_s, w_t)}{C^s(y_s, w_s)} \leq \frac{\sum_{j=1}^N w_{jt} x_{js}}{\sum_{j=1}^N w_{js} x_{js}} \equiv \mathcal{P}_{i,st}^L, \tag{7.8.8}$$

and

$$\mathcal{P}_i^t(w_s, w_t, y_t) \equiv \frac{C^t(y_t, p_t)}{C^t(y_t, p_s)} \geq \frac{\sum_{j=1}^N w_{jt} x_{jt}}{\sum_{j=1}^N w_{js} x_{jt}} \equiv \mathcal{P}_{i,st}^P. \tag{7.8.9}$$

In words, the Laspeyres and Paasche input price indexes provide the upper and the lower bounds for the true input price indexes, respectively. More importantly, and similar to the output prices, there is also an exact relationship between the true input price indexes and their statistical counterparts. Specifically, if in addition to the standard regularity conditions of production theory, one assumes cost-minimizing behavior and that the cost functions for both periods t and s are characterized by the translog functions with certain restrictions on coefficients, then the geometric mean of the two true price indexes is exactly equal to the Törnqvist input price index, i.e.,

$$\left(\mathcal{P}_i^s(p_s, p_t, x_s) \times \mathcal{P}_i^t(p_s, p_t, x_t)\right)^{1/2} = \prod_{j=1}^N \left(\frac{w_{jt}}{w_{js}}\right)^{\frac{v_{jt} + v_{js}}{2}} \equiv \mathcal{P}_{i,st}^T. \tag{7.8.10}$$

Similarly as for the output-price case, this important result is due to Diewert (1983b). The importance of this result is based on the fact that there is no need to know (or estimate) the coefficients of the cost function – just a need to believe it is of the translog form (with certain restrictions) – then the true but unknown in practice input price indexes can be computed via the formulas of the Törnqvist price indexes. Again, since the translog functional form is the second-order approximation to virtually any unknown functional form (that has a second-order Taylor's series approximation), this theorem also essentially says that the Törnqvist price indexes are the (second-order) approximations to the geometric mean of the *true* price indexes, for any underlying technology, i.e.,

$$\mathcal{P}_{i,st}^T \approx \left(\mathcal{P}_i^s(w_s, w_t, y_s) \times \mathcal{P}_i^t(w_s, w_t, y_t) \right)^{1/2}. \tag{7.8.11}$$

These are indeed powerful results that justify the use of the Törnqvist price indexes for estimation of the true economic price indexes. Because of the results stated in (7.8.6) and (7.8.10), the Törnqvist index is referred to as the *exact* index for the translog revenue and cost functions. And, because the translog functional form is a *flexible* functional form, the Törnqvist index is also called *superlative* (see Diewert, 1976 for a detailed discussion of these notions).

Similar results can be shown for the Fisher ideal price index. In fact, even without imposing any functional form, an immediate conclusion one could guess from the two inequalities (7.8.4) and (7.8.5) is that if we take the geometric average of these two bounds – of the Laspeyres and Paasche output price indexes, and so get the Fisher ideal price index – we would get something that is less extreme and so potentially closer to the true price indexes for outputs, especially when their geometric average is considered. A formal and exact relationship between the Fisher ideal output (input) price index is established somewhat similarly as was done for the Törnqvist index case, and can be found in Diewert (1992a).

7.8.3 Relationships for the Quantity Indexes

Recalling that the revenue and cost functions (used to define the price indexes) are dual to the distance functions (used to define the quantity indexes), one expects that similar relationships outlined in the previous subsection must exist for the quantity indexes as well. This is indeed true, and here we summarize these relationships in more detail, because the quantity indexes often serve as building blocks for defining the productivity indexes.[13]

Theorem. *Assume the cost-minimizing behavior in both periods. Then, the geometric mean of the two Malmquist input quantity indexes is equal to the Törnqvist input quantity index, i.e.,*

$$\left(Q_i^s(x_s, x_t, y_s) \times Q_i^t(x_s, x_t, y_t) \right)^{1/2} = \prod_{j=1}^N \left(\frac{x_{jt}}{x_{js}} \right)^{\frac{v_{jt}+v_{js}}{2}} =: Q_{i,st}^T, \tag{7.8.12}$$

if the input distance functions for both periods s and t are characterized by the translog functions with identical coefficients between periods s and t for the second-order input terms, i.e., for $\tau = s, t$

---

[13] In the rest of the chapter we also assume appropriate differentiability of the cost and revenue and distance functions, to be able to use the Hotelling–Shephard lemma.

$$\ln \psi^\tau(x, y) = a_o^\tau + \sum_{m=1}^{M} \alpha_m^\tau \ln y_m + \sum_{j=1}^{N} \beta_j^\tau \ln x_j + \frac{1}{2} \sum_{m=1}^{M} \sum_{r=1}^{M} \alpha_{mr}^\tau \ln y_m \ln y_r$$

$$+ \frac{1}{2} \sum_{l=1}^{N} \sum_{j=1}^{N} \beta_{lj}^\tau \ln x_l \ln x_j + \frac{1}{2} \sum_{m=1}^{M} \sum_{j=1}^{N} \gamma_{mj}^\tau \ln y_m \ln x_j,$$

$$(7.8.13)$$

where $\beta_{lj}^s = \beta_{lj}^t$ in addition to the symmetry conditions $\beta_{lj}^\tau = \beta_{jl}^\tau$ and $\alpha_{mr}^\tau = \alpha_{rm}^\tau$, for all m, r, l, and j.

This important result is from the seminal work of Caves et al. (1982a), where its original proof can be found, along with analogous results for the output quantity indexes, which we summarize in the next theorem.

Theorem. *Assume the revenue maximizing behavior in both periods. Then, the geometric mean of the two Malmquist output quantity indexes is equal to the Törnqvist output quantity index, i.e.,*

$$\left(Q_o^s(y_s, y_t, x_s) \times Q_o^t(y_s, y_t, x_t)\right)^{1/2} = \prod_{m=1}^{M} \left(\frac{y_{mt}}{y_{ms}}\right)^{\frac{v_{mt} + v_{ms}}{2}} =: Q_{st}^T,$$

$$(7.8.14)$$

if the output distance *functions for both periods s and t are characterized by the* translog *functions with identical coefficients between periods s and t for the second-order output terms, i.e., for $\tau = s, t$*

$$\ln \psi^\tau(x, y) = a_o^\tau + \sum_{m=1}^{M} \alpha_m^\tau \ln y_m + \sum_{j=1}^{N} \beta_j^\tau \ln x_j + \frac{1}{2} \sum_{m=1}^{M} \sum_{r=1}^{M} \alpha_{mr}^\tau \ln y_m \ln y_r$$

$$+ \frac{1}{2} \sum_{l=1}^{N} \sum_{j=1}^{N} \beta_{lj}^\tau \ln x_l \ln x_j + \frac{1}{2} \sum_{m=1}^{M} \sum_{j=1}^{N} \gamma_{mj}^\tau \ln y_m \ln x_j,$$

$$(7.8.15)$$

where $\alpha_{mr}^s = \alpha_{mr}^t$, in addition to the symmetry conditions $\beta_{lj}^\tau = \beta_{jl}^\tau$ and $\alpha_{mr}^\tau = \alpha_{rm}^\tau$, for all m, r, l, and j.

These fundamental results can in turn be used to establish a relationship between the Hicks–Moorsteen productivity index and the Törnqvist Productivity index, as we summarize in the next subsection. Meanwhile, in the next two theorems we summarize relationships between the Fisher and the Malmquist quantity indexes. The first to establish such fundamental results was Diewert (1992a) and the theorems below are their slight extensions.

Theorem. *Assume the cost minimizing behavior in both periods. Then, the two Malmquist input quantity indexes are equal to the Fisher ideal output quantity index, i.e., we have*

$$Q_{i,st}^{F} = Q_i^s(x_s, x_t, y_s) = Q_i^t(x_s, x_t, y_t) = \left[\frac{y_t' A_t y_t}{y_s' A_s y_s} \gamma_t \right]^{1/2}, \quad (7.8.16)$$

if the input distance functions for both periods $\tau = s, t$ are characterized by the Diewert functions of the following form

$$D_i^{\tau}(y, x) = [(y' A_\tau y)^{-1}(x' C_\tau x) + (\alpha_\tau' y^{-1})(\beta_\tau' x)((y^{-1})' B_\tau x)]^{\frac{1}{2}}, \quad (7.8.17)$$

where $y^{-1} = (1/y_1, \ldots, 1/y_M)'$, $A_\tau = A_\tau'$, $C_\tau = C_\tau'$, B_τ are the parameter matrices and α_τ, β_τ are (column) parameter vectors, all conformable with (column) vectors x and y, and satisfies the following constraints

$$(y_\tau' A_\tau y_\tau)^{-1}(x_\tau' C_\tau x_\tau) = 1, \quad \tau = s, t, \quad (7.8.18)$$

$$(y_s^{-1})' B_s = 0_N', \quad (7.8.19)$$

$$(\alpha_t' y_t^{-1}) = 0, \quad (7.8.20)$$

$$C_t = \gamma_t C_s. \quad (7.8.21)$$

Theorem. *Assume revenue maximizing behavior in both periods. Then, the two Malmquist output quantity indexes are equal to the Fisher ideal output quantity index, i.e., we have*

$$Q_{o,st}^{F} = Q_o^s(y_s, y_t, x_s) = Q_o^t(y_s, y_t, x_t) = \left[\frac{x_t' C_t x_t}{x_s' C_s x_s} \frac{1}{\lambda_t} \right]^{1/2}, \quad (7.8.22)$$

if the output distance *functions for both periods* $\tau = s, t$ *are characterized by the Diewert function of the following form*

$$D_o^{\tau}(x, y) = [(y' A_\tau y)(x' C_\tau x)^{-1} + (\alpha_\tau' y)(\beta_\tau' x^{-1})(y' B_\tau x^{-1})]^{\frac{1}{2}}, \quad (7.8.23)$$

where $x^{-1} = (1/x_1, \ldots, 1/x_N)'$, $A_\tau = A_\tau'$, $C_\tau = C_\tau'$, B_τ *are the parameter matrices and* α_τ, β_τ *are (column) parameter vectors, all conformable with (column) vectors* x *and* y, *and satisfies the following constraints*

$$(y_\tau' A y_\tau)(x_\tau' C_\tau x_\tau)^{-1} = 1, \quad \tau = s, t, \quad (7.8.24)$$

$$B_\tau x_\tau^{-1} = 0_M, \quad \tau = s, t, \quad (7.8.25)$$

$$\beta_\tau' x_\tau^{-1} = 0, \quad \tau = s, t, \quad (7.8.26)$$

$$A_t = \lambda_t A_s, \quad \lambda_t > 0. \quad (7.8.27)$$

These fundamental results, for cases when $C_t = C_s = C$ in the context of input indexes and when $A_t = A_s = A$ in the context of output indexes, appeared in the seminal work of Diewert (1992a), who provided the first proof for the case of input orientation and noted that the proof for the output indexes is analogous. For pedagogical reasons, below we use a similar line of proof applied to the case of output indexes and do so for a slightly more general case – when the matrices transforming inputs into outputs (and thus defining the technology) are allowed to change between periods in the Hicks-neutral technological change manner, i.e., as characterized by (7.8.21) and (7.8.27).[14]

Proof. First, note that

$$Q_{o,st}^F := \left(Q_{o,st}^L \times Q_{o,st}^P \right)^{1/2}$$

$$:= \left(\frac{p_s y_t}{p_s y_s} \times \frac{p_t y_t}{p_t y_s} \right)^{1/2} = \left(\frac{(\frac{p_s}{p_s y_s}) y_t}{(\frac{p_t}{p_t y_t}) y_s} \right)^{1/2}$$

$$= \left(\frac{\nabla_y' D_o^s(x_s, y_s) y_t}{\nabla_y' D_o^t(x_t, y_t) y_s} \right)^{1/2} \quad (Hotelling-Shephard\ lemma)$$

$$= \left(\frac{(x_s' C_s x_s)^{-1} (y_s' A_s y_t)}{(x_t' C_t x_t)^{-1} (y_t' A_t y_s)} \right)^{1/2}$$

$$= \left(\frac{(x_s' C_s x_s)^{-1} (y_s' A_s y_t)}{(x_t' C_t x_t)^{-1} (y_t' A_s y_s) \lambda_t} \right)^{1/2}$$

$$= \left(\frac{(x_s' C_s x_s)^{-1}}{(x_t' C_t x_t)^{-1}} \frac{1}{\lambda_t} \right)^{1/2} \quad (because\ y_s' A y_t = (y_s' A y_t)' = y_t' A y_s),$$

where we used the fact that, under the condition of the theorem (7.8.23), (7.8.24), (7.8.25), and (7.8.26), we have

$$D_o^\tau(x_\tau, y_\tau) = \left((y_\tau' A_\tau y_\tau)(x_\tau' C_\tau x_\tau)^{-1} \right)^{1/2} = 1, \quad \tau = s, t, \quad (7.8.28)$$

and so, with appropriate differentiability assumptions, also

$$\nabla_y' D_o^\tau(x_\tau, y_\tau) = (x_\tau' C_\tau x_\tau)^{-1} (y_\tau' A_\tau), \quad \tau = s, t. \quad (7.8.29)$$

Meanwhile,

$$Q_o^s := D_o^s(x_s, y_t)/D_o^s(x_s, y_s) = D_o^s(x_s, y_t) \quad (because\ D_o^s(x_s, y_s) = 1)$$

$$= \left((y_t' A_s y_t)(x_s' C_s x_s)^{-1} \right)^{1/2}$$

$$= \left(\frac{(y_t' A_s y_t)(x_s' C_s x_s)^{-1}}{(y_t' A_t y_t)(x_t' C_t x_t)^{-1}} \right)^{1/2} \quad (since\ (y_t' A y_t)(x_t' C_t x_t)^{-1} = D_o^t(x_t, y_t) = 1)$$

$$= \left(\frac{(y_t' A_s y_t)(x_s' C_s x_s)^{-1}}{\lambda_t (y_t' A_s y_t)(x_t' C_t x_t)^{-1}} \right)^{1/2} \quad (because\ A_t = \lambda_t A_s, \ \lambda_t > 0)$$

$$= \left(\frac{1}{\lambda_t} \frac{(x_s' C_s x_s)^{-1}}{(x_t' C_t x_t)^{-1}} \right)^{1/2}.$$

[14] Note that a similar generalization can be also made for the case of establishing relationships with the Törnqvist indexes, and we leave this to the readers as an exercise.

And, similarly,

$$Q_o^t = D_o^t(x_t, y_t)/D_o^t(x_t, y_s) = 1/D_o^t(x_t, y_s) \ (because \ D_o^t(x_t, y_t) = 1)$$

$$= \left(\frac{1}{(y_s' A_t y_s)(x_t' C_t x_t)^{-1}} \right)^{1/2}$$

$$= \left(\frac{(y_s' A_s y_s)(x_s' C_s x_s)^{-1}}{(y_s' A_t y_s)(x_t' C_t x_t)^{-1}} \right)^{1/2} \ (since \ (y_s' A y_s)(x_s' C_s x_s)^{-1} = D_o^s(x_s, y_s) = 1)$$

$$= \left(\frac{(y_s' A_s y_s)(x_s' C_s x_s)^{-1}}{\lambda_t (y_s' A_s y_s)(x_t' C_t x_t)^{-1}} \right)^{1/2} \ (because \ A_t = \lambda_t A_s, \ \lambda_t > 0)$$

$$= \left(\frac{1}{\lambda_t} \frac{(x_s' C_s x_s)^{-1}}{(x_t' C_t x_t)^{-1}} \right)^{1/2}. \qquad \square$$

In summary, the four theorems above say that when the distance functions are the Diewert functions or translog functional forms with certain restrictions on coefficients, then the *true* output or input quantity indexes can be estimated *exactly* through the corresponding Fisher Ideal or the Törnqvist output or input quantity indexes, respectively. Importantly, this means that, due to these theoretical results, there is no need to know or even to estimate the coefficients of the distance functions in such cases as long as one is comfortable assuming or believing their functional form is Diewert function or translog (with certain restrictions on coefficients) – then the true but unknown in practice quantity indexes are computed by applying the formulas of the Fisher Ideal or the Törnqvist quantity indexes, respectively.

Thus, as before, we can also say that because the Diewert functional forms or translog functional forms are the second-order approximations to virtually any unknown functional form, these theorems imply that the Fisher Ideal or the Törnqvist quantity indexes are *superlative* – they give the (second-order) approximations to the geometric mean of the *true* quantity indexes, for virtually any underlying technology. That is, formally, we have

$$Q_{o,st}^F \approx \left(Q_o^s(y_s, y_t, x_s) \times Q_o^t(y_s, y_t, x_t) \right)^{1/2} \approx Q_{o,st}^T, \qquad (7.8.30)$$

and

$$Q_{i,st}^F \approx \left(Q_i^s(x_s, x_t, y_s) \times Q_i^t(x_s, x_t, y_t) \right)^{1/2} \approx Q_{i,st}^T. \qquad (7.8.31)$$

These results give a strong economic theory justification for the use of the Fisher Ideal or the Törnqvist quantity indexes for practical estimation of changes in quantities as well as laying out the road to justifying the use of the Fisher and Törnqvist *productivity* indexes as outlined in the next subsection.

7.8.4   Relationships for the Productivity Indexes

Because the productivity indexes are either directly defined in terms of quantity indexes (as the Hicks–Moorsteen productivity indexes) or in terms of distance functions (as the Malmquist productivity indexes), the reader might expect that similar relationships as those derived above for the distance functions and quantity indexes must exist for the productivity indexes as well. We summarize some of these relationships below.

Theorem. *Assume revenue- (or profit-)maximizing and cost-minimizing behavior in both periods. Also let* $\varpi_j^* = (\varpi_{jt}(1 - \epsilon^t) + \varpi_{js}(1 - \epsilon^s))/2$, *while* $\varpi_{j\tau} = (w_{j\tau}x_{j\tau})/\sum_{j=1}^N w_{j\tau}x_{j\tau}$ *and* ϵ^τ *be the (local) input-oriented measure of scale elasticity in period* $\tau = s, t$. *Then we have*

$$MPI_o := \left(M_o^s(x_s, x_t, y_s, y_t) \times M_o^t(x_s, x_t, y_s, y_t) \right)^{1/2} \qquad (7.8.32)$$

$$= \frac{Q_{o,st}^T}{Q_{i,st}^T} \times \prod_{j=1}^N \left(\frac{x_{jt}}{x_{js}} \right)^{\varpi_j^*} =: TPI_{st},$$

if the output distance functions for both periods s and t be characterized by the translog functions with the second-order coefficients being equal for periods s and t, i.e., for $\tau = s, t$

$$\ln \psi^\tau(x, y) = a_o^\tau + \sum_{m=1}^M \alpha_m^\tau \ln y_m + \sum_{j=1}^N \beta_j^\tau \ln x_j + \frac{1}{2} \sum_{m=1}^M \sum_{r=1}^M \alpha_{mr}^\tau \ln y_m \ln y_r$$

$$+ \frac{1}{2} \sum_{l=1}^N \sum_{j=1}^N \beta_{lj}^\tau \ln x_l \ln x_j + \frac{1}{2} \sum_{m=1}^M \sum_{j=1}^N \gamma_{mj}^\tau \ln y_m \ln x_j,$$

$$(7.8.33)$$

where $\alpha_{mr}^s = \alpha_{mr}^t$, $\beta_{lj}^s = \beta_{lj}^t$ *and* $\gamma_{mj}^s = \gamma_{mj}^t$ *(in addition to the symmetry conditions* $\beta_{lj}^\tau = \beta_{jl}^\tau$ *and* $\alpha_{mr}^\tau = \alpha_{rm}^\tau$*), for all m, r, l, and j.*

This fundamental result and its original proof appeared in the seminal work of Caves et al. (1982a). In essence, this theorem tells us that we can obtain the theoretically appealing Malmquist Productivity Index even without full knowledge of the distance functions, as long as they are of the translog form with certain restrictions. One just has to apply the simple formula for the Törnqvist productivity index, and adjust them for the scale of input usage, as suggested in (7.8.32). In addition, similar to the previous cases, since the translog functional form is the second-order approximations to any unknown (twice-differentiable) functional form, this theorem also says that the Malmquist Productivity Index can be approximated by the Törnqvist productivity index, adjusted for the change in scale of input usage, and this holds for virtually any underlying technology (as long as it satisfies standard regularity conditions).

Moreover, Caves et al. (1982a) also pointed out formally that the measure of scale elasticity can be obtained without knowledge of the distance functions. Specifically, by assuming profit maximization behavior and decreasing returns to scale, one can estimate the scale elasticity as follows:[15]

$$\varepsilon_\tau = \frac{p_\tau y_\tau}{w_\tau x_\tau}, \quad \tau = s, t. \tag{7.8.34}$$

Note also that under CRS, which is a common assumption in empirical studies, and assuming profit maximizing behavior, which is also a very common assumption in empirical studies in economics, the expression in (7.8.34) yields unity and the last term in (7.8.32) disappears, making the output-oriented Malmquist productivity index exactly equal to the Törnqvist productivity index under the conditions stated in the theorem just above.

It should be clear that analogous results can be established for the input-oriented Malmquist productivity index, in which case the translog input distance functions with proper restrictions on coefficients would be involved. Moreover, analogous results can also be derived for other indexes, e.g., for the consumption price indexes, such as the Konüs cost-of-living index, etc. We leave these derivations to the readers as exercises (and see Caves et al., 1982a for details).

Meanwhile, note that similar results can also be established for the Fisher productivity index, in which case one would involve Diewert functional forms for the distance functions, as was originally proved by Diewert (1992a), and below we state and sketch a similar proof for a slightly generalized case, where the matrices augmenting inputs and outputs are allowed to change over time in the Hicks-neutral fashion.

Theorem. *Assuming revenue (or profit) maximizing and cost minimizing behavior in both periods, we have*

$$FPI_{st} = \left(\gamma_t \times \frac{1}{\lambda_t} \right)^{1/2} = MPI_o \tag{7.8.35}$$

$$= M_o^s(x_s, x_t, y_s, y_t) = M_o^t(x_s, x_t, y_s, y_t)$$

if the output distance functions for both periods $\tau = s, t$ are characterized by the Diewert functions of the following form

$$D_o^\tau(x, y) = \left((y' A_\tau y)(x' C_\tau x)^{-1} + (\alpha_\tau' y)(\beta_\tau' x^{-1})(y' B_\tau x^{-1}) \right)^{1/2}, \tag{7.8.36}$$

where $x^{-1} = (1/x_1, \ldots, 1/x_N)'$, $A_\tau = A_\tau'$, $C_\tau = C_\tau'$, B_τ are the parameter matrices and α_τ, β_τ are (column) parameter vectors, all conformable with (column) vectors x and y, satisfying the following sets of constraints

---

[15] Also see Zelenyuk (2013a) for related results and discussions.

$$\left((y_\tau' A_\tau y_\tau)(x_\tau' C_\tau x_\tau)^{-1}\right)^{1/2} = 1, \quad \tau = s, t, \tag{7.8.37}$$

and

$$A_t = \lambda_t A_s, \ \lambda_t > 0, \ C_t = \gamma_t C_s, \ \gamma_t > 0, \tag{7.8.38}$$

and either

$$B_s x_s^{-1} = \mathbf{0}_M, \ y_s' B_s = \mathbf{0}_N,$$
$$y_s' B_t x_s^{-1} = \beta_t' x_t^{-1} = \alpha_t' y_t = (\alpha_s' y_t)(\beta_s' x_t^{-1}) = 0, \tag{7.8.39}$$

or

$$B_t x_t^{-1} = \mathbf{0}_M, \ y_t' B_t = \mathbf{0}_N,$$
$$y_t' B_s x_t^{-1} = \beta_s' x_s^{-1} = \alpha_s' y_s = (\alpha_t' y_s)(\beta_t' x_s^{-1}) = 0. \tag{7.8.40}$$

Intuitively, this theorem says that we can obtain the theoretically appealing Malmquist Productivity Index even without full knowledge of the distance functions, as long as they are Diewert functions with certain restrictions. Indeed, one can apply the simple formula for the Fisher productivity index. Moreover, similar to the previous cases, since the Diewert functions is the second-order approximation to any unknown (twice-differentiable) functional form, this theorem also says that the Malmquist Productivity Index can be approximated by the Fisher productivity index, and this holds for essentially any underlying technology satisfying standard regularity conditions.

Proof. To sketch the proof of the previous theorem, first, note that we have

$$
\begin{aligned}
M_o^s(x_s, x_t, y_s, y_t) &:= D_o^s(x_t, y_t)/D_o^s(x_s, y_s) \\
&= D_o^s(x_t, y_t) \ (since \ D_o^s(x_s, y_s) = 1) \\
&= \left((y_t' A_s y_t)(x_t' C_s x_t)^{-1}\right)^{1/2} \\
&= \left((y_t' A_t y_t)(x_t' C_t x_t)^{-1} \frac{\gamma_t}{\lambda_t}\right)^{1/2} \\
&\quad (A_t = \lambda_t A_s, \ \lambda_t > 0, \ C_t = \gamma_t C_s, \ \gamma_t > 0) \\
&= \left(\frac{\gamma_t}{\lambda_t}\right)^{1/2}, \\
&\quad (because \left((y_t' A y_t)(x_t' C x_t)^{-1}\right)^{1/2} = D_o^t(x_t, y_t) = 1)
\end{aligned}
$$

and, similarly,

$$
\begin{aligned}
M_o^t(x_s, x_t, y_s, y_t) &:= D_o^t(x_t, y_t)/D_o^t(x_s, y_s) \\
&= 1/D_o^t(x_s, y_s) \ (because \ D_o^t(x_t, y_t) = 1) \\
&= 1/\left(\left((y_s' A_t y_s)(x_s' C_t x_s)^{-1}\right)^{1/2}\right)
\end{aligned}
$$

$$= 1 / \left(\left(\frac{\lambda_t}{\gamma_t} (y_s' A_s y_s)(x_s' C_s x_s)^{-1} \right)^{1/2} \right)$$

$$(A_t = \lambda_t A_s, \lambda_t > 0, \ C_t = \gamma_t C_s, \gamma_t > 0)$$

$$= \left(\frac{\gamma_t}{\lambda_t} \right)^{1/2}$$

$$(because \ \left((y_s' A y_s)(x_s' C x_s)^{-1} \right)^{1/2} = D_o^s(x_s, y_s) = 1).$$

I.e., we arrive to the same result, as is also the case for FPI_{st}, because

$$FPI_{st} := \frac{Q_{o,st}^F}{Q_{i,st}^F}$$

$$:= \left(\frac{p_s y_t}{p_s y_s} \times \frac{p_t y_t}{p_t y_s} \right)^{1/2} \Big/ \left(\frac{w_s x_t}{w_s x_s} \times \frac{w_t x_t}{w_t x_s} \right)^{1/2}$$

$$= \left(\frac{(\frac{p_s}{p_s y_s}) y_t}{(\frac{p_t}{p_t y_t}) y_s} \right)^{1/2} \Big/ \left(\frac{(\frac{w_s}{w_s x_s}) x_t}{(\frac{w_t}{w_t x_t}) x_s} \right)^{1/2}$$

$$= \left(\frac{\nabla_y' D_o^s(x_s, y_s) y_t}{\nabla_y' D_o^t(x_t, y_t) y_s} \right)^{1/2} \Big/ \left(\frac{\nabla_x' D_o^s(x_s, y_s) x_t}{\nabla_x' D_o^t(x_t, y_t) x_s} \right)^{1/2}$$

$$(using \ Hotelling - Shephard \ lemma)$$

$$= \left(\frac{(x_s' C_s x_s)^{-1}(y_s' A_s y_t)}{(x_t' C_t x_t)^{-1}(y_t' A_t y_s)} \right)^{1/2} \Big/ \left(\left(\frac{(x_t' C_s x_t)(y_s' A_s y_s)(x_s' C_s x_s)^{-2}}{(x_s' C_t x_t)(y_t' A_t y_t)(x_t' C_t x_t)^{-2}} \right)^{1/2} \right)$$

$$= \left(\frac{(y_s' A_s y_t)}{(y_t' A_s y_s) \lambda_t} \right)^{1/2} \Big/ \left(\left(\frac{(y_s' A_s y_s)(x_s' C_s x_s)^{-1}}{(y_t' A_t y_t)(x_t' C_t x_t)^{-1}} \right)^{1/2} \left(\frac{x_t' C_s x_s}{\gamma_t x_s' C_s x_t} \right)^{1/2} \right)$$

$$= \left(\frac{\gamma_t}{\lambda_t} \right)^{1/2}, \ (since \ x_t' C_\tau x_s = x_s' C_\tau x_t, \ y_s' A_\tau y_t = y_t' A_\tau y_s, \ and$$

$$since \ D_o^\tau(x_\tau, y_\tau) = [(y_\tau' A_\tau y_\tau)(x_\tau' C_\tau x_\tau)^{-1}]^{\frac{1}{2}} = 1, \ \tau = s, t).$$

$\square$

Note that an analogous result can be derived for the case of HMPI. This can be done directly as for the theorems above as well as indirectly, by involving the general result we stated in Chapter 4, about equivalence of MPI and HMPI, and showing that a particular distance function of interest, under certain restrictions, satisfies inverse homotheticity and CRS. Another indirect way is to involve the theorem above on equivalence of HMPI and FPI and then show that for the same technology, MPI and HMPI are equivalent. For pedagogical purposes, we summarize this special case below and include a sketch of the proof of it in the appendix.

Theorem. *Assuming revenue maximizing and cost minimizing behavior in both periods, we have*

$$M_o^\tau(x_s, x_t, y_s, y_t) = HM^\tau(x_s, x_t, y_s, y_t) = 1/M_i^\tau(y_s, y_t, x_s, x_t), \quad \tau = s, t,$$
(7.8.41)

for the case when the input distance functions for both periods s and t are characterized by the (simplified) Diewert functions of the following form

$$D_i^\tau(y, x) = \left((y' A_\tau y)^{-1} (x' C_\tau x) \right)^{1/2}, \quad \tau = s, t,$$
(7.8.42)

where $A_\tau = A_\tau'$, $C_\tau = C_\tau'$, are the parameter matrices all conformable with (column) vectors x and y, satisfying the following sets of constraints

$$\left((y_\tau' A_\tau y_\tau)(x_\tau' C_\tau x_\tau)^{-1} \right)^{1/2} = 1, \quad \tau = s, t.$$
(7.8.43)

It is worth noting that, unlike the previous theorem, this last theorem does not require Hicks-neutrality, yet it restricts the distance function to be a simplified Diewert function, which makes it inverse homothetic. If we also assume Hicks-neutrality, then due to the previous theorem we obtain an equivalence with the Fisher productivity index, implying that the Fisher productivity index can be used to compute HMPI exactly if one is willing to believe in the assumptions underlying the theorem (and Hicks-neutrality) or approximately, due to the approximation nature of the Diewert functions. One can use similar logic to show the equivalence between the MPI and HMPI via the Törnqvist productivity index (under translog functional form), as was done in Mizobuchi (2017b). Also, see Mizobuchi and Zelenyuk (2018) for some recent developments involving Quadratic-mean-of-order-r Indexes for productivity analysis.

Finally, note that the results in this chapter assumed no technical inefficiency and so, in a sense, should be viewed as benchmark or "idealist" cases. In practice, the existence of inefficiency and its variation across firms can hardly be denied and often is too naive to assume. Therefore, it is very important to know the ways to estimate the true productivity indexes like MPI, HMPI, etc. in a framework that admits the possibility of inefficiency, and we discuss this in Chapter 8.

7.9 CONCLUDING REMARKS ON THE LITERATURE

The origins of the theory of index numbers go back to at least the nineteenth century, to the seminal works of Laspeyres (1871), Paasche (1874), as well as the early twentieth-century fundamental contributions of Fisher (1921, 1922), Frisch (1930, 1936), Törnqvist (1936). We only briefly outlined this approach here, focusing on the relationship of indexes in the statistical approach to the indexes developed within the economic approach, which we also briefly considered in Chapter 4.

Interestingly, the statistical approach to index numbers preceded the economic approach by about a century. The estimators proposed in the statistical approach were grounded mainly in mathematical properties, but from the economic point of view they were in some sense *ad hoc*, until the fundamental studies on economic index numbers in 1970s, 1980s and 1990s – especially due to the seminal works of Diewert (1971, 1974c, 1976, 1980, 1981, 1983a, 1992a,b), Caves et al. (1982a,b), and Diewert (1992a,b), to mention just a few. Also see the classical works of Diewert (1981), Diewert and Nakamura (1993) and Balk (1998, 2004), Balk and Diewert (2001), Balk (2008), and Mizobuchi and Zelenyuk (2018) for some recent developments, as well as "The Lectures of Diewert" where more formal and historical details can be found.[16]

Here, we gave a summary of some of the main results on this subject – covering it in more detail would require a separate book, or even several books, so we leave it for future endeavors, while in the meantime we recommend learning the details from the works we cite here and references therein.

7.10 EXERCISES

1. Prove that $Q_{st}^{F\ indirect} = Q_{st}^{F}$.
2. Prove that $Q_{st}^{P\ indirect} = Q_{st}^{L}$.
3. Prove that $Q_{st}^{L\ indirect} = Q_{st}^{P}$.
4. Prove that $Q_{st}^{T\ indirect} \neq Q_{st}^{T}$.
5. Prove that the only price index that satisfies the positivity (7.6.1a), quantity reversal (7.6.15a), time reversal (7.6.14a), and factor reversal (7.6.17a) properties is the Fisher ideal price index defined in (7.2.5).
6. Prove that the Laspeyres and Paasche price and quantity indexes do not satisfy the
   (a) reversal properties (7.6.14a), (7.6.17a) and (7.6.14b), (7.6.17b),
   (b) transitivity property (7.6.20a) and (7.6.20b),
   (c) other tests listed above.
7. Prove that the Törnqvist (or translog) price and quantity indexes do not satisfy
   (a) the constant weight tests (7.6.4a), (7.6.4b),
   (b) the Paasche and Laspeyres bounding property (7.6.13a),
   (c) the reversal properties (7.6.15a), (7.6.17a) and (7.6.15b), (7.6.17b),
   (d) all the monotonicity properties (7.6.18a), (7.6.19a) and (7.6.18b), (7.6.19b),
   (e) the transitivity property (7.6.20a), (7.6.20b),
   (f) the product test (7.4.1).

---

[16] http://economics.ubc.ca/faculty-and-staff/w-erwin-diewert/ (accessed on 15/9/2017).

8. Prove that the indirect Törnqvist price and quantity indexes fail
   (a) the identity property (7.6.3a)–(7.6.3b),
   (b) the mean value properties (7.6.12a), (7.6.13a) and (7.6.12b), (7.6.13b).
9. Prove (7.8.4).
10. Prove (7.8.5).
11. Prove (7.8.8).
12. Prove (7.8.9).
13. Prove (7.8.12).
14. Prove (7.8.14).
15. Prove (7.8.32).

7.11 APPENDIX

Here we sketch a proof (in the spirit of Diewert (1992a) of equivalence of Fisher input quantity indexes and the Malmquist input quantity indexes.

Proof. First of all, note that

$$Q_i^F = \left(Q_i^L \times Q_i^P\right)^{1/2} = \left(\frac{w_s x_t}{w_s x_s} \times \frac{w_t x_t}{w_t x_s}\right)^{1/2} = \left(\frac{(\frac{w_s}{w_s x_s})x_t}{(\frac{w_t}{w_t x_t})x_s}\right)^{1/2}$$

$$= \left(\frac{\nabla_x' D_i^s(y_s, x_s)x_t}{\nabla_x' D_i^t(y_t, x_t)x_s}\right)^{1/2}$$

$$(using\ the\ Hotelling-Shephard\ lemma)$$

$$= \left(\frac{\nabla_x'\left([(y_s'A_s y_s)^{-1}(x_s'C_s x_s)]^{\frac{1}{2}}\right)x_t}{\nabla_x'\left([(y_t'A_t y_t)^{-1}(x_t'C_t x_t)]^{\frac{1}{2}}\right)x_s}\right)^{1/2}$$

$$= \left(\frac{(y_s'A_s y_s)^{-1}(x_s'C_s x_t)}{(y_t'A_t y_t)^{-1}(x_t'C_t x_s)}\right)^{1/2}$$

$$= \left(\frac{y_t'A_t y_t}{y_s'A_s y_s}\frac{1}{\gamma_t}\right)^{1/2},$$

$$(because\ x_t'C_t x_s = x_s'\gamma_t C_s x_t),$$

where we used the fact that, under the condition of the theorem, $\forall(x, y) \in T^\tau$, $\tau = s, t$ we have

$$D_i^\tau(y_\tau, x_\tau) = \left((y_\tau'A_\tau y_\tau)^{-1}(x_\tau'C_\tau x_\tau)\right)^{1/2} = 1, \quad \tau = s, t,$$

and so, with appropriate differentiability, we have

$$\nabla_x' D_i^\tau(y_\tau, x_\tau) = (y_\tau'A_\tau y_\tau)^{-1}x_\tau'C_\tau, \quad \tau = s, t.$$

Furthermore, note that

$$Q_i^s = D_i^s(y_s, x_t)/D_i^s(y_s, x_s) = D_i^s(y_s, x_t) \ (because \ D_i^s(y_s, x_s) = 1)$$

$$= \left((y_s' A_s y_s)^{-1}(x_t' C_s x_t) + (\alpha_s' y_s^{-1})(\beta_s' x_t)((y_s^{-1})' B_s x_t) \right)^{1/2}$$

$$= \left((y_s' A_s y_s)^{-1}(x_t' C_s x_t) \right)^{1/2}$$

$$= \left[\frac{(y_s' A_s y_s)^{-1}(x_t' C_s x_t)}{(y_t' A_t y_t)^{-1}(x_t' C_t x_t)} \right]^{1/2} \quad (since \ (y_t' A_t y_t)^{-1}(x_t' C x_t) = D_i^t(y_t, x_t) = 1)$$

$$= \left[\frac{(y_s' A_s y_s)^{-1}(x_t' C_s x_t)}{(y_t' A_t y_t)^{-1}(x_t' \gamma_t C_s x_t)} \right]^{1/2} \quad (because \ C_t = \gamma_t C_s)$$

$$= \left[\frac{(y_s' A_s y_s)^{-1}}{(y_t' A_t y_t)^{-1}} \frac{1}{\gamma_t} \right]^{1/2},$$

and, similarly, we also have

$$Q_i^t = D_i^t(y_t, x_t)/D_i^t(y_t, x_s) = 1/D_i^t(y_t, x_s) \ (because \ D_i^t(y_t, x_t) = 1)$$

$$= \frac{1}{\left[(y_t' A_t y_t)^{-1}(x_s' C_t x_s) + (\alpha_t' y_t^{-1})(\beta_t' x_s)((y_t^{-1})' B_t x_s) \right]^{1/2}}$$

$$= \frac{1}{\left[(y_t' A_t y_t)^{-1}(x_s' C_t x_s) \right]^{1/2}} \quad (imposing \ constraints)$$

$$= \left[\frac{(y_s' A_s y_s)^{-1}(x_s' C_s x_s)}{(y_t' A_t y_t)^{-1}(x_s' C_t x_s)} \right]^{1/2} \quad (since \ (y_s' A_s y_s)^{-1} x_s' C x_s = D_i^s(y_s, x_s) = 1)$$

$$= \left[\frac{(y_s' A_s y_s)^{-1}(x_s' C_s x_s)}{(y_t' A_t y_t)^{-1}(x_s' \gamma_t C_s x_s)} \right]^{1/2} \quad (because \ C_t = \gamma_t C_s)$$

$$= \left[\frac{(y_s' A_s y_s)^{-1}}{(y_t' A_t y_t)^{-1}} \frac{1}{\gamma_t} \right]^{1/2}.$$

$\square$

Below we sketch a proof of equivalence of MPI and HMPI under the Diewert functions.

Proof. Using the same logic as in the proofs above, we first arrive at

$$HMPI^s = \frac{Q_o^s}{Q_i^s} = \frac{D_o^s(x_s, y_t)/D_o^s(x_s, y_s)}{D_i^s(y_s, x_t)/D_i^s(y_s, x_s)}$$

$$= \frac{D_o^s(x_s, y_t)}{D_i^s(y_s, x_t)} = \left(\frac{(y_t' A_s y_t)(x_s' C_s x_s)^{-1}}{(y_s' A_s y_s)^{-1}(x_t' C_s x_t)} \right)^{1/2}$$

$$= \left((y_t' A_s y_t)(x_t' C_s x_t)^{-1} \right)^{1/2},$$

and

$$
\begin{aligned}
HMPI^t &= \frac{Q_o^t}{Q_i^t} = \frac{D_o^t(x_t, y_t)/D_o^t(x_t, y_s)}{D_i^t(y_t, x_t)/D_i^t(y_t, x_s)} \\
&= \frac{1/D_o^t(x_t, y_s)}{1/D_i^t(y_t, x_s)} = \left(\frac{1/((y_s' A_t y_s)(x_t' C_t x_t)^{-1})}{1/((y_t' A_t y_t)^{-1}(x_s' C_t x_s))} \right)^{1/2} \\
&= \left(\frac{(y_t' A_t y_t)^{-1}(x_t' C_t x_t)}{(y_s' A_t y_s)(x_s' C_t x_s)^{-1}} \right)^{1/2} = \left(\frac{1}{(y_s' A_t y_s)(x_s' C_t x_s)^{-1}} \right)^{1/2},
\end{aligned}
$$

and therefore

$$
\begin{aligned}
HMPI^{st} &= \left(HMPI^s \times HMPI^t \right)^{1/2} \\
&= \left(\frac{\left((y_t' A_s y_t)(x_t' C_s x_t)^{-1} \right)^{1/2}}{\left((y_s' A_t y_s)(x_s' C_t x_s)^{-1} \right)^{1/2}} \right)^{1/2} \\
&= \left(\frac{D_o^s(x_t, y_t)}{D_o^t(x_s, y_s)} \right)^{1/2} \\
&= \left(\frac{D_o^s(x_t, y_t)}{D_o^s(x_s, y_s)} \times \frac{D_o^t(x_t, y_t)}{D_o^t(x_s, y_s)} \right)^{1/2} \\
&= MPI_o.
\end{aligned}
$$

$\square$

CHAPTER 8

Envelopment-Type Estimators

One of the most popular approaches in the theoretical measurement and empirical estimation of the efficiency of various economic systems is known as *Data Envelopment Analysis*, abbreviated as DEA. This approach is rooted in and cohesive with theoretical economic modeling via the so-called *Activity Analysis Models* and is estimated via the powerful linear programming approach.[1]

In this chapter, we consider a variety of models that can be used to estimate particular types of technologies: constant, nonincreasing and variable returns to scale, convex and non-convex technologies. This chapter does not exhaust everything that has been suggested in the literature – fulfilling such a task would be practically impossible in one chapter. The goal is more modest, yet practically valuable: we focus on the most popular methods and consider their "step-by-step construction," intuition, some of the most important properties, some interesting variations and modifications, etc. We pay attention to aspects that we consider very useful for a reader to advance in his/her own research and, possibly, advance the frontier of the research.

8.1 INTRODUCTION TO ACTIVITY ANALYSIS MODELING

An economist's approach to thinking about nonparametric efficiency measurement can be viewed through the so-called *Activity Analysis Models* – a way of mathematically modeling production relationships. An activity analysis model (AAM) can be defined as a set of mathematical formulations designed to mimic a technology set from the observed data of some real-world production process

---

[1] The name DEA was coined in the seminal paper of Charnes et al. (1978), who used a mathematical programming perspective to refine and generalize the Debreu–Shephard–Farrell approach to estimation of production efficiency. It is their seminal work that appears to have done the most to popularize this method all over the world, especially in the business/management research community. We give more remarks on the related literature below, especially at the end of this chapter.

of interest. The best way to understand such modeling is to actually build a few AAMs.

There are two fundamental assumptions behind most AAMs. The first fundamental assumption we will always make for AAMs in this book is that all decision making units (DMUs) have *access* to the *same technology* (which can be characterized by the technology set T that satisfies the main regularity axioms; see Chapter 1). This assumption is important to justify the estimation of *one frontier* from the full sample – often called the (observed) *best practice frontier* for the population represented by that sample. Note that this assumption does not imply that all firms have the same access, nor does it imply that all firms use this technology to full capacity. On the contrary, it is allowed that, for various reasons, each particular firm may not be on the frontier. The reasons for "deviations" from the technology frontier are well-explained by asymmetric information and behavioral economics theories and are documented in many empirical studies.[2] These could be managerial reasons (lack of full information and related principal-agent problems, poor self-control, limited cognitive abilities, etc.), due to exogenous regulator policy that may also involve unconscious or ideology-driven mistakes, various macroeconomic factors, etc. The goal of a researcher then is to estimate such deviations from the frontier and analyze their specific reasons, to understand and recommend how to improve the performance of particular DMUs, industries, countries, the entire world.

The second fundamental assumption of most AAMs is that all observed input–output combinations (x^k, y^k), $k = 1, \ldots, n$ are *feasible* under T, i.e., $(x^k, y^k) \in T$ for every observation or DMU $k = 1, \ldots, n$. Together, these two fundamental assumptions can be formally stated as,

$$\Pr\{(x^k, y^k) \in T\} = 1, \ \forall k = 1, \ldots, n, \tag{8.1.1}$$

where $\Pr\{A\}$ means probability of the event A. Therefore, with such assumptions, no errors of the type that would make an observation go outside of the technology set are allowed. In the case when such errors are expected, a check for the so-called "super-efficient" outliers is recommended before using an AAM approach.[3] All the deviations from an estimated frontier can then be viewed as estimates of technical inefficiency relative to an observed best-practice frontier, i.e., a frontier constructed from observed data. These estimates are therefore understood as stochastic and further statistical analysis on them can be performed.[4]

---

[2] E.g., see Greenwald and Stiglitz (1986), Thaler and Sunstein (2009), Bloom et al. (2016), to mention just a few.

[3] E.g., standard statistical procedures for checking for outliers is usually recommended, such as starting from the simplest ones like box-plots and histograms for each variable. One can also use stochastic versions of DEA (see Simar, 2007 and Simar and Zelenyuk, 2011).

[4] Note that while the true (and usually unobserved) frontier is viewed here as a "deterministic" object, the AAM-implied frontier depends on a sample and thus inherits random nature (and related sampling and asymptotic distributions) from the randomness of the sample.

Suppose at this stage that we believe the production process that we want to analyze exhibits constant returns to scale (CRS), at least in the neighborhood of interest and for the observed data. This means that, for any DMU $k \in \{1, \ldots, n\}$, any *radial* expansion or contraction made via an arbitrary non-negative scalar $z^k \geq 0$ will remain in T.[5] Formally, this would mean,

$$(x^k, y^k) \in T \implies z^k(x^k, y^k) \in T, \forall z^k \geq 0, \ k = 1, \ldots, n. \quad (8.1.2)$$

Suppose, in addition, that the technology we want to analyze also exhibits the *additivity property*, which says that if two activities (say k and j) are *feasible* then their sum is also feasible. Formally, if $(x^k, y^k) \in T$ and $(x^j, y^j) \in T$ then $(x^k + x^j, y^k + y^j) \in T$, for any $k, j = 1, \ldots, n$, or more generally:

$$\text{if } (x^k, y^k) \in T, \quad \forall k = 1, \ldots, n \text{ then } \left(\sum_{k=1}^{n} x^k, \sum_{k=1}^{n} y^k \right) \in T. \quad (8.1.3)$$

The CRS and additivity assumptions together, then imply that

$$\left(\sum_{k=1}^{n} z^k x^k, \sum_{k=1}^{n} z^k y^k \right) \in T, \ z^k \geq 0. \quad (8.1.4)$$

Finally, let us also impose the property of *free (strong) disposability* of all inputs and all outputs on this technology. To do so, recall that the free input disposability was theoretically defined (in Chapter 1) as

$$x^o \in L(y) \implies x \in L(y), \quad \forall x \geq x^o, \ y \in \mathfrak{R}_+^M. \quad (8.1.5)$$

So, let $x^o = \sum_{k=1}^{n} z^k x^k$ then (8.1.5) says $\sum_{k=1}^{n} z^k x^k \in L(y) \implies x \in L(y)$ for *all* x that satisfy

$$x \geq \sum_{k=1}^{n} z^k x^k. \quad (8.1.6)$$

Similarly, the free (strong) output disposability was defined as

$$y^o \in P(x) \implies y \in P(x), \quad \forall y \leq y^o, \ x \in \mathfrak{R}_+^N. \quad (8.1.7)$$

So, let $y^o = \sum_{k=1}^{n} z^k y^k$ then (8.1.7) says $\sum_{k=1}^{n} z^k y^k \in P(x) \implies y \in P(x), \forall y \in \mathfrak{R}_+^M$ such that

$$y \leq \sum_{k=1}^{n} z^k y^k. \quad (8.1.8)$$

---

[5] Note that the original definition of CRS requires $z^k > 0$ and for the computational convenience (yet without any practical loss) we extend this to $z^k \geq 0$ in AAM contexts. This will also ensure the origin is in the technology set estimated via this AAM, as required by the full singularity condition discussed in Chapter 1.

Overall, our technology so far is mimicked by some set $\hat{T}$ that allows all the combinations (x, y) that satisfy (8.1.1), (8.1.2), (8.1.3), (8.1.6), and (8.1.8) that we have imposed on the technology from our knowledge (expectations, beliefs) about it. In fact, only three of these restrictions – (8.1.2), (8.1.6), and (8.1.8) – are enough, since the rest were just auxiliary. Formally, our technology set that satisfies (8.1.2), (8.1.6), and (8.1.8) is defined as

$$\hat{T} \equiv \{(x, y) \in \Re_+^N \times \Re_+^M : y \leq \sum_{k=1}^{n} z^k y^k, \sum_{k=1}^{n} z^k x^k \leq x, z^k \geq 0, k = 1, \ldots, n\},$$

(8.1.9)

and is the smallest *convex free disposal cone* that fits the observed data $\{(x^k, y^k) : k = 1, \ldots, n\}$.[6]

If we do not know any other property of the technology set T, then $\hat{T}$, in some sense, summarizes our "best" understanding about T. As we will discuss in the next chapter, under certain assumptions it is a consistent estimator of T, belonging to the class of (nonparametric) maximum likelihood estimators.

In terms of the output sets, the technology can be estimated with

$$\hat{P}(x) \equiv \{y \in \Re_+^M : y \leq \sum_{k=1}^{n} z^k y^k, \sum_{k=1}^{n} z^k x^k \leq x, z^k \geq 0, k = 1, \ldots, n\},$$

(8.1.10)

and in terms of the input requirement set, the technology is estimated with

$$\hat{L}(y) \equiv \{x \in \Re_+^N : y \leq \sum_{k=1}^{n} z^k y^k, \sum_{k=1}^{n} z^k x^k \leq x, z^k \geq 0, k = 1, \ldots, n\}.$$

(8.1.11)

The intuition of imposing assumptions (8.1.2), (8.1.6), and (8.1.8) is easier to understand through geometry. Figure 8.1 illustrates a one-input–one-output example and only two activities (observations), k and j. The CRS assumption imposes that all the points on the rays from the origin and through the observed points must be in T, e.g., as points $z^k(x^k, y^k)$ and $z^j(x^j, y^j)$, $\forall z^k, z^j \geq 0$. The additivity assumption, when added to the CRS assumption, implies that all the points "in-between" any two rays in T (as for example point A, for which z^j, z^k happen to be 1) must also be in T. Finally, the assumption of free disposability of inputs and outputs implies that all the points to the right (or down) from these rays are also in T – so here, in fact, the "steepest" ray defines the frontier of the technology in this two-dimensional case.

The formulation (8.1.9) is often referred to as the Data Envelopment Analysis model, or the DEA-*estimator*, for technology under the assumption of CRS and (although rarely mentioned, yet also assumed) additivity and free disposability assumptions. We will refer to it as DEA-CRS formulation.

---

[6] Note that convexity of T here is not assumed directly but is implied by CRS and additivity assumptions – check!

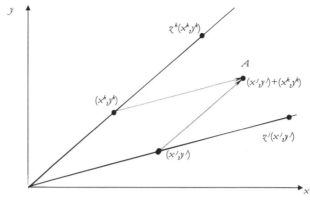

Figure 8.1 One-input–one-output example of constructing AAM under CRS.

In turn, this estimator can be used to formulate the DEA-*estimator of the Farrell output-oriented technical efficiency* score of any (x, y) allocation (e.g., a real or a hypothetical observation), under the assumptions of CRS (along with free disposability of all inputs and all outputs and the additivity), as follows:

$$\widehat{TE}(x, y) \equiv \max_{\theta, z^1, \ldots, z^n} \theta \tag{8.1.12a}$$

s.t.

$$\sum_{k=1}^{n} z^k y_m^k \geq \theta \, y_m, \; m = 1, \ldots, M, \tag{8.1.12b}$$

$$\sum_{k=1}^{n} z^k x_l^k \leq x_l, \; l = 1, \ldots, N, \tag{8.1.12c}$$

$$\theta \geq 0, \; z^k \geq 0, \; k = 1, \ldots, n. \tag{8.1.12d}$$

A few important remarks are in order. First, note that for better clarity we have written the constraints (8.1.12b)–(8.1.12d) in a more explicit form than before in (8.1.9) – using scalar rather than vector notation.

Second, note that inputs and outputs enter this formulation not as optimization variables, but as constants – actual observations on inputs and outputs ($k = 1, \ldots, n$).

Third, note that if we want to estimate the efficiency score of a particular DMU from the data, e.g., for some (x^j, y^j), $j \in \{1, \ldots, n\}$, then (x^j, y^j) would enter the formulation twice: once with all the data, on the l.h.s. of the constraints, where it is used in "forming the technology set," and the second time as the observation on the r.h.s. of (8.1.12b) and (8.1.12c), where it is used as a starting point of measuring efficiency towards the estimated frontier.

Fourth, note that the optimizing variables in (8.1.12a)–(8.1.12d) are of two types: (i) θ, which also happens to be the entire objective function here, whose optimal value will give the estimated efficiency score, and (ii) the intensity variables, $z^k \geq 0$, $k = 1, \ldots, n$, that help to form the frontier. In fact, the optimal values of the intensity variables carry valuable information about the optimal (from the observed activities) peers for an allocation (x, y). For example, if optimization of (8.1.12a)–(8.1.12d) for a particular sample $\{(x^k, y^k) : k = 1, \ldots, n\}$ gave $z^3 = 0.3$, $z^5 = 0.2$ and $z^7 = 0.5$, while all other intensity variables are zeros, then the observations 3, 5, and 7 in that sample are the optimal peers for the activity (x, y), in the sense that they serve as the weights in a linear combination that determine coordinates of the radial projection of (x, y) onto the frontier of the output sets, while keeping x fixed. Formally, we will have here $y \times \widehat{TE}(x, y) \leqq 0.3y^3 + 0.2y^5 + 0.5y^7$, i.e., none of the observations here is an "exact peer" (in the sense of radial projection of y onto the frontier of the output set), yet observation 7 here can be viewed as the closest peer since it has the largest value of z, followed by observation 3 and then observation 5.[7] Upon obtaining such information, the empirical researcher may look in more detail into the case studies for each peer, to better understand the reasons for the inefficiency of an allocation (x, y) and make recommendations on how to improve performance of a DMU of interest.[8]

Fifth, as the reader might have noticed already, the objective function in this formulation and all the constraints are linear! That is, the optimization problem (8.1.12a)–(8.1.12d) is a linear programming (LP) problem – a "well-behaved" and well-studied optimization problem that can be (relatively) easily solved with any LP-solver (e.g., Simplex method, interior point method, etc.), incorporated in many mathematical/statistical software packages (e.g., MATLAB, Gauss, SAS, Excel, etc.).[9]

Sixth, note that $\widehat{TE}(x, y) \geq 1$ for any allocation $(x, y) \in \hat{T}$, and so unless it equals one and thus indicates 100 percent technical efficiency in a Farrell sense, it actually gives an "inefficiency score" for (x, y) if $\widehat{TE}(x, y) > 1$, while its reciprocal $(1/\widehat{TE}(x, y))$ gives the corresponding efficiency score. For this reason, some researchers prefer starting with $1/\widehat{TE}(x, y)$. Both approaches are correct as long as they are defined and explained clearly and used consistently.

---

[7] Note that in the cases when CRS and NIRS are assumed, the sum of the intensity variables may or may not sum to unity, and so to interpret the weights of peers in percentage terms one may need to normalize the intensity variables by the sum $\sum_{k=1}^{n} z^k$.

[8] Importantly, note that in general there might be different combinations of peers, i.e., the intensity variables are not unique and considering other possible combinations may shed additional light in an empirical analysis.

[9] The LP method has been well described and illustrated in many books and articles (e.g., see Dantzig, 1963). To promptly get a taste of its power, it is insightful to recall a famous example from Dantzig (1982), where he pointed out the complexity of what these days seems to be a simple problem of optimal assigning 70 workers to 70 jobs: solving such a problem would be impossible even if many powerful computers were working in parallel on comparing each combination with another, even if they started at the time of the "big bang" – because it involves comparing 70! possible combinations: a number larger than 10^{100}. On the other hand, this task can be solved rather quickly when formulated as a linear programming problem and then approached with the Simplex method he invented. Clearly, the activity analysis/DEA models that involve many firms using many inputs and outputs in different combinations are much harder problems than Dantzig's example, yet the formulation via a linear programming problem helps in solving them within seconds on modern computers.

Finally, note that the constraints in (8.1.12a)–(8.1.12d) are inequalities and, while optimal solutions may turn some of them into equalities, others may (and often do) remain inequalities. The values that can be added to turn each of the remaining inequalities in (8.1.13b) into equalities are referred to as output slacks for the particular allocation (x, y) and under the particular assumptions on technology. Similarly, the values that can be subtracted to turn each of the remaining inequalities in (8.1.13c) into equalities are referred to as input slacks for the particular allocation (x, y) and under the particular assumptions on technology. Sometimes these slacks are written out explicitly in the AAM formulation and sometimes not (as in a canonical LP formulation), yet they are typically available in the standard output of an LP problem solver. While most of the empirical research appears to focus on the estimates of technical efficiency, the estimates of the slacks (both output and inputs) and analysis of their reasons is also important to understand the ways to improve the efficiency of individual units or their groups. Indeed, as we have seen in Chapter 3, an allocation (x, y) can have full Farrell-type efficiency, yet may still have quite large slacks in some outputs or some inputs. By removing these slacks, the DMUs may gain further efficiency, e.g., hospitals may cure more patients to reduce their suffering and potentially save more lives, banks may provide more loans to people and firms, universities, energy generators and distributors, water suppliers and other businesses may lower costs and their fees for consumers while delivering the same or greater quantity and quality of services.

A similar discussion holds for the input orientation. Specifically, here, the DEA-*estimator of the Farrell input-oriented technical efficiency* score of a DMU with an allocation (x, y), under the assumption of CRS (along with additivity and free disposability of all inputs and all outputs), is obtained from

$$\widehat{TE}_i(y, x) \equiv \min_{\theta, z^1, \dots, z^n} \theta \tag{8.1.13a}$$

s.t.

$$\sum_{k=1}^{n} z^k y_m^k \geq y_m, \quad m = 1, \dots, M, \tag{8.1.13b}$$

$$\sum_{k=1}^{n} z^k x_l^k \leq \theta\, x_l, \quad l = 1, \dots, N, \tag{8.1.13c}$$

$$\theta \geq 0, \quad z^k \geq 0, \quad k = 1, \dots, n. \tag{8.1.13d}$$

Again, this is an LP problem that can be solved via any standard LP solver. Also note that here we have $\widehat{TE}_i(y, x) = 1/\widehat{TE}(x, y)$ due to CRS (see the theoretical discussions in Chapter 1 and Chapter 3 and check!).[10]

---

[10] In the literature, the DEA approach with CRS assumption is often referred to as the CCR model/approach, due to the seminal work of Charnes et al. (1978), who considered the input-oriented version, while the single output case of this approach was considered by Farrell (1957). See the end of this chapter for more details on this.

Analogous remarks we made about the output-oriented DEA estimator apply for the input-oriented DEA estimator. Importantly, note that the two orientations generally may yield different peers and different slacks, which should not be surprising since they presume different objectives.

Meanwhile, it is also worth noting that some regularity conditions on the data need to be imposed for (8.1.9)–(8.1.11), and typically on other AAMs, namely:

$$i. \quad \sum_{k=1}^{n} x_l^k > 0, \quad l = 1, \ldots, N, \tag{8.1.14}$$

$$ii. \quad \sum_{k=1}^{n} y_m^k > 0, \quad m = 1, \ldots, M, \tag{8.1.15}$$

$$iii. \quad \sum_{l=1}^{N} x_l^k > 0, \quad k = 1, \ldots, n, \tag{8.1.16}$$

$$iv. \quad \sum_{m=1}^{M} y_m^k > 0, \quad k = 1, \ldots, n. \tag{8.1.17}$$

In words, the first and second conditions say that at least one *activity* (i.e., observation: firm, plant, etc.) uses some positive amount of *each* input and produces some positive amount of *each* output. Meanwhile, the third and fourth conditions say that at least one input and at least one output must be used in each activity.[11]

Note that these conditions effectively remove the problematic singularity points (see Chapter 1) from consideration, yet also have a practical appeal. Indeed, if some inputs were not used or some outputs were not produced by any activity (firm), there is usually no practical reason to treat it as an (active) input or output, respectively, in the AAM. Similarly, if there is an observation that used no input or produced no output, then there is no reason to treat it as an (active) observation and it can be removed from the working sample used for AAM.

In principle, one can also impose various additional constraints onto an AAM, with a goal to better mimic the real production process. This, however, should be done carefully – because it may (and typically does) compromise other desirable properties implied by previously added constraints, e.g., convexity, CRS, additivity, free disposability, etc.

Some constraints may also substantially complicate the corresponding mathematical programming problems, turning them into nonlinear problems, possibly making them hybrids with integer-programming problems, and potentially making them much harder to compute and less resistant to problems of infeasibility, selection of inferior local optima and degenerate solutions.[12]

---

[11] See Karlin (1959) for more discussions.

[12] By degenerate solutions we mean here solutions that are correct, yet of little practical value, but an optimization routine is stuck there.

Moreover, in general, note that additional constraints on an optimization problem never lead to more optimal solutions and, in fact, often lead to suboptimal solutions.[13] In the case of the DEA approach for efficiency estimation, this means that adding constraints to an AAM never lead to lower efficiency (higher inefficiency) estimates of any particular DMU, and often (though not always) lead to an increase of efficiency (decrease of inefficiency) estimates. In extreme cases, when "too many constraints" are imposed, then too many (or even all) DMUs may look 100 percent efficient, while in reality some of them may be very inefficient.[14]

As a result, adding constraints to AAM typically lowers the discriminative power of the DEA method, potentially misrepresenting the reality as much more efficient than it is. All of these caveats suggest that any constraint in AAM should be added with a good judgment, based on well-grounded justifications.

Despite these caveats, additional constraints sometimes may help in better modeling real production processes and so this topic received substantial attention in the literature and in the next sections we will consider the most popular example of additional constraints – imposing a non-CRS structure.

8.2 NON-CRS ACTIVITY ANALYSIS MODELS

The AAM in the previous section imposed constant returns to scale on technology – a property that is very common in theoretical models in economics, yet it may not always be a relevant assumption to impose on technology. Indeed, the scale properties of technology are often what researchers want to estimate and test. In this section, we discuss how to relax the CRS assumption.

Let us suppose now that we believe the technology satisfies nonincreasing returns to scale (NIRS; see Chapter 1). This means that for any observation, (x^k, y^k), $k = 1, \ldots, n$, all of which are in the technology set T *by assumption* (8.1.1), any *radial* contraction (but not any expansion) made via multiplying by a scalar $z^k \in [0, 1]$ will also remain in T. Intuitively, this means that equiproportional divisibility of activities is always feasible.[15] Formally, this can be stated as

$$(x^k, y^k) \in T \;\Rightarrow\; z^k(x^k, y^k) \in T, \; \forall z^k : 0 \leq z^k \leq 1, \; k = 1, \ldots, n. \quad (8.2.1)$$

The assumption of *additivity* that we made in our first AAM must now be modified to be coherent with the NIRS condition. This can be done by imposing (instead of (8.1.3)) a property that we will refer to as *sub-additivity* of activities, formally defined as a situation where $(x^k, y^k) \in T$ and $(x^j, y^j) \in T$ together, imply that $(z^k x^k + z^j x^j, z^k y^k + z^j y^j) \in T$, for any z^k, z^j such that $0 \leq z^k + z^j \leq 1$, $z^k, z^j \geq 0$, or more generally,

---

[13] Only non-binding constraints will not lead to any change in the optimal values.

[14] Of course, how many is "too many" varies across different samples, different dimensions, and different production processes.

[15] Note that the original definition of NIRS would require $0 < z^k \leq 1$, and again, the strict inequality is weakened here for the AAM for computational convenience.

$$(x^k, y^k) \in T, \ \forall k = 1, \ldots, n \Rightarrow \left(\sum_{k=1}^{n} z^k x^k, \sum_{k=1}^{n} z^k y^k \right) \in T, \ \forall z^k :$$

$$\sum_{k=1}^{n} z^k \leq 1, \ z^k \geq 0, \ k = 1, \ldots, n.$$

$$(8.2.2)$$

Imposing the free disposability of inputs and outputs on this technology, results in the same conditions as in the previous AAM, namely conditions (8.1.6) and (8.1.8). Overall, the resulting technology would be that which satisfies (8.2.2), (8.1.6), and (8.1.8), i.e.,

$$\hat{T} \equiv \{(x, y) \in \Re_{+}^{N} \times \Re_{+}^{M} : y \leq \sum_{k=1}^{n} z^k y^k, \ \sum_{k=1}^{n} z^k x^k \leq x,$$

$$\sum_{k=1}^{n} z^k \leq 1, \ z^k \geq 0, \ k = 1, \ldots, n\}, \tag{8.2.3}$$

and we will refer to it as the DEA-NIRS formulation. As for the previous AAM, the intuition of imposing sub-additivity instead of additivity is easier to understand through geometry. Figure 8.2 illustrates a one-input–one-output example and four activities (observations), k, j, g, and r. The sub-additivity assumption only guarantees that the points "in-between" any two vectors $((x^k, y^k)$ and (x^j, y^j), (x^j, y^j) and (x^g, y^g), etc.) – i.e., points formed by linear combinations of vectors, with the sum of coefficients of the combination restricted to be within the unit interval – must also belong to T. The point (x^r, y^r), for example, cannot be obtained via a radial contraction of some of the existing activities, but it can be formed from the two activities (x^j, y^j) and (x^g, y^g) for some $0 \leq z^j, z^g \leq 1$, with $\sum_{k=1}^{n} z^k \leq 1$. As before, the free

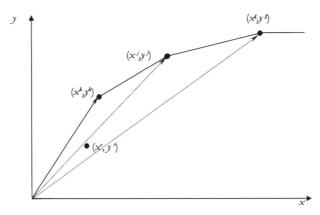

Figure 8.2 One-input–one-output example of constructing AAM under NIRS.

disposability of inputs and outputs would imply that all the points to the right of (or down from) these vectors are also in T. For this example, the technological frontier would therefore be formed from (convex combinations of) the points $(0, 0)$, (x^k, y^k), (x^j, y^j), (x^g, y^g), and $(+\infty, y^g)$.

It must be evident by now what the corresponding estimates of $P(x)$, $L(y)$ and of technical efficiency would be – one just needs to add the constraint $\sum_{k=1}^{n} z^k \leq 1$ to the AMM formulation under CRS assumptions. That is, the DEA-estimate of the output-oriented Farrell technical efficiency score, under the assumption of NIRS (along with sub-additivity and free disposability of all inputs and all outputs) for a DMU with an allocation (x, y) is therefore

$$\widehat{TE}(x, y) \equiv \max_{\theta, z^1, \ldots, z^n} \theta \tag{8.2.4a}$$

s.t.

$$\sum_{k=1}^{n} z^k y_m^k \geq \theta \, y_m, \quad m = 1, \ldots, M, \tag{8.2.4b}$$

$$\sum_{k=1}^{n} z^k x_l^k \leq x_l, \quad l = 1, \ldots, N, \tag{8.2.4c}$$

$$\sum_{k=1}^{n} z^k \leq 1, \tag{8.2.4d}$$

$$\theta \geq 0, \ z^k \geq 0, \ k = 1, \ldots, n. \tag{8.2.4e}$$

Similarly, the DEA-estimate of the *input-oriented* Farrell technical efficiency score, assuming NIRS (along with sub-additivity and free disposability of all inputs and all outputs) for a DMU with an allocation (x, y) is

$$\widehat{TE}_i(y, x) \equiv \min_{\theta, z^1, \ldots, z^n} \theta \tag{8.2.5a}$$

s.t.

$$\sum_{k=1}^{n} z^k y_m^k \geq y_m, \quad m = 1, \ldots, M, \tag{8.2.5b}$$

$$\sum_{k=1}^{n} z^k x_l^k \leq \theta \, x_l, \quad l = 1, \ldots, N, \tag{8.2.5c}$$

$$\sum_{k=1}^{n} z^k \leq 1, \tag{8.2.5d}$$

$$\theta \geq 0, \ z^k \geq 0, \ k = 1, \ldots, n. \tag{8.2.5e}$$

The resulting technology (by definition) does not allow increasing returns to scale at any region of production. This may be inconsistent with many real-world technologies. Indeed, many economists and engineers believe that at some (usually low) scales of production there often may exist some economies of scale – a situation that corresponds to (at least locally) *increasing returns to scale*. The two AAMs we have built above do not allow for measuring such a phenomenon.

Let us now build another AAM, relaxing some of the assumptions that we have imposed thus far on previous AAMs, to allow for local increasing returns to scale. To do so, we take the assumption of *sub-additivity* of activities from the previous AAM and turn it into what we refer to as *convexity of (observed) activities* – formally defined as a situation where $(x^k, y^k) \in T$ and $(x^j, y^j) \in T$ imply $(z^k x^k + z^j x^j, z^k y^k + z^j y^j) \in T$, $\forall z^k, z^j \geq 0 : z^k + z^j = 1$, or more generally,

$$\text{if } (x^k, y^k) \in T, \quad \forall k = 1, \ldots, n \implies \left(\sum_{k=1}^{n} z^k x^k, \sum_{k=1}^{n} z^k y^k \right) \in T, \forall z^k$$

$$\text{such that } \sum_{k=1}^{n} z^k = 1, \; z^k \geq 0, \; k = 1, \ldots, n. \tag{8.2.6}$$

Again, if we desire to impose the free disposability of inputs and outputs on this technology, this would result in the same conditions as in the previous AAMs, namely conditions (8.1.6) and (8.1.8). Overall, technology would then satisfy

$$\hat{T} \equiv \{(x, y) \in \mathfrak{R}_+^N \times \mathfrak{R}_+^M : y \leq \sum_{k=1}^{n} z^k y^k, \; \sum_{k=1}^{n} z^k x^k \leq x,$$

$$\sum_{k=1}^{n} z^k = 1, \quad z^k \geq 0, \; k = 1, \ldots, n\}. \tag{8.2.7}$$

The resulting set is referred to as the *smallest convex free disposal hull* that fits all of the observations on production activities, $\{(x^k, y^k) : k = 1, \ldots, n\}$. Also note that the technology set estimated via DEA-CRS is a *conical closure* of the technology set estimated via (8.2.7).

Again, the geometric intuition of imposing the assumption of convexity of activities may help in unveiling the mystery of (8.2.7). Figure 8.3, for example, illustrates a one-input–one-output example and four activities (observations), $k, j, r,$ and g. The convexity of activities assumption would only guarantee that the points formed by the convex combination of all the activities also belong to T. In Figure 8.3, this means that points in the convex hull formed by activities (x^k, y^k), (x^j, y^j), (x^r, y^r), and (x^g, y^g) belong to the set T, but note that *not* all radial contractions (and expansions) are guaranteed to belong to T. When the free disposability of inputs and outputs is imposed, then all of the points to the right of and down from this convex hull would also belong to T. For this example, the technological frontier is formed from (convex combinations of) the points $(x^r, 0)$, (x^r, y^r), (x^k, y^k), (x^j, y^j), (x^g, y^g), and $(+\infty, y^g)$. The resulting technology set would then appear as the one that,

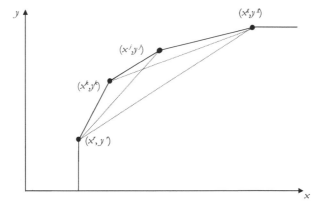

Figure 8.3 One-input–one-output example of constructing AAM under VRS.

for some levels of operation, allows the returns to scale to be greater than those from a CRS technology formed by the smallest convex cone that fits the same data. E.g., in Figure 8.3, operation anywhere at the linear segment from x^r to x^k gives greater returns to scale (which here can be measured by the slope of the linear segment) than that achieved at (x^k, y^k), which in turn is greater than that at (x^j, y^j), which in turn is greater than that at (x^g, y^g), where the returns from the increasing scale become zero.

This type of technology in efficiency analysis is conventionally referred to as the Variable Returns to Scale (VRS) technology, although this name is a bit misleading since it is just *one* (simple) example of a possible technology that allows for variable returns to scale (e.g., recall other examples considered in Chapter 1).

Again, it must be clear what the corresponding estimates of $P(x)$ and $L(y)$ and of technical efficiency would be – just add the constraint $\sum_{k=1}^{n} z^k = 1$ to the corresponding formulations under CRS. Meanwhile, the DEA-estimate of the *output*-oriented Farrell technical efficiency score, under the assumption of VRS imposed by assuming convexity of observed activities (along with free disposability of all inputs and all outputs) for an allocation (x, y) is

$$\widehat{TE}(x, y) \equiv \max_{\theta, z^1, \ldots, z^n} \theta \tag{8.2.8a}$$

s.t.

$$\sum_{k=1}^{n} z^k y_m^k \geq \theta\, y_m, \ m = 1, \ldots, M, \tag{8.2.8b}$$

$$\sum_{k=1}^{n} z^k x_l^k \leq x_l, \ l = 1, \ldots, N, \tag{8.2.8c}$$

$$\sum_{k=1}^{n} z^k = 1, \tag{8.2.8d}$$

$$\theta \geq 0, \; z^k \geq 0, \; k = 1, \ldots, n. \tag{8.2.8e}$$

Similarly, the DEA-estimate of the *input-oriented* Farrell technical efficiency score, under the assumption of VRS (along with free disposability of all inputs and all outputs) for an allocation (x, y) is

$$\widehat{TE}_i(y, x) \equiv \min_{\theta, \, z^1, \ldots, z^n} \theta \tag{8.2.9a}$$

s.t.

$$\sum_{k=1}^{n} z^k y_m^k \geq y_m, \; m = 1, \ldots, M, \tag{8.2.9b}$$

$$\sum_{k=1}^{n} z^k x_l^k \leq \theta \, x_l, \; l = 1, \ldots, N, \tag{8.2.9c}$$

$$\sum_{k=1}^{n} z^k = 1, \tag{8.2.9d}$$

$$\theta \geq 0, \; z^k \geq 0, \; k = 1, \ldots, n. \tag{8.2.9e}$$

Finally, analogous remarks we made about the DEA-CRS estimator in the previous section (about optimization variables, peers, slacks, etc.) apply to the DEA-NIRS and DEA-VRS estimators. In the next section, we discuss how these measures can be used to measure local economies of scale.[16]

8.3   MEASURING SCALE

It is a good moment now to talk about measuring scale economies using the Data Envelopment Analysis estimators. This concept was briefly mentioned in Chapter 4 in the context of decomposing MPI and the logic here is actually similar to the logic we used when discussing the overall efficiency measures – e.g., when we decomposed the cost efficiency into the technical efficiency and a residual that we called the allocative efficiency measure. Here we decompose the "technical efficiency under CRS" into the "pure technical efficiency" and the "scale efficiency" components. Formally, the Farrell-type *output-oriented scale efficiency measure* can be defined as

$$\widehat{SE}(x, y) \equiv \frac{\widehat{TE}(x, y | T^{CRS})}{\widehat{TE}(x, y | T^{VRS})}, \tag{8.3.1}$$

---

[16] In the literature, the DEA model with VRS assumption is sometimes referred to as the "BCC model" due to the seminal work of Banker et al. (1984). It would be fair to also acknowledge the less cited, yet earlier breakthrough contribution in this vein by Afriat (1972) and especially Färe et al. (1983).

where $\widehat{TE}(x, y|T^{CRS})$ is the DEA-estimator of $TE(x, y)$ when CRS is assumed (i.e., model (8.1.12a–8.1.12d) is used), and $\widehat{TE}(x, y|T^{VRS})$ is the DEA-estimator of $TE(x, y)$ when VRS is assumed (i.e., model (8.2.8a–8.2.8e) is used).

Using the homogeneity property of the Farrell measure of technical efficiency, and letting $\tilde{y} = y\,\widehat{TE}(x, y|T^{VRS})$, we can also rewrite (8.3.1) as

$$\widehat{SE}(x, y) = \widehat{TE}(x, \tilde{y}|T^{CRS}). \tag{8.3.2}$$

Intuitively, expression (8.3.2) says that the scale efficiency of a point (x, y) is measured by first "correcting" this point for the technical inefficiency with respect to the VRS technology and then estimating the *technical efficiency* with respect to the CRS technology of this "corrected" observation, $(x, \tilde{y})$. Expression (8.3.1), can also be rewritten as a useful decomposition:

$$\widehat{TE}(x, y|T^{CRS}) \equiv \widehat{TE}(x, y|T^{VRS}) \times \widehat{SE}(x, y). \tag{8.3.3}$$

The geometric intuition of the scale efficiency measure (8.3.1), as well as expressions (8.3.2) and (8.3.3), is revealed by Figure 8.4. Let us consider the observation at point A first. Intuitively, the scale efficiency measure would first "correct" observation A for (output-oriented *à la Farrell*) technical inefficiency by "bringing" it to point B, and then measure the distance from point B to point C using the usual Farrell output-oriented technical efficiency measure. In this case, we have $\widehat{SE}(x, y) > 1$, which indicates scale inefficiency and from the picture we know that this inefficiency is due to operating at (and not fully exploiting) the increasing returns to scale portion of the technology. Similarly, the scale efficiency measure at point E is the Farrell output-oriented measure of technical efficiency from point F to point G. It is also true here that $\widehat{SE}(x, y) > 1$, but from the picture we know that this inefficiency is due to operating at the decreasing returns to scale level of technology. Clearly, for a point like Q, the scale efficiency measure (8.3.1) would indicate no scale inefficiency, since in this case $\widehat{TE}(x, y|T^{CRS}) = \widehat{TE}(x, y|T^{VRS})$, although the pure technical inefficiency would be identified there.

Furthermore, note that while the true technology could be non-CRS (and potentially more complicated than the VRS technology), its conical closure as the one constructed via DEA-CRS, gives a very useful hypothetical or counterfactual CRS technology that can be used as a reference to identify and benchmark against, because this reference represents what is often perceived as the (observed) *socially optimal scale*. In Figure 8.4, the points of coincidence of the frontiers under CRS and VRS assumptions (e.g., point D, H, and all points on the line segment between them) indicate the optimal scale that firms may reach even when employing T^{VRS}. Importantly, note that the connotation "socially" or "from society's point of view" is important here because this type of scale is optimal in the sense of using minimal input per unit of output or maximal rate of output from given input. It is also sometimes referred to as the *most productive scale size* (MPSS). This socially optimal scale or MPSS can be different (and possibly very different) from points of *privately*

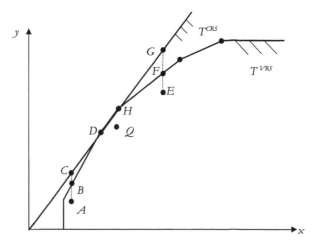

Figure 8.4 Intuition of the output-oriented scale efficiency measure.

optimal scale depending on the goals of the private individual (e.g., the scale that maximizes profit of that individual).[17]

The reader may wonder how one could identify the source of scale inefficiency in a general case, e.g., in many dimensions it is quite difficult to imagine the geometric aspect of it! There is a simple way of getting information on the source of inefficiency. It is based on auxiliary estimation of efficiency scores under NIRS, i.e., from model (8.2.4a)–(8.2.4e), denoted with $\widehat{TE}(x, y | T^{NIRS})$. Specifically, the following rule can be used to identify the source of scale inefficiency:

- If $\widehat{SE}(x, y) > 1$ and $\widehat{TE}(x, y | T^{NIRS}) = \widehat{TE}(x, y | T^{CRS})$ $\Rightarrow$ the scale inefficiency is due to local increasing returns to scale (IRS), i.e., the firm observed at (x, y) is underexploiting the economies of scale in production at that allocation (x, y).
- If $\widehat{SE}(x, y) > 1$ and $\widehat{TE}(x, y | T^{NIRS}) < \widehat{TE}(x, y | T^{CRS})$ $\Rightarrow$ the scale inefficiency is due to decreasing returns to scale (DRS), i.e., the firm observed at (x, y) is having *diseconomies* of scale in production at that allocation (x, y).

The logic of this rule must be evident from Figure 8.4.

Remark. For the sake of convenience, one may also redefine the scale efficiency measure such that it indicates the source of the scale inefficiency being IRS for values bigger than 1 and being DRS for values less than 1, e.g., by adopting the *multiplicatively reflected output-oriented scale efficiency measure*, defined as

---

[17] An alternative definition of optimal scale for society can also be defined via a formal definition of the (aggregate) welfare or utility function of society, which may give different points than the socially optimal scale we refer to here, depending on those functions.

$$\widetilde{SE}(x, y) = \begin{cases} \widehat{SE}(x, y) & \text{if } \widehat{TE}(x, y|T^{NIRS}) = \widehat{TE}(x, y|T^{CRS}) \\ 1/\widehat{SE}(x, y) & \text{if } \widehat{TE}(x, y|T^{NIRS}) < \widehat{TE}(x, y|T^{CRS}) \end{cases}$$

or the *additively reflected output-oriented scale efficiency measure*, defined as

$$\check{SE}(x, y) = \begin{cases} 2 - 1/\widehat{SE}(x, y) & \text{if } \widehat{TE}(x, y|T^{NIRS}) = \widehat{TE}(x, y|T^{CRS}) \\ 1/\widehat{SE}(x, y) & \text{if } \widehat{TE}(x, y|T^{NIRS}) < \widehat{TE}(x, y|T^{CRS}). \end{cases}$$

The reader should have realized by now that there also must exist an input-oriented analogue of (8.3.1) – indeed, the Farrell-type *input-oriented scale efficiency measure*, is defined as

$$\widehat{SE}_i(y, x) \equiv \frac{\widehat{TE}_i(y, x|T^{CRS})}{\widehat{TE}_i(y, x|T^{VRS})}, \tag{8.3.4}$$

where $\widehat{TE}_i(y, x|T^{CRS})$ is the DEA-estimator of $TE_i(y, x)$ when CRS is assumed (i.e., model (8.1.13a–8.1.13d) is used), and $\widehat{TE}_i(y, x|T^{VRS})$ is the DEA-estimator of $TE_i(y, x)$ when VRS is assumed (i.e., model (8.2.9a–8.2.9e) is used). Again, using the homogeneity property of the Farrell measure of technical efficiency, and letting $\tilde{x} = x\widehat{TE}_i(y, x|T^{VRS})$, we can rewrite (8.3.4) as

$$\widehat{SE}_i(y, x) = \widehat{TE}_i(y, \tilde{x}|T^{CRS}), \tag{8.3.5}$$

as well as rewrite it as a useful decomposition:

$$\widehat{TE}_i(y, x|T^{CRS}) \equiv \widehat{TE}_i(y, x|T^{VRS}) \times \widehat{SE}_i(y, x). \tag{8.3.6}$$

The reader is now encouraged to visualize the geometric intuition of this measure and develop a general rule for identifying the sources of scale inefficiency and the reflected versions of this measure, as well as for the scale efficiency measure based on other tools (directional and hyperbolic distance functions, Russell-type and slack-based measures, etc.) – analogous to developments for the output orientation. While performing this exercise, the reader may notice a problem with this measure of scale – a potential ambiguity due to the choice of orientation.

Indeed, Figure 8.5 demonstrates cases when the output-oriented scale efficiency is telling a completely different story than the input-oriented one. For example, for point A we have $\widehat{SE}(x, y) = 1$, indicating perfect scale efficiency, while $\widehat{SE}_i(y, x) < 1$, indicating scale inefficiency. For the point E, it is the opposite. A peculiar situation occurs with point Q, where $\widehat{SE}_i(y, x) < 1$ and $\widehat{SE}(x, y) > 1$, but the sources of scale inefficiency are clearly different: the observation at Q is scale inefficient due to IRS from the input orientation, but scale inefficient due to DRS from the output orientation.

Such a problem deserves some discussion. First of all, such an ambiguity due to the choice of orientation is pertinent not only to the scale efficiency measurement, but also (to a somewhat smaller extent) to the technical efficiency measurement. A general response to this problem is that the orientation of measurement must be chosen *a priori*, based on some theory or industry specifics

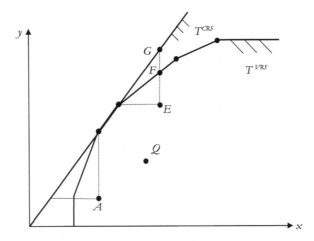

Figure 8.5 Output- vs. input-oriented scale efficiency measures.

or aims of researchers, and conveyed clearly to readers. For example, electricity companies may be required by a regulator to produce a certain level of output and producing more might be undesirable (e.g., costly to store/dispose). In this case, choosing the input orientation of measurement might be better than choosing the output orientation. On the other hand, when measuring efficiency of hospitals, it is natural to expect (or hope!) that hospitals are aiming to maximize their output of healthcare services from given (e.g., budgeted in the past) inputs and so output orientation measurement might be more natural there.[18]

It might also be the case that in the banking industry all (or the majority of) banks pursue goals that are close to maximizing the outputs, given the endowment of funds, buildings, labor, etc., since the profit is often computed (planned, etc.) as a percentage of outputs that banks conduct, while many of the inputs are fixed or quasi-fixed (on a contract, etc.) in a short-run.[19]

It may also happen that the same industry, or a set of firms within it, pursues goals that are "consistent" with different orientations of measurement in different periods of the industry's evolution (its business cycles, etc.). Farmers in agriculture, for instance, may pursue goals that are more "consistent" with revenue maximization (i.e., output orientation) during an economic booms – in order to produce and sell as much output as possible with given inputs. The same farmers may also behave the opposite way during economic recessions – by using as few inputs as possible to produce a given level of output (e.g., guaranteed to be purchased by government or futures options), which might be more consistent with the input orientation. It may even happen that different

---

[18] E.g., for related discussion, see Chowdhury and Zelenyuk (2016) and references therein.

[19] E.g., for related discussion, see Curi et al. (2015) and references therein.

(e.g., strategic, geographic, etc.) groups of firms in an industry pursue goals that are consistent with different orientations.

Ideally, a researcher is encouraged to get relevant out-of-sample information on the firm's orientation – by interviewing some of their representatives, independent experts, etc. If such information is unavailable or very costly, a researcher may try comparing the estimates of (8.3.1) and (8.3.4) – to see if there is any ambiguity in practice; often there is no ambiguity, or very little of it.

If the ambiguity is present and the researcher cannot decide which orientation to choose, it might be useful to report results from both measures, and to try to analyze why the difference is present and for which firms – this may shed some useful light on the phenomenon and trigger further interesting investigations. Researchers may also report an "average measure of efficiency," defined for the scale efficiency case as

$$\widehat{ASE}_i(y, x) = \left(\widehat{SE}_i(y, x) \times (\widehat{SE}(x, y))^{-1}\right)^{1/2}, \tag{8.3.7}$$

or, alternatively as[20]

$$\widehat{ASE}(x, y) = \left(\widehat{SE}(x, y) \times (\widehat{SE}_i(y, x))^{-1}\right)^{1/2} = (\widehat{ASE}_i(y, x))^{-1}, \tag{8.3.8}$$

along with information on the source of scale inefficiency out of three (or more) options: DRS, VRS, Ambiguous. In a similar fashion, one may also combine the reflected scale efficiency measures for both orientations.

8.4 ESTIMATION OF COST, REVENUE, AND PROFIT FUNCTIONS AND RELATED EFFICIENCY MEASURES

The AAMs discussed above (and below) can also be used to model cost, revenue and profit. In fact, if relevant and accurate price information is available, then it is usually advised to use a corresponding dual approach, because it contains richer information and helps revealing behavior or preferences of economic agents or DMUs. Specifically, if information on input prices is available, in addition to the output levels for each DMU, and the assumptions of VRS and free disposability of inputs and outputs is adequate, then a researcher can estimate the *(minimal) cost function* for a DMU with an allocation (y, w) via

---

[20] Note that the reciprocal of one of the measures in (8.3.7) and (8.3.8) is taken to have both components of the average use the same units of measurement.

$$\hat{C}(y, w) \equiv \min_{\substack{x_1,\ldots,x_N \\ z^1,\ldots,z^n}} \sum_{l=1}^{N} w_l x_l, \tag{8.4.1a}$$

s.t.

$$\sum_{k=1}^{n} z^k y_m^k \geq y_m, \quad m = 1, \ldots, M, \tag{8.4.1b}$$

$$\sum_{k=1}^{n} z^k x_l^k \leq x_l, \quad l = 1, \ldots, N, \tag{8.4.1c}$$

$$\sum_{k=1}^{n} z^k = 1, \tag{8.4.1d}$$

$$z^k \geq 0, \quad k = 1, \ldots, n. \tag{8.4.1e}$$

Note that here, unlike in the AAM formulations above, the input vector $x = (x_1, \ldots, x_l, \ldots, x_N)$ that appears in the objective function and in the r.h.s. of one of the constraints, serves as one of the intensity variables over which optimization is made. It should be clear by now that CRS can be imposed on this formulation by removing the constraint $\sum_{k=1}^{n} z^k = 1$, while NIRS can be imposed by replacing this constraint with $\sum_{k=1}^{n} z^k \leq 1$.

The results of the AAM-based cost optimization problem can then be used to construct the DEA-based cost efficiency measure, defined for an allocation (x, y, w) as the ratio of the estimated minimal cost to the actual cost, i.e.,

$$\widehat{CE}(y, w, x) \equiv \frac{\hat{C}(y, w)}{wx}, \quad \text{for } wx \neq 0. \tag{8.4.2}$$

On a theoretical level, this measure and its geometric intuition were discussed in Chapter 3, and (8.4.2) is the corresponding DEA estimator. From discussions in Chapter 3, it should also be clear that

$$\widehat{CE}(y, w, x) \leq \widehat{TE}_i(y, x), \quad \forall x \in \hat{L}(y), \ w \in \Re_+^N, \tag{8.4.3}$$

i.e., the estimated cost efficiency score is always lower (or equal) than the estimated technical input efficiency score. This inequality is also known as Mahler's inequality, which can be closed by introducing the (multiplicative) residual – that would indicate about the estimated *allocative (in)efficiency* of an allocation (x, y, w), after correcting it for the estimated technical inefficiency using $\widehat{TE}_i(y, x)$. Formally, the estimated input-oriented allocative efficiency is defined as

$$\widehat{AE}_i(y, w, x) \equiv \frac{\widehat{CE}(y, w, x)}{\widehat{TE}_i(y, x)} \tag{8.4.4}$$

and so we have

$$\widehat{CE}(y, w, x) \equiv \widehat{TE}_i(y, x) \times \widehat{AE}_i(y, w, x), \tag{8.4.5}$$

which is a famous decomposition of the *cost efficiency* measure, or the Farrell *input-oriented overall efficiency* measure. The decomposition is into two sources: (i) inefficiency due to underutilizing technological capacity and (ii) inefficiency due to misallocation of inputs with respect to the prices faced by the DMU and under the assumption of cost minimizing behavior.

If information on output prices is available, in addition to the input levels for each DMU, then similar arguments can be made about the *overall* output efficiency, or just the *revenue efficiency* measure, that can be defined as

$$\widehat{RE}(x, p, y) \equiv \frac{\hat{R}(x, p)}{py}, \ \text{for } py \neq 0, \tag{8.4.6}$$

where, for example, when the assumptions of VRS and free disposability of inputs and outputs is adequate, a researcher can estimate the *(maximal) revenue function* for an allocation (x, p) via

$$\hat{R}(x, p) \equiv \max_{\substack{y_1, \dots, y_M, \\ z^1, \dots, z^n}} \sum_{m=1}^{M} p_m y_m, \tag{8.4.7a}$$

s.t.

$$\sum_{k=1}^{n} z^k y_m^k \geq y_m \geq 0, \ m = 1, \dots, M, \tag{8.4.7b}$$

$$\sum_{k=1}^{n} z^k x_l^k \leq x_l, \ l = 1, \dots, N, \tag{8.4.7c}$$

$$\sum_{k=1}^{n} z^k = 1, \tag{8.4.7d}$$

$$z^k \geq 0, \ k = 1, \dots, n. \tag{8.4.7e}$$

Note that here, unlike in the AAM formulations above, the output vector $y = (y_1, \dots, y_m, \dots, y_M)$ that appears in the objective function and in the r.h.s. of one of the constraints, plays a role of one of the intensity variables over which maximization is made. The CRS or NIRS can be imposed on this formulation by removing the constraint $\sum_{k=1}^{n} z^k = 1$ or replacing it with $\sum_{k=1}^{n} z^k \leq 1$, respectively.

On theoretical grounds, this measure and its geometric intuition were discussed in Chapter 3 (and other chapters) and $\widehat{RE}(x, p, y)$ in the formulation above is its corresponding DEA estimator. It should also be clear that

$$\widehat{RE}(x, p, y) \geq \widehat{TE}(x, y), \ \forall y \in \hat{P}(x), \ p \in \Re_{++}^{M}, \tag{8.4.8}$$

i.e., that the revenue efficiency score is always greater than the technical output-oriented efficiency score. This is known as output-oriented Mahler's inequality, which can be closed by introducing the (multiplicative) residual, which would indicate about the estimated *allocative (in)efficiency* of a point (x, p, y), after correcting it for technical inefficiency using $\widehat{TE}(x, y)$. Formally, the estimated output-oriented allocative efficiency is defined as

$$\widehat{AE}(x, p, y) \equiv \frac{\widehat{RE}(x, p, y)}{\widehat{TE}(x, y)}, \tag{8.4.9}$$

and so we have

$$\widehat{RE}(x, p, y) \equiv \widehat{TE}(x, y) \times \widehat{AE}(x, p, y), \tag{8.4.10}$$

which is a famous decomposition of the *revenue efficiency* measure, or the Farrell *output-oriented overall efficiency* measure. Similarly as for (but alternatively to) the case of input orientation, the decomposition is also into two sources: (i) inefficiency due to underutilizing technological capacity and (ii) inefficiency due to the misallocation of inputs with respect to the prices faced by DMU and under the assumption of revenue maximizing behavior.

Furthermore, let us now consider the case of profit function estimation via DEA – this is advised when information on input and output prices is available, in addition to the input and output levels for each DMU. For example, when the assumptions of VRS and free disposability of inputs and outputs is adequate, a researcher can estimate the *(maximal) profit function* for any realization of prices (w, p) via

$$\hat{\pi}(w, p) \equiv \max_{\substack{(x,y), \\ z^1,\dots,z^n}} \sum_{m=1}^{M} p_m y_m - \sum_{l=1}^{N} w_l x_l, \tag{8.4.11a}$$

s.t.

$$\sum_{k=1}^{n} z^k y_m^k \geq y_m \geq 0, \ m = 1, \dots, M, \tag{8.4.11b}$$

$$\sum_{k=1}^{n} z^k x_l^k \leq x_l, \ l = 1, \dots, N, \tag{8.4.11c}$$

$$\sum_{k=1}^{n} z^k = 1, \tag{8.4.11d}$$

$$z^k \geq 0, \ k = 1, \dots, n. \tag{8.4.11e}$$

Note that here, and unlike in the AAM or DEA formulations above, both vectors $x = (x_1, \dots, x_N)$ and $y = (y_1, \dots, y_M)$ that appear in the objective function and in the r.h.s. of two of the constraints, play the roles of intensity variables (along with $z_1, \dots, z_n$) over which the maximization is made. As before, the CRS or NIRS can be imposed on this formulation by removing the constraint $\sum_{k=1}^{n} z^k = 1$ or replacing it with $\sum_{k=1}^{n} z^k \leq 1$, respectively.[21]

We have discussed the profit function and its geometric intuition in previous chapters, starting from Chapter 2 and $\hat{\pi}(x, p, y)$ represents its corresponding DEA estimator (with certain assumptions on technology made in AAM). From those theoretical discussions, recall that the profit function was related to the directional distance function in general theoretical context, and the DEA-estimated version of this relationship for any allocation (x, y, w, p) can be expressed as

$$\hat{\Pi}(w, p, x, y| -d_x, d_y) \equiv \frac{\hat{\pi}(w, p) - (py - wx)}{(pd_y + wd_x)} \geq \hat{D}_d(x, y| -d_x, d_y),$$

(8.4.12)

where the l.h.s. of this (Mahler-type) inequality is the DEA-estimate of a directional (Nerlovian) profit efficiency measure, $\hat{\Pi}(w, p, x, y| - d_x, d_y)$, while the r.h.s. of it is the DEA-estimated directional distance function. Specifically, for an allocation (x, y) and for a specific direction $d = (-d_x, d_y)$, the DEA-estimated directional distance function is given by

$$\hat{D}_d(x, y| - d_x, d_y) \equiv \max_{\theta, z^1, \ldots, z^n} \theta,$$

(8.4.13a)

s.t.

$$\sum_{k=1}^{n} z^k y_m^k \geq y_m + \theta d_{y_m}, \quad m = 1, \ldots, M,$$

(8.4.13b)

$$\sum_{k=1}^{n} z^k x_l^k \leq x_l - \theta d_{x_l}, \quad l = 1, \ldots, N,$$ (8.4.13c)

$$\sum_{k=1}^{n} z^k = 1,$$

(8.4.13d)

$$\theta \geq 0, \ z^k \geq 0, \ k = 1, \ldots, n.$$ (8.4.13e)

which assumes VRS and free disposability of inputs and outputs while, as before, the CRS or NIRS assumptions can be imposed on this formulation by removing the constraint $\sum_{k=1}^{n} z^k = 1$ or replacing it with $\sum_{k=1}^{n} z^k \leq 1$, respectively.

The Mahler-type inequality can be closed by introducing the residual (and here we choose it to be additive), which would indicate about the estimated *allocative (in)efficiency* of an allocation (x, y) facing prices (w, p), after

---

[21] Note that for CRS, profit maximization will yield profit to be 0 or ∞, unless some additional constraints (e.g., limits on inputs) are imposed.

correcting it for technical inefficiency using $\hat{D}_d(x, y| - d_x, d_y)$. Formally, the estimated profit-oriented directional allocative efficiency is defined as

$$\widehat{AE}_\pi(w, p, x, y| - d_x, d_y) \equiv \hat{\Pi}(w, p, x, y| - d_x, d_y) - \hat{D}_d(x, y| - d_x, d_y),$$
(8.4.14)

and so we have

$$\hat{\Pi}(w, p, x, y| - d_x, d_y) = \hat{D}_d(x, y| - d_x, d_y) + \widehat{AE}_\pi(w, p, x, y| - d_x, d_y),$$
(8.4.15)

which is a decomposition of the *profit efficiency* measure into two sources: (i) inefficiency due to underutilizing directional technological capacity and (ii) inefficiency due to the misallocation of inputs with respect to the prices faced by the DMU and under the assumption of revenue maximizing behavior and, importantly, for a particular direction of measurement specified by $d = (-d_x, d_y)$.[22]

Furthermore, a somewhat more intuitive profit efficiency measure – the output-oriented Farrell-type profit efficiency measure of Färe et al. (2018) that we discussed in Chapter 3 can be estimated as

$$\hat{\mathscr{E}}_o(x, y; w, p|Z) \equiv \frac{\hat{\pi}(w, p)}{py} + \frac{wx}{py},$$

where $\hat{\pi}(w, p)$ is the DEA-estimated profit function as described above (possibly with some additional constraints specified by Z and wx and py are the actual costs and revenues. This profit efficiency measure can be further decomposed into revenue efficiency, Farrell technical efficiency (output-oriented) and a new allocative efficiency measure, and each can be estimated via a selected DEA or other estimators, as detailed in Färe et al. (2018).

Similar remarks that we outlined for the estimation of technical efficiency (about optimization variables, peers, slacks, etc.) hold for these estimators as well, up to some modifications. For example, note that for strictly positive prices, the DEA for cost minimization should give no input slacks and the DEA revenue maximization should give no output slacks; meanwhile the DEA for the profit optimization should give no slacks at all and in this sense the efficiency measure based on the profit function is the most comprehensive among all, satisfying the so-called Pareto–Koopmans efficiency criterion.

Again, note that solutions to those different LP problems for any DMU, may generally yield different sets of peers and different slacks (which may not be unique for any particular optimization), which should not be surprising since these are based on different optimization behaviors.

Finally, note that the estimates based on the dual (cost, revenue, and profit) efficiency measures can also be used for measuring the scale economies. Such

---

[22] Indeed, note that different choices of direction (i.e., orientation) may imply results that are different not only quantitatively but also qualitatively. Therefore, a well-justified choice of the direction, complemented with a sensitivity analysis with respect to its variation, is important in the practical use of this approach.

approaches will be alternative and complementary to approaches described in the previous subsection (see Zelenyuk, 2014b and Färe et al., 2016a for some examples and related theory).

8.5 ESTIMATION OF SLACK-BASED EFFICIENCY

In Chapter 3 we discussed the so-called slack-based efficiency measures that have their own appeal and some advantages over other efficiency measures. The AAM or DEA models discussed above can easily be adapted to estimate these measures. We will consider these methods in the context of the slack-based directional distance function measure, introduced by Färe and Grosskopf (2010) and elaborated in Färe et al. (2015, 2016a). This measure can be estimated, for any allocation $(x, y) \in \hat{T}$, via

$$\overrightarrow{SBD}_{\hat{T}}(x, y; 1_{N+M}) = \max_{\substack{\beta_1, \ldots, \beta_N, \gamma_1, \ldots, \gamma_M \\ z^1, \ldots, z^n}} \sum_{l=1}^{N} \beta_l + \sum_{m=1}^{M} \gamma_m$$

$$s.t.$$

$$\sum_{k=1}^{n} z^k y_m^k \geq y_m + \gamma_m \cdot 1, \ m = 1, \ldots, M, \quad (8.5.1a)$$

$$\sum_{k=1}^{n} z^k x_l^k \leq x_l - \beta_l \cdot 1, \ l = 1, \ldots, N, \quad (8.5.1b)$$

$$\sum_{k=1}^{n} z^k = 1, \quad (8.5.1c)$$

$$z^k \geq 0, \ k = 1, \ldots, n, \quad (8.5.1d)$$

$$\beta_l \geq 0, \ l = 1, \ldots, n, \quad (8.5.1e)$$

$$\gamma_m \geq 0, \ m = 1, \ldots, M, \quad (8.5.1f)$$

if one assumes VRS and free disposability of inputs and outputs. As before, the CRS or NIRS assumptions can be imposed on this formulation by removing the constraint $\sum_{k=1}^{n} z^k = 1$ or replacing it with $\sum_{k=1}^{n} z^k \leq 1$, respectively.[23]

Now, let $(\beta_1^*, \ldots, \beta_N^*)$ and $(\gamma_1^*, \ldots, \gamma_M^*)$ be the optimizers in (8.5.1d), then under standard regularity conditions with free disposability of inputs and outputs, $\overrightarrow{SBD}_{\hat{T}}(x, y; 1_{N+M}) = 0$ if and only if $(\beta_1^*, \ldots, \beta_N^*, \gamma_1^*, \ldots, \gamma_M^*) = 0_{N+M}$. Note that (x, y) is on the efficient subset of the frontier of the DEA estimated technology set, denoted with $\partial \hat{T}$, i.e., it is Pareto–Koopmans efficient relative to $\hat{T}$.

---

[23] Recall that 1_{N+M} in $\overrightarrow{SBD}_{\hat{T}}(x, y; 1_{N+M})$ stands for the vector defining units of measurement for each element of x and y.

Färe et al. (2015) noted a useful relationship between this measure and the profit function, when the latter is normalized with the value of the directional vector $(\sum_{m=1}^{M} p_m \cdot 1 + \sum_{l=1}^{N} w_l \cdot 1)$. The estimated version of this relationship says that, $\forall (x, y) \in \hat{T}$ we have

$$
\frac{\hat{\pi}(w, p) - (py - wx)}{(\sum_{m=1}^{M} p_m \cdot 1 + \sum_{l=1}^{N} w_l \cdot 1)} \geqq \sum_{m=1}^{M} \frac{p_m \gamma_m^* \cdot 1}{\sum_{m=1}^{M} p_m \cdot 1 + \sum_{l=1}^{N} w_l \cdot 1}
$$
$$
+ \sum_{l=1}^{N} \frac{w_l \beta_l^* \cdot 1}{\sum_{m=1}^{M} p_m \cdot 1 + \sum_{l=1}^{N} w_l \cdot 1}.
$$
(8.5.2)

Note that the measure is now represented as an aggregation of individual "slacks" weighted by the observed price-share weights

$$
S_m = \frac{p_m \cdot 1}{\sum_{m=1}^{M} p_m \cdot 1 + \sum_{l=1}^{N} w_l \cdot 1}, \quad m = 1, \ldots, M,
$$

and

$$
W_l = \frac{w_l \cdot 1}{\sum_{m=1}^{M} p_m \cdot 1 + \sum_{l=1}^{N} w_l \cdot 1}, \quad l = 1, \ldots, N.
$$

Also note that $S_m \geqq 0$ and $W_l \geqq 0$ for all $m = 1, \ldots, M$ and $l = 1, \ldots, N$ and $\sum_{m=1}^{M} S_m + \sum_{l=1}^{N} W_l = 1$. So, for all $(x, y) \in \hat{T}$ we have

$$
\frac{\hat{\pi}(w, p) - (py - wx)}{(\sum_{m=1}^{M} p_m \cdot 1 + \sum_{l=1}^{N} w_l \cdot 1)} \geqq \sum_{m=1}^{M} S_m \gamma_m^* + \sum_{l=1}^{N} W_l \beta_l^*. \quad (8.5.3)
$$

Moreover, if $\overrightarrow{SBD}_{\hat{T}}(x, y; \mathbf{1}_{N+M}) > 0$ one can also state, $\forall (x, y) \in \hat{T}$, that

$$
\frac{\hat{\pi}(w, p) - (py - wx)}{(\sum_{m=1}^{M} p_m \cdot 1 + \sum_{l=1}^{N} w_l \cdot 1)} \geqq \overrightarrow{SBD}_{\hat{T}}(x, y; \mathbf{1}_{N+M})
$$
$$
\times \left(\sum_{m=1}^{M} S_m \tilde{\gamma}_m + \sum_{l=1}^{N} W_l \tilde{\beta}_l \right), \quad (8.5.4)
$$

where

$$
\tilde{\gamma}_m = \frac{\gamma_m^*}{\sum_{m=1}^{M} \gamma_m^* + \sum_{l=1}^{N} \beta_l^*}, \quad m = 1, \ldots, M, \quad (8.5.5)
$$

and

$$
\tilde{\beta}_l = \frac{\beta_l^*}{\sum_{m=1}^{M} \gamma_m^* + \sum_{l=1}^{N} \beta_l^*}, \quad l = 1, \ldots, N. \quad (8.5.6)
$$

In words, the l.h.s. of (8.5.4) is a DEA estimate of the normalized profit efficiency, while the r.h.s. is a DEA estimate of the slack-based directional technical efficiency. The difference between the two gives a DEA estimate of allocative inefficiency measure that closes the inequality in (8.5.4) and provides a decomposition of the DEA-estimate of the (normalized) profit efficiency.

The representation in (8.5.4) allows for identifying the potential individual contributions of each output and each input as shares of the total technical inefficiency, given by (8.5.5) and (8.5.6), respectively.[24]

8.6 TECHNOLOGIES WITH WEAK DISPOSABILITY

Empirical modeling of technologies with weak disposability of undesirable (or "bad") outputs or weak disposability of inputs is a subject in itself and separate chapters or even books can be written on it. The importance of such modeling is emphasized by – and is in line with the priorities of humanity for – sustainable development, desires to produce good outputs with fewer (or ideally no) bad outputs, such as CO_2, NO_x, non-performing loans, side effects in healthcare, etc. In Chapter 1, we briefly discussed the fundamentals of how to theoretically model such technologies and here we will briefly outline key fundamentals for their estimation in practice and refer readers to where more details can be found.

To modify the AAMs presented above to allow for only the weak disposability of all outputs, recall from Chapter 1 that theoretically this means that

$$y^o \in P(x) \Rightarrow y = \lambda y^o \in P(x), \ \forall \lambda \in [0, 1], \ x \in \mathfrak{R}_+^N, \tag{8.6.1}$$

and so if we let $y^o = \sum_{k=1}^{n} z^k y^k \in P(x)$, then (8.6.1) implies

$$y = \lambda \sum_{k=1}^{n} z^k y^k \in P(x), \ \forall \lambda \in [0, 1]. \tag{8.6.2}$$

Thus, an AAM of technology that mimics a VRS technology with all inputs being freely disposable, but all the outputs as only weakly disposable is given by

$$\hat{T} \equiv \{(x, y) \in \mathfrak{R}_+^N \times \mathfrak{R}_+^M :$$

$$x \geq \sum_{k=1}^{n} z^k x^k,$$

$$y = \lambda \sum_{k=1}^{n} z^k y^k, \ 0 \leq \lambda \leq 1,$$

$$\sum_{k=1}^{n} z^k = 1, \ z^k \geq 0, \ k = 1, \dots, n\}. \tag{8.6.3}$$

---

[24] See Färe et al. (2015) and Pham and Zelenyuk (2019) for related results and more discussions on this type of measurement.

That is, the only difference is in the constraints on the outputs, which are now equalities and, note, they are all connected via the same *scaling factor* $\lambda \in [0, 1]$, which will enter into optimization for a particular efficiency measure as an additional optimization variable.[25]

Now, suppose some of the outputs are freely disposable – call them g – while others are only weekly disposable jointly with (or conditional on) g – call them b, i.e., $y = (g, b) \in \mathfrak{R}_+^{M_g} \times \mathfrak{R}_+^{M_b}$. Then, the AAM in (8.6.3) can be adjusted as follows:

$$
\hat{T} \equiv \{(x, g, b) \in \mathfrak{R}_+^N \times \mathfrak{R}_+^{M_g} \times \mathfrak{R}_+^{M_b} :
$$
$$
x \geq \sum_{k=1}^n z^k x^k,
$$
$$
g \leq \lambda \sum_{k=1}^n z^k g^k,
$$
$$
b = \lambda \sum_{k=1}^n z^k b^k, \ 0 \leq \lambda \leq 1,
$$
$$
\sum_{k=1}^n z^k = 1, \ z^k \geq 0, \ k = 1, \dots, n\}, \tag{8.6.4}
$$

i.e., the constraints for the freely disposable outputs are inequalities, while for the weakly disposable outputs they are equalities, yet all are still connected via the common scaling factor $\lambda \in [0, 1]$. The idea of such AAMs goes back to at least Shephard (1974), with recent refinements by Färe and Grosskopf (2003, 2004, 2009), to mention a few. Since (8.6.4) appears to be the most popular in practice; we will focus on it here, although note there are many ways to generalize it.[26,27] In turn, the DEA-estimate of the input-oriented Farrell technical efficiency score of any particular allocation (x, y), under the assumption of VRS, free disposability of all inputs x and good outputs g and weak disposability of bad outputs b is given by

---

[25] Some studies call it the "abatement factor." While there is some resemblance of it to the notion of the abatement factor in regulatory economics and environmental economics, it is not exactly the same and so we will refer to it more precisely as the scaling factor.

[26] For example, it is quite natural to expect that different good outputs are associated with different bad outputs, and likely with different relationships. So, a natural generalization is to allow for different factors, $\lambda_{mm'} \in [0, 1]$, connecting different bad outputs to different good outputs, reflecting different relationships among them. Another related case is where some of the good outputs are not connected to any of the bad outputs, i.e., (8.6.4) where some of the good outputs do not have the scaling factors (λ) in their constraints.

[27] Note that the technology set characterized by AAM (8.6.4) is not necessarily convex, yet the output sets are convex; some studies allowed for the scaling factor to vary across DMUs within one AAM formulation, i.e., have $\lambda^1, \dots, \lambda^n$ instead of one λ in (8.6.3), which in turn ensured that the technology set is convex (see Kuosmanen, 2005; Kuosmanen and Podinovski, 2009). On the other hand, convexity of the entire technology set might also be viewed as too restrictive, and just convexity of output (and/or input) sets may be sufficient (Färe and Grosskopf, 2009). Also see the related discussion and comparisons in Pham and Zelenyuk (2019).

$$\widehat{TE}_i(g, b, x) \equiv \min_{\theta, z^1, \ldots, z^n, \lambda} \theta$$

$$x\theta \geq \sum_{k=1}^{n} z^k x^k, \ 0 \leq \theta \leq 1,$$

$$g \leq \lambda \sum_{k=1}^{n} z^k g^k,$$

$$b = \lambda \sum_{k=1}^{n} z^k b^k, \ 0 \leq \lambda \leq 1,$$

$$\sum_{k=1}^{n} z^k = 1, \ z^k \geq 0, \ k = 1, \ldots, n. \tag{8.6.5}$$

Note that while for a particular AAM there is a single λ, using this AAM for estimating the efficiency scores for different DMUs, one at a time, allows for different estimates of λ for different DMU.[28]

By now, the reader should also be able to write out the DEA-estimate of the output-oriented Farrell technical efficiency. However, would it be an adequate measure here? Indeed, recall that such a measure expands *all* the outputs equi-proportinately (or radially) and such an increase is considered as an improvement for the good outputs, but not so for the bad outputs. What should one do? There are many ways to handle this situation. For example, one may fix the bad outputs and only measure the radial expansion of the good outputs, giving rise to what we will refer to as *the good-output-oriented Farrell technical efficiency*, defined for the DEA-VRS estimator as

$$\widehat{TE}_g(x, g, b) \equiv \max_{\theta, z^1, \ldots, z^n, \lambda} \theta$$

$$x \geq \sum_{k=1}^{n} z^k x^k,$$

$$g\theta \leq \lambda \sum_{k=1}^{n} z^k g^k, \ \theta \geq 1,$$

$$b = \lambda \sum_{k=1}^{n} z^k b^k, \ 0 \leq \lambda \leq 1,$$

$$\sum_{k=1}^{n} z^k = 1, \ z^k \geq 0, \ k = 1, \ldots, n. \tag{8.6.6}$$

---

[28] On the other hand, allowing for different λ's within AAM (8.6.4) and using it for estimating efficiency for different DMUs may give n estimates of λ for *each* DMU, i.e., $n \times n$ estimates of λ for the sample of size n, which may lead to ambiguity regarding interpretations of λ's. See Färe and Grosskopf (2009) and Pham and Zelenyuk (2019) for more details and more variations, comparisons and references.

Another natural and common approach is to radially contract the bad outputs (and, possibly, the inputs) while radially expanding the good outputs, giving rise to what we refer to as *the generalized hyperbolic technical efficiency measure* (see Chapter 3 for related discussion), defined for the DEA-VRS estimator as

$$\widehat{GHTE}(x, g, b) \equiv \max_{\theta_g, \theta_b, \theta_x, z^1, \dots, z^n, \lambda} f(\theta_g, \theta_b, \theta_x)$$

$$x/\theta_x \geq \sum_{k=1}^{n} z^k x^k, \ \theta_x \geq 1,$$

$$g\,\theta_g \leq \lambda \sum_{k=1}^{n} z^k g^k, \ \theta_g \geq 1, \ 0 \leq \lambda \leq 1,$$

$$b/\theta_x = \lambda \sum_{k=1}^{n} z^k b^k, \ \theta_x \geq 1,$$

$$\sum_{k=1}^{n} z^k = 1, \ z^k \geq 0, \ k = 1, \dots, n, \tag{8.6.7}$$

where, note, we allow for different proportionality factors for radially contracting inputs (via θ_x), bad outputs (via θ_b) and radially expanding good outputs (via θ_g), and where $f(\theta_g, \theta_b, \theta_x)$ is a suitable aggregating function (e.g., geometric mean, possibly with different weights, specified by the researcher).

A simpler special-case version of this formulation (8.6.7) is the case restricted to equi-proportionate changes, i.e., $\theta_g = \theta_b = \theta_x = \theta$. Many other interesting special cases can be obtained from (8.6.7). E.g., one may set $\theta_x = 1$, in which case the inputs are kept fixed while the good outputs are radially expanded and the bad outputs are radially contracted (here one may allow θ_g and θ_b to be different or restrict them to being the same).[29] One may also set $\theta_b = 1$, to keep the bad outputs fixed and radially contract inputs and radially expand good outputs, with the same or different factors. For this last case, if one also sets $\theta_x = 1$ with $f(\theta_g, \theta_b, \theta_x) = \theta_g$ or, alternatively, $\theta_g = 1$ with $f(\theta_g, \theta_b, \theta_x) = \theta_x$, then (8.6.6) or (8.6.5), respectively, are obtained.

One may also generalize (8.6.7) further and allow for different scaling for each output and each input, i.e., deploy the Russell-type measurement discussed in Chapter 3. Yet another alternative is to reduce the inputs and bad outputs and increase good outputs via subtracting/adding individual slacks, i.e., using the additive-type or the slack-based efficiency measures; or one may apply the directional distance function, the cost function, the revenue function or the profit functions and the related to them efficiency measures. We discussed these measures extensively in Chapter 3 and briefly discussed their

---

[29] In this peculiar case, if the objective function is multiplicative, one can (and in fact needs to) set $\lambda = 1$, for identification purposes, which also simplifies the optimization problem. See Zhou et al. (2008) for related discussion.

estimation via an AAM in the previous section, and the method of adapting them to the case with undesirable outputs should be clear by now.[30]

A few important remarks are in order. First, note that the last three formulations are not LP problems and so, in general, they may be not as easy to compute. These problems are substantially simplified when one assumes CRS or NIRS technology, in which case not only the constraint $\sum_{k=1}^{n} z^k = 1$ is removed or replaced with $\sum_{k=1}^{n} z^k \leq 1$, respectively, but also one can then set $\lambda = 1$ without changing the optimal value of the objective function (e.g., see Färe and Grosskopf, 2003; Färe and Grosskopf, 2004 for details). This makes (8.6.6) or (8.6.5) LP problems.

In case one wants to preserve VRS, and thus keep λ as one of the optimization variables, or in general formulations like (8.6.7), or its further generalizations, one may need to resort to a nonlinear optimization approach. This typically involves an iterative numerical optimization method such as sequential quadratic programming algorithm, interior point algorithm, etc.[31,32]

Finally, note that all of these approaches can be adapted to the case where some of the inputs are weakly disposable, while the other inputs and all of the outputs are freely disposable or cases that combine these with the above approaches. We leave these interesting cases for the readers to explore as exercises, possibly resulting in new papers or books in this important area for future research.

8.7 MODELING NON-CONVEX TECHNOLOGIES

All estimates of the technologies we have studied through AAMs so far satisfy the convexity assumption imposed on technology set T. (The proof of this statement will be clear in a moment.) This is substantially more restrictive than what we imposed in Chapter 1. In fact, it is even more restrictive than imposing convexity on only $L(y)$ and/or only on $P(x)$. Indeed, in theoretical

---

[30] For details on some of these and a comparison, see Pham and Zelenyuk (2019).

[31] For some special cases, certain transformations of constraints are also possible to convert a nonlinear problem into linear, e.g., see Zhou et al. (2008); Sahoo et al. (2011) for related discussion. For computational details and references, see Pham and Zelenyuk (2019), who recommend *inter alia* sequential quadratic programming algorithm for these problems.

[32] When the objective function is nonlinear, one may also resort to its first-order approximation to linearize it and thus simplify the optimization problem. Such approximation is often sufficient in practice and certainly valuable, at least as the starting point for initiating the iterative numerical optimization. Indeed, one must remember that such optimization in practice may also give "spurious optima" (local optima, degenerate solutions, etc.), and so it is recommended to try different starting values, especially (yet not only) the one supported by some theoretical arguments, such as certain types of approximations, prior knowledge, etc. In a similar vein, for VRS cases where constraints cannot be transformed into linear, $\lambda = 1$ appears to be a good starting value to initiate the iterative optimization algorithms, while a good choice for starting values for the intensity variables are their DEA-NIRS estimates. See Pham and Zelenyuk (2019) for this and more on computational matters.

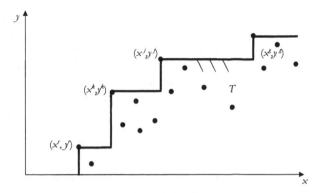

Figure 8.6 An example of AAM for T that only imposes Free Disposability.

Figure 8.7 An example of AAM for $L(y)$ that only imposes Free Disposability.

economics, one often considers the technology with convex $L(y)$ and $P(x)$, yet may view the convexity of T as too restrictive.

An AAM that does not impose convexity was suggested in the seminal work of Deprins et al. (1984).[33] All that such an AAM consists of is the manifestation of free disposability of inputs and outputs. Not surprisingly, it is referred to as the *Free Disposal Hull* (FDH) estimator, which can be formally defined as

$$\hat{T} \equiv \cup_{k=1}^{n}\{(x, y) \in \mathfrak{R}_{+}^{N} \times \mathfrak{R}_{+}^{M} : y \leq y^{k}, x^{k} \leq x\}. \qquad (8.7.1)$$

Figure 8.6 gives a geometric illustration of such a technology in the two-dimensional (x, y)-space, while Figure 8.7 and 8.8 give it for the two-dimensional input and output spaces, respectively. The geometric intuition is that now all the points to the right and down for Figure 8.6 (to the right and up for Figure 8.7 and to the left and down for Figure 8.8) from any

---

[33] Some roots of this concept can also be found in Afriat (1972).

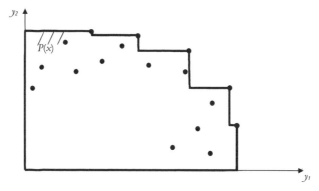

Figure 8.8 An example of AAM for $P(x)$ that only imposes Free Disposability.

observed activity must belong to T, but this is not guaranteed for any convex combinations of points in those sets.

There are various ways to implement the FDH in practice. One particular formulation of the FDH estimator is via the hybrid of integer programming and linear programming – such a formulation is the same as the DEA-VRS, but where the constraints "$z^k \geq 0$, $k = 1, \ldots, n$" are replaced with "$z^k \in \{0, 1\}$, $k = 1, \ldots, n$." In a sense, this formulation emphasizes the relationship between the two approaches: the technology set estimated via the DEA-VRS approach is the *convex closure* of the FDH-estimated technology set. Specifically, for any allocation (x, y), the FDH-estimate of the *output-oriented* Farrell technical efficiency score, under the assumption of free disposability of all outputs and all inputs can be stated as

$$\widehat{TE}(x, y) \equiv \max_{\theta} \theta \tag{8.7.2a}$$

s.t.

$$\sum_{k=1}^{n} z^k y_m^k \geq \theta \, y_m, \; m = 1, \ldots, M, \tag{8.7.2b}$$

$$\sum_{k=1}^{n} z^k x_l^k \leq x_l, \; l = 1, \ldots, N, \tag{8.7.2c}$$

$$\sum_{k=1}^{n} z^k = 1, \tag{8.7.2d}$$

$$\theta \geq 0, \; z^k \in \{0, 1\}, \; k = 1, \ldots, n. \tag{8.7.2e}$$

Similarly, for an allocation (x, y), the FDH-estimate of the *input-oriented* Farrell technical efficiency score under the assumption of free disposability of all inputs and all outputs is given by

$$\widehat{TE}_i(x, y) \equiv \min_{\theta} \theta \qquad (8.7.3a)$$

s.t.

$$\sum_{k=1}^{n} z^k y_m^k \geq y_m, \quad m = 1, \ldots, M, \qquad (8.7.3b)$$

$$\sum_{k=1}^{n} z^k x_l^k \leq \theta x_l, \quad l = 1, \ldots, N, \qquad (8.7.3c)$$

$$\sum_{k=1}^{n} z^k = 1,$$

$$\theta \geq 0, \quad z^k \in \{0, 1\}, \quad k = 1, \ldots, n. \qquad (8.7.3d)$$

An alternative (and equivalent) formulation of the FDH estimator can be given via the min–max optimization problem, which is typically faster to compute as it essentially involves only sorting procedures (e.g., see Simar and Wilson, 2013 for more details).[34]

Complete abandoning of the convexity assumption might not be desirable, however. Convexity of the input requirement set has quite strong economic appeal and often is well justified on an intuitive basis. In producer theory, for example, convexity of the input requirement set is often motivated by beliefs that an average is often viewed to be at least as good as the extremes and the desire to have a nonincreasing marginal rate of technical substitution ($\partial x_i / \partial x_j |_{D_i(y,x)=1}$) between any two inputs. Convexity of the technology set is clearly a sufficient condition for convexity of the input requirement set, yet it is not necessary and, in some sense, may be "too much": a very "non-convex" technology set T can still allow for convexity of input requirement sets or convexity of output sets or both.[35]

Non-convex technologies that have convex input requirements sets are sometimes referred to as *quasi-concave technologies*. In particular, the output correspondence P characterizing technology T is called quasi-concave if and only if

$$P(x') \cap P(x^o) \subseteq P(tx' + (1-t)x^o), \quad \forall x', x^o \in \mathfrak{R}_+^N, \quad \forall t \in [0, 1],$$

and, the input requirement correspondence is called quasi-concave if and only if

$$L(y') \cap L(y^o) \subseteq L(ty' + (1-t)y^o), \quad \forall y', y^o \in \mathfrak{R}_+^M, \quad \forall t \in [0, 1].$$

---

[34] For a stochastic version of FDH, see Simar and Zelenyuk (2011).

[35] Also note that in statistical terms, imposing the assumption of convexity on the technology set T when the true T is not convex may lead to an inconsistent estimation of T and the related measures.

The following lemma clarifies the relationship between quasi-concavity and convexity.[36]

Theorem. *Let technology be characterized by T with associated output correspondence P that defines output sets $P(x)$ and input requirement correspondence L that defines input requirement sets $L(y)$. We have:*

> (i) *$L(y)$ is convex for all $y \in \mathfrak{R}_+^M$ if and only if P is quasi-concave for all $x \in \mathfrak{R}_+^N$.*
>
> (ii) *$P(x)$ is convex for all $x \in \mathfrak{R}_+^N$ if and only if L is quasi-concave for all $y \in \mathfrak{R}_+^M$.*

The AAMs discussed above can be modified to estimate the quasi-concave technologies and we leave these as exercises (see Petersen, 1990; Bogetoft, 1996; Bogetoft et al., 2000, and, more recently, Pham and Zelenyuk, 2019 for a related discussion). Meanwhile, note that graphically, technology with a quasi-concave P would look like that in Figure 8.6 and Figure 8.8, but $L(y)$ would be the convex hull of the $L(y)$ in Figure 8.7. Similarly, technology with a quasi-concave L would look like that in Figure 8.6 and Figure 8.7, but $P(x)$ would be the convex hull of the $L(y)$ in Figure 8.8.

8.8 INTERTEMPORAL CONTEXT

All of the AAMs presented above can be easily cast in the intertemporal context – when one wants to estimate an efficiency score (or a value of the distance function) for a firm in one period relative to the frontier in a different period, e.g., as is required by some of the productivity indexes considered in Chapter 4. For example, the *output*-oriented Shephard's distance function under the assumption of VRS (along with free disposability of all inputs and all outputs), for an allocation (x_s, y_t) relative to the (estimated) technology for period τ can be estimated via

$$\left(\hat{D}_o^\tau(x_s, y_t) \right)^{-1} \equiv \max_{\theta, z^1, \dots, z^n} \theta \tag{8.8.1a}$$

s.t.

$$\sum_{k=1}^n z^k y_{m\tau}^k \geq \theta\, y_{mt}, \quad m = 1, \dots, M, \tag{8.8.1b}$$

$$\sum_{k=1}^n z^k x_{l\tau}^k \leq x_{ls}, \quad l = 1, \dots, N, \tag{8.8.1c}$$

---

[36] See Shephard (1953, 1970) and Pham and Zelenyuk (2019) for more details and proofs.

$$\sum_{k=1}^{n} z^k = 1, \tag{8.8.1d}$$

$$\theta \geq 0, \; z^k \geq 0, \; k = 1, \ldots, n. \tag{8.8.1e}$$

In words, because the measurement is from an allocation (x_s, y_t), on the r.h.s. of the constraints we have x appearing with time-subscript s and y appearing with time-subscript t. Moreover, note that the l.h.s. of the constraints uses the data on (x, y) with subscript τ because the measurement is with respect to the technology estimated as the observed best-practice in the period τ. As before, the CRS or NIRS assumptions can be added to this formulation by removing the constraint $\sum_{k=1}^{n} z^k = 1$ or replacing it with $\sum_{k=1}^{n} z^k \leq 1$, respectively. Similar formulations can be stated for many other cases of AAMs and for many other efficiency measures that we considered above (and those omitted) and we leave these tasks to the readers as fruitful exercises.

8.9   RELATIONSHIP BETWEEN CCR AND FARRELL

In their seminal work, Charnes et al. (1978) suggested the following approach of estimating the efficiency score of a DMU $j \in \{1, \ldots, n\}$:

$$E_{i,CCR}^{j} = \max_{\substack{v_1,\ldots,v_N \\ u_1,\ldots,u_M}} \left\{ \frac{\sum_{m=1}^{M} u_m y_m^{j}}{\sum_{l=1}^{N} v_l x_l^{j}} : \frac{\sum_{m=1}^{M} u_m y_m^{k}}{\sum_{l=1}^{N} v_l x_l^{k}} \leq 1, \; k = 1, \ldots, n, \right.$$

$$\left. u_m \geq 0, \; v_l \geq 0, \; l = 1, \ldots, N; \; m = 1, \ldots, M \right\}, \tag{8.9.1}$$

and in the operations research literature, this formulation is often referred to as the "CCR model," to honor the authors who proposed it.

Let us now try to understand the intuition behind this expression. Firstly, note that the objective function here is an *aggregate output* for DMU j divided by an *aggregate input* for the same DMU j, and so in this sense it is a productivity measure or productivity score.

Secondly, note that the aggregation in this productivity score is done via a weighted summation of outputs and inputs in much the same way as one would compute revenues and costs, respectively, except that instead of actual output and input prices this aggregation is using weights $u_1, \ldots, u_M$ and $v_1, \ldots, v_N$. Importantly, note that these weights serve as intensity variables in this optimization problem (8.9.1), so they are determined in this optimization.

Thirdly, note that the optimization problem (8.9.1) has n constraints, where the l.h.s. has the same form as the objective function, i.e., the productivity score, for every DMU $k = 1, \ldots, n$, and it is required to be less than one, implying that the $E_{i,CCR}^{j}$ would be valued between zero and one.

Fourthly, note that the weights $u_1, \ldots, u_M$ used to construct the output index for *each* DMU, and the weights $v_1, \ldots, v_N$ used to construct the input index, are all required to be nonnegative and to be the same across all DMUs within the estimation of (8.9.1) for DMU j. In a sense, these weights are like prices and, in fact, they are referred to as the "shadow prices."

Thus, the solution to (8.9.1) would carry an intuition of some type of "normalized productivity measure" for DMU j because, essentially, it gives information on aggregate output per aggregate input, normalized by selecting aggregation weights that make this DMU look the best it could given the data on all other DMUs. Indeed, since the problem (8.9.1) is a *maximization* over the aggregation weights, this optimization problem can be intuitively interpreted as a search for the *most favorable* weights for DMU j so that the resulting productivity measure for DMU j is as high as possible and consistent with the constraints requiring the same productivity measures for all other DMUs to be bounded from above by unity. In other words – in fact, in the words of Charnes et al. (1978): "Under these observations and constraints, no other set of common weights will give a more favorable rating relative to the reference set."[37]

What we show below, following Charnes et al. (1978), is that the efficiency score $E^j_{i,CCR}$, obtained from problem (8.9.1) is actually the same as the Farrell input-oriented technical efficiency score based on the activity analysis model with the CRS and additivity assumptions as well as free disposability of all inputs and outputs assumptions imposed on the technology set, which we considered in this chapter earlier. Moreover, the weights in this problem have a meaningful economic interpretation of being the (normalized) shadow prices, i.e., the Lagrange-multipliers for (input and output) constraints in the optimization problem for the estimation of Farrell efficiency scores based on the activity analysis model we considered earlier.

To see the relationship, let us first rewrite (8.9.1) in an equivalent but more compact vector-matrix form

$$E^j_{i,CCR} = \max_{v,u} \left\{ \frac{u'y^j}{v'x^j} \quad : \quad \frac{u'y^k}{v'x^k} \leq 1, \quad k = 1, \ldots, n, \quad u \geq 0, v \geq 0 \right\},$$
(8.9.2)

where $u' = (u_1, \ldots, u_M)$ and $v' = (v_1, \ldots, v_N)$. Clearly, this problem is *not* a LP problem – it is what is called the *fractional* programming problem, yet it is equivalent to the following LP problem

$$E^j_{i,CCR} = \max_{v,u} \left\{ U'y^j \quad : \quad V'x^j = 1, U'y^k - V'x^k \leq 0, \right.$$

$$\left. k = 1, \ldots, n, \ U \geq 0, V \geq 0 \right\},$$
(8.9.3)

---

[37] Although, note that there might be other sets of common weights that give an equally favorable rating, i.e., the optimal weights here are not unique in general.

where $U' = (u'_1, \ldots, u'_M)$ and $V' = (v'_1, \ldots, v'_N)$ is another set of weights (intensity variables) to be optimized over.[38]

Remarkably, this last LP problem in (8.9.3) is dual to the model we used above to estimate the Farrell input-oriented technical efficiency score of the DMU j via the activity analysis model assuming CRS, additivity and free disposability of all inputs and all outputs. That is, (8.9.3) is dual to

$$\widehat{TE}_i(y^j, x^j) := \min_{\lambda, z^1, \ldots, z^n} \left\{ \lambda : \sum_{k=1}^n z^k y^k \geq y^j, \ \sum_{k=1}^n z^k x^k \leq \lambda x^j, \right.$$

$$\left. z^k \geq 0, \ \lambda \geq 0, \ k = 1, \ldots, n \right\}, \qquad (8.9.4)$$

which is sometimes referred to as the "envelopment form of DEA" (although we prefer calling it the "AAM form"), while its dual, (8.9.3), is sometimes referred to as the "multiplier form" of DEA.

Below we sketch a proof of this fundamental for the theory of efficiency and productivity analysis result. To do so, we need to recall the duality theory in linear programming. To facilitate our discussion, let us denote the (intensity) variables in the primal LP with the (H by 1) vector ξ, and the (intensity) variables in the dual LP with the (L by 1) vector Z. Also, denote A as a (H by L) matrix of constants, as well as b and c as (H by 1) and (L by 1) vectors of constants. These vectors and matrices will be used to define the objective functions and constraints in the primal and dual LP problems.[39] Also, recall the following well-known theorem in mathematics (e.g., see Dantzig, 1963).

Theorem. *(Duality in LP): For any LP problem, given by*

$$b'\xi^* = \max_{\xi} \{b'\xi \ : \ A' \times \xi \leq c, \ \xi \geq 0\}, \qquad (8.9.5)$$

one can always construct dual LP problem given by

$$c'Z^* = \min_{Z} \{c'Z \ : \ A \times Z \geq b, \ Z \geq 0\}, \qquad (8.9.6)$$

that will ensure that the optimal value of the objective function in the primal is the same as that in the dual (i.e., $b'\xi^* = c'Z^*$). Moreover, the optimal values of the variables in the primal LP, ξ^*, are (normalized and potentially non-unique) shadow prices of the corresponding constraints in the dual LP (i.e., $A \times Z \geq b$) and vice versa.

---

[38] Check the relationship of (8.9.3) and (8.9.2) by letting $U = tu$, $V = tv$, for any $t > 0$, plugging them into (8.9.3), and after simple algebraic rearrangements one gets (8.9.2).

[39] Note that the dual to the dual of any primal returns back to the original primal. Therefore, the choice of which formulation is called dual and which one is called primal is arbitrary, although some conventions may exist in the literature. Usually, (8.9.4) is referred to as the primal DEA-CRS formulation while (8.9.3) is its dual, although it can also be the opposite.

This fundamental theorem says exactly what we want to show: that the optimal value of the objective function in (8.9.3), and therefore in (8.9.1), is the same as that in (8.9.4). Moreover, in order to get information about the shadow prices for each constraint in the activity analysis model (here with the CRS, additivity and free disposability assumptions), we just need to get solutions to the primal model (8.9.3), ξ^*.[40]

So, let us convince ourselves that (8.9.4) is indeed dual to (8.9.3). For this, note that we can rewrite (8.9.3) as

$$E_{i,CCR}^{j} = \max_{U,V} U'y^j + V' \cdot 0 \qquad E_{i,CCR}^{j} = \max_{U,V} \underbrace{\begin{bmatrix} y^j & 0 \end{bmatrix}}_{b'} \times \underbrace{\begin{bmatrix} U & V \end{bmatrix}'}_{\xi'}$$

s.t. $\qquad\qquad\qquad\qquad\qquad\qquad$ s.t.

$$
\begin{aligned}
U' \cdot 0 + V'x^j &\leq 1 \\
U' \cdot 0 - V'x^j &\leq \text{-}1 \\
U'y^1 + V'x^1 &\leq 0 \\
\cdots\cdots\cdots\cdots\cdots\cdots \\
U'y^n - V'x^n &\leq 0 \\
U \geq 0, \quad V &\geq 0
\end{aligned}
\quad\Longleftrightarrow\quad
\underbrace{\begin{bmatrix} 0 & (x^j)' \\ 0 & (-x^j)' \\ (y^1) & (-x^1)' \\ \cdots & \cdots \\ (y^n)' & (-x^n)' \end{bmatrix}}_{A'} \times \underbrace{\begin{bmatrix} U \\ V \end{bmatrix}}_{\xi} \leq \underbrace{\begin{bmatrix} 1 \\ -1 \\ 0 \\ \cdots \\ 0 \end{bmatrix}}_{c},
$$

$$U \geq 0, \qquad V \geq 0.$$

Or, more, compactly it can be stated as

$$E_{i,CCR}^{j} = \max_{\xi} \{b'\xi \quad : \quad A' \times \xi \leq c, \quad \xi \geq 0\}. \tag{8.9.7}$$

Applying the duality theorem stated in (8.9.5)–(8.9.6), one must see the dual to (8.9.7) is given by

$$E_{i,CCR}^{j} = \min_{Z} \{c'Z \quad : \quad A \times Z \geq b, \quad Z \geq 0\}, \tag{8.9.8}$$

where, in our context, $Z = (\lambda^1, \lambda^2, z^1, \ldots, z^n)'$.

Now, to see what expression (8.9.8) implies, let us fill out the matrices in (8.9.8), and we get

---

[40] To clarify further, note that here, as would be in general in a LP problem, the optimal solutions ξ^* and Z^* can be, and often are, non-unique, yet when they enter the objective functions of the LP problems they yield unique optimal values of the objective functions, $b'\xi^*$ and $c'Z^*$, which happen to be equal, due to the duality theorem. This means that DEA estimates of efficiency scores are unique and can be computed either via the dual or the primal LP problems, whichever is easier. In practice, it is usually the dual formulation of DEA given in (8.9.3) that is faster to compute, especially for large data sets with many DMUs.

$$E_{i,CCR}^{j} = \min_{Z} c'Z = \min_{Z} \begin{bmatrix} 1 & -1 & 0 & \cdots & 0 \end{bmatrix} \times \begin{bmatrix} \lambda^1 & \lambda^2 & z^1 & \cdots & z^n \end{bmatrix}'$$

$$= \min_{Z} \lambda^1 - \lambda^2$$

s.t.

$$\begin{bmatrix} 0 & 0 & y^1 & \cdots & y^n \\ x^j & -x^j & -x^1 & \cdots & -x^n \end{bmatrix} \times \begin{bmatrix} \lambda^1 \\ \lambda^2 \\ z^1 \\ \cdots \\ z^n \end{bmatrix} \geq \begin{bmatrix} y^j \\ 0 \end{bmatrix}.$$

Now, multiply the matrices through and let $\lambda \equiv \lambda^1 - \lambda^2$, and obtain the following optimization problem,

$$E_{i,CCR}^{j} = \min_{\lambda, z^1, \ldots, z^n} \left\{ \lambda : \sum_{k=1}^{n} z^k y^k \geq y^j, \sum_{k=1}^{n} z^k x^k \leq \lambda x^j, z^k \geq 0, k = 1, \ldots, n \right\},$$

which is the LP that estimates the Farrell input-oriented technical efficiency score (under CRS, additivity and free disposability of inputs and outputs) for the DMU j, restated in (8.9.4), as we wanted to show.

The bottom line of these derivations is that the two approaches – one proposed in a seminal work of Farrell (1957) and the other one proposed by Charnes et al. (1978) – are equivalent ways of estimating technical efficiency. Some researchers, especially those in business, operations research/management science and engineering tend to prefer the CCR formulation, while others, mainly those from economics and the econometrics areas tend to refer to formulation (8.9.4) that is based on the economic activity analysis models, although the two approaches are equivalent ways of modeling the same phenomenon – input-oriented technical efficiency of a DMU. Similar arguments, with some modifications, can be made for NIRS and VRS models, which we leave to the readers.[41]

Also note that one can impose additional constraints onto the multiplier form of the DEA (which, in turn, will modify the envelopment form), with a goal to better mimic the real production process: e.g., to incorporate some out-of-sample knowledge from experts, engineering requirements, regulator's restrictions, etc.

The sub-area of DEA dealing with such constraints is often referred to as the study of "weight-restrictions in DEA," which has been extensively explored in the operations research/management science side of the DEA literature.

Importantly, note that (unlike additional constraints in the AAM or envelopment form of DEA) the weight restrictions in the multiplier form of DEA would never lead to an increase of efficiency scores, and in fact they often decrease them (i.e., increase inefficiency scores). As a result, the discriminative

---

[41] E.g., see Färe et al. (1983), Banker et al. (1984) and textbook discussions in Charnes et al. (1994), Ray (2004), Cooper et al. (2007b) and Cooper et al. (2011b).

power of the approach may, and often does, increase due to such additional weight-restrictions in the multiplier form of DEA, besides potentially more realistic modeling of the production process.

However, note that the caveats we discussed for the additional restrictions in the AAM framework (higher computational complexity, lower resistance to problems of infeasibility, selection of inferior local optima and degenerate solutions) also apply here, for the weight restrictions in the multiplier form of DEA. Therefore, the general advice is the same: such restrictions must be added with care, based on well-grounded judgments.

Separate chapters can be written on this topic and it is outside of the scope of this more generally targeted book. For a reader interested in this topic, we recommend to start with such classical works as Dyson and Thanassoulis (1988); Charnes et al. (1990); Thompson et al. (1990). More recent and fundamental developments that gave new interpretations (as "technological trade-offs") of various weight restrictions in DEA can be found in Podinovski (2004), Podinovski and Bouzdine-Chameeva (2013), Atici and Podinovski (2015), to mention just a few. Also see reviews on this topic by Allen et al. (1997), Thanassoulis et al. (2004), Podinovski (2015) for more details and many useful references on the topic.

8.10 CONCLUDING REMARKS

As mentioned at the beginning of the chapter, we did not attempt to exhaust everything that has been suggested in the literature on the topic – realizing such a task would be practically infeasible. The goal was much more modest: we focused on a few of the most popular methods, considering their "step-by-step construction," intuition, key properties and some modifications – the aspects that we consider very useful for a reader to start and advance in her/his own research and, possibly, advance the frontier of the research.

A few remarks on the literature are in order. Undoubtedly, the two most influential for the origins of envelopment-type estimators were the seminal works of Farrell (1957) and Charnes et al. (1978), which deservingly attract most citations in the area.[42] However, it is also important to recognize that the roots for this approach also go back to the seminal works of Leontief (1925), von Neumann (1945),[43] Kantorovich (1960)[44] and Dantzig (1949, 1955).[45] These works formed the inspiration and the foundation of DEA and many other approaches, including the duality theory and the linear programming method.

Among these (and likely in general), von Neumann (1945) appears to be the first among the most rigorous mathematical treatments (in a general equilibrium set up, with use of his duality theory and his generalized version

---

[42] E.g., Google Scholar reports (on 11/10/2017) over 18,500 and 28,600 citations, respectively.

[43] This is the English version of his article published in 1938.

[44] This is the English version of his article published in 1939.

[45] Also see Dantzig (1963, 1982).

of the fix-point theorem to establish equilibrium) that explicitly recognized that an economic system can have production inefficiency, reflected by his *coefficient of expansion* of the economy (an analogue of what later was called Farrell efficiency measure) being less than 1. This and other works of von Neumann (1945) have influenced many scholars in various fields of economics. Among the most important of these for the productivity and efficiency analysis are the fundamental contributions from Debreu (1951), Koopmans (1951a,b) and Shephard (1953) that also preceded and influenced Farrell (1957) and then Charnes et al. (1978).

Initially, Farrell's work has been to some extent largely ignored by mainstream research, with the exception of a few works (e.g., Seitz, 1970; Timmer, 1971; Afriat, 1972). This changed with the seminal work of Charnes et al. (1978) that generalized Farrell's ideas (to multi-output context), mathematically established duality results and equivalence with the alternative (and often more convenient) interpretation – as the estimation of an optimal productivity score (aggregate output to aggregate input ratio). Charnes et al. (1978) also coined this approach as the DEA and their inspiring and now seminal work essentially opened a new and important interdisciplinary area of research, known these days as the DEA field, attracting attention from not only economists but also many statisticians and, importantly, business and management scientists and practitioners from many industries and government agencies.

The important extensions of the Farrell/CCR approach, such as DEA with non-CRS assumptions and the non-convex activity analysis modeling via FDH and modeling of non-discretionary inputs formed what perhaps can be called the second important wave of research in the area, especially influenced by the seminal works of Afriat (1972) and followed up by Färe et al. (1983), Banker et al. (1984), Deprins et al. (1984), Färe and Grosskopf (1985) and Banker and Morey (1986a,b).

An important stream of DEA literature has been dedicated to estimating technologies with weak disposability of inputs or (and especially) outputs. The origin of this modeling goes back to at least Shephard (1974), which inspired the first wave in this stream, e.g., Färe and Svensson (1980), Färe and Grosskopf (1983), Grosskopf (1986), Tyteca (1996), Chung et al. (1997b), Tyteca (1997), among others, as well as a more recent wave in this stream, Scheel (2001), Seiford and Zhu (2002), Färe and Grosskopf (2003, 2004), Kuosmanen (2005), Färe and Grosskopf (2009), Førsund (2009), Kuosmanen and Podinovski (2009), Zhou et al. (2008), Sahoo et al. (2011), Podinovski and Kuosmanen (2011), Pham and Zelenyuk (2019), to mention just a few. Some of the recent surveys on this topic are Dakpo et al. (2017) and Sueyoshi et al. (2017), where more useful references on the topic can be found. Other important contributions to DEA modeling under different types of technologies include works of Petersen (1990), Bogetoft (1996), Bogetoft et al. (2000), to mention a few.

There are other streams and branches of DEA (and, more generally, envelopment estimators) research, which, due to space limitations, we omitted here.

One of them focuses on modeling network technologies (static and dynamic) – originating with the seminal works of Färe and Grosskopf (1996), Färe et al. (1996) and elaborated on in many other works more recently (e.g., see Tone and Tsutsui, 2010, 2014 and Kao, 2009a,b, 2014 and references therein). Another is about the game theory connection and interpretation of the DEA approach. Implicit roots of this stream (as of many others) can be found in the seminal work of von Neumann (1945), while more explicit examples can be found in Hao et al. (2000), Nakabayashi and Tone (2006), Liang et al. (2008), Lozano (2012), and more about this can be learned from recent reviews, e.g., by Cook et al. (2010) and Lozano et al. (2016).

Other valuable references include textbooks on DEA by Charnes et al. (1994), Ray (2004), Cooper et al. (2007b) and Cooper et al. (2011b), reviews by Boussofiane et al. (1991), Førsund and Sarafoglou (2002), Cook and Seiford (2009) and Emrouznejad et al. (2008), to mention just a few.

Finally, another important wave of research that brought DEA and FDH to a completely different level is the work on statistical analysis for these estimators, due to the seminal works of Léopold Simar and many of his co-authors, including famous mathematical statisticians of these days, as will be discussed in greater detail in the next chapter.

8.11 EXERCISES

1. Show that (8.1.9) satisfies CRS and prove that $\widehat{TE}_i(y, x) = 1/\widehat{TE}(x, y)$.
2. Prove the *homogeneity* properties of $\widehat{TE}_i(y, x)$ and $\widehat{TE}(x, y)$ in general and under CRS.
3. Are the technology characterizations obtained via the various AAMs above closed sets? Prove it.
4. Are the technology characterizations obtained via the various AAMs above convex sets? Prove it.
5. Write the dual LP for the VRS formulation (see Banker and Morey, 1986a,b).
6. Build AAMs that allow for weak (but not free) disposability of inputs or/and outputs and formulate estimators of various efficiency measures for such AAM. (See Pham and Zelenyuk, 2018 for some solutions and references for related works.)
7. Write out AAM/DEA formulation that accounts for a network nature (static or dynamic) of a production process, e.g., in banking or insurance business. (See Färe and Grosskopf, 1996; Färe et al., 1996; Tone and Tsutsui, 2010, 2014; and Kao (2009a,b, 2014) and references there.)
8. Write out AAM/DEA formulations for estimating scale elasticity based on Farrell-type measures and based on the directional distance function. (See Zelenyuk, 2013a for some solutions and references for related works.)

CHAPTER 9

Statistical Analysis for DEA and FDH: Part 1

9.1 STATISTICAL PROPERTIES OF DEA AND FDH

The goal of this section is to summarize the main statistical properties of the DEA and FDH estimators that lay out a foundation for further statistical analysis involving the DEA and FDH scores. The first aspect to note is that the two fundamental assumptions of DEA and FDH, postulating that all DMUs have access to the same technology and no noise[1] (and so $\Pr\{(x^k, y^k) \in T, \forall k = 1, \dots, n\} = 1$), imply that, for the DEA and FDH estimators, we always have $\hat{T} \subseteq T$. This means that $\hat{T}$ is a downward biased estimate of the technology set $T = \{(x, y) : x$ can produce $y\}$. Consequently, the DEA or FDH also give a biased estimate of the true efficiency scores. Specifically, at any fixed points $(x, y) \in T$, for the output-oriented (Farrell measure of technical) efficiency, the bias is always downward, i.e.,

$$1 \leq \widehat{TE}(x, y) \leq TE(x, y) \leq \infty, \tag{9.1.1}$$

and for the input-oriented analogue, the bias is always upward, i.e.,

$$0 \leq TE(x, y) \leq \widehat{TE}(x, y) \leq 1. \tag{9.1.2}$$

Thus, the first question of interest is whether this bias disappears asymptotically or, more importantly, whether these estimators are consistent in the sense of mathematical statistics.

More formally, can we say that $\widehat{TE}(x, y) \rightarrow TE(x, y)$ in probability (weakly or strongly or uniformly) as $n \rightarrow \infty$? Of course, the sample size going to infinity never happens with real-world data, so this is an abstract theoretical property. Nevertheless, it also has an important practical meaning: intuitively, consistency means that an estimator gets close to the truth with a relatively large sample. In a sense, consistency is a minimal property that an estimator should have. An estimator that does not possess it can be doubted

---

[1] If one suspects there is noise or especially outliers, then it is advised to filter the data to remove the noise and outliers, e.g., by using the Stochastic DEA or Stochastic FDH approach of Simar and Zelenyuk (2011) or other methods.

as an appropriate one in a statistical sense (although it might still be useful in another sense).

A closely related property is the rate or speed of convergence (to the truth) of an estimator. Indeed, not only is it critical to have a consistent estimator but also one that converges to the truth reasonably fast, or faster than others. It is also important to know if, and how, the convergence rates depend on aspects of the model, e.g., its dimension (number of inputs and outputs).

The first breakthrough for the statistical properties of DEA was made by Banker (1993), who sketched a proof that, for the single-output case (in output-oriented context), under certain regularity conditions, the DEA approach provides a consistent estimator for the technical efficiency score and pointed out that it belongs to the class of maximum likelihood estimators. This result was then substantially empowered by Korostelev et al. (1995b,a), who also showed convergence of the estimated technology to the true technology for both DEA and FDH estimators. More importantly, they also derived precise rates of convergence of both estimators, showing that they depend on the dimension of the production model, as well as share some optimality properties under fairly general conditions of nonparametric estimation.

The convergence properties, including the rates of convergence, for the fully multivariate (multi-input–multi-output) case were first established in the seminal work of Kneip et al. (1998). Meanwhile, the first breakthrough on the limiting distribution of the DEA estimator was made by Gijbels et al. (1999), but only for the one-input–one-output case. About a decade later, Kneip et al. (2008) extended this result to the fully multivariate case for DEA with VRS assumption and, importantly, also proved consistency of various bootstrap procedures. Soon after, the asymptotic distribution for the case of DEA with CRS was established by Park et al. (2010). Meanwhile, the limiting distribution of FDH estimator for the fully multivariate case was pioneered by Park et al. (2000), while consistency of the bootstrap for the FDH estimator was established by Jeong and Simar (2006).

To summarize and employ these key statistical results in our further discussions, we will follow the above-mentioned papers and first outline the data generating process (DGP). Note that most of the results in the literature were explicitly derived for the input-oriented case, with a note that the output-oriented case is similar. Meanwhile, more recently it appears that the output-oriented case has gained greater popularity in practice, and so for pedagogical purposes we will mostly focus on the output-oriented context in our formal discussions, while the input-oriented case is similar and often can be found in the original papers.

9.1.1 Assumptions on the Data Generating Process

Different results found in the literature generally required somewhat different assumptions on the DGP, but their essence can be grasped with, for example, statistical assumptions (SA) taken from Simar and Zelenyuk (2006, 2007), which were in turn adapted (to the group-wise heterogeneous case in the output-oriented context) from the seminal works of Kneip et al. (1998) and Korostelev et al. (1995b,a).[2] These assumptions are usually stated after transforming variables into a (partially) polar coordinates system. Specifically, let $\omega(y) \in \mathfrak{R}_+^1$ denote the modulus of $y \in \mathfrak{R}_+^M$, with $\omega(y) = \sqrt{y'y}$, and $\eta = \eta(y) \in [0, \pi/2]^{M-1}$ denote the angle of $y \in \mathfrak{R}_+^M$, where $\eta_m = \arctan(y_{m+1}/y_1)$, if $y_1 > 0$ or $\eta_m = \pi/2$ if $y_1 = 0$ for $m = 1, \ldots, M-1$. For any (x, y), let $y^\partial(x)$ denote the radial projection of y (keeping x fixed) onto the frontier of the technology set, i.e.,

$$y^\partial(x) = y \times TE(x, y).$$

Assume:

SA1 The data set on input–output observations, denoted as $\mathscr{S}_n = \{(x^k, y^k) : k = 1, \ldots, n\}$, is a sample of independent random variables on technology set T, which is assumed to satisfy the regularity conditions of production theory (including free disposability of inputs and outputs and, if DEA is used, convexity of T). All observations in $\mathscr{S}_n$ can be partitioned to L subsamples so that each subsample l represents a distinct subgroup l in the population, thus $\mathscr{S}_n = \{(x^{l,k}, y^{l,k}) : k = 1, \ldots, n_l; \ l = 1, \ldots, L\}$, and $n_1 + \ldots + n_L = n$.

SA2 For all $l \in \{1, \ldots, L\}$, the input vector $x \in \mathfrak{R}_+^N$ is governed by some probability density function, $f_{x,l}(x)$, with compact support $\mathbb{X} \subseteq \mathfrak{R}_+^N$.

SA3 For all $l \in \{1, \ldots, L\}$ and all $x \in \mathbb{X}$, the vector $\eta = (\eta_1, \ldots, \eta_{M-1})$ has some conditional density, $q_l(\eta|x)$, on $[0, \pi/2]^{M-1}$, while the modulus ω has some conditional density, $f_l(\omega|\eta, x)$, where the support of ω is $[0, \omega(y^\partial(x))]$.[3]

SA4 For all $l \in \{1, \ldots, L\}$, $\forall x \in \mathbb{X}$, and $\forall \eta \in [0, \pi/2]^{M-1}$ there exist some constants, $\varepsilon_1 > 0$ and $\varepsilon_2 > 0$, such that $\forall \omega \in [\omega(y^\partial(x)), \omega(y^\partial(x)) + \varepsilon_2]$, $f_l(\omega|\eta, x) \geq \varepsilon_1, l \in \{1, \ldots, L\}$.

SA5 The efficiency measure $TE(x, y)$ is differentiable in x and y.

These assumptions are additional (to those from production theory) regularity conditions that define the DGP, ensuring such statistical properties of DEA and FDH estimators as convergence in probability (consistency) and convergence in distribution. We will refer to them as statistical regularity conditions for DEA and FDH and accept them for our further discussions (unless stated otherwise). Also note that since all the groups are assumed to have access to the same technology set T, the upper boundary of the support of $f_l(\omega|\eta, x)$ is the same for each group $l \in \{1, \ldots, L\}$, and so

$$\omega(y^\partial(x)) = \sup\left\{\omega \in \mathfrak{R}_+^1 : f_l(\omega|\eta, x) > 0\right\}. \tag{9.1.3}$$

---

[2] Also see a nice review and explanations in Simar and Wilson (2008).

[3] Note that this assumes that all the groups share the same technology set, though they may have different distributions of inefficiency with respect to the frontier of this same set and, of course, different realizations of the efficiency levels for each observation.

Accordingly, the relation between $\omega(y)$ and the technical efficiency measure at (x, y) can be rewritten as

$$TE(x, y) = \omega(y^{\partial}(x))/\omega(y). \tag{9.1.4}$$

Furthermore, in the DGP outlined by the SA1–SA5, although the same efficiency measure (9.1.4) is applied to all firms in the population, the resulting efficiency scores for particular DMUs and groups may still have different distributions across the different subgroups, $l \in \{1, \ldots, L\}$, within the populations.

The distribution of inputs and outputs is also allowed to vary across the groups. To keep track of this variety we will use superscripts k and l to denote that a variable or a measure is referring to a DMU $k \in \{1, \ldots, n_l\}$ that belongs to group $l \in \{1, \ldots, L\}$. Also note that SA3, along with (9.1.4), implies the existence of a conditional (on (η, x)) density for technical efficiency of a group $l \in \{1, \ldots, L\}$, with the support $[1, \infty]$, and we will denote it with $g_l(TE|\eta, x)$.

Furthermore, note that SA4, along with (9.1.4), implies that $g_l(TE|\eta, x) \geq \varepsilon_1$, $\forall TE \in [1, 1 + \varepsilon_2]$ for any group $l \in \{1, \ldots, L\}$.

All in all, with assumptions SA1–SA5, the DGP, which we denote with $\mathscr{P} = \mathscr{P}(T, \mathbb{G}_l(TE, \eta, x), l = 1, \ldots, L)$, is well defined through the joint densities of (TE, η, x), for all subgroups $l \in \{1, \ldots, L\}$, given by

$$\mathbb{G}_l(TE, \eta, x) = g_l(TE|\eta, x)q_l(\eta|x)f_{x,l}(x), \ l \in \{1, \ldots, L\}, \tag{9.1.5}$$

each with support $\Omega = [1, \infty) \times [0, \pi/2]^{M-1} \times \mathbb{X}$.

The DGP described above is assumed to generate our sample of input–output observations, $\mathscr{S}_n := \{(x_i, y_i) : i = 1, \ldots, n\}$, which are identically distributed within each subgroup $l \in \{1, \ldots, L\}$, yet not necessarily identically distributed across the groups. Also note again that the DGP described above preserves the assumption that all DMUs have access to the same technology, yet it also allows for the conditions of this access (i.e., level of ability to get to its frontier) to be different for different subgroups, and different realizations of inefficiency for each DMU.

Examples of such a DGP in economics may include cases when different subgroups (e.g., public vs. private firms, etc.) might have considerably different regulation regimes, different operational, and/or cultural environments that determine different economic incentives, etc. So, the marginal densities that generate the technical (in)efficiency scores of DMUs (and the densities generating the inputs and outputs) for these DMUs might be different across the subgroups, while the technology can still be the same for all the DMUs.

9.1.2 Convergence Rates of DEA and FDH

Given the statistical regularity conditions outlined in previous subsections and following the seminal works of Kneip et al. (1998), Park et al. (2000),

Kneip et al. (2008) and Park et al. (2010), it is now known that the rates of convergence of DEA and FDH estimators are given by

$$\widehat{TE}(x, y \mid \mathscr{S}_n) - TE(x, y) = O_p(n^{-\kappa}), \tag{9.1.6}$$

where for DEA-VRS we have $\kappa = 2/(N + M + 1)$, while for DEA-CRS we have $\kappa = 2/(N + M)$ and for FDH, we have $\kappa = 1/(N + M)$. Though originally, these rates were derived for the case of one group in a population, they are also preserved for the group-wise heterogeneous DGP characterized in the previous subsection, as was pointed out and adapted by Simar and Zelenyuk (2006, 2007).

Let us pause here for a bit and give some intuition for these somewhat theoretical statements. Intuitively, (9.1.6) says that the DEA and FDH estimators are practically close to the truth that they try to estimate (under the statistical regularity conditions for DEA and FDH listed above), if the sample size is large enough.

Moreover, note that despite there being only $n_l \leq n$ observations in any group $l \in \{1, \ldots, L\}$ of the sample, the convergence rate in this DGP depends on n rather than on n_l. This is because of the ("feasibility") assumption that all firms have access to the same technology, so all n observations were used to estimate individual technical efficiency of a DMU in any group relative to the DEA or FDH estimated best-practice frontier.

An alternative approach would be to allow different groups to have different technologies, $T^l, l \in \{1, \ldots, L\}$, which would require slight modifications of the assumptions listed above, and then the convergence rates will depend on n_l, $l \in \{1, \ldots, L\}$, i.e., the sample sizes of the groups used to estimate the group technologies.

9.1.3   The Dimensionality Problem

A very important point to note regarding the convergence rates summarized in the previous subsection is that, not only is there no precise rule as to what sizes of a sample shall be considered as "large enough," the larger the dimension of the production model estimated with DEA or FDH, the larger must be the sample to get accurate results.

This problem can be seen from (9.1.6), which says that the rates of convergence to the truth of both estimators negatively depend on the dimension of the production model (i.e., on the number of inputs and outputs) that one wants to estimate with the DEA or FDH. The higher the dimension, the slower the rate of convergence to the truth.

For example, for the case of one input and one output technology, (9.1.6) tells us that the rate of convergence of DEA-VRS is $n^{-2/3}$, which is in fact faster than the usual parametric rate ($n^{-1/2}$), and, in the case of $N + M = 3$, the DEA-VRS estimator attains the same rate as the usual parametric rate. However, the higher the dimension of the production model gets, the lower the rate of convergence becomes. A similar argument holds for the FDH estimator, whose rate is even slower as clarified by (9.1.6), and for the DEA under CRS, whose rate is slightly faster than under VRS assumption.

The phenomenon when the rate of convergence of an estimator negatively depends on the dimension of the estimated model is known in statistics as the "curse of dimensionality" problem and is quite common for nonparametric estimators, the class to which DEA and FDH belong. In some sense, this problem is the main price to pay for avoiding parametric assumptions.[4] We will see some Monte Carlo evidence of this problem in the context of density estimation below.

In practice, this problem means that, to have reliable results in using a nonparametric method, one would usually need to have more data than for the case of using a parametric estimator. Or, to put it another way, when the sample size is relatively small and the dimension of the model is relatively large, a nonparametric estimator (DEA, FDH, etc.) might be not very reliable and putting in some relevant parametric structure might be a safer way to go.

To minimize the curse of dimensionality, it is recommended that the dimension of the DEA/FDH model be kept at a minimum, i.e., parsimonious, as long as the production model is adequate to the empirical context. For this, one may consider combining some of the inputs (outputs) into more aggregate inputs (outputs). For example, different types of labor inputs can be aggregated into total labor costs, while different types of products can be aggregated into revenue for a group of such products, etc.[5]

As explained in Färe and Zelenyuk (2002, 2012), such aggregation typically introduces an aggregation bias relative to the disaggregated case (except for some special cases), yet such an aggregated approach often still bears the essence of the phenomenon of interest.

Interestingly, the aggregation bias partially compensates for the estimation bias since they often work in opposite directions. Indeed, while the estimated technical inefficiency scores are downward biased (i.e., showing less inefficiency than the true scores), the aggregation of inputs or outputs into sub-costs and sub-revenues, respectively, leads to part of the allocative inefficiency being counted in the technical inefficiency, which typically increases inefficiency scores, and thus usually leads to increasing the discriminative power of such an approach.[6]

---

[4] Generally it is impossible to say where the boundary for the choice of parametric vs. nonparametric is, mainly because it often depends on the context and data. Some Monte Carlo evidence on the impact of the "curse of dimensionality" onto inference is also available and can give useful insights into the problem (e.g., see Simar and Zelenyuk, 2006; Kneip et al., 2008, 2015, 2016; Simar and Zelenyuk, 2017, etc.).

[5] Ideally, one should use individual (for each DMU) prices for such aggregation, but if they are not available then one may use market or average prices. Often, however, already aggregated information is actually easier to obtain than the disaggregate one, so the aggregated approach is often a necessity and the important question is how far aggregated one shall go.

[6] See detailed discussion on the nature and the bounds of the aggregation bias in Färe and Zelenyuk (2002, 2012).

Aggregation of inputs into sub-costs and outputs into sub-revenues is not the only viable approach to meaningfully reduce the dimension of the DEA or FDH models. Alternatively, or additionally, one may also adapt the Principal Component Analysis (PCA), as was described in Daraio and Simar (2007a). One may (and in fact is recommended to) also use a parametric approach such as stochastic frontier analysis (see Chapter 11 and on) where the curse of dimensionality is typically not a problem (besides a small loss of degrees of freedom), although one may still experience the multicollinearity problem there and have to resolve it also via the aggregation approach or via PCA or both.

Finally, whichever way is used to reduce the dimensions, we also recommend performing a sensitivity analysis, to verify the robustness of the conclusions wrt small variations in specifications of production models used for DEA/FDH.[7]

9.2 INTRODUCTION TO BOOTSTRAP

Especially before (and to some extent after) the statistical properties of the DEA and FDH estimators were known, researchers usually resorted to the standard inference techniques to analyze the (estimates of) efficiency scores obtained from DEA and FDH. The most popular examples of such uses include a test on the means of efficiency scores as well as the regression analysis of efficiency, as the dependent variable, on some explanatory (or, as they are sometimes called, environmental) variables, using the (asymptotic) normality argument. Earlier studies that performed such analysis usually ignored the problems of bias of the estimated efficiency scores as well as the inherent dependency of the scores. The next wave of studies tried to address these problems by suggesting various types of bootstrap for correcting the intrinsic drawbacks of the DEA and FDH estimators, as well as to empower their advantages. We summarize some of these developments in this book, but to help to grasp the ideas better we feel obliged to give a brief overview or refresh some of the key ideas and formulas of the general bootstrap approach.

9.2.1 Bootstrap and the Plug-In Principle

In a nutshell, statistical bootstrap is a method of estimation of the sampling distribution of an estimator or statistic by resampling from the original data. The idea of the bootstrap was first laid out with a well-developed theory in the seminal work of Efron (1979), although some related ideas were proposed before that and much of the theory was developed later.[8]

Among the most encouraging conclusions from the bootstrap theory is that a consistent bootstrap can give an approximation to a sampling distribution

---

[7] E.g., see Zelenyuk and Zelenyuk (2015) and Chowdhury and Zelenyuk (2016) for some recent examples.

[8] E.g., for a survey of some key results and references, see Horowitz (2002).

of an estimator even if this distribution is unknown (even asymptotically) or difficult to estimate. Moreover, such approximation is at least as good as the approximation provided by the (first-order) asymptotic theory, under fairly moderate assumptions on the data-generating process. Moreover, the bootstrap can give an even more accurate approximation if the estimator (statistic) is asymptotically pivotal.[9]

Most importantly, for the case where the limiting distribution is unknown, an appropriate bootstrap procedure could provide the only adequate inference for the unknown true parameters.

For the context of efficiency analysis, the bootstrap was introduced by Simar (1992), further developed by Simar and Wilson (1998, 2000b,a), and more recently studied by Kneip et al. (2008), Simar and Zelenyuk (2007), to mention a few, whose work we follow here.

To understand the general bootstrap method intuitively, recall that classical statistics is based on learning about the population of interest based on analyzing the sample drawn from the population of interest.

For example, the point of interest could be some unknown population parameter (potentially a vector), call it $\theta \in \Theta$, where Θ is the space of possible parameters. Suppose we have some appropriate (at least consistent) estimator of θ based on the observed data, i.e., a sample $\{\xi_1, \xi_2, \ldots, \xi_n\}$ from the population of interest, and we denote this estimator with $\hat{\theta}_n = \hat{\theta}(\xi_1, \xi_2, \ldots, \xi_n)$.[10]

Researchers usually assume that there is some data generating process (DGP) that governs the realizations of a random variable into the observed data, which can be characterized by some distribution given the parameter θ, denoted by $F = F(\xi|\theta)$.[11] If we were to know F, then for some simple cases we could derive the sampling distribution of $\hat{\theta}_n$ and use it to do precise inference about the true θ.[12] Let us denote this sampling distribution with $\mathbb{G}_n(\theta|F) = \Pr(\hat{\theta}_n \leq \theta|F)$. When the sampling distribution is unknown, sometimes it is possible to derive the limiting or asymptotic distribution of $\hat{\theta}_n$, call it $\mathbb{G}_\infty(\theta|F)$, which one may use to do asymptotic inference.[13]

---

[9] A statistic (estimator) is asymptotically pivotal if its asymptotic distribution is independent from the unknown population parameters.

[10] In the context of frontier estimation, it could be that $\xi_i = (x^i, y^i)$, i.e., observation on input–output allocation of DMU i or $\xi_i = (x^i, y^i, Z_i)$, when there is also a vector of environmental variables, Z_i, that influences production. Meanwhile, $\hat{\theta}_n = \hat{\theta}(\xi_1, \xi_2, \ldots, \xi_n)$ could stand for the DEA or FDH estimator of efficiency scores, etc.

[11] For the efficiency context, this could be (9.1.5) that defines the DGP used to justify the DEA and FDH estimators.

[12] An example would be when $\hat{\theta}_n$ is a sample mean of iid observations from $\mathcal{N}(\mu, \sigma^2)$, implying that the sampling distribution of $\hat{\theta}_n$ would be $\mathcal{N}(\mu, \sigma^2/n)$, which can be used to do precise inference about θ.

[13] E.g., in the simplest case when $\hat{\theta}_n$ is the sample mean of a random sample from an unknown distribution with a finite mean and variance μ and σ^2, then under mild conditions, the central limit theorem ensures the limiting distribution of $\sqrt{n}(\hat{\theta}_n - \mu)/\sigma$ would be $\mathcal{N}(0, 1)$, which can be used for the asymptotic inference.

Now, suppose that we can draw not just one random sample, but many (e.g., some number B) random samples, and for each of them we would apply our estimator $\hat{\theta}_n$ to get a sequence of estimates $\{\hat{\theta}_{n,b} : b = 1, \ldots, B\}$ for θ. This sequence of estimates of θ would then allow us to obtain a numerical approximation of the sampling distribution of our estimator $\hat{\theta}_n$, i.e., of $\mathbb{G}_n(\theta|F)$. Of course, this would not give an analytical form of the sampling distribution, yet the numerical approximation can be made as precise as one wants by increasing the number of random samples, B, that we take from the population. Knowledge of such numerical approximation of the distribution of $\hat{\theta}_n$, may allow inferring on the true θ. For example, we can estimate confidence intervals, any quantile or percentile of this distribution, a p-value of a test about θ, etc., as will be described later. So in principle, this is an alternative way of getting information about the sampling distribution of an estimator or a statistic, $\mathbb{G}_n(\theta|F)$, not analytically but in a numerically approximated form. This way, however, is practically possible only in a controlled experiment that can be repeated a large number of times – as in the Monte Carlo experiments.

The idea of the bootstrap method is similar to the just described process, except that in the bootstrap, the resampling is done not from the population (which is usually impossible or too expensive to do in practice) but from the original sample treated as if it were the population (or resample from the true distribution, if it is known, with parameters estimated from the sample), and so it is practically feasible. More precisely, we can state the following definition of the bootstrap:

Definition. Statistical bootstrap is a *method of estimation of the sampling distribution*, and of related properties, of an estimator through resampling from the original sample. This resampling is done either (i) by using some appropriate nonparametric estimator of the DGP that produced the original sample, or (ii) by using the DGP itself, if its parametric form is known with the true parameters replaced by their consistent estimates from the original sample.

Alternatively, we can also say that $\mathbb{G}_n(\theta|F)$ is estimated by "plugging-in" an "appropriate" parametric or nonparametric estimator of F (call it $\hat{F}_n$), into $\mathbb{G}_n(\theta|F)$ and so we will denote the bootstrap estimator of the sampling distribution with $\mathbb{G}_n(\theta|\hat{F}_n)$. For this reason, the bootstrap method is sometimes referred to as an example of using the "plug-in" principle in statistics.

9.2.2   Bootstrap and the Analogy Principle

Let us give another interpretation of the bootstrap method – as an application of the analogy principle in statistics. Here, the analogy is between the "true world" and the "bootstrap world" or, perhaps more precisely, the "virtual world" that we generate using computers to mimic the true world. The true world here consists of the population (usually not entirely observed) and an observed sample based on which we get the estimates of the true characteristics or some parameters.

Meanwhile, in the bootstrap world, the same original sample is treated as the pseudo-population, while the estimates of its characteristics (mean, variance, quantiles, etc.) are treated as true characteristics of the pseudo-population. Furthermore, since this pseudo-population is fully observed, this means that, at least in principle, we have all the information about it. Specifically, we also know (or at least can approximate with any degree of accuracy) the relationship between the (pseudo) true parameters and their estimates. This relationship will then mimic or approximate the relationship between the true parameters and their estimates in the true world – which is of the main interest.

More formally, let us denote the data set with $S_n := \{\xi_1, \xi_2, \ldots, \xi_n\}$, which we assume was generated from some DGP characterized by some distribution function $F(\xi | \theta)$ where θ is the parameter of interest and $\hat{\theta}_n$ is its consistent estimator. The idea of the bootstrap method is to approximate the sampling distribution of $\hat{\theta}_n$ or of $(\hat{\theta}_n - \theta)$ by treating S_n as if it were the population (or, call it pseudo-population) and from which, using appropriate $\hat{F}_n$, we randomly draw the pseudo-samples or bootstrap-samples, which we denote with $S_{n*}^* = \left\{\xi_1^*, \xi_2^*, \ldots, \xi_{n*}^*\right\}$. Depending on the circumstances (which we discuss later), the random drawing can be done with replacement ("WR-design") or without replacement ("WOR-design"), which is with or without returning the drawn observation back before drawing another observation.

Moreover, the sample size in the pseudo-samples, n^*, is not necessarily the same as the original sample size, n, although most frequently, except for some particular cases, both are made to be the same and the WR-design is used – as we will also consider here, and so to simplify notation we will have $n^* = n$, and we explicitly note when it is theoretically needed otherwise.

Also note that since we have all the observations on the pseudo-population, S_n, we therefore have all the information about the distribution of S_n^*, at least in principle. In particular, we can use the same formula for estimating θ as the one used to the original sample, but now we apply it to each pseudo-sample $S_{n,b}^*$, where b is the subscript for particular bootstrap replication ($b = 1, \ldots, B$). By doing this, we will obtain $\left\{\theta_{n,b}^* : b = 1, \ldots, B\right\}$ – the set of B bootstrap estimates of pseudo-true parameter $\hat{\theta}_n$ of the pseudo-population. The main value of the bootstrap is in the fact that, if it is consistent (which we later define more formally) then the relationship between the bootstrap-based estimate (the pseudo-estimate) $\hat{\theta}_{n,b}^*$ and the original estimate $\hat{\theta}_n$ will mimic (or be an analog of) the relationship between the original estimate $\hat{\theta}_n$ and the (unobserved) true parameter θ. In other words, the bootstrap provides a valid (and sometimes the best available) asymptotic approximation of the sampling distribution if and only if we have

$$\hat{\theta}_{n,b}^* - \hat{\theta}_n | \hat{F}_n \overset{asy.}{\sim} \hat{\theta}_n - \theta | F. \tag{9.2.1}$$

Note, again, the analogy in the argument in (9.2.1): $\hat{\theta}_n$ is an empirical analogue of θ in the "true world." Similarly, $\hat{\theta}^*_{n,b}$ is an empirical analogue of $\hat{\theta}_n$ but in the pseudo (or bootstrap/virtual) world. Most importantly, the relationship of interest, $\hat{\theta}_n - \theta \,|\, F$, can be inferred from or mimicked by its analogue given by $\hat{\theta}^*_{n,b} - \hat{\theta}_n \,|\, \hat{F}_n$. Thus, statistical bootstrap can be understood as an application of the analogy principle in statistics. Indeed, in addition to the classical analogy between a population and its sample, bootstrap considers analogy between the sample and a resample from it, and the information inferred from the latter relationship (which is known) is then used to understand better the relationship between the population and its sample. If the relationship (9.2.1) is formally established, the rest is a matter of technicality. Specifically, since we have all the information about the distribution of S^*_n (because we have all the pseudo-population S_n), at least in principle, we also have all the information about the sampling distribution of $\hat{\theta}_n$ and, while its analytical form might be unknown, it can still be approximated by the Monte Carlo simulations from the original sample S_n, with an arbitrary degree of accuracy.

9.2.3   Practical Implementation of Bootstrap

While there are many types and sub-types of bootstrap methods, most of them follow similar steps when applied in practice and below we present a typical algorithm of a statistical bootstrap.

Step 1 *Estimation of the quantity of interest*: Compute the estimator $\hat{\theta}_n$ of the true parameter θ using the true sample $S_n = \{\xi_1, \xi_2, \dots, \xi_n\}$.

Step 2 *Generation of bootstrap samples*: Use an appropriate estimator of DGP, $\hat{F}_n$, to generate bootstrap samples $S^*_{n,b} = \left\{\xi^*_{1,b}, \xi^*_{2,b}, \dots, \xi^*_{n,b}\right\}$, where $b = 1, \dots, B$, denotes bootstrap replications.

Step 3 *Estimation of appropriate bootstrap analogue of the quantity of interest*: Compute the bootstrap estimate $\hat{\theta}^*_{n,b}$ of $\hat{\theta}_n$ via the same formula as $\hat{\theta}_n$ was computed in Step 1, but now use the bootstrapped sample $S^*_{n,b}$ obtained from Step 2, instead of S_n.

Step 4 *Replication*: Repeat Steps 2–3 B times to obtain and save $\hat{\theta}^*_{n,b}$ from all $b = 1, \dots, B$ iterations for further use.

Step 5 *Inference*: Use $\left\{\hat{\theta}^*_{n,b} - \hat{\theta}_n \,:\, b = 1, \dots, B\right\}$ from Step 4 to approximate the sampling distribution of $\hat{\theta}_n - \theta \,|\, F$ and then to infer about θ, e.g., construct confidence intervals, estimate and correct for bias of $\hat{\theta}_n$, perform statistical tests about θ or some functions of it.

The reader will already have a sense that the key in the bootstrap is to "appropriately" mimic the data generating process, and in particular the distribution $F(\xi|\theta)$, for "appropriately" drawing the bootstrap or the pseudo-samples from the original sample. That is, the key is the choice of $\hat{F}_n$ in Step 2 of the algorithm above that will ensure (9.2.1) holds, and there are several common choices of it, which can be classified into four cases.[14]

The first (and very special) case in choosing $\hat{F}_n$ is when one completely knows (or assumes) what the true $F(\xi|\theta)$ is (e.g., Normal, Chi-squared, Logistic, etc.) and then for obtaining the bootstrap or pseudo-samples one could draw from this very distribution – as in a Monte Carlo experiment.

The second, and more realistic, case is when one knows the distribution but not some of its parameters (e.g., σ^2 is unknown, etc.) – then one can draw from this known distribution with the unknown parameters replaced by their consistent estimates (which, remember, are treated as true parameters in the bootstrap world). Such a bootstrap is referred to as a *parametric bootstrap*—because it relies on the knowledge or assumption of the parametric form of $F(\xi|\theta)$.

The third and perhaps most realistic of the three cases is when $F(\xi|\theta)$ is completely unknown – then one must replace it with some "appropriate" estimator. There exists a number of nonparametric methods for estimating $F(\xi|\theta)$ and such bootstraps is referred to as a *nonparametric bootstrap*. In many cases in practice (yet not always!), the empirical distribution function (EDF), which is a consistent and the simplest estimator of an unknown distribution function under fairly general assumptions, would be an appropriate nonparametric estimator. In other cases, some smooth estimators of the density of distribution can be used to generate the pseudo-samples, in which case it would be called the (nonparametric) *smooth bootstrap*.

The fourth case is a combination of the previous cases, where some parts can be nonparametric while some other parts of the algorithm may involve parametric assumptions, in which case it would be appropriate to call it a semiparametric (or semi-nonparametric) bootstrap.

To summarize our brief introduction into general bootstrap method, in all cases, the bootstrap principle is essentially the same: characteristics of the original population are inferred from the sampling distribution of their estimators, which, in turn, approximated by estimates from pseudo-samples obtained by resampling from the original sample or from the known distribution that ensure appropriate mimicking of the original data generating process. We shall defer the discussion of the choice of the estimator of $F(\xi|\theta)$ to further sections, after we discuss more about the benefits of bootstrap.

9.2.4 Bootstrap for Standard Errors of an Estimator

In this section, we will consider some popular bootstrap-based methods of estimating standard errors and bias of an estimator. Recall that the standard error is one of the most commonly used measures of statistical accuracy, which, for an estimator $\hat{\theta}_n$, is defined as

---

[14] Jumping slightly ahead of the discussion here, note that merely using a consistent estimator of $F(\xi|\theta)$ is not sufficient to ensure consistency of the bootstrap, although it is certainly a necessary condition.

$$se_F(\hat{\theta}_n) = \left(V(\hat{\theta}_n)\right)^{1/2} = \left(E_F\left((\hat{\theta}_n)^2\right) - (E_F(\hat{\theta}_n))^2\right)^{1/2}, \quad (9.2.2)$$

where E_F indicates that the mathematical expectation is taken with respect to the original distribution, F, that generated the data used in the estimator $\hat{\theta}_n$. Although for some simple estimators (e.g., such as the sample mean, etc.), the variance can be easily estimated, for many useful yet complex estimators or statistics, a good estimator of their variance (or standard error) might be available only in the limiting case and so might be unreliable for a small sample or even not available at all. In such circumstances, a good way out could be to use an appropriate bootstrap procedure. Indeed, using the analogy principle, the bootstrap analogue of (9.2.2) is

$$se_{\hat{F}_n}(\hat{\theta}^*_{n,b}) = \left(E_{\hat{F}_n}\left((\hat{\theta}^*_{n,b})^2\right) - (E_{\hat{F}_n}(\hat{\theta}^*_{n,b}))^2\right)^{1/2}, \quad (9.2.3)$$

where $\hat{\theta}^*_{n,b}$ (for $b = 1, \ldots, B$) are obtained using $\hat{F}_n$ as an estimator of F, and so, note, the mathematical expectation now is to be taken with respect to $\hat{F}_n$. Importantly, note that although $E_{\hat{F}_n}(\hat{\theta}^*_{n,b})$ and $E_{\hat{F}_n}((\hat{\theta}^*_{n,b})^2)$ are usually unknown, they can be approximated with any level of precision by their Monte Carlo analogues by using bootstrap estimates from Step 4 of the algorithm presented above. Indeed, in general, under fairly mild regularity conditions and relying on the Weak Law of Large Numbers, for any continuous function G of a random variable with finite mean(s) and variance(s), we have

$$\frac{1}{B}\sum_{b=1}^{B} G\left(\hat{\theta}^*_{n,b}\right) - E_{\hat{F}_n}\left(G(\hat{\theta}^*_{n,b})\right) \xrightarrow{p} 0. \quad (9.2.4)$$

And so, we can get numerical approximation of each component of (9.2.3) by just taking the sample means over all the bootstrap replications, i.e.,

$$\frac{1}{B}\sum_{b=1}^{B} \hat{\theta}^*_{n,b} \xrightarrow{p} E_{\hat{F}_n}\left(\hat{\theta}^*_{n,b}\right), \quad (9.2.5)$$

and

$$\frac{1}{B}\sum_{b=1}^{B} \left(\hat{\theta}^*_{n,b}\right)^2 \xrightarrow{p} E_{\hat{F}_n}\left(\left(\hat{\theta}^*_{n,b}\right)^2\right). \quad (9.2.6)$$

Importantly, note that the degree of accuracy of this approximation would depend on the number of replications, B, which is completely under the researcher's control. Thus, the bootstrap estimate of the standard error of an estimator $\hat{\theta}_n$ can be obtained as

$$\hat{se}^*_{\hat{F}_n}(\hat{\theta}_n) = \left(\frac{1}{B}\sum_{b=1}^{B}\left(\hat{\theta}^*_{n,b}\right)^2 - \left(\frac{1}{B}\sum_{b=1}^{B}\hat{\theta}^*_{n,b}\right)^2\right)^{1/2}, \quad (9.2.7)$$

which, if (9.2.1) is true, is a consistent estimate of the true standard error (9.2.2).

9.2.5 Bootstrapping for Bias and Mean Squared Error

To understand how to use bootstrap to estimate the bias of an estimator, let us first recall that the bias of an estimator $\hat{\theta}_n$ for the true θ is defined as

$$Bias_F(\hat{\theta}_n) = E(\hat{\theta}_n) - \theta. \tag{9.2.8}$$

Some simple estimators (e.g., the sample mean, the least squares estimates of linear models, etc.) are unbiased, yet many useful but somewhat complicated estimators are biased, and DEA and FDH are examples of such estimators. Moreover, often a closed analytical form of bias of an estimator might be available only in limited cases and might be questionable for a small sample or even unavailable at all. Again, in such circumstances, a rescue way out could come from an appropriate bootstrap procedure. Indeed, using the analogy principle, we can approximate (9.2.8) with its bootstrap analogue

$$Bias_{\hat{F}_n}\left(\hat{\theta}_{n,b}^*\right) = E_{\hat{F}_n}\left(\hat{\theta}_{n,b}^*\right) - \hat{\theta}_n. \tag{9.2.9}$$

The intuition of the method is again based on the fundamental expression (9.2.1): when it is true, i.e., $\hat{\theta}_{n,b}^* - \hat{\theta}_n | \hat{F}_n \sim \hat{\theta}_n - \theta | F$, then it would also ensure $E_{\hat{F}_n}\left(\hat{\theta}_{n,b}^*\right) - \hat{\theta}_n \sim E_F(\hat{\theta}_n) - \theta$ and so $Bias_{\hat{F}_n}\left(\hat{\theta}_{n,b}^*\right) \approx Bias_F(\hat{\theta}_n)$. In turn, the unknown $E_{\hat{F}_n}\left(\hat{\theta}_{n,b}^*\right)$ can be approximated with any level of precision by its Monte Carlo analogue, via (9.2.5), and so, the bootstrap estimated bias of $\hat{\theta}_n$ with respect to θ would be

$$\widehat{Bias}_{\hat{F}_n}^*\left(\hat{\theta}_n\right) = \frac{1}{B}\sum_{b=1}^{B}\hat{\theta}_{n,b}^* - \hat{\theta}_n. \tag{9.2.10}$$

And, the resulting bias corrected estimate of θ would be

$$\hat{\theta}_n^{bcor} = \hat{\theta}_n - \widehat{Bias}_{\hat{F}_n}^*\left(\hat{\theta}_n\right) = 2\hat{\theta}_n - \frac{1}{B}\sum_{b=1}^{B}\hat{\theta}_{n,b}^*. \tag{9.2.11}$$

A common confusion is to call (9.2.11) an unbiased estimator. This would be incorrect because (9.2.10) does not give us an expression for the true bias, but only its estimate and so the procedure in (9.2.11) does not remove the bias, but only corrects for it with an estimated bias. That is why we refer to the resulting estimator $\hat{\theta}_n^{bcor}$ not as unbiased but as biased-corrected.

Recall now that, for a biased estimator, a more appropriate measure of statistical accuracy is not the variance (or standard error) but the mean squared error (MSE), defined as

$$MSE_F(\hat{\theta}_n) = E_F\left((\hat{\theta}_n - \theta)^2\right) \tag{9.2.12}$$

$$= V_F(\hat{\theta}_n) + \left(Bias_F(\hat{\theta}_n)\right)^2.$$

So, a bootstrap estimate of MSE of $\hat{\theta}_n$ relative to θ can be obtained as

$$\widehat{MSE}^*_{\hat{F}_n}(\hat{\theta}_n) = \left(\hat{se}^*_{\hat{F}_n}(\hat{\theta}_n)\right)^2 + \left(\widehat{Bias}^*_{\hat{F}_n}(\hat{\theta}_n)\right)^2. \tag{9.2.13}$$

It is worth noting here that a number of other methods for estimating statistical bias of an estimator have been suggested in the literature, some of which can be found in Efron and Tibshirani (1993) and Davison and Hinkley (1997), yet it is important to remember that there are cases when it is not advised to use the bias corrected estimate but better to rely on the original estimate, even if we know for sure that it is biased.

Indeed, note that correction for bias introduces additional noise of estimation so it might happen that the estimator $\hat{\theta}_n^{bcor}$ is actually inferior to $\hat{\theta}_n$ in terms of statistical accuracy. A popular rule of thumb that helps in deciding whether bootstrap bias correction is useful in a particular context or not was suggested by Efron and Tibshirani (1993) and is based on the following argument. Using (9.2.12), note that the first-order approximation to the square root of MSE (RMSE) is given by

$$\left(MSE_F(\hat{\theta}_n)\right)^{1/2} = se_F(\hat{\theta}_n)\left(1 + \left(\frac{Bias_F(\hat{\theta}_n)}{se_F(\hat{\theta}_n)}\right)^2\right)^{1/2} \tag{9.2.14}$$

$$\approx se_F(\hat{\theta}_n)\left(1 + \frac{1}{2}\left(\frac{Bias_F(\hat{\theta}_n)}{se_F(\hat{\theta}_n)}\right)^2\right).$$

Suppose now that the researcher knows or suspects that the estimator is biased, yet the bias could be very small in the sense that RMSE of the estimator is not much different than its standard error. For example, the researcher might choose the level of "comfort" and denote it with α (%), for not correcting for the bias if RMSE of an estimator is not larger than the standard error of this estimator by α. Then, according to (9.2.14) we should require, approximately, that

$$\left(1 + \frac{1}{2}\left(\frac{Bias_F(\hat{\theta}_n)}{se_F(\hat{\theta}_n)}\right)^2\right) \approx \frac{\left(MSE_F(\hat{\theta}_n)\right)^{1/2}}{se_F(\hat{\theta}_n)} \leq 1 + \frac{\alpha}{100}. \tag{9.2.15}$$

Solving this inequality would suggest that for the cases when

$$Bias_F(\hat{\theta}_n) \leq \frac{\sqrt{2\alpha}}{10}se_F(\hat{\theta}_n), \tag{9.2.16}$$

the researcher should not correct for the bias since it is "comfortably" small enough in the sense that RMSE is no more than α larger than the standard error of the estimator, because correction for the bias might introduce additional noise to it, making it inferior to the original estimator $\hat{\theta}_n$. The true quantities in (9.2.15) or (9.2.16) are usually unknown, yet they can be estimated via bootstrap methods as we described above, using (9.2.5) and (9.2.3). Also, a

common choice is to set $\alpha = 3$ (%), then $\sqrt{2\alpha}/10 \approx 0.245$ and so using
(9.2.16) would suggest that the researcher is not advised to do bias correction
if the bootstrap-estimated bias of the estimator is smaller than the quarter of
the standard deviation (or its bootstrap estimated version), i.e.,

$$\widehat{Bias}^*_{\hat{F}_n}\left(\hat{\theta}_n\right) \leq \frac{1}{4}\hat{se}^*_{\hat{F}_n}(\hat{\theta}_n). \tag{9.2.17}$$

The inequality (9.2.17), usually referred to as the "Efron–Tibshirani rule-of-thumb," is what is often used in practice for deciding if it is reasonable to correct for the bias of an estimator.

9.2.6 Bootstrap Estimation of Confidence Intervals

In this subsection we consider several bootstrap-based methods for confidence intervals estimation. All of them are also based on the analogy principle used above with the difference being the focus of the analogy. To outline the methods, let us recall that the true confidence interval is given by

$$\Pr\left(\hat{\theta}_n - c_l(\alpha/2) \leq \theta \leq \hat{\theta}_n + c_u(\alpha/2)|F\right) = 1 - \alpha, \tag{9.2.18}$$

where α is the level of significance chosen by a researcher (e.g., $\alpha = 0.05$) and $c_u(\alpha/2)$ and $c_l(\alpha/2)$ are the corresponding true critical values defining the upper and lower bounds, respectively. The point of interest of the estimation here are these critical values, which, in general, are completely determined by the sampling distribution of $\hat{\theta}_n$, i.e., by $\mathbb{G}_n(\theta|F) = \Pr(\hat{\theta}_n \leq \theta|F)$, or, asymptotically, by its limit when $n \to \infty$, i.e., by $\mathbb{G}_\infty(\theta|F)$.

For example, often $\mathbb{G}_\infty(\theta|F)$ is a Normal distribution, and so for say $\alpha = 0.05$ we have $c_u(\alpha/2) = c_l(\alpha/2) \approx 1.96se(\hat{\theta}_n)$, i.e.,

$$\Pr\left(\hat{\theta}_n - 1.96se(\hat{\theta}_n) \leq \theta \leq \hat{\theta}_n + 1.96se(\hat{\theta}_n)|F\right) \to 0.95, \tag{9.2.19}$$

meaning the confidence intervals constructed as $[\hat{\theta}_n - 1.96se(\hat{\theta}_n), \hat{\theta}_n + 1.96se(\hat{\theta}_n)]$ will cover the true parameter θ (that we try to estimate with $\hat{\theta}_n$) by about 95 percent, if the sampling and estimation were conducted a large number of times (e.g., 1000).

However, even for simple examples the true $se(\hat{\theta}_n)$ is rarely known. More commonly it must be consistently estimated. Indeed, recall that even for such a simple estimator as $\hat{\theta}_n = \frac{1}{n}\sum_{i=1}^n \xi_i$, where we have $se(\hat{\theta}_n) = \sqrt{\frac{1}{n}V(\xi_i)}$, the exact value of $V(\xi_i)$ may be unknown and must be consistently estimated, e.g., with $s_n^2 = \frac{1}{n-1}\sum_{i=1}^n(\xi_i - \frac{1}{n}\sum_{i=1}^n \xi_i)^2$. To use s_n^2 instead of $V(\xi_i)$ one shall rely on one of the laws of large numbers, which presumes a fairly large sample size n. Indeed, the fact that the true variance (or the standard error) is estimated with a relatively small sample might endanger the reliability of the confidence interval estimates based on the limiting distribution $\mathbb{G}_\infty(\theta|F)$ or even on the sampling distribution, if the latter is known, whether they are normal or not.

Moreover, sometimes even limiting distributions might be unknown for some estimators. In all these cases a consistent bootstrap might be the only way out. Let us first consider the case when the sampling or limiting distribution is known to be normal, but the true standard error of the estimator is unknown and the small size of the sample gives doubts on the reliability of its estimate. Here, a natural way would be to use the bootstrap estimates of the standard errors $\hat{s}e_{\hat{F}_n}(\hat{\theta}_n)$ we discussed above. Then, for $\alpha = 0.05$, we have $c_u^*(\alpha/2) = c_l^*(\alpha/2) = 1.96\hat{s}e_{\hat{F}_n}(\hat{\theta}_n)$ and so, if the bootstrap is consistent, we would have

$$\Pr\left(\hat{\theta}_n - 1.96\hat{s}e(\hat{\theta}_n) \le \theta \le \hat{\theta}_n + 1.96\hat{s}e(\hat{\theta}_n)|\hat{F}_n\right) \to 0.95, \quad (9.2.20)$$

where $\hat{F}_n$ is an appropriate estimator of F, used to get the bootstrap samples. Now, let us consider a more general case: when the sampling or limiting distribution is not necessarily normal, complicated or not known at all, the entire probability statement (9.2.18) can be approximated relying on the fundamental expression (9.2.1). For this, we can rewrite (9.2.18) as

$$\Pr\left(-c_u(\alpha/2) \le \hat{\theta}_n - \theta \le c_l(\alpha/2)|F\right) = 0.95. \quad (9.2.21)$$

From (9.2.1), we know that the distribution of $\hat{\theta}_n - \theta$ can be approximated by the distribution of its bootstrap analogue, $\hat{\theta}_{n,b}^* - \hat{\theta}_n$, i.e., by $\mathbb{G}_\infty(\theta_0|F)$, if the employed bootstrap is consistent. Therefore, the true statement (9.2.18) can also be approximated by its bootstrap analogue

$$\Pr\left(-c_u^*(\alpha/2) \le \hat{\theta}_{n,b}^* - \hat{\theta}_n \le c_l^*(\alpha/2)|\hat{F}_n\right) \approx 0.95, \quad (9.2.22)$$

where $\hat{F}_n$ is an appropriate estimator of F, used to get the bootstrap samples, $c_l^*(\alpha/2)$ and $c_u^*(\alpha/2)$ are the resulting bootstrap analogues of $c_l(\alpha/2)$ and $c_u(\alpha/2)$, respectively. Although, the exact analytical expression for (9.2.22) might be unknown (sometimes even when F is known), it can be well approximated with any degree of accuracy via Monte Carlo methods, by using the bootstrap estimates $\left\{(\hat{\theta}_{n,b}^* - \hat{\theta}_n) : b = 1, \ldots, B\right\}$. In fact, in practice, $-c_u^*(\alpha/2)$ and $c_l^*(\alpha/2)$ can be obtained as the left and right endpoints of the trimmed sorted (in ascending order) list of $\left\{(\hat{\theta}_{n,b}^* - \hat{\theta}_n) : b = 1, \ldots, B\right\}$ where the trimming is done by deleting $(\alpha/2) \times 100\%$ of the elements at each end of the sorted list. The resulting bootstrap-based estimate of the confidence interval for the true parameter, θ, with significance level α, therefore can be given by

$$[\hat{\theta}_n - c_l^*(\alpha/2), \hat{\theta}_n + c_u^*(\alpha/2)], \quad (9.2.23)$$

which, in a large number of repeated sampling, must cover the true parameter θ, about 95 percent of times, if the employed bootstrap approach is consistent. This second way of constructing confidence intervals just described is often referred to as the equal-tailed *basic bootstrap confidence interval method*. A particular strength of it is that the knowledge on the limiting distribution as well as prior correction for the bias (if any) are not required. A weakness of this approach is that it usually gives wider confidence intervals than those based on knowledge of the limiting distribution (e.g., as the previous method), which is in a sense a price paid for the greater generality.

It is also worth noting that although the two methods described above are, perhaps, the most popular in practice, the literature on other methods for bootstrap estimation of confidence intervals is rich, and considers various context-specific issues. Other popular methods, for example, include the so-called percentile method, t-bootstrap method (e.g., see Efron and Tibshirani (1993) and Davison and Hinkley (1997) for this and other methods). All of the methods, however, share the same essence of the bootstrap described in the earlier sections of this chapter, i.e., the use of analogy and the plug-in principles to the context of resampling from a sample to learn about the population.

9.2.7 Consistency of Bootstrap

All of the above discussions about the use of bootstrap for estimation of bias, standard errors, confidence intervals, etc. was done relying on the fundamental expression (9.2.1), saying that $(\hat{\theta}^*_{n,b} - \hat{\theta}_n)|\hat{F}_n$ has the same limiting distribution as $(\hat{\theta}_n - \theta)|F$, which we said is true when the bootstrap is consistent. But, when is it true that a particular bootstrap estimator is consistent? The goal of this subsection is to give some understanding of this important matter.

9.2.7.1 *Some General Results on Consistency of Bootstrap*

Let us first clarify precisely what we mean by consistency of bootstrap.

Definition. (Consistency of bootstrap) Let θ be the parameter of interest (in the parameter space Θ) and $\hat{\theta}_n$ be its estimator of interest constructed from a random sample generated from a DGP characterized by some distribution function $F(.|\theta)$, whose sampling cdf is given by $\mathbb{G}_n(\theta|F)$ and limiting distribution given by $\mathbb{G}_\infty(\theta|F)$. Then, the bootstrap estimator $\mathbb{G}_n(\theta|\hat{F}_n) = \Pr(\hat{\theta}_n \le \theta|\hat{F}_n)$ is consistent if and only if $\forall \varepsilon > 0$, $\theta \in \Theta$, we have

$$\lim_{n \to \infty} \Pr(\sup_\theta |\mathbb{G}_n(\theta|\hat{F}_n) - \mathbb{G}_\infty(\theta|F(.|\theta))| > \varepsilon) = 0. \quad (9.2.24)$$

Intuitively, this definition says that if the bootstrap estimator of the sampling distribution of $\hat{\theta}_n$, i.e., $\mathbb{G}_n(\theta|\hat{F}_n)$, is practically the same, uniformly over $\theta \in \Theta$, as the limiting distribution of $\hat{\theta}_n$, given by $\mathbb{G}_\infty(\theta|F)$, then the bootstrap is consistent (and so statement (9.2.1) holds). A natural question is: when does this consistency requirement hold? A general answer to this question was given by Beran and Ducharme (1991) and is summarized in the next theorem.[15]

---

[15] For stating this theorem we use slightly more precise notation than the simplified notation above: we must distinguish between all permitted distribution functions, denoted here as $F := F(\xi|\theta)$, and its particular member, for a particular $\theta = \theta_o$, denoted with $F_o := F(\xi|\theta_o) \in \mathbb{F}$.

Theorem. *(Sufficient Condition for Consistency of Bootstrap) Let $\mathbb{F}$ be a space of permitted distribution functions $F := F(\xi|\theta)$, where $F_o := F(\xi|\theta_o) \in \mathbb{F}$ is its particular member (for a particular $\theta = \theta_o$) and let $\mathfrak{m}$ be a metric on this space. The bootstrap estimator $\mathbb{G}_n(\theta_o|\hat{F}_n)$ is consistent if, for any $\varepsilon > 0$ and $F_o \in \mathbb{F}$, all three conditions listed below are satisfied:*

1. $\lim_{n\to\infty} \Pr(\mathfrak{m}(\hat{F}_n, F_o) > \varepsilon) = 0$,
2. $\mathbb{G}_\infty(\theta_o|F)$ *is a continuous function of* θ_o, $\forall F \in \mathbb{F}$,
3. $\mathbb{G}_n(\theta_o|H_n) \to \mathbb{G}_\infty(\theta_o|F_o)$, $\forall \theta_o$, $\forall \{H_n\} \in \mathbb{F} :$
   $\lim_{n\to\infty} \mathfrak{m}(H_n, F_o) = 0$.

The proof of this theorem can be found in Beran and Ducharme (1991). The intuition, however, is important to highlight here. The theorem lists three conditions that are not required but are sufficient to ensure consistency of bootstrap. Roughly speaking, the first condition essentially requires that $\hat{F}_n$ is a consistent estimator of F_o.[16] The second condition requires that the limiting distribution of $\hat{\theta}_n$ is a continuous function, which holds in most situations yet not always. Finally, because $\hat{F}_n$ changes with n, and so does $\mathbb{G}_n(\theta_o|\hat{F}_n)$, the third condition, together with the second, essentially requires that the functional representing the bootstrap estimator converges to the limiting distribution of $\hat{\theta}_n$ (for *any* possible sequence H_n in the permitted functional space that converges to the true distribution F_o in terms of a metric $\mathfrak{m}$).

The advantage of the last theorem is that it is fairly general, in particular for a general $\hat{F}_n$ and for a general $\mathbb{G}_\infty(\theta_o|F_o)$. One drawback of this theorem is that these three conditions are not always easy to check, and might require tedious derivations to check them in practice. Another drawback of this theorem is that it only gives sufficient conditions, and so if some of them fail, it is not always clear if a particular bootstrap is still consistent or not.

9.2.7.2 EDF and Consistency of Naive Bootstrap

In most econometric applications, the role of $\hat{F}_n$ can be well played by the empirical distribution function (EDF). For a univariate random variable U with cdf $F(u)$ at a point u, observed through a random sample $\{u_1, \ldots, u_n\}$, the EDF at the point u is given by

$$EDF_n(u) = \frac{1}{n} \sum_{i=1}^{n} \mathbb{I}(u_i \leq u), \tag{9.2.25}$$

where $\mathbb{I}(A)$ is the indicator function that yields value 1 if statement A is true and value 0 otherwise. Intuitively, (9.2.25) gives a proportion of observations

---

[16] This requirement is about weak convergence in probability in a metric sense, where $\mathfrak{m}$ is a suitable metric, e.g., Mallow's metric of order r: $\mathcal{M}_r(F_X, F_Y) := \inf_{\mathscr{C}(X,Y)} \left\{ (E(|X - Y|^r))^{1/r} : X \sim F_X, Y \sim F_Y \right\}$ where $\mathscr{C}(X, Y)$ is a set of pairs of random variables (X, Y).

from the sample $\{u_1, \ldots, u_n\}$ that are not greater than the value u, at which cdf is estimated. Clearly, the larger u is the more observations fall below it and so the closer the value of EDF would be to unity. Although very simple, the EDF is a very powerful estimator of a cdf F, in the sense that it has nice properties under fairly mild conditions. In particular, it is strongly (almost surely) and uniformly consistent (due to Glivenko-Cantelli theorem) and its limiting distribution is normal with mean and variance given by $E(EDF_n(u)) = F(u)$ and $V(EDF_n(u)) = F(u)(1 - F(u))/n$, respectively, which are estimated by plugging $EDF_n(u)$ instead of $F(u)$.

Besides the use in the basic bootstrap and in the Kolmogorov–Smirnov test, both of which we will discuss below, the EDF also stays at the foundation of many estimators. For example, take the population mean of a continuous function g of a random variable U with distribution function at u given by $F(u)$, defined as

$$E(g(U)) := \int_u g(u) dF(u). \tag{9.2.26}$$

Then, its estimator can be obtained using the analogy and the "plug-in principle," where in place of the true cdf $F(u)$ in (9.2.26) we plug-in its empirical analogue, $EDF_n(u)$, given in (9.2.25), to get

$$\hat{E}(g(U)) := \int_u g(u) d EDF_n(u) = \frac{1}{n} \sum_{i=1}^{n} g(u_i).$$

This is another way to formally motivate the method of moments estimator – the replacement of the true moments with their sample or empirical analogues is justified due to the replacement of the true distribution with the EDF.[17]

The bootstrap based on EDF is very simple and is usually referred to as basic or simple or naive bootstrap – one simply assigns an equal probability weight of $1/n$ for drawing any observation of the sample in a given resampling. One of the most fundamental results in the bootstrap theory that gives both *necessary and sufficient* conditions for the naive bootstrap of a "t-type" statistic is due to Mammen (1992), which we summarize below.

Theorem. *(Consistency of Naive Bootstrap) Let*

$$\mathcal{T}_n := \frac{\overline{g_n} - \mu_n}{\sigma_n}, \tag{9.2.27}$$

where $\overline{g_n} = \frac{1}{n} \sum_{i=1}^{n} g_n(\xi_i)$ is the statistic of interest constructed from a random sample $\{\xi_1, \ldots, \xi_n\}$ from a population, where g_n is a sequence of functions of observations in the random sample and μ_n and σ_n are some sequences of numbers. Let the bootstrap sample $\{\xi_1^*, \ldots, \xi_n^*\}$ be obtained using the EDF,

---

[17] The last equality above is obtained using the Lebesgue–Stieltjes integral (which generalizes the Riemann integral, in particular, yielding the summation for the step functions).

and let $\overline{g_n}^* = \frac{1}{n}\sum_{i=1}^n g_n(\xi_i^*)$ and $T_n^* := (\overline{g_n}^* - \overline{g_n})/\sigma_n$ be the bootstrap analogues of $\overline{g_n}$ and T_n, respectively. Then, the EDF-based (or naive) bootstrap estimator of $\mathbb{G}_n(\tau|F) = \Pr(T_n \le \tau|F)$, denoted as $\mathbb{G}_n(\tau|EDF_n)$, is consistent if and only if

$$T_n \xrightarrow{d} \mathcal{N}(0, 1). \tag{9.2.28}$$

The proof of this result is not difficult (and can be found in Mammen, 1992), but its intuition is important here and quite straightforward. In words, the theorem says that the naive bootstrap estimator of the sampling distribution of a "t-type" statistic is consistent if and only if the limiting distribution of this statistic is standard normal (assuming other conditions of the theorem are also satisfied).

The reasoning behind this fundamental result should not be very surprising. Specifically, note that if the statistic of interest in this theorem has the standard Normal limiting distribution (which due to the central limit theorem is true under quite mild assumptions), the same should hold for its bootstrap analogue and so (9.2.24) will be satisfied. On the other hand, if (9.2.28) is satisfied for bootstrap based on EDF, then it means that $\mathbb{G}_n(\tau|EDF_n)$ is practically the same as $\mathbb{G}_\infty(\tau|F)$, uniformly over τ, which in turn would be the standard Normal, due to the usual central limit theorem argument (e.g., due to Lyapunov) for a "t-type" statistic (9.2.27).

Notably, one of the implications of this theorem is that if the limiting distribution of the "t-type" statistic is not standard normal, then the naive (i.e., EDF-based) bootstrap of this statistic is not guaranteed to be consistent and so some other appropriate estimators of F must be found for a consistent bootstrap procedure. However, also note that most econometric applications lead to statistics that (immediately or after applying the Delta-method) are asymptotically normally distributed so, after appropriate standardization, the condition (9.2.28) would be satisfied and then the naive bootstrap would be consistent and estimation and inference based on it shall be reliable.

A natural question now is: "Why would one need to use the naive bootstrap for a 't-type' statistic such as T_n which, for ensuring consistency of this bootstrap, must necessarily have the asymptotic standard normal distribution – would not it be better to use this asymptotic distribution without going to the bootstrap?!" Of course, one can. Yet, it has been formally shown (and confirmed in many Monte Carlo experiments) that a consistent bootstrap approximation of the sampling distribution is at least as good as the first-order asymptotic theory approximation. Moreover, for relatively small samples, a consistent bootstrap often gives more accurate approximation than the first-order asymptotic theory approximation, and so is more reliable. Furthermore, in cases when the limiting distribution of a statistic does not depend on parameters of the distribution that generated the data, in which case the statistic is called "asymptotically pivotal", the bootstrap approximation is theoretically better in the sense of giving higher- (than the first-)order asymptotic theory approximation. Therefore, for cases like the one described in the Mammen (1982) theorem, the bootstrap-based confidence intervals, the p-values of tests, etc. are usually expected to be more accurate than those based on standard normal tables.

9.2.7.3   Other Types of Bootstrap

Since the seminal paper of Efron (1979), many different bootstrap procedures have been introduced addressing various issues for peculiar DGPs that do not comply with assumptions of the Beran–Ducharme theorem or Mammen theorem. The case of bounded support, which is very relevant to the efficiency analysis, is one such case, and one solution is the smooth bootstrap via a kernel density estimator (KDE) that properly accounts for the boundary. We will consider this bootstrap in the context of DEA and FDH in the next section. Another important type of bootstrap is the so-called "wild" bootstrap, originally introduced to handle heteroscedasticity (Wu, 1986; Mammen, 1993) and is particularly useful for nonparametric kernel-based estimators and tests. In time series contexts where dependency across time is relevant, the so-called block-bootstrap or its variations can be used (Künsch, 1989).

9.3   BOOTSTRAP FOR DEA AND FDH

Bootstrap for DEA and FDH inherited the essence of the general statistical bootstrap approach, but with some specifics, some of which are critical. Indeed, within the context of technology frontier estimation is a case where some of the most commonly used bootstrap approaches are inconsistent. In particular, the simplest or the so-called naive bootstrap does not account for the main feature of the problem – the estimation of the (upper) boundary of the unknown (technology) set, which leads to inconsistency. This section aims to briefly outline these specifics with references where further details can be found.

9.3.1   Bootstrap for Individual Efficiency Estimates

The first rigorous bootstrap treatment in efficiency and productivity analysis goes back to at least Simar (1992) and then was elaborated on further in a number of important works, mainly by Léopold Simar and his many co-authors (especially Alois Kneip and Paul Wilson). The first breakthrough work in this line of research was the seminal paper of Simar and Wilson (1998), where using theoretical reasoning supported by convincing Monte Carlo evidence, they pointed out the incorrectness of the naive bootstrap in the context of bootstrapping individual efficiency scores and proposed an alternative that performed fairly well. This alternative was a version of the *smooth* bootstrap. We briefly discuss this and related approaches in the next subsection.

9.3.1.1 Smooth Bootstrap for DEA and FDH

As with any type of bootstrap, the idea of the smooth bootstrap is also based on resampling. Here, however, the resampling is done not from the original sample and certainly not from the true distribution or density, but from the kernel-estimated density that characterizes the sample. An important element of such a version of the smooth bootstrap was that the kernel density estimator (KDE) properly accounts for the boundary issue. The boundary issue here arises because efficiency scores are bounded (between 0 and 1 or between 1 and ∞ for the Farrell measure with input or output orientation, respectively), with most observations observed near the bound since, naturally, the DMUs are striving to be as efficient as possible. Such a boundary issue was handled via the Silverman (1986) reflection method, although other suitable methods could be used as well.

Specifically, Simar and Wilson (1998) suggested the smooth homogeneous bootstrap for DEA and FDH, and shortly after, Simar and Wilson (2002) extended those ideas to offer the smooth heterogeneous bootstrap for DEA and FDH. Formally, in the homogeneous case it is assumed that $g(TE|\eta, x) = g(TE)$ and so the random drawing simplifies to drawing from the KDE of $g(TE)$, the unconditional density of the technical efficiency scores. As a matter of fact, in practice, the drawing is actually done from the normal density (when the Gaussian kernel is chosen) with some noise perturbation added with the help of an optimal smoothing parameter, and with the application of the Silverman's reflection method to account for the bounded support.

The smooth homogeneous bootstrap (as well as its group-wise heterogeneous version) became a better alternative to the standard procedures of estimation of standard errors or related statistical tests because they accounted for the specifics (boundedness, bias and dependency) of efficiency estimates in the DEA and FDH contexts. Simar and Wilson (1998) supported this with extensive Monte Carlo evidence about the good performance and advantages of these methods over the standard inference. This bootstrap approach made a true breakthrough at the time, yet the authors did acknowledge its limitations. The major limitations included the fact that it was assuming that all DMUs have the same distribution (characterized by the density) of efficiency and, importantly, so that it was independent from inputs and outputs. More precisely, their approach assumed that the conditional density of true efficiency scores was the same as the marginal density of the true efficiency scores, and the same for all DMUs, and therefore was referred to as the smooth homogeneous bootstrap for individual Farrell efficiency.

The homogeneity assumption of the smooth bootstrap for DEA (or FDH) was soon relaxed in the seminal work of Simar and Wilson (2002), which gave rise to the smooth heterogeneous bootstrap for DEA. On the other hand, the heterogeneous bootstrap for DEA and FDH, proposed by Simar and Wilson (2002), relaxes the restrictive assumption of independence of efficiency from the inputs and outputs, but does so at the substantial price of becoming much more complex, requiring estimation of the joint density $G_l(TE, \eta, x)$ or its analogue in the Cartesian space. Moreover, one should remember that the KDE, as most nonparametric estimators, suffers from the "curse of dimensionality" problem arising in the multivariate context, which would be in addition to the "curse of dimensionality" problem faced by the DEA and FDH estimators. Another related complexity of this method is due to the need to select a multivariate bandwidth, a challenging problem fraught with practical difficulties even in standard cases.

All in all, the dramatic increase of the complexity of the smoothed heterogeneous bootstrap for DEA and FDH obstructed its popularity in practice. For practitioners, this means that one must be careful when choosing between the two versions of the smooth bootstrap, paying attention to the sample size. Sometimes, for a relatively small sample (relative to the dimension of the production model), where the accuracy of the multivariate KDE applied to DEA or FDH estimates may be doubtful, it might be safer to accept the assumption of homogeneity to get more accurate results, unless there is strong evidence or strong belief that technical efficiency depends on the input and output-mix. Ideally, of course, one should try to find a larger sample and apply a technique that fits best to the problem, but this is not always feasible. Therefore, a compromise might be better than nothing or even better than an extreme such as the full heterogeneity case or the case of full homogeneity. Such a compromise can be, for example, reducing the dimension of the assumed production model by merging some inputs, if it is not critical to consider them separately for theoretical or research focus reasoning. E.g., different types of labor expenses might be merged into one, and also, perhaps, with administrative expenses. Similarly, different types of output, if measured in the same (e.g., monetary) units, can be merged into fewer or even one output, as is done for measuring the "total output" of a country via GDP, etc.[18]

A compromise between the homogeneous and heterogeneous versions of the smooth bootstraps is when one assumes the same technology for all groups, yet allows for different distributions for different groups – an algorithm of such a group-wise heterogeneous smooth bootstrap is summarized below.[19]

Step 1 *Estimation of the quantity of interest*: Apply DEA or FDH to the original sample $\mathscr{S}_n = \{(x^k, y^k) : k = 1, \ldots, n\}$ to obtain estimates of the true efficiency scores $\mathscr{E} = \{TE(x^k, y^k) : k = 1, \ldots, n\}$, further denoted as $\hat{\mathscr{E}} = \{\widehat{TE}^k : k = 1, \ldots, n\}$. Partition the original sample

---

[18] Some of these assumptions or dimension reductions can be statistically tested, e.g., see Simar and Wilson (2001) for one of the first works on this that uses homogeneous bootstrap and Schubert and Simar (2011) that used a subsampling approach. Such types of tests usually have very low power in rejecting a false null hypothesis (of homogeneity or smaller dimensions), meaning that one may need to have very large samples to be able to reject a false null hypothesis.

[19] This approach is inspired by Simar and Zelenyuk (2006, 2007) and first applied in Henderson and Zelenyuk (2007), although the algorithm was not fully outlined there and so we state it below for the output-oriented case.

and the estimates into distinct (sub-)groups $\mathscr{S}_{n_l}^l = \{(x^k, y^k) : k = 1, \ldots, n_l\}$ and $\hat{\mathscr{E}}_l = \{\widehat{TE}^{l,k} : k = 1, \ldots, n_l\}$, for all $l \in \{1, \ldots, L\}$ representing the corresponding (sub-)groups within the population.

Step 2 *Estimation of the quantity of interest*: Use a proper KDE to generate the bth bootstrap sample for each group $l = 1, \ldots, L$ separately. Denote these samples as $\mathscr{S}_{n_l,b}^{*l} = \{(x_b^{*l,k}, y_b^{*l,k}) : k = 1, \ldots, n_l\}$, $l \in \{1, \ldots, L\}$ and the pooled sample as $\mathscr{S}_{n,b}^{*} = \{(x_b^{*l,k}, y_b^{*l,k}) : k = 1, \ldots, n_l, \ l = 1, \ldots, L\} = \{\mathscr{S}_{n_1,b}^{*l} : l = 1, \ldots, L\}$. To obtain them, do the following steps for each group $l = 1, \ldots, L$:

Step 2.1 resample via EDF from $\hat{\mathscr{E}}_l$ to get $\hat{\mathscr{E}}_{lb}^{*} = \{\widehat{TE}_b^{*l,k} : k = 1, \ldots, n_l\}$.

Step 2.2 draw $\hat{\varepsilon}_{l,k}^b$ from $\mathcal{N}(0, 1)$, for $k = 1, \ldots, n_l$, if Gaussian density is chosen for KDE.

Step 2.3 compute the bootstrap analogues of the efficiency scores as $\widetilde{TE}_b^{*l,k} = \widehat{TE}_b^{*l,k} + h_l\hat{\varepsilon}_{l,k}^b$ if $\widehat{TE}_b^{*l,k} + h_l\hat{\varepsilon}_{l,k}^b \geq 1$ and $\widetilde{TE}_b^{*l,k} = 2 - \widehat{TE}_b^{*l,k} - h_l\hat{\varepsilon}_{l,k}^b$ if otherwise, where h_l is a suitable bandwidth for the KDE of density of the true efficiency scores for group l.[20]

Step 2.4 refine the bootstrap analogues of the efficiency scores as $TE_b^{*l,k} = \overline{TE}_b^{*l} + (\widetilde{TE}_b^{*l,k} - \overline{TE}_b^{*l})/\sqrt{1 + h_l^2/\hat{\sigma}_l^2}$, for all $i = 1, \ldots, n_l$, where $\overline{TE}_b^{*l} = \frac{1}{n_l}\sum_{k=1}^{n_l} \widetilde{TE}_b^{*l,k}$ and $\hat{\sigma}_l$ is the sample standard deviation computed from $\{\widehat{TE}^{l,k} : k = 1, \ldots, n_l\}$.

Step 2.5 define $x_b^{*l,k} = x^{l,k}$, $y_b^{*l,k} = (\widehat{TE}_b^{l,k}/TE_b^{*l,k}) \times y^{l,k}$, for all $k = 1, \ldots, n_l$.

Step 3 *Estimation of appropriate bootstrap analogue of the quantity of interest*: Apply DEA or FDH using the same formulas as in Step 1, but for the *pooled* bootstrap sample $\mathscr{S}_{n,b}^*$, to obtain bootstrap analogues (or pseudo-estimates) of the estimated (or pseudo-true) efficiency scores of observations of interest; denote and save these estimates as $\mathscr{E}_b^* = \{\widehat{\widetilde{TE}}_b^{*l,k} : k = 1, \ldots, n_l, \ l = 1, \ldots, L\}$.

Step 4 *Replication*: Repeat Steps 2–3, B times.

Step 5 *Inference*: Use $\{\mathscr{E}_b^* : b = 1, \ldots, B\}$ from Step 4 to infer about the true efficiency score at a fixed point, $TE(x, y)$, or a function of it, e.g., construct confidence intervals, estimate the bias or perform statistical tests about it, etc.

---

[20] Here, note, the bandwidth h_l is to be chosen for the set of all DEA estimates of efficiency scores in the group l that are not equal to unity. See Simar and Wilson (2008) and the next chapter for more details and references on KDE and bandwidth selection.

In the special case when $L = 1$, this algorithm coincides with the smooth homogeneous bootstrap for output-oriented efficiency. The algorithm for the input-oriented case is similar and was presented in Simar and Wilson (1998, pp. 56–57) for the homogeneous case.[21] For an application of this approach to cross-country performance analysis, see Henderson and Zelenyuk (2007).

9.3.1.2 Subsampling Bootstrap for DEA and FDH

Perhaps the main limitation of the smooth bootstrap was that no theoretical proof was found about the consistency of such an approach, in fact to date, although this was the only justified practical approach for that time. The first proof of consistency of a bootstrap approach for DEA and FDH came with the seminal work of Kneip et al. (2008) and Jeong and Simar (2006), respectively, where they proposed a new alternative, the so-called "subsampling bootstrap." This type of bootstrap is, in fact, much simpler than the smooth bootstrap and is very similar to the simple or naive bootstrap, using the same resampling function but for drawing samples of a smaller size than the original sample, e.g., of the size $m = \lfloor n^\gamma \rfloor < n$, for $\gamma \in (0, 1)$, where $\lfloor c \rfloor$ denotes the integer part of a real positive number c.

To grasp the essence of the validity of this bootstrap, it is worth first grasping the essence of invalidity of the naive bootstrap for the context of boundary estimations. For this, consider a classic example of using a random sample $\{\xi_1, \ldots, \xi_n\}$ to estimate the upper bound of the support of a univariate random variable, e.g., from the uniform distribution on $[0, \theta]$. It is well known that the maximum likelihood estimator (MLE) for θ is $\hat{\theta}_{(n)} := \max\{\xi_1, \ldots, \xi_n\}$. If we want to resample naively from $\{\xi_1, \ldots, \xi_n\}$ then, on a single draw, the probability that $\hat{\theta}_{(n)}$ is drawn is $1/n$ and that it is not drawn is $(1 - 1/n)$. Thus, the probability of never drawing $\hat{\theta}_{(n)}$ in all the n independent draws is $(1 - 1/n)^n$, while the probability of the opposite event (drawing $\hat{\theta}_{(n)}$ at least once in the n draws) is $1 - (1 - 1/n)^n$. Recalling that $e = \lim_{n \to \infty}(1 + 1/n)^n$, we get

$$\lim_{n \to \infty}(1 - (1 - 1/n)^n) = 1 - 1/e \approx 0.632,$$

i.e., even in a hypothetical case when $n \to \infty$ (i.e., perfect representation of the population), over 60 percent of the bootstrap samples will contain at least one observation of $\hat{\theta}_{(n)}$ and so the bootstrap estimates $\hat{\theta}^*_{(n)}$ for all these bootstrap samples will be identical to the original estimate $\hat{\theta}_{(n)}$. On the other hand, the probability of observing the event $\hat{\theta}_{(n)} = \theta$ in any sample is zero, by definition (because it is a continuous random variable). Thus, such naive resampling will not be an adequate mimicking of the true DGP.

---

[21] I.e., for the group-wise heterogeneous case with input orientation, Step 2.3 should change to
$$\widehat{TE}_b^{*l,k} = \widehat{TE}^{*l,k} + h_l \hat{\varepsilon}_{l,k}^b \text{ if } \widehat{TE}^{*l,k} + h_l \hat{\varepsilon}_{l,k}^b \le 1 \text{ and } \widehat{TE}_b^{*l,k} = 2 - \widehat{TE}^{*l,k} - h_l \hat{\varepsilon}_{l,k}^b$$
otherwise, while Step 2.5 should change to $x_b^{*l,k} = x^{l,k}(\widehat{TE}_b^{l,k}/TE_b^{l,k*})$, $y_b^{*l,k} = y^{l,k}$.

The idea of subsampling is very simple: if only m out of n random draws (independently, uniformly, with replacement) are made, such that $m < n$ and $m/n \to 0$ as $n \to \infty$, then we have

$$\lim_{n \to \infty} \Pr\left(\hat{\theta}^*_{(n)} = \hat{\theta}_{(n)}\right) = \lim_{n \to \infty} (1 - (1 - 1/n)^m) = 0,$$

which is coherent with the true DGP. The formal proofs of consistency of the m out of n bootstrap in general context is much more involved and more details can be found in Bickel and Freedman (1981), Beran and Ducharme (1991), Hall (1992), Bickel and Sakov (2008) to mention a few.[22] Its extension (and in some sense a generalization) to the case of multivariate estimation of a boundary was given by Kneip et al. (2008) for DEA and by Jeong and Simar (2006) for FDH, who proved that under certain regularity conditions (similar to those discussed above) such a bootstrap is consistent in the DEA and FDH context, for any $\gamma \in (0, 1)$.

Kneip et al. (2008) also proposed another alternative and also proved its consistency – the so-called "double-smooth" bootstrap, where in addition to smoothing the distribution of observations (as discussed above), they also smooth the initial estimates of the frontier. However, this alternative appears to be much more complex and so is rarely used in practice.[23] Kneip et al. (2011) also provided extensive Monte Carlo evidence, confirming good performance of their new bootstrap approaches.

More recently, Kneip et al. (2011) proposed a computationally much more efficient and simpler than the double-smooth bootstrap, where only some observations (at and "near" the boundary) required the computationally more intensive smoothing, while the rest of the observations are resampled naively. This approach also appears to be more complex than the m out of n bootstrap and so the latter appears to be more popular in practice.

A slightly generalized version of subsampling bootstrap for DEA and FDH was proposed by Simar and Zelenyuk (2007), and applied in Henderson and Zelenyuk (2007). Such a version allows for different groups within the population to have different distributions, where the resampling is done separately for each group, while the DEA estimation is done on the pooled sample if all groups share the same frontier, often referred to as the "grand frontier" or "meta-frontier." The algorithm for such a group-wise heterogeneous version of the subsampling bootstrap for DEA and FDH can be summarized as follows:

Step 1 Obtain an estimate of $TE(x, y|\mathscr{P})$, a true *individual* efficiency score evaluated *at a fixed point* (x, y) relative to the technology frontier characterized by some data generating process

---

[22] Another alternative is random resampling m out of n *without replacement*, e.g., see Politis and Romano (1994) and Politis et al. (2001).

[23] The single smooth bootstrap described above can be considered as a simplification (and in this sense an approximation) of the double-smooth bootstrap.

$\mathscr{P}$ (see (9.1.5)) using DEA or FDH to the original sample $\mathscr{S}_n = \{(x^k, y^k) : k = 1, \ldots, n\}$; denote this estimate as $\widehat{TE}(x, y|\mathscr{S}_n)$. Partition the original sample into (sub-)groups $\mathscr{S}_{n_l}^l = \{(x^k, y^k) : k = 1, \ldots, n_l\}$ for all $l \in \{1, \ldots, L\}$ representing the corresponding (sub-)groups in the population.

Step 2 Obtain the bth bootstrap sample: For each group l, make a choice of $\gamma_l \in (0, 1)$ to determine m_l and do the resampling (independently, uniformly, with replacement) of m_l out of n_l pairs (x^k, y^k) from the original samples for each group $l \in \{1, \ldots, L\}$, separately, to generate corresponding bootstrap samples $\mathscr{S}_{m_l,b}^{*l} = \{(x_b^{*l,k}, y_b^{*l,k}) : k = 1, \ldots, m_l\}, l \in \{1, \ldots, L\}$. Denote the *pooled* bootstrap sample as $\mathscr{S}_{m,b}^* = \{\mathscr{S}_{m_1,b}^{*1}, \ldots, \mathscr{S}_{m_L,b}^{*L}\}, m = m_1 + \ldots + m_L$.

Step 3 Obtain the bth bootstrap estimates of interest: Use the same formulas as in Step 1, but with respect to the frontier constructed from the *pooled* bootstrap sample $\mathscr{S}_{m,b}^*$ obtained in Step 2; denote them as $\widehat{TE}(x, y|\mathscr{S}_{m,b}^*)$.

Step 4 Repeat Steps 2–3 B times to obtain and save $\widehat{TE}(x, y|\mathscr{S}_{m,b}^*)$ from all $b = 1, \ldots, B$ iterations.

Step 5 Use $\{\widehat{TE}(x, y|\mathscr{S}_{m,b}^*) : b = 1, \ldots, B\}$ from Step 4 to make inferences about $TE(x, y \mid \mathscr{P})$, e.g., construct confidence intervals for $TE(x, y \mid \mathscr{P})$, the bias corrected estimate of $TE(x, y \mid \mathscr{P})$, perform statistical tests about $TE(x, y \mid \mathscr{P})$ or some functions of it, etc.

To be more specific, a symmetric confidence interval for $TE(x, y \mid \mathscr{P})$, for a fixed point (x, y), can be constructed as

$$\left[\frac{\widehat{TE}(x, y \mid \mathscr{S}_n)}{1 + n^{-\kappa}\delta_{1-\alpha/2,m}}, \frac{\widehat{TE}(x, y \mid \mathscr{S}_n)}{1 + n^{-\kappa}\delta_{\alpha/2,m}} \right],$$

where $\delta_{\alpha/2,m}$ and $\delta_{1-\alpha/2,m}$ are the bootstrap-based estimates of the quantiles of interest, with $\alpha/2$ and $1 - \alpha/2$ respectively, for a selected significance level $\alpha \in (0, 1)$, defined by

$$\Pr\left[m^\kappa \left(\frac{\widehat{TE}(x, y|\mathscr{S}_{m,b}^*)}{\widehat{TE}(x, y \mid \mathscr{S}_n)} - 1 \right) \le \delta_{\alpha/2,m}|\mathscr{S}_n \right] = \frac{\alpha}{2}$$

and

$$\Pr\left[m^\kappa \left(\frac{\widehat{TE}(x, y|\mathscr{S}_{m,b}^*)}{\widehat{TE}(x, y \mid \mathscr{S}_n)} - 1 \right) \le \delta_{1-\alpha/2,m}|\mathscr{S}_n \right] = 1 - \frac{\alpha}{2},$$

where recall that $\kappa = 2/(N + M + 1)$ for DEA-VRS, $\kappa = 2/(N + M)$ for DEA-CRS, and $\kappa = 1/(N + M)$ for FDH.

Importantly, Kneip et al. (2008) proved that the conditional distribution of $m^\kappa \left(\frac{\widehat{TE}(x,y|\mathscr{S}_{m,b}^*)}{\widehat{TE}(x,y|\mathscr{S}_n)} - 1 \right)$ given $\mathscr{S}_n$ converges to the sampling distribution of $n^\kappa \left(\frac{\widehat{TE}(x,y|\mathscr{S}_n)}{TE(x,y|\mathscr{P})} - 1 \right)$ given $\mathscr{P}$, implying that $\delta_{\alpha/2,m}$ and $\delta_{1-\alpha/2,m}$ give consistent estimates of the true quantiles of interest $\delta_{\alpha/2}$ and $\delta_{1-\alpha/2}$ defined by

$$\Pr \left[n^\kappa \left(\frac{\widehat{TE}(x, y \mid \mathscr{S}_n)}{TE(x, y \mid \mathscr{P})} - 1 \right) \leq \delta_{\alpha/2} | \mathscr{P} \right] = \frac{\alpha}{2}$$

and

$$\Pr \left[n^\kappa \left(\frac{\widehat{TE}(x, y \mid \mathscr{S}_n)}{TE(x, y \mid \mathscr{P})} - 1 \right) \leq \delta_{1-\alpha/2} | \mathscr{P} \right] = 1 - \frac{\alpha}{2},$$

thus ensuring consistency of the confidence intervals constructed in this way.

While relatively simple to implement and a theoretically powerful approach, the main complication of the subsampling bootstrap, in general and in the DEA context in particular, is that the choice of the exact size of the subsample is important in practice. Indeed, while in their fundamental work, Kneip et al. (2008) derived the theoretical consistency results for any $\gamma \in (0, 1)$, the choice of γ in practice is important in the sense that different choices of γ can lead to different quantitative and even qualitative conclusions.

This problem of choosing γ (or more generally m) is somewhat similar to the problem of choosing the level of smoothing (bandwidth) in the density estimation. Here, the smaller m is relative to n the more information from the original sample is lost, while for m closer to n the bootstrap distribution can be too concentrated, thus jeopardizing accurate inference in both cases, and the desired m that yields accurate inference is somewhere in-between these cases. Earlier studies (e.g., see Simar and Zelenyuk, 2007) simply used a rule-of-thumb choice of γ, such as $\gamma = 2/3$ or $\gamma = 0.7$, combined with a sensitivity analysis to check if and how results are changing for small deviations from such choice.

In a related and more general context, Politis et al. (2001) and Bickel and Sakov (2008) showed that the subsampling inference typically works well for a fairly wide range of values m, thus suggesting that one should look for m that yields the lowest volatility (e.g., measured by standard deviation) in estimates of the objects of interest, such as quantiles (confidence intervals), etc. Simar and Wilson (2011a) carefully adapted their method to selection of m in the sub-sampling bootstrap for DEA and FDH and presented convincing Monte Carlo evidence of its good performance.

The subsampling bootstrap can also be used in the context of estimation and inference of aggregates of efficiency scores, e.g., when one wants to estimate an average efficiency of an industry, and we discuss this in the next chapter.

9.4 CONCLUDING REMARKS

Although somewhat extensive and detailed, this chapter gave only a brief intro-duction to bootstrap and its adaptation to DEA and FDH contexts. We mainly focused on the Farrell measures of technical efficiency, because it appears to be the most popular measure of technical efficiency in practice (although not without caveats, as we discussed in the previous chapters), and we will continue focusing on it in the next chapter. Meanwhile, readers interested in bootstrap for other alternatives in measuring efficiency, such as the directional distance function and the hyperbolic efficiency measure, are referred to Simar and Vanhems (2012) and Simar et al. (2012).

9.5 EXERCISES

1. Implement the naive bootstrap to estimate standard errors and construct confidence intervals for a sample mean of various distributions.
2. Implement the naive bootstrap to estimate standard errors and construct confidence intervals for regression coefficients of various distributions.
3. Implement the naive bootstrap to estimate standard errors and construct confidence intervals maximum of data from $uniform(0, \theta)$.
4. Implement the m out of n bootstrap to estimate standard errors and construct confidence intervals maximum of data from $uniform(0, \theta)$.
5. Implement the smooth homogeneous bootstrap for the DEA context; try several simple scenarios and then real data.
6. Implement the smooth group-wise heterogeneous bootstrap for the DEA context; try several simple scenarios and then real data.
7. Implement the m out of n bootstrap for the DEA context; try several simple scenarios and then real data; and try different choices of m to check the sensitivity of results to the choice of m.

CHAPTER 10

Statistical Analysis for DEA and FDH: Part 2

Estimation of *individual* efficiency scores, correcting them for the bias and estimating their standard errors and confidence intervals are very useful when the focus is on particular DMUs. In most applications, however, the main focus is often on the big picture, i.e., on the overall tendencies of the population or its sub-populations of interest rather than (or in addition to) some individual DMUs. Such analysis can be done through various approaches, most popular of which are analysis of means, distributions or densities and a regression analysis, and the goal of this chapter is to outline these approaches and their *caveats*.

10.1 INFERENCE ON AGGREGATE OR GROUP EFFICIENCY

A common starting point of such aggregate analysis is to look at the aggregate efficiency and aggregate productivity measures. The simplest examples of such aggregate measures would be the sample means of the individual estimates. Such measures would be estimators of the population means. By the laws of large numbers, because the individual measures are consistent estimators of the true efficiency scores, the average of them is also a consistent estimator of the true mean of the population distribution of efficiency scores (under certain regularity conditions similar to those described in the previous chapter).

An important question, however, is whether the population mean is what should be of primary interest. As we discussed in Chapter 5, the equally weighted mean is a useful characteristic of a distribution, but just relying on that can misrepresent the situation dramatically. Indeed, when we look at the real world, one can see that many (if not most) industries are dominated by just a few firms, although they may also have many other small firms trying to have their place under the sun. For example, take the banking industry: in most countries just a few banks have a larger share of the industry (e.g., in terms of assets, loans, deposits, etc.) than the hundreds of remaining small banks. Imagine, hypothetically, if all those small banks have very high efficiency levels, say

316

very close to 100 percent, while those few gigantic banks have low efficiency levels, say close to 50 percent, although they control most of the industry share, say at 90 percent. In such an example, even though the industry is clearly dominated by the very inefficient banks, the equally weighted mean of efficiency (and the sample mean that represents it) would be close to 100 percent, suggesting an almost perfect efficiency situation in the industry! Would the equally weighted mean adequately describe the situation in such an industry, though? Clearly, the efficiency or productivity scores that enter the averaging should be adequately weighted, with weights reflecting the economic importance of each DMU that generated those scores. In Chapter 5 we described this in more detail, outlining the aggregation theory and how those weights are derived in various cases and here we will briefly discuss how to do inference on them.

The first attempt to do inference on the unequally weighted aggregate efficiency and contrasting it to the inference on equally weighted aggregate efficiency (i.e., the sample means) is found in Simar and Zelenyuk (2003, 2007). It might be also worth noting that their project originally started with an endeavor to adapt the *smooth* bootstrap, yet eventually converged to deploying the subsampling bootstrap, inspired and based upon a working paper at that time that eventually became the seminal work of Kneip et al. (2008).[1]

To briefly refresh the notation of the aggregation method, assume that we focus on a group within a population, e.g., group $l \in \{1, \ldots, L\}$, represented by n_l DMUs of the original sample of n DMUs. Recall from Chapter 5 that the aggregate technical efficiency of group l is the weighted average of individual technical efficiency scores within the group l, where the weights are the observed revenue shares of each DMU in group $l \in \{1, \ldots, L\}$, i.e.,

$$\overline{TE}^l = \sum_{k=1}^{n_l} TE^{l,k}(x^{l,k}, y^{l,k}) \times S^{l,k}, \qquad (10.1.1)$$

$$S^{l,k} = \frac{py^{l,k}}{p \sum_{k=1}^{n_l} y^{l,k}}, \qquad (10.1.2)$$

where p is the row vector of corresponding output prices. Similarly, the efficiency for the entire population would aggregate exactly into the weighted sum of the aggregate efficiency scores for each group, where the weights are the group's output shares, i.e.,

$$\overline{TE} = \sum_{l=1}^{L} \overline{TE}^l \times S^l, \qquad (10.1.3)$$

---

[1] It is also worth noting that in early studies, while judging on efficiency of certain groups after using DEA or FDH estimations, researchers usually used the Kruskal–Wallis and other standard statistical tests, but these tests ignored the effect of DEA on the inference, besides failing to account for economic weights associated with the efficiency scores.

$$S^l = p \sum_{k=1}^{n_l} y^{l,k} / \left(p \sum_{l=1}^{L} \sum_{k=1}^{n_l} y^{l,k} \right), \ l = 1, \dots, L. \tag{10.1.4}$$

The true aggregate efficiency scores outlined above are typically not observed in practice and must be estimated, e.g., one typically replaces the true individual efficiency scores with their consistent estimates from DEA or FDH. Such estimates of $\overline{TE}^l$ ($l = 1, \dots, L$) and of $\overline{TE}$ would have the same issues as the individual efficiency estimates (bias and dependency, in finite samples), and a bootstrap procedure can be used to correct for the bias and to estimate the confidence intervals and (in a similar fashion as outlined in the previous chapter).

To perform inference on such aggregate efficiency measures, Simar and Zelenyuk (2003, 2007) extended the subsampling bootstrap of Kneip et al. (2008) to the group-wise heterogeneous case and its algorithm is summarized below.

Step 1 Estimate the quantities of interest – the true aggregate efficiency scores relative to common technology frontier T characterized by some data generating process $\mathscr{P}$, denoted as $\overline{TE}$ and $\overline{TE}^l$, $l = 1, \dots, L$. Use the DEA-VRS (or DEA-CRS or FDH) estimator utilizing the original sample on inputs and outputs for all DMUs, $\mathscr{S}_n = \{(x^k, y^k) : k = 1, \dots, n\}$ to obtain estimates of individual efficiency scores, and aggregate them according to formulas explained in (10.1.1)–(10.1.4). Denote these estimate as $\widehat{\overline{TE}}(\mathscr{S}_n)$ and $\widehat{\overline{TE}}^l(\mathscr{S}_n)$, $l = 1, \dots, L$. Obtain related functions of them that are of interest for testing, e.g., for comparing efficiency of group A relative to group Z ($A, Z \in \{1, \dots, L\}$), compute $\widehat{RD}_{A,Z} = \widehat{\overline{TE}}^A / \widehat{\overline{TE}}^Z$ as an estimator of $RD_{A,Z} = \overline{TE}^A / \overline{TE}^Z$, etc.

Step 2 Obtain the bth bootstrap sample: For each group, l, make a choice of $\gamma_l \in (0, 1)$ to determine m_l, and do the resampling (independently, uniformly, with replacement) of m_l out of n_l pairs (x^k, y^k) from the original samples for each group $l \in \{1, \dots, L\}$, separately, to generate corresponding bootstrap samples $\mathscr{S}_{m_l,b}^{*l} = \{(x_b^{*j}, y_b^{*j}) : j = 1, \dots, m_l\}$, $l \in \{1, \dots, L\}$. Denote the *pooled* bootstrap sample as $\mathscr{S}_{m,b}^* = \{\mathscr{S}_{m_1,b}^{*1}, \dots, \mathscr{S}_{m_L,b}^{*L}\}$, $m = m_1 + \dots + m_L$.

Step 3 Obtain the bth bootstrap estimates of interest: Use the same formulas as in Step 1 to compute the bootstrap estimate of $\overline{TE}$ and $\overline{TE}^l$, $l \in \{1, \dots, L\}$, and the related functions of interest (e.g., $RD_{A,Z} = \overline{TE}^A / \overline{TE}^Z$) but with respect to the frontier constructed from the *pooled* bootstrap sample $\mathscr{S}_{m,b}^*$ obtained in Step 2; denote them as $\widehat{\overline{TE}}_b^*$ and $\widehat{\overline{TE}}_b^{*l}$, $l \in \{1, \dots, L\}$, $\widehat{RD}_{A,Z,b}^* = \widehat{\overline{TE}}_b^{*A} / \widehat{\overline{TE}}_b^{*Z}$.

Step 4 Repeat Steps 2–3 B times to obtain and save the estimates of interest for all $b = 1, \dots, B$ replications.

Step 5 Achieve the bootstrap goals: Use results from Step 4 to infer about the true quantities of interest. For example, construct confidence intervals for $\overline{TE}, \overline{TE^l}, RD_{A,Z}$, etc., obtain their bias corrected estimates or perform statistical tests about them, using the general formulas described in the previous chapter.

For example, suppose we want to test whether the aggregate efficiency of two groups, say groups A and Z, are different from one another, i.e., the null hypothesis of interest is H_0: $\overline{TE}^A = \overline{TE}^Z$, or in terms of the relative difference statistics, H_0: $RD_{A,Z} \equiv \overline{TE}^A/\overline{TE}^Z = 1$. The quantity $RD_{A,Z}$ is not observed but can be estimated by replacing the unobserved true efficiencies, $\overline{TE}^A$ and $\overline{TE}^Z$, with their DEA or FDH estimates. The bootstrap confidence interval for $RD_{A,Z}$ constructed in Step 5 will help empirically verify this null hypothesis – it should be rejected if such confidence interval (at a selected significance level α) does not contain unity, and not rejected otherwise.

It is worth noting that one could also use the smooth bootstrap here. However, the subsampling bootstrap has important advantages over the smooth bootstrap. As we discussed in the previous chapter, the main advantage is that it is able to account for heterogeneity, and another is that it does not require estimation of (the smoothing parameter for) the multivariate density estimation as the heterogeneous smooth bootstrap does. Another and a related advantage is that the subsampling bootstrap is much simpler and much faster to implement than the smooth (even homogeneous) bootstrap.

In their work, Simar and Zelenyuk (2007) tried their methodology with many simulations and presented some of them in their paper. Here we closely follow them and reproduce one of their examples, to illustrate the method in practice. An advantage of using a simulated data set rather than a real one is that in our simulated example we know the "truth" and thus can get a sense of the performance of a considered technique (the DEA estimator, its bias corrected version, the confidence intervals, etc.).

In the example below, technology frontier is characterized by the output distance function given by $D_o(x, y) = (y_2 + y_1)/x_1^{0.2}x_2^{0.3} = 1$, where the inputs are generated as iid from Uniform(0,1), the inefficiency is generated as $TE^{l,k} = 1 + u^{l,k}$, and $(u^{l,k}|x) \sim N^+(\mu, \sigma_l^2(x))$ for all $k \in \{1, \ldots, n_l\}$ and all $l \in \{A, Z\}$. Moreover, the inefficiency here is assumed to be heteroskedastic for both types of DMUs, yet they are heteroskedastic in different ways: for the Z-type DMUs we have $\sigma_Z(x) = \sigma_Z(1-x_1)^{\lambda_Z}$, while for the A-type DMUs it is $\sigma_A(x) = \sigma_A x_1^{\lambda_A}$.[2] Intuitively, this form of heteroskedasticity implies that the A-type DMUs tend to have more inefficiency the more they use the input x_1.

---

[2] The outputs are obtained by first drawing $\widetilde{y}_1^{l,k}$ and $\widetilde{y}_2^{l,k}$, from $Uniform(0.2, 1)$, for each subgroup, and these are used to generate random rays in the output space characterized by the slopes $\varphi^{l,k} = \widetilde{y}_2^{l,k}/\widetilde{y}_1^{l,k}$ for all k in every group $l \in \{A, Z\}$, and these in turn are used to simulate the efficient outputs (i.e., where $D_o(x, y) = 1$) as: $y_{1,eff}^{l,k} = x_1^{0.2}x_2^{0.3}/(\varphi^{l,k} + 1)$

Table 10.1 *Bootstrapping aggregate efficiency results for a simulated example.*

	DEA Estim.	True Estim.	Bias Corr. Estim.	Estim. Bias	Estim. St. Dev.	Est. lower CI bound	Est. upper CI bound
AgEf. A	1.21	1.27	1.28	−0.07	0.03	1.21	1.34
AgEf. Z	1.11	1.16	1.16	−0.05	0.02	1.01	1.20
AgEf.	1.16	1.21	1.22	−0.06	0.02	1.17	1.25
MeEf. A	1.27	1.31	1.32	−0.08	0.04	1.24	1.38
MeEf. Z	1.30	1.31	1.29	−0.09	0.05	1.17	1.37
MeEf.	1.21	1.31	1.30	−0.09	0.03	1.23	1.35
$RD_{A,Z;Ag}$	1.09	1.10	1.11	−0.02	0.04	1.03	1.19
$RD_{A,Z;Mean}$	0.97	0.998	0.91	0.07	0.06	1.80	1.02

Notes: CI = Confidence Intervals (0.95 level); MeEf = mean efficiency; AgEf. = aggregate efficiency; $RD_{A,Z;Ag}$ and $RD_{A,Z;Mean}$ are $RD_{A,Z}$ statistics for weighted and non-weighted average efficiencies; for choosing subsample sizes we have $\gamma_A = \gamma_Z = 0.7$. $B = 2000$. 'True' estimates are obtained by aggregating the "true" efficiency scores drawn from the specified above densities.

An example of it could be that an increase in the number of employees may increase the so-called principal-agent problem (due to the larger asymmetric information problem), causing the firm's efficiency to deteriorate.[3]

Table 10.1 presents the results of the bootstrap application (with 2,000 replications) for this scenario (and thus replicates those in Simar and Zelenyuk, 2007). The first important thing to note is that the aggregate efficiency estimates are fairly far from the "true" ones and the bootstrap-based bias correction substantially improves the DEA estimates. The next thing to note is that the estimated confidence intervals also cover the true quantities. Interestingly, the point-estimates tell us that the aggregate efficiency of the two subgroups are quite similar when the non-weighted means are used and fairly different when the weighted means are used. In turn, the bootstrap confidence intervals for these aggregate efficiency scores and for the RD-statistics suggest that the non-weighted averages are not significantly different from each other. Meanwhile, the aggregate efficiency based on weighted averages are significantly different from each other.

The MATLAB code for this and other scenarios and for the bootstrap procedure is available in the archive of the *Journal of Applied Econometrics,* in reference to the paper of Simar and Zelenyuk (2007). An application of this

---

and $y_{2,eff}^{l,k} = x_1^{0.2} x_2^{0.3} - y_{1,eff}^{l,k}$. The "realized" (observed) outputs are then constructed as $y_1^{l,k} = y_{1,eff}^{l,k}/TE^{l,k}$, and $y_2^{l,k} = y_{2,eff}^{l,k}/TE^{l,k}$.

[3] While many parameters were tried and the results were similar qualitatively, for the results presented here we have $\mu_A = -0.1$ and $\mu_Z = 0$, while $\sigma_A = 0.5$, $\sigma_Z = 1.7$ and $\lambda_A = 3$ and $\lambda_Z = 0.2$. We also assume that information on prices is not available so that we have to construct the price-independent weights as described in Chapter 5.

approach to study performance across countries and efficiency catch-up in particular can be found in Henderson and Zelenyuk (2007), while Shiu and Zelenyuk (2012) used it to study efficiency of regions in China, while Curi et al. (2015) used it to analyze efficiency of banks, to mention a few.[4]

10.2 ESTIMATION AND COMPARISON OF DENSITIES OF EFFICIENCY SCORES

Here we consider another way of analyzing efficiency scores obtained from DEA or FDH estimators – based on estimation and testing about densities of efficiency scores, and we follow the work of Simar and Zelenyuk (2006). Just as in the previous example, for simplicity, we will consider the example of two subgroups, A and Z.

10.2.1 Density Estimation

First of all, recall that for a density, f_U, of a random variable, U, whose realizations are observed in a random sample $\{u_1, \ldots, u_n\}$, the KDE (Rosenblatt, 1956) at a point u, is given by

$$\hat{f}_h(u) = \frac{1}{nh} \sum_{j=1}^{n} K\left(\frac{u_j - u}{h}\right), \tag{10.2.1}$$

where $K(u)$ is a suitable kernel and h is a suitably selected bandwidth. It is well known that the estimator (10.2.1) is consistent and asymptotically normal, under fairly mild regularity conditions. In most situations, the particular type of kernel is not very important, and it is usually either Gaussian (i.e., standard normal density) or Epanechnikov, although many other alternatives exist.

The choice of the bandwidth, h (also referred to as the tuning parameter), is much more important: although the asymptotic theory typically requires only a certain order, e.g., usually $h = cn^{-1/5}$ for *any* positive constant, c, the particular estimates may differ substantially for substantial differences in h (or in c). The simplest, yet very useful, approach to selecting h is known as the robust (or adaptive) rule-of-thumb, given by

$$\hat{h}_{AROT} = 1.06 \min\left\{\hat{\sigma}_u, \; iqr(u)/1.349\right\} n^{-1/5}, \tag{10.2.2}$$

where $\hat{\sigma}_u$ and $iqr(u)$ are the sample standard deviation and the interquartile range of U, respectively. Though simple, this approach often gives a fairly good fit for many densities and is also often used as a starting point in more sophisticated selection procedures such as the cross-validation approach, the method of Sheather and Jones (1991), etc.[5]

---

[4] The choice of m_l can be made by adapting the approach of Simar and Wilson (2011a), which in turn is based on ideas from Politis et al. (2001) and Bickel and Sakov (2008).

[5] See Silverman (1986), Pagan and Ullah (1999), Henderson and Parmeter (2015) for details and further references.

The first issue of concern in the context of DEA and FDH, which we have mentioned already, is the fact that the efficiency score is bounded with many of the observations tending towards the bound. In statistics, this situation is known as the problem of bounded support, and in this situation the usual KDE could be substantially biased near the boundary (i.e., where most of the observations in efficiency analysis tend to be) and, in fact, is inconsistent at the boundary. As was mentioned above, one remedy for this problem that was used by Simar and Wilson (1998) is to use the so-called Silverman's reflection method (popularized by Silverman, 1986; also see Schuster, 1985), which ensures consistent estimation.[6] The idea of this approach is to modify the KDE as follows: for the cases when the random variable is *bounded from below* by some constant c_1 (e.g., for the output-oriented technical efficiency, $c_1 = 1 \leq TE$), use

$$\hat{f}_{h,c_1}^R(u) = \begin{cases} \frac{1}{nh_R} \sum_{j=1}^n \left[K\left(\frac{u_j-u}{h_R}\right) + K\left(\frac{(2c_1-u_j)-u}{h_R}\right) \right], & u \geq c_1 \\ 0 & otherwise, \end{cases}$$

(10.2.3)

and when the random variable is *bounded from above* by some constant c_2 (e.g., for the input-oriented technical efficiency, $c_2 = 1 \geq TE \geq 0$), use

$$\hat{f}_{h,c_2}^R(u) = \begin{cases} \frac{1}{nh_R} \sum_{j=1}^n \left[K\left(\frac{u_j-u}{h_R}\right) + K\left(\frac{(2c_2-u_j)-u}{h_R}\right) \right], & u \leq c_2 \\ 0 & otherwise, \end{cases}$$

(10.2.4)

where $K(.)$ is a suitable symmetric kernel and h_R is a suitable bandwidth for the *reflected* sample (i.e., $\{u_1, \ldots, u_n, 2c - u_1, \ldots, 2c - u_n\}$ where $c = c_1$ for (10.2.3) and $c = c_2$ for (10.2.4)).[7] This approach is easily adapted when a variable is bounded from both sides. However, in the efficiency analysis context, when the inefficiency is measured on the scale $[0, 1]$, it usually suffices to account only for the relevant bound where DMUs are expected to strive to and so most observations are typically observed near it.

Figures 10.1 and 10.2 illustrate the boundary problem, presenting examples of densities of *true* efficiency scores and of their kernel-based estimates with and without reflection, for $n = 100$ and $n = 1000$, respectively. Here, the inefficiency is generated as $TE^{l,k} = 1 + u^{l,k}$, and $(u^{l,k}|x) \sim N^+(\mu_l, \sigma_l^2)$, for all $k \in \{1, \ldots, n\}$ and all $l \in \{1, 2\}$, where $\mu_1 = 0$, $\mu_2 = 0.2$ and $\sigma_1 = \sigma_2 = 0.2$. From these figures, one can see that ignoring reflection indeed introduces bias and inconsistency, because the KDE always assigns some mass outside of the bound, and this happens for both small samples like $n = 100$ and fairly

---

[6] An alternative remedy would be to use special "boundary" kernels.

[7] E.g., if one uses a rule-of-thumb like (10.2.2) or the method of Sheather and Jones (1991) for selecting h_R, then it is desirable to correct such bandwidth by $2^{1/5} \approx 1.1487$ to preserve their optimality because the real sample size is n rather than $2n$.

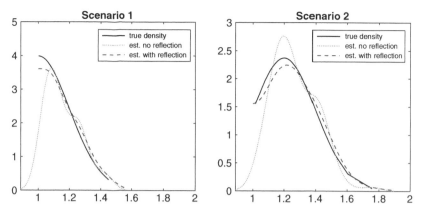

Figure 10.1 True and estimated densities ($n = 100$).

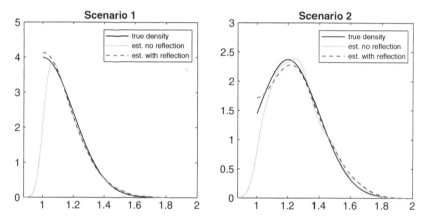

Figure 10.2 True and estimated densities ($n = 1000$).

large samples such as $n = 1000$. One can also see from the figures that the reflection method is particularly more helpful for the first scenario than for the second. This is because the mode is at the bound in the former and away from the bound (at 1.2) in the latter, and so relatively more mass of the density is near the bound in the first scenario than in the second, implying that the boundary problem is more pronounced in the first case than in the second. Indeed, even if the density is nonzero at the bound but very little mass is near it, and so very few or no observations are found there, then the boundary problem can be (and often is) ignored for practical simplicity. This is, however, not the case in efficiency analysis, where one naturally expects DMUs to strive to be near the 100 percent efficiency bound.

Another issue is the discontinuity problem: by virtue of DEA and FDH, in practice at least one observation in a sample (and usually several of them) must have 100 percent estimated efficiency score, i.e., be on the estimated frontier. However, in theory, because technical efficiency is assumed to be a continuous random variable, the probability of observing the event that the (true) technical efficiency is 100 percent is zero! For this reason, the DEA or FDH estimated efficiency scores of 1 are sometimes referred to as "spurious ones" or "spuriously efficient," and if one uses them in the density estimation, one gets "spurious" mass at and near unity. The simplest way to deal with them is to ignore them for the sake of KDE (with reflection), though this leads to some loss of information from the sample.

Another natural way to deal with the "spurious ones" for KDE is to first do the bootstrap-based bias correction (via the smooth or subsampling bootstrap) and then apply KDE for them rather than for the original DEA or FDH estimates. This approach seems more appealing than just ignoring the "spurious ones," yet sometimes it can actually add too much noise, exaggerating the inefficiency of some or all DMUs or the variation among them. There is no precise theory on whether one should prefer to use bias corrected scores or original scores with the "spurious ones" ignored; one may use the Efron rule-of-thumb, discussed in the previous chapter, to decide on this dilemma, though it also has an *ad hoc* element.

Figures 10.3 and 10.4 illustrate the problem for $n = 100$ and $n = 1000$, respectively.[8] They present typical plots of densities of the true efficiency scores, their kernel-based estimates (with reflection) when the true efficiency scores are used and when they are replaced with their DEA estimates without the "spurious ones" and when using the bias-corrected estimates based on group-wise heterogeneous smooth bootstrap (with 1000 replications), discussed in the previous chapter.[9] One can see that using DEA estimates in place of the true scores may introduce substantial bias, whether in small samples like $n = 100$ or in a fairly large sample such as $n = 1000$. One can also see from the figures that the problem is also substantial whether the mode of the density is at 1 (i.e., 100 percent efficiency) or away from it, making it hard to accurately identify and test the location of the true mode and, consequently, the number of true modes in distributions of efficiency.

The bottom line here is that while presenting plots of estimated densities (or other plots, e.g., box-plots, etc.) is very useful to get a visual sense of the results, one should take them with "a pinch of salt," so to speak, and be

---

[8] The same scenario is used for Figures 10.1 and 10.2, but where the frontier $y = x_1^{0.3} x_2^{0.5}$ (with inputs from $Uniform(0.2, 1)$) is estimated via DEA-VRS.

[9] Another alternative, explained by Simar and Wilson (2008), is to remove the "spurious ones" only for the sake of selection of bandwidths (e.g., as was described for the smooth bootstrap). We do not present this alternative because when a substantial number of "spurious ones" are present (e.g., even for 10–20 percent of the sample, as is often the case in practice), such an approach often leads to even greater overestimation near the boundary than in the presented figures, placing too much mass (or even a spike) near it. Smoothing the "spurious ones" in the way discussed in the next section (using (10.2.12)) usually brings an improvement, especially for testing, though it still may be problematic for plotting the estimated densities, leaving too much mass near the bound. Future research may need to be conducted to clarify this matter.

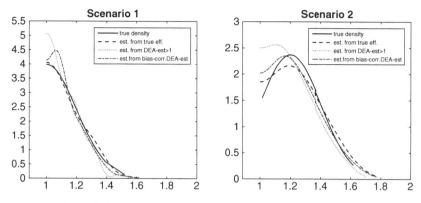

Figure 10.3 True and estimated densities ($n = 100$).

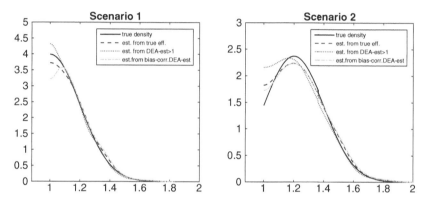

Figure 10.4 True and estimated densities ($n = 1000$).

careful when interpreting their shape in the sense that it could be fairly far from the shape of the true densities, due to the inherent bias of the DEA and FDH estimators or due to the noise introduced with correction of this bias. It is also advised to complement the visual analysis with a more formal analysis based on statistical testing – the topic we briefly discuss in the next subsection.

10.2.2 Statistical Tests about Distributions of Efficiency

Various tests can be performed about the distributions of efficiency scores: testing for their equality among groups or relative to a particular distribution or testing for stochastic dominance, etc. One could use various methods to do such testing, and tests based on KDE constitute one (yet not the only) natural approach and we will focus on it here. We will also focus on what seems to be the most popular test in practice: the test of equality of two distributions of true efficiency scores, while noting that other tests will share a lot of similarity on how they can be adapted to DEA and FDH context.

Suppose one uses KDE (with reflection), gets estimated densities of efficiencies for each group and plots them, as we did above, and notices that for some groups the densities are more similar than for others and then wonders if the difference is significant or whether it is due to the randomness of the sample. To perform such testing, Simar and Zelenyuk (2006) proposed adapting the Li (1996b) test to the peculiar context of efficiency estimation, and we follow them here.

To fix ideas formally, suppose we are interested in testing equality of densities of two random variables, which we denote as U^A and U^Z, for which the random samples, $\{u_j^A : j = 1, \ldots, n_A\}$ and $\{u_j^Z : j = 1, \ldots, n_Z\}$, representing the two populations or two sub-populations, A and Z, of a population, respectively, are available. Formally, let $f_A(u)$ and $f_Z(u)$ denote the probability density functions of the distributions of random variables, U^A and U^Z, respectively, at a fixed point, u, our null and alternative hypotheses can be stated as:

$H_0 : f_A(u) = f_Z(u), \forall u$ in the support of the random variables U^A and U^Z,

vs.

$H_1 : f_A(u) \neq f_Z(u)$, on a set of positive measures.

A criterion particularly convenient for the context of comparing densities is the integrated square difference, defined as

$$ISD = \int (f_A(u) - f_Z(u))^2 du. \tag{10.2.5}$$

Clearly, $ISD = 0$ if H_0 is true and $ISD > 0$ if H_1 is true. This criterion was used for developing a test for equality of densities by various authors, e.g., Mammen (1992), Anderson et al. (1994), Li (1996b, 1999) and Fan and Ullah (1999), who proposed slightly different empirical analogues of (10.2.5). A set of particularly convenient empirical analogues, or test statistics, was proposed by Li (1996b, 1999) and later extended by Fan and Ullah (1999) and Simar and Zelenyuk (2006), who adapted their approach to DEA and FDH and similar adaptation can be done to other tests.[10]

The idea of the empirical analogue of ISD is based on first noting that $dF_A(u) = f_A(u)du$ and $dF_Z(u) = f_Z(u)du$, and so we can rewrite (10.2.5) as:

---

[10] Particular assumptions for each of these tests vary and, for these details, see the corresponding papers we cited. In a nutshell, note that most of these tests require no serial correlation within a group, yet allow for contemporaneous correlation between the two groups, which could be the case, for example, when one group of DMUs are trying to learn from or mimic the actions and experience of another group of DMUs. A real world example of such contemporaneous correlation could be a know-how diffusion phenomenon – e.g., when local firms are learning from foreign firms about the new business processes, while the foreign firms might be learning from local firms about successful local business traditions.

$$ISD = \int f_A(u)\,dF_A(u) + \int f_Z(u)\,dF_Z(u)$$
$$- \int f_A(u)\,dF_Z(u) - \int f_Z(u)\,dF_A(u)$$

and then replace $f_A(u)$ and $f_Z(u)$ with their consistent KDEs, for each observed point $j = 1, \ldots, n_A$ and $k = 1, \ldots, n_Z$, and also replace the distribution functions $F_A(u)$ and $F_Z(u)$ with respective empirical distribution functions, $EDF_n(u)$, for each observation (i.e., replace the integral with simple arithmetic averaging over the observations). This gives an empirical analogue of (10.2.5):

$$\widehat{ISD}_{n_A,n_Z,h} = \frac{1}{n_A^2 h} \sum_{j=1}^{n_A} \sum_{k=1}^{n_A} K\left(\frac{u_{A,j} - u_{A,k}}{h}\right)$$
$$+ \frac{1}{n_Z^2 h} \sum_{j=1}^{n_Z} \sum_{k=1}^{n_Z} K\left(\frac{u_{Z,j} - u_{Z,k}}{h}\right)$$
$$- \frac{1}{n_A n_Z h} \sum_{j=1}^{n_A} \sum_{k=1}^{n_Z} K\left(\frac{u_{A,j} - u_{Z,k}}{h}\right)$$
$$- \frac{1}{n_Z n_A h} \sum_{j=1}^{n_Z} \sum_{k=1}^{n_A} K\left(\frac{u_{Z,j} - u_{A,k}}{h}\right). \tag{10.2.6}$$

Li (1996b) noted that one could also use a related test statistic – the one constructed by removing the "diagonal" terms from (10.2.6), i.e.,

$$\widehat{ISD}^{nd}_{n_A,n_Z,h} = \frac{1}{n_A(n_A - 1)h} \sum_{j=1}^{n_A} \sum_{k=1,k\neq j}^{n_A} K\left(\frac{u_{A,j} - u_{A,k}}{h}\right)$$
$$+ \frac{1}{n_Z(n_Z - 1)h} \sum_{j=1}^{n_Z} \sum_{k=1,k\neq j}^{n_Z} K\left(\frac{u_{Z,j} - u_{Z,k}}{h}\right)$$
$$- \frac{1}{n_Z(n_A - 1)h} \sum_{j=1}^{n_Z} \sum_{k=1,k\neq j}^{n_A} K\left(\frac{u_{Z,j} - u_{A,k}}{h}\right)$$
$$- \frac{1}{n_A(n_Z - 1)h} \sum_{j=1}^{n_A} \sum_{k=1,k\neq j}^{n_Z} K\left(\frac{u_{A,j} - u_{Z,k}}{h}\right). \tag{10.2.7}$$

Using the central limit theorem for degenerate U-statistics from Hall (1984), Li (1996b) showed that, after appropriate "standardization," the limiting distribution of both (10.2.6) and (10.2.7) are standard normal; specifically (under certain regularity conditions), we have

$$n_A h^{1/2} \widehat{ISD}_{n_A,n_Z,h} \xrightarrow[\text{under } H_0]{d} \mathcal{N}(0, \sigma_{\lambda,h}^2), \tag{10.2.8}$$

where

$$\sigma_{\lambda,h}^2 = 2(\int f_A(u)dF_A(u) + \lambda^2 \int f_Z(u)dF_Z(u)$$
$$+ \lambda \int f_A(u)dF_Z(u) + \lambda \int f_Z(u)dF_A(u)) \int K^2(u)du.$$
(10.2.9)

Because the true densities are unknown, the asymptotic variance of the above statistics, $\sigma_{\lambda,h}$, is also unknown, but Li (1996b) showed that it can be consistently estimated by replacing the true densities in (10.2.9) by their consistent kernel-based estimates at the observed data points, i.e., via

$$\hat{\sigma}_{\lambda,h}^2 = 2 \left\{ \frac{1}{n_A^2 h} \sum_{j=1}^{n_A} \sum_{k=1}^{n_A} K\left(\frac{u_{A,j} - u_{A,k}}{h}\right) \right.$$
$$+ \frac{\lambda_n^2}{n_Z^2 h} \sum_{j=1}^{n_Z} \sum_{k=1}^{n_Z} K\left(\frac{u_{Z,j} - u_{Z,k}}{h}\right)$$
$$+ \frac{\lambda_n}{n_A n_Z h} \sum_{j=1}^{n_A} \sum_{k=1}^{n_Z} K\left(\frac{u_{A,j} - u_{Z,k}}{h}\right)$$
$$+ \frac{\lambda_n}{n_Z n_A h} \sum_{j=1}^{n_Z} \sum_{k=1}^{n_A} K\left(\frac{u_{Z,j} - u_{A,k}}{h}\right) \right\} \int K^2(u)du,$$
(10.2.10)

where $\lambda_n = n_A/n_Z$ and $n = n_A + n_Z$ provided that $\lambda_n \to \lambda \in (0, \infty)$ as $n_A \to \infty$ and where $\int K^2(u)du = 1/(2\sqrt{\pi})$ when K is the Gaussian kernel.

Although both statistics, (10.2.6) and (10.2.7), are asymptotically equivalent, the latter appears to have slightly better performance in various Monte Carlo experiments.[11] Moreover, Li (1999), showed that the naive (EDF-based) bootstrap is consistent and yields better performance both in terms of size and in terms of the power of the test than the first-order asymptotic results stated in (10.2.8). This is not surprising given that these test statistics are asymptotically standard normal (and asymptotically pivotal), and so the seminal Mammen (1992) theorem can be adapted here.

Well before the KDE-based tests were invented, one of the most popular tests for the same types of hypotheses was the Kolmogorov–Smirnov (KS) test, which is based on the KS distance criterion, given by

$$KS_{n_A,n_Z} = \sup_u | EDF_{n_A}^A(u) - EDF_{n_Z}^Z(u) |,$$
(10.2.11)

---

[11] Note however that for relatively small samples, (10.2.7) might be sensitive to the order of observations and so should be applied with caution, replaced or complemented with (10.2.6) (see Li and Racine, 2007, pp. 363–364 for related discussion).

where $EDF_{n_A}^A(u)$ and $EDF_{n_Z}^Z(u)$ are the empirical distribution functions applied for estimating distributions of random variables U^A and U^Z from the random samples, $\{u_j^A : j = 1, \ldots, n_A\}$ and $\{u_j^Z : j = 1, \ldots, n_Z\}$.

By the Glivenko–Cantelli theorem, this statistic converges almost surely to zero under the null hypothesis and to a constant characterizing the largest difference between the two distributions. The distribution of this statistic is not normal, and in fact is quite complicated, and its discovery and derivations under different assumptions are due to Kolmogorov (1933) and Smirnov (1939), to mention just a few. The null hypothesis with this test is rejected if the value of KS_{n_A, n_Z} is larger than $cr(\alpha)\sqrt{(n_A + n_Z)/n_A n_Z}$, where $cr(\alpha)$ is the critical value from the asymptotic distribution of KS_{n_A, n_Z}, which depends on the chosen level of significance, e.g., for $\alpha \in \{0.01, 0.05, 0.1\}$, we have $cr(\alpha) \in \{1.63, 1.36, 1.22\}$, respectively. An advantage of this test is that it does not need an assumption about the existence of densities for the random variables of interest and so is more general than a test based on KDE. Another advantage of this approach is that it does not require estimation of a bandwidth and so is somewhat simpler, although with modern computers and new algorithms, bandwidth estimation became simpler, especially for a univariate case such as this one.[12]

It is worth noting here that, as for any statistical test, especially a general one with very little structure imposed, the power of these tests might be very low for relatively small samples (e.g., 20 observations). Thus, one should be very careful when interpreting the results of the test, when for a given data set the null hypothesis cannot be rejected – it may be just because the sample size is relatively low to identify small or complex differences in the distributions.

More importantly, whether employing the kernel-based tests or the KS test or any other test, one should be careful adapting this and other tests to the context of DEA and FDH. In particular, the first natural question is whether one also needs to use some methods for accounting for the boundary problem in the DEA or FDH context, as most of the mass of the distribution is likely to be very close to the bound and, as we saw in the figures above, the usual KDE for such a case can give a very poor fit. Simar and Zelenyuk (2006) discussed the asymptotic properties of the reflected version of the Li test, confirming it is also asymptotically normal. Their general conclusion was that despite the fact that the reflection method is very useful in the estimation of density with bounded support, it is not needed for adapting the original Li-test as it does not make any improvement over the original test. Their Monte Carlo evidence also

---

[12] The asymptotic theory for the Li-test and its adapted version is valid for any bandwidth of appropriate order, while the finite sample results appear to be insensitive to small variation in the bandwidth, and in fact appears to work well even with the robust Silverman rule of thumb, sometimes even better (and certainly faster) than when more complicated bandwidth selection methods are used. This is because what is more important for the sake of the test, is that the same bandwidth of appropriate order (and reasonable magnitude suggested by some optimal criteria) is used for both densities, in the bootstrapping under the null hypothesis.

showed that both versions of the test have a similar performance. An intuitive explanation for this phenomenon is related to the fact that the bias incurred due to ignoring the reflection appears in estimates of both $f_A(u)$ and $f_Z(u)$, and it gets asymptotically canceled out (under H_0) in the square of the difference, $f_A(u) - f_Z(u)$. Clearly, there is also no need for the reflection method for the KS test application.

The second and more important issue is that we are not using the true random variables, whose densities we wish to test for equality, but their DEA or FDH estimates, that have finite-sample bias and dependency, and the structure of this dependency is unknown. Although these problems vanish asymptotically, the convergence rate depends on the dimension of the DEA (or FDH) model, so the convergence rate in the original distribution of the Li-test (which is $O_p((n^2h)^{-1/2})$ where an optimal h is $O(n^{-1/5})$) would not be preserved in general, but may depend on the dimension of the production model and the type of DEA (or FDH) estimator employed. In such situations, bootstrap can help by opening a practical and improved way of conducting inference, and Simar and Zelenyuk (2006) suggested two algorithms of this adapted-to-DEA bootstrap-based Li test. A similar approach can be applied for the FDH case, as well as for adapting the Kolmogorov–Smirnov test to the DEA or FDH context.

Another issue for the application of the test is the discontinuity problem: note that we observe "spurious" mass at unity, since at least one observation is on the frontier constructed by DEA or FDH, while the probability of drawing an observation on the true frontier is zero. In principle, one could use a two-step approach to tackle this issue: (i) correct for the bias in the efficiency estimates via the subsampling bootstrap or the smooth bootstrap, as described above, and (ii) use these bias-corrected estimates in the test of interest. An important complication, however, for the first step is that the bias correction is likely to depend on the choice of the subsample or the bandwidth of KDE, respectively, both suffering from the "curse of dimensionality" problem, and so such bias correction might add more noise and so may actually jeopardize performance of the tests. Moreover, analyzing such an approach under various Monte Carlo scenarios would be very computationally intensive, even with computers today (e.g., one bootstrap-based bias-correction estimation procedure may take hours, since it requires LP optimization for an efficiency score of each DMU in each bootstrap replication). Furthermore, similarly as for ignoring the reflection, what matters for the test is the difference, $f_A(u) - f_Z(u)$, over all the possibilities of u, and the bias appearing in estimates of $f_A(u)$ and $f_Z(u)$ eventually gets asymptotically canceled out (under H_0) and approximately canceled out in a finite sample.

All in all, after experimenting with many different approaches, Simar and Zelenyuk (2006) proposed two simple algorithms to remedy the problem, which also circumvent the discontinuity problem without the computationally intensive bias correction:

Algorithm I was based on bootstrapping of a statistic using the sample of DEA-estimates where $\widehat{TE}^i > 1$ (or $\widehat{TE}^i < 1$ for input orientation or when the scale is converted to [0, 1] interval), to avoid the "spurious ones" discussed above.[13]

Meanwhile, Algorithm II was based on bootstrap for the sample of DEA-estimates where the scores that equal unity are "smoothed away" from the bound by adding a small uniform noise. Specifically, they suggested for this noise to be within the 5 percent quantile of the empirical distribution of $\left\{ \widehat{TE}^{l,k} : \widehat{TE}^{l,k} > 1, k = 1, \ldots, n_l, l = 1, \ldots, L \right\}$, but of order no larger than the estimation noise implied by the rate of convergence of the deployed estimator. Formally, such smoothing is made by assigning[14]

$$
\widetilde{TE}^{l,k} = \begin{cases} \widehat{TE}^{l,k} + \epsilon^k, & \widehat{TE}^{l,k} = 1 \\ \widehat{TE}^{l,k} & otherwise \end{cases}, \tag{10.2.12}
$$

where $\epsilon^k := Uniform\left(0, \min\left\{n^{-2/(M+N+1)}, a - 1\right\}\right)$ and a is the α-quantile (e.g., 5 percent) of the empirical distribution of $\{\widehat{TE}^{l,k} : \widehat{TE}^{l,k} > 1, k = 1, \ldots, n_l, l = 1, \ldots, L\}$.[15] A summary of both bootstrap algorithms for Li-statistic adapted to DEA context is given below.

Step 1 Apply DEA or FDH to the original sample, $\mathscr{S}_n = \{(x^k, y^k) : k = 1, \ldots, n\}$, to obtain estimates of the true efficiency, $\mathscr{E} = \{TE(x^k, y^k) : k = 1, \ldots, n\}$, further denoted as $\hat{\mathscr{E}} = \{\widehat{TE}^k : k = 1, \ldots, n\}$. Deal with the "spurious ones" either via Algorithm I (trimming the sample of original estimated efficiency scores from those equal unity) or Algorithm II (smoothing the estimates of original efficiency scores according to (10.2.12)). Partition the original sample and the estimates into distinct (sub-)groups of interest, $\hat{\mathscr{E}}_l = \{\widetilde{TE}^{l,k} : k = 1, \ldots, m_l\}$, for all $l \in \{1, \ldots, L\}$ representing the corresponding (sub-)groups within the population, where $m_l \leq n_l$ for Algorithm I (considering only $\widetilde{TE}^{l,k} = \widehat{TE}^{l,k} \neq 1$) and $m_l = n_l$ for Algorithm II. Estimate the test statistic for comparing $\hat{\mathscr{E}}_A$ to $\hat{\mathscr{E}}_Z$, $A, Z \in \{1, \ldots, L\}$ denote it by $\hat{\mathscr{T}}_{n_A, n_Z}$ (e.g., (10.2.6) or (10.2.7) with (10.2.10) for Li, 1996b or (10.2.11) for KS-test).

---

[13] This approach is also used in the Algorithm I in the truncated regression context of Simar and Zelenyuk (2007) discussed below.

[14] This approach, in essence and in different context, has later been justified in a more formal set up by Kneip et al. (2011).

[15] Again, another alternative is to remove the "spurious ones" only for the sake of selection of bandwidths (Simar and Wilson, 2008). We do not present this alternative here for the test because when a substantial number of "spurious ones" are present (e.g., even for 10–20 percent of the sample, as is often the case in practice), such approach leads to the two samples persistently looking much more similar than they really are (relative to comparing the true efficiency scores in a Monte Carlo), which in turn distorts both the size and especially the power of the test.

Step 2 Resample from $\hat{\mathscr{E}}_A$ or $\hat{\mathscr{E}}_Z$, whichever is larger, using the EDF, to obtain the bootstrap analogues, denoted as $\hat{\mathscr{E}}^*_{l,b} = \{\widetilde{TE}^{*l,k}_b : k = 1,\ldots,m_l\}$, $A, Z \in \{1,\ldots,L\}$.

Step 3 Estimate the test statistic of interest using the same formulas as in Step 1 (e.g., (10.2.6) or (10.2.7) for Li, 1996b or (10.2.11) for KS-test) for comparing $\hat{\mathscr{E}}_A$ to $\hat{\mathscr{E}}_Z$, $A, Z \in \{1,\ldots,L\}$, but using the bootstrap samples $\hat{\mathscr{E}}^*_{A,b}$ and $\hat{\mathscr{E}}^*_{Z,b}$, $A, Z \in \{1,\ldots,L\}$ to obtain bootstrap analogues (or pseudo-estimates) of the test statistics, denote it as $\hat{\mathscr{T}}^{*b}_{n_A,n_Z}$.

Step 4 *Replication*: Repeat Steps 2–3, B times to obtain and save $\hat{\mathscr{T}}^{*b}_{n_A,n_Z}$ from all $b = 1,\ldots,B$.

Step 5 *Inference*: Use $\{\hat{\mathscr{T}}^{*b}_{n_A,n_Z} : b = 1,\ldots,B\}$ from Step 4 and $\hat{\mathscr{T}}^b_{n_A,n_Z}$ to compute the p-values of the test.

A simple way to get the bootstrap estimates of p-values is to compute the number of times the bootstrap values of the statistic ($\hat{\mathscr{T}}^{*b}_{n_A,n_Z}$) exceed the original value of the statistic $\hat{\mathscr{T}}_{n_A,n_Z}$, i.e.,

$$\hat{\mathsf{p}}_{n,B} = \frac{1}{B}\sum_{b=1}^{B} \mathbb{I}\left(\hat{\mathscr{T}}^{*b}_{n_A,n_Z} > \hat{\mathscr{T}}_{n_A,n_Z}\right),$$

where the bootstrapping or resampling is done under H_0 (which can be done by either drawing from the pooled sample (with both groups A and Z) or drawing from one sample, e.g., the largest of the two).[16]

Monte Carlo results from various scenarios provided evidence of good performance of such algorithms for moderate dimensions of DEA models, requiring much less computing time than (and no additional estimation noise from) the tests that would involve bias correction of DEA scores. Simar and Zelenyuk (2006) also provided figures that can serve as a useful visual reference regarding the impact of the "curse of dimensionality." Using the same DGPs as them, we replicated the power functions for the Li-test under different dimensions of the DEA model and Figure 10.5 and Figure 10.6 present them for 20 and 100 observations in each group, respectively.

The first point to note from the figures is that the power function for the two-input–one-output DEA-estimates is very similar to that based on true efficiencies, even for the case with only 20 observations, and especially with 100 observations. One can also see a manifestation of the curse of dimensionality of the DEA estimator: the higher the dimension, the worse the power. Indeed, with 20 observations in each group, the power function based on the DEA-estimates in the four-input case is fairly poor (and far from that based on the true efficiencies) and is almost flat for the five-input case with 20 observations.

---

[16] Li (1999) proved the consistency of both approaches in the standard context and found that the latter often attains slightly higher power and so is often preferred. This slight superiority of drawing from one sample rather than a pooled sample appears to hold in the context when the true efficiency scores are replaced with those estimated via DEA or FDH.

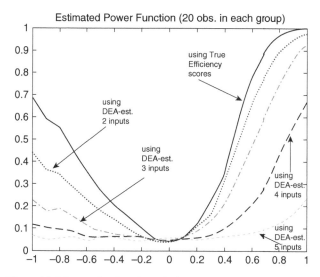

Figure 10.5 Power for the adapted Li-test, with Alg. II ($n_A = n_Z = 20$).

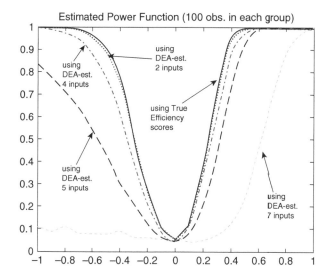

Figure 10.6 Power for the adapted Li-test, with Alg. II ($n_A = n_Z = 100$).

The increase in the sample, however, helps to mitigate the curse of dimensionality. With 100 observations, the power for the four-input case and even the five-input case is fairly close (and for the two-input case it is practically identical) to that based on the true efficiency scores, although larger samples are needed to achieve good power for the seven-input case.

This test found many applications in practice, including Zelenyuk and Zheka (2006) for testing sensitivity of removing outliers (very inefficient

DMUs) from their sample, in Henderson and Zelenyuk (2007) for studying catching-up and convergence of countries, in Chowdhury and Zelenyuk (2016) to study efficiency of hospitals, Curi et al. (2015) and Kenjegalieva et al. (2009) to analyze efficiency of banks, to mention a few.

10.3 REGRESSION OF EFFICIENCY ON COVARIATES

Besides analyzing unconditional means (weighted or non-weighted) and distributions of efficiency, it is also very useful to analyze their *conditional* means and their derivatives (marginal effects, elasticities, etc.), where conditioning is done on various factors that are deemed or expected to have a substantial influence on inefficiency. In the DEA literature, such factors are usually referred to as the "environmental" variables (although such a choice of wording is probably unlucky). This approach is sometimes referred to as the "two-stage DEA," because the employed strategy consists of two stages: the DEA is used in the first stage to estimate the true efficiency scores, which are then, at the second stage, used in a regression analysis on covariates. For example, one may want to estimate an econometric model of the following form:

$$TE^i = \psi(Z_i) + \varepsilon_i, \quad i = 1, \ldots, n, \tag{10.3.1}$$

where Z_i stands for a d-variate row-vector of covariates, for DMU i, which are expected to influence the (in)efficiency score of this DMU, TE^i, via some functional relationship ψ, and ε_i is a statistical noise (unexplained random residual term).

An early and frequently used practice in the DEA literature was to estimate a model like (10.3.1) via the so-called Tobit approach, or even simply using an OLS (possibly with a robust estimator for standard errors), and usually assuming that ψ is some known function, usually assumed to be a linear one. This common practice started to change (although still happens) after Simar and Wilson (2007), hereafter SW2007, vividly showed that such approaches have serious issues, and also proposed an alternative based on truncated regression with bootstrap, suitable under certain regularity conditions.[17]

The reason why truncated regression is considered as more appropriate than Tobit is because both sides of (10.3.1) are bounded by 1, and so the distribution of ε_i is also bounded. In the particular case of *output-oriented* Farrell-type efficiency, we have $TE^i \geq 1$ implying $\varepsilon_i \geq 1 - \psi(Z_i)$ and thus implying a condition with left-tail truncation at $1 - \psi(Z_i)$, which is different from the censoring model (where the Tobit model is a particular

---

[17] The first empirical application (besides the empirical examples in Simar and Wilson, 2007) appears to be due to Zelenyuk and Zheka (2006), who analyzed the dependency of (in)efficiency of firms on various factors, with a focus on corporate governance, in several industries. Also see Demchuk and Zelenyuk (2009), Curi et al. (2015), Chowdhury and Zelenyuk (2016), Du et al. (2017b) for other applications of this approach.

example).[18] A natural way to approach such a model is via a truncated regression approach.[19]

For simplicity of computation, SW2007 assumed that the distribution of ε_i is normal with zero mean and unknown variance, σ_ε^2, and truncation on the left (when $TE^i \geq 1$) determined by $\varepsilon_i \geq 1 - \psi(Z_i)$. Also for simplicity, they mostly focused on the case when ψ is linear, i.e., $\psi(Z_i) = Z_i\beta$, as were also most of the applications before and after their work. Here, for pedagogical reasons, we will keep the notation with a general parametric form $\psi(Z_i) = \psi(Z_i|\beta)$ where the form of ψ is known but β needs to be estimated. Thus, the truncated (normal, parametric) regression model is given by

$$TE^i = \psi(Z_i|\beta) + \varepsilon_i, \quad \varepsilon_i \sim \mathcal{N}(0, \sigma_\varepsilon^2) : \varepsilon_i \geq 1 - \psi(Z_i|\beta), \quad i = 1, \ldots, n$$
$$(10.3.2)$$

and so the corresponding likelihood function is given by

$$\mathscr{L}_n = \prod_{i=1}^{n} \frac{1}{\sigma_\varepsilon} \phi\left(\frac{TE^i - \psi(Z_i|\beta)}{\sigma_\varepsilon}\right)\left[1 - \Phi\left(\frac{TE^i - \psi(Z_i|\beta)}{\sigma_\varepsilon}\right)\right]^{-1}, \quad (10.3.3)$$

where ϕ and Φ are standard normal pdf and cdf respectively. Optimizing (10.3.3) numerically (e.g., in MATLAB or other suitable software) one can get MLE estimates of β and of σ_ε.

SW2007 proposed two algorithms for their framework. In a nutshell, their Algorithm 1 uses the standard DEA estimates in place of the true (in)efficiency scores, only bootstrapping the parameters of the second-stage regression. Meanwhile, Algorithm 2 is more elaborate and uses the bias-corrected estimates of efficiency scores, obtained using the auxiliary cycle of heterogeneous parametric bootstrap that accounted for the assumed regression dependency (10.3.2). The next two subsections summarize these two approaches.

10.3.1 Algorithm 1 of SW2007

Algorithm 1 in SW2007 can be summarized as follows:

Step 1 Use the original data in $\mathscr{S}_n := \{(x^i, y^i) : i = 1, \ldots, n\}$ to compute $\widehat{TE}^i$ for all $i = 1, \ldots, n$ using a preferred DEA or FDH approach.

---

[18] Recall that the Tobit estimator is designed to tackle a "censoring" problem (i.e., when the observations beyond the bound exist but are not observed and replaced with values on the bound, and thus called censored values). On the other hand, in the case with the efficiency scores and their DEA and FDH estimates, which are greater or equal to 1 (for the output-oriented efficiency) or in [0,1] interval if the reciprocal or input orientation is taken, the observations do not exist beyond the bound by construction.

[19] Another way of handling such a boundary problems is to use a suitable transformation, e.g., the double-log transformation, $\ln(\ln(TE))$, for $TE > 1$, yet such approach appears to suffer from bias-inflation: taking an anti-log of the fitted values of $\ln(\ln(TE))$ "exponentiate" the bias and potentially jeopardizes the accuracy of the fit and the related inference. Another approach is to use the "DEA+OLS" approach of Banker and Natarajan (2008) that relies on a different set of assumptions (e.g., see related discussion by Simar and Wilson, 2011b).

Step 2 Apply the MLE to obtain the estimates of $\beta, \sigma_\varepsilon$ in the truncated regression of $\widehat{TE}^i$ on Z_i (given by (10.3.2) with specified form for ψ); denote them as $\hat{\beta}, \hat{\sigma}_\varepsilon$. Obtain other related functions of interest (likelihood-ratio statistics, etc.). **NB**: At this step, SW2007 used only observations where $\widehat{TE}^i > 1$, thus reducing the original sample size to some $m < n$ (potentially much smaller than n).

Step 3 For a replication b, obtain the bootstrap analogues of efficiency scores as follows: $TE^{*i} = \psi(Z_i|\hat{\beta}) + \hat{\varepsilon}_i$, where $\hat{\varepsilon}_i \sim \mathcal{N}(0, \hat{\sigma}_\varepsilon^2) : \hat{\varepsilon}_i \geq 1 - \psi(Z_i|\hat{\beta})$, for each $i = 1, \ldots, m$. Use the MLE method to estimate the truncated regression, as in Step 2, regressing TE^{*i} on Z_i, yielding bootstrapped estimates of $(\beta, \sigma_\varepsilon)$; denote them as $(\beta_b^*, \sigma_{b,\varepsilon}^*)$. Obtain the bootstrap analogues of other related functions of interest.

Step 4 Repeat Steps 2–3 B times, to get a set of bootstrap analogues of parameters of the truncated regression.

Step 5 Use the estimates of the true parameters of interest and their bootstrap analogues from Step 4, to perform inference, such as constructing the bootstrap-based confidence intervals and performing various statistical tests.

An advantage of this procedure is its relative simplicity, and, as a result, it is also relatively fast to compute, particularly because it does not require DEA estimation in the bootstrap loops. Monte Carlo results show that for moderate dimensions of the DEA model, this approach typically give reasonable approximations (sometimes even better than Algorithm II).

A drawback of this algorithm is the loss of part of the sample, due to trimming observations where $\widehat{TE}^i = 1$. Indeed, such observations are the most efficient peers and thus contain valuable information about efficiency! In some cases, the number of such observations to trim could be very large, especially for the FDH estimator, and so trimming all of them might lead to a substantial loss of information.[20] As an alternative, rather than losing such information, one may adapt the approach proposed by Simar and Zelenyuk (2006), which we discussed above in the context of testing the equality of densities. That is, instead of trimming such observations, one may smooth them away from the boundary by adding a sufficiently small noise – a uniform noise of order smaller than the estimation noise of a chosen estimator (see (10.2.12) and related discussion).

10.3.2   Algorithm 2 of SW2007

Besides the drawbacks mentioned above, the major disadvantage of Algorithm 1 is that it essentially ignores the fact that the DEA (or FDH) are actually biased and dependent estimates. These issues, at least to some extent, can be

---

[20] In particular, note again that the larger the dimension of the DEA or FDH model the higher such number is likely to be, implying greater loss of observations in greater dimensions, while one actually needs the opposite to mitigate the "curse of dimensionality."

taken into account via Algorithm 2 from SW2007, which can be summarized in the following steps:

Step 1 Use the original data in $\mathscr{S}_n := \{(x^i, y^i) : i = 1, \dots, n\}$ to compute $\widehat{TE}^i$ for all $i = 1, \dots, n$ using a preferred DEA or FDH estimator.

Step 2 Apply the MLE to obtain the estimates of $\beta, \sigma_\varepsilon$ in the truncated regression of $\widehat{TE}^i$ on Z_i given by (10.3.2) with specified form for ψ; denote them as $\hat{\beta}, \hat{\sigma}_\varepsilon$.[21]

Step 3 Loop over the next four sub-steps, $b = 1, \dots, B_1$ times, to obtain a set of bias-corrected estimates of inefficiency scores:

    Step 3.1 For each $i = 1, \dots, n$, draw $\hat{\varepsilon}_{i,b}$ from $\mathcal{N}(0, \hat{\sigma}_\varepsilon^2)$ distribution with truncation on the left at $(1 - \psi(Z_i|\hat{\beta}))$.

    Step 3.2 For each $i = 1, \dots, n$, compute the bootstrap analogues of the efficiency scores as $TE_b^{i*} = \psi(Z_i|\hat{\beta}) + \hat{\varepsilon}_{i,b}$.

    Step 3.3 Define $x_b^{i*} = x^i$, $y_b^{i*} = (\widehat{TE}_b^i / TE_b^{i*}) \times y^i$, $Z_i^* = Z_i$ for all $i = 1, \dots, n$.

    Step 3.4 For each $i = 1, \dots, n$, compute $\widehat{TE}_b^{i*}$ via the same estimator as in Step 1, but using the bootstrapped data $\mathscr{S}_{n,b}^* := \{(x_b^{i*}, y_b^{i*}) : i = 1, \dots, n\}$ from Step 3.3.

Step 4 For each $i = 1, \dots, n$, compute the bias-corrected estimates $\widehat{TE}_{bc}^i$ defined as $\widehat{TE}_{bc}^i = \widehat{TE}^i - \widehat{Bias}(\widehat{TE}^i)$, where $\widehat{Bias}(\widehat{TE}^i)$ is the bootstrap-based estimate of the bias of $\widehat{TE}^i$ wrt TE^i, obtained using the bootstrapping estimates from Step 3 (using the general procedure for bias correction described in the previous chapter).

Step 5 Apply MLE to the truncated regression model of $\widehat{TE}_{bc}^i$ on Z_i to get the refined estimates; denote them $(\hat{\hat{\beta}}$ and $\hat{\hat{\sigma}}_\varepsilon)$.

Step 6 Loop over the next three sub-steps, $b = 1, \dots, B_2$ times, to get a set of bootstrap analogues of parameters of the truncated regression:

    Step 6.1 For each $i = 1, \dots, n$, draw $\hat{\hat{\varepsilon}}_{i,b}$ from $\mathcal{N}(0, \hat{\hat{\sigma}}_\varepsilon^2)$ with left-truncation at $(1 - \psi(Z_i|\hat{\beta}))$.

    Step 6.2 Obtain the double-bootstrap analogues of efficiency scores via: $TE_b^{i**} = \psi(Z_i|\hat{\beta}) + \hat{\hat{\varepsilon}}_{i,b}$, for each $i = 1, \dots, n$.

    Step 6.3 Use MLE, as in Step 2, to estimate truncated regression of TE_b^{i**} on Z_i, yielding bootstrapped estimates $(\beta_b^{**}, \sigma_{\varepsilon,b}^{**})$.

Step 7 Use the refined estimates, $\hat{\hat{\beta}}$ and $\hat{\hat{\sigma}}_\varepsilon$, of the true parameters of interest and their (double-)bootstrap analogues from Step 6, $\{(\beta_b^{**}, \sigma_{\varepsilon,b}^{**}), b = 1, \dots, B_2\}$, to construct the bootstrap-based confidence intervals for each element of β and σ_ε, and for other functions of interest involving them, using the general procedures described in the previous chapter.

---

[21] Again, at this step it is advised to use a "trimmed" sample, where $\widehat{TE}^i > 1$, i.e., without the "spurious ones" or, alternatively, smooth them away from the boundary by adding uniform noise of an order smaller than the estimation noise, similar to Simar and Zelenyuk (2006).

Comparing the two algorithms from SW2007, one must see that the essence of difference between them is in the two new steps in Algorithm 2: (i) Steps 3 and 4 are used to obtain the bias-corrected estimates of efficiency scores with an additional bootstrap cycle that were not present in their Algorithm 1, and (ii) Step 5 is used to refine and replace the estimates of the regression from Step 2, to be further bootstrapped in Step 6, which is the second bootstrap cycle, thus the term "double-bootstrap." Although Algorithm 1 is simpler and may even sometimes (for small dimensions) provide more accurate inference, Algorithm 2 is expected to take into account the bias and dependency more adequately and so most studies appear to have preferred using it.[22]

10.3.3 Inference in SW2007 Framework

Most studies using SW2007 approach based their inference mainly on checking whether or not the bootstrap-estimated confidence interval (CI) for a coefficient of interest covers zero (or another hypothesized value). Specifically, for testing $H_0 : \beta_r = 0$ against $H_1 : \beta_r \neq 0$, one can check if the estimated CI for an rth element of β covers zero or not. If so, then the corresponding explanatory variable, Z_r, is considered as not statistically significant as an explanatory variable for inefficiency at the chosen significance level (e.g., $\alpha = 0.05$) for which the CI was estimated. If the CI does not cover zero, then the variable is considered as significant (from zero, at the chosen significance level).

Standard *caveats* of interpreting results of regression analysis apply here. In particular, statistical significance (insignificance) of β_r does not necessarily imply that Z_r is relevant (irrelevant) for explaining inefficiency, but rather implies there is (not) enough evidence to significantly doubt otherwise, on average and *ceteris paribus* (all other aspects fixed), at the chosen significance level (although this might be different at another level) and provided all the other assumptions about the model and data generating process hold. These are a lot of conditions and, in principle, violation of any of them may jeopardize validity of the inference, as is the case pertinent to any statistical inference, not just the SW2007 approach.

To be more precise, note that what is estimated is the conditional mean, so all the interpretations of significance of coefficients should be "on average" and "*ceteris paribus*" style (and with regard to the units of measurement of the involved variables). Indeed, for some particular firm, the influence of a covariate may be very different from what is seen as an average tendency

---

[22] Naturally, and at least in principle, one may try to adapt such or other bootstrap algorithms for the alternative ways to handle the truncated nature of the error, such as log–log transformation or using the "DEA+OLS" approach of Banker and Natarajan (2008), after careful adaptation to the different set of assumptions on the DGP and accounting for the caveats discussed in Simar and Wilson (2011b), and some of these works appear to be underway by Rajiv Banker and his team.

for all observations. Moreover, even for the average tendency, a statistically insignificant covariate may have a significant impact in tandem with another variable (i.e., when "*ceteris paribus*" does not hold fully).

Furthermore, all the conclusions are also conditional on the chosen functional form of ψ – typically, researchers assume it is linear, thus implicitly imposing the meaning of the linear approximation (around the mean of data), unless the true ψ is exactly linear. The degree of approximation depends on how close the assumed functional form for the estimation is relative to the true ψ in the neighborhood of a point of interest. Thus, for substantial departures from the mean of the data, the interpretation of the estimated coefficients should be made very carefully (or not at all), unless there is high certainty that the true ψ is exactly the assumed form. Alternatively, one can estimate ψ nonparametrically (see comments in the next subsection).

Also note that, whatever ψ is, the model (10.3.2) presumes only one-way causality, from Z_i and ε_i onto TE^i, which is fine if Z_i and ε_i are exogenous wrt TE^i. In reality, however, the relationship could happen to be opposite or mutual (e.g., with a feedback from inefficiency onto Z or even onto ε, immediate or perhaps lagged) implying a much more complex DGP than the one originally assumed in SW2007, potentially a complex system of equations (see below for more discussion on this issue).

One shall also remember that the size of the estimated coefficient also matters. For example, an estimated coefficient could be statistically significant yet still negligible from an economic or practical point of view. It could also be relatively large, but with very wide CI so that one of the CI bounds is very close to zero, meaning that the true value is also likely to be near zero. Of course, one should also keep in mind that the size of the coefficient is related to the units of measurement of the corresponding covariate and of the dependent variable, and so it is usually desirable to standardize the variables (e.g., by subtracting their sample means and dividing by their sample standard deviations) or take logs (for strictly positive variables) before the estimations, to make them unit invariant.

As in other regression analysis contexts, it is also useful to do a sensitivity analysis, checking the robustness of regression results to the dropping of various variables from the starting general specification and, possibly, selecting the most parsimonious model. For this one can follow the standard practice in regression analysis, e.g., by using various criteria, such as AIC or BIC, and paying attention to what happens to the estimates of σ (e.g., sudden changes in estimates of σ or their relatively large values may indicate numerical convergence problems or, perhaps, model mis-specifications).[23]

One can also use the likelihood-ratio (LR) test, especially for testing more complex hypotheses and for navigating towards a more parsimonious model via testing nested models. For example, if one observes that some coefficients appeared significant while others as insignificant, say denoted respectively by

---

[23] E.g., see Zelenyuk and Zelenyuk (2015), Chowdhury and Zelenyuk (2016).

β_1 and β_2, being sub-vectors of β, one can test a hypothesis that $H_0 : \beta_2 = 0$ against $H_1 : \beta_2 \neq 0$, considering the LR test statistic

$$\widehat{\mathcal{LR}}_n = 2 \ln \left(\frac{\widehat{\mathscr{L}_n}}{\widehat{\mathscr{L}_n}(H_0)} \right), \tag{10.3.4}$$

where $\widehat{\mathscr{L}_n}$ and $\widehat{\mathscr{L}_n}(H_0)$ are the estimated likelihood functions of the unrestricted and restricted (via imposing $\beta_2 = 0$) models, respectively. Note that because the true efficiency scores in (10.3.3) are replaced with their estimates (with or without bias correction), this as well as any other test may also inherit similar issues as those described above and so using bootstrap can also help here. In particular, the bootstrap-based p-value can be computed as the number of times the original value of the statistic $\widehat{\mathcal{LR}}_n$ is smaller than its bootstrap analogues ($\widehat{\mathcal{LR}}_n^{*b}$), i.e.,

$$\hat{\mathsf{p}}_{n,B} = \frac{1}{B} \sum_{b=1}^{B} \mathbb{I} \left(\widehat{\mathcal{LR}}_n^{*b} > \widehat{\mathcal{LR}}_n \right), \tag{10.3.5}$$

where the resampling must be done under H_0.[24]

Finally, note that one can also use this test (as well as AIC and BIC criteria) to explore the statistical differences of various (and nested) DEA or FDH models used at the first stage. For example, one can compare results from one DEA or FDH model with its reduced version (which has a lower "curse of dimensionality" problem), where some of the inputs or outputs are aggregated or omitted. Or, one can compare the results from the pooled or grand frontier to results with group frontiers. These tests can be useful for exploring the data and navigating a search for a more parsimonious model, although more work is clearly needed to establish precise statistical properties of such tests, taking into account the recent breakthrough by Kneip et al. (2015), and to analyze their performance in finite samples via Monte Carlo studies.[25]

10.3.4   Extension to Panel Data Context

When utilizing panel data, researchers using SW2007 often pooled the data over several periods at the first stage to estimate the pooled or grand frontier for a certain time span. Such a step is usually motivated by the need to have as large a sample as possible to wrestle with the "curse of dimentionality" of DEA or FDH performed at the first stage. With such an approach, one effectively ignores possible changes in the frontier between the periods that were pooled. Even if a time dummy is included in the second stage, the fact that time is not modeled at the first stage implies that the "separability" assumption is imposed with respect to the time dummy.

---

[24] This can be done by imposing $\beta_2 = 0$ in the algorithms above for the estimation of bootstrap analogues of the likelihood function of the restricted and the unrestricted models.

[25] See Du et al. (2017a) for some explorations on this matter.

This approach can be relaxed by extending the SW2007 method to allow for different frontiers, estimating them separately by DEA or FDH for different periods (or groups) at the first stage, and then, in the second stage, regressing the estimated efficiency scores on covariates with all the sample. Specifically, one may consider the following general model

$$TE_t^i = \psi(Z_{it}, t) + \varepsilon_{it}, \quad i = 1, \ldots, n_t; \ t = 1, \ldots, T, \qquad (10.3.6)$$

or its simplified linear form, with the time entering the model only as an intercept time-dummy,

$$TE_t^i = Z_{it}\beta + D_t\gamma + \varepsilon_{it}, \quad i = 1, \ldots, n_t; \ t = 1, \ldots, T, \qquad (10.3.7)$$

where Z_{it} is a row-vector of covariates expected to influence or correlate with the efficiency of DMU i in year t via a vector of parameters β to be estimated, and D_t is a vector of year dummies (from 1 to T, with one period dropped to be the reference period) and γ is the corresponding vector of parameters to be estimated that represent the annual (or group) effects on inefficiency. This model can also be approached either with the truncated regression approach, with appropriate modification of the original SW2007 algorithms or by carefully adapting the ideas from the "OLS+DEA" approach of Banker and Natarajan (2008).[26]

One can also adapt the LR-test statistic (10.3.4) with bootstrapped p-values (10.3.5) to test the hypothesis of one frontier vs. group frontiers (see Du et al., 2017b,a for more details on this approach).

Other special cases of (10.3.6) (and generalization of (10.3.7)) are also possible; e.g., one could consider

$$TE_t^i = \alpha_i + Z_{it}\beta + D_t\gamma + \varepsilon_{it}, \quad i = 1, \ldots, n_t; \ t = 1, \ldots, T, \qquad (10.3.8)$$

where α_i models the time-invariant heterogeneity in inefficiency across DMUs, which can be assumed as the fixed effect (FE) or as a random effect (RE), depending on which one is more appropriate for the empirical context, thus giving rise to, respectively, the FE and the RE two-stage DEA panel data frameworks.[27] Finally, one can also allow for some elements in β to vary over time, e.g., via slope dummies, or add polynomial terms to capture possible nonlinearity. Although relatively simple, all these modifications must be made with care, presenting a valid theory or at least Monte Carlo evidence that they perform well under certain assumptions.

---

[26] See the related discussion in Simar and Wilson (2011b) and our discussion below.

[27] Just as in the general panel data contexts, RE framework would not be suitable if α_i is (or expected to be) correlated with some of the variables in the vector Z_{it} and in this case FE would be more suitable, however it will not give estimates of coefficients of the time-invariant covariates in Z_{it}, if any, accumulating their influence into estimates of α_i.

10.3.5 *Caveats* of the Two-Stage DEA

The approach of Simar and Wilson (2007) is very useful to start with and, in fact, appears to be one of the most popular to date and was applied in many contexts.[28] Nevertheless, as for any method, it is important to realize and acknowledge its limitations. Indeed, as with any method it also relies on a certain set of assumptions, which were explicitly listed in Simar and Wilson (2007, p. 34-37) and explained and emphasized further in their follow up paper, Simar and Wilson (2011b).[29] Most of these assumptions are somewhat natural simplifications of reality and are further generalizations of those from Korostelev et al. (1995a,b) and Kneip et al. (1998), yet some are new and deal with the structure of influence of Z onto inefficiency. Specifically, one of them involves parametric assumption for $\psi(Z_i|\beta)$ and the other one is the so-called "separability assumption," both of which deserve special attention.

10.3.5.1 *Parametric Assumptions*

Recall that one of the strengths of DEA and FDH approaches is that they are nonparametric. That is, no parametric assumption was imposed on technology or on the distribution of (x, y) or on the inefficiency in the first stage, but in the second stage, one is asked to believe and impose some particular form on how inefficiency depends on Z and on noise (truncated normality). To mitigate this restriction, one can use a nonparametric version of their method, e.g., adopting the local likelihood approach to truncated regression proposed by Park et al. (2008), and inspired by Tibshirani and Hastie (1987).

The local likelihood approach allows for practically any nonlinear (and smooth) regression function ψ in (10.3.2) (and its derivatives) to be estimated at any point of interest, without requiring one to assume a parametric form of ψ. In essence, the trick is based on approximating ψ with a polynomial of some degree, locally at any point of interest, via the kernel weights with suitable bandwidth (e.g., selected via the maximum likelihood cross-validation method).

More specifically, in this approach, for a d-variate point of interest z, the (conditional) log-likelihood function with a qth-order local polynomial for approximating ψ and the shape functional τ of the distribution of ε, is given by

$$
\ln \mathscr{L}_n(\theta_0, \ldots, \theta_{r(q)-1}, \tau_0, \ldots, \tau_{r(q)-1}|z)
$$
$$
= \sum_{i=1}^{n} \ell \left(TE_i, \theta_0 + \theta_1(Z_{i1} - z_1) + \cdots + \theta_{r(q)-1}(Z_{id} - z_d)^q, \right.
$$
$$
\left. \tau_0 + \tau_1(Z_{i1} - z_1) + \cdots + \tau_{r(q)-1}(Z_{id} - z_d)^q \right) K_h(Z_i - z),
$$
$$
(10.3.9)
$$

---

[28] E.g., their seminal paper was ranked by Scopus as the "Last 5 Years Most Cited Article" in 2011 and 2012 in the Journal of Econometrics.

[29] This subsection is largely inspired by these seminal works, through the prism of our understanding and with some additions.

where $\ell(TE, v, \omega) = \ln\left[g_\varepsilon(TE - v, \omega)\mathbb{I}(TE \geq 1)/(1 - G(1 - v, \omega))\right]$ with density $g_\varepsilon(\varepsilon, \tau) = \partial G(\varepsilon, \tau)/\partial \varepsilon$, for some distribution function G, and $r(q) - 1$ is the total number of partial derivatives up to order q, i.e., $r(q) = \sum_{j=0}^{q} \binom{j+d-1}{d-1}$. The term $K_h(u)$ is a d-variate kernel function weight, typically a symmetric density function defined on $\mathfrak{R}^d$, where h is a matrix of suitable bandwidths corresponding to each continuous variable in Z.[30]

The local MLE of $\psi(z)$ and of the vector of its d partial derivatives, $\nabla_z \psi(z)$, are obtained respectively as the optimal values of θ_0 and $(\theta_1, \ldots, \theta_d)$ in the maximization of (10.3.9) numerically (e.g., in MATLAB or other suitable software), at any point of interest z and so they may and usually do vary with z.[31]

Park et al. (2008) derived asymptotic theory for such an approach, proving that it provides consistent estimates that are asymptotically normal, and so the normal inference can be used for standard cases, although bootstrap can provide a better alternative. They also presented a bit of Monte Carlo evidence suggesting that substantial improvements can be reached in the accuracy of estimation of coefficients representing magnitudes and significance of drivers of efficiency and productivity of individual economic agents (e.g., hospitals, banks, etc.). As is often the case, however, the gains are "not free" and come at a price of not only much greater complexity (theoretical and computational) but also in the requirement for larger samples to mitigate the "curse of dimensionality" pertinent to the kernel-based methods even in the standard context when the true efficiency scores are observed. Of course, in reality, the true efficiency scores are not observed and must be replaced with their estimates, e.g., via DEA or FDH (thus adding another "curse of dimensionality," at the first stage), which are typically biased and dependent. Thus, one needs to adapt the versions of algorithms for SW2007 to the approach of Park et al. (2008) and to study their asymptotic properties and finite sample performances.

10.3.5.2 Separability

Let $\mathcal{Z}$ be the space of possible values of Z. Considering a general case when Z may influence both (in)efficiency and technology, define the *conditional technology set* (conditional on Z realized at some particular values in vector $z \in \mathcal{Z}$) as

---

[30] If some variables in Z are discrete then they can be handled via the discrete kernels, e.g., in the spirit of Aitchison and Aitken (1976) or its generalizations (e.g., Li et al., 2016). The asymptotic theory for such cases follows from Park et al. (2015).

[31] Note that increasing the order of the polynomial approximation can bring higher theoretical accuracy of estimation, yet it also increases the computational burden because the number of variables to optimize over grows rapidly. Fortunately, the choice of the order of the polynomial is not very important, both in theory and in practice, because the approximation is local, in the neighborhood defined by h which goes to zero as (and slower than) n goes to infinity. So, in practice, it is typically selected to be linear or even the local constant to simplify the optimization, and hardly ever beyond the local quadratic (e.g., useful if the focus is on the first partial derivatives of ψ).

$$T(z) = \{(x, y) \; : \; x \text{ can produce } y \text{ under conditions } Z = z \in \mathcal{Z}\}, \tag{10.3.10}$$

then the technology set T that we used before $(T = \{(x, y) \; : x \text{ can produce } y\})$ can be called *the unconditional technology set*. We can also define T as the union of $T(z)$ for all the possibilities of $z \in \mathcal{Z}$, i.e.,

$$T = \bigcup_{z \in \mathcal{Z}} T(z). \tag{10.3.11}$$

The "separability assumption" in SW2007 simply says that Z, whatever values it takes, is not influencing $T(z)$ in the sense that it remains the same as the unconditional technology set for all possibilities of Z, i.e.,

$$T(z) = T, \; \forall z \in \mathcal{Z}. \tag{10.3.12}$$

Importantly, note that whether the separability assumption is true or not, the standard DEA and FDH approaches are estimating the technology set (or its frontier) without considering Z. That is, they always estimate the unconditional technology set T (with certain assumptions imposed), whether (10.3.12) is true or not.[32] So, if one is interested in measuring (in)efficiency wrt frontier of the conditional technology set, for some $z \in \mathcal{Z}$, then the DEA or FDH estimates at the first stage would not represent what one is looking for, unless (10.3.12) holds. Indeed, a DMU with an allocation (x, y, z) might even be fully efficient with respect to $T(z)$, yet (x, y) may still be very inefficient wrt T.[33]

Whether (10.3.12) holds or not is an empirical question that, ideally, needs to be tested.[34] On the other hand, whether to choose conditional or unconditional technology as a benchmark against which to measure the efficiency is often (if not always) a conceptual question that may depend on the research question and the research goals (which need to be made explicit). For example, consider measuring the efficiency of some DMUs (banks, hospitals, sports-people, economists, etc.): Conceptually, one can say that the performance of American, Australian, ..., Ukrainian DMUs should be only benchmarked against their "national" frontiers, constructed respectively from American, Australian, ..., Ukrainian observations. This might be justified by some research goals, e.g., national rather than international competitions.[35]

---

[32] The unconditional technology set/frontier was also sometimes called the "grand" or "meta" technology set/frontier in various contexts in the literature.

[33] Importantly, note that in general (in multi-variate setting), measuring with respect to the unconditional frontier still allows comparison with respect to closest peers rather than just one best peer.

[34] Earlier studies did not test it mainly due to the absence of reliable testing procedures. Recently important progress on this matter was made by Daraio et al. (2017).

[35] E.g., also note that some variables in Z might be outside the control of DMUs, and if they also happen to influence conditional technology, it may then be unfair, in some respects, to measure inefficiency of such DMUs relative to the unconditional technology that may be unattainable for values of Z pertinent to those DMUs. On the other hand, a caveat here is that pushing such reasoning further, one could argue that every DMU can be unique in its own ways and

On the other hand, one can also have more egalitarian or agnostic views with respect to nationality or geography (race or other conditions) and thus have a research goal to measure performance of everyone with respect to the same criterion – the frontier of the unconditional technology set.

Therefore, when using SW2007, it is useful to acknowledge that either the separability condition is assumed (and ideally confirmed to hold with a statistical test), or be explicit that all the analysis and related conclusions are made for measuring with respect to the unconditional rather than conditional frontier(s), with all the *caveats* attached to it. In the former case, there is no difference between the conditional and unconditional technology sets, so the analysis is the same, while in the latter the results and qualitative conclusions may differ.

If, for whatever reasons, one is interested in measuring efficiency wrt conditional rather than unconditional frontiers, yet cannot admit the separability condition, then one must use alternative approaches. One of such recently developed approaches is based on the concept of partial frontiers and conditional efficiency measures, pioneered by Cazals et al. (2002) and further developed by Daraio and Simar (2005, 2007b,a, 2014) and Bădin et al. (2010, 2012), to mention a few key works. In essence, the idea of this approach is also based on two stages: In the first stage one uses a version of the so-called m-frontier or α-frontier estimators, with explicit conditioning on realizations of Z, and then, in the second stage, one uses the kernel-based regression to disentangle the influence on covariates in Z onto the conditional efficiency scores. By using the method of Cazals et al. (2002) at the foundation, this approach avoids the "curse of dimensionality" at its first stage and attains the parametric ($\sqrt{n}$) rate at the first stage. However, it is not immune from the "curse of dimensionality" problem completely because it is pertinent to any kernel-based method, and so it arises here at the second stage, when the continuous variables in Z are smoothed via a kernel-based method.[36] The theoretical validity of the inference in this framework is proven in Daraio and Simar (2014).[37]

Another appealing approach to mitigate the "separability" assumption is based on the nonparametric stochastic frontier approach (SFA). For example, one can use the local likelihood approach, introduced to SFA by Kumbhakar et al. (2007b), or its generalization proposed by Park et al. (2015) to allow for discrete variables among covariates. Another, somewhat simpler, yet also very powerful approach was proposed by Simar et al. (2014, 2017), which also tackles the stochastic frontier non- and semiparametrically, but via combining the

---

have their own individually conditioned frontiers. Even in such a case, however, the DEA still provides a valid way of performance comparison of DMUs, but it is wrt the unconditional frontier, while an appropriate second stage analysis can then help in explaining the variation in such performance (relative to the unconditional frontier) vs. the variation in Z.

[36] As in other contexts of kernel-based methods, this problem can be mitigated to some extent by imposing more structure, for example the generalized-additive nonparametric structure.

[37] As with any methods, this one also has some *caveats*, one of which is the arbitrariness of the choice of the order (i.e., level of m or α), because the results may depend on it and so robustness or sensitivity checks about how the choice influences conclusions are important.

local least squares and the method of moments approaches. Again, as with any kernel-based methods, these approaches are also not immune from the "curse of dimensionality," although it can be mitigated to some extent by imposing some structure, e.g., the generalized-additive nonparametric structure.

An important advantage of the Kumbhakar et al. (2007b) and Park et al. (2015) approaches is that they model the frontier relationship and the inefficiency relationship in one stage. Their main disadvantage (with the current state of computing) is their high computational intensity, especially to estimate an optimal bandwidth, requiring many rounds of multivariate optimization of a complicated likelihood function, which can be especially difficult for large data sets. The approach of Simar et al. (2014, 2017) is much simpler computationally and allows for nonparametric estimation of elasticities of inefficiency wrt covariates, with or without conditioning the frontier on realizations of Z (and so is less restrictive than the local-likelihood approaches). The main price for this flexibility and simplicity is that the approach is implemented in two stages, yet it still avoids the explicit separability assumption by involving less stringent conditions about the structure of influence of Z onto inefficiency.

Finally, an important *caveat* for all the mentioned methods that are based on kernels is that the choice of the bandwidths can be very critical to the results and even for the qualitative conclusions and so this should be done very carefully, with various robustness or sensitivity checks.[38]

10.3.5.3   Endogeneity

Finally, all of the methods described so far have basically ignored the potential endogeneity and reverse causality problems, e.g., the case when inefficiency might influence or have feedback onto some elements in Z. While in principle, one can adapt the described approaches to handle such a problem (at least to some extent and under additional assumptions), doing so in practice appears to be very complex and besides extra information (that might be infeasible) often may require additional assumptions that are not necessarily more "innocent" than the assumption of exogeneity of Z.

Indeed, one may try to generalize the truncated regression model and involve the full information MLE approach, which however will require specification of additional equation(s) characterizing the endogeneity or the reverse causality. In some sense easier looking approach would be to use the least squares approach of Banker and Natarajan (2008) and combine it with the standard instrumental variables approach in econometrics; but one would then

---

[38] While the theory usually requires only a proper rate of convergence of these bandwidths, in practice the same rate with different constants can lead to dramatically different conclusions. Some optimal methods of selection, e.g., cross-validation methods, are usually advised, yet even then may often yield multiple solutions, some of which may be "spurious" and so a careful selection with various starting values and various optimization algorithms is recommended. See Hall and Marron (1991) for a related discussion in a more general context.

need to find suitable instruments, which might be very difficult in practice.[39] Even if such instruments are found in principle, the validity of statistical inference in such a framework is still under question, as we explain in the next section.

All in all, methods for proper handling of potential endogeneity problems is a natural direction for future research in the field.

10.3.5.4 Asymptotic Theory

Despite being the most popular to date (and probably for many years to come), SW2007 have not presented an asymptotic theory to fully justify their approach. Their more recent work with Alois Kneip, in Kneip et al. (2015), has made a breakthrough on the matter, explicitly proving (and confirming via Monte Carlo) that the standard central limit theorems cannot be trusted in the context when the true efficiency scores in an average are replaced by their DEA or FDH estimates. Since the regression approach, whether via the least squares or via the MLE, also involves averaging, their important findings also have an implication here, and we briefly summarize Kneip et al. (2015) in the next section, after we conclude this *"caveats"* discussion with the following subsection.

10.3.5.5 So, Can One Still Use SW2007?

The answer to the question stated in the title of this subsection probably depends on the tastes and views. Our subjective view is as follows: the progress of knowledge and related technology often comes in the pattern of Heraclitus-Hegelian dialectics, and including the law of 'the negation of the negation'. Indeed, what we see suggested today may soon be negated by new and better methods, which then again will be negated by newer and even better methods. Take, for example, such a simple concept as the wheel – it has been improving over thousands of years and if humanity had chosen to wait for the finally perfect wheel to be offered, rather than using what was practically feasible and useful, though clumsy and ridiculous in hindsight, then humanity would never progress from the Stone Age! The same essence is with all the methods we discuss here, including SW2007: The researchers are advised to use all methods to the best capacity they can (and this depends on the availability of software, training, etc.), yet take any of them with a grain of salt, understanding and acknowledging their limitations, and performing robustness and sensitivity checks to attain greater confidence in conclusions for today, while being ready and encouraging for these conclusions to be challenged tomorrow.

---

[39] An interesting alternative to the instrumental variables approach was proposed by Ashley and Parmeter (2015), and it potentially can be adapted to the context of two-stage DEA/FDH analysis as well.

10.4 CENTRAL LIMIT THEOREMS FOR DEA AND FDH

At the time of finalizing this book, a few important breakthroughs were made with respect to the understanding of limiting distributions of aggregates of efficiency scores estimated via DEA or FDH. The starting point and the very key paper in this vein is due to Kneip et al. (2015), promptly followed by its further important extensions due to Kneip et al. (2016), Daraio et al. (2017) and Simar and Zelenyuk (2017). In a nutshell, these papers showed that the standard central limit theorems cannot be relied upon when the true efficiency scores are replaced with their DEA or FDH estimates in various contexts. More importantly, they also derived new central limit theorems that form the foundation for many useful statistical tests involving DEA or FDH estimators in various contexts. The goal of this section is to briefly summarize key results, leaving more details in the cited papers and in future works.

10.4.1 Bias vs. Variance

In a nutshell, the main focus of Kneip et al. (2015), hereafter KSW, was the simple (equally weighted) average of efficiency scores estimated via DEA or FDH, $\widehat{TE}(x^k, y^k \mid \mathscr{S}_n)$, $k = 1, \ldots, n$. While analyzing the applicability of the standard central limit theorem (CLT) for these scores, KSW noticed theoretically that the average of the scores has substantial bias that may dominate the variance. Metaphorically, KSW called this phenomenon as "bias killing the variance" and proposed some solutions to it – through correction for the bias and refinement of the estimate – formally proving their theoretical validity.

To be more precise, the first key result established in KSW can be summarized in the following theorem.

Theorem. *Under the regularity conditions in KSW,[40] as $n \to \infty$, for the DEA and FDH estimators, for all $k \in \{1, \ldots, n\}$ we have*

$$E\left(\widehat{TE}(x^k, y^k \mid \mathscr{S}_n) - TE(x^k, y^k)\right) = C_0 n^{-\kappa} + R_{n,\kappa},$$

$$VAR\left(\widehat{TE}(x^k, y^k \mid \mathscr{S}_n) - TE(x^k, y^k)\right) = o\left(n^{-\kappa}\right),$$

where $C_0 \in (0, \infty)$ and $R_{n,\kappa} = o\left(n^{-\kappa}\right)$, and $\forall k, j \in \{1, \ldots, n\}$, $k \neq j$, we have

$$\left|COV\left(\widehat{TE}(x^k, y^k \mid \mathscr{S}_n) - TE(x^k, y^k), \widehat{TE}(x^j, y^j \mid \mathscr{S}_n) - TE(x^j, y^j)\right)\right| = o\left(n^{-1}\right).$$

---

[40] The regularity conditions are similar to those we discussed above, assuming smoothness of the frontier and of the joint density $f(x, y)$ of (X, Y) on T and that $f(x, y)$ is strictly positive in a neighborhood of the frontier of T. For precise details, see in KSW, especially their Theorems 3.1, 3.2, and 3.3.

While the proof of this important result can be found in KSW, let us focus on its intuition here. Firstly, this theorem clarifies that the bias is of order $O(n^{-\kappa})$ while, secondly, its variance is $\sigma_{TE}^2 + o(n^{-\kappa})$, where σ_{TE}^2 is the true variance of the efficiency score, and κ depends on the chosen estimator and, importantly, reduces with the dimension of the production model. Thirdly, and fortunately, the covariances are of order $o(n^{-1})$, i.e., independent of κ. Comparing these orders suggests that while there is no problem with covariances, the order of the bias can be larger than (and thus dominating the order of) the variance, thus invalidating the application of the standard CLT.

Specifically, note that the rate κ and the remainder term $R_{n,\kappa}$ (as well as the constant C_0) generally depend on the dimension of the production model and on which particular estimator is used:

- for DEA-CRS it is $\kappa = 2/(N+M)$ and $R_{n,\kappa} = O(n^{-3\kappa/2}(\ln(n))^{\delta_1})$,
- for DEA-VRS it is $\kappa = 2/(N+M+1)$ and $R_{n,\kappa} = O(n^{-3\kappa/2}(\ln(n))^{\delta_2})$,
- for FDH it is $\kappa = 1/(N+M)$ and $R_{n,\kappa} = O(n^{-2\kappa}(\ln(n))^{\delta_3})$, where the values of $\delta_1, \delta_2, \delta_3$ are given in KSW.[41]

Thus, already for $\kappa \leq 1/2$ the bias dominates the variance (e.g., for DEA-VRS, this happens already when $N + M \geq 3$).

Furthermore, KSW use this key result for deriving new fundamental CLT for the simple averages of the efficiency scores and we summarize this result in the following corollary.

Corollary. *Under the regularity conditions in KSW, as $n \to \infty$, we have*

$$\sqrt{n}\left(\overline{\widehat{TE}}_n - E(TE(x^k, y^k)) - Cn^{-\kappa} - o(n^{-\kappa})\right) \xrightarrow{d} \mathcal{N}(0, \sigma_{TE}^2), \quad (10.4.1)$$

where

$$\overline{\widehat{TE}}_n = n^{-1} \sum_{k=1}^{n} \widehat{TE}(x^k, y^k \mid \mathscr{S}_n). \quad (10.4.2)$$

The CLT result in (10.4.1) suggests that there is a problem of bias dominating the variance (and the standard CLT fails) even for moderate dimensions when $\kappa \leq 1/2$. Indeed, as mentioned above, for the case of DEA-VRS this phenomenon of bias dominating the variance (due to $\kappa \leq 1/2$) already occurs when $N + M \geq 3$, which is a fairly small dimension of the production model.

Based on these two results and related reasoning, KSW proposed solutions involving a version of the generalized jackknife to correct for the bias and control the variance. They formalized their solutions in two new CLTs and presented MC evidence that the confidence intervals based on the standard

---

[41] As pointed out by KSW, $\ln(n)$ appearing in $R_{n,\kappa}$ is not crucial for deriving the CLT and can be ignored for practical purposes of implementing related statistical inference.

CLT gave very poor coverage even when $N + M = 2$, while their approaches provided much better (close to nominal) coverage.

The work of KSW is fundamentally important because it provides the foundation for many useful statistical tests involving DEA or FDH estimators, including the two-stage "DEA+regression" context discussed above. Specifically, while this book was finalized, Kneip et al. (2016) and Daraio et al. (2017) proposed several statistical tests based on results from KSW. Meanwhile, Simar and Zelenyuk (2017) have extended the results from KSW to develop two new central limit theorems specifically for the aggregate efficiency scores (industry efficiency, etc.) of the type described above. More results along these lines are expected to come, and we leave their detailed discussion for the future.

10.5   CONCLUDING REMARKS

This and previous chapters had a challenging task of concisely summarizing the state of the art for statistical analysis for DEA and FDH approaches, doing it in a textbook style. Part of the challenge is to be precise yet concise. Indeed, while originally planned as one chapter, an early draft went well beyond 100 pages and still had not provided a complete picture with all the details – something that perhaps can be done in a separate book fully dedicated to such a topic. To our knowledge, such a book has been in preparation for several years, by Léopold Simar and Paul Wilson, and we are looking forward to it and would encourage readers to visit it for more details.[42] In the meantime, we hope we achieved the minimal yet important goal of providing a big picture of the popular methods in practice for a relatively wide audience, with some key details, while for further nuances we refer to the original papers we cited in the text.

10.6   EXERCISES

1. Implement the naive bootstrap to estimate standard errors and construct confidence intervals for a sample mean of efficiency and aggregate efficiency (e.g., replicate scenarios from Simar and Zelenyuk, 2007).

2. Implement the m out of n bootstrap to estimate standard errors and construct confidence intervals for a sample mean of efficiency and aggregate efficiency (e.g., replicate scenarios from Simar and Zelenyuk, 2007) and compare your results with those in the previous exercise. Check the sensitivity of results with respect to different choices of m.

3. Implement the adapted to DEA or FDH Li-test and KS-test for various scenarios (e.g., replicate scenarios from Simar and Zelenyuk, 2006).

---

[42] We also highly encourage one to read the excellent reviews by Simar and Wilson (2013, 2015).

4. Implement Algorithm 1 of the truncated regression with bootstrap for the two-stage DEA (e.g., replicate scenarios from Simar and Wilson, 2007).
5. Implement Algorithm 2 of the truncated regression with bootstrap for the two-stage DEA (e.g., replicate scenarios from Simar and Wilson, 2007).
6. Implement Algorithm 2 of the truncated regression with bootstrap for the two-stage DEA allowing for different frontiers between two groups (or two periods).
7. Implement the bootstrap-based LR-test for testing restrictions in Algorithm 2 of the truncated regression with bootstrap for the two-stage DEA, e.g., for testing the restriction of the common frontier for two groups in a population (see Du et al., 2017b,a).

CHAPTER 11

Cross-Sectional Stochastic Frontiers: An Introduction

As we first pointed out in Chapter 1, the distance function or a single output production function indicates the maximum output vector or level of single output that can be produced given inputs. Chapter 2 introduced the cost function, which gives the minimum cost of producing a given output vector or a single output. Chapter 3 discussed the modeling and formulation of production and the related relationships of cost, revenue, and profit and the measurement of various aspects of efficiency.

These formulations allow one to transition from a purely technical radial measure to one that incorporates two different costs on inefficiency. One measures the reduced costs associated with movements to the frontier from a position of technical inefficiency. Another measures the reduced costs associated with movements from the frontier to a point on the frontier that corresponds to minimum efficient cost. In this chapter we discuss in more detail some of the issues involved with specifying and actually estimating the functions that we discussed in Chapter 6 in order to measure potential shortfalls in technical efficiency and the costs associated with such suboptimal business practices.

Recall from Chapter 1 that the *output set* is defined as

$$P(x) \equiv \{y \in \Re_+^M : y \text{ is producible from } x \in \Re_+^N\}, \tag{11.0.1}$$

while the *production function* $f : \Re_+^N \to \Re_+^1$ is defined as $f(x) \equiv \max\{y: (x, y) \in T\} = \max\{y: y \in P(x)\}$. Since $P(x)$ is a compact set, we are sure that the maximum exists and is unique. For multiple outputs we can define the *output-oriented* Shephard (1970) distance function $D_o : \Re_+^N \times \Re_+^M \to \Re_+^1 \cup \{+\infty\}$ as $D_o(x, y) \equiv \inf\{\theta > 0 : (x, y/\theta) \in T\} = \inf\{\theta > 0 : y/\theta \in P(x)\}$. When we consider a single output technology, D_o is the ratio of actual output to the potential (maximal) output that can be produced with the same level of input and thus for some observation (y^o, x^o) we can write the frontier production relationship as $f(x^o) = y^o/D_o(x^o, y^o)$. For the multiple-output case, the Shephard output distance function provides the smallest scalar necessary to radially expand all outputs until they reach the frontier of the output set.

This expansion is accomplished for inputs set at their initial levels. We also pointed out that a scalar measure such as this will allow us to ultimately identify the frontier of the set and distances from a position inside the set to the frontier. This, in turn, will make it possible to develop a relatively straightforward empirical strategy to identify and estimate the level of productivity (technical efficiency) for a multi-output (or single-output) firm.

In Chapter 6, we discussed how the role of technical efficiency can be motivated from a functional representation for the output distance function. For example, the M-output, N-input deterministic Cobb–Douglas output distance function $D_o(x, y)$ could be derived by first writing it as the ratio of two geometric means.[1,2] As we explained in Chapter 6, this is consistent with the presentation of the original stochastic frontier model by Aigner et al. (1977). Schmidt and Sickles (1984) maintained this convention in their fixed effects panel stochastic frontier that we will discuss in Chapter 12. A straightforward logarithmic transformation of an output distance function expressed as the ratio of a geometric mean of outputs and the geometric mean of the inputs along with a reparameterization of the index weights gives rise to the following equation:

$$- \ln y_1 = \sum_{j=2}^{M} \theta_j \ln(y_j/y_1) - \sum_{k=1}^{N} \beta_k \ln(x_k) + u, \ u \geq 0. \qquad (11.0.2)$$

If we multiply the expression by -1 and set $M = 1$, then we have our familiar Cobb–Douglas frontier production function. The term u is non-negative owing to the inequality in the definition of the distance function that allows for technical inefficiency. Inefficiency is measured by inefficiency $u = 1 - D_o(x, y)$. The nonnegative difference $1 - D_o(x, y)$ is often approximated by $u \approx 1 - \exp(-u)$. We promised in Chapter 6 to revisit this modeling issue explicitly in Chapter 11. The remainder of this chapter is devoted to how the term u can be specified and estimated.

In Chapter 8, we also considered one of the more popular estimation approaches in efficiency and productivity analysis – Data Envelopment Analysis (DEA), which constructs a piecewise linear convex hull to envelope input–output data and thus determine the boundary of the level sets. We can illustrate the estimation problem by considering how one could estimate such a boundary in the case of a one-output–two-input technology with constant returns to scale. Suppose that we have data (e.g., different firms) for the input/output ratios x_1/y and x_2/y, in which case the convex hull of the data defines the boundary of the level sets and thus defines f. All measurements of the relevant distances are carried out by comparisons to the convex hull of the

---

[1] We note that the Cobb–Douglas distance function violates the regularity conditions but we use it here simply to illustrate how a functional representation may be derived from a simple index number aggregator of outputs and inputs. More flexible functional representations such as the translog that preserve regularity over a portion of the sample space can be derived analogously.

[2] The output-distance function defined above can hypothetically take on values greater than one.

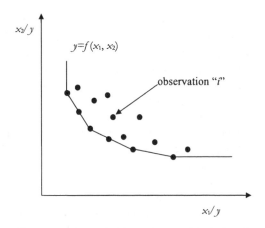

Figure 11.1 Input requirement set and boundary for a CRS technology.

data with free disposability of the inputs providing us with the vertical and horizontal portions in this simple two-dimensional case (Figure 11.1).

Of course, the technology may not exhibit constant returns to scale (Charnes et al., 1978) and thus alternative approaches may be needed in order to allow for returns to scale to vary as output varies (Banker et al., 1984). If constant returns to scale is not a maintained hypothesis, then f can still be identified. Let's say we have $i = 1, \ldots, n$ observations. Then for a particular firm or decision making unit (DMU) (x_{1i}, x_{2i}, y_i) one takes the convex hull of (x_{1j}, x_{2j}) such that $y_j \geq y_i$, $i, j = 1, \ldots, n$ (since the $x's$ that produce $y_j \geq y_i$ could presumably produce y_i due to free disposability of outputs) and this gives us f, which is the upper bound of the efficiency measure or the boundary of the level set. Varian (1983) showed how to bound possible technologies that "rationalize" the data by assuming cost-minimizing behavior given a revealed preference condition: if $y_j \geq y_i$, then $wx_j \geq wx_i$. This convex hull is one of the Varian bounds.

One of the major drawbacks of the original or canonical form of the DEA problem is its failure to accommodate statistical noise that can be present in real data sets. This drawback encouraged researchers to look for alternative methods, the most successful of which, at least so far, became what is now known as the stochastic frontier model discovered independently by Aigner et al. (1977) and Meeusen and van den Broeck (1977) and which has broadened into the field referred to as Stochastic Frontier Analysis (SFA). This approach allowed for statistical noise in the data, although the SFA had its own drawbacks. We will also touch on these drawbacks, among its many advantages, in this chapter.

As we pointed out in Chapter 6, Cobb and Douglas (1928) were the pioneers among the early empirical researchers who promoted the paradigm of the so-called average production function. Their conceptual approach – statistical estimation of an explicitly imposed functional form of a production relationship, assuming no inefficiency but acknowledging the presence of a statistical error – was the general path to follow for applied productivity researchers for almost a half a century. The stochastic error in these models was symmetric. Non-symmetries were recognized but viewed as misspecification errors that were (hopefully) swept into the constant term. As an alternative to the average production function, the stochastic frontier specification of the error term recognizes the crucial role that such potential non-symmetries in the error distribution of the production function may have. By exploiting the implications of economic theory such a model of production has provided researchers with a deeper understanding of the measured production process and its adoption.

11.1 THE STOCHASTIC FRONTIER PARADIGM

In the SFA paradigm, there remains a crucial role for the idiosyncratic error disturbance specified in the average production model. Such a disturbance term is typically appended to the production function or some other functional representation of the technology to represent latent factors like measurement error, misspecification of the underlying functional form, and inherent randomness of the production process. However, in the SFA paradigm an additional source of error, an additional latent variable, is added to the production model to account for *technical inefficiency*. Due to the interpretation of this latent variable as the technical inefficiency that reduces actual output from the average frontier output specified by the production function's parametric (or nonparametric) econometric form, the additional random component has only positive support.[3] Such a two-component error mixture results in a nonsymmetric error and it is this non-symmetry that is a key to the SFA literature. To be more concrete, consider the Cobb–Douglas production model (or linear in logs) with such a two-component error structure,

$$\ln(y) = \beta_0 + \sum_{k=1}^{N} \beta_k \ln(x_k) + \varepsilon, \qquad (11.1.1)$$

$$\varepsilon = v - u, \qquad (11.1.2)$$

---

[3] It is clear that the rationale for inefficiency that we evaluate in this chapter in the stochastic frontier model suggests not only radial technical inefficiency but also inefficiencies due to improper allocations, given output and input prices. We do not take up this very important topic of allocative inefficiency, which is a topic whose empirical and theoretical treatment would take up many, many additional chapters. Perhaps it is best left for another book. The literature on the topic of allocative inefficiency is vast and deep. Interested readers can easily search online for the term "allocative efficiency." When this was done in January 2017, over 90,000 hits came up on Google. The approaches used to identify and estimate such inefficiencies in multiple output, multiple input technologies using both regression and index number approaches can be found in Lovell and Sickles (1983), Sickles et al. (1986), Kumbhakar (1987), Kumbhakar (1997), Getachew and Sickles (2007), and O'Donnell (2016), among many other studies, many of which are referenced in those studies.

where v is the usual random disturbance with mean zero and variance σ_v^2 and u is the technical efficiency term that has only positive support with a mean $\mu > 0$ and a variance σ_u^2. This is the canonical form of the stochastic frontier model (SFM). Under varying assumptions about the errors u and v and their moments, weak exogeneity of the xs, and different correlation structures among the various sources of randomness and the regressors, the canonical form of the SFM nests almost all of the methods introduced to date in the literature on the SFM. We will discuss the SFM in depth in this chapter.

We will now backtrack a bit to discuss the historical context into which SFA was introduced. In so doing, we will discuss a number of technical and conceptual issues that have arisen as productivity researchers did what researchers do: provide better and more robust methods to measure productivity. In the remainder of this chapter, we will often use ε to denote the random error that is appended to the production relationship and will not distinguish between it and its component terms. Until we formally introduce the stochastic frontier model we implicitly set $\sigma_v^2 = 0$ and thus disregard the possibility of measurement error and other sources of randomness that are distinct from latent sources of inefficiency.

To fix ideas about the econometric problem that is intrinsic to the SFM, recall that the most ubiquitous estimating procedure used in empirical analysis, least squares regression, fits a line through the data by minimizing the sum of squared deviations between the observed and the fitted values of the dependent variable. With no statistical assumptions, this exercise is purely a graphical, or descriptive one. If one is trying to explicitly model a single output production process in terms of the inputs that are at the discretion of the firm to change, then such a curve- or line-fitting exercise does not give proper scope to the fact that there should be an envelope to the estimated regression line representing the maximum output obtainable from any given set of inputs. This is a direct result of the definition of the technology set and its functional representation given above. Farrell (1957)[4] appears to have been the first to point out how this issue could be logically addressed at an empirical level. We have shown how this was accomplished in earlier chapters, but we repeat a bit of that discussion in the context of the canonical stochastic frontier model.

We begin with a homogeneous constant returns to scale technology with two inputs and one output. We represent the production function in a typical equation such as $y = f(x_1, x_2)$. Linear homogeneity means that the function possesses the property that $f(\lambda x_1, \lambda x_2) = \lambda f(x_1, x_2)$ for $\lambda > 0$ and thus the unit isoquant $1 = f(x_1/y, x_2/y)$ can be used to represent the technology. The production isoquant and the isocost line are given in the figure below.

---

[4] Michael James Farrell was a remarkable intellectual figure and made a number of important contributions during his distinguished academic career at Cambridge in economic theory. His lasting legacy, however, was his formal treatment of the efficiency of business performance, its measurement and methods to compare the technical and allocative efficiency performance of businesses (Grifell-Tatjé and Lovell, 2004).

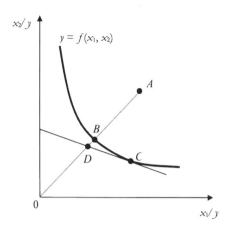

Figure 11.2 Production isoquant and the isocost line.

Assuming that a firm is operating at point A we can define technical efficiency as the ratio OB/OA. If input prices are such that the optimum is at C, then allocative efficiency at point D is measured as the ratio OD/OB (i.e., ratio of cost at C to cost at B) and cost efficiency would be measured as the ratio OD/OA. In order to estimate these important measures of efficiency one needs to find f. How is that done? We have already shown graphically above and in terms of the linear program developed in Chapter 9 how this can be accomplished by DEA. However, how can this be accomplished using a regression-based approach? There are several answers. Each of these answers leads to a different estimator and each of these different estimators has its own set of shortcomings.

11.2 CORRECTED OLS

Among the first to challenge those who estimated an average production function and thus offer a more compelling and theoretically consistent estimation approach, one that was *non-stochastic/nonparametric* but yet allowed for *technical inefficiency* – was Farrell (1957). As discussed in more detail in Chapter 8, Farrell used a linear programming-based technique, which in turn was rooted in earlier work of von Neumann (1938, 1945), Debreu (1951), Koopmans (1951a), and Shephard (1953), to construct what has come to be referred to as a Debreu–Shephard–Farrell efficiency measure. This was later reformulated into the DEA methodology by Charnes et al. (1978), as we have discussed in detail in previous chapters. Such a fundamentally different view inspired many researchers to reconsider the standard paradigm of the *average* production functions. One of them was Winsten (1957) who in a discussion note on Farrell's (1957) paper was perhaps the first to suggest a way to incorporate the inefficiency concept into the *regression* analysis paradigm. In particular, Winsten noted that

> It would also be interesting to know whether in practice this [Farrell's] efficient production function turned out to be parallel to the average production function, and whether it might not be possible to fit a line to the averages, and shift it parallel to itself to estimate the efficient production function. (Winsten, 1957, p. 283)

Although Winsten had not put his curiosity into practice, he influenced others to do so. His suggestion later grew into a variation of methods that generally adopt a *three-stage* algorithm:

(1) Use ordinary least squares (OLS) to estimate an average production relationship based on a prespecified or assumed functional form.
(2) Take the OLS residuals from the first stage to "correct" the OLS estimated intercept obtained in the first stage, thus making a parallel shift in the estimated average production function that is everywhere above all the observations. This is referred to as the *estimated production* or *technology frontier*.
(3) Estimate individual inefficiencies as the distance from the observations to the estimated frontier obtained in stage 2.

This approach was given the name "Corrected OLS" or COLS. Graphically, COLS leads to the following approach depicted in Figure 11.3 to developing an estimator of f and of estimating technical efficiency for a single output/single input technology $y = f(x)$.

Utilizing a regression approach and simply shifting the intercept term so that all estimated residuals are non-positive provides us with the COLS estimator (Waldman, 1982; Aigner et al., 1977; Olson et al., 1980; Kopp and Mullahy, 1993). Under standard conditions consistent with the Gauss–Markov theorem, ordinary least squares estimates of the production parameters of such a model are unbiased and have minimum variance in the space of linear estimators. With fairly mild assumptions on the error process on the error term, the usual tests based on standard limiting normal distributions can be carried out on model parameters.

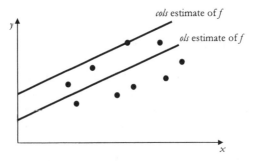

Figure 11.3 Average and frontier production function for a linear technology.

We can outline this approach more formally in a relatively simple version of the method applied to the Cobb–Douglas model in logarithmic form. In the first step we use OLS to estimate the following regression

$$\ln(y_i) = \beta_0 + \beta_1 \ln(x_{i1}) + \cdots + \beta_N \ln(x_{iN}) + \varepsilon_i, \quad i = 1, \ldots, n, \quad (11.2.1)$$

where y_i is (single-valued) output, $x_i = (x_{i1}, \cdots, x_{iN})$ is a vector of inputs for production unit i, and $\beta = (\beta_0, \beta_1, \cdots, \beta_N)$ is the vector of parameters (common for all i) that we need to estimate and ε_i is statistical noise. This step would give OLS estimates, which we denote $\hat{\beta} = (\hat{\beta}_0, \hat{\beta}_1, \cdots, \hat{\beta}_N)$. At the second step, one would then correct the intercept as

$$\hat{\beta}_0^{cols} = \hat{\beta}_0 + \max_i\{\hat{\varepsilon}_i\}, \; i = 1, \ldots, n, \quad (11.2.2)$$

where $\hat{\varepsilon}_i$ are OLS residuals. Then, at the third step of the COLS procedure, one can estimate the technical inefficiency for each observation as the *deviation* from the frontier, or equivalently as the difference between the maximal OLS residual and the OLS residual corresponding to a particular observation, i.e.,

$$Technical\,Inefficiency = \hat{\varepsilon}_i^{cols} = \max_i\{\hat{\varepsilon}_i\} - \hat{\varepsilon}_i, \quad i \in \{1, \ldots, n\}. \quad (11.2.3)$$

Such a procedure will ensure that no observation is above the estimated and corrected, or shifted, production function. Thus the shifted or corrected production function becomes the production *frontier*, formally defined as

$$\ln(y_i) = \hat{\beta}_0^{cols} + \hat{\beta}_1 \ln(x_{i1}) + \cdots$$
$$+ \hat{\beta}_N \ln(x_{iN}) - \hat{\varepsilon}_i^{cols}. \quad (11.2.4)$$

One conceptual problem with this version of COLS in this simple Cobb–Douglas case is that it does not envelope (using DEA terminology) the data from above in the closest way possible but rather the closest way possible for a linear in logarithms technology. This is because by correcting only the estimated intercept (but not all estimated parameters) it merely makes a parallel shift of the average production function obtained from a linear (in logs) statistical model via OLS. However, even with this caveat, it was the first step in a progression of developments that pointed researchers in the direction of parametric regression methods that eventually led to SFA.

11.3 PARAMETRIC STATISTICAL APPROACHES TO DETERMINE THE BOUNDARY OF THE LEVEL SETS: THE "FULL FRONTIER"

Another answer to the question of how to locate the deterministic boundary of the level sets leads us to the parametric statistical approach introduced by Aigner and Chu (1968) to estimate the frontier technology and thus deviations below it in the form of technical inefficiency. What is meant by a deterministic frontier? This is really an unfortunate term to use as it suggests that there is not a statistical underpinning to the modeling exercise. Such a distinction has hindered researchers for decades in their communication about the many linear programming, econometric and statistical treatments to the identification and estimation of the frontier function and the radial measure of technical inefficiency attached to a particular firm or DMU. The approach introduced by Farrell (1957) and generalized by Charnes et al. (1978) (CCR) has often been referred to as a nonparametric method resulting in a deterministic frontier.

In reality, the CCR method utilizes a parametric function, albeit one that is piecewise linear, which is just another parametric model. Moreover, as the piecewise convex envelope of the data is a solution to an optimization problem involving random variables (y, x), the resulting measure of technical efficiency is clearly an estimator and thus statistical, not deterministic. Such a link to a statistical estimation problem, akin to OLS or MLE was met with substantial skepticism by many in the field of operational research. In order to justify an alternative view that the model is intrinsically non-statistical, one would need to view a sample of data as the population (Rosenbaum, 2002) and not a sample of firms that could be augmented by new firms or reduced in size by firms leaving the industry. However, the view that such programming methods do in fact result in an estimator has become the prevalent scientific perspective through the substantial contributions of Léopold Simar and his many colleagues and students. Simar (1996) first made the argument that DEA could be viewed as an estimator and over the last three decades the work by Simar and Wilson (1998, 1999, 2000b, 2007), Kneip et al. (1998), Gijbels et al. (1999), Cazals et al. (2002), Florens and Simar (2005), and Daouia and Simar (2005), among many others, have made it clear that DEA can be interpreted as a statistical construct and thus an estimator with finite and asymptotic properties grounded in standard statistical theory.

Some two decades before Simar began his work on the statistical interpretation of DEA, Schmidt (1976) pointed out the equivalence of the linear programming solution of Aigner and Chu (1968) and the solution of the likelihood equations when the technical efficiency term was drawn from an exponential distribution. Schmidt's work meant that the technical efficiencies from DEA were in fact statistics based on parametric MLE. In regard to linear programming approaches being in some sense nonparametric, it also should be recognized that a piecewise linear functional form is no less parametric than a second-order Taylor series approximation in natural logarithms, the familiar translog production function of which the Cobb–Douglas is a special case.

11.3.1   Aigner–Chu Methodology

Returning to the Aigner and Chu (1968) contribution, a goal of productivity researchers at the time of their study was to model a specific parametric production function while also allowing all the observations to be enveloped. This did not seem feasible until the influential work of Aigner and Chu (1968), who suggested a new methodology that allowed estimation of parameters of a *pre-specified* functional form (e.g., Cobb–Douglas, as in their example).

This was accomplished, however, not via the OLS but via the mathematical programming formulations that restricted all observations to be bounded from above in a closest possible way, given the chosen functional form for the production function. More formally, for the example of the assumed Cobb–Douglas production function, they suggested to use

$$\ln(y_i) = \hat{\beta}_0^* + \hat{\beta}_1^* \ln(x_{i1}) + \cdots + \hat{\beta}_N^* \ln(x_{iN}) - \hat{\varepsilon}_i^*, \quad i = 1, \ldots, n, \quad (11.3.1)$$

where the estimated parameters $\hat{\beta}^* = (\hat{\beta}_0^*, \hat{\beta}_1^*, \cdots, \hat{\beta}_N^*)$ were obtained by solving the quadratic programming problem, defined as

$$(\hat{\beta}_0^*, \hat{\beta}_1^*, \cdots, \hat{\beta}_N^*, \hat{\varepsilon}_1^*, \cdots, \hat{\varepsilon}_n^*) = \operatorname{argmin} \left\{ \sum_{i=1}^{n} \varepsilon_i^2 : \varepsilon_i \geq 0, \forall i, \right.$$

$$\left. \beta = (\beta_0, \beta_1, \cdots, \beta_N) \geq 0 \right\},$$

or, alternatively, the linear programming problem

$$(\hat{\beta}_0^*, \hat{\beta}_1^*, \cdots, \hat{\beta}_N^*, \hat{\varepsilon}_1^*, \cdots, \hat{\varepsilon}_n^*) = \operatorname{argmin} \left\{ \sum_{i=1}^{n} \varepsilon_i : \varepsilon_i \geq 0, \forall i, \right.$$

$$\left. \beta = (\beta_0, \beta_1, \cdots, \beta_N) \geq 0 \right\}. \quad (11.3.2)$$

For both problems, $\varepsilon_i := \ln(y_i) - \beta_0 - \beta_1 \ln(x_{i1}) - \cdots - \beta_N \ln(x_{iN})$, and optimization is carried out over $(\varepsilon_1, \cdots, \varepsilon_n)$ and $(\beta_0, \beta_1, \cdots, \beta_N)$. Only about a decade later, the statistical interpretation to this methodology (when a specific one-sided error term is added) was discovered by Schmidt (1976), via the maximum likelihood theory.

As with many new approaches in this literature, the Aigner and Chu methodology, while solving one aspect of the envelopment drawback of COLS, still had problems. For example, the estimator is rather sensitive to outliers (points lying significantly distant from the rest of the observations), and it is possible for a single observation to cause the entire frontier to be ill-behaved. Simple DEA and COLS also suffer from this problem. In addition to this undesirable property, there was another and that was the lack of an important aspect of statistical uncertainty provided by the standard random disturbance term. This is to be distinguished from the uncertainty that may drive a manager to make decisions that are not optimal, which may also be considered separate from inefficiencies that are under the control of the firm and its management. The substantive implications of uncertainty due to asymmetric information for the measurement of inefficiency is discussed in O'Donnell et al. (2010). For the Aigner–Chu model all sources of randomness are due to inefficiency. An important development in the field was needed that specified a technology frontier that allowed for both inefficiency and for statistical error. This became possible with the introduction of SFA, but a few important contributions preceded it, which we discuss in the next section.

11.3.2   Afriat–Richmond Methodology

Another fundamental contribution that moved the profession closer to the discovery of SFA was proposed by Afriat (1972). In his seminal work, Afriat defined the technical efficiency measure as

$$\varepsilon_i(y, x) \equiv \frac{y_i}{f(x_{i1}, \cdots, x_{iN})}, \quad i = 1, \cdots, n, \tag{11.3.3}$$

where y_i and x_i are the observed output and input vector of firm i, $f(\cdot)$ is the production frontier utilized by firm i, and the random variable ε_i takes on values between 0 and 1. Afriat also pointed out that the natural choice of the probability distribution for the error term ε_i would be a Beta distribution. He also suggested an alternative for a Cobb–Douglas production function wherein $\ln(1/\varepsilon)$ takes on the Gamma distribution. This apparently was the first explicit assignment of a specific probability distribution to the inefficiency component. While Afriat did not implement this idea in his 1972 study, his idea was drawn on and elaborated by Richmond (1974), who also appears to have been the first to explicitly implement a version of COLS to a real data set. Greene (1990) was later to incorporate this distribution into the one-sided efficiency term in his gamma-distributed SFA model.

Richmond pointed out that the Afriat suggestion implied that

$$\ln(y_i) = \beta_0 + \beta_1 \ln(x_{i1}) + \ldots + \beta_N \ln(x_{iN}) - u_i, \quad i = 1, \ldots, n, \tag{11.3.4}$$

where the inefficiency component is now defined as $u_i \equiv -\ln(\varepsilon_i)$ and is assumed to be iid gamma distributed as $G(u|\mu, 1)$ with shape parameter μ and scale parameter normalized to 1, i.e.,

$$u_i \sim_{iid} G(u; \mu) \equiv \begin{cases} \frac{1}{\Gamma(\mu)}(u)^{\mu-1}\exp(-u), & 0 < u < \infty, \quad \mu > 0 \\ 0 & otherwise, \end{cases}$$
$$\tag{11.3.5}$$

where $\Gamma(\mu) = \int_0^\infty u^{\mu-1}\exp(-u)du$. With the scale parameter normalized at unity, the mean and variance of the one-sided random variable u_i that represents a measure of efficiency are both equal to the shape parameter μ.

As a result of such a distributional assumption, the expectation of Afriat's definition for a (Cobb–Douglas) stochastic technical efficiency measure becomes[5]

$$E(\varepsilon) \equiv E(\exp(-u)) = \int_0^\infty \exp(-u)G(u; \mu)du = 2^{-\mu}. \tag{11.3.6}$$

It would be convenient to use OLS to estimate the model. The only problem that arises with OLS in this context is that the error term has a nonzero

---

[5] See Appendix for details.

mean. Based on the distributional assumptions the only issue is the non-zero mean of the inefficiency term but a simple correction can be applied via a reparameterization of the original model as

$$\ln(y_i) = (\beta_0 - \mu) + \beta_1 \ln(x_{i1}) + \ldots + \beta_N \ln(x_{iN}) + (\mu - u_i) \tag{11.3.7}$$

$$\equiv \beta_0^* + \beta_1 \ln(x_{i1}) + \ldots + \beta_N \ln(x_{iN}) + u_i^*, \tag{11.3.8}$$

where the properties of the new error term u_i^* in this model are

$$E(u_i^*) = 0, \quad V(u_i^*) = \mu, \text{ and } Cov(u_i^*, u_{j \neq i}^*) = 0.$$

Assuming that u_i^* is not correlated with any of the regressors, we can obtain the OLS estimates, denoted here as $\hat{\beta} \equiv (\hat{\beta}_0^*, \hat{\beta}_1, \ldots, \hat{\beta}_N)$. From the basics of regression analysis, we know that these estimates are unbiased and consistent estimates of the true parameters $\beta \equiv (\beta_0^*, \beta_1, \ldots, \beta_N)$. In order to recover the original production model first note that all the parameters of the re-parameterized model are the same as those of the original model, except for the intercept, and thus our OLS estimates of the re-parameterized model are also unbiased and consistent estimates, except for the intercept. That is,

$$E(\hat{\beta}_k) = \beta_k \text{ and plim } \hat{\beta}_k = \beta_k, \forall k \tag{11.3.9}$$

and

$$E(\hat{\beta}_0^*) = \beta_0^* \equiv \beta_0 - \mu \text{ and plim}(\hat{\beta}_0^*) = \beta_0^* \equiv \beta_0 - \mu. \tag{11.3.10}$$

As the last equation shows, we now require an estimate of μ – the mean of inefficiency – to correct the OLS estimated intercept and to thus provide an estimate of the true intercept – the intercept of the original production model.

Recall that $\mu = V(u_i^*)$. Thus we can use the OLS estimate of $V(u_i^*)$ as an estimate of μ, i.e.,

$$\hat{\mu} \equiv \frac{\sum_{i=1}^n (\hat{u}_i^*)^2}{n - N - 1} \equiv \frac{\sum_{i=1}^n (\ln y_i - \hat{\beta}_0^* - \hat{\beta}_1 \ln(x_{i1}) - \ldots - \hat{\beta}_N \ln(x_{iN}))^2}{n - N - 1}, \tag{11.3.11}$$

where $\hat{u}_i^* (i = 1, \ldots, n)$ are the OLS residuals from the re-parameterized model.

Since we know that the OLS estimator of the variance is a consistent estimator of the true variance under the conditions of the model assumptions, it follows that

$$E(\hat{\mu}) = \mu \text{ and plim } \hat{\mu} = \mu.$$

And, therefore, the corrected intercept is also consistent, i.e.,

$$E(\hat{\beta}_0^* + \hat{\mu}) = \beta_0 \text{ and plim}(\hat{\beta}_0^* + \hat{\mu}) = \beta_0.$$

Let us now investigate the properties of the Afriat measure of random technical efficiency, $\hat{E}(\varepsilon_i) = 2^{-\hat{\mu}}$. Using Slutsky's theorem, it can be shown that the estimator is consistent, since

$$\text{plim}(\hat{E}(u_i)) = \text{plim}\, 2^{-\hat{\mu}} = 2^{-(\text{plim}\,\hat{\mu})} = 2^{-\mu}. \tag{11.3.12}$$

This estimate, however, can be shown via Jensen's inequality[6] to have an upward bias as

$$E(2^{-\hat{\mu}}) \geq 2^{E(-\hat{\mu})}.$$

It may also be important to measure the aggregate efficiency in an industry in which the sample of firms operate. The distribution of efficiency within the industry – the proportion of observation with efficiency at least equal to some given value c, $(0 < c < 1)$ – can be defined as

$$\Pr(\varepsilon \geq c) = \Pr(u \leq -\ln c) = \int_{0}^{-\ln c} G(u; \mu)du. \tag{11.3.13}$$

The Afriat–Richmond methodology has much in common with the methodology proposed by Aigner and Chu (1968). However, the novelty brought by Afriat and Richmond was an explicit assumption of a specific probability distribution for the inefficiency term. Further work on this issue was pursued by Schmidt (1976) who showed that if u is distributed as exponential (a special case of the gamma distribution), then the Aigner and Chu deterministic frontier based on a linear programming estimator is the maximum-likelihood estimator. The Aigner and Chu quadratic programming estimator is also the maximum-likelihood estimator for u with a half-normal distribution. However, as Schmidt noted, although these were the maximum likelihood estimators (MLE), their asymptotic properties were questionable. In particular, the range of the random variable y is parameter dependent, which violates one of the regularity conditions for maximum likelihood since integral and differential operators are no longer interchangeable (Schmidt, 1976). Greene (1980a) provided sufficient conditions on the density of the inefficiency distribution under which the regularity conditions for maximum likelihood were not violated. These are restrictive properties and are not shared by many standard one-sided distributions.

As we will see shortly, these two discoveries – that Aigner and Chu estimators were MLEs and that some adjustment is needed for these estimators to satisfy the usual desired properties of MLE – were the last two important links in the intellectual chain of research discoveries that led to SFA. It is interesting that the stochastic frontier model of Aigner et al. (1977) was introduced

---

[6] Recall that Jensen's inequality (stated for convex functions) implies that, $E(g(x)) \leq g(E(x))$, for any concave function g. Also, note that $E(g(x)) \cong g(E(x))$, in the sense of a first-order Taylor's series approximation for any differentiable g, which certainly applies to our case.

through the joint efforts of Aigner and Schmidt, who had worked separately on earlier links in the chain, together with the efforts of Lovell, who along with Afriat and Schmidt were professors at UNC-Chapel Hill.

Before we move to the paradigm of stochastic frontiers, we acknowledge one more contribution of the Afriat and Richmond methodology. Because of their specific distributional assumption, advantageously, their version of COLS became much less sensitive to outliers. However, this came with a price as the corrected relationship does not envelop the data. Since the correction uses the estimated mean of the one-sided errors, there are necessarily observations that are above the production frontier. No explanation is given for such observations by Afriat or Richmond, except for the implication that they are more than efficient, which contradicts the original Afriat definition of efficiency.[7] A natural way to interpret these observations above the frontier would be to acknowledge that there may be other error processes in addition to the error process generating the inefficiency error. This of course was assumed when researchers estimated average production functions but ignored inefficiency.

The defects of the full frontier specification of inefficiency not only involve statistical properties and the substantial leverage that outliers may have on the identification of inefficient observations, but the full frontier also does not allow for a role for measurement error on the dependent variable. All stochastic noise is subsumed in the stochastic inefficiency term and thus no acknowledgment is given to the possibility that other sources of non-systematic error exist. This is probably the biggest drawback of the full frontier model and led to the development of the stochastic frontier model which we discuss next.

11.4 PARAMETRIC STATISTICAL APPROACHES TO DETERMINE THE STOCHASTIC BOUNDARY OF THE LEVEL SETS: THE "STOCHASTIC FRONTIER"

The *stochastic frontier* methodology was introduced independently and almost simultaneously on two different continents by Aigner et al. (1977) (hereafter ALS)[8] in the USA and Meeusen and van den Broeck (1977) (hereafter MvB) in Europe. These studies laid out a foundation for what is now referred to as Stochastic Frontier Analysis. Both methodologies are based on the assumption that randomness in the production function is composed of two independent terms: one is responsible for *inefficiency*, the other represents the usual disturbance in a regression model and is interpreted as simply statistical *noise*. The

---

[7] Another problem with their COLS method is that they correct only for the intercept and thus do not allow for the technology among the most efficient observations to differ from that obtained from the "average" of all the observations. Empirically, however, this problem seems not to be significant (e.g., see Olson et al., 1980).

[8] The authors actually note that their idea was inspired by Aigner, Amemiya, and Poirier (1976).

statistical noise component is viewed as a zero mean symmetric random error that allows for random variation in the frontier across observational units, e.g., over time for a firm or across firms in an industry at a point in time.

The statistical noise component captures random shocks to the production process such as weather and macroeconomic events, that are typically assumed to be exogenous to the firm. The latent term that captures inefficiency has historically been assumed to be one-sided and asymmetric. Symmetric (uniform) inefficiency distributions were introduced by Li (1996a) but the widely used specifications of inefficiency have always stressed the lack of symmetry due to a variety of factors owing to the market incentives of efficient production. These include unobserved internal production factors that are manifested by poor management or questionable labor quality that may not permit firms to reach their best practice levels of production given the common technology they adopt in an industry or that a firm utilizes over time. Under such a formulation it is still the production frontier that is modeled, but unlike the average production function approach the formulation is of maximal outputs, given certain levels of inputs. With the addition of a symmetric random component, this maximum is *not deterministic* but *random*.

Average inefficiency in this model is identified relative to a best-practice firm. However, it should be noted that the technology used by all of the firms in the reference set, that is the sample of firms under study, is assumed to be the same. This of course may not be the case. Mundlak (1988) and many others have examined heterogeneous production technologies and have developed estimating approaches for such settings. An alternative approach in the productivity and efficiency literature is the metafrontier of Battese et al. (2004). This paradigm allows for firms utilizing different technologies to be evaluated in terms of their efficiencies in a manner that makes possible the establishment of a comparable efficiency metric. Moreover, gaps in the technologies relative to an industry benchmark can be estimated. The metafrontier shares much of its motivation with the latent-class model of Greene (2002) that we will take up in Chapter 13.

To proceed with the estimation of this model, both errors are assumed to follow some specific distributions with some unknown parameters. For the pure statistical noise term, both ALS and MvB assumed a normal distribution with zero mean. It is a natural assumption that economists are comfortable with in many contexts and can be justified by using many arguments, among them the classic central limit theorem. However, the choice of the distribution for inefficiency is not that simple, and although many distributions may seem reasonable, none in particular can be motivated on the basis of economic/statistical theory, context, etc. The choice of the distribution for the *inefficiency* term is arbitrary and in practice often is based on computational simplicity.

ALS considered a half-normal (equivalent to the truncated normal with their parameterization) and the exponential for the inefficiency distribution, while MvB considered the exponential distribution. A series of studies also considered other distributions, e.g., the truncated normal with a non-zero mode (ALS assumed a mode of zero) (Stevenson, 1980), and gamma (Greene, 1980a,b; Stevenson, 1980) and found that in most cases the results, at least qualitatively, are fairly similar. For whatever distribution assumed for the one-sided inefficiency distribution, the parametric error structure is then used to obtain the maximum likelihood estimators for the parameters of the assumed production model and, importantly, the variances of both error terms, which are then used to obtain the estimated mean of the inefficiency-error component.

In our discussion of the SFM, we consider the ALS parameterization. The production model is assumed to be

$$y_i = f(x_i|\beta) \exp(\varepsilon_i), \quad i = 1, \cdots, n, \tag{11.4.1}$$

where the dependent variable, y, represents output for observation i in the sample, the vector of regressors, $x_i = (x_{i1}, \ldots, x_{iK})'$, represents inputs, and the relationship between them is assumed to be characterized by some *known* function f with *unknown* parameters β to be estimated. The error term ε_i is assumed to be *composed* of two *independent* components: v_i is (two-sided) *statistical noise* and u_i is one-sided, nonnegative, error term representing *technical inefficiency*, i.e.,

$$\varepsilon_i = v_i - u_i, \quad i = 1, \cdots, n. \tag{11.4.2}$$

With such a model formulation we are still modeling a *frontier* as Farrell (1957), Aigner and Chu (1968), Afriat (1972), Richmond (1974), and others were striving to model, and not an *average* production function. However, the *frontier* is now *stochastic* as the maximal output, $f(x_i) \exp(v_i)$, is stochastic due to the randomness of v_i. The inefficiency of firm i now can be measured as

$$\exp(-u_i) \equiv \frac{y_i}{f(x_i) \exp(v_i)}, \quad i = 1, \cdots, n. \tag{11.4.3}$$

Note that the way in which the error term ε_i enters the production model is just a convenient way to allow the error term to have unbounded support (more will be said about this later when we discuss the bounded inefficiency model), but also allows the dependent variable, the output, still to be nonnegative, given $f(x_i) \geq 0$. Estimation is typically performed on the log-transformed model:

$$\ln y_i = \ln f(x_i|\beta) + v_i - u_i, \quad i = 1, \cdots, n. \tag{11.4.4}$$

Following ALS, we assume that

$$v_i \sim_{iid} \mathcal{N}(0, \sigma_v^2)$$

and

$$u_i \sim_{iid} |\mathcal{N}(0, \sigma_u^2)|.$$

The probability density function $f_v(\cdot)$ for each random variable v_i at a point v is given by

$$f_v(v) = \frac{1}{\sqrt{2\pi}\sigma_v} \exp\left\{-\frac{1}{2}\frac{v^2}{\sigma_v^2}\right\} \equiv \frac{1}{\sigma_v}\phi\left(\frac{v}{\sigma_v}\right), \quad -\infty \le v \le +\infty,$$

$$(11.4.5)$$

while the probability density function for each random variable u_i at a point u is given by

$$f_u(u) = \frac{2}{\sqrt{2\pi}\sigma_u} \exp\left\{-\frac{1}{2}\frac{u^2}{\sigma_u^2}\right\} \equiv 2\frac{1}{\sigma_u}\phi\left(\frac{u}{\sigma_u}\right), \quad 0 \le u \le +\infty, \quad (11.4.6)$$

where $\phi(\cdot)$ is the standard normal probability density. Although it was not known at the time the product distribution of the normal and the half-normal distribution has a classical distributional heritage as pointed out by Azzalini (1985, 2013) that can be traced to much earlier work by De Helguero (1908) and Birnbaum (1950) and is referred to as the skew-normal distribution in the statistics literature.[9] William Greene has been instrumental in popularizing this class of distribution, especially in the context of his work on persistent and transitory inefficiency that we will pursue in Chapter 13. Filippini and Greene (2016) provides an insightful and up to date survey of competing methods that utilize the skew-normal to effectively decompose transitory and persistent inefficiencies and also provides numerical approaches based on simulated maximum likelihood to estimate these decompositions.

In order to specify the likelihood equations for the maximum likelihood estimator (MLE) of the production model and to estimate the unknown β together with σ_v, and σ_u, one needs to specify the distribution of ε_i. Since $\varepsilon_i := v_i - u_i$, its distribution can be obtained from the assumptions on the distributions of u_i and v_i. In particular, given the assumption that u_i and v_i are independent, it follows that the density of ε_i is:[10]

$$f_{\varepsilon_i}(\varepsilon) = \frac{2}{\sigma}\phi\left(\frac{\varepsilon}{\sigma}\right)\left[1 - \Phi\left(\frac{\varepsilon\lambda}{\sigma}\right)\right], \quad -\infty \le \epsilon \le +\infty, \quad (11.4.7)$$

where $\Phi(\cdot)$ is the standard normal distribution function, $\sigma^2 = \sigma_v^2 + \sigma_u^2$, and $\lambda = \sigma_u/\sigma_v$. The composite errors, $\varepsilon_1, \ldots, \varepsilon_n$, are of course not observed, but from our model we know that

$$\varepsilon_i = \ln y_i - \ln f(x_i), \quad i = 1, \ldots, n. \quad (11.4.8)$$

The function $\ln f(x_i)$ is assumed to belong to a class of known parametric functions with a finite number of unknown parameters, the elements of vector β that are the parameters to be estimated. The observations are contained in the data set $\{(y_i, x_i) : i = 1, \ldots, n\}$. The log-likelihood function can be written in terms of the production model and its parameterization as

---

[9] The derivation of the moments of the half-normal, shown originally by Elandt (1961) and the distribution for the mixture of the normal and the half-normal by Azzalini (1985) are given in the Appendix to this chapter.

[10] See the Appendix for a formal derivation.

$$\ell(y_1, \ldots, y_n \mid \beta, \lambda, \sigma^2) = \frac{n}{2} \ln\left(\frac{2}{\pi}\right) - \frac{n}{2} \ln\left(\sigma^2\right)$$

$$-\frac{1}{2\sigma^2} \sum_{i=1}^{n} (\ln y_i - \ln f(x_i))^2 + \sum_{i=1}^{n} \ln\left(1 - \Phi\left(\frac{(\ln y_i - \ln f(x_i))\lambda}{\sigma}\right)\right).$$

$$(11.4.9)$$

Note that the log-likelihood appears to be similar to the usual log-likelihood function for the average production function except for the second term in the second line, very much like the correction for a truncated sample that has proven so important in labor economics and models therein in which sample selection or limitations on the observables are addressed formally via a skew-normal type composite error structure (Sickles and Schmidt, 1978). Note also that as the parameter λ becomes smaller, which occurs when the variance of the inefficiency term relative to the variance of the noise term becomes smaller, the likelihood function for the stochastic frontier model becomes indistinguishable from the corresponding likelihood function for the average production model. Computational problems that plague empirical/numerical identification can arise when the variance of inefficiency becomes large relative to the variance of idiosyncratic noise as the third term in the above equation would involve evaluating the natural log of an expression very close to 0.

Given these assumptions, the mean and variance of the inefficiency component of the error u_i are respectively

$$E(u_i) \equiv \mu = \frac{\sqrt{2}}{\sqrt{\pi}}\sigma_u, \tag{11.4.10}$$

and

$$V(u_i) = \left(\frac{\pi - 2}{\pi}\right)\sigma_u^2, \tag{11.4.11}$$

and as a result,

$$E(\varepsilon_i) = E(v_i - u_i) = E(-u_i) = -\mu = -\frac{\sqrt{2}}{\sqrt{\pi}}\sigma_u, \tag{11.4.12}$$

$$V(\varepsilon_i) = V(v_i - u_i) = V(v) + V(u) = \sigma_v^2 + \left(\frac{\pi - 2}{\pi}\right)\sigma_u^2, \tag{11.4.13}$$

and

$$\text{cov}(\varepsilon_i, \varepsilon_j) = 0, \forall i \neq j. \tag{11.4.14}$$

The scores of the log-likelihood function are:

$$\frac{\partial}{\partial \beta}\ell(y_1, \ldots, y_n \mid \beta, \lambda, \sigma^2) = \frac{1}{\sigma^2}\sum_{i=1}^{n}(\ln y_i - \ln f(x_i))\frac{\partial}{\partial \beta}\ln f(x_i)$$

$$+\frac{\lambda}{\sigma}\sum_{i=1}^{n}\frac{\phi((\ln y_i - \ln f(x_i))\lambda\sigma^{-1})}{(1 - \Phi((\ln y_i - \ln f(x_i))\lambda\sigma^{-1}))}\frac{\partial}{\partial \beta}\ln f(x_i). \quad (11.4.15)$$

$$\frac{\partial}{\partial \lambda} \ell(y_1, \ldots, y_n \mid \beta, \lambda, \sigma^2) = -\frac{1}{\sigma} \sum_{i=1}^{n} \frac{\phi((\ln y_i - \ln f(x_i))\lambda \sigma^{-1})}{(1 - \Phi((\ln y_i - \ln f(x_i))\lambda \sigma^{-1}))}$$

$$\times (\ln y_i - \ln f(x_i)), \tag{11.4.16}$$

$$\frac{\partial}{\partial \sigma^2} \ell(y_1, \ldots, y_n \mid \beta, \lambda, \sigma^2) = -\frac{n}{2\sigma^2} + \frac{1}{2\sigma^4} \sum_{i=1}^{n} (\ln y_i - \ln f(x_i))^2$$

$$+ \frac{\lambda}{2\sigma^3} \sum_{i=1}^{n} \frac{\phi((\ln y_i - \ln f(x_i))\lambda \sigma^{-1})}{(1 - \Phi((\ln y_i - \ln f(x_i))\lambda \sigma^{-1}))}(\ln y_i - \ln f(x_i)).$$

$$\tag{11.4.17}$$

The maximum-likelihood estimates are obtained by setting the scores equal to zero and solving the set of $K + 2$ normal equations above simultaneously. Alternatively one could utilize the generalized method of moments (GMM) on the scores. The proposed estimator possesses the usual desired asymptotic properties of conventional MLE in that they are consistent and asymptotically efficient estimates of the true parameters $(\beta, \lambda, \sigma^2)$. The variances of the MLEs are derived in the usual manner, i.e., from the Fisher information matrix.

In order to estimate the mean μ of the inefficiency term u, first note that we can rewrite this expression for $\sigma^2 = \sigma_v^2 + \sigma_u^2$ and $\lambda = \sigma_u/\sigma_v$ as:

$$E(u_i) \equiv \mu = \frac{\sqrt{2}}{\sqrt{\pi}} \sigma_u = \frac{\sqrt{2}}{\sqrt{\pi(1 + \lambda^2)}} \sigma \lambda, \tag{11.4.18}$$

and thus based on consistent estimates of σ and λ we can utilize Slutsky's theorem to obtain a consistent estimate of μ as

$$\widehat{\mu} = \frac{\sqrt{2}}{\sqrt{\pi \left(1 + \widehat{\lambda}^2\right)}} \widehat{\sigma}\widehat{\lambda}. \tag{11.4.19}$$

ALS noted that an alternative (statistically inefficient) technique to estimate the stochastic frontier model would be to apply a two-stage approach. In the first stage, one would estimate the parameters of the production function using an OLS regression and consistently estimate the composite error term ε_i. In the second stage, one would then correct the regression intercept by a consistent estimate of μ obtained using the method of moments together with the assumptions on the distribution of each part of the composite error term. This idea was formalized in a later paper by Olson et al. (1980), which we discuss in the next section.

Before turning to the Olson et al. (1980) method, we need to mention an alternative to the SFA (and DEA) model introduced by Kuosmanen and Kortelainen (2012). Kuosmanen and Kortelainen developed a model that they consider to lie between the SFA and DEA models. They refer to this as the Stochastic Non-smooth Envelopment of Data (StoNED) model. The model utilizes a semiparametric frontier production function with the composed error structure of ALS and is constrained to meet the monotonicity and concavity conditions that are satisfied by the DEA estimator. Extensions to panel data are relatively straightforward. Their estimator is available on the web and offers a workable, innovative, and underappreciated approach to evaluating the technical efficiency of a production unit.

11.4.1 Olson, Schmidt, and Waldman (1980) Methodology

If we take the same regression model as in ALS and re-parameterize it by subtracting $E(u) = \mu$ from the intercept and adding μ to the composite error term, then this yields the following model:

$$\ln y_i = [\ln f(x_i|\beta) - \mu] + [v_i - u_i + \mu], \quad i = 1, \cdots, n \quad (11.4.20)$$

or

$$\ln y_i = \ln f_i^*(x_i|\beta) + \varepsilon_i^*, \quad i = 1, \cdots, n, \quad (11.4.21)$$

where $\ln f_i^*(x_i|\beta) = \ln f(x_i|\beta) - \mu$ and $\varepsilon_i^* = v_i - u_i + \mu$. The transformed model has an error with mean zero, the same variance and covariance structure, and carries with it the same assumptions in regard to the regressors and their independence with the stochastic error terms. Thus the OLS (or NLS if $g(\cdot)$ is nonlinear in β) estimator will possess the usual desired properties (unbiased, consistent, efficient, and asymptotically normally distributed), even without the distributional assumptions on the composite error of ALS.

Now note that the second and third central moments of ε_i^*, are given by

$$\mu_2 = \sigma_v^2 + \left(\frac{\pi - 2}{\pi}\right)\sigma_u^2, \quad (11.4.22)$$

$$\mu_3 = \sqrt{\frac{2}{\pi}}\left(\frac{\pi - 4}{\pi}\right)\sigma_u^3. \quad (11.4.23)$$

Using these expressions for the moments and solving them as a system of equations, explicit expressions for the variances of both components can be derived as:

$$\sigma_u^3 = \left[\sqrt{\frac{2}{\pi}}\left(\frac{\pi}{\pi - 4}\right)\mu_3\right], \quad (11.4.24)$$

and

$$\sigma_v^2 = \mu_2 - \frac{\pi - 2}{\pi}\sigma_u^2. \quad (11.4.25)$$

The variances can be consistently estimated by the plug-in method using the consistent moment estimates:

$$\hat{\sigma}_u^3 = \left[\sqrt{\frac{2}{\pi}}\left(\frac{\pi}{\pi - 4}\right)\hat{\mu}_3\right], \quad (11.4.26)$$

and

$$\hat{\sigma}_v^2 = \hat{\mu}_2 - \left(\frac{\pi - 2}{\pi}\right)\hat{\sigma}_u^2, \tag{11.4.27}$$

where $\hat{\mu}_2$ and $\hat{\mu}_3$ are the sample second and third moments (about the origin) constructed from the residuals, $\hat{\varepsilon}_i^*$, obtained from the OLS estimation of the transformed regression. These can be used as the basis of a test for the existence of the correct skewness of the composed error term, an issue we address later in this chapter.

Once the variance of the inefficiency term u is found, we can obtain an estimate of the mean of inefficiency by recalling that, as before

$$\mu \equiv \frac{\sqrt{2}}{\sqrt{\pi}}\sigma_u, \tag{11.4.28}$$

and therefore a consistent estimator would be

$$\hat{\mu} = \frac{\sqrt{2}}{\sqrt{\pi}}\hat{\sigma}_u. \tag{11.4.29}$$

This estimate can then be used to correct the intercept and the composite error and ultimately retrieve consistent estimates of the parameters of the original stochastic frontier model. It represents yet another version of corrected ordinary squares (COLS).

Olson et al. (1980) conducted a number of Monte Carlo simulations of this modification in the usual deterministic COLS method and compared the ALS methodology with their version of COLS, which is often referred to as *modified* OLS or simply MOLS. They found that their "corrected least squares estimator [with the ALS error structure] does quite well, in most cases, and is thus a reasonable alternative to maximum likelihood" (Olson et al., 1980, p. 68).

11.4.2   Estimation of Individual Inefficiencies

The two approaches we have discussed so far, ALS and MOLS, are alternative (but asymptotically equivalent) ways of estimating the same stochastic frontier. They both give estimates of the parameters of the production function, the variances of the statistical noise and, unlike the average production function approach, the estimate of the *mean* of the inefficiency term and the estimate of its variance. This is certainly a fundamental contribution to the field of applied production analysis. However, what many researchers also require are estimates of the *inefficiencies* of *each observation* (plant, firm, region, country, etc.) in the sample. This was not given in any of the methodologies presented so far in this chapter. In fact, at one point this was considered a major drawback of the SFA approach relative to others and was even considered an impossible task by many working in this field. A simple, yet ingenious solution to this quandary was provided by Materov (1981) and elaborated in Jondrow et al. (1982), henceforth JLMS. JLMS suggested that one could use $E(u_i|\varepsilon_i)$ as a point estimate of u_i.

To see that this is a reasonable estimator, first recall that from the law of iterated expectations we have

$$E(u_i) = E_\varepsilon[E(u_i|\varepsilon_i)]. \tag{11.4.30}$$

Next, recall that a consistent estimator of the left-hand side of the equation above can be obtained from $\hat{\mu}$, as we have discussed above using either the ALS or MOLS approach. Moreover, a natural consistent estimator of the right-hand side of this expression, motivated by the law of large numbers, is $\frac{1}{n}\sum_{i=1}^{n}E(u_i|\varepsilon_i)$, which is the sample average of the individual inefficiency esti-mates. Thus, all one needs is to construct a consistent estimator of $E(u_i|\varepsilon_i)$ and for this, recalling from the definition of *conditional* expectation, we have

$$E(u_i|\varepsilon_i) \equiv \int_0^\infty u f_{u_i|\varepsilon_i}(u|\varepsilon)du, \tag{11.4.31}$$

where, from definition of the conditional density,

$$f_{u_i|\varepsilon_i}(u|\varepsilon) \equiv \frac{f_{u_i,\varepsilon_i}(u,\varepsilon)}{f_{\varepsilon_i}(\varepsilon)}. \tag{11.4.32}$$

Notice that the denominator and the numerator were specified in the derivation of the joint density of u and ε. All that is left to do is to manipulate the expression with a bit of algebra to obtain the distribution for u, conditional on $\varepsilon_i = \varepsilon$, which brings us to the expression

$$f_{u_i|\varepsilon_i}(u|\varepsilon) \equiv \frac{1}{1-\Phi(-\mu_*/\sigma_*)}\phi\left(\frac{u-\mu_*}{\sigma_*}\right), \quad \mu_* = \frac{-\sigma_u^2\varepsilon}{\sigma^2},$$

$$\sigma_*^2 = \frac{\sigma_v^2\sigma_u^2}{\sigma^2}, \quad u \geq 0, \tag{11.4.33}$$

where $\sigma^2 = \sigma_u^2+\sigma_v^2$, $\lambda = \frac{\sigma_u}{\sigma_v}$, $\Phi(\cdot)$ is the standard normal distribution function and $\phi(\cdot)$ is the corresponding probability density function. Notice that this is the density of a normally distributed random variable *truncated* at zero with nonzero mean, μ_*. Thus, the mean of this random variable is given by

$$E(u_i|\varepsilon_i) = \mu_* + \sigma_*\frac{1}{1-\Phi(-\mu_*/\sigma_*)}\phi\left(\frac{-\mu_*}{\sigma_*}\right), \tag{11.4.34}$$

or

$$E(u_i|\varepsilon_i) = \sigma_*\left[\frac{\mu_*}{\sigma_*} + \frac{1}{1-\Phi(-\mu_*/\sigma_*)}\phi\left(\frac{-\mu_*}{\sigma_*}\right)\right]. \tag{11.4.35}$$

Now, noting that $-\frac{\mu_*}{\sigma_*} = \frac{\sigma_u^2 \varepsilon}{\sigma^2 \frac{\sigma_v \sigma_u}{\sigma}} = \frac{\sigma_u \varepsilon}{\sigma \sigma_v} = \frac{\varepsilon \lambda}{\sigma}$, we can write the conditional expectation as:

$$E(u_i|\varepsilon_i) = \frac{\sigma_v \sigma_u}{\sigma} \left[-\frac{\varepsilon_i \lambda}{\sigma} + \frac{\phi(\varepsilon_i \lambda/\sigma)}{1 - \Phi(\varepsilon_i \lambda/\sigma)} \right]. \tag{11.4.36}$$

Note that we can replace the true parameters in this last expression with their consistent estimates (e.g., obtained via ML or MOLS) and thus obtain an estimator for an *individual inefficiency*, conditional on statistical noise, for each observation i, $i \in \{1, \cdots, n\}$.

Recently, Horrace and Parmeter (2018) study a standard production frontier model, but deviate from two-sided shocks being distributed as normal, instead allowing for Laplace-type errors. The Laplace distribution has a different shape than the normal distribution and with this new shape, several interesting properties emerge surrounding the stochastic production frontier model, notably, the lack of a wrong skewness issue. Parmeter et al. (2017b), assuming access to determinants of inefficiency, demonstrate that distributional assumptions on inefficiency can be eschewed by writing the model in partly linear form after a mean correction in the spirit of Wang and Schmidt (2002). Such a correction provides a natural way to specify the heteroskedastic patterns often associated with the efficiency error that were first considered by Caudill et al. (1995). This offers a robust alternative to the stochastic frontier model to consider while avoiding one of its most commonly criticized assumptions. In their application to financing constraints of Taiwanese firms, Parmeter et al. (2017b) find substantial differences across parametrically specified models and the partly linear model. Parmeter and Zelenyuk (2018) further extend this model to the setting where the production frontier can also be nonparametrically specified. Finally, Parmeter et al. (2017b) propose discrete approximations to the standard parametric stochastic frontier model. Their work demonstrates that the distributional assumptions on the inefficiency term can be dispensed by taking on some finite sample bias. Their method leverages latent class mixture modeling, but using binomial distributions as opposed to the more commonly used normal classes. We will discuss the latent class model in more depth in Chapter 13.

11.4.3   Hypothesis Tests and Confidence Intervals

One of the major advantages of the stochastic frontier approach is that its framework allows for the application of statistical tests that are well known to empirical researchers. In particular, the hypothesis that there is no inefficiency can be naturally formulated as a one-sided test wherein $H_0 : \sigma_u^2 = 0$, or equivalently, $H_0 : \lambda := \sigma_u/\sigma_v = 0$, for $\sigma_v^2 > 0$ tested against the alternative hypothesis $H_1 : \sigma_u^2 > 0$. In order to test this hypothesis one can use the

ML estimate of λ and it's asymptotic variance (from the Fisher information matrix) and form the usual test statistic

$$\frac{\widehat{\lambda}}{se(\widehat{\lambda})} \xrightarrow{d} \mathcal{N}(0, 1). \tag{11.4.37}$$

However, this is a test that has significant problems as under the null hypothesis the parameter is on the boundary of the parameter space. This is a comparable problem to one addressed in the panel data literature when tests for the significance of the error components were first developed (see, for example, Breusch and Pagan, 1980; Chesher, 1984; Lee and Chesher, 1986; Kiefer, 1982). Coelli (1995) pointed out this problem and showed that standard t-type tests for the existence of inefficiency have poor size. He also showed in a series of Monte Carlo simulations that one-sided generalized likelihood-ratio tests appeared to perform best in terms of size and power. In such tests, the constrained (H_0) and unconstrained (H_1) values of the log-likelihood were calculated and the standard LR-test statistic constructed as:

$$LR_\lambda = -2[\ln(l(H_0)) - \ln(l(H_1))]. \tag{11.4.38}$$

The test statistic does not have a limiting distribution that is $\chi^2_{(1)}$ under the null hypothesis of $\lambda = 0$ but rather is a mixture of two Chi-squared distributions with 1 and 0 degrees of freedom, each weighted equally with weights equal to $\frac{1}{2}$. Thus the proper test statistic to use if one is testing for the presence of inefficiency is:

$$LR_\lambda \xrightarrow{d} \frac{1}{2}\chi^2_{(1)} + \frac{1}{2}\chi^2_{(0)}. \tag{11.4.39}$$

Another test for the presence of inefficiency is one based on the skewness of the composite errors ε. We will discuss this in much more depth in the next section when we introduce the bounded inefficiency model, but point out at this juncture that a well-defined test for skewness would involve the use of the third moments of the composite (OLS) errors for the re-parameterized SFM. The first of these tests is based on the statistic $\sqrt{b_1} := \frac{m_3}{m_2^{2/3}}$. This test has long been used in the statistics literature to test for skewness but the first SFA application appears to have been due to Schmidt and Lin (1984). The critical values for this test are not readily available in most statistical textbooks, but only in selected sources (e.g., D'Agostino and Pearson, 1973), which makes its application less convenient relative to other available tests.

Coelli (1995) has also made a strong case via Monte Carlo simulations that another test statistic that was often used in other contexts, referred to as the M3T statistic (Pagan and Hall, 1983) performs much better in finite samples.

It has higher power and is asymptotically normally distributed under the null of no skewness. The test statistic is given by:

$$M3T := \frac{m_3}{\sqrt{\frac{6m_2^3}{n}}} \xrightarrow{d} \mathcal{N}(0, 1). \tag{11.4.40}$$

The conclusion of this testing procedure is that if the null hypothesis of symmetry of the distribution of the composite errors is not rejected, then there is no need to resort to stochastic frontier analysis, as OLS (or GLS) may do the job. Although Coelli (1995) also reported that the power of this test is slightly less than the power of the one-sided generalized likelihood-ratio test, the test does not require maximum likelihood estimation and so is highly recommended before starting SFA estimation as the first step in the analysis.

The distribution of an estimate $(\widehat{u}_i)$ of $E(u_i|\varepsilon_i)$ is needed in order to construct confidence intervals for the firm inefficiencies in the classical cross-sectional (or time-series) ALS model. Much of the brief discussion below is based on Wang and Schmidt (2009), which in turn is based on earlier work by Horrace and Schmidt (1996). The estimate $\widehat{u}_i$ is of course a statistic since it is a function of ε_i, which is a random variable. In the cross-sectional (time-series) case, the conditioning expression is needed as we do not have a consistent estimate for u_i. As we shall see later, such an issue is not particularly relevant when we move to the panel setting, for in that case in most specifications of cross-sectionally and time-varying efficiencies we no longer need the conditioning distribution in order to construct a consistent estimate of firm-specific inefficiency. Thus, when large n and T asymptotics apply, we no longer need to rely on the Jondrow et al. (1982) estimate. As in Wang and Schmidt (2009), we do not consider the error in the estimation of β, although such additional sources of error can be addressed. This can be done with bootstrapping algorithms or by using standard transformations in random variables based on truncated series approximations of the nonlinear functions. Wang and Schmidt (2009) point out that the reason for treating the estimated parameters as known in the construction of the distribution of firm-specific inefficiency is that much more of the randomness in $E(u_i|\varepsilon_i)$ is due to ε_i than any additional errors due to the estimation of the parameters. In particular, the error in the former is $O_p(1)$ while the error in the latter is $O_p(1/\sqrt{n})$. It should be clear that the distribution of u_i and the distribution of the estimate of u_i based on the Jondrow et al. (1982) conditional mean $\widehat{u}_i = E(u_i|\widehat{\varepsilon}_i)$ are not the same under standard conditions. Wang and Schmidt (2009) point out that $\widehat{u}_i$ is a shrinkage of u_i towards its mean since the conditional expectation is less variable than its unconditional estimate if an optimal forecast is used on which to condition the inefficiency component in the composed error $v - u$ used in the ALS stochastic frontier. A similar point extends to the Pitt and Lee (1981) and the Battese and Coelli (1988, 1992, 1995) random effects panel data estimators of the stochastic frontier using a similar composed error structure. In their derivation of the distribution of $\widehat{u}_i$ and in a series of numerical simulations, Wang and Schmidt (2009) make it clear that using $\widehat{u}_i$ to test for the proper specification of the underlying inefficiency distribution of u_i is misguided. Only if $\sigma_v^2 \to 0$ (with fixed σ_u^2) will the two distributions converge, while when $\sigma_v^2 \to \infty$ (with fixed σ_u^2) the distribution of the estimated inefficiency $\widehat{u}_i$ degenerates to a point $E(u)$. Goodness-of-fit tests based on their derivations for the distribution of estimated (conditional) efficiency can be found in Wang et al. (2011). Horrace and Schmidt (1996, pp. 261–262) provide lower (L_i) and upper (U_i) bounds for a $(1 - \lambda)$-confidence interval for $TE_i|\varepsilon_i$. An alternative derivation that leads to an equivalent expression for the $(1 - \lambda)$-confidence interval for $TE_i|\varepsilon_i^*$ was developed by Bera and Sharma (1999). [11]

As a practical matter, when looking at means and variances of the inefficiency estimates we have discussed, one must characterize the distribution of the inefficiency for a firm at a point in time. To construct confidence intervals for u_i, one can use the methods discussed in Horrace and Schmidt (1996) and base the confidence interval on the distribution of inefficiency conditional on stochastic noise. Moreover, if one specifies the distribution of efficiency using a parametric panel stochastic frontier model, then it is straightforward to utilize the estimated distribution to simulate the moments of the distribution by standard numerical integration methods of the estimated densities given the estimated parameters and thus consistently estimate the mean and variance. This would allow one to test hypotheses and to generate confidence intervals for the efficiency estimates or rankings based on simulated quantiles or other approaches (see, for example, Horrace, 2005; Newson, 2006). [12]

Belotti et al. (2013), in their package on panel frontiers, have provided Stata code that utilizes methods based on the Horrace and Schmidt (1996, 2000) method for constructing confidence intervals for the conditional distribution of inefficiency given statistical noise. We will take up the panel frontier in more detail in Chapters 12 and 13 but we can anticipate things a bit here in regard to the distributions of panel estimates of the efficiency effects. What might one use for a general treatment to construct test statistics based on a point estimate of firm inefficiency in a panel data setting? If one is unwilling to make an assumption on the distributions of u and v in a panel, then the Schmidt and Sickles (1984) point estimate of inefficiency based on the within estimate of the effects (α_t), constructed as $\max_j\{\alpha_j\} - \alpha_j$, can be used and

---

[11] Simar and Wilson (2010) have also pursued the construction of confidence intervals but rather for $E(u|\varepsilon)$ instead of confidence intervals for $(u|\varepsilon)$ or the corresponding estimate of technical inefficiency, $1 - \exp(-u|\varepsilon)$.

[12] Horrace and Schmidt (1996) show the confidence intervals for inefficiencies in the panel data setting we pursue in Chapters 12 and 13 based on MLE or GLS. The random error components frontier model considered in Pitt and Lee (1981), Schmidt and Sickles (1984) and Battese and Coelli (1988) can also be constructed using a straightforward extension of the cross-sectional Jondrow et al. (1982) approach. We discuss this briefly in Chapter 12.

bootstrapped distributions can be constructed (Kim, et al., 2007) or standard central limit theorems can be utilized to approximate the asymptotic distributions for the inefficiency estimates. Marginal confidence intervals can be based on the constructions given in Kim and Schmidt (2008), while multiple comparisons require the use of methods detailed in Horrace and Schmidt (1996, 2000). In these latter two cases, however, a normality assumption is required on the distribution of the individual point estimates of inefficiency, leading to critical values drawn from a multivariate normal.

Neither Horrace and Schmidt (1996, 2000) nor Wang and Schmidt (2009) pursue issues involving the estimation error of β in their discussion of confidence intervals for the technical efficiency term $\widehat{u}_i = E(u_i|\varepsilon_i)$, a statistic that, although unbiased, is not consistent for the standard cross-sectional setting in which it was introduced. They point out that the actual calculation of the inefficiency estimate is based on the estimated residual $\widehat{\varepsilon}_i$, which is based on the estimates of β. They note as well that the randomness in $E(u_i|\varepsilon_i)$ is $O_p(1)$ while that of $\widehat{\beta}$ is $O_P(1/\sqrt{n})$ and thus is relatively unimportant in the construction of confidence intervals for the efficiency estimates.

Simar and Wilson (2010) and Wheat et al. (2014), on the other hand, focus on just such error in their studies of confidence intervals in the SFA model. Wheat et al. also develop what they refer to as minimum width prediction intervals instead of the two-sided intervals developed by Horrace and Schmidt (1996). These prediction intervals, in addition to being smaller than two-sided intervals, are also the highest posterior density (HDP) interval in Bayesian inference. The minimum width prediction interval takes advantage of the non-symmetry in inefficiency estimate and as they point out is also the one-sided interval considered by Taube (1988).

Wheat et al. (2014) develop their prediction intervals for the inefficiency estimate by simulating draws from the asymptotic distribution of the estimates of β while Simar and Wilson (2010) provide a bootstrap aggregating, or bagging algorithm based on draws from the estimated distribution of the model parameters to construct their prediction intervals. The explicit algorithms to construct these prediction intervals can be found in these two papers and we do not repeat them here.

11.4.4   The Zero Inefficiency Model

Kumbhakar et al. (2013) propose a zero inefficiency stochastic frontier (ZISF) model that can accommodate a sample including both efficient and inefficient firms. The authors derive the corresponding log-likelihood function to estimate observation-specific inefficiency. They also discuss testing for the presence of fully efficient firms and provide simulated and empirical examples to demonstrate applications for the model.

For the Cobb–Douglas production function their model takes the form

$$\ln(y_i) = \beta_0 + \beta_1 \ln(x_{i1}) + \ldots + \beta_N \ln(x_{iN}) + v_i - u_i, \quad i = 1, \ldots, n,$$
(11.4.41)

$$\varepsilon_i = v_i - u_i.$$
(11.4.42)

Again, v_i is random noise, and u_i denotes technical inefficiency. The authors assume some firms are fully efficient while others are inefficient, which is information that is not available to the econometrician. The goal is then to classify each firm as efficient or inefficient. To accomplish this, the authors formulate their ZISF model as

$$ZISF \longrightarrow \ln(y_i) = \beta_0 + \beta_1 \ln(x_{i1}) + \ldots + \beta_N \ln(x_{iN}) + v_i,$$
(11.4.43)

with probability p and

$$ZISF \longrightarrow \ln(y_i) = \beta_0 + \beta_1 \ln(x_{i1}) + \ldots + \beta_N \ln(x_{iN}) + v_i - u_i$$
(11.4.44)

with probability $(1 - p)$, where p is the probability of a firm being fully efficient.

Assuming $u_i \sim iid \, \mathcal{N}_+(0, \sigma_u^2)$ and $v_i \sim iid \, \mathcal{N}(0, \sigma_v^2)$, the density of the error term is given by

$$(p/\sigma_v)\phi(\varepsilon/\sigma_v) + (1 - p)\left[\frac{2}{\sigma}\phi\left(\frac{\varepsilon}{\sigma}\right)\Phi\left(\frac{-\varepsilon}{\sigma_0}\right)\right],$$
(11.4.45)

where $\phi(\cdot)$ and $\Phi(\cdot)$ are the pdf and cdf for the standard normal distribution, and $\lambda = \sigma_u/\sigma_v$, $\sigma^2 = \sigma_v^2 + \sigma_u^2$, and $\sigma_0 = \sigma/\lambda$. The authors choose an extension of the model that makes the probability of full efficiency a parametric function of observables

$$p_i = \frac{\exp(z_i'\gamma)}{1 + \exp(z_i'\gamma)}, \quad \text{or} \quad p_i = \Phi(z_i'\gamma), \quad i = 1, \ldots, n,$$
(11.4.46)

where z_i is an $m \times 1$ vector of exogenous variables influencing whether a firm is inefficient and γ is an $m \times 1$ vector of parameters.

To test for full efficiency, one needs more than a t-test since the null hypothesis of full efficiency lies on the boundary of the parameter space. To test $p = 1$, one can use the pseudo-likelihood ratio test

$$PLR = -2(L_N - L_{ZI}),$$
(11.4.47)

where L_N is the log-likelihood of the normal linear model and L_{ZI} is the log-likelihood of the ZISF model. Furthermore, one can show

$$\frac{\partial \ln f(\varepsilon)}{\partial p} = \frac{1}{f(\varepsilon)}\left[\sigma_v^{-1}\phi(\varepsilon/\sigma_v) - \frac{2}{\sigma}\phi(\varepsilon/\sigma_v)\Phi(-\varepsilon/\sigma_0)\right],$$
(11.4.48)

which has expectation zero under $p = 1$. The PLR test has an asymptotic distribution which is a 50–50 mixture of χ_0^2 and χ_1^2 distributions.[13] The conditional density of u given ε is zero with probability p and

---

[13] See Chen and Liang (2010).

$$\frac{\phi((u - \mu_*)/\sigma_*)}{\sigma_* \Phi(-\varepsilon/\sigma_0)}, \tag{11.4.49}$$

with probability $(1 - p)$, where $\sigma_*^2 = \frac{\sigma_v^2 \sigma_u^2}{\sigma_v^2 + \sigma_u^2} = \frac{\sigma_v^2 \sigma_u^2}{\sigma^2}$ and $\mu_* = -\varepsilon \sigma_*^2/\sigma_v^2 = -\varepsilon \sigma_u^2/\sigma^2$. The conditional mean estimator for u in the ZISF model is

$$E[u_i|\varepsilon_i] = (1 - p)\frac{\sigma_u^2}{\sigma_u^2 + \sigma_v^2}\left[\sigma_0 \frac{\phi(\varepsilon/\sigma_0)}{\Phi(-\varepsilon/\sigma_0)} - \varepsilon\right]. \tag{11.4.50}$$

11.4.5   The Stochastic Frontier Model as a Special Case of the Bounded Inefficiency Model

In a series of papers Qian and Sickles (2008), Almanidis and Sickles (2012), and Almanidis et al. (2014) pointed out that, not unlike the various nested functional forms we discussed in Chapter 6 or the various treatments for time-varying and cross-sectionally varying efficiency models we consider next in the following two chapters, a more general framework exists for analyzing the SFM. Such a general framework also elucidates the particular problems that incorrect skewness in the residuals of the SFM model can cause and also provides a more general identification strategy for such models.

Instead of allowing unbounded support for the distribution of the productive (cost) inefficiency term in the right (left) tail, the bounded efficiency model introduces an unobservable upper bound to inefficiencies or a lower bound to the efficiencies, referred to as the *inefficiency bound*. Such an inefficiency bound gives the parametric stochastic frontier model more appeal as a robust empirical vehicle for analyzing for firm performance on the grounds of economic and econometric theory. In fact, the empirical settings in which a bounded inefficiency support is the only reasonable specification would appear to be the norm, consistent with the implications from the Industrial/Organization literature on the dynamics of market structure and entry/exit (see, for example, Handbook chapters by Ackerberg et al., 2007; Reiss and Wolak, 2007).

The presence of inefficiency with unbounded support would seem to be the rarity, yet this is the assumption in the standard SFM. Competition would be expected to weed out extremely inefficient firms. The inefficiency bound is informative in many applications as it indicates how binding are the constraints of competition or supervision. It also can provide indirect measures of the strength of market power or the extent of a market niche. The inefficiency bound for the general stochastic frontier model can be used for gauging the tolerance for or ruthlessness against inefficient firms in a particular market or industry. Using this bound as the inefficient frontier, we also may define inverted efficiency scores in the same spirit of Inverted Data Envelopment Analysis IDEA described in Entani et al. (2002).

The bounded inefficiency model (BIM) also provides the researcher with an explanation for the causes of wrong skewness (Carree, 2002; Simar and Wilson, 2010). In work on productive efficiency, researchers have often found positive instead of negative skewness in their residuals using traditional SFA methods. This has two implications if the traditional stochastic frontier model is utilized. The first is that the model is not point identified (Waldman, 1982). The second is that the first problem may be addressed if one is able to acquire more data, as the improper skewness may be simply a finite sample problem (Simar and Wilson, 2010). The BIM, however, allows the distribution of the inefficiency term itself to be negatively skewed. Such a distributional pattern may occur when the tail of the distribution is truncated. The normal distribution, for example, is symmetric, but the doubly truncated normal distribution can have negative skewness when the right tail's truncation point is closer to the mode than the left tail's truncation point. Hafner et al. (2016) have recently provided other generalization of the efficiency distributions to address the problem of wrong skewness. Horrace and Wright (2017) also have recently generalized the results of Waldman (1982) for the normal–half-normal stochastic frontier model using the theory of the Dirac delta (Dirac, 1930), and distribution-free conditions are established to ensure a stationary point in the likelihood as the variance of the inefficiency distribution tends to zero. Stability of the stationary point and "wrong skew" results are derived or simulated for common parametric assumptions on the model. They find that all specifications of the parametric model with normal errors possess this stationary point, so many models are observationally equivalent as the inefficiency variance goes to zero. Stability must be explored on a case by case basis. Other distributions considered by Qian and Sickles (2008), Almanidis and Sickles (2012), and Almanidis et al. (2014) (AQS) to address the "skewness" problem are the truncated half-normal distribution and the truncated exponential distribution. They discuss both local and global identifiability conditions as well as point and set identification and also discuss in depth both method of moments and maximum likelihood estimators of the bounded stochastic frontier production function. We briefly outline their models and estimators in the next section.

11.4.5.1 The Model

The bounded inefficiency model nests the canonical SFM in that u_i can have bounded support from both above and from below. The lower bound in inefficiency is of course zero. The lower bound of inefficiency identifies the frontier on average. If the upper bound on inefficiency is set at some value, say B, then a generalization of the ALS model would have u_i distributed as

$$f_u(u) = \frac{\frac{1}{\sigma_u}\phi(\frac{u-\mu}{\sigma_u})}{\Phi(\frac{B-\mu}{\sigma_u}) - \Phi(\frac{-\mu}{\sigma_u})} 1_{[0,\,B]}(u), \quad \sigma_u > 0, \ B > 0. \quad (11.4.51)$$

Here $\Phi(\cdot)$ and $\phi(\cdot)$ are the standardized normal distribution and density functions and $1_{[0,\,B]}$ is the usual indicator function. When $B \rightarrow \infty$ the doubly truncated normal becomes the usual truncated normal distribution. When $\mu = 0$ and $B \rightarrow \infty$ the doubly truncated distribution becomes the half-normal. When $\mu = 0$ the doubly truncated normal distribution becomes the truncated half-normal distribution. The doubly truncated normal distribution can have positive or negative skewness, depending on the parameter B.

AQS provide detailed properties for these generalizations of the canonical stochastic frontier model. A variety of results from Almanidis et al. (2014) for the truncated normal, the truncated half-normal model, and the exponential model that are useful in reporting efficiency measures in such models are reproduced in the table below. In particular, we reproduce the expressions for the conditional mean of the error given the stochastic disturbance that is the typical estimate used for firm inefficiency in cross-sectional studies. This term, $(E[u_i|\varepsilon_i])$, can be shown to be the best predictor of the inefficiency term u_i under their assumptions.[14]

11.4.5.2   Method of Moments Estimation

Olson et al. (1980) considered the method of moments (MOM) estimator for the ALS model and we can easily modify their approach to estimate the BIM. Moreover, the MOM estimates can also be used in a one-step Newton-Raphson estimator (the so-called "method scoring" introduced by Rothenberg and Leenders (1964)). The approach introduced by Olson et al. (1980) has been referred to as the modified corrected least squares (MOLS) estimator to distinguish it from one used to identify inefficiency from a deterministic frontier, the corrected ordinary least squares (COLS) estimator we discussed earlier in this chapter. The estimator utilizes two steps. One first estimates the frontier production function using ordinary least squares or instrumental variables if endogeneity may be an issue with potentially endogenous inputs. Only the constant term cannot be consistently estimated by a least squares or instrumental variables regression. The second step uses the distributional assumptions on the residual to specify the moments and the moment conditions are used to identify the parameters.

To see how this can be accomplished, rewrite the SFM as a standard Cobb–Douglas production frontier

$$\ln y_i = (\beta_0 - E(u_i)) + \sum_{j=1}^{N} \beta_j \ln x_{i,\,j} + \varepsilon_i^*, i = 1, \ldots, n, \quad (11.4.52)$$

where $\varepsilon_i^* = \varepsilon_i + E(u_i)$. The error term ε_i^* has zero mean and we maintain the assumption that the regressors are weakly exogenous. Hence OLS yields consistent estimates for ε_i^* and the β_j, $j = 1, \ldots, N$. We can match the sample

---

[14] We thank Springer Publishing Co. for allowing us to reproduce this table from the original Almanidis et al. (2014) study.

Table 11.1 *Key results.*

$f(\varepsilon)$ is the density of $\varepsilon = v - u$, $\mathbb{E}(u|\varepsilon)$ is the conditional mean of u given ε, and $f(u|\varepsilon)$ is the conditional density of u given ε. $\phi(\cdot)$, and $\Phi(\cdot)$ are the pdf and cdf of the standard normal distribution, respectively. And $\mathbf{1}_{[0,B]}(\cdot)$ is an indicator function.

Model	$f(\varepsilon)$	$\mathbb{E}(u|\varepsilon)$	$f(u|\varepsilon)$
Doubly truncated normal	$\left[\Phi\left(\frac{B-\mu}{\sigma_u}\right)-\Phi\left(\frac{-\mu}{\sigma_u}\right)\right]^{-1}\cdot\left[\frac{1}{\sigma}\phi\left(\frac{\mu+\varepsilon}{\sigma}\right)\right]\cdot$ $\left[\Phi\left(\frac{(B+\varepsilon)\lambda+(B-\mu)\lambda^{-1}}{\sigma}\right)-\Phi\left(\frac{\varepsilon\lambda-\mu\lambda^{-1}}{\sigma}\right)\right]$ $\sigma=\sqrt{\sigma_u^2+\sigma_v^2},\ \lambda=\sigma_u/\sigma_v$	$\mu_*+\sigma_*\dfrac{\phi\left(-\frac{\mu_*}{\sigma_*}\right)-\phi\left(\frac{B-\mu_*}{\sigma_*}\right)}{\Phi\left(\frac{B-\mu_*}{\sigma_*}\right)-\Phi\left(-\frac{\mu_*}{\sigma_*}\right)}$ $\mu_*=\dfrac{\mu\sigma_v^2-\varepsilon\sigma_u^2}{\sigma^2},\ \sigma_*=\dfrac{\sigma_u\sigma_v}{\sigma}$	$\dfrac{\frac{1}{\sigma_*}\phi\left(\frac{u-\mu_*}{\sigma_*}\right)}{\Phi\left(\frac{B-\mu_*}{\sigma_*}\right)-\Phi\left(-\frac{\mu_*}{\sigma_*}\right)}\mathbf{1}_{[0,B]}(u)$
Truncated half-normal	$\left[\Phi\left(\frac{B}{\sigma_u}\right)-1/2\right]^{-1}\cdot\frac{1}{\sigma}\phi\left(\frac{\varepsilon}{\sigma}\right)\cdot$ $\left[\Phi\left(\frac{(B+\varepsilon)\lambda+B\lambda^{-1}}{\sigma}\right)-\Phi\left(\frac{\varepsilon\lambda}{\sigma}\right)\right]$	$\mu_*+\sigma_*\dfrac{\phi\left(-\frac{\mu_*}{\sigma_*}\right)-\phi\left(\frac{B-\mu_*}{\sigma_*}\right)}{\Phi\left(\frac{B-\mu_*}{\sigma_*}\right)-\Phi\left(-\frac{\mu_*}{\sigma_*}\right)}$ $\mu_*=-\dfrac{\varepsilon\sigma_u^2}{\sigma^2},\ \sigma_*=\dfrac{\sigma_u\sigma_v}{\sigma}$	$\dfrac{\frac{1}{\sigma_*}\phi\left(\frac{u-\mu_*}{\sigma_*}\right)}{\Phi\left(\frac{B-\mu_*}{\sigma_*}\right)-\Phi\left(-\frac{\mu_*}{\sigma_*}\right)}\mathbf{1}_{[0,B]}(u)$
Truncated exponential	$\dfrac{e^{\frac{\varepsilon}{\sigma_u}+\frac{\sigma_v^2}{2\sigma_u^2}}\left[\Phi\left(\frac{B+\varepsilon}{\sigma_v}+\frac{\sigma_v}{\sigma_u}\right)-\Phi\left(\frac{\varepsilon}{\sigma_v}+\frac{\sigma_v}{\sigma_u}\right)\right]}{\sigma_u\left(1-e^{-B/\sigma_u}\right)}$	$\mu_*+\sigma_v\dfrac{\phi\left(-\frac{\mu_*}{\sigma_v}\right)-\phi\left(\frac{B-\mu_*}{\sigma_v}\right)}{\Phi\left(\frac{B-\mu_*}{\sigma_v}\right)-\Phi\left(-\frac{\mu_*}{\sigma_v}\right)}$ $\mu_*=-\varepsilon-\dfrac{\sigma_v^2}{\sigma_u}$	$\dfrac{\frac{1}{\sigma_v}\phi\left(\frac{u-\mu_*}{\sigma_v}\right)}{\Phi\left(\frac{B-\mu_*}{\sigma_v}\right)-\Phi\left(-\frac{\mu_*}{\sigma_v}\right)}\mathbf{1}_{[0,B]}(u)$

Reprinted by permission from Springer Nature: Springer, Festschrift in Honor of Peter Schmidt: Econometric Methods and Applications by Sickles, R. C. and Horrace, W. C., editors (2014).

moments based on $\widehat{\varepsilon}_i^*$ with expressions for the population moments and thus estimate the parameters of the distribution of ε_i^*.

11.4.5.3 Maximum Likelihood Estimation

Maximum likelihood estimation is based on the log-likelihood for the doubly truncated normal. Derivations for the truncated half-normal and the truncated exponential as well as the scores for the three models can be found in Almanidis et al. (2014). The log-likelihood is

$$\ell(\beta, \lambda, \sigma^2, \mu, B \,|x_1, \ldots, x_n; y_1, \ldots, y_n) =$$

$$-n \ln \left[\Phi\left(\frac{B - \mu}{\sigma_u(\sigma, \lambda)}\right) - \Phi\left(\frac{-\mu}{\sigma_u(\sigma, \lambda)}\right) \right] \tag{11.4.53}$$

$$-n \ln \sigma - \frac{n}{2} \ln(2\pi) - \sum_{i=1}^{n} \frac{(\varepsilon_i + \mu)^2}{2\sigma^2}$$

$$+ \sum_{i=1}^{n} \ln \left\{ \Phi\left(\frac{(B + \varepsilon_i)\lambda + (B - \mu)\lambda^{-1}}{\sigma}\right) - \Phi\left(\frac{\varepsilon_i\lambda - \mu\lambda^{-1}}{\sigma}\right) \right\},$$

where $\varepsilon_i = \ln y - \beta_0 - \sum_{k=1}^{K} \ln x_{i,k}\beta_k$ and $\sigma_u(\sigma, \lambda) = \sigma/\sqrt{1 + 1/\lambda^2}$ and where $\lambda = \sigma_u/(\sigma_u^2 + \sigma_v^2)^{1/2}$. Almanidis et al. (2014) also use a reparameterization of the bound parameter B that makes it much easier to address numerical issues and prove the asymptotic normality of their estimates. They use the reparameterization $\hat{B} = \exp(-B)$. The estimate of the composite error term is $\hat{\varepsilon}_i = \ln y_i - \hat{\beta}_0 - \sum_k \ln x_{i,k}\hat{\beta}_k$, $i = 1, \cdots, n$ and from this they estimate the inefficiency term u_i using the formula for $E(u_i|\varepsilon_i)$ found in Almanidis et al. (2014). Let $\beta = (\beta_0, \beta_1, \ldots, \beta_k)'$. In their calculation of the scores, Almanidis et al. use the γ-parameterization in their derivation of the scores, where $\gamma = \sigma_u^2/\sigma^2$ and thus $\gamma(\lambda) = \lambda^2/(1 + \lambda^2)$. The scores for the log-likelihood are given by:

$$\frac{\partial \ell}{\partial \beta} = \sum_{i=1}^{n} \frac{(\varepsilon_i + \mu) \ln(x_i)}{\sigma^2} + \frac{\sqrt{\gamma/(1 - \gamma)}}{\sigma} \sum_{i=1}^{n} x_i \frac{\phi(z_{4i}) - \phi(z_{3i})}{\Phi(z_{3i}) - \Phi(z_{4i})},$$

$$\tag{11.4.54}$$

$$\frac{\partial \ell}{\partial \lambda} = \frac{n}{\gamma} \frac{[z_1\phi(z_1) - z_2\phi(z_2)]}{\Phi(z_1) - \Phi(z_2)}$$

$$+ \frac{1}{\sigma} \sum_{i=1}^{n} \frac{1}{\Phi(z_{3i}) - \Phi(z_{4i})} \{((-\ln(\tilde{B}) + \varepsilon_i) \frac{1}{(1 - \gamma)^2} \sqrt{(1 - \gamma)/\gamma}$$

$$+ (\ln(\tilde{B}) + \mu) \frac{1}{\gamma^2} \sqrt{\gamma/(1 - \gamma)})\phi(z_{3i})$$

$$- (\varepsilon_i \frac{1}{(1 - \gamma)^2} \sqrt{(1 - \gamma)/\gamma} - \mu\lambda \frac{1}{\gamma^2} \sqrt{\gamma/(1 - \gamma)})\phi(z_{4i})\}$$

$$\tag{11.4.55}$$

$$\frac{\partial \ell}{\partial \sigma^2} = \frac{n}{2\sigma^2} \frac{[(z_1\phi(z_1) - z_2\phi(z_2)]}{\Phi(z_1) - \Phi(z_2)} - \frac{n}{2\sigma^2} + \sum_{i=1}^{n} \frac{(\varepsilon_i + \mu)^2}{2\sigma^4}$$

$$+ \frac{1}{2\sigma^2} \sum_{i=1}^{n} \frac{z_{4i}\phi(z_{4i}) - z_{3i}\phi(z_{3i})}{\Phi(z_{3i}) - \Phi(z_{4i})}, \tag{11.4.56}$$

$$\frac{\partial \ell}{\partial \mu} = \frac{n}{\sigma\sqrt{\gamma}} \frac{\phi(z_1) - \phi(z_2)}{\Phi(z_1) - \Phi(z_2)} - \sum_{i=1}^{n} \frac{(\varepsilon_i + \mu)}{\sigma^2} + \frac{\sqrt{(1-\gamma)/\gamma}}{\sigma}$$

$$\sum_{i=1}^{n} \frac{\phi(z_{4i}) - \phi(z_{3i})}{\Phi(z_{3i}) - \Phi(z_{4i})}, \tag{11.4.57}$$

$$\frac{\partial \ell}{\partial \tilde{B}} = \frac{n}{\tilde{B}\sigma\sqrt{\gamma}} \frac{\phi(z_1)}{\Phi(z_1) - \Phi(z_2)} - \frac{1}{\tilde{B}\sigma\sqrt{(1-\gamma)\gamma}} \sum_{i=1}^{n} \frac{\phi(z_{3i})}{\Phi(z_{3i}) - \Phi(z_{3i})}, \tag{11.4.58}$$

where $z_1 = -\frac{(\ln(\tilde{B}) + \mu)}{\sigma\sqrt{\gamma}}$, $z_2 = \frac{-\mu}{\sigma\sqrt{\gamma}}$, $z_{3i} = -\frac{(\ln(\tilde{B}) - \varepsilon_i)\sqrt{\gamma/(1-\gamma)} + (\ln(\tilde{B}) + \mu)\sqrt{(1-\gamma)/\gamma}}{\sigma}$, $z_{4i} = \frac{\varepsilon_i(\sqrt{\gamma/(1-\gamma)}) - \mu\sqrt{(1-\gamma)/\gamma}}{\sigma}$, and ε_i is given above.

11.4.5.4 The Skewness Issue

The stochastic frontier model without bounded inefficiency and with the composed error term $(-u + v)$ should have negative skewness if the technical inefficiency term u has only positive support. However, it may be the case in applied work that the OLS residuals show positive skewness. The existence of positively skewed residuals may be due to several different factors. First, as samples are just that, one may have drawn a non-representative random sample when the underlying model does have the correct population skewness (see Carree, 2002; Greene, 2007; Simar and Wilson, 2010). One suggestion to this problem is to go out and get a larger sample, or at least a different one that does not present this particular problem. If one wishes to continue to use the canonical stochastic frontier model in this situation, then there are standard default options in most programs to address this problem. One simply treats all of the firms in the sample as fully efficient by setting the variance $\sigma_u^2 = 0$ and proceed with OLS as indicated in Olson et al. (1980) and Waldman (1982). Simar and Wilson (2010) suggest a bagging method to overcome the inferential problems when a half-normal distribution for inefficiencies when skewness is positive instead of negative. However, positive skewness is perfectly consistent with a model specified by bounded inefficiency.

The skewness of the doubly truncated normal distribution is given by $S_u = \frac{2\eta_0^3 - \eta_0(3\eta_1 + 1) + \eta_2}{(1 - \eta_0^2 + \eta_1)^{3/2}}$, where $\eta_k \equiv \frac{\xi_1^k\phi(\xi_1) - \xi_2^k\phi(\xi_2)}{\Phi(\xi_2) - \Phi(\xi_1)}$, $k = 0, 1, \ldots, 4$, and $\xi_1 =$

$\frac{-\mu}{\sigma_u}$, and $\xi_2 = \frac{B-\mu}{\sigma_u}$. As η_0, the inverse Mill's ratio, is given by $\sqrt{2/\pi}$ in the half-normal model, and ξ_1 and ξ_2 are the lower and upper truncation points of the standard normal density, it is clear that when $B > 2\mu$, $S_u > 0$, and when $B < 2\mu$, $S_u < 0$. Since $B > 0$ by definition, only when $\mu > 0$ can u_i be negatively skewed. As μ increases, the range of values taken by B that are consistent with a u_i that is negatively skewed increases. If we begin with a normal distribution with $\mu \to \infty$ that is truncated at zero and $B > 0$ then there is essentially no truncation on the left at all. Any finite truncation on the right gives rise to a negative skewness. That is not the case for the truncated half-normal model ($\mu = 0$) and the truncated exponential model, wherein the skewness of u_i is always positive.

Almanidis et al. (2014) use Monte Carlo simulations to show that the BIM generalization of the canonical SFM is capable of generating residuals from a production-based representation of technology much more often than would be the case with the traditional SFM (Simar and Wilson, 2010). Almanidis et al. (2014) note that skewness is not necessarily a sample size issue, since when $B < 2\mu$ the proportion of samples with positive skewness converges to one. One implication of their analysis is that the finding of skewness at variance with the stochastic frontier model with no lower bound in inefficiency may be a finding that the BIM model should in fact be consistent with the underlying DGP and that, if a researcher finds a skewness statistic with the "wrong" sign, then she may erroneously reject her model. The bounded inefficiency model, the doubly truncated normal model in particular, avoids this problem.

11.4.5.5   Identification and Estimation

Almanidis and Sickles (2012) and Almanidis et al. (2014) discuss in depth the set identification of the parameters of the bounded inefficiency model. They first analyze identification of the parameters describing the technology. Next, they examine the identification of the distributional parameters of the bounded inefficiency term using the information contained in the distribution of the residual. The identification conditions for the first part are well known and are satisfied in most of the cases. Identification of the distributional parameters of the bounded inefficiency model is not as straightforward. Their approach is to partition the distributional parameters into the mutually exclusive sets I_1, I_2, I_3, and I_4, defined as

$$I_1 \equiv \{(\mu, B) | \mu \leq 0, B > 0\},$$
$$I_2 \equiv \{(\mu, B) | \mu > 0, B \in (0, 2\mu)\},$$
$$I_3 \equiv \{(\mu, B) | B = 2\mu > 0\},$$
$$I_4 \equiv \{(\mu, B) | \mu > 0, B > 2\mu\}. \tag{11.4.59}$$

They note that the line $I_3 \equiv \{\mu, B) | B = 2\mu > 0\}$ corresponds to the case in which $B = 2\mu$ and the skewness measure $\psi_3 = 0$. For I_3 the implicit function theorem that they utilize to examine the invertibility of the mappings from sample moments to the distributional parameters is not applicable. However, their simulation results show that even when the true values of B and μ satisfy the relationship $B = 2\mu$, both B and μ appear to be consistently estimated. If one views the doubly truncated normal model as a collection of different sub-models corresponding to the different domains of parameters, then they show that conditions appear to indicate that each sub-model may be globally identified. They also note that on the line of $\{(\mu, B)|\mu = 0, B > 0\} \subset I_1$, the doubly truncated normal model reduces to the truncated half-normal model and that for the sub-model corresponding to the line I_2 positive skewness is displayed as sample size continues to grow.

11.5 CONCLUDING REMARKS

In this chapter we have concentrated on the intellectual developments that lead to the Canonical Stochastic Frontier Model. We have discussed this model at length and have also considered a generalized form based on the possibility that the stochastic frontier has an upper (lower) bound on the inefficiency (efficiency). The model parameters of the more general bounded inefficiency model can be estimated by maximum likelihood, including the inefficiency bound. We have also pointed out that a standard problem with the Canonical Stochastic Frontier Model, known in the literature as the "wrong" skewness problem, can be avoided when both lower and uppers bounds are taken into account.

However, we should not ignore the possibility that regression-based alternatives such as corrected least squares may have advantages in estimating the deep parameters of the technology nor the advantages provided by different types of data, such as panel data and frontiers based on them which we develop in the following chapter. The following quote from Olson et al. (1980) is instructive and appears somewhat timeless: "the corrected least squares estimator [with the ALS error structure] does quite well, in most cases, and is thus a reasonable alternative to maximum likelihood."

The SFA model has some technical complications and modeling drawbacks as MLE requires specification of the density of $\varepsilon_i = v_i - u_i$, which may be difficult for certain one-sided distributions. Moreover, for cross-section (or time-series) applications, unlike in the full frontier model, point estimates of inefficiency for each observation are not consistent. However, Jondrow et al. (1982) pointed out that $E(u_i|v_i - u_i)$ can be consistently estimated. This conditional expectation of technical inefficiency for a particular observation is contaminated by non-systematic elements that impact output but are uncorrelated with (in)efficiency *per se*. Although the Jondrow et al. (1982) estimator has been the mainstay of stochastic frontier applications, it is hampered by strong parametric distributional assumptions, which are needed to disentangle the moments of the two errors, by strong assumptions about the independence of inefficiency levels and levels of certain inputs, and cannot consistently estimate observation specific efficiency levels. Robustness of estimates to violations of these strong assumptions is also questionable. In the next two chapters we move to a panel data setting and introduce the panel stochastic frontier to mitigate these particular problems with the Canonical SFM.

11.6 EXERCISES

1. The stochastic frontier production model is distinguished by the presence of a nonsymmetric error term, which is the result of the linear combination of a symmetric error for idiosyncratic measurement error in the model and a one-sided error that represents the latent technical inefficiency in production. What might be the source of other unobserved components whose distribution is one-sided that could explain the nonsymmetric residuals of a standard production function estimated by standard regression techniques?

2. Derive the expression for the conditional mean of the stochastic frontier latent inefficiency measure conditional on the idiosyncratic error when the distribution of inefficiency is truncated normal and the distribution of the idiosyncratic error is normal.

3. The stochastic frontier production model is assumed to take on the following general form

$$y_i = \psi(x_i|\beta)\exp(\varepsilon_i),$$

where

$$\varepsilon_i = v_i - u_i, \quad i = 1, \cdots, n.$$

The variables are measured in level form and the function $\psi(x_i|\beta)$ can be any convenient parametric function. Instead of the model above you estimate the model

$$y = \psi(x_i|\beta) + \varepsilon_i.$$

Under suitable assumptions about the distribution of the composed error terms, can you establish any relationship between the estimated average technical efficiency for the two specifications?

4. The use of third moments to identify the parameters in the stochastic frontier model using the method of moments estimator of Olson et al. (1980) and Almanidis et al. (2014) has been criticized for requiring identifying information that may not be reliable in finite samples. Perform a small Monte Carlo experiment that examines the robustness of the conditional mean estimator based on COLS to deviations in the true skewness of the distribution of the composed error of 20 percent and 50 percent.

5. Explain how you may test for the presence of technical efficiency in SFA and why the test under the null hypothesis of technical efficiency is not well defined and leads to a degenerate statistic under the null

hypothesis. Discuss the similarities of this statistical problem with those faced in the panel data literature when testing for the presence of random effects.

11.7 APPENDIX

11.7.1   Derivation of $E(\varepsilon_i)$

Let $\varepsilon_i = \exp(-u_i)$. Recall that

$$E(\exp(-u)) = \int_0^\infty \exp(-u)G(u; \mu)du$$

$$= \int_0^\infty \exp(-u)\frac{1}{\Gamma(\mu)}u^{\mu-1}\exp(-u)du.$$

Collecting like terms, we get

$$E(\exp(-u)) = \int_0^\infty \frac{1}{\Gamma(\mu)}u^{\mu-1}\exp(-2u)du$$

$$= \frac{1}{\Gamma(\mu)}\int_0^\infty u^{\mu-1}\exp(-2u)du.$$

Now, let $y = 2u$; therefore, $u = \frac{y}{2}$ and $du = \frac{1}{2}dy$. Making the substitutions for u and du into the integral, we obtain

$$E(\exp(-u)) = \frac{1}{\Gamma(\mu)}\int_0^\infty \left(\frac{y}{2}\right)^{\mu-1}\exp(-y)\frac{1}{2}dy$$

$$= \left(\frac{1}{2}\right)^\mu \frac{1}{\Gamma(\mu)}\int_0^\infty y^{\mu-1}\exp(-y)dy$$

$$= \left(\frac{1}{2}\right)^\mu$$

$$= E(\varepsilon) = 2^{-\mu}$$

since $\int_0^\infty y^{\mu-1}\exp(-y)dy = \Gamma(\mu)$.

11.7.2   Derivation of the Moments of a Half-Normal Random Variable

If $u_i \sim |\mathcal{N}(0, \sigma_u^2)|$ then it has a probability density function given by

$$f_u(u) = \frac{2}{\sqrt{2\pi}\sigma_u}\exp\left\{-\frac{1}{2}\frac{u^2}{\sigma_u^2}\right\} = 2\frac{1}{\sigma_u}\phi\left(\frac{u}{\sigma_u}\right), \qquad 0 \le u \le +\infty.$$

The moment-generating function of this variable is given by

$$E[\exp(tu)] = \int_0^\infty \exp(tu)f_u(u)du.$$

We then have:

$$
\begin{aligned}
m(t) &= 2 \int_0^\infty \exp(tu) \frac{1}{\sqrt{2\pi}\sigma_u} \exp\left\{-\frac{(u)^2}{2\sigma_u^2}\right\} du \\
&= 2 \int_0^\infty \frac{1}{\sqrt{2\pi}\sigma_u} \exp\left\{\frac{-u^2 + 2\sigma_u^2 tu + (t\sigma_u^2)^2 - (t\sigma_u^2)^2}{2\sigma_u^2}\right\} du \\
&= 2 \int_0^\infty \frac{1}{\sqrt{2\pi}\sigma_u} \exp\left\{\frac{-u^2 + 2\sigma_u^2 tu - (t\sigma_u^2)^2}{2\sigma_u^2} + \frac{(t\sigma_u^2)^2}{2\sigma_u^2}\right\} du \\
&= 2 \int_0^\infty \frac{1}{\sqrt{2\pi}\sigma_u} \exp\left\{\frac{-u^2 + 2\sigma_u^2 tu - (t\sigma_u^2)^2}{2\sigma_u^2}\right\} du \, \exp\left\{\frac{(t\sigma_u^2)^2}{2\sigma_u^2}\right\}.
\end{aligned}
$$

Letting $z = \frac{(u - t\sigma_u^2)}{\sigma_u}$, we then have $du = \sigma_u dz$, then $u = 0 \implies z = -t\sigma_u$, $u \to \infty \implies z \to \infty$ and we have:

$$
\begin{aligned}
m(t) &= 2 \int_{-t\sigma_u}^\infty \frac{1}{\sqrt{2\pi}\sigma_u} \exp\left\{-\frac{1}{2}z^2\right\} \sigma_u dz \, \exp\left\{\frac{t^2\sigma_u^2}{2}\right\} \\
&= 2\left[1 - \int_{-\infty}^{-t\sigma_u} \frac{1}{\sqrt{2\pi}} \exp\left\{-\frac{1}{2}z^2\right\} \right] dz \, \exp\left\{\frac{t^2\sigma_u^2}{2}\right\} \\
&= 2\left[1 - \Phi(-t\sigma_u)\right] \exp\left\{\frac{t^2\sigma_u^2}{2}\right\} \\
&= 2\Phi(t\sigma_u) \exp\left\{\frac{t^2\sigma_u^2}{2}\right\},
\end{aligned}
$$

where $\Phi(z)$ is the standard normal distribution function with corresponding probability density function $\phi(z)$. Given the moment generating function $m(t)$, we can then generate any moment m_k' for the random variable. Specifically, the first moment is given by:

$$
\begin{aligned}
\left.\frac{dm(t)}{dt}\right|_{t=0} = m_1' &= \left.\frac{d[2\Phi(t\sigma_u)]}{dt} \exp\left\{\frac{t^2\sigma_u^2}{2}\right\} + 2\Phi(t\sigma_u) \frac{d\left[\exp\left\{\frac{t^2\sigma_u^2}{2}\right\}\right]}{dt}\right|_{t=0} \\
&= \left.2\phi(t\sigma_u)\sigma_u \exp\left\{\frac{t^2\sigma_u^2}{2}\right\} + 2\Phi(t\sigma_u)\exp\left\{\frac{t^2\sigma_u^2}{2}\right\} t\sigma_u^2\right|_{t=0} \\
&= \left.2\frac{\sigma_u}{\sqrt{2\pi}} + 2\Phi(t\sigma_u)\exp\left\{\frac{t^2\sigma_u^2}{2}\right\} t\sigma_u^2\right|_{t=0} \\
&= 2\frac{\sigma_u}{\sqrt{2\pi}} + 2\Phi(0)\exp\{0\} \cdot 0 \cdot \sigma_u^2 \\
&= E(u) = \sqrt{\frac{2}{\pi}}\,\sigma_u.
\end{aligned}
$$

Similarly, the second moment (around zero) is given by:

$$
\left.\frac{d^2 m(t)}{dt^2}\right|_{t=0} = m'_2
$$

$$
= 2 \frac{d[\Phi(t\sigma_u)]}{dt} \exp\left\{\frac{t^2\sigma_u^2}{2}\right\} t\sigma_u^2
$$

$$
+ 2\Phi(t\sigma_u)\frac{d[\exp\{\frac{t^2\sigma_u^2}{2}\}]}{dt} t\sigma_u^2 + 2\Phi(t\sigma_u)\exp\left\{\frac{t^2\sigma_u^2}{2}\right\}\frac{d[t\sigma_u^2]}{dt}\Bigg|_{t=0}
$$

$$
= 2\phi(t\sigma_u)\sigma_u \exp\left\{\frac{t^2\sigma_u^2}{2}\right\} t\sigma_u^2 + 2\Phi(t\sigma_u)\exp\left\{\frac{t^2\sigma_u^2}{2}\right\}(t\sigma_u^2)t\sigma_u^2
$$

$$
+ 2\Phi(t\sigma_u)\exp\left\{\frac{t^2\sigma_u^2}{2}\right\}\sigma_u^2\Bigg|_{t=0}
$$

$$
= 2\Phi(0)\exp\{0\}\sigma_u^2 = 2(1/2) \cdot 1 \cdot \sigma_u^2
$$

$$
= \sigma_u^2.
$$

The variance is then given by:

$$
m_2 = m'_2 - (m'_1)^2 = \sigma_u^2 - \left(\sqrt{\frac{2}{\pi}}\sigma_u\right)^2 = \left(\frac{\pi}{\pi} - \frac{2}{\pi}\right)\sigma_u^2 = Var(u)
$$

$$
= \left(\frac{\pi - 2}{\pi}\right)\sigma_u^2.
$$

11.7.3 Derivation of the Distribution of the Stochastic Frontier Normal–Half-Normal Composed Error

Consider the distributions of the random variables that make up the stochastic frontier composed error $\varepsilon = v - u$: $v_i \sim \mathcal{N}(0, \sigma_v^2)$ and $u_i \sim |\mathcal{N}(0, \sigma_u^2)|$, i.e.,

$$
f_v(v) = \frac{1}{\sqrt{2\pi}\sigma_v}\exp\left\{-\frac{1}{2}\frac{v^2}{\sigma_v^2}\right\} = \frac{1}{\sigma_v}\phi\left(\frac{v}{\sigma_v}\right), \quad -\infty \le v \le +\infty,
$$

$$
f_u(u) = \frac{2}{\sqrt{2\pi}\sigma_u}\exp\left\{-\frac{1}{2}\frac{u^2}{\sigma_u^2}\right\} = 2\frac{1}{\sigma_u}\phi\left(\frac{u}{\sigma_u}\right), \quad 0 \le u \le +\infty,
$$

where $\phi(\cdot)$ stands for the standard normal probability density. We denote the distribution function for the standard normal density as $\Phi(\cdot)$. Here we show that

$$
f_\varepsilon(\varepsilon) = \frac{2}{\sigma}\phi\left(\frac{\varepsilon}{\sigma}\right)\left[1 - \Phi\left(\frac{\varepsilon\lambda}{\sigma}\right)\right], \quad -\infty \le \varepsilon \le +\infty.
$$

To do this we must first find the joint density of v and u:

$$f_{vu}(v,u) = f_v(v)f_u(u) = \frac{1}{\sqrt{2\pi}\,\sigma_v}\exp\left\{-\frac{1}{2}\frac{v^2}{\sigma_v^2}\right\}\frac{2}{\sqrt{2\pi}\,\sigma_u}\exp\left\{-\frac{1}{2}\frac{u^2}{\sigma_u^2}\right\}$$

$$= \frac{1}{\sqrt{2\pi}\,\sigma_v}\frac{2}{\sqrt{2\pi}\,\sigma_u}\exp\left\{-\frac{1}{2}\frac{v^2}{\sigma_v^2}-\frac{1}{2}\frac{u^2}{\sigma_u^2}\right\}.$$

Next express v in terms of ε and u, thus getting the joint distribution of ε and u (Note that determinant of the Jacobian of the transformation is unity):

$$f_{vu}(v,u) = f_{vu}(\varepsilon+u,u)$$

$$= \frac{1}{\sqrt{2\pi}\,\sigma_v}\frac{2}{\sqrt{2\pi}\,\sigma_u}\exp\left\{-\frac{1}{2}\left(\frac{(\varepsilon+u)^2}{\sigma_v^2}+\frac{u^2}{\sigma_u^2}\right)\right\}$$

$$= \frac{1}{\sqrt{2\pi}\,\sigma_v}\frac{2}{\sqrt{2\pi}\,\sigma_u}\exp\left\{-\frac{1}{2}\left(\frac{\varepsilon^2+u^2+2\varepsilon u}{\sigma_v^2}+\frac{u^2}{\sigma_u^2}\right)\right\}$$

$$= \frac{(\sigma_v^2+\sigma_u^2)}{\sqrt{2\pi}\,\sigma_v\sigma_u}\frac{2}{\sqrt{2\pi}(\sigma_v^2+\sigma_u^2)}$$

$$\times\exp\left\{-\frac{1}{2}\left(\frac{\varepsilon^2(\sigma_v^2+\sigma_u^2)}{\sigma_v^2(\sigma_v^2+\sigma_u^2)}+\frac{\frac{2\varepsilon u}{\sqrt{\sigma_v^2+\sigma_u^2}}\frac{\sqrt{\sigma_v^2+\sigma_u^2}}{(\sigma_v\sigma_u)}}{\sigma_v^2/(\sigma_v\sigma_u)}+\frac{u^2(\sigma_u^2+\sigma_v^2)}{\sigma_u^2\sigma_v^2}\right)\right\}.$$

Letting $\sigma^2 = (\sigma_v^2+\sigma_u^2)$, $\lambda = \sigma_u/\sigma_v$, and $\delta^2 = (\sigma_v^2+\sigma_u^2)/\sigma_v^2\sigma_u^2$, we simplify to

$$\frac{\delta}{\sqrt{2\pi}}\frac{2}{\sqrt{2\pi}\,\sigma}\exp\left\{-\frac{1}{2}\left(\frac{\varepsilon^2\lambda^2}{\sigma^2}+\frac{\varepsilon^2}{\sigma^2}+\frac{2\varepsilon\lambda}{\sigma}\delta u+u^2\delta^2\right)\right\}$$

$$= \frac{\delta}{\sqrt{2\pi}}\frac{2}{\sqrt{2\pi}\,\sigma}\exp\left\{-\frac{1}{2}\left(\frac{\varepsilon^2\lambda^2}{\sigma^2}+\frac{2\varepsilon\lambda}{\sigma}\delta u+u^2\delta^2\right)\right\}\exp\left\{-\frac{1}{2}\frac{\varepsilon^2}{\sigma^2}\right\}$$

$$= \frac{2\delta}{\sqrt{2\pi}}\exp\left\{-\frac{1}{2}\left(\frac{\varepsilon\lambda}{\sigma}+u\delta\right)^2\right\}\frac{1}{\sqrt{2\pi}\,\sigma}\exp\left\{-\frac{1}{2}\frac{\varepsilon^2}{\sigma^2}\right\}$$

$$= h_{\varepsilon,u}(\varepsilon,u).$$

This is the joint distribution of ε and u. Now we can integrate over u to get the marginal distribution of ε:

$$f_\varepsilon(\varepsilon) = \int_0^\infty h_{\varepsilon,u}(\varepsilon,u)du$$

$$= \frac{1}{\sqrt{2\pi}\,\sigma}\exp\left\{-\frac{1}{2}\frac{\varepsilon^2}{\sigma^2}\right\}\int_0^\infty\frac{2\delta}{\sqrt{2\pi}}\exp\left\{-\frac{1}{2}\left(\frac{\varepsilon\lambda}{\sigma}+u\delta\right)^2\right\}du.$$

Using a change of variable technique, let $\gamma = \left(\frac{\varepsilon\lambda}{\sigma} + u\delta\right)$. Then $u = 0 \implies$ $\gamma = \frac{\varepsilon\lambda}{\sigma}$, $u \to \infty \implies \gamma \to \infty$, and $d\gamma = \delta\,du$. Thus

$$
= \frac{1}{\sqrt{2\pi}\sigma} \exp\left\{-\frac{1}{2}\frac{\varepsilon^2}{\sigma^2}\right\} 2\delta \int_{\frac{\varepsilon\lambda}{\sigma}}^{\infty} \frac{1}{\sqrt{2\pi}} \exp\left\{-\frac{1}{2}(\gamma)^2\right\} \frac{1}{\delta} d\gamma
$$

$$
= \frac{2}{\sqrt{2\pi}\sigma} \exp\left\{-\frac{1}{2}\frac{\varepsilon^2}{\sigma^2}\right\} \left[1 - \int_{-\infty}^{\frac{\varepsilon\lambda}{\sigma}} \frac{1}{\sqrt{2\pi}} \exp\left\{-\frac{1}{2}(\gamma)^2\right\} d\gamma\right]
$$

$$
f_\varepsilon(\varepsilon) = \frac{2}{\sigma}\phi\left(\frac{\varepsilon}{\sigma}\right)\left[1 - \Phi\left(\frac{\varepsilon\lambda}{\sigma}\right)\right], \qquad -\infty \le \varepsilon \le +\infty.
$$

A useful transformation suggested by Battese and Coelli (1988) will also prove useful in optimizing the likelihood function. If we let $\xi = \frac{\sigma_u^2}{\sigma^2}$, then $\xi/(1-\xi) = \frac{\sigma_u^2}{\sigma_v^2} \equiv \lambda^2$. This transforms the density function to be

$$
f_\varepsilon(\varepsilon) = \frac{2}{\sigma}\phi\left(\frac{\varepsilon}{\sigma}\right)\left[1 - \Phi\left(\frac{\varepsilon}{\sigma}\sqrt{\frac{\xi}{1-\xi}}\right)\right], \qquad -\infty \le \varepsilon \le +\infty.
$$

This reparameterization is particularly useful to ensure that in the MLE iterations the value of the parameter ξ is always positive since λ may sometimes be set equal to a negative trial value, causing severe numerical problems.

Panel Data and Parametric and Semiparametric Stochastic Frontier Models: First-Generation Approaches

In this chapter, we discuss different economic models of growth and production that make it possible to decompose productivity growth into such sources of growth as innovation and catch-up. Again, we return to our old friend, the Solow residual (Solow, 1957; Griliches, 1996) for the information needed to identify and measure these dynamical aspects of production. We also discuss the initial technical developments in the panel data literature by those working in the field of productivity and efficiency dynamics that anticipated, and in many cases preceded years earlier, the relatively recent contributions of panel data econometricians (Baltagi, 2014). The productivity and efficiency literature has stressed the importance of flexibility in measuring productivity change and firm-specific and time-varying changes in technical efficiency, or catch-up. Of course if catch-up is measured as cross-sectional and temporally varying heterogeneity, then it is easy to show that such general forms of heterogeneity are just normalized panel data measures of time-varying fixed or random effects. We explain why the identification and measurement of productive efficiency and innovation often require panel data. In the next chapter, we extend our coverage to more recent contributions to modeling productivity and efficiency using factor models, Bayesian techniques, and more recent developments in semi-nonparametric estimation methods. Some of the material in this and the next chapter also can be found in Sickles et al. (2015) and Shang (2015).

12.1 PRODUCTIVITY GROWTH AND ITS MEASUREMENT

12.1.1 Residual-Based Productivity Measurement

Productivity estimates used by central governments and statistical agencies are usually measured by expressing total factor productivity (TFP) as the ratio of a weighted average of M-outputs (y_i) to a weighted average of N-inputs (x_i). In modern index number analyses, the weights are usually chosen to address changing input mix. When there is a single output y (or output index, such as gross output), *TFP* can be expressed as

$$TFP = \frac{y}{\sum_{j=1}^{N} a_j x_j}. \tag{12.1.1}$$

The weights used to aggregate the outputs and inputs are chosen based on a variety of criteria (see, for example, Good et al., 1997) but the actual aggregating functions can usually be parsed into either an arithmetic (Kendrick, 1961) or a geometric (Solow, 1957) average. The former uses input prices as the weights while the latter relies on input expenditure shares as the weights. The Solow-type *TFP* measure is used by central governments in most countries and can be linked to a Cobb–Douglas production function with constant returns to scale, $y = A x_L^{\alpha} x_K^{1-\alpha}$, and expressed as,

$$TFP = \frac{y}{x_L^{\alpha} x_K^{1-\alpha}}, \tag{12.1.2}$$

where x_L and x_K are labor and capital services and y is real GDP. Assuming cost minimization, the expenditure shares used in forming the geometric average of inputs are the output elasticities for the respective inputs. The growth rates in the level of *TFP*, or total factor productivity growth, are given by the time derivative of *TFP* and leads to the familiar expression for *TFP* growth

$$\dot{TFP} = \frac{dy/y}{dt} - \left[\alpha \frac{dx_L/x_L}{dt} + (1-\alpha) \frac{dx_K/x_K}{dt} \right]. \tag{12.1.3}$$

Chapter 4 provided an in-depth technical discussion of Solow growth accounting and we refer the interested reader back to that discussion. Since $\dot{TFP}$ is a function (ratio) of index numbers, it derives its properties from the properties of its underlying aggregator functions. These can be traced back to the pioneering work of Fisher (1921), who discussed many of the desirable properties for such index numbers, some of which are relatively easily met and others of which are not – issues that have been addressed in more technical detail in Chapter 7. The *TFP* index used in the vast majority of applied and empirical work in productivity can be found in the original contributions by Jorgenson and Griliches (1967) and Jorgenson and Griliches (1972).

12.2 INTERNATIONAL AND US ECONOMIC GROWTH AND DEVELOPMENT

The achievements of Krugman, Kim and Lau, Young and many others motivated many researchers to uncover the sources of the strong economic growth in Asia and elsewhere. Debates among researchers on the primary sources of economic growth and development were centered on two basic explanations that are rooted in the decomposition of economic growth sources: factor-accumulation and productivity-growth components. According to Kim and Lau (1994), Young (1992, 1995), and Krugman (1994), rapid economic growth in such emerging areas as East Asia was largely explained by the mobilization of resources. Alternative explanations to the neoclassical growth model explain economic growth not only in terms of intensive and extensive utilization of input factors but also due to factors that impact the degree to which countries can appropriate the productivity potential of world technical innovations. Factors such as governmental industrial policies, trade liberalization policies, and political, religious, and cultural institutions are often viewed as central to the ability of countries to catch up with a shifting world production possibilities frontier.

12.2.1   The Neoclassical Production Function and Economic Growth

Stiroh (2001) provides a very coherent treatment that frames the problem of measuring sources of *TFP* growth in the context of the neoclassical production $y = f(x_K, x_L, T)$. As noted by Stiroh (2001, p. 37) and paraphrased by countless others:

> The striking implication of the neoclassical model is that, in the long run, per capita output and productivity growth are driven entirely by growth in exogenous technical progress and they are independent of other structural parameters like the savings rate. If the savings rate and investment share increase, for example, the long-run level of productivity rises but the long-run growth rate eventually reflects only technical progress. In this sense, the neoclassical growth model is not really a model of long-run growth at all since productivity growth is due to exogenous and entirely unexplained technical progress.

12.2.2   Modifications of the Neoclassical Production Function and Economic Growth Model: Endogenous Growth

Exogenous productivity growth was the prevailing modeling assumption until the endogenous growth model was put forth by Romer (1986) and took hold in the late 1980s. The source of the endogenous growth, often expressed in a reduced form equation that shifts the production function over time were typically spillovers of one sort or another. We will focus on spillovers due to spatial effects and supply chain networks in production later in the book. If we simply alter the specification of the level of technology A to allow it to vary according to some model and some set of variables that are determined within the model itself, then technology would be considered endogenously determined. For example, if R is such a variable or set of variables, then the production function can be written as

$$y = A(R)f(x_K, x_L, R). \qquad (12.2.1)$$

The various possible sources of the spillover differentiate much of the endogenous growth literature, at least at the macroeconomic level. For example, Arrow (1962) emphasized learning by doing. For Romer (1986) the endogeneity came from the stock of research and development. For Lucas (1988) it was the stock of human capital. A major source of post-World War II economic growth has been innovation in the form of technological change. Coe and Helpman (1995) bring in trade spillovers by showing that the rate of return on research and development investment is not limited to performing countries but extends to their trade partners. Coe et al. (1997) analyzed a set of less developed countries and again found trade playing an important role in transmitting technology. Diao et al. (2005) examined the role of technology spillovers in stages-of-growth transitions and also noted that the lack of advanced skills in a developing country often hampers the adoption of new technologies. They also examined the openness, concluding that reduced openness had a negative impact on overall productivity growth and economic development.

There is, however, another interpretation for the reduced form endogenous technology term in the modern productivity model, specifically the presence of inefficiency. Suppose one defines the endogenous factor in productivity growth as simply a country's or firm's differential ability to loosen the constraints on the utilization of the existing world technology. With this interpretation of endogenous productivity effects, *TFP* growth is determined by the efficiency with which the existing technology (inclusive of innovations) is utilized (see, e.g., Sickles and Cigerli, 2009).

Production spillovers have important implications for economic growth and for its management. If any type of investment whose gains are not internalized by private agents impacts long-run growth, then there is no unique long-run growth path and thus no so-called "golden rule." From a public policy perspective, spillovers provide a clear role for government intervention. Government intervention may take many forms if investment is too low from society's perspective. Investment tax credits or research and development grants are two traditional forms of government intervention. However, government intervention may also take the form of relaxing constraints on businesses via deregulatory reforms, reduced red tape, private sector market reforms, or any other aspect of the institutional and political mechanism established in a country and its markets that increase A. The later set of external effects can be summed up as governmental actions that reduce constraints, or efficiency enhancing investments. If one examines the new growth model more closely it must be recognized that it is indistinguishable empirically from the stochastic frontier model wherein A is an efficiency term. A substantial engine of economic growth has been efficiency change. As pointed out by Abramovitz (1986), Dowrick and Nguyen (1989), and Nelson and Wright (1992), among many others, the major sources of country growth differentials in the developed countries after World War II can be explained by the neoclassical growth model amended to conclude such endogenous factors as knowledge spillovers, technological diffusion, and convergence to a best practice production process (Smolny, 2000). The "new growth theory" implicitly recognizes the role of efficiency in production. One set of papers that provides an explicit efficiency interpretation of this growth process is Hultberg et al. (1999, 2004), and Ahn et al. (2000), who introduce inefficiency into the growth process. Of course the standard neoclassical model without explicit treatment of efficiency has been used by many authors in examining growth and convergence.

Endogenous growth also has been addressed using formal spatial econometric specializations based on both average production/cost models as well as frontier production/cost models. Models that extend the multiplicative spillover effects by expanding $A(R)$ by framing production in a spatial autoregressive setting in order to address network effects or trade flows among countries have been formulated by Ertur and Koch (2007) and Behrens et al. (2010). In the Ertur and Koch (2007) panel model of spillovers the aggregate level of technology for country i at time t is specified as a function of three components

$$A_i(t) = \Omega(t) k_i^{\phi}(t) \prod_{j \neq i}^{n} A_j^{\gamma w_{ij}}(t). \tag{12.2.2}$$

Following Solow (1956) and Swan (1956), the first term $\Omega(t) = \Omega(0)e^{\mu t}$ captures standard exogenous technical change, the second term $k_i^{\phi}(t), 0 \leq \phi < 1$, where $k_i(t) = x_{K,i}(t)/x_{L,i}(t)$, captures the contribution of country i's capital accumulation, and the third term addresses the formal spillovers across countries. This model can be shown to result in a spatial autoregressive specification. More general stochastic frontier treatments that do not force efficiency on the productive units, whether they are countries, states, or firms, have been introduced by Druska and Horrace (2004) in the cross-sectional setting and for the panel model in a series of papers by Glass et al. (2013, 2014, 2016) and Han et al. (2016a,b).

It should be pointed out that the endogenous growth paradigm can also have a structural model interpretation wherein the spillovers are generated by a formal endogenous variable with stochastic terms that need to be specified by the modeler. Such structural models are considered in our chapter on endogeneity. The panel stochastic frontier model we turn to soon can be interpreted as a structural model in which the latent efficiency term is viewed as a placeholder for technical efficiency effects, such as in the Aigner et al. (1977) model, for cost efficiency effects as in Olley and Pakes (1996), for the effects of intangible capital as in Corrado et al. (2009), for unobserved organizational capital as in Brynjolfsson and Hitt (2003), or simply for an unobservable factor as in Levinsohn and Petrin (2003).

12.3 THE PANEL STOCHASTIC FRONTIER MODEL: MEASUREMENT OF TECHNICAL AND EFFICIENCY CHANGE

Cross-sectional models in general are unable to capture growth dynamics. Cross-sectional models of productivity are no different. Separating catch-up from shifts in the available frontier technology cannot be accomplished using the static stochastic frontier model of Aigner et al. (1977) and Meeusen and van den Broeck (1977). Researchers recognized this shortcoming and developed alternatives that utilized panel treatments relatively soon after, such as Pitt and Lee (1981) and Schmidt and Sickles (1984). These, however, did not allow the country (or productive unit under study, such as a firm) effects to vary over time and the innovations by Cornwell et al. (1990) and Kumbhakar (1990), Battese and Coelli (1992), Lee and Schmidt (1993) addressed this shortcoming. Kim and Lee (2006) also generalized the Lee and Schmidt (1993) model to allow for temporal patterns of inefficiency to vary by the productive unit under study. Many empirical settings have been examined using these time-varying effects models. At a country level, Kim and Lee (2006) decomposed total factor growth of 49 countries into technological change and technical efficiency change components and estimated productivity changes over certain regions and compared their regional characteristics. The results of their study show that technical efficiency had a significant positive effect on productivity growth. East Asia led the world in total factor productivity growth because technical efficiency gain is much faster than that of other countries. Kalirajan et al. (1996) note that the key determinant of economic growth is not the level of input use but rather the method of application of inputs. They are able not only to rank *TFP* but also the technical efficiency over 45 countries. Findings from these many studies made it clear that technical efficiency, as a separate and contributing factor to innovation in determining productivity growth, was often a significant determinant of productivity growth and that a failure to properly distinguish between a shift in the technology and a movement to the best practice of that technology could seriously bias productivity measurement.

Regression-based approaches for estimating sources of time-varying and country-specific total factor productivity growth utilize panel data methods in specifying time-varying technical inefficiency captured by normalized (possibly time-varying) intercepts or fixed effects. Technical inefficiency can also be identified through normalized within residuals from error components models with the technical inefficiency effects. Moreover, parametric distributions can be assumed for such panel random effect models and maximum likelihood can be used. For example, a truncated normal distribution with time-varying means can be specified as the one-sided error process for technical efficiency (Battese and Coelli, 1992). Cuesta (2000) also generalized the Battese and Coelli (1992) model by allowing each country to have its own time path of technical inefficiency. The assumption of independence between inputs and technical efficiency is problematic as is the incidental parameters problem of MLE when fixed effects are assumed since the number of parameters increases with the sample size. Kim et al.'s (2008) model provides a solution to the Cuesta (2000) large sample size problem by grouping the firms. Kim et al. (2008) apply their model to estimate frontier production functions for a 57-country sample grouped over four time periods: 1970–75, 1975–80, 1980–85 and 1985–90. Their results indicate country groups have different time-varying technical efficiencies. Between the early 1970s and late 1980s the East Asia region had one of the fastest growth rates in technical efficiency.

Differentiating productivity growth into catch-up (efficiency change) and innovation (technical change) can also provide modelers with methods to explain relative speeds of catch-up and thus better understand the mechanisms and constraints that impact how quickly and to what extent the productive units under study can access the existing (and changing) technology. Hultberg et al. (1999, 2004) provided such linkages in their work on aggregate economic growth and sectoral growth within the OECD countries. Among other things, these studies found that upward of 60 percent of the variation in efficiency could be explained by factors of economic, political, and social institutions of a country. These were the factors that constrained countries and the sectors within them to move to and adopt the frontier technology.

12.4   INDEX NUMBER DECOMPOSITIONS OF ECONOMIC GROWTH-INNOVATION AND EFFICIENCY CHANGE

One common approach to decompose *TFP* into sources due to innovation and efficiency change based on the economic theory of index numbers is presented in a study of productivity growth in the OECD by Färe et al. (1989a) using an innovation and efficiency change decomposition based on the Malmquist productivity index. Alam (2001) utilized such a decomposition in a study of the banking industry and found that technical change was the dominant component of productivity change during the 1980s, dominating the contributions from scale or efficiency effects. The Färe et al. (1989a) method has been widely used although its statistical properties illustrate the difficulties in identifying significant sources of productivity growth while at the same time being sensitive to overly parametric assumptions. For example, utilizing bootstrapping techniques introduced by Simar and Wilson (2000a), Jeon and Sickles (2004) found that there was no statistical significance to the productivity decompositions at standard nominal significance levels using the OECD data. Førsund and Hjalmarsson (2008) point out what they consider to be the main problem with the Malmquist index and its decomposition. The Malmquist productivity index blurs the distinction between the *ex ante* micro function relevant for investments and the short-run production possibilities for the industry as a unit. When estimating technological change and technical efficiency change with the Malmquist productivity index, it is assumed that any producing firm may potentially produce at the frontier. According to Førsund and Hjalmarsson (2008), this would be the case only when there are no vintage effects, an assumption that could hold in industries where capital has a minor role, unlike paper, pulp, cement, etc. where the Malmquist productivity index has been used to study productivity growth. In the case of disembodied technical change, wherein the shift in the production function over time is not incorporated into a specific best practice production function, the technical change in principle can only be relevant for existing units and thus the index cannot discriminate between efficiency change and disembodied technical change.

Grosskopf and Self (2006) calculate the Malmquist productivity index and its decomposition into technical and efficiency change. They also provide estimates based on a neoclassical production approach with embodied technical change. In summarizing their findings, Grosskopf and Self note that country differences are crucial in developing the proper structural interpretations for what are essentially reduced form correlations between factor accumulation and TFP growth on the one hand and economic growth in the region on the other. They also point out the complicated dynamic of postwar growth that appears at times to be unique to each country's historical experiences and institutions.

12.4.1 Index Number Procedures

The Malmquist TFP index (also referred to as Hicks–Moorsteen productivity index) was given its name by Bjurek (1996). It has been discussed in depth in Chapter 4. In order to construct the Malmquist TFP index and decompose it into sources of technological change and technical efficiency change panel data is needed. Färe et al. (1994a), among others, develop the methodology to construct and decompose a TFP measure based on the output-oriented Shephard's distance function $D_o(x_t, y_t)$. A special case of this multi-output distance function is the single output production function that we will discuss at length in this and subsequent chapters. An output efficient firm has a distance function score of unity and it is not possible for the firm to increase its output vector radially without increasing one or more of its inputs or changing the technology. Conversely, an output inefficient firm has a distance function score that is less than one. The Malmquist productivity index uses data from two adjacent periods. When the index is above 1, it signals growth and when it is below 1, it signals regress. Førsund and Hjalmarsson (2008) have questioned its widespread use as a transparent method to identify the major contributions to productivity growth, technical change and efficiency change, due to potential vintage capital effects. Jeon and Sickles (2004) have questioned its appeal and usefulness based on inferential shortcomings, especially when data is highly aggregated.

12.5 REGRESSION-BASED DECOMPOSITIONS OF ECONOMIC GROWTH-INNOVATION AND EFFICIENCY CHANGE

There are many contributions to the efficiency and productivity literature that offer up different ways to estimate this canonical panel model and to decompose TFP growth into a catch-up and innovation component. These include models introduced by Cornwell et al. (1990), Kumbhakar (1990), Battese and Coelli (1992), Lee and Schmidt (1993), Park et al. (1998, 2003, 2007), Greene

(2005a), Kneip et al. (2004), Kneip and Sickles (2011), and Kneip et al. (2012). Space limits the possibility of dealing with the many other approaches that have been proposed to estimate the panel stochastic frontier and provide a decomposition of *TFP* growth into innovative and catch-up, or technical efficiency. For a more detailed account of these and other statistical treatments see Sickles et al. (2015). Some of the more general purpose estimators that have been proposed for panel stochastic frontiers that are also very appropriate to estimate the canonical panel productivity model are the Bayesian Stochastic Frontier Model (Liu et al., 2013), the Bounded Inefficiency Model of Almanidis et al. (2014) and related models of Lee (1996), Lee and Lee (2014), and Orea and Steinbuks (2012), and the "true" fixed effects model of Greene (2004, 2005a,b). Related work that we pursue in the next chapter also includes relatively recent extensions to the Greene models by Tsionas and Kumbhakar (2014) who use Bayesian methods to decompose the error term into a four-way error component model of persistent and time-varying inefficiency, random firm effects and statistical noise.

A recent theoretical treatment of growth dynamics that we take up in more detail in Chapter 15 and that mirrors the decompositions we provide in this chapter can be found in the work of König et al. (2016). In their theoretical treatment of the dynamics of productivity and growth, enhancements in productivity come about as profit-maximizing firms either endogenously invest in R&D or imitate/appropriate the technologies of other firms. The balanced-growth equilibrium of their model is characterized by essentially the same considerations as Ahn et al. (2000). In Ahn et al. the adjustment speeds in the movement to the frontier for firms that were closer to the frontier was relatively slower than those for firms that were further from the frontier. In (König et al., 2016) firms that are closer to the technological frontier tend to invest in R&D instead of imitation, while firms that are farther from the efficient frontier are more prone to imitate/appropriate the existing technology. The use of existing productivity enhancing technologies to increase production results in a convergence of firms to the existing frontier, which is efficiency change. The shifting out of the technology frontier by new in-house R&D investments shifts out the frontier. The overall movement in productivity due to these two dynamic factors is productivity change, a portion of which is efficiency change and a portion of which is technical change or innovation. An interesting implication of the König et al. (2016) analysis is that productivity's long-run distribution has a particular pattern with tail properties that are best described by a Pareto distribution, which is usually observed in the empirical record.

When describing a production process, it's inevitable that the key elements such as the number and the nature of inputs and outputs, the form of innovation, and the potential that the decision-making unit, or firm, fails to utilize all inputs efficiently given market prices, be considered. To generate more output, a firm can use more inputs, or if technically inefficient, increase productivity with inputs kept fixed. Though in many cases, the two words "productivity" and "efficiency" are interchangeable and often used to express the same concept, they are not the same concept in the production theory. Productivity is a broader term and depends on various factors, such as technology, productive efficiency, environmental influences, unexpected incidents, and so on. Productive efficiency can be decomposed into many components, but its two most important, given a constant returns to scale technology, are: 1) technical efficiency, which measures the capability to produce as much output as possible with given inputs or utilize as few inputs as possible to obtain a certain output level; 2) allocative efficiency, which refers to the attempt to adjust the proportion of inputs and outputs according to the price faced, in order to achieve a certain maximum or minimum objective, such as revenue or profit maximization, or cost minimization.

12.6 ENVIRONMENTAL FACTORS IN PRODUCTION AND INTERPRETATION OF PRODUCTIVE EFFICIENCY

Environmental factors have been addressed in the productivity and efficiency literature in somewhat straightforward regression-based treatments wherein the mean and variance of efficiency is parameterized as a function of the environmental factors. Models that utilize such reduced form specifications of the determinants of efficiency have a long life in the productivity and efficiency literature, both in regard to deterministic frontier methods utilized in DEA and stochastic frontiers employed in SFA. Contributions to this literature based on stochastic frontier methods have appeared in Pitt and Lee (1981) and Kalirajan (1981), who appear to be the first to raise the issue of why such environmental effects are important in their two-step analyses. Other studies, among many, can be found in Cornwell et al. (1990), Battese and Coelli (1995), Good et al. (1995), Wang and Schmidt (2002), Simar and Wilson (2008), Kim and Schmidt (2008), and in Mastromarco and Simar (2015) who utilize the Bădin et al. (2010, 2012) nonparametric conditional frontier estimator for their conditional efficiency estimator. In the panel data stochastic frontier paradigm one can interpret the estimates from standard production functions that control for environmental factors as additional regressors (institutional factors in aggregate studies, regulatory regimes and oversight in firm-level studies, especially in banking and finance) as representing a set of period specific (think dummies for each period to represent change across time, which also could be approximated by a series expansion in time) optimal instructions available to all firms. If we consider that a firm's ability to take advantage of the existing technology relative to other firms is its relative efficiency, then a time trend or powers of time common to all productive units under study and individual unit-specific time-varying effects would identify the common technical change and unit-specific efficiency change in a standard neoclassical production function. We will adopt this interpretation of the production technology and the environmental factors that impact it in our analysis below.

An alternative perspective is that environmental factors in production are not determinants of efficiency, or simply heterogeneity controls as they would be interpreted in a standard production function estimated by regression-based methods, but rather are inputs in firm production, along with what economists would view as classical inputs such as labor, capital, energy, services, and materials. The treatment of environmental factors in productive efficiency carried out in Simar et al. (2014, 2017) allowed environmental factors to influence both efficiency and the frontier as is also done in the conditional frontier approaches of Daraio and Simar (2007a,b) and Bădin et al. (2010, 2012). This has much in common with the tenants of the state-contingent technology developed and extended in a series of contributions by Chambers and Quiggin (2000, 2002), Quiggin and Chambers (2006) and by O'Donnell et al. (2010) and suggests, among other things, that each firm's production function is based on an environment-specific set of instructions.

In a similar vein but one that is motivated in quite a different fashion researchers have extended and improved on the weak disposability model that Färe et al. (1989b) used to address the presence of bad outputs (or inputs) in production. The technology contains (y, x, z), where z is not an environmental variable but rather a variable that negatively affects the environment, or what's referred to as a "bad" output. Forsund (2009, 2010, 2017) has contributed much to this literature that addresses the materials balancing that must be preserved in any production system by considering the same technology containing (y, x, z) but parsing the inputs into those such as materials inputs that contribute to pollution and non-material inputs, such as labor and capital services that do not. Thus not all inputs have positive marginal products nor do all outputs have positive marginal valuations. A recent work by Hampf (2015) focuses on these issues as well in the stochastic frontier model in which the stochastic formulation of the materials balance condition imposes physical constraints on production technologies. Although the use of the term "environment" is of course not the same as its use as the conditioning variables that may define a state-contingent technology or simply be considered as heterogeneity controls, there is much similarity between the two perspectives: what is the environment in which the firm is operating and how the operation of the firm affects the environment.

12.7 THE STOCHASTIC PANEL FRONTIER

Chapter 11 discussed various approaches to estimating technical efficiency and we left with a specification of the stochastic frontier that incorporated a bound on inefficiency. The bounded inefficiency model not only generalized the canonical stochastic frontier model but also provided another step in the evolution of productivity and efficiency modeling, answering in part the question posed in Chapter 11 of how to specify the boundary of the level sets and thus construct a metric for evaluating a firm's absolute or relative efficiency (inefficiency). An answer to the question of how we specify the boundary of the level sets leads to the stochastic panel frontier.

The stochastic frontier model based on a single cross-section suffers from at least three serious difficulties. The first is that the technical efficiency of a particular firm (observation) can be estimated but not consistently. That is, although we can consistently estimate the composed error (distributed as the skew-normal or more generally using the bounded inefficiency model specification that nests the skew-normal) for a given observation, we cannot consistently estimate its components. Moreover, the variance of the non-symmetric technical inefficiency term conditional on the symmetric random disturbance does not vanish when the sample size increases (Jondrow et al., 1982). The second is that the model is not point identified without relatively strong parametric assumptions. The third is that inefficiency is assumed to be independent of the regressors. However, if the firm knows its level of performance relative to other firms then it is reasonable to assume that this should affect its input decisions. The problem of endogeneity is not intrinsically solved by the presence of panel data, but as we discuss in Chapter 14, panel data may help in addressing this sort of dependency under certain circumstances.

These problems are potentially avoidable if one has panel data (Pitt and Lee, 1981; Schmidt and Sickles, 1984). For a panel stochastic frontier, the technical efficiency of a particular firm can be estimated consistently for large T. Also, evidence of persistent underperformance would show up in the effects as well as in the skewness of the within residuals and thus it may not be necessary to impose strong parametric assumptions on the distributions of inefficiency and stochastic noise. Finally, estimation of parameters and of the firm's inefficiency levels can be obtained without assuming that technical inefficiency is uncorrelated with the regressors. We use the general treatment of Schmidt and Sickles (1984) (SS) as it nests the special case of random effects considered by Pitt and Lee (1981) who first considered such a model. We can write the model as

$$y_{it} = \alpha + x'_{it}\beta + v_{it} - u_i, \quad i = 1, \ldots, n; t = 1, \ldots, T,$$

or as

$$y_{it} = \alpha^* + x'_{it}\beta + v_{it} - u_i^*, \tag{12.7.1}$$

where $\alpha^* = \alpha - \mu$; $u_i^* = u_i - \mu$; $E(u_i) = \mu \geq 0$, and where x_{it} is a vector of K inputs.[1]

Next define $\alpha_i = \alpha^* - u_i^*$ and the model becomes

$$y_{it} = \alpha_i + x'_{it}\beta + v_{it}, \tag{12.7.2}$$

---

[1] Unless stated otherwise, we may dispense with the notational convention used in earlier chapters wherein N indicated the number of inputs and M the number of outputs in the production technology. The set of regressors for the many estimators we discuss in this and in subsequent chapters may include inputs, outputs, and other controls. Thus we turn to a more general notation and simply let the set of parameters be K or some other convenient label we establish as the number of parameters to be estimated in order to estimate the underlying technology and the role other conditioning factors and characteristics may play in affecting it.

which is the standard panel model with cross-sectional effects that can be specified as random or fixed, or simply ignored. SS discussed five estimators for this stochastic panel frontier model that mirror the standard literature on linear panel data models.

The first approach considered by SS is simple ordinary least squares. If we treat $(v_{it} - u_i^*)$ as the disturbance and assume weak exogeneity of the disturbance and the regressors, then estimates of α^* and β are consistent for large n, although the consistency is lost for fixed n and large T.

The second approach is the within (dummy variable) estimator. If we suppress the constant term and add dummies for each of the n cross-sections, then estimates of β are consistent for large n or large T. Consistency of the α_i requires large T. One can use the one-sided (or two-sided in the case of the BIM) bound on the support of the technical inefficiency term, which in the case of a one-sided production frontier requires that $u_i \geq 0$, to normalize the effects and the overall constant term. This measure is constructed as $\hat{\alpha} \equiv \max\{\hat{\alpha}_i\}$ and define $\hat{u}_i = \hat{\alpha} - \hat{\alpha}_i$. The most efficient firm in the sample is thus normalized to have 0 percent inefficiency. The use of the order statistic to construct a consistent estimate of relative efficiency was introduced by Greene (1980a). Greene showed that if the density of u is nonzero in some neighborhood of $(0, \varsigma)$ for some $\varsigma > 0$, then the inefficiency of the most efficient firm in the sample will approach 0 percent for large n. The within estimates of firm-specific efficiencies are consistent for large T. Park et al. (1998) have shown this to be the semiparametric efficient estimator of the stochastic frontier when the efficiency distribution is not specified parametrically. Thus, the consistency of the slope coefficients and the relative efficiencies require large n and T.

The third approach is generalized least squares (GLS) or a random effects estimator based on a composed error. This is the model considered by Pitt and Lee (1981), who used parametric MLE to estimate the random effects stochastic frontier. If both variances σ_u^2 and σ_v^2 are known and the effects are uncorrelated with the regressors, then the GLS estimates of α^* and β are consistent for either large n or T. If the variances are not known and must be estimated then consistent estimation of σ_u^2 requires large n. For large T, GLS and within are equivalent. Moreover, with GLS we can recover estimates of the individual firm intercepts by calculating each cross-section's residual mean. These estimates are consistent for large T, provided that β is consistently estimated and as Schmidt and Sickles (1984) point out this requires large n. Thus GLS requires the same large sample asymptotics for both n and T as does the within estimator in order to consistently estimate the relative efficiencies.

A middle ground between the random effects and the fixed effects estimators wherein the effects and some of the regressors are weakly exogenous and some are not is the Hausman and Taylor (1981) estimator. We will consider this estimator in more detail when we next examine the time-varying efficiency version of the SS model that was introduced by Cornwell et al. (1990). It is instructive to note at this juncture that orthogonality conditions imposed on the effects and the regressors with the random effects composed error treatment is often rather important empirically, as there may be a number of trending inputs, which when transformed into logs in the use of a Cobb–Douglas or translog functional form often become highly collinear and may not have much independent variability. This is because the alternative within estimator cannot identify the coefficients on regressors that are time–invariant or linear combinations of regressors that do not vary much over time. A parsimonious use of orthogonality conditions may allow one to either identify factors that differ among the cross-sections but do not vary over time, such as the state in which a firm resides to control for state-specific regulations, tax policies, etc., or to substantially reduce the collinearity problem caused by relatively little independent variability over time by particular regressors or by linear combinations of regressors.

A final estimator considered by SS is the parametric maximum likelihood estimator given independence and a distribution for the one-sided technical efficiency error and the random disturbance. Pitt and Lee (1981) considered a half-normal technical efficiency error and an independent normal random disturbance. The maximum likelihood estimates are consistent and asymptotically efficient for large n and fixed T.

Although the SS estimator does provide the researcher with considerable latitude in specifying a stochastic panel frontier, there is an important shortcoming with the specification and that is the assumption that inefficiency is time–invariant. Cornwell et al. (1990) (CSS) freed up the assumption of temporal invariance by allowing time heterogeneity in slopes and in intercepts and allowing orthogonality between inefficiency and some of the regressors. When one of the regressors is time and when heterogeneity is interpreted as efficiency, then CSS showed how their model could be consistently estimated by a more efficient IV estimator than within. Park et al. (1998) showed that this estimator was semiparametric efficient. They also developed the GLS estimator for this particular error covariance structure. We now turn to the CSS extensions of the SS model and to other specifications that address the possible time-varying nature of productive efficiency.

12.7.1 Cornwell, Schmidt, and Sickles (1990) Model

Cornwell et al. (1990) extended the panel data model of Schmidt and Sickles (1984) to allow for heterogeneity in slopes as well as intercepts. A particular parameterization of these heterogeneities allowed them to replace the time-invariant normalized effects $\alpha_i = \alpha - u_i$, where u_i is technical inefficiency, with time-varying effects $\alpha_{it} = \alpha - u_{it}$, where u_{it} is the time-varying level in firm-specific inefficiency. Their general model is

$$y_{it} = x'_{it}\beta + z'_i\gamma + w'_{it}\delta_i + v_{it} \quad i = 1, \cdots, n; \ t = 1, \cdots, T, \quad (12.7.3)$$

where x_{it}, z_i and w_{it} are $K \times 1$, $J \times 1$ and $L \times 1$ vectors, respectively, and the parameter vectors β, γ and δ_i are dimensioned conformably. Note that 1) variables in z do not vary over time; 2) coefficients of w, δ_i, change across different units, thus representing heterogeneity in slopes.

A common construction can relate this model to the standard panel data model. Let $\delta_0 = E[\delta_i]$, and $\delta_i = \delta_0 + u_i$. Then the model can be written as

$$y_{it} = x'_{it}\beta + z'_i\gamma + w'_{it}\delta_0 + \varepsilon_{it},$$

where

$$\varepsilon_{it} = v_{it} + w'_{it}u_i. \tag{12.7.4}$$

Here u_i is assumed to be an iid zero mean vector of random variables with covariance matrix Δ while the disturbances v_{it} are assumed to be iid, with zero mean and constant variance σ_v^2 and to be uncorrelated with regressors and the u_i. Recall that the panel data stochastic frontier model of Schmidt and Sickles (1984) is

$$y_{it} = \alpha + x'_{it}\beta + v_{it} - u_i = \alpha_i + x'_{it}\beta + v_{it}. \tag{12.7.5}$$

To relax the assumption that the firm effects are time-invariant, Cornwell et al. (1990) replaced the time–invariant effects α_i with time-varying effects by letting

$$\alpha_{it} = \theta_{i1} + \theta_{i2}t + \theta_{i3}t^2, \tag{12.7.6}$$

which is a model with heterogeneous slope parameters for the intercept, t, and t^2. Thus time-varying inefficiency can take on a different quadratic pattern for each firm. This particular parameterization can be modified to include any of what have been termed "environmental" variables as well. If we let $w'_{it} = (1, t, t^2)$ and $\delta'_i = (\theta_{i1}, \theta_{i2}, \theta_{i3})$, then it is clear that this particular parameterization can be estimated by their general model.

The Cornwell et al. (1990) (CSS) model can be written in matrix form as

$$y = X\beta + Z\gamma + W\delta_0 + \varepsilon, \tag{12.7.7}$$
$$\varepsilon = Qu + v, \tag{12.7.8}$$

where W is a $nT \times L$, $Q = diag(w_i)$, $i = 1, \cdots, n$ is an $nT \times nL$ matrix, and δ_0 is the associated $L \times 1$ coefficient vector. To identify each δ_i, we require Q to be of full column rank, i.e., $L \leq T$.

12.7.1.1 Implementation

Depending on the level of correlation between the error term and regressors, three cases with different assumptions can be considered. The estimation methods can be seen as a modification of fixed-effects, random-effects and Hausman-Taylor approaches, respectively.

"Within" Estimator: Allow for Correlation between All Regressors and the Effects

Let $P_Q = Q(Q'Q)^{-1}Q'$ and $M_Q = I - P_Q$. Then P_Q projects matrices onto the column space of Q, and M_Q projects matrices onto the null space of Q. The within estimator of β is given by

$$\hat{\beta}_w = (X'M_Q X)^{-1}X'M_Q y. \tag{12.7.9}$$

Recall that because Z does not vary with time, $M_Q Z = 0$, and γ cannot be estimated. However, $\hat{\beta}_w$ is consistent even if (X, Z) and Q_u are correlated.

GLS: No Correlation between Regressors and Effects

The GLS estimator of $(\beta, \gamma, \delta_0)$ is the solution to

$$\left[(X, Z, W)'\Omega^{-1}(X, Z, W)\right]^{-1}(X, Z, W)'\Omega^{-1}y, \tag{12.7.10}$$

where $\Omega = \sigma^2 I_{nT} + Q(I_n \otimes \Delta)Q'$. Equivalently, we can first make a transformation of the equation such that covariance of the transformed error term satisfies the assumption of the standard linear regression model, and then apply the standard OLS method. The transformed equation can be written as

$$\Omega^{-1/2}y = \Omega^{-1/2}X\beta + \Omega^{-1/2}Z\gamma + \Omega^{-1/2}W\delta_0 + \Omega^{-1/2}\varepsilon. \tag{12.7.11}$$

It can be shown that

$$\Omega^{-1/2} = \frac{1}{\sigma}M_Q + F, \tag{12.7.12}$$

with $F = Q(Q'Q)^{-1/2}\left[\sigma^2 I_{nL} + (Q'Q)^{1/2}(I_n \otimes \Delta)(Q'Q)^{1/2}\right]^{-1/2}(Q'Q)^{-1/2}Q'$. In this case, γ can be estimated and the GLS estimator is more efficient than that within estimator for fixed T. One drawback is that consistency requires (x, z, w) and Qu to be uncorrelated.

Extended Hausman–Taylor Estimator: Correlation between Some of the Regressors and the Effects

Consider the case in which some of the regressors are correlated with the effects. Following Hausman and Taylor (1981), partition the regressors and assume that (X_1, Z_1, W_1) are uncorrelated with the effects in the sense that their sample covariance converges to zero in probability, while (X_2, Z_2, W_2) are correlated with the effects. Dimensions are denoted k_1, j_1, l_1, k_2, j_2, and l_2 respectively. The general idea is to use uncorrelated variables as instruments and we can identify and consistently estimate all the coefficients if certain rank and corresponding order requirements, such as those required for identification in the linear simultaneous equations model, are met.

We start with the within estimator. Recall that the within method only identifies β, whose estimate can be used to construct the within residuals that can be used as the left-hand side variable in the following regression:

$$(y - X\hat{\beta}_w) = Z\gamma + W\delta_0 + [Qu + v + X(\beta - \hat{\beta}_w)]. \quad (12.7.13)$$

Premultiplying this equation by $\Omega^{-1/2}$, we get

$$\Omega^{-1/2}(y - X\hat{\beta}_w) = \Omega^{-1/2}Z\gamma + \Omega^{-1/2}W\delta_0 + \Omega^{-1/2}[Qu + v + X(\beta - \hat{\beta}_w)]. \quad (12.7.14)$$

Using instruments $B^* = \Omega^{-1/2}B = \Omega^{-1/2}(X_1, W_1, Z_1)$ instead of B to prevent possible collinearity between (Z_2, W_2) and (X_1, W_1, Z_1).[2] This gives the simple consistent estimator

$$\begin{bmatrix} \hat{\gamma}_w \\ \hat{\delta}_{0w} \end{bmatrix} = \left[(Z, W)'\Omega^{-1/2}P_{B^*}\Omega^{-1/2}(Z, W) \right]^{-1}$$
$$\times (Z, W)'\Omega^{-1/2}P_{B^*}\Omega^{-1/2}(y - X\hat{\beta}_w). \quad (12.7.15)$$

Enough instruments are needed to identify all the coefficients, that is, $k_1 + j_1 + l_1 \geq J + L$, or equivalently $k_1 \geq j_2 + l_2$. The efficient instrumental variables (IV) estimator can be obtained by using instruments $A^* = \Omega^{-1/2}A = \Omega^{-1/2}(M_Q, X_1, Z_1, W_1)$ to estimate all of the parameters jointly. Denoting $G = (X, Z, W)$, the efficient IV estimator is given by:

$$\begin{bmatrix} \tilde{\beta}^* \\ \tilde{\gamma}^* \\ \tilde{\delta}_0^* \end{bmatrix} = (G'\Omega^{-1/2}P_{A^*}\Omega^{-1/2}G)^{-1}G'\Omega^{-1/2}P_{A^*}\Omega^{-1/2}y. \quad (12.7.16)$$

Expressions for consistent (for large n) estimates of the covariance terms σ_v^2 and Δ can be found in Cornwell et al. (1990). Extensions that generalize the time-varying nature of the unobserved efficiency effects in the CSS model can be found in Almanidis et al. (2015). Estimators for generalized parameter heterogeneity based on a random coefficients SFA model also can be found in Tsionas (2002) and Huang and Wang (2004).

It remains to use these general estimators to estimate the time-varying efficiencies for each firm. We can do this in a way that's analogous to the methods utilized in Schmidt and Sickles (1984). As with Schmidt and Sickles (1984), the parameter δ_i is estimated by regressing the residuals $(y_{it} - x_{it}'\beta)$ for firm i on w_{it}, which in the parameterization for the quadratic time-varying inefficiency Cornwell et al. (1990) is simply used as a constant, a time trend, and the square of the time trend. The fitted values of $\hat{\alpha}_{it}$ are consistent estimates of α_{it} for large T. The frontier intercept is then estimated for each time period as

$$\hat{\alpha}_t = \max_{j=1,\dots,n} (\hat{\alpha}_{jt}), \quad (12.7.17)$$

and then the individual (in)efficiency term for an observation i in a period t is estimated as

$$\hat{u}_{it} = \hat{\alpha}_t - \hat{\alpha}_{it}, i = 1, \dots, n; t = 1, \dots, T. \quad (12.7.18)$$

---

[2] This is based on an argument by White (1984, pp. 95–99) and repeated in Cornwell et al. (1990, pp. 189) that assumes a reduced form for (Z_2, W_2) exists that is linear in (X_1, Z_1, W_1).

12.7.2 Alternative Specifications of Time-Varying Inefficiency: The Kumbhakar (1990) and Battese and Coelli (1992) Models

12.7.2.1 Kumbhakar's Specification

Kumbhakar (1990) considered a general model of both allocative inefficiency and time-varying technical efficiency. As this book focuses only on the estimation of technical efficiency, we do not consider his general model, nor the many other models of allocative efficiency in this rather dense literature. We instead focus on how his model of time-varying efficiency can be viewed in the production function setting, without side-conditions based on the inefficient application of first-order conditions for cost-minimization discussed first in the literature by Schmidt and Lovell (1979). The Kumbhakar (1990) model of time-varying technical efficiency in the stochastic frontier production setting specifies inefficiency as firm–specific and varying according to an exponential function of time given by

$$u_{it} = (1 + \exp(bt + ct^2))^{-1} \tau_i, \tag{12.7.19}$$

where a and b are parameters to be estimated and where τ_i's distribution is assumed to be iid $N^+(0, \sigma_\tau^2)$ and where the usual disturbance term v_{it} is iid $\mathcal{N}(0, \sigma_v^2)$.

In the Kumbhakar model of time-varying technical inefficiency the error process is specified parametrically and the composed error is the sum of a normal error v_{it} and a truncated normal u_{it}. In this sense, it extends the parametric random effects model of Pitt and Lee (1981) by allowing the firm–specific efficiency effect to have a mean that varies over time. It is a parsimonious model in that the temporal variations in inefficiency are functions of only two additional parameters, a and b, but of course this constrains the possible temporal patterns on inefficiency that different firms can exhibit and relies on parametric MLE for its consistency properties.

12.7.2.2 Battese and Coelli's Specification

Battese and Coelli (1992) considered a different time-varying path for the firm effects

$$u_{it} = \eta_t \tau_i = \{\exp[-\eta(t - T)]\} \tau_i, \quad t = 1, \dots, T; \ i = 1, \dots, n. \tag{12.7.20}$$

In their model v_{it} is assumed to be iid $\mathcal{N}(0, \sigma_v^2)$ random variables; τ_i is assumed to be iid and again follows a nonnegative truncated distribution $\mathcal{N}(\mu, \sigma^2)$; η is set to be a scalar parameter. The movement of firm-specific effects u_{it} depends on the sign of η. The time-invariant case corresponds to $\eta = 0$. To allow for more flexible temporal changing patterns of the firm effects, one can specify η Battese and Coelli (1992) as $\eta_{it} = 1 + \eta_1(t - T) + \eta_2(t - T)^2$, allowing the effects to be convex or concave rather than simply increasing or decreasing with a constant rate. Parametric MLE is also used in the Battese and Coelli (1992) model. Again, parsimony is assured as the model is a function of only two additional parameters η_1 and η_2 but of course this also constrains the temporal patterns of inefficiency exhibited by firms over time and its consistency is usually assured when the parametric assumptions for the composed error distributions are correct.

12.7.3   The Lee and Schmidt (1993) Model

The model proposed in Lee and Schmidt (1993) is a one component factor model that nests any specification with an identical temporal pattern, such as Kumbhakar (1990) and Battese and Coelli (1992). Extensions to multiple factor models for time-varying efficiency modeling are pursued in the next chapter. They consider a situation in which n is large and T is relatively small, which is the standard panel data setting in most productivity studies. The model they consider is a variant of the linear production model we have considered above

$$y_{it} = \alpha_t + x'_{it}\beta + v_{it} - u_{it}, \quad i = 1, \ldots, n; \, t = 1, \ldots, T. \quad (12.7.21)$$

With $\alpha_{it} = \alpha_t - u_{it}$ specified as the firm-specific effects that change over time, the model can then be rewritten as

$$y_{it} = x'_{it}\beta + \alpha_{it} + v_{it}. \quad (12.7.22)$$

The one component factor model considered by Lee and Schmidt (1993), and discussed in more detail in Lee (1991), assumes that

$$\alpha_{it} = \eta_t \delta_i, \quad (12.7.23)$$

where η_t, $\{t = 1, \ldots, T\}$, are the the time-varying effects to be estimated and δ_i, $\{i = 1, \ldots, n\}$, are the firm effects. The scale of δ cannot be determined until the scale of η is set. The normalization used by Lee and Schmidt (1993) is to set the time-varying effects at period 1 to be 1, that is, $\eta_1 = 1$. If we let $y_i = (y_{i1}, \ldots, y_{iT})'$, $X_i = (x_{i1}, \ldots, x_{iT})'$, $\theta' = (1, \eta_2, \ldots, \eta_T)$, and $v_i = (v_{i1}, \ldots, v_{iT})'$, where v_{is} is assumed to be iid with mean 0 and variance σ^2, not necessarily normal, then the model for firm i over all observed periods is

$$y_i = X_i\beta + \theta\delta_i + v_i. \quad (12.7.24)$$

The model for all observations can be expressed in the following matrix form as

$$y = X\beta + (I_n \otimes \theta)\delta + v. \quad (12.7.25)$$

Here y and v are $nT \times 1$ block vectors whose ith block is y_i or v_i, respectively, $\delta' = (\delta_1, \ldots, \delta_n)$ are the fixed effects, and X is $nT \times k$. In addition to the parameters already specified, there is an additional random effects parameter σ_δ^2 considered by Lee and Schmidt (1993) as an alternative to the fixed effects treatment that utilizes $\delta' = (\delta_1, \ldots, \delta_n)$.

12.7.3.1 Implementation

Fixed-Effects Approach

In the fixed-effects case, δ is estimated along with the other parameters. These include β, θ, and σ_v^2. If θ were known, one could apply OLS after utilizing some standard transformations. Let's assume for the moment that θ is known. Then following usual approaches to deal with the incidental parameters problem using a within-type transformation, define the projection matrix $P_\theta = \theta(\theta'\theta)^{-1}\theta'$ and its orthogonal complement $M_\theta = I_T - P_\theta$. Both P_θ and M_θ are idempotent, and $M_\theta\theta = 0$. By utilizing the properties of such matrices, the fixed effects can be removed by transforming the model to get

$$M_\theta y_i = M_\theta X_i \beta + M_\theta v_i$$
$$(I_n \otimes M_\theta)y = (I_n \otimes M_\theta)X\beta + (I_n \otimes M_\theta)v. \qquad (12.7.26)$$

Without the individual effects, standard least squares can be applied to estimate β. The sum of square errors for the model is

$$SSE_F(\beta, \theta) \equiv \sum_i (M_\theta y_i - M_\theta X_i \beta)'(M_\theta y_i - M_\theta X_i \beta)$$
$$= [(I_n \otimes M_\theta)y - (I_n \otimes M_\theta)X\beta]'[(I_n \otimes M_\theta)y$$
$$- (I_n \otimes M_\theta)X\beta]. \qquad (12.7.27)$$

Then, given θ, we know SSE_F is minimized by $\hat{\beta}$ from the properties of OLS estimator. Since θ is not known in practice estimates of β and θ must be jointly determined by minimizing the SSE_F. The minimization problem can be solved numerically as an iterative algorithm based on the relation between $\hat{\beta}$ and $\hat{\theta}$ and was given in Lee (1991) as

$$\hat{\beta} = \left(\sum_i X'_i \hat{M}_\theta X_i\right)^{-1} \sum_i X'_i \hat{M}_\theta y_i$$
$$= [X'(I_n \otimes \hat{M}_\theta)X]^{-1} X'(I_n \otimes \hat{M}_\theta)y, \qquad (12.7.28)$$

where $\hat{M}_\theta$ is the expression for M_θ evaluated at $\theta = \hat{\theta}$. The estimates obtained are consistent and asymptotically normal given standard regularity conditions for large n and finite T. After determining the estimates of β and θ the remaining parameters can be derived recursively as: $\hat{\delta}_i = \hat{\theta}'(y_i - X_i\hat{\beta})/\hat{\theta}'\hat{\theta}$ and $\hat{\alpha}_{it} = \hat{\theta}_t\hat{\delta}_i$.

Random-Effects Approach

In the random-effects case, the δs are assumed to be random variables instead of fixed parameters and are uncorrelated with other explanatory variables. Denote $\mu = E(\delta_i)$, and let $\delta_i^* = \delta_i - \mu$ be the centered variable. Here the δ_i^*s are assumed to be iid with mean zero and variance σ_δ^2 while μ is constant so that the δ_i^*s are also uncorrelated with other explanatory variables. The model can be rewritten as

$$y_i = X_i\beta + \theta\mu + \varepsilon_i, \quad \varepsilon_i = \theta\delta_i^* + v_i. \tag{12.7.29}$$

For all nT observations the model is

$$y = X\beta + (\mathbf{1} \otimes \theta)\mu + \varepsilon, \tag{12.7.30}$$

where $\mathbf{1}$ is an $n \times 1$ vector of ones. The new error vector ε does not satisfy the standard assumption that all entries are independently and identically distributed as the covariance is given by

$$\Omega = \text{Cov}(\varepsilon) = \sigma_v^2 I_{nT} + \theta'\theta\sigma_\delta^2(I_n \otimes P_\theta). \tag{12.7.31}$$

The inverse of Ω will be needed to implement the GLS estimator. We can write the inverse of Ω as:

$$\Omega^{-1} = \sigma_v^{-2}(M_\theta + q^2 P_\theta), \tag{12.7.32}$$

where

$$q^2 = \sigma_v^2/(\sigma_v^2 + \theta'\theta\sigma_\delta^2). \tag{12.7.33}$$

Since the covariance is a non-scalar and non-diagonal matrix, GLS is used as the efficient estimator. As with the fixed-effects case, estimates of (β, θ, μ) are obtained by minimizing the sum of squared errors:

$$SSE_G(\beta, \theta, \mu) = \sum_i (y_i - X_i\beta - \theta\mu)'(M_\theta + q^2 P_\theta)(y_i - X_i\beta - \theta\mu)$$

$$= [y - X\beta - (\mathbf{1} \otimes \theta)\mu]'[(I_n \otimes M_\theta) + q^2(I_n \otimes P_\theta)]$$

$$[y - X\beta - (\mathbf{1} \otimes \theta)\mu]. \tag{12.7.34}$$

Denoting the estimates as $\tilde{\beta}$, $\tilde{\theta}$, and $\tilde{\mu}$, Lee (1991) then derives a solution for the GLS estimate $\tilde{\beta}$, in terms of $\tilde{\theta}$ and $\tilde{\mu}$, similar to that in the fixed-effects case

$$\tilde{\beta} = \{X'[(I_n \otimes \tilde{M}_\theta) + q^2(M_1 \otimes \tilde{P}_\theta)]X\}^{-1}X'[(I_n \otimes \tilde{M}_\theta) + q^2(M_1 \otimes \tilde{P}_\theta)]y, \tag{12.7.35}$$

where $\tilde{P}_\theta = \tilde{\theta}(\tilde{\theta}'\tilde{\theta})^{-1}\tilde{\theta}'$, $\tilde{M}_\theta = I_T - \tilde{\theta}(\tilde{\theta}'\tilde{\theta})^{-1}\tilde{\theta}'$ and $M_1 = I_n - \mathbf{1}(\mathbf{1}'\mathbf{1})^{-1}\mathbf{1}'$. The GLS estimator is more efficient than the fixed effects estimator, but only when all the effects are not correlated with the explanatory variables. The remaining unknown parameters can then be estimated by letting $e_i = y_i - X_i\tilde{\beta}$ and $\bar{e} = \sum_i e_i/n$. $\tilde{\theta}$ is the eigen-vector corresponding to the largest eigenvalue of

$$\sum_i \left\{ (1-q^2)^{-1/2}e_i + [1 - (1-q^2)^{-1/2}]\bar{e} \right\} \left\{ (1-q^2)^{-1/2}e_i \right.$$

$$\left. + [1 - (1-q^2)^{-1/2}]\bar{e} \right\}' \tag{12.7.36}$$

and

$$\tilde{\mu} = (\mathbf{1} \otimes \tilde{\theta})'(y - X\tilde{\beta})/(n\tilde{\theta}'\tilde{\theta}). \tag{12.7.37}$$

As with other uncorrelated random effects specifications of the stochastic frontier production model consistency of the GLS estimates rests on the assumed uncorrelatedness of the effects and the regressors, in which case they are consistent, asymptotically normal and more efficient than the fixed effects estimator as they use both between and within variation of the data. If the effects and regressors are uncorrelated then GLS in this setting is more efficient than the fixed effects estimate but the efficiency gain diminishes as T gets large.

Estimates of the parameters of interest, the firm efficiencies, are solved recursively as

$$\tilde{\delta}_i^* = \frac{\tilde{\theta}'(y_i - X_i\tilde{\beta} - \tilde{\theta}\tilde{\mu})}{\tilde{\theta}'\tilde{\theta}} \tag{12.7.38}$$

$$\tilde{\delta}_i = \tilde{\delta}_i^* + \tilde{\mu} = \frac{\tilde{\theta}'(y_i - X_i\tilde{\beta})}{\tilde{\theta}'\tilde{\theta}} \tag{12.7.39}$$

$$\tilde{\alpha}_{it} = \tilde{\eta}_t \tilde{\delta}_i, \tag{12.7.40}$$

where

$$(1, \tilde{\eta}_2, \ldots, \tilde{\eta}_T) = \tilde{\theta}'.$$

Since the covariance matrix of the error term is usually unknown in practice, one must first estimate the covariance matrix, or the value of q^2, which is extensively used in estimation, in order to obtain the feasible GLS estimator. In the case of a non-scalar covariance matrix, the simple OLS method can give consistent estimators of β and θ, which can then be used to estimate q^2. Expressions for the feasible GLS estimation of the parameters based on initial consistent estimates of q^2 are given in Lee (1991).

12.7.4 Panel Stochastic Frontier Technical Efficiency Confidence Intervals

Horrace and Schmidt (1996) discuss the construction of confidence intervals for inefficiencies in the panel data setting. Confidence intervals can also be developed for the random error components frontier model considered in Pitt and Lee (1981), Schmidt and Sickles (1984), and Battese and Coelli (1988) using a straightforward extension of the cross-sectional Jondrow et al. (1982) approach. For example, if inefficiency is time–invariant and we let $\varepsilon_i = (\varepsilon_{i1}, \ldots, \varepsilon_{iT}) = (v_{i1} - u_i, \ldots, v_{iT} - u_i)$, then by defining $\bar{\varepsilon}_i = (1/T)\sum_{t=1}^{T} e_{it}$, $\mu_i^* = \sigma_u^2\bar{\varepsilon}_i(\sigma_u^2 + \sigma_v^2/T)^{-1}$, $\sigma_*^2 = \sigma_v^2\sigma_u^2(\sigma_v^2 + T\sigma_u^2)^{-1}$, the distribution of $u_i|\varepsilon_i$ is $\mathcal{N}(\mu_i^*, \sigma_*^2)$ and the corresponding confidence intervals are constructed in the same way as the cross-section ALS model except that ε_i has been replaced with $\bar{\varepsilon}_i$ and σ_v^2 with σ_v^2/T. The Battese and Coelli (1988) approach to establishing confidence intervals for inefficiency can also be extended to deal with unbalanced panels. Hjalmarsson et al. (1996) provide expressions for extending the Horrace and Schmidt (1996) approach to various time-varying efficiency models for the panel frontier.

12.7.5   Fixed versus Random Effects: A Prelude to More General Panel Treatments

One of the modeling issues in panel data analysis of the stochastic frontier model concerns the implications of including fixed effects in the stochastic frontier production function. Standard results have held that a MLE-based estimator of the panel stochastic frontier is subject to the "incidental parameters" (IP) problem that induces a serious bias in estimated coefficients in the production function (Chamberlain, 1980). Greene (2005b) has analyzed and proposed a generalization to the parametric MLE-based estimators developed in Pitt and Lee's (1981) time-invariant inefficiency model and Battese and Coelli's (1992) narrowly structured time-varying inefficiency model. Such an incidental parameters problem does not exist with the regression-based approaches proposed in Schmidt and Sickles (1984) and Cornwell et al. (1990). The possibility of this bias in parametric MLE-based estimation of fixed-effects stochastic frontiers was thought to severely taint this otherwise attractive specification, but Greene has shown that the bias in the model slopes in the stochastic frontier context has been greatly exaggerated. Moreover, Greene has also shown that the force of the IP problem is actually exerted on the variance of the noise component of the composed error – much more so than on other model components. Taken together, these findings would seem to indicate that researchers should focus on how the IP problem may impact estimated inefficiency in the SF model, not on the estimated parameters. This is what motivated Greene to refocus attention on how the effects themselves should be decomposed. One such decomposition is to view the standard fixed effects as the true fixed effects and those that change over time as what one would normally think of as (suitably normalized) technical efficiency effects. Indeed, Wang and Ho (2010) and Chen et al. (2014) developed several estimation methods to deal with the IP problem. One particularly effective approach based on the method of moments has recently been developed by Wikström (2015). We discuss this issue in more depth in the next chapter and in our chapter on endogeneity.

Greene (2005b) and Filippini and Greene (2016), among others, have stressed the methodological ambiguity in the specification of the panel data models with composed error, $\varepsilon_{it} = v_{it} - u_i$. The time-invariant component has heretofore been identified with inefficiency. Greene (2005b) argued that in many contexts, it would be more appropriate to identify time invariant variation as cross-sectional heterogeneity. The large cross-country variation in the World Health Organization's (WHO) study of national health care systems provides a clear example. Greene (2005b) considers the stochastic frontier model with time-invariant heterogeneity and time-varying inefficiency (labeled a "true random effects" model). The use of the term "true" in this framework relates to the specific use of the stochastic frontier as the platform for the models, rather than a reinterpretation of the linear regression model. The structural random element of the stochastic frontier model in this context is $\varepsilon_{it} = w_i + v_{it} - u_{it}$, where w_i is the (time-invariant) heterogeneity term (either fixed effect or random effect) and $v_{it}-u_{it}$ represent the "true" stochastic frontier. Greene (2005b) discussed identification of the maximum simulated likelihood estimator for this class of models. Such "true random effects" and "true fixed effects" estimators are now widely used platforms for panel data applications of the stochastic frontier model. Wang and Ho (2010) solve the IP problem faced with Greene's true fixed effects model by model transformations. Kutlu et al. (2018) solve this problem in a way similar to Wang and Ho (2010) by using model transformations, but they allow the heterogeneity term (individual effects term) to be time-varying along the lines of the CSS fixed effects estimator. Hence, these two papers are able to avoid the IP problem in panel data context.

12.8 CONCLUDING REMARKS

The first generation of panel data estimators provided researchers with a number of approaches to evaluate time-varying and cross-sectionally varying efficiency and productivity measures, freeing up the rather limited possibilities that existed before the 1990s in evaluating such dynamic productivity trends. It became clear, however, that there were limitations in these early approaches in terms of their relatively strong reliance on parametric distributional assumptions as well as on parametric assumptions about the nature of evolving patterns of efficiency and productivity change. Moreover, various forms of heterogeneity and their sources could be better explained by extensions in these first generation models to the second generation models we consider in the following chapter.

12.9 EXERCISES

1. Show under what conditions the Kumbhakar (1990) estimator is a special case of the Cornwell et al. (1990) estimator.
2. The Battese and Coelli (1992) and Kumbhakar (1990) panel frontier estimators rely on parametric assumptions to identify and estimate the production (cost) function and technical efficiency. The Cornwell et al. (1990) and the Lee and Schmidt (1993) models identify and estimate the parameters of the production (cost) function and technical efficiency using moment conditions. Discuss the advantages of estimators based on parametric distributional assumptions versus estimators that rely on moment conditions in terms of robustness to misspecified distribution assumptions.
3. What is the advantage of a Jondrow et al. (1982)-type estimator in the panel stochastic frontier model?
4. Show under what conditions the Lee and Schmidt (1993) model nests both the Kumbhakar (1990) and the Battese and Coelli (1992) models.

5. The Kumbhakar (1990) and the Battese and Coelli (1992) panel frontier estimators assume that the temporal patterns of efficiency are the same for every firm. Cornwell et al. (1990) and the Lee and Schmidt (1993) do not. In what institutional settings would you find the assumptions of temporal patterns of efficiency to be shared by all firms in the industry and in what institutional setting would you not?

CHAPTER 13

Panel Data and Parametric and Semiparametric Stochastic Frontier Models: Second-Generation Approaches

In this chapter, we discuss more recent methods to model and estimate productivity and efficiency utilizing semi-nonparametric efficient econometric estimators, latent class and factor models, and Bayesian methods. These approaches offer the modeler substantial improvements in robustness properties and flexibility and can nest many of the more classical methods developed in the previous chapter. The material in this and the previous chapter can also be found in Sickles et al. (2015) and Shang (2015).

13.1 THE PARK, SICKLES, AND SIMAR (1998, 2003, 2007) MODELS

A series of papers by Park et al. (1998, 2003, 2007) (PSS) considered a stochastic frontier model in which the firm inefficiency effects are correlated with other explanatory variables but where the joint distribution of the effects and the regressors was not parametrically specified. Models in which the mean function was also nonparametrically specified using kernel smoothers and where the random disturbance was similarly nonparametrically specified can be found in Adams et al. (1997, 1999), and Adams and Sickles (2007). Three different patterns of correlation are discussed in the three Park, Sickles, and Simar papers corresponding to cases in which the random disturbance is serially uncorrelated, serially correlated with an AR(1) specification, and in which the panel model is dynamic. We consider only the case in which the random disturbance is serially uncorrelated considered in Park et al. (1998).

The basic setting of Park et al. (1998) is the familiar panel model

$$y_{it} = \alpha_i + x'_{it}\beta + v_{it} \quad \text{for } i = 1, \cdots, n; t = 1, \cdots, T, \quad (13.1.1)$$

where y_{it} represents output level of firm i at time t, x_{it} is a $k \times 1$ vector of regressors, and v_{it} is the statistical noise that is independently and identically distributed with $\mathcal{N}(0, \sigma_v^2)$, and α_i is the firm–specific effect that is bounded above (or below for the cost frontier model). The link between this generic panel specification and the stochastic panel frontier model we considered in

Chapter 12 is based on a normalization wherein $\alpha_i = \alpha^* - u_i^*$, where $\alpha^* = \alpha - \mu$; $u_i^* = u_i - \mu$; $E(u_i) = \mu \geq 0$. Thus the model can be respecified as

$$y_{it} = \alpha + x_{it}'\beta + v_{it} - u_i, \quad i = 1, \ldots, n; t = 1, \ldots, T, \quad (13.1.2)$$

which is the stochastic panel frontier model. With different levels of dependency between the firm effects, α, and the regressors, x, three cases are considered by Park et al. (1998). Model 1 does not assume any specific pattern of dependency between α and x, which leads to the semiparametric efficient within estimator. Model 2 assumes that the effects are correlated with a subset of the explanatory variables, $z \in x$. We leave it to the interested reader to pursue the details of this estimator that can be found in Park et al. (1998). Model 3 assumes that α affects z only through its long run changes (average movements in $\bar{z}$). The semiparametric efficient estimators for Models 2 and 3 are analogous to those proposed in Hausman and Taylor (1981). This is actually a semiparametric efficient version of the correlated random effects model wherein the effects are a function of only a subset of the regressors.

13.1.1   Implementation

In the parametric model, an estimator is asymptotically efficient when its covariance attains the asymptotic lower bound. The lower bound can be calculated as the inverse of the Fisher information, $I = E(S^*S^{*'})$, where S^* is the efficient score function. With P representing the class of semiparametric models, we can calculate Fisher-like information, $I(P)$, in a similar way, using adjusted efficient score functions. The semi-nonparametric efficient estimator would attain the asymptotic lower bound.

13.1.1.1   PSS Model 1: No Specific Dependency Structure

We first introduce some notation and assumptions. Denote $x_i = (x_{it}', \ldots, x_{iT}')' \in \mathbb{R}^{kT}$. The (α_i, x_i)'s are assumed to be independently and identically distributed with some joint density $h(\cdot, \cdot)$. The support of the marginal density of α is assumed to be bounded from above and the bound B sets the upper level of the average production frontier. Also assumed is that the v's and the (α, x)'s are independent. The generic observations for (y, x) are $y = (y_1, \ldots, y_T)'$, where $y_t = (y_{1t}, \ldots, y_{nt})'$, and $x = (x_1, \ldots, x_T)$, where $x_t = (x_{1t}, \ldots, x_{nt})$. Let $S_t(\beta) = y_t - x_t'\beta$, $\bar{S}(\beta) = \frac{1}{T}\sum_{t=1}^{T} S_t(\beta)$ and $U_t(\beta) = S_t(\beta) - \bar{S}(\beta)$. Let $\Sigma_w = E[\frac{1}{T}\sum_{t=1}^{T}(x_t - \bar{x})(x_t - \bar{x})']$, where $\bar{x} = \frac{1}{T}\sum_{t=1}^{T} x_t$, $\bar{y} = \frac{1}{T}\sum_{t=1}^{T} y_t$, $\bar{\sigma}_v = \sigma_v/\sqrt{T}$, and Σ_w is assumed to be non-singular.

One can derive the efficient score function and the information bound for estimates of β as (for a detailed proof, see Park et al., 1998):

$$S^* = \sigma_v^{-2} \sum_{t=1}^{T} x_t U_t(\beta), \tag{13.1.3}$$

$$I(P) = \bar{\sigma}_v^{-2} \Sigma_w. \tag{13.1.4}$$

The information bound $I(P)$ above corresponds to the information bound of the least favorable regular parametric sub-model that can be obtained after the density of (α, x) is parameterized by $h_\eta(\alpha, x) = h(\alpha - \eta, x)$, where $h(\cdot, \cdot)$ is some (unknown) joint density of the effects and the regressors, and where η is a nuisance parameter (e.g., a bandwidth). Using this information bound, it can be shown that the within estimator given below is semiparametric efficient:

$$\hat{\beta} = \frac{1}{nT} \hat{\Sigma}_w^{-1} \sum_{i=1}^{n} \sum_{t=1}^{T} (x_{it} - \bar{x})(y_{it} - \bar{y}_i), \tag{13.1.5}$$

$$\hat{\Sigma}_w = \frac{1}{nT} \sum_{i=1}^{n} \sum_{t=1}^{T} (x_{it} - \bar{x}_i)(x_{it} - \bar{x}_i)'. \tag{13.1.6}$$

When the effects and the regressors are not correlated, the semiparametric efficient within estimator is no longer semiparametric efficient, but the semiparametric efficient random effects estimator of Park and Simar (1994) is.

13.1.1.2 PSS Model 3: Dependency between Firm Effects and Average Movements of a Subset of Regressors

We first rewrite the model as

$$y_{it} = \alpha_i + x_{it}' \beta_{(1)} + z_{it}' \beta_{(2)} + v_{it}. \tag{13.1.7}$$

Here x_{it} is a $p \times 1$ vector, z_{it} is a $q \times 1$ vector, and $p + q = k$. Assume that α_i and x_i are conditionally independent in the sense that any dependence between x and α is through the variable z. In this case, the firm inefficiency effects only influence the correlated regressors (z) through their long-run movements ($\bar{z}$), and thus the joint density of (α_i, z_i, x_i) is

$$f(\alpha, z, x) = h(\alpha, z)g(x|z), \tag{13.1.8}$$

where

$$h(\alpha, z) = h_M(\alpha, \bar{z})p(z). \tag{13.1.9}$$

The density $g(\cdot|\cdot)$ represents the density of x_i conditioned on z_i. Let $\beta = (\beta_{(1)}', \beta_{(2)}')'$. We can then similarly define $S_t(\beta) = y_t - x_t' \beta_{(1)} - z_t' \beta_{(2)}$, $U_t(\beta) = S_t(\beta) - \bar{S}(\beta)$, $\bar{z} = \frac{1}{T} \sum_{t=1}^{T} z_t$, and $\bar{\sigma}_v = \sigma_v / \sqrt{T}$. The joint density of $(\bar{S}(\beta), \bar{z})$ is then denoted as

$$w(s, \bar{z}) = \int \phi_{\bar{\sigma}_v}(s - u) h_M(u, \bar{z}) du = \phi_{\bar{\sigma}_v} \cdot h(\cdot, \bar{z})(s), \tag{13.1.10}$$

where $\phi_{\bar{\sigma}_v}$ is the $\mathcal{N}(0, \bar{\sigma}_v^2)$ density of the within errors and

$$w'(s, \bar{z}) = \frac{\partial}{\partial s} w(s, \bar{z}). \tag{13.1.11}$$

Next define

$$\Sigma_w(x) = E\left(\frac{1}{T} \sum_{t=1}^{T} (x_t - \bar{x})(x_t - \bar{x})'\right) \tag{13.1.12}$$

$$\Sigma_w(z) = E\left(\frac{1}{T} \sum_{t=1}^{T} (z_t - \bar{z})(z_t - \bar{z})'\right) \tag{13.1.13}$$

$$\Sigma_w(x, z) = E\left(\frac{1}{T} \sum_{t=1}^{T} (x_t - \bar{x})(z_t - \bar{z})'\right) \tag{13.1.14}$$

$$\Sigma_B(x|\bar{z}) = E\left[\frac{1}{T} (\bar{x} - E(\bar{x}|\bar{z}))(\bar{x} - E(\bar{x}|\bar{z}))'\right] \tag{13.1.15}$$

$$I_0 = \int \left[\frac{w'(s, \bar{z})}{w(s, \bar{z})}\right]^2 ds d\bar{z}. \tag{13.1.16}$$

Similar results for the efficient score function, $l^{*'} = (l^{*'}_{\beta_{(1)}}, l^{*'}_{\beta_{(2)}})$, and the information bound for Model 2 are used to construct the efficient score function and the information bound for the semiparametric efficient estimator for Model 3. These are

$$l^*_{\beta_{(1)}} = \sigma_v^{-2} \sum_{t=1}^{T} x_t U_t(\beta) - (\bar{x} - E(\bar{x}|\bar{z})) \frac{w'(s, \bar{z})}{w(s, \bar{z})} (\bar{S}(\beta), \bar{z}), \tag{13.1.17}$$

$$l^*_{\beta_{(2)}} = \sigma_v^{-2} \sum_{t=1}^{T} z_t U_t(\beta), \tag{13.1.18}$$

$$I(P) = \begin{pmatrix} \bar{\sigma}_v^{-2} \Sigma_w(x) + I_0 \Sigma_B(x|\bar{z}) & \bar{\sigma}_v^{-2} \Sigma_w(x, z) \\ \bar{\sigma}_v^{-2} \Sigma'_w(x, z) & \bar{\sigma}_v^{-2} \Sigma_w(z) \end{pmatrix}. \tag{13.1.19}$$

The semiparametric efficient estimator β then can be determined in the following steps:

(a) Obtain a consistent estimator $\tilde{\beta}$ of β (for example, the within estimator);[1]
(b) Set $\tilde{l} = I^{-1}l^*$, which is called the efficient influence function;
(c) Construct the efficient estimator as

$$\hat{\beta} = \tilde{\beta} + \frac{1}{n} \sum_{i=1}^{n} \tilde{l}(x_i, z_i, y_i, \tilde{\beta}; x_1, z_1, y_1, \dots, x_n, z_n, y_n).$$

$$\tag{13.1.20}$$

[1] Park, et al. (1998) discuss consistent estimation of the other parameters σ_v^2 and the nonparametric multivariate density h.

The estimator is consistent for large n and asymptotically $\mathcal{N}(\beta, I^{-1})$, where $E(\tilde{l}) = 0$ and $E(\tilde{l}\tilde{l}') = I^{-1}$. Estimates of relative efficiency follow the conventions of Schmidt and Sickles (1984) and Cornwell et al. (1990) discussed above and require large T and large n for consistency. The relative technical efficiency of a particular firm is calculated as

$$\widehat{TE}_i = \exp[-\{\max(\widehat{\alpha}_i) - \widehat{\alpha}_i\}], \qquad (13.1.21)$$

where $\widehat{\alpha}_i = \overline{S}_i(\widehat{\beta})$.

13.2 THE LATENT CLASS MODELS

In all the stochastic frontier models that we have discussed thus far, with the exception of the metafrontier, the production function is set uniformly for all units, which implies that all the firms share the same technology and only differ in the level of efficiency. Heterogeneity has been captured by the efficiency term in the panel applications we briefly touched on in Chapter 12 and in this chapter up to this point, with the exception of the metafrontier discussed briefly in Chapters 9 and 11 and which we treat more extensively in Chapter 15. This assumption may not be true in practice. The heterogeneities among firms due to different sizes, innovation abilities, targeting groups, etc. will lead to different operating strategies and may result in firms adopting different technologies. Imposing the same functional form in the model may incorrectly identify differences in the utilized production technology as inefficiency.

One straightforward way to deal with this problem is to group the firms into different categories based on some observable criteria, such as country, region, epoch, size, etc., and then conduct the analysis separately for each group. Alternatively, one can group the observations based on the results from some clustering analysis. A shortcoming of these methods is that we cannot utilize information contained in the correlation between different groups, since the analyses are typically conducted separately. Moreover, it is difficult in practice to collect enough exogenous information to accurately identify distinct categories and it is often hard to evaluate the suitability of the grouping criteria.

By combining the latent structure and stochastic frontier model, Greene (2002), Orea and Kumbhakar (2004), and Greene (2005b) generalized the panel frontier model to allow for such a set of groupings. Assume that there exist J finite but unobserved classes in the panel data and that class heterogeneity shows up as heterogeneity in the slope parameters of the stochastic panel frontier and in the variances of the disturbance terms but not in the function form of the frontier technology. We will discuss the random effects specification of the Latent Class Model. The model is discussed thoroughly in Greene (2005b) and for the stochastic production frontier can be written as

$$y_{it} = \alpha + x_{it}'\beta_j + v_{it|j} - u_{i|j}, \quad i = 1, \ldots, n; t = 1, \ldots, T; j = 1, \ldots, J,$$
$$(13.2.1)$$

where the half-normal inefficiency term u_i has positive support and moments $E(u_i) = \mu \geq 0$, and $V(u_{i|j}) = \sigma^2_{u|j}$, and where $v_{it|j}$ is assumed to be iid $\mathcal{N}(0, \sigma^2_{v|j})$. The composed error term is $\varepsilon_{it|j} = v_{it|j} - u_{i|j} = y_{it} - \alpha - x'_{it}\beta_j$. The density for an observation i, t for a particular latent class j is given by

$$P(i, t|j) = f(y_{it}|x_{it}; \beta_j, \sigma_j, \lambda_j) = \frac{\Phi(\lambda_j \varepsilon_{it|j}/\sigma_j)}{\Phi(0)} \frac{1}{\sigma_j} \phi\left(\frac{\varepsilon_{it|j}}{\sigma_j}\right),$$

(13.2.2)

where $\lambda_j = \sigma_{u|j}/\sigma_{v|j}$ and $\sigma_j = \sqrt{\sigma^2_{v|j} + \sigma^2_{u|j}}$. Since the inefficiency terms are assumed to be independently distributed over time, the conditional likelihood for firm i given class j is

$$\mathcal{L}(i|j) = \prod_{t=1}^{T} P(i, t|j)$$

(13.2.3)

and the unconditional likelihood function for firm i averaged over the j classes is

$$\mathcal{L}(i) = \sum_{j=1}^{J} \pi(i, j) P(i|j) = \sum_{j=1}^{J} \pi(i, j) \prod_{t=1}^{T} P(i, t|j).$$

(13.2.4)

Here $\pi(i, j)$ is a prior probability describing the distribution of firms in different classes. The simplest specification would be a uniform probability for all observations or $\pi(i, j) = \pi(j)$, for $i = 1, \ldots, n$. An alternative is to allow heterogeneity in the probabilities by adopting a multinomial logit form,

$$\pi(i, j) = \frac{\exp(z'_i \pi_j)}{\sum_{l=1}^{J} \exp(z'_i \pi_l)}, \quad \pi_J = 0,$$

(13.2.5)

where $\pi_J = 0$ is a normalization and the z variables may represent firm-specific characteristics.

In the Greene (2005b) model the inefficiency term is assumed to be independent over time. The latent class model proposed by Orea and Kumbhakar (2004) allows the inefficiency term to change over time by following a deterministic path: $u_{it|j} = \gamma_{it}(\cdot) u_{i|j}$, where $\gamma_{it}(\cdot)$ is assumed to be an exponential function to incorporate a vector of firm – specific characteristics that might also change over time:

$$u_{it|j} = z^*_{it}(\eta_j) u_{i|j} = \exp(z^*_{it}\eta_j) u_{i|j},$$

(13.2.6)

where $z^*_{it} = (z^*_{1it}, \ldots, z^*_{Hit})'$ is a vector of time-varying variables and $\eta_j = (\eta_{1j}, \ldots, \eta_{Hj})'$ is the the associated parameter vector. With such a temporal changing path, the individual likelihood in their model is defined directly over all the time periods.

13.2.1 Implementation

One can maximize the log-likelihood to solve for the parameter vector $\Theta_j = \{\alpha, \beta_j, \lambda_j, \sigma_j\}$ and π_j with J finite and known. A number of methods have been proposed to select the finite number of latent classes using cross-validation and specification metrics, such as the Akaike and Bayes information criteria. An alternative to maximizing the log-likelihood function directly was proposed by Greene (2005b) and utilizes the Expectation-Maximization (EM) algorithm. Based on Bayes' rule, the posterior probability of a firm i belonging to class j is

$$w(j|i) = \frac{P(i|j)\pi(i, j)}{\sum_{l=1}^{J} P(i|l)\pi(i, l)}. \tag{13.2.7}$$

Two portions of the optimization problem can be considered separately using these posterior probabilities in order to solve for the estimated parameter vectors $\{\hat{\Theta}_j, \hat{\pi}_j\}, (j = 1, \ldots, J)$, which are

$$\hat{\Theta}_j = \arg\max_{\Theta_j} \left[\sum_{i=1}^{n} w(j|i) \ln P(i|j) \right], \quad j = 1, \ldots, J, \tag{13.2.8}$$

$$(\hat{\pi}_1, \ldots, \hat{\pi}_J) = \arg\max_{(\pi_1, \ldots, \pi_J)} \left[\sum_{i=1}^{n} \sum_{j=1}^{J} w(j|i) \ln \pi(i, j) \right], \quad \hat{\pi}_J = 0. \tag{13.2.9}$$

Iteratively optimizing the two problems in a zig-zag search and updating the posterior probability $w(j|i)$, one can solve for the ML estimates of Θ_j and π_j. Greene (2005b) used the multinomial logit specification of $\pi(i, j)$. An alternative estimation method using a Bayesian approach also can be used. If we denote the results from the optimization as $\{\hat{\Theta}_j, \hat{\pi}_j), \hat{w}(j|i)\}$, then $\hat{w}(j|i)$ provides the best estimate of the probability of individual i being in class j, and thus one can estimate the class of individual i to be the one with the largest probability. After classifying firms into different groups, firm-specific parameters can be estimated by $\hat{\Theta}_j$ or $[\hat{\Theta}|i] = \sum_{j=1}^{J} \hat{w}(j|i)\hat{\Theta}_j$.

Relative technical efficiency of firm i is estimated as

$$\widehat{TE}_i = \exp[-\{\max(\hat{\alpha}_i) - \hat{\alpha}_i\}], \tag{13.2.10}$$

where $\hat{\alpha}_i$ can be retrieved from $[\hat{\Theta}|i]$.

The latent class model has been used in many empirical contexts. One of the more interesting early applications in the context of productivity measurement for multi-input and multi-output firms can be found in Kumbhakar et al. (2007a) who discuss how to estimate a mixture/latent class model (LCM) involving multi-output and multi-input distance functions in their panel study of European railways. Su et al. (2016) provide an exhaustive theoretical treatment of structures such as these in general econometric modeling contexts.

Latent class production techniques that suggest heterogeneity in technologies being utilized by firms in the same industry recently has been studied in Triebs et al. (2016) who model type-specific technologies used in US publicly owned electric utilities. Heterogeneity in a firm's adoption of technology clearly may not be captured by simple additive fixed or random effects but may suggest a broader set of heterogeneities. They model these using linear parametric forms that share much with the Cornwell et al. (1990) general heterogeneity model discussed in Chapter 12.

13.3   THE AHN, LEE, AND SCHMIDT (2007) MODEL

Ahn et al. (2007) considered a "multiple time-varying individual effects" model, in which firm-specific efficiencies are described by multiple factors that change over time, and the number of factors can be obtained in the estimation. The production frontier model is specified as

$$y_{it} = \delta_t + x'_{it}\beta + v_{it} - u_{it} \tag{13.3.1}$$

$$= x'_{it}\beta + \eta_{it} + v_{it}, \quad i = 1, 2, \ldots, n, \ t = 1, 2, \ldots, T, \tag{13.3.2}$$

where v_{it} is the stochastic noise, and $u_{it} \geq 0$ is the inefficiency term of firm i at time t; δ_t represents the time-varying intercept, and it is assumed that there is no time-invariant intercept term contained in $x'_{it}\beta$. Put together, $\eta_{it} \equiv \delta_t - u_{it}$ is interpreted as firm i's efficiency level at time t. The efficiency terms η_{it} are assumed to be explained by p unrestricted components,

$$\eta_{it} = \theta_{1t}\alpha_{1i} + \theta_{2t}\alpha_{2i} + \cdots + \theta_{pt}\alpha_{pi} = \sum_{j=1}^{p} \theta_{jt}\alpha_{ji}. \tag{13.3.3}$$

Note that the model reduces to the Lee and Schmidt (1993) model when we set $p = 1$. This model also nests the model of Cornwell et al. (1990) in that we can set $p = 3$ and $\theta_{1t} = 1$, $\theta_{2t} = t$, and $\theta_{3t} = t^2$. The correct number of efficiency components, denoted by p_0, is needed for the consistent estimation. If $p > p_0$, the estimators of θ_{jt} are inconsistent; if $p < p_0$, the estimators of both β and θ_{jt} are inconsistent. The detailed procedure of estimating p as well as all other parameters will be described below.

13.3.1   Implementation

Restate the model for firm i in matrix form:

$$y_i = x_i\beta + \eta_i + v_i, \quad \eta_i = \Theta\alpha_i, \tag{13.3.4}$$

where $y_i = (y_{i1}, \ldots, y_{iT})'$ is the dependent variable vector, $x_i = (x_{i1}, \ldots, x_{iT})'$ is the $T \times k$ matrix of regressors, and Θ is a $T \times p$ matrix of time-varying factors. The parameters to be estimated are β, Θ and the true number of efficiency components p, and the αs are regarded as random variables. A nonlinear least squares method can be used to consistently estimate the model if both n and T are large. Here a GMM method is utilized to analyze data with large n and small T.

It is assumed that Θ is of full column rank, and that for purposes of identification, a further normalization is made wherein $\Theta = (\Theta'_1, \Theta'_2)'$, with $\Theta_2 = -I_p$ and Θ_1 is a $(T - p) \times p$ matrix consisting of the unrestricted parameters. In the case of $p = 1$, i.e., the Lee and Schmidt (1993) model, it is equivalent to the normalization of θ_1 to -1.

In this model specification, all regressors vary across both firms and time and there are no time-invariant regressors included, although such regressors may be included if there is no time-invariant common factor. Though not contained in the model, the firm-specific time-invariant characteristics are used as instruments in the estimation. Denote $z_i = (x'_{i1}, \ldots, x'_{iT}, f'_i)'$ to be the set of instruments, where f_i is a vector of time-invariant factors. It is assumed that z_i and v_i are uncorrelated. More formally, $E(v_{it}|z_i, \alpha'_i) = 0$, $t = 1, \ldots, T$ and $E(v_i v'_i|z_i, \alpha'_i) = \Sigma_v$, $i = 1, 2, \ldots, n$. This assumption is used to build the moment conditions in GMM. Other regularity conditions are specified, details of which can be found in Ahn et al. (2007).

Additional notations are needed before explaining the estimation method. Denote $H_0 = (H'_{1,0}, H'_{2,0})'$ to be a $T \times (T - p)$ matrix of full column rank. It is constructed in a manner that $H_{1,0}$ is a $(T - p) \times (T - p)$ matrix and $H'_0 \Theta_0 = 0_{(T-p) \times p}$. Θ_0 is the normalized matrix we described before, i.e., $\Theta_0 = (\Theta'_{1,0}, -I_p)'$. Note H_0 is not unique in the sense that $(H_0 B)' \Theta_0 = 0_{(T-p) \times p}$ for any non-singular matrix B. Thus a further normalization is made that $H_{1,0} = I_{T-p}$. Then $H'_{2,0} = \Theta_{1,0}$, resulting from the condition that $H'_0 \Theta_0 = 0_{(T-p) \times p}$.

The model is then transformed by pre-multiplying by H'_0 to

$$H'_0 y_i = H'_0 x_i \beta_0 + H'_0 v_i. \tag{13.3.5}$$

Here β_0 is the true value of the parameter. Now α_i is removed through the transformation while Θ_0 remains (in H_0). Let w_i be a $q \times 1$ vector of instruments (it may contain only some of the variables in z_i). Using the weak exogeneity assumption, the moment conditions are stated as

$$E(H' u_i(\beta) \otimes w_i) = 0_{(T-p)q \times 1}, \tag{13.3.6}$$

where $u_i(\beta) = y_i - x_i \beta$. For a given p, the parameters can be obtained by the continuous-updating GMM estimator developed in Ahn et al. (2007) and further refined in Ahn et al. (2013). Note that for identification, the number of moment conditions must be greater than or equal to the number of parameters in θ and β, which requires $(T - p)q - [(T - p)p + k] \geq 0$. The true value of p can be estimated by utilizing an χ^2 statistic developed in Ahn et al. (2007) and Ahn et al. (2013). We do not repeat the details of their derivations here.

Technical efficiency is measured using the approaches of Cornwell et al. (1990) and Lee and Schmidt (1993). With $\hat{\alpha}_i = (\hat{\Theta}'\hat{\Theta})^{-1}\hat{\Theta}' u(\hat{\beta})$ we can write

$$\hat{\delta}_t = \max_i \hat{\eta}_{it} = \max_i \hat{\Theta}_t \hat{\alpha}_i, \tag{13.3.7}$$

and technical efficiency when output is measured in natural log form is estimated as:

$$\widehat{TE}_{it} = \exp(-\hat{u}_{it}) = \exp[-(\hat{\delta}_t - \hat{\Theta}_t \hat{\alpha}_i)], \tag{13.3.8}$$

where the inefficiency component of the stochastic panel frontier is estimated as $\hat{u}_{it} = \hat{\delta}_t - \hat{\eta}_{it}$. Consistency of the technical efficiencies and the slope parameters requires large n and T.

13.4   BOUNDED INEFFICIENCY MODEL

This model can be extended to the panel data setting:

$$y_{it} = \alpha_0 + x'_{it}\beta + v_{it} - u_{it}, \tag{13.4.1}$$

where u_{it} is assumed to be the positive inefficiency term and follows a time-varying distribution with upper bound B_t. We can impose different structures for the changing path of B_t to fit different circumstances. A generic setup can be

$$B_t = \sum_{i=1}^{n} b_i(t/T)^i, \ t = 1, \ldots, T, \tag{13.4.2}$$

where b_i represents individual effects, and B_t would be the weighted sum of influences from all firms at period t.

13.5   THE KNEIP, SICKLES, AND SONG (2012) MODEL

Similar to the setting in Ahn et al. (2007), the model proposed in Kneip et al. (2012) (KSS) assumed that the individual effects are influenced by a set of time-varying factors, which are represented by some smooth functions of time t.

No assumptions are imposed on the functional form of the effects and thus the model allows for arbitrary patterns of temporal change. The KSS model is given by

$$y_{it} = \beta_0(t) + \sum_{j=1}^{k} \beta_j x_{itj} + u_i(t) + v_{it}, \ i = 1, \ldots, n; \ t = 1, \ldots, T, \tag{13.5.1}$$

where $u_i(t)$s are assumed to be smooth time-varying individual effects, and it's required for identifiability that $\sum_i u_i(t) = 0$. $\beta_0(t)$ is some average function and can be eliminated by transforming the model to the centered form

$$y_{it} - \bar{y}_t = \sum_{j=1}^{k} \beta_j(x_{itj} - \bar{x}_{tj}) + u_i(t) + v_{it} - \bar{v}_i,$$

$$i = 1, \ldots, n; \ t = 1, \ldots, T, \tag{13.5.2}$$

where $\bar{y}_t = \frac{1}{n}\sum_i y_{it}$, $\bar{x}_{tj} = \frac{1}{n}\sum_i x_{itj}$, and $\bar{v}_i = \frac{1}{n}\sum_i v_{it}$. We can see that all the time-invariant effects are incorporated in $u_i(t)$. Here $u_i(t)$ is assumed to be a linear combination of $L < T$ basis functions (common factors) $g_1, \ldots, g_L$:

$$u_i(t) = \sum_{r=1}^{L} \theta_{ir} g_r(t). \tag{13.5.3}$$

Kneip et al. (2012) interpreted the individual effects factors $u_i(t)$ as technical efficiency for a particular firm i at time t, which is calculated as $TE_i(t) = \exp\{u_i(t) - \max_{j=1,\ldots,n}(u_j(t))\}$, just as it is calculated with the CSS estimator. This semiparametric construction is more flexible and realistic than parametric models, which presume a fixed functional form for the changing path of the individual effects. However, as KSS point out, identifiability requires that all variables $x_{itj}, \{j = 1, \ldots, k\}$ possess considerable variation relative to the factors. Compared with a fully nonparametric econometric model the existence of some common structure leads to much faster rates of convergence in estimation as well as makes it easier to form socioeconomic interpretations about underlying influencing factors.

The full model can be rewritten as

$$\begin{aligned} y_{it} - \bar{y}_t = \sum_{j=1}^{k} \beta_j (x_{itj} - \bar{x}_{tj}) \\ + \sum_{r=1}^{L} \theta_{ir} g_r(t) + v_{it} - \bar{v}_i, \quad i = 1, \ldots, n; \, t = 1, \ldots, T. \end{aligned} \tag{13.5.4}$$

Parameters β_j, θ_{ir}, the basis functions $g_1, \ldots, g_L$, and the dimension of the space spanned by these functions are unknown and remain to be estimated.

There exists an identifiability problem with such a specification for the individual effects. Given a set of basis functions, only the spanned linear space can be identified. To deal with this problem, KSS utilize a normalization under which the g_rs are orthogonal and the θ_{ir}s are uncorrelated with each other in the sample. This set of basis can be estimated by principal components from the sample of all individual effects,

$$u_1 = (u_1(1), \cdots, u_1(T))'$$
$$\cdots$$
$$u_n = (u_n(1), \cdots, u_n(T))'. \tag{13.5.5}$$

If we denote the empirical covariance matrix of $u_1, \ldots, u_n$ as

$$\Sigma_{n,T} = \frac{1}{n}\sum_i u_i u_i' \tag{13.5.6}$$

and let $\lambda_1 \geq \lambda_2 \geq \cdots \geq \lambda_T$ be the eigenvalues of the matrix and $\gamma_1, \gamma_2, \cdots, \gamma_T$ be the corresponding eigenvectors, then:

$$g_r(t) = \sqrt{T}\gamma_{rt} \quad \text{for all } r = 1, \ldots, L; \, t = 1, \ldots, T, \tag{13.5.7}$$

$$\theta_{ir} = \frac{1}{T}\sum_t u_i(t)g_r(t) \text{ for all } r = 1, \ldots, L; \, i = 1, \ldots, n, \tag{13.5.8}$$

$$\lambda_r = \frac{T}{n}\sum_i \theta_{ir}^2 \quad \text{for all } r = 1, \ldots, L, \tag{13.5.9}$$

and where for all $l = 1, 2, \ldots$

$$\sum_{r=l+1}^{T} \lambda_r = \frac{1}{n}\sum_{i,t}\left(u_i(t) - \sum_{r=1}^{L}\theta_{ir}g_r(t)\right)^2. \tag{13.5.10}$$

We can see that $u_i(t) \approx \sum_{r=1}^{L}\theta_{ir}g_r(t)$ will be the best L-dimensional linear estimate, and the dimension L, where $(n > L, T > L)$ is naturally equal to $rank(\Sigma_{n,T})$.

13.5.1   Implementation

The KSS method first estimates β by penalized least squares using smoothing splines to approximate the factors, then obtains the approximations to the u_is and its covariance structure, and finally determines the estimates of the basis functions $\hat{g}_r$ through the empirical covariance matrix $\hat{\Sigma}_{n,T}$, which is estimated by the empirical covariance of the $(\hat{u}_1, \ldots, \hat{u}_n)$. The corresponding coefficients of the basis functions are obtained by least squares. In the last step, one updates the estimate of u_i by $\sum_{r=1}^{L}\hat{\theta}_{ir}\hat{g}_r$.

The KSS estimation algorithm entails the following three steps.

Step 1 Obtain estimates $\hat{\beta}_1, \ldots, \hat{\beta}_k$ and nonparametric approximations $\hat{u}_1, \ldots, \hat{u}_n$ by least squares.

$$\min_{\beta, u} \sum_i \frac{1}{T}\sum_t \left(y_{it} - \bar{y}_t - \sum_{j=1}^{k}\beta_j(x_{itj} - \bar{x}_{tj}) - u_i(t)\right)^2$$
$$+ \sum_i \kappa \frac{1}{T}\int_1^T \left(u_i^{(m)}(s)\right)^2 ds, \tag{13.5.11}$$

where $u_i^{(m)}$ is the mth derivatives of u_i, and $\kappa > 0$ is a prespecified smoothing parameter. According to spline theory (see Eubank, 1988), any $\hat{u}_i$ obtained from this minimization problem can be expressed as a linear combination of a set of natural spline basis $z_1, \ldots, z_T$ of order $2m$, $\hat{u}_i(t) = \sum_j \hat{\zeta}_{ji}z_j(t)$; $m = 2$ is a typical choice, which results in cubic smoothing splines. If we let Z and A be $T \times T$ matrices with entries $\{z_j(t)\}_{j,t=1,\ldots,T}$ and $\{\int_1^T z_j^{(m)}(s)z_k^{(m)}(s)ds\}_{j,k=1,\ldots,T}$, and let

$\hat{\beta} = (\hat{\beta}_1, \ldots, \hat{\beta}_k)'$ and $\hat{\zeta}_i = (\hat{\zeta}_{1i}, \ldots, \hat{\zeta}_{Ti})'$, then this is equivalent to the following problem:

$$\min_{\beta, \zeta} \sum_i (\| y_i - \bar{y} - (x_i - \bar{x})\beta - Z\zeta_i \|^2 + \kappa \zeta'_i A \zeta_i), \qquad (13.5.12)$$

where $\| \cdot \|$ is the usual Euclidean norm. The solutions are then given by

$$\hat{\beta} = \left(\sum_i (x_i - \bar{x})'(I - Z_\kappa)(x_i - \bar{x}) \right)^{-1}$$

$$\sum_i (x_i - \bar{x})'(I - Z_\kappa)(y_i - \bar{y}) \qquad (13.5.13)$$

and

$$\hat{\zeta}_i = (Z'Z + \kappa A)^{-1} Z'(y_i - \bar{y} - (x_i - \bar{x})\hat{\beta}), \qquad (13.5.14)$$

where

$$Z_\kappa = Z(Z'Z + \kappa A)^{-1} Z' = \left(I - \kappa (Z')^{-1} A Z^{-1} \right)^{-1}. \qquad (13.5.15)$$

From the above results, we can get the estimates of u_i as

$$\hat{u}_i = Z\hat{\zeta}_i = Z_\kappa \left(y_i - \bar{y} - (x_i - \bar{x})\hat{\beta} \right). \qquad (13.5.16)$$

Step 2 Obtain the empirical covariance matrix

$$\hat{\Sigma}_{n,T} = \frac{1}{n} \sum_i \hat{u}_i \hat{u}'_i, \qquad (13.5.17)$$

where $\hat{u}_i = (\hat{u}_i(1), \ldots, \hat{u}_i(T))'$ for $i = 1, \ldots, n$. One can then calculate the eigenvalues

$$\hat{\lambda}_1 \geq \hat{\lambda}_2 \geq \cdots \geq \hat{\lambda}_T$$

and the corresponding eigen vectors

$$\hat{\gamma}_1, \hat{\gamma}_2, \cdots, \hat{\gamma}_T.$$

Step 3 Determine the basis functions and corresponding coefficients. It follows from the analysis of the identifiability problem that $\hat{g}_r(t) := \sqrt{T} \cdot \hat{\gamma}_{rt}$, for $r = 1, 2, \ldots, L$; $t = 1, 2, \ldots, T$. The coefficients $(\hat{\theta}_{1i}, \ldots, \hat{\theta}_{Li})$ can be obtained from the following minimization problem

$$\min_{\theta_{1i}, \ldots, \theta_{Li}} \sum_{t=1}^{T} \left(y_{it} - \bar{y}_t - \sum_{j=1}^{k} \hat{\beta}_j (x_{itj} - \bar{x}_{tj}) - \sum_{r=1}^{L} \theta_{ri} \hat{g}_r(t) \right)^2. \qquad (13.5.18)$$

This provides an update of the estimate of u_i by utilizing the terms $\sum_{r=1}^{L} \hat{\theta}_{ir} \hat{g}_r$.

Returning to the non-centered model, the general average function $\beta_0(t)$ is left to be estimated. A nonparametric method similar to Step 1 can be applied to get an approximation. An alternative is to assume $\beta_0(t)$ also lies in the space spanned by the set of basis functions, that is, $\beta_0(t) = \sum_{r=1}^{L} \bar{\theta}_r g_r(t)$. The coefficients can then be estimated by a similar minimization problem as Step 3 with objective function $\sum_{t=1}^{T} (\bar{y}_t - \sum_{j=1}^{k} \hat{\beta}_j \bar{x}_{tj} - \sum_{r=1}^{L} \theta_r \hat{g}_r(t))^2$. Once the parameters of the model and the factors are estimated (the number of factors can be estimated as in the KSS model), it is straightforward to utilize the methods we outlined at the beginning of our discussion of the KSS estimator to develop estimates of time-varying and firm-specific technical efficiency.[2]

13.6   THE AHN, LEE, AND SCHMIDT (2013) MODEL

The model setting in Ahn et al. (2013) is more general than in Ahn et al. (2007). The former allows for serially correlated disturbances and also considers the case of weak exogeneity. More interest also is placed on the consistent estimation of slope coefficients β when there exists correlation between the individual effects and the regressors. The focus remains on large n and small T asymptotics. Using the notation of Ahn et al. (2013) we write their model as

$$y_{it} = x_{it}'\beta + \sum_{j=1}^{p} \xi_{tj}\alpha_{ij} + \varepsilon_{it}, \qquad (13.6.1)$$

where the correlation between the regressors and individual effects motivates the use of a fixed-effects type approach. To emphasize this feature, the model interprets ξ_{tj} as macro shocks and α_{ij} as random coefficients instead of factors and factor loadings, though the model itself resembles a factor model.

The model can be rewritten for firm i in matrix form

$$y_i = X_i\beta + u_i; \qquad u_i = \eta_i + \varepsilon_i = \Xi\alpha_i + \varepsilon_i, \qquad (13.6.2)$$

where $y_i = (y_{i1}, \ldots, y_{iT})'$ is the $(T \times 1)$ dependent variable vector, $X_i = (x_{i1}, \ldots, x_{iT})'$ is the $T \times k$ matrix of regressors, and β is conformable $(k \times 1)$ coefficient vector. The error term u_i is composed of the random noise $\varepsilon_i = (\varepsilon_{i1}, \ldots, \varepsilon_{iT})'$ and the unobservable individual effects $\eta_i = \Xi\alpha_i$ is a $(T \times 1)$ vector composed of p unobservable firm-specific variables contained in the $(p \times 1)$ vector $\alpha_i = (\alpha_{i1}, \ldots, \alpha_{ip})'$ and p unobservable macro shocks contained in the $(T \times p)$ matrix Ξ, which contains elements ξ_{ij} that are the same for all firms. The errors (ε) and the regressors (x) are assumed to be uncorrelated. Ahn et al. (2013) consider the case of large n and small T, in

---

[2] The KSS estimator, as well as the estimators considered by Bai and Ng (2002) and Bai (2009), can be implemented using the software documented and referenced in Bada and Liebl (2014). The KSS estimator is also one of the estimators in the suite of estimators considered in Chapter 17 and is also available on the website listed there.

which case the true fixed effect estimator is not consistent unless the error is iid. Their model relaxes this assumption in that it allows any kind of autocorrelation of ε_i and only assumes that ε_i is uncorrelated with regressors x_{it} while α_{ij} might be correlated with x_{it}. Then for identification, it is assumed that there exist instrument variables that are correlated with α_{ij} but not with ε_{it}.

13.6.1 Implementation

It is not possible to separate the effects of Ξ and α without some normalization as the terms appear multiplicatively. For identification, Ξ is normalized such that $\Xi = (\Theta', -I_p)'$ with Θ an unrestricted $(T - p) \times p$ matrix of parameters. With instruments, the GMM method proposed in Ahn et al. (2001) is extended to incorporate multiple time-varying effects and two methods are proposed to estimate the true number of individual effects. We will outline the two-step process in which one first obtains consistent estimators of β and Θ assuming the true number of effects p_0 is known. An estimate of p_0 is based on a sequential testing method. Details on their assumptions and further discussion of their implications can be found in Ahn et al. (2013).

The basic GMM estimator they employ is based on a set of moment conditions defined for a given p by $H(\theta) = (H_1(\theta_1), \ldots, H_{T-p}(\theta_{T-p})) = (I_{T-p}, \Theta)'$, where $\theta_j, j = 1, \ldots, T - p$, is the jth column of Θ', $\theta = vec(\Theta')$, and $H_j(\theta_j)$ is the jth column of $H(\theta)$. $H(\theta)$ is constructed in this form so that $H(\theta)'\Xi = 0_{(T-p) \times p}$ and so unobservable individual effects α can be removed by premultiplying the model by $H(\theta)$

$$H(\theta_0)'y_i = H(\theta_0)'X_i\beta_0 + H(\theta_0)'\varepsilon_i, \quad (13.6.3)$$

where the subscript 0 is used to represent the true value of parameters.

Ahn et al. (2013) consider two cases of their model that depending on the strong or weak exogeneity of the instruments used informing the orthogonality conditions embedded in $H(\theta)$.

13.6.1.1   Case 1: Strictly Exogenous Instruments

Denote z_i to be the column vector with all the distinct elements in $(x_{i1}, \ldots, x_{iT})$ in the sense that any time-invariant regressors appear only once. Let τ_t be the vector of variables shared by all firms at time t and let $\tau = (\tau'_1, \ldots, \tau'_T)'$. Then we can represent the strict exogeneity of the regressors as $E(\varepsilon_i \mid z_i, \tau) = 0_{T \times 1}$. Assume that there are other variables not in X_i but uncorrelated with ε_i that can be used as instruments. Let these be denoted as f_i and augment the strictly exogenous regressors z_i with these additional instruments to form the $q \times 1$ vector $w_{S,i} = (z'_i, f'_i)'$, where S is used to distinguish that these are strictly exogenous instruments. The moment conditions that result from these strict exogeneity assumptions can be simply stated as

$$E(\varepsilon_i \otimes w_{S,i} \mid \tau_0) = 0_{Tq \times 1}. \quad (13.6.4)$$

Assuming $p = p_0$, the moment conditions used in their GMM method are expressed as

$$E[m_{S,i}(\delta_0)|\tau_0] = E[H(\theta_0)'u_i(\beta_0) \otimes w_{S,i}|\tau_0] = 0_{(T-p)q \times 1}, \quad (13.6.5)$$

where $\delta = (\beta', \theta')'$, and $u_i(\beta) = y_i - X_i\beta$. The optimal GMM estimator is then obtained by iteratively solving the following problem

$$\min_{\delta} J(\delta|p) = n\left(\frac{1}{n}\sum_{i=1}^{n}m_{S,i}(\delta)\right)'\left(\frac{1}{n}\sum_{i=1}^{n}m_{S,i}(\hat{\delta})m_{S,i}(\hat{\delta})'\right)^{-1}\left(\frac{1}{n}\sum_{i=1}^{n}m_{S,i}(\delta)\right),$$

$$(13.6.6)$$

where $[n^{-1}\sum_{i=1}^{n}m_{S,i}(\hat{\delta})m_{S,i}(\hat{\delta})']^{-1}$ is the weighting matrix and $\hat{\delta}$ is an initial consistent estimator of δ.

The identification condition for δ requires $p = p_0$, i.e., p is specified correctly. Two methods are considered to estimate the true value. One utilizes the Hansen–Sargan statistic of the over-identification test. It is shown in the paper that this statistic is equivalent to the minimized value of $J(\tilde{\delta}|p)$, where $\tilde{\delta}$ is the optimal GMM estimator. The property of the Hansen–Sargan statistic implies that when $p = p_0$, $J(\tilde{\delta}|p)$ follows a χ^2 distribution with degree of freedom being $(T - p_0)(q - p_0) - k$, and when $p < p_0$, $J(\tilde{\delta}|p)$ goes to infinity. Thus, we can start by setting null hypothesis $p_0 = 0$, and sequentially increase the testing number of p until the null is not rejected. Another method for selecting p follows Bai and Ng (2002) and Bai (2009) and is detailed in Ahn et al. (2013).

13.6.1.2   Case 2: Weakly Exogenous Instruments

The paper also considered consistent estimation of parameters when some regressors are only weakly exogenous. Let $x_{W,it}$ and $x_{S,it}$ represent the weakly and strictly exogenous regressors, respectively, and let $w_{S,i}$ be the set of the leads and lags of $x_{S,it}$. Denote the q_j variables $w_{j,i} = (w'_{S,i}, x'_{W,i1}, \ldots, x'_{W,ij})'$, where $j = 1, \ldots, T - p$. The modified weak exogeneity condition can be stated as

$$E(\varepsilon_{is}|w_{j,i}, \tau_0) = 0, \quad s \geq j, \quad j = 1, \ldots, T - p. \quad (13.6.7)$$

To avoid further complexity it is assumed that τ_t is strictly exogenous and the moment conditions for $p_0 = p$ thus become

$$E(m_{W,i}(\delta_0)|\tau_0) = E\left(\begin{array}{c|c} H_1(\theta_{1,0})'u_i(\beta_0)w_{1,i} \\ H_2(\theta_{2,0})'u_i(\beta_0)w_{2,i} \\ \vdots \\ H_{T-p}(\theta_{T-p,0})'u_i(\beta_0)w_{T-p,i} \end{array} \middle| \tau_0 \right) = 0. \quad (13.6.8)$$

Note that the moment conditions here are a subset of those stated in the strictly exogenous case and thus most results follow from that case and we can use the same methods to estimate p consistently.

Once the model parameters have been estimated one can form the technical efficiency estimates and proceed with $\Xi\alpha_{it}$ as the technical efficiency measure for firm i. The relative technical efficiency of firm i at time t therefore, can be measured as

$$\widehat{TE}_{it} = \exp[-\{\max_i(\widehat{\Xi\alpha}_{it}) - \widehat{\Xi\alpha}_{it}\}]. \tag{13.6.9}$$

13.7 THE LIU, SICKLES, AND TSIONAS (2017) MODEL

According to the estimation method, panel stochastic frontier models can generally be grouped into two categories. One is the traditional method using least squares estimation or the maximum likelihood techniques (MLE), which relies on certain specifications of the distribution of the error term. The other is the Bayesian method that emerged in the 1990s, which treats all the parameters randomly and usually makes use of Markov Chain Monte Carlo (MCMC) techniques and the Gibbs sampling algorithm in estimation.

Liu et al. (2017) consider two Bayesian stochastic panel frontier models that do not rely on restrictive conjugate prior information for the individual effects that evolve over time. In their Model 1, they specify the production model with time-varying effects as

$$y_{it} = x'_{it}\beta + \gamma_{it} + v_{it}, \quad i = 1, \ldots, n; \ t = 1, \ldots, T. \tag{13.7.1}$$

Here x_{it} is the k-dimensional vector of regressors, β is the corresponding k-dimensional vector of slope parameters, v_{it} is assumed to be iid following a $\mathcal{N}(0, \sigma_v^2)$ distribution, and γ_{it} is some firm-specific effect that changes over time. Denote $\gamma_i = (\gamma_{i1}, \ldots, \gamma_{iT})'$. In order to implement the Bayesian analysis of this model, prior distributions for the parameters $(\beta, \gamma, \sigma_v^2)$ and the sample likelihood are needed in order to calculate the posterior. The prior for the parameter γ_i is not specified but the first-order or second-order differences of γ_i are assumed to follow a normal prior given by

$$p(\gamma) \propto \prod_{i=1}^{n} \exp\left(-\frac{\gamma_i' Q \gamma_i}{2\omega^2}\right) = \exp\left(-\frac{1}{2\omega^2}\gamma'(I_n \otimes Q)\gamma\right), \tag{13.7.2}$$

where ω is some smoothness parameter. $Q = D'D$ and D is a $(T-1) \times T$ matrix with $D_{tt} = 1$ for all $t = 1, \ldots, T-1$, $D_{t-1,t} = -1$ for all $t = 2, \ldots, T$, and zero otherwise. This sets the prior on the smoothness for the time-varying effects and implies that $\gamma_{i,t} - \gamma_{i,t-1} \sim \mathcal{N}(0, \omega^2)$, or equivalently $D\gamma_i \sim \mathcal{N}(0, \omega^2 I_{T-1})$. We can alternatively assume a normal prior for the second-order difference: $\gamma_{i,t} - 2\gamma_{i,t-1} + \gamma_{i,t-2} \sim \mathcal{N}(0, \omega^2)$ or, in matrix form, $D^{(2)}\gamma_i \sim \mathcal{N}(0, \omega^2 I_{T-2})$. In both cases, the smoothness priors are assumed to be iid.

The parameters β and σ_v are specified with a non-informative joint prior distribution: $p(\beta, \sigma_v) \propto \sigma_v^{-1}$. The joint prior of all unknown parameters $(\beta, \sigma_v, \gamma_v)$ is then obtained as

$$p(\beta, \sigma_v, \gamma) \propto \sigma_v^{-1} \prod_{i=1}^{n} \exp\left(-\frac{\gamma'_i Q \gamma_i}{2\omega^2}\right)$$

$$= \sigma_v^{-1} \exp\left(-\frac{1}{2\omega^2} \gamma'(I_n \otimes Q)\gamma\right). \tag{13.7.3}$$

The sample likelihood function is

$$\mathscr{L}(y, x, \beta, \gamma, \sigma_v) \propto \sigma_v^{-nT} \exp\left\{-\frac{1}{2\sigma_v^2}(y - x\beta - \gamma)'(y - x\beta - \gamma)\right\}. \tag{13.7.4}$$

The posterior based on Bayesian learning is given in the classical relationship

$$p(\beta, \gamma, \sigma_v | y, x, \omega) \propto p(\beta, \gamma, \omega) \cdot l(y, x; \beta, \gamma, \omega), \tag{13.7.5}$$

and is calculated via the MCMC algorithm for Model 1 via the posterior distribution:

$$p(\beta, \gamma, \sigma_v | y, x, \omega) \propto \sigma_v^{-(nT+1)} \exp\left\{-\frac{1}{2\sigma_v^2}(y - x\beta - \gamma)'(y - x\beta - \gamma)\right\}$$

$$\times \exp\left(-\frac{1}{2\omega^2} \gamma'(I_T \otimes Q)\gamma\right). \tag{13.7.6}$$

13.7.1 Implementation

Gibbs sampling is employed to simulate the joint posterior distribution based on conditional posterior distributions of blocks of parameters. The conditional posterior distributions for $(\beta, \gamma, \sigma_v)$ are given in Liu et al. (2017). With the conditional distribution for each parameter, one takes draws of one parameter per time cyclically from their respective conditional distribution. That is, with the kth draw in hand, the $(k+1)$th draw will be obtained in the following order:

1) Draw $\beta^{(k+1)}$ from $p(\beta | \sigma_v = \sigma_v^{(k)}, \gamma = \gamma^{(k)})$;
2) Draw $\sigma_v^{(k+1)}$ from $p(\sigma_v | \beta = \beta^{(k+1)}, \gamma = \gamma^{(k)})$;
3) Draw $\gamma^{(k+1)}$ from $p(\gamma | \beta = \beta^{(k+1)}, \sigma_v = \sigma_v^{(k+1)})$.

The choice of smoothing parameter ω can be determined through Bayesian cross-validation. The Gibbs sampler takes draws from the conditional distributions until they converge to the joint posterior distribution of $(\beta, \gamma, \sigma_v)$.

Model 2 of Liu et al. (2017) follows the setup of Kneip et al. (2012) and treats the effects as linear combinations of a finite number of basis functions. Their derivation of the conditional posteriors and the use of the Gibbs sampler and the MCMC algorithm to generate joint posterior distributions are detailed in their paper. We do not reproduce the results here but encourage the interested reader to examine the derivations from the original source.

Once the model parameters and the unit specific time-varying effects are estimated, the relative efficiency level is measured as

$$\widehat{TE}_{it} = \exp[-\{\max_i(\widehat{\gamma}_{it}) - \widehat{\gamma}_{it}\}]. \tag{13.7.7}$$

13.8 THE TRUE FIXED EFFECTS MODEL

Greene (2005a,b) discussed the characteristics of the fixed-effects method, and proposed a "true" fixed effects model. The basic setting is the classic panel data stochastic frontier model,

$$y_{it} = \alpha_i + x'_{it}\beta + v_{it} - u_{it}, \tag{13.8.1}$$

$$\varepsilon_{it} = v_{it} - u_{it}, \tag{13.8.2}$$

or

$$y_{it} = \alpha_i + x'_{it}\beta + \varepsilon_{it}. \tag{13.8.3}$$

We can see that the standard fixed effects estimates cannot distinguish the individual time-invariant effects and the inefficiency. Another problem is that the estimators are consistent when $T \to \infty$, but there may exist persistent biases when T is small due to the incidental parameter problem. To deal with these problems and to examine the seriousness of the biases in the case of a finite and small T, Greene (2005a,b) proposed the "true" fixed effects (TFE) model and considered an alternative method for estimation. In the TFE model, v_{it} is assumed to be iid with a normal distribution $\mathcal{N}(0, \sigma_v^2)$ and u_{it} is iid with distribution $F_u(\sigma_u)$. F_u represents some one-parameter distribution defined on $\mathbb{R}^+$ and σ_u is its scale parameter. The half-normal and the exponential are two commonly used distributions in this family. Utilizing the ML technique and estimating the individual fixed effects along with other parameters, Greene developed a maximum likelihood dummy variable estimator (MLDVE). One drawback of MLDVE is that the covariance parameter cannot be consistently estimated with a short panel. The detailed examination of the incidental problem can be found in Greene (2005b).

Wang and Ho (2010) solved the incidental parameters problem in the true fixed effects context by the use of de-meaning and first-differences and also utilize the scaling property, an essential property of the stochastic frontier model pointed out by Wang and Schmidt (2002) and Alvarez et al. (2006). Belotti and Ilardi (2012) proposed two new approaches for this TFE model, and both give consistent estimates for fixed T and large n. Their methods utilize the first difference transformation of the model, where $y_i = (y_{i1}, \ldots, y_{iT})'$ is the vector of observations for the dependent output variable (or cost if we reverse the sign of u_{it}), $x_i = (x_{i1}, \ldots, x_{iT})'$ are the regressors (usually inputs but may contain additional controls and environmental variables), $\Delta y_i = [(y_{i2} - y_{i1}), \ldots, (y_{iT} - y_{i,T-1})]'$, $\Delta x_i = [(x_{i2} - x_{i1}), \ldots, (x_{iT} - x_{i,T-1})]'$, and the first-differenced errors are constructed accordingly.

$$\Delta y_i = \Delta x_i' \beta + \Delta \varepsilon_i, \tag{13.8.4}$$

$$\Delta \varepsilon_i = \Delta v_i - \Delta_i u_i. \tag{13.8.5}$$

Belotti and Ilardi (2012) show that Δv_i is iid with distribution given by a $\mathcal{N}_{T-1}(0, \Sigma_v)$. The covariance matrix is $\Sigma_v = \sigma_v^4 \Lambda_{T-1}$, where

$$\Lambda_{T-1} = \begin{pmatrix} 2 & -1 & 0 & \cdots & 0 \\ -1 & 2 & -1 & \cdots & 0 \\ 0 & -1 & \ddots & \cdots & \vdots \\ \vdots & \vdots & \cdots & \ddots & 1 \\ 0 & 0 & \cdots & -1 & 2 \end{pmatrix}.$$

The marginal likelihood is straightforward to construct if one uses the Wang and Ho (2010) specification of a deterministic time-varying inefficiency model with $u_{it} = h_{it} u_i$ and $h_{it} = \exp(x_{it}' \delta)$, where z_{it} are environmental variables and u_i is assumed to be iid $\mathcal{N}^+(0, \sigma_u^2)$. This is because the differencing operation does not impact u_i. However, without such an assumption the expression for the marginal likelihood is not at all straightforward unless one adopts the approach of Belotti and Ilardi (2012), who do not impose any constraint on the variability of the inefficiency term. Denoting the unknown conditional distribution of Δu_i as $f(\Delta u_i | \sigma)$, one can define the marginal likelihood contribution as

$$\mathcal{L}_i(\theta) = \int f(\Delta v_i, \Delta u_i | \theta) d \Delta u_i = \int f(\Delta v_i | \theta) f(\Delta u_i | \sigma_u) d \Delta u_i \tag{13.8.6}$$

$$= \int f(\Delta y_i | \beta, \sigma_v^2, \Delta X_i, \Delta u_i) f(\Delta u_i | \sigma_u) d \Delta u_i, \tag{13.8.7}$$

where the second equality comes from the independence of Δv_i and Δu_i and where $\theta = (\beta', \sigma_u, \sigma_v^2)'$.

13.8.1   Implementation

There are several approaches to estimating the model. One approach is to maximize the marginal likelihood function, which can be obtained by simulation. We can see that the marginal likelihood function is the conditional expectation of some function of the differenced inefficiency vector Δu_i, which can be consistently estimated by its simulated counterpart under some regularity conditions for the distribution of u_i (both half-normal and exponential distributions satisfy these regularity conditions). The marginal likelihood and its simulated counterpart are given by

$$\mathcal{L}_i(\theta) = \int f(\Delta y_i | \theta, \Delta x_i, \Delta u_i) f(\Delta u | \sigma_u) d \Delta u_i \tag{13.8.8}$$

$$= E_{\Delta \tilde{u}} \left[\phi_{T-1}(\Delta y_i - \Delta x_i' \beta + \sigma_u \Delta \tilde{u}_i; 0, \Sigma_v) \right] \tag{13.8.9}$$

$$\approx \frac{1}{M} \sum_{m=1}^{M} \left[\phi_{T-1}(\Delta y_i - \Delta x_i'\beta + \sigma_u \Delta \tilde{u}_{im}; \ 0, \ \Sigma_v) \right].$$

(13.8.10)

Here $\phi_{T-1}(\cdot; \ \mu, \ \Sigma)$ is the $(T-1)$-dimensional Gaussian density with mean μ and covariance matrix Σ and M denotes the number of draws taken from the distribution of the inefficiency vector $\Delta \tilde{u}$. Instead of simulating from the multivariate distribution, one can simply draw from the univariate distribution of each element and form the differenced inefficiency error

$$\Delta \tilde{u}_{im} = (\tilde{u}_{i2m} - \tilde{u}_{i1m}, \ldots, \tilde{u}_{iTm} - \tilde{u}_{i(T-1)m})'.$$

(13.8.11)

It can be shown that when the number of draws $M \to \infty$ and sample size $n \to \infty$, the simulated marginal maximum likelihood estimator converges to the marginal maximum likelihood estimator. Thus M needs to be large enough to ensure that the simulated expectation is a good approximation and the requirement for a large number of draws results in a trade-off between the computational complexity of this new approach and the inconsistency of MLDVE developed in Greene (2005a,b).

The second approach derives a closed form expression of the marginal likelihood function of the differenced model under the assumption that inefficiency term u_i has an exponential distribution and the number of time series is $T = 2$. As Belotti and Ilardi (2012) point out, the difference between two iid exponential random variables with scale parameter σ_u is Laplace with density

$$f(\Delta u \mid \sigma_u) = \frac{1}{2\sigma} \exp\left(\frac{|\Delta u|}{\sigma_u} \right)$$

(13.8.12)

and thus the marginal likelihood in closed-form can be written as

$$\mathcal{L}(\theta) = \prod_{i=1}^{n} f(\Delta y_{it} | \theta, \ \Delta x_{it})$$

(13.8.13)

$$= \prod_{i=1}^{n} \left\{ \frac{1}{2\sigma_v} \left[\exp\left(\frac{\sigma_v^4}{\sigma_u^2} - \frac{\Delta \mu_{it}}{\sigma_u} \right) \Phi\left(\frac{\Delta \mu_{it}}{\sqrt{2\sigma_v^2}} - \frac{\sqrt{2}\sigma_v^2}{\sigma_u} \right) \right. \right.$$

$$\left. \left. + \exp\left(\frac{\sigma_v^4}{\sigma_u^2} + \frac{\Delta \mu_{it}}{\sigma_u} \right) \Phi\left(-\frac{\Delta \mu_{it}}{\sqrt{2\sigma_v^2}} - \frac{\sqrt{2}\sigma_v^2}{\sigma_u} \right) \right] \right\},$$

(13.8.14)

where $\Delta \mu_{it} = \Delta y_{it} - \Delta x_{it}\beta$ and $\Phi(\cdot)$ is the cdf of standard normal. The likelihood function can be seen as a marginal likelihood function of a subsample subtracted from the whole panel data with only two periods. There are, in total, $B = \binom{T}{2}$ such subsamples, and each provides a consistent subsample estimator. To exploit the information of the entire sample, we can combine the B marginal likelihood functions into one single objective function.

$$U_n(\theta) = n^{-1} \binom{T}{2}^{-1} \sum_{i=1}^{n} \sum_{t=2}^{T} \sum_{s<t} \ln f(\Delta_t^s y_i | \theta, \Delta_t^s x_i), \qquad (13.8.15)$$

where $\Delta_t^s y_i = y_{it} - y_{is}$ and $\Delta_t^s x_i = x_{it} - x_{is}$. The resulting estimator based on maximizing this expression is named the Pairwise Difference Estimator by Belotti et al. (2012), who show that under either n or T growing without limit for fixed T or n, the estimator is consistent. Once the estimates of the parameters have been generated, estimates of the inefficiency terms can be generated using the methods we have already discussed above.

The relative technical efficiency can also be measured as

$$\widehat{TE}_{it} = \exp[-\{\max(\widehat{u}_{it}) - \widehat{u}_{it}\}]. \qquad (13.8.16)$$

13.9   TRUE RANDOM EFFECTS MODELS

In what might be viewed as the logical limit of the progression in model development of heterogeneous effects models, Colombi et al. (2011) proposed what has come to be labeled the "generalized true random effects model." Tsionas and Kumbhakar (2014) have further developed this model, which extends the model introduced at the end of the last chapter to one in which there is a four-way decomposition of the error term into $\varepsilon_{it} = w_i - h_i + v_{it} - u_{it}$. In this framework, $w_i - h_i$ represents a permanent heterogeneous stochastic frontier effect while $v_{it} - u_{it}$ represents a transitory counterpart. This generalized model captures both the time-invariant aspect of the original Pitt and Lee model and the extension of Greene's true random effects model. The models proposed by Colombi et al. (2011) and by Colombi et al. (2014) provide an attractive general framework for the analysis of panel data with stochastic frontier models. However, the implementation of the model as proposed is severely limited because estimation requires T-variate normal integration, which is essentially impractical with T (number of periods) more than 4 or 5, although the authors did develop a method of moments (MOM) estimator based on least squares, MOM estimation of the stochastic frontier model may have computational limitations in such highly nonlinear models than full information maximum likelihood estimation because the results of estimates of deep parameters such as the variance of the inefficiency are often quite volatile. Filippini and Greene (2016) developed a maximum simulated likelihood method that has substantial computational advantages over brute force MLE and that has made the generalized true random effects model a practical contender for the SF specification.

13.9.1   The Tsionas and Kumbhakar Extension of the Colombi, Kumbhakar, Martini, and Vittadini (2014) Four Error Component Model

The persistent and time-varying inefficiency model with four error components, an assumed closed-skew normal distribution for the stochastic frontier, and individual effects and long-/short-run efficiency was discussed in Colombi et al. (2014). The Bayesian version of it is presented in Tsionas and Kumbhakar (2014) wherein they propose a panel data stochastic frontier model that disentangles firm heterogeneity from long-run and short-run technical inefficiency. The authors use Bayesian methods to provide robust treatments for estimating the inefficiency components in a four-way error component model. Although the original model was presented for a cost function, we will discuss this model in the context of the production function

$$y_{it} = x'_{it}\beta + \alpha_i + v_{it} - u_{it} - \eta_i. \tag{13.9.1}$$

Let $\varepsilon_{it} = \alpha_i + v_{it} - u_{it} - \eta_i$ represent the composed error and assume that both u_{it} and η_i are nonnegative random variables that capture firm-specific random effects, random noise, short-run technical inefficiency, and long-run technical inefficiency.[3]

Rewriting the model in (13.9.1) as short-run and long-run technical inefficiency

$$y_{it} = (\alpha_i - \eta_i) + x'_{it}\beta + (v_{it} - u_{it}) \equiv \delta_i + x'_{it}\beta + v_{it} - u_{it}, \tag{13.9.2}$$

and treating δ_i as random firm-specific effects, one obtains Green's random-effects model. Greene, however, models δ_i as nuisance parameters, focusing on estimating the β parameters and time-varying technical inefficiency, u_{it}. In (13.9.1), α_i are nuisance parameters, and η_i and u_{it} are the variables of interest, along with the β parameters. However, if one rewrites the model in (13.9.1) as

$$y_{it} = x'_{it}\beta - \eta_i - u_{it} + (v_{it} + \alpha_i) \equiv x'_{it}\beta - \eta_i - u_{it} + \xi_{it}, \tag{13.9.3}$$

one obtains a model that resembles the one proposed by Kumbhakar and Heshmati (1995). However, Kumbhakar and Heshmati (1995) assume ξ_{it} is iid, whereas ξ_{it} is not iid in (13.9.3).

13.9.1.1 Bayesian Numerical Inference

The authors assume the following about the iid error components

$$v_{it} \sim \mathcal{N}(0, \sigma_v^2), \ u_{it} \sim \mathcal{N}^+(0, \sigma_u^2), \ \alpha_i \sim \mathcal{N}(0, \sigma_\alpha^2), \ \eta_i \sim \mathcal{N}^+(0, \sigma_\eta^2). \tag{13.9.4}$$

For Bayesian analysis, one needs to specify a prior for the parameter vector. The authors choose priors that are flexible, yet they are still conditionally conjugate[4]

$$p(\beta, \sigma_v, \sigma_u, \sigma_\eta, \sigma_\alpha) = p(\beta)p(\sigma_v)p(\sigma_u)p(\sigma_\eta)p(\sigma_\alpha). \tag{13.9.5}$$

---

[3] See Tsionas and Kumbhakar (2014) for a discussion on the rationale for including four error components.

[4] See Koop et al. (1995).

The authors assume $\beta \sim N_k(\bar{\beta}, \mathbf{A}^{-1})$, where N_k denotes the k-variate normal distribution with mean vector $\bar{\beta}$ and prior precision matrix $\mathbf{A}$. By stacking the time series observations, the model in (13.9.1) becomes

$$y_{it} = (\alpha_i - \eta_i) \otimes \iota_T + x'_{it}\beta + (v_{it} - u_{it}) \equiv \delta_i \otimes \iota_T + x'_{it}\beta + \varepsilon_{it}, \quad (13.9.6)$$

where ι_T is a vector of ones, $\otimes$ denotes the Kronecker product, and $\varepsilon_{it} = v_{it} - u_{it}$. Letting $\delta_i = \alpha_i - \eta_i$, the density function is given by

$$f_\delta(\delta_i) = \frac{2}{\sigma_\delta}\phi\left(\frac{\delta_i}{\sigma_\delta}\right)\Phi\left(\frac{\lambda_\delta\delta_i}{\sigma_\delta}\right), \quad (13.9.7)$$

where $\sigma_\delta^2 = \sigma_\alpha^2 + \sigma_\eta^2$ and $\lambda_\delta = \frac{\sigma_\eta}{\sigma_\alpha}$. Accordingly, the likelihood for firm i becomes

$$\mathscr{L}(y_i, X_i; \theta) = \frac{4}{\sigma\sigma_\delta}\int_{-\infty}^{\infty}\phi\left(\frac{r_i - \delta_i \otimes \iota_T}{\sigma_\delta}\right)\phi\left(\frac{\delta_i}{\sigma_\delta}\right)\Phi\left(\lambda\frac{r_i - \delta_i \otimes \iota_T}{\sigma_\delta}\right)$$
$$\times \Phi\left(\frac{\lambda_\delta\delta_i}{\sigma_\delta}\right)d\delta_i, \quad (13.9.8)$$

where $r_i = y_i - X_i\beta$ and where $\sigma^2 = \sigma_v^2 + \sigma_u^2$ and $\lambda = \frac{\sigma_u}{\sigma_v}$.

The overall inefficiency in the four error component model is given by the sum of short-run and long-run technical inefficiency components. The relative technical efficiency can be estimated by the usual approach where:

$$\widehat{TE}_{it} = \exp[-\{\max(\widehat{u}_{it} + \hat{\eta}_i) - (\widehat{u}_{it} + \hat{\eta}_i)\}].$$

13.9.2   Extensions on the Four Error Component Model

Recent work on this class of models has involved extensions to accommodate determinants of both persistent and time-varying inefficiency by Badunenko and Kumbhakar (2017) and endogeneity by Kumbhakar and Lai (2017), who consider a stochastic frontier panel data model with correlated random firm-effects introduced along with the persistent and transient technical inefficiency that allow firm-effects and persistent inefficiency to be jointly determined along with the regressors. They also allow for determinants of both persistent and transient inefficiency in their two-step MLE estimation procedure.

13.10   SPATIAL PANEL FRONTIERS

Models with spatial structures are found in fields such as regional science, economic geography and urban economics, but relatively recently the methodology has been applied in many panel data studies in international economics, public economics, and agricultural economics. The approach captures the structure of cross-sectional correlation with the exogenous spatial weights matrix and estimates the spatial effects by spatial parameters. The spatial weights matrix is usually formed based on spatial (geographical) characteristics, but the characteristics also can be based on economic or socio-economic distance among units. A distinctive feature of the spatial econometric approach is that the spatial weights matrix is generally specified a priori based on an exogenous conceptualization of the structure of spatial dependence. Hence, the right choice of a spatial weights matrix is crucial for the correct model specifications.

Han and Sickles (2019) examined productivity at the sectoral level in the USA taking into consideration the possibility that a productivity shock in one sector may result in a reallocation of inputs in other sectors due to production linkages via the production supply chain. Such linkages have been studied extensively in the literature. Recent works by Timmer et al. (2014, 2015) and Timmer (2017) provide new insights and an excellent summary of many of the productivity aspects of supply chain networks. Jones (2012) recognizes the possibility that the effects of misallocation can be amplified through the input–output structure. He points that the contagion of the negative effects caused by misallocations can reduce total factor productivity. Acemoglu et al. (2012) also have a similar idea that microeconomic idiosyncratic shocks can lead to aggregate fluctuations through the input–output linkages. In other words, the productivity of each industry may be dependent on the productivity of other industries. Such linkages among industries using the US input–output matrix in 1997 is found in Figure 13.1.

Measurement of industry-level productivity has been examined in many studies with a variety of methodologies, but most studies do not take possible cross-sectional dependencies into account. Much of the current research focuses on the contributions of industries to aggregate productivity. Growth accounting techniques and index-number approaches are widely used in many statistical agencies, but these approaches estimate the productivity growth of each industry separately assuming industries are independent and do not consider possible interdependencies among them. However, interdependency is inevitable, especially among industries of an economy since the outputs of many sectors are used as the inputs of many others. Han and Sickles (2019) propose a novel approach for creating a spatial weights matrix based on economic distance when physical distance does not properly capture the spatial linkages. The data they examine comes from the KLEMS database and they study the industry-level productivity of the USA during the period 1947–2010. As the data is industry-specific and a formal distance metric based on geographical distance has no obvious appeal. Instead, they define economic distance, analogous to geographic distance, using the supply flows that can be found from input–output tables. They specify both a spatial frontier production model utilizing spatial autoregressive models (SAR) and a spatial Durbin model (SDM) and estimate them with Cornwell et al. (1990) type stochastic frontier approaches. They also utilize alternative methods suggested by Levinsohn and Petrin (2003) that are based on a different set of instruments to handle potential endogeneity of the factor inputs.

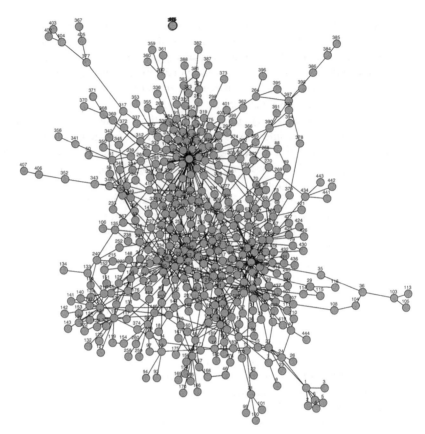

Figure 13.1 Industry linkages. Reproduced from Acemoglu, D., Carvalho, V. M., Ozdaglar, A., & Tahbaz-Salehi, A. (2012). The network origins of aggregate fluctuations. *Econometrica, 80*(5), 1977–2016. © 2012 The Econometric Society. Reprinted with permission of John Wiley & Sons, Inc.

The SAR stochastic frontier model for panel data developed by Glass et al. (2016) has been augmented with random effects to account for latent heterogeneity and by distinguishing between net time-invariant inefficiency and net time-variant inefficiency by Glass et al. (2018).

Maximum likelihood is often the basis for the development of estimation procedures for other spatial stochastic frontier-type models, one of which we discuss below in more detail. These models can be developed by extending spatial non-frontier specifications such as a spatio-temporal model (e.g., Elhorst, 2001), a higher-order SAR model (e.g., Badinger and Egger, 2011; Elhorst et al., 2012) or a model with SAR and spatial autocorrelated error terms (e.g., Kelejian and Prucha, 1998, 2010) to a stochastic frontier setting.

13.10.1 The Han and Sickles (2019) Model

In order to outline one approach to modeling spatial effects in the stochastic frontier model developed by Han and Sickles (2019), we consider our familiar panel frontier

$$y_{it} = \alpha + x'_{it}\beta - u_{it} + v_{it}. \qquad (13.10.1)$$

As we have noted, Cornwell et al. (1990) extended this model to allow for heterogeneity in slopes and intercepts. They modeled the time-dependent individual effects α_{it} as

$$\alpha_{it} = \alpha - u_{it} = R'_t\delta_i. \qquad (13.10.2)$$

Here we use R_t for the $L \times 1$ time-varying component that globally affects all individual units. The δ_i are its $L \times 1$ coefficients that depend on i. The time dependent individual effect, α_{it}, can be assumed to be decomposed into a common time trend $R'_t\delta_0$ and a unit-specific term $R'_t\xi_i$. After adding a time-invariant fixed effects variable z_i for a more general model specification the standard log-linear production function can be written as

$$y_{it} = x'_{it}\beta + z'_i\gamma + R'_t\delta_0 + R'_t\xi_i + v_{it}, \qquad i = 1, \cdots, n, \quad t = 1, \cdots, T, \qquad (13.10.3)$$

where z_i is a $J \times 1$ vector, the ξ_i are assumed to be iid zero mean random variables with covariance matrix Δ, and v_{it} is the random error term that is assumed to be iid with zero mean and variance σ_v^2. If R contains only a constant, then the above equation reduces to the standard panel data model that we have shown can be reparameterized into the Schmidt and Sickles (1984) stochastic panel frontier.

13.10.1.1 Generalization of the CSS Model-A Spatial Autoregressive and Spatial Durbin Stochastic Frontier

The spatial autoregressive generalization of the Cornwell et al. (1990) model is

$$y_{it} = \rho \sum_{j=1}^{n} w_{ij} y_{jt} + x'_{it}\beta + z'_i\gamma + R'_t\delta_0 + R'_t\xi_i + v_{it}, \qquad (13.10.4)$$

where w_{ij} is the ijth element of an exogenous ($n \times n$) spatial weights matrix W_n. The spatial Durbin specification is

$$y_{it} = \rho \sum_{j=1}^{n} w_{ij} y_{jt} + x'_{it}\beta + \lambda \sum_{j=1}^{n} w_{ij} x'_{jt} + z'_i\gamma + R'_t\delta_0 + R'_t\xi_i + v_{it}. \qquad (13.10.5)$$

Estimation of these two models and the calculation of efficiency can be carried out by making distributional assumptions on the error terms (ξ_i, v_{it}) and utilizing MLE. Expressions for the likelihood equations and algorithms for a two-step quasi-MLE procedure are given in Han and Sickles (2019). Of particular interest is difference between the structural models above and their reduced forms, which provide a much richer parameterization of the spillovers from inefficient neighbors either due to direct or indirect effects from changes in a neighbor's outputs or by changes in a neighbor's inputs.

13.10.1.2 Spatial Weights Matrix: Economic Distance

The spatial weights matrix is an important part of a spatial panel frontier or any spatial econometric model. It is often specified a priori and assumed to be an exogenous representation of the structure of spatial dependence. Getis and Aldstadt (2004) point out that a model with a wrong choice of spatial weights matrix is essentially misspecified. Unlike the spatial weights matrix in a typical spatial analysis that relies on geographic relationships, such a measure is often not relevant when, for example, we study the aggregate production function at the industry level. In this setting we would need to define an economic distance measure for the construction of the spatial weights matrix. Such a measure was constructed by Han and Sickles (2019) using input–output tables and the multiplier product matrix and represented a measure of economic distance that exploited the interconnectivity between sectors. An alternative by Han et al. (2016b) used the relative bilateral trade volume of a country as an economic distance measure.

Sonis and Hewings (1999) proposed an index called the Multiplier Product Matrix (MPM), which connects the properties of backward and forward linkages constructed from the input–output tables to measure the impacts of an industry on other industries in an economy. Han and Sickles (2019) utilized the multiplier product matrix to create a spatial weights matrix based on economic distance as geographic distance is not a meaningful spatial concept linking the supply chains embedded in the sectoral flows among industries. A heat map of the MPM that represents the relationships between the supplying and demanding sectors used in the Han and Sickles (2019) study of US sectoral productivity is given in Figure 13.2.

One can define a measure of economic distance between industry i and j as

$$d_{ij} \equiv \max_{i'} m^E_{i'j} - m^E_{ij}, \tag{13.10.6}$$

where m^E_{ij} is the element of the multiplier matrix MPM. The diagonal elements of the MPM are nonzero and in fact are usually the largest element in their columns (or rows). Thus we need to set the diagonals to zero in order to satisfy the regularity assumption that an observation does not feed back spatially to itself. Once we have constructed our measure of economic distance, we can assign weights according to the distance. There are several schemes to assign weights, such as contiguous neighbors, inverse distances, lengths of shared borders divided by the perimeter, bandwidth, centroid distance, and k nearest neighbors. A widely used weighting scheme for a spatial weights matrix excludes observations that are further than a threshold distance d^*, that is,

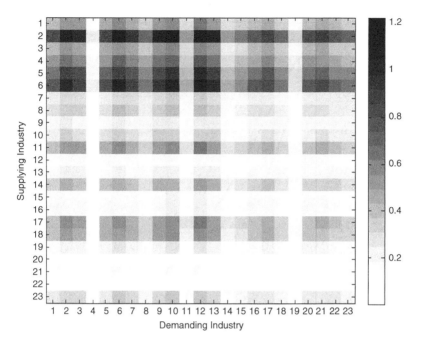

Figure 13.2 Multiplier product matrix heat map.

$$w_{ij} = \left\{ \begin{array}{ll} 1 & \text{if } d_{ij} < d^*; \\ 0 & \text{otherwise.} \end{array} \right. \tag{13.10.7}$$

The spatial weighting function suffers from the problem of discontinuity. One way to circumvent this is to assume a continuous function, d_{ij}. For continuous weighting schemes, application of distance decay function or distance decline function is suggested, which allows more weights for nearby units than areas that are far from one another (Brunsdon et al., 1996; LeSage, 2004; McMillen and McDonald, 2004). A negative exponential function is suggested by Brunsdon et al. (1996) as follows:

$$w_{ij} = \exp(-\eta d_{ij}^2), \tag{13.10.8}$$

where η is the spatial scale parameter which determines the degree of distance decay. The larger the value of η, the more abrupt is the cut-off of the influence of distant economic units. The distance-decay varies between different concepts of distance, for different groups of economic units, and also for different estimation approaches. Various decay profiles for different values of η are found in Figure 13.3. Han and Sickles (2019) detail a cross-validation two-step quasi-MLE approach to estimate the parameters of the weighting matrix along with the parameters of the spatial panel frontier. Conditions that the spatial weights matrix W should satisfy are discussed in Han and Sickles (2019) who also discuss the two-step methods for the estimation of the stochastic

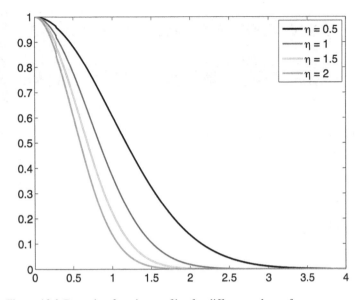

Figure 13.3 Decaying function profiles for different values of η.

spatial panel frontier and the calculation of direct and indirect spillovers from inefficient and spatially linked sectors of the US economy.

13.11 CONCLUDING REMARKS

The stochastic frontier panel data models that we have detailed in this and the previous chapter were developed to address a variety of problems and specifications in applied productivity modeling. There are many methods and of course many authors whose research efforts have been focused on particular approaches and each of these authors believes their model to be the best or at least an improvement on earlier methods. However, it is not at all clear at this juncture which method is the best and thus which method(s) should be viewed as the gold standard for panel efficiency analyses. As with any set of modeling approaches we would recommend analyses using a number of these approaches, possibly utilizing the model averaging methods adopted in other relatively recent productivity studies using a variety of these models. We discuss such approaches in depth in Chapter 16.

13.12 EXERCISES

1. Aggregate economy wide analyses using the Penn World Tables or aggregate sectoral data based on the World KLEMS Initiative often lead to productivity decompositions into factors such as technology change (innovation) and efficiency. However, micro or

firm-/establishment-level data may allow researchers to uncover other factors that constrain or contribute to productivity growth, such as distortions in output–input mix, incorrect scale, and optimization errors, among other things. How would you modify the methods utilized in the panel data stochastic frontier models to differentiate among such factors in aggregate and micro firm analyses?

2. In the stochastic frontier panel data model the composed error is (ignoring subscripts) $\varepsilon = v - u$. Let $\tau = E(u|\varepsilon)$. Since τ is a random variable, and not a parameter, then ignoring for the moment the estimation error in generating τ, explain why τ is a point estimate ("prediction") of u and it is the optimal (minimum mean squared error) estimate based on the usual argument that a "rational expectation" is equivalent to the optimal forecast.

3. Explain why one would use τ to predict efficiency when panel data is available instead of the unconditional estimate of u.

4. Standard distribution theory for estimation of the coefficients in panel stochastic frontier models is usually based on large N, T asymptotics. Derive the convergence rates for the parameters of the Ahn et al. (2013) estimator for fixed T and large N as well as the corresponding rates of convergence for the estimates of $\tau = E(u|\varepsilon)$.

5. For each of the models discussed in this chapter find examples of data that are publicly available and replicable that would allow one to justify, based on institutional knowledge of the industry, sector or country, that the underlying assumptions of the models were correct. Absent this, how would you test the identifying assumptions of each of these models? Can you construct a nonparametric identification criterion for any of these models to either set or point identify the parameters, even at infinity?

CHAPTER 14

Endogeneity in Structural and Non-Structural Models of Productivity

In this chapter, we discuss a variety of issues, some of which have been taken up in previous chapters, involving the causal linkages between input decisions and the productive output that is generated by these input decisions. Although we do not spend the considerable time and effort it would take to explore this issue in depth, we do feel that it is important to devote an entire chapter to the issues surrounding endogeneity and the various approaches in the productivity literature that have been taken to address it.

14.1 THE ENDOGENEITY PROBLEM

Consider the simple Cobb–Douglas production function (we will use this functional form throughout this discussion)

$$Y_i = e^\alpha L_i^{\beta_l} K_i^{\beta_k} e^{u_i}. \tag{14.1.1}$$

Here Y_i is the output of firm i, L_i is labor, K_i is the capital stock, u_i is a disturbance term, and α, β_l, and β_k are parameters to be estimated. The term $e^{\alpha+u_i}$ is interpreted as the Hicksian neutral efficiency level of firm i, which is unobservable by the econometrician but known to the firm, α is interpreted as the mean efficiency level across firms, while u_i is the deviation from the mean for firm i; u_i includes left out factors, efficiency differences, functional form discrepancies, and errors of measurement. By taking natural logs, we obtain

$$y_i = \alpha + \beta_l l_i + \beta_k k_i + u_i. \tag{14.1.2}$$

Marschak and Andrews (1944) pointed out that one cannot estimate this model by ordinary least squares because the model is likely to suffer from an endogeneity problem. Griliches and Mairesse (1995), Ackerberg et al. (2015) and many, many others subsequently have also pointed this out. The assumption that the explanatory variables and the disturbance term are uncorrelated in the model is crucial when we estimate the model with the ordinary least squares.

The reason that the least squares estimators are biased and inconsistent can be attributed to many factors, among which are: (1) endogenous right-hand-side variables due to omitted variables; (2) endogenous treatment effects; (3) simultaneous equations bias; (4) ignored dynamics in a panel data setting; (5) ignored parameter heterogeneity; (6) measurement error on the independent and dependent variable; (7) non-random sampling; and (8) attrition bias. Although each of these problems is no less likely to occur than another, and each results in inconsistent parameters estimation if ignored, two problems appear to have been the focus of much attention in production function estimation. They are simultaneity and attrition. Both constitute what has become known as the "endogeneity problem" in production function estimation.

14.2   SIMULTANEITY

Estimation of the simple production function is likely to be biased because of the possible correlation between unobserved productivity shocks and input levels. As Marschak and Andrews (1944) pointed out, input usage is determined by the firm with its knowledge of own productivity, u_i, not by the economist. If the firm knows its productivity (albeit not perfectly), its input choices are likely to be correlated with its productivity.

For instance, suppose a firm operates under perfect competition. Each firm can choose its input amounts to maximize profit, all the prices are given, and we will assume that only labor can be varied in the short run. The firm has perfect knowledge of u_i. The firm's short-run optimal choice of labor input is then given by

$$L_i = \left(\frac{p_i}{w_i} \beta_l e^{\alpha + u_i} K_i^{\beta_k} \right)^{\frac{1}{1 - \beta_l}} . \tag{14.2.1}$$

Here p is the output price and w is the wage. Since L_i depends on u_i, ordinary least squares (OLS) estimates of the production function are biased.

Even though the possible simultaneity problem was pointed out as early as 1944, the problem has often been ignored. One reason is because in many cases researchers thought the problem did not apply to their data. For example, if the disturbance term contains factors that are not known with certainty by producers, such as weather or disease, input choices are determined in advance of the shock. This is the source, in part, of the rationale given by Zellner et al. (1966) in their expected profit-maximizing device used to justify consistency of average production parameter estimates by OLS or MLE under normality. However, for firms or industries not affected by those factors, this assumption may not hold. Another reason why the problem of simultaneity was often ignored was the development of duality approaches to modeling productivity outlined in earlier chapters, wherein dual forms such as cost functions were estimated. In regulated industries, for example, where data was often available in the public record, cost functions could be estimated with little attention given to endogeneity as the regressors output and input prices could safely be assumed exogenous (Christensen and Greene, 1976).

14.3 SELECTION BIAS

One of the limitations of many production data sets, specifically ones that are used to estimate productivity, is the problem of attrition. Aw et al. (2001) indicate that firm entry and exit rates in most countries tend to exceed 10 percent per year. They pointed out that in Taiwan, e.g., the turnover rate of firms is high owing to low sunk entry and exit costs resulting from low capital intensities and sector-specific dense networks of subcontracting relationships (supply chains). Moreover, they found that firms that survived at the end of the survey period were likely to be those firms that performed better. Similar findings have been noted by Olley and Pakes (1996) for the telecommunications equipment industry and in many other studies since.

In such a case, simple least squares estimation may suffer from selection bias if the factors that influence selection are correlated with outcomes of interest (typically production or any of the dual measures of cost, revenue, profit, or input requirements) and/or with selected regressors (Heckman, 1976). If there is selection bias, the distribution of outcomes of surviving firms' performances may be systematically higher than for a random sample from the population of firms if the firms that did not survive left the sample due to low levels of efficiency. Firms that survive will have u_i draws from a selected sample if firms know about some part of their productivity before deciding to exit.

This is clearer if we were to suppose that firms have some monopoly power and are endowed with different fixed levels of capital. Assume that firms observe their productivity and then decide to exit or not, and if they do not then choose the level of input use. If we ignore the issue of timing for the moment, then we can simplify the problem a bit by assuming that a firm makes a decision to exit or not after assessing its current profits and market value. Since the market value of a firm tends to be highly correlated with its level of capital, then the data from the survived firms will display a negative correlation between productivity and capital. The reason is that relatively less productive firms are able to stay in the market if they have more capital and/or more market protection, or protected niches (Kutlu and Sickles, 2012). This means that even if K_i is exogenous in the entire population, we may still have selection. Endogenous input decisions will cause an upward bias since there is usually positive correlation between inputs (especially those that are more easily adjusted, e.g., labor) and unobserved productivity. This is the traditional reason for positive bias in the ordinary least squares estimate of the labor coefficient in production function estimations. Panel data approaches, such as the within (fixed effects) estimator only addresses the bias if a plant's productivity is constant over time. Therein lies the one reason for utilizing methods that allow for firm-specific and time-varying latent productivity, such as those put forth by Cornwell et al. (1990), Lee and Schmidt (1993), Kneip et al. (2012), and Ahn et al. (2013), and many others for stochastic frontier models of efficiency and productivity. Finally, if selection is based only on surviving firms, then there is the possibility of a downward bias in the capital coefficient. This is because firms with larger capital stocks will survive even with lower levels of productivity, thus inducing a negative correlation between the disturbance term in the selected sample and the level of the capital input.

14.4 TRADITIONAL SOLUTIONS TO THE ENDOGENEITY PROBLEM CAUSED BY INPUT CHOICES AND SELECTIVITY

The traditional solutions to these two problems have often involved the use of panel data at the firm or plant level. Again, consider the linear in logs Cobb–Douglas production function

$$y_{it} = \alpha + \beta_l l_{it} + \beta_k k_{it} + w_{it} + \eta_{it}. \tag{14.4.1}$$

Here w_{it} is observed by the firm, but not by econometricians and η_{it} is not observed at all. Olley and Pakes (1996) interpreted w_{it} as the productivity of firms and η_{it} as either measurement error or a productivity shock that cannot affect input choice decisions by the firm. The typical solutions to the endogeneity problem caused by the correlation of productivity and input are to use standard instrumental variables based on predicting the endogenous variables into the column space of the predetermined variables, or by using fixed effects, which of course is just instrumental variables using within deviations of the exogenous variables as instruments.

As the basic idea of the method of instrumental variables is to find a variable correlated with the inputs, but not with the disturbance term, input prices are often suggested as possible instrument variables because they influence choices of inputs but are uncorrelated with the disturbance term if we assume the input markets are perfectly competitive. However, input prices have some drawbacks as instruments. First, input prices are not always available. For example, Ackerberg et al. (2015) point out that firms often do not report input prices and the reported labor costs that are reported are difficult to use in practice since they are reported as average wage per worker (actually as total labor expenditure divided by headcounts). Since the average wage contains some of the unknown worker's characteristics unobserved worker's quality differences will contaminate the productivity term, w_{it}, and thus the use of input prices as instrument variables for inputs cannot resolve the problem of endogeneity fully. Moreover, input prices often do not have enough variation across firms to identify production function coefficients.

In a dynamic panel setting we can difference out the time–invariant latent productivity:

$$
\begin{aligned}
y_{it} - y_{it-1} = {} & \beta_l(l_{it} - l_{it-1}) + \beta_k(k_{it} - k_{it-1}) \\
& + (w_{it} - w_{it-1}) + (\eta_{it} - \eta_{it-1}).
\end{aligned} \tag{14.4.2}
$$

Since $(w_{it} - w_{it-1})$ is correlated with $(l_{it} - l_{it-1})$, one can use an instrument variable approach. Arellano and Bond (1991) used lagged values of output and the inputs as instruments, while Blundell and Bond (1998) suggested using both lagged differences and lagged levels as instruments for the level equation and the differenced equation, respectively. Unfortunately, lagged variables tend to be rather weak instruments, especially when the degree of autocorrelation is high, which it often is in these panel settings.

14.5   STRUCTURAL ESTIMATION

The approach introduced by Olley and Pakes (1996) (OP) and developed by Levinsohn and Petrin (2003) and Ackerberg et al. (2006, 2015) is one solution to endogeneity caused by selection and endogenous input decisions. The OP approach uses investment to control for correlation between input choices and the unobserved productivity of a firm in their study of the dynamics of productivity in the telecommunications industry.

The OP method can be briefly outlined using the Cobb–Douglas production function analyzed in the previous section and repeated here:

$$y_{it} = \alpha + \beta_l l_{it} + \beta_k k_{it} + w_{it} + \eta_{it}. \qquad (14.5.1)$$

Here again, w_{it} is productivity unobserved by the econometrician but observed by the firm. OP assume that productivity shocks follow an exogenous first-order Markov process and that η_{it} is an error term not observed by the firm or, of course, the econometrician. The OP method relies on a set of assumptions. The first is that labor choice is non-dynamic. The second is that the capital choice is dynamic and evolves according to a standard perpetual inventory accumulation equation given by $k_{it} = K(k_{it}, i_{i,t-1})$, where $i_{i,t-1}$ is firm $i's$ investment at time $t - 1$. The third is that productivity is the only unobservable in the function aside from the usual idiosyncratic error term. Ackerberg et al. (2015) refer to this as the "scalar unobservable" assumption. The fourth is one of the most contentious, and is that there is strict monotonicity in the investment decision. That is, $i_{it} = i_t(k_{it}, w_{it})$ is strictly increasing in w_{it}. If one is willing to make these assumptions, then the investment function can be inverted and written as

$$w_{it} = i_t^{-1}(k_{it}, i_{it}). \qquad (14.5.2)$$

In order to estimate the parameters of the production function, one must estimate the inverse investment function. No particular functional form is given and thus nonparametric econometric procedures are pursued. Such procedures to estimate efficiency and productivity in the stochastic frontier panel paradigm using semiparametric methods has been explored by many authors. We have discussed several semi-nonparametric and nonparametric methods to estimate relationships such as this using penalized smoothing splines, kernel smoothers, Taylor-series, and general sieve-type estimators.

If we substitute the expression for the investment function into the production function we have

$$y_{it} = \alpha + \beta_l l_{it} + \beta_k k_{it} + i_t^{-1}(k_{it}, i_{it}) + \eta_{it}. \tag{14.5.3}$$

The functional form for the unobservable productivity function (14.5.2) is of course unknown since productivity itself is unobservable and thus some sort of series expansion or other asymptotic approximation is specified to model the unobservable function. OP use polynomials (up to fourth order). Cornwell et al. (1990) use second-order polynomials to model efficiency, although they do not need the monotonicity assumption to justify the use of their instruments. We can simply rewrite this expression as

$$y_{it} = \beta_l l_{it} + \phi_t(k_{it}, i_{it}) + \eta_{it}, \tag{14.5.4}$$

where $\phi_t(k_{it}, i_{it}) = \alpha + \beta_k k_{it} + w_{it}$. By estimating this last equation by OLS one obtains $\hat{\beta}_l, \hat{\phi}_t$. This is the first step in the OP algorithm.

The second step in the OP algorithm identifies β_k by using information from the first step and by exploiting the first-order Markov process assumption on w_{it}. From the relation, $\phi_t(k_{it}, i_{it}) = \alpha + \beta_k k_{it} + w_{it}$, we have $w_{it} = \phi_t(k_{it}, i_{it}) - \alpha - \beta_k k_{it}$ and the first-order Markov process assumption on w_{it} implies that $w_{it} = g(w_{i,t-1}) + \xi_{it}$. With these expressions they rewrite the original production function as

$$
\begin{aligned}
y_{it} - \beta_l l_{it} &= \alpha + \beta_k k_{it} + i_t^{-1}(k_{it}, i_{it}) + \eta_{it} \\
&= \alpha + \beta_k k_{it} + g(w_{i,t-1}) + \xi_{it} + \eta_{it} \\
&= \alpha + \beta_k k_{it} + g(\phi_{t-1} - \alpha - \beta_k k_{i,t-1}) + \xi_{it} + \eta_{it} \\
&= \beta_k k_{it} + \tilde{g}(\phi_{t-1} - \beta_k k_{i,t-1}) + \xi_{it} + \eta_{it}. \tag{14.5.5}
\end{aligned}
$$

Estimates of β_l and ϕ_t obtained in the first step then allow one to construct an estimate of β_k using nonlinear least squares on this last equation.

The OP approach is relatively straightforward to implement and takes into account both selection and the dynamics of entry and exit. However, investment might not be appropriate for the proxy variable since in practice, firms with only occasional investments will have zero quantity of investment for some periods. Levinsohn and Petrin (2003) (LP) pointed out that this can occur for a large portion of data for manufacturing censuses and proposed using intermediate inputs, such as materials, fuel or electricity, as proxies. They begin with the production function

$$y_{it} = \alpha + \beta_l l_{it} + \beta_k k_{it} + \beta_m m_{it} + w_{it} + \eta_{it}. \tag{14.5.6}$$

Here m_{it} represents intermediate inputs. They then specify a demand function for the intermediate inputs as

$$m_{it} = m_t(k_{it}, w_{it}). \tag{14.5.7}$$

Similar to the assumptions in the OP approach, the intermediate input demand function also is assumed to be monotonic in w_{it} for all k_{it}:

$$w_{it} = m_t^{-1}(k_{it}, m_{it}). \tag{14.5.8}$$

Levinsohn and Petrin (2003) utilize an estimation procedure (GMM) analogous to OP.

Ackerberg et al. (2006, 2015) have criticized OP and LP regarding a possible collinearity problem. Especially for the LP approach, collinearity arises in the first stage of the estimation. Moreover, they question whether l_{it} is in fact independent of the nonparametric terms $\phi_t(k_{it}, i_{it})$ or $\phi_t(k_{it}, m_{it})$. They consider possible scenarios causing collinearity problems depending on the timing of input decisions. First, they supposed the case where l_{it} is chosen at the same time as m_{it}. Since m_{it} is assumed to be chosen by $m_{it} = m_t(k_{it}, w_{it})$, l_{it} might be chosen according to

$$l_{it} = l_t(k_{it}, w_{it}). \tag{14.5.9}$$

One can rewrite this expression using $w_{it} = m_t^{-1}(k_{it}, m_{it})$ to express the labor term as

$$l_{it} = l_t(k_{it}, m_t^{-1}(k_{it}, m_{it})) = h_t(k_{it}, m_{it}). \tag{14.5.10}$$

Since, l_{it} is a function of m_{it} and k_{it}, there is collinearity between l_{it} and the nonparametric function, $\phi_t(k_{it}, m_{it})$. Thus β_l may only be weakly identified.

Second, they conjectured the case that l_{it} is chosen either before or after m_{it}. If, for example, l_{it} is chosen before m_{it}, $m_{it} = m_t(l_{it}, k_{it}, w_{it})$, not $m_{it} = m_t(k_{it}, w_{it})$. If, on the other hand, l_{it} is chosen after m_{it}, w_{it} evolves after the choice of m_{it} so we will have variation in l_{it}. However, in this case, the inverted demand function cannot reflect the correct productivity shock.

They next consider measurement error or optimization error, where either error m_{it} implies the existence of another unobservable in the equation for m_{it}. This of course violates the scalar unobservable assumption and one cannot invert the equation. Moreover, if there is measurement error in l_{it}, one can find independent variation in l_{it} but this variation is just noise and is not meaningful or helpful in identification. For this reason, they proposed an alternative procedure to deal with the collinearity problem. The procedure does not estimate any coefficients in the first stage but instead estimates all of the coefficients in the second stage. The production function to be estimated then becomes

$$y_{it} = \beta_l l_{it} + \beta_k k_{it} + w_{it} + \eta_{it}. \tag{14.5.11}$$

Consideration on the timing of input decisions is crucial. They assumed that k_{it} is chosen at time $t - 1$, and m_{it} is chosen at time t while l_{it} is chosen in-between, say, $t - b(0 < b < 1)$. They also assumed that w_{it} evolves according to a first-order Markov process as OP and LP but also considered two different sub-periods of time: periods between $t - 1$, $t - b$ and t, i.e.,

$$p(w_{it}|I_{i,t-b}) = p(w_{it}|w_{i,t-b})$$
$$p(w_{i,t-b}|I_{i,t-1}) = p(w_{i,t-b}|w_{i,t-1}). \tag{14.5.12}$$

With these assumptions the materials demand function is

$$m_{it} = m_t(l_{it}, k_{it}, w_{it}). \tag{14.5.13}$$

Substituting the inverse demand function (14.5.8) into the production function (14.5.11) gives

$$y_{it} = \beta_l l_{it} + \beta_k k_{it} + m_t^{-1}(l_{it}, k_{it}, m_{it}) + \eta_{it}. \tag{14.5.14}$$

Ackerberg et al. (2006, 2015) examine the following composite term to assess identification of β_l and β_k:

$$\Phi_t(l_{it}, k_{it}, m_{it}) = \beta_l l_{it} + \beta_k k_{it} + m_t^{-1}(l_{it}, k_{it}, m_{it}). \tag{14.5.15}$$

In the second stage of their procedure they exploit two independent moment conditions. One is a first-order Markov assumption on w_{jt} that can be written as

$$w_{it} = E(w_{it}|I_{i,t-1}) + \xi_{it} = E(w_{it}|w_{i,t-1}) + \xi_{it}. \tag{14.5.16}$$

Since capital input choices are assumed to be decided at $t-1$, we have $E(\xi_{it}|k_{it}) = 0$. To this moment condition they then add a second moment condition given l_{it-1}, i.e., $E(\xi_{it}|l_{i,t-1}) = 0$ and using $\hat{\Phi}_{it}$ from the first stage, we have

$$w_{it}(\beta_l, \beta_k) = \hat{\Phi}_{it} - \beta_l l_{it} - \beta_k k_{it}. \tag{14.5.17}$$

They obtained $\xi_{it}(\beta_l, \beta_k)$ by nonparametrically regressing $w_{it}(\beta_l, \beta_k)$ on $w_{it-1}(\beta_l, \beta_k)$. With these two moment conditions they then could form

$$\frac{1}{T}\frac{1}{n}\sum_t\sum_i \xi_{it}(\beta_l, \beta_k) \cdot \begin{pmatrix} k_{it} \\ l_{i,t-1} \end{pmatrix}, \tag{14.5.18}$$

and by minimizing (14.5.18) under the moment conditions, one can estimate (β_l, β_k) and thus the production process using GMM.

This entire exercise is leveraged by moment conditions and other assumptions for identification and it is reasonable to question when such assumptions are valid. Recall that the assumptions underlying the identification and consistency of this method relies on: (1) monotonicity of certain input levels (investment for OP and investment and labor for LP); (2) timing of input decisions; (3) a particular specification of the conditions under which firms leave the sample–note there is apparently no control for firms that enter the industry; (4) lack of a neoclassical underpinning for what a production function is defined to be–frontier production function; (5) particular moment conditions that are based on the relative timing of different input choices; (6) a related but often separate issue of the sources endogeneity that are often much broader than simply attrition bias and endogeneity; (7) presence of supply chains at the micro firm level; and (8) the use of a single output technology, among other things. This later assumption has been recently lifted by De Loecker et al. (2016) but their framework assumes that multiple output decisions are independent, which runs counter to the typical reasons why a firm produces multiple outputs, namely that there are shared inputs.

14.6 ENDOGENEITY IN NONSTRUCTURAL MODELS OF PRODUCTIVITY: THE STOCHASTIC FRONTIER MODEL

Until recently both empirical and theoretical stochastic frontier models often assumed away potential endogeneity issues that may arise. This may indeed surprise some of the researchers outside the field, as endogeneity problems for production functions have been viewed as a serious concern in other contexts, e.g., Olley and Pakes (1996), Levinsohn and Petrin (2003). Indeed, it appears that endogeneity may be a more serious problem in the stochastic frontier model compared to the standard average production/cost function models due to additional complications introduced by the presence of the one-sided inefficiency term, which is generally assumed to be independent from the two-sided error term. In the context of health care cost function estimation, Mutter et al. (2013) give a good example of why endogeneity can arise in stochastic frontier models. Their argument is as follows. Assume that quality and quantity are jointly determined by the hospitals and that quality is cost-enhancing. If the quality variable is included in the health care cost frontier equation, then the two-sided error term would be correlated with the quality. This would lead to inconsistent parameter and efficiency estimates. If the researcher omits the quality variable from the cost frontier to avoid this problem, then a high-quality health care provider would be incorrectly considered as less efficient compared to a low-quality health care provider. In this example, endogeneity arises when any one of the regressors is not independent from the two-sided error term, which we call a type I endogeneity problem. Another type of endogeneity arises when the one-sided error term is not independent from the two-sided error term, which we call endogeneity problem of type II. For example, Gronberg et al. (2011), Kutlu and Nair-Reichert (2018), and Kutlu et al. (2018) model inefficiency by Herfindahl–Hirshman Index, executive remuneration, and return on revenue, respectively. They argue that these variables are not independent from the two-sided error term, which would cause inconsistent parameter and efficiency estimates. Selectivity issues have been addressed in a non-structural stochastic frontier setting by Greene (2010) who developed a full information "true" sample selection model for the stochastic frontier specification based on the Heckman (1979) framework.

It appears that Guan et al. (2009) is one of the earliest papers that attempted to solve the endogeneity issue in the stochastic frontier context. They follow a two-step estimation methodology to handle the type I endogeneity problem. In the first step, they consistently estimate the frontier parameters using the GMM method. In the second step, they use the residuals from the first stage as the dependent variable and apply standard stochastic frontier methods to obtain efficiency estimates. One issue with this method is that the dependent variable in the second stage is an estimate from the first stage, which may cause less precise efficiency estimates compared to methods that get the estimates in a single stage. A more serious issue is that if the model is subject to endogeneity of type II, then the second stage estimates would give inconsistent inefficiency estimates as the standard stochastic frontier models do not handle endogeneity. In a panel data context, Kutlu (2010) proposes solutions to the type I endogeneity problem using a control function approach.[1] The first solution involves estimating a limited information maximum likelihood model in a single stage. The second solution is a two-stage approach. Kutlu (2010) presents his ideas using a production function setting.

We follow the notation and exposition of Kutlu et al. (2018), which generalizes Kutlu (2010). For productive unit i, $y_{i.} = (y_{i1}, y_{i2}, \ldots, y_{iT})'$ is a $T \times 1$ vector and $x_{1i.} = (x_{1i1}, x_{1i2}, \ldots, x_{1iT})'$ is a $T \times k_1$ matrix where T is the number of time periods for productive unit i. We use similar notation for other vectors and matrix variables. The production model of Kutlu (2010) is given by

$$y_{i.} = x_{1i.}\beta - u_{i.} + v_{i.} \tag{14.6.1}$$
$$x_{i.} = z_{i.}\Delta + \varepsilon_{i.}$$
$$\begin{bmatrix} \varepsilon_{it}^* \\ v_{it} \end{bmatrix} = \begin{bmatrix} \Omega^{-1/2}\varepsilon_{it} \\ v_{it} \end{bmatrix} \sim \mathcal{N}\left(\begin{bmatrix} 0 \\ 0 \end{bmatrix}, \begin{bmatrix} I_p & \sigma_v\rho \\ \sigma_v\rho' & \sigma_v^2 \end{bmatrix} \right)$$
$$u_{it} = h_{i.}u_i^*$$
$$h_{it} = \exp(-\tau(t - T))$$
$$u_i^* \sim \mathcal{N}^+\left(\mu, \sigma_u^2\right),$$

where y_{it} is the logarithm of the output for the ith productive unit at time t; x_{1it} is a vector of variables that can contain endogenous variables; x_{it} is a $p \times 1$ vector of all endogenous variables (excluding y_{it}); z_{it} is a $q \times 1$ vector of all exogenous variables; v_{it} is the two-sided error term; $u_{it} \geq 0$ is a one-sided error term capturing the inefficiency; $u_i^* \geq 0$ is a productive unit specific random component independent from v_{it} and ε_{it}; Δ is a $q \times p$ matrix of coefficients; Ω is the $p \times p$ variance–covariance matrix of ε_{it}; σ_v^2 is the variance of v_{it}; ρ is the vector representing the correlation between ε_{it}^* and v_{it}; and I_p is the $p \times p$ identity matrix. Kutlu (2010) assumes that v_{it} may be not independent of some of the regressors but it is independent of u_{it}. It can be shown by using a Cholesky decomposition of the variance–covariance matrix of $\left(\text{vec}\left(\varepsilon_{i.}^{*\prime}\right)', v_{i.}' \right)'$ that

$$v_{i.} = \varepsilon_{i.}\eta + w_{i.}, \tag{14.6.2}$$

---

[1] Kutlu and Sickles (2012) use a very similar approach in the Kalman filter setting to estimate a dynamic game.

where $\sigma_w = \sigma_v\sqrt{1-\rho'\rho}$, $\eta = \sigma_w\Omega^{-1/2}\rho/\sqrt{1-\rho'\rho}$, $w_{i.} = \sigma_w w_{i.}^*$, and $\varepsilon_{i.}^*$ and $w_{i.}^* \sim \mathcal{N}(0, I_T)$ are independent. Then, the frontier and endogenous variable prediction equations can be written as

$$y_{i.} = x_{1i.}\beta + (x_{i.} - z_{i.}\Delta)\eta + e_{i.} \tag{14.6.3}$$

$$x_{i.} = z_{i.}\Delta + \varepsilon_{i.},$$

where $e_{i.} = w_{i.} - u_{i.}$ and $(x_{i.} - z_{i.}\Delta)\eta$ is a bias correction term. In this setting, Kutlu (2010) estimates efficiency by

$$E\left[u_{it} \mid e_{i.}\right] = h_{it}\left[\mu_{i*} + \frac{\sigma_{i*}\phi\left(\frac{\mu_{i*}}{\sigma_{i*}}\right)}{\Phi\left(\frac{\mu_{i*}}{\sigma_{i*}}\right)}\right] \tag{14.6.4}$$

$$TE_{it} = \exp\left(-E\left[u_{it} \mid e_{i.}\right]\right),$$

where ϕ and Φ are the standard normal probability density and cumulative density functions and where $\mu_{i*} = \frac{-\sigma_u^2 e_{i.}'h_{i.}+\mu\sigma_w^2}{\sigma_u^2 h_{i.}'h_{i.}+\sigma_v^2}$, $\sigma_{i*}^2 = \frac{\sigma_w^2\sigma_u^2}{\sigma_u^2 h_{i.}'h_{i.}+\sigma_w^2}$.

The LIML method of Kutlu (2010) estimates equation (14.6.3) simultaneously by the maximum likelihood estimation method. This method is LIML in the sense that it does not specify a structural specification for the distribution of the endogenous variables. The two-stage control function approach of Kutlu (2010) first gets the reduced form residuals $\hat{\varepsilon}_{i.}$ and enters them as a control function in the regression

$$y_{i.} = x_{1i.}\beta + \hat{\varepsilon}_{i.}\eta + e_{i.} \tag{14.6.5}$$

The conventionally calculated standard errors from the second stage estimation need to be adjusted to reflect the fact that Δ and η have been estimated. Kutlu (2010) proposes using a proper bootstrapping procedure to get the corrected standard errors. Alternatively, one can use analytical approaches such as Murphy and Topel (1985). While the two-stage control function approach is less efficient compared to LIML method, the required assumptions may be further relaxed, e.g., normality of $\left(\text{vec}\left(\varepsilon_{i.}^{*\prime}\right)', v_{i.}'\right)'$ is less essential for the two-stage control function approach. For both LIML and two-stage control function approaches, exogeneity of a variable can be tested by checking the significance of the corresponding component of η. In what follows, whenever we refer to Kutlu (2010), we will mean the one-stage LIML method that he proposed. Tran and Tsionas (2013) consider a GMM procedure based on the score of the likelihood of this model.

In the cross-sectional data framework, Karakaplan and Kutlu (2017a) propose a similar model that can solve the endogeneity problem of both type I and type II. They achieve this by modifying some of the assumptions on error variables. We continue to use the same notation but drop t as their model is in cross-sectional data framework. Karakaplan and Kutlu (2017a) assume that $h_i = \sqrt{\exp\left(x_{2i}'\varphi_u\right)}$, where the term x_{2it}' is used for modeling the heterogeneity of the u_{it} term, φ_u is a comfortable vector of parameters, and where x_{2i} is a vector of variables that can contain endogenous variables and u_i^* is independent of other error terms, i.e., ε_i and v_i. Hence, in contrast to Kutlu (2010), $u_i = h_i u_i^*$ is no longer necessarily independent of v_i unconditionally. The modified assumption is that u_i and v_i are conditionally independent given all explanatory variables, i.e., x_i and z_i. Karakaplan and Kutlu (2017b) propose a panel data counterpart of this model so that $u_{it} = h_{it} u_i^*$ and $h_{it} = \sqrt{\exp\left(x'_{2it} \varphi_u\right)}$. In the Bayesian econometrics context, Griffiths and Hajargasht (2016) propose another model that handles endogeneity problems of both type I and type II.

When estimating a translog model where the endogenous variables enter as cross products with other variables, the number of endogenous variables may grow very rapidly. Amsler et al. (2016) provide a good discussion of this matter. They give an example of translog cost function model where there are two endogenous input prices. In the translog setting, this implies that there are five endogenous variables. The two-stage least squares estimation of such a model requires at least five instruments. Although it is possible to generate five instruments using two existing instruments, the strength of these generated instruments may be questionable. The models of Kutlu (2010) and Karakaplan and Kutlu (2017a,b) are particularly useful when estimating a translog model that involves cross products of endogenous variables. Under the assumptions described above, it is enough to use only two control functions, i.e., two instruments.

By using a copula approach, Amsler et al. (2016) relax not only the assumption that regressors are independent of v_{it}, but also that regressors and u_i^* are independent. One difficulty with this approach is that the researcher has to pick a copula. Amsler et al. (2016) pick the Gaussian copula for convenience and technical reasons. Another difficulty is that the application of this copula may be computationally demanding. Amsler et al. (2016) do not allow environmental variables in the model. Amsler et al. (2017) introduce environmental variables in the same framework. Tran and Tsionas (2015) is another study that uses the copula approach in the stochastic frontier context. They propose a model that does not require the availability of outside information to obtain the instruments by constructing a flexible joint distribution of the endogenous variables and the composed error.

So far the models discussed only consider the extensions of standard stochastic frontier models to allow for endogeneity. Greene (2005a,b) argues that if the researcher does not consider firm–specific heterogeneity, the heterogeneity may be confused with inefficiency. Greene suggests controlling firm–specific heterogeneity by including a fixed effects term. However, this method is subject to the incidental parameters problem. Wang and Ho (2010) address the incidental parameters problem by either using first difference or within transformations. Kutlu et al. (2018) generalize Greene's and Wang and Ho's models to allow the heterogeneity term to depend on time or other variables and solve endogeneity problems of type I and type II in this context. Their model does not suffer from the incidental parameters problem. In particular, they keep the other parts of the model the same as Kutlu (2010) and Karakaplan and Kutlu (2017a,b) and suggest modeling the frontier equation as follows:

$$y_{i.} = x_{3i.}\alpha_i + x_{1i.}\beta - u_{i.} + v_{i.} \qquad (14.6.6)$$

$$x_{i.} = z_{i.}\Delta + \varepsilon_{i.}$$

$$\begin{bmatrix} \varepsilon_{it}^* \\ v_{it} \end{bmatrix} = \begin{bmatrix} \Omega^{-1/2}\varepsilon_{it} \\ v_{it} \end{bmatrix} \sim \mathcal{N}\left(\begin{bmatrix} 0 \\ 0 \end{bmatrix}, \begin{bmatrix} I_p & \sigma_v\rho \\ \sigma_v\rho' & \sigma_v^2 \end{bmatrix} \right)$$

$$u_{it} = h_{i.}u_i^*$$

$$h_{it} = \sqrt{\exp\left(x_{2it}'\varphi_u\right)}$$

$$u_i^* \sim \mathcal{N}^+\left(\mu, \sigma_u^2\right),$$

where α_i is a productive unit specific parameter vector and $x_{3i.}$ is a matrix of variables that determine heterogeneity. In line with Cornwell et al. (1990), Kutlu et al. (2018) suggest using $x_{3it} = \left(1, t, t^2\right)'$. They also argue that $x_{3i.}$ can contain some product characteristics terms that help to control for heterogeneity of the products. They transform this model by orthogonal projections, i.e., $M_{x_3} = I_{T_i} - x_{3i.}\left(x_{3i.}'x_{3i.}\right)^{-1}x_{3i.}'$, and estimate the transformed model:

$$M_{x_3}y_{i.} = M_{x_3}x_{1i.}\beta - M_{x_3}u_{i.} + M_{x_3}v_{i.}$$

Kutlu et al. (2018) also relate their model with Olley and Pakes (1996) (OP) and Levinsohn and Petrin (2003) (LP) type of models. One potential problem with the standard production function or stochastic frontier production function is that some of the determinants of the production may be observable to the firms but not to the econometrician. This would mean that some of the input choices may be endogenous. OP–LP and others propose control function approaches to overcome this issue where the control function is constructed by modeling the inputs under different settings. However, these models make strong assumptions about the market structure (e.g., competitive environment and the level of investment), the monotonicity of intermediate input demand function, etc. Moreover, in this framework, providing sound solutions when the production function has translog functional form seems to be a difficult task. In the stochastic frontier context, Shee and Stefanou (2015) provide a mechanism that can solve the endogeneity problem using a methodology that closely follows LP's solution.

In contrast to OP–LP-type solutions, the solution of Kutlu et al. (2018) can attack the endogeneity problem in a variety of ways. Unlike the earlier fixed effects solutions to this type of endogeneity problem, their model allows a flexible effects term that can vary based on time and other variables. Hence, their model is less prone to the standard criticisms for the fixed effects approach. Moreover, their method can utilize the instruments from the standard literature to solve the endogeneity problems of prices. Another advantage of this method is that the estimation of translog production functions is easier. Recall that cross products of endogenous variables do not require additional instruments. Finally, both OP–LP approaches are intrinsically control function approaches. Hence, under suitable conditions, it can even be desirable to combine the control functions of both approaches to get models that are robust to many different kind of endogeneity problems. For example, the approach of Shee and Stefanou (2015) does not solve the endogeneity problem of type II. It is a trivial practice to incorporate control functions of Kutlu and others to modify Shee and Stefanou (2015) so that it becomes robust to the endogeneity problem of type I and type II.

14.7 ENDOGENEITY AND TRUE FIXED EFFECTS MODELS

What are "true" fixed effects? How do we distinguish unobserved heterogeneity from inefficiency in the panel stochastic frontier model? In the panel stochastic frontier production function, output (or its log) for firm i at time t is a function of measures of inputs and observable variables to control for production environment. We will continue to use the linear form of the production function (or distance function, recognizing that in the latter case x will contain right-hand-side endogenous multiple outputs):

$$y_{it} = x'_{it}\beta + \eta_i(t) + v_{it}. \tag{14.7.1}$$

In order to make the point about what are or are not "true" fixed effects (of course this is just a semantic term of art as "truth" in the context of unobserved heterogeneity is a misnomer), we first decompose $\eta_i(t)$ into two terms, call them a_i and b_i, where for the sake of this argument, we ignore the possible time varying nature of $\eta_i(t)$. Differences across firms in the value of b_i reflect differences in the technical efficiency of production, and as in Schmidt and Sickles (1984) a conceptual measure of inefficiency can be measured as

$$RIE_i = \max_{i,i=1,\dots,n} b_i - b_i \geq 0. \tag{14.7.2}$$

Differences in the value of a_i, however, reflect differences in the production environment that are beyond the control of the firm and which we do not wish to include in our efficiency measures.

Amsler and Schmidt (2017) use the following argument to make the point about how the interpretation of the effects, as well as the modeling scenario, are essential in decomposing and giving meaning to the a_i and b_i measures. Suppose that the firms are farms, in which case a natural interpretation of b_i would be a measure of the skill of the farmer. On the other hand, a_i would represent relevant but unobserved features of the production environment like soil quality or microclimate. It is clear that without additional assumptions, typically in the form of some type of orthogonality assumption, a_i and b_i cannot be separately point identified. The identification strategy of Amsler and Schmidt (2017) is to assume that there are some observable variables that are correlated with a_i but not b_i and some other variables that are correlated with b_i but not a_i. Staying with their agricultural example, assume that the education of the farmer is correlated with the ability of the farmer but not with soil quality or microclimate. Define an indicator variable for the physical location of the farm that is correlated with soil quality or microclimate but not with the ability of the farmer. Then such a variable can be used as an instrument for b_i. Orthogonality conditions such as this, stated in terms of both simple and partial correlations, are used by Amsler and Schmidt (2017) to develop identification conditions for the inefficiency and heterogeneity effects. For example, their first model assumes that the ability of the farmer is uncorrelated with the physical location of the farm, whereas the second model assumes that, conditional on education of the farmer, the ability of the farmer is uncorrelated with the physical location of the farm. Using these assumptions various point identification results follow. Amsler and Schmidt (2017) seek to distinguish between time-invariant heterogeneity (e.g., soil quality) and time-invariant inefficiency (e.g., skill of the farmer). The previous literature, such as Colombi et al. (2014), accomplishes this by relying on strong distributional assumptions. Amsler and Schmidt (2017) wish to avoid such strong assumptions. The identification strategy is to find variables that can be assumed to be uncorrelated with heterogeneity but correlated with inefficiency, and vice versa. This model can be used in a wide variety of settings besides stochastic frontier models, for example, to distinguish the effects of genetics from those of environment, or to distinguish the effects of innate ability and socioeconomic background.

14.8 ENDOGENEITY IN ENVIRONMENTAL PRODUCTION AND IN DIRECTIONAL DISTANCE FUNCTIONS

Kumbhakar and Tsionas (2016) model a production process that produces an undesirable (bad) output in addition to the desirable (good) output. These models are known as by-production (or BP) models and include technical inefficiency. They argue that neither the directional distance function approach nor the transformation function approach for modeling a technology that generates both good and bad outputs using good and bad inputs can distinguish between technical efficiency and environmental efficiency. They utilize Bayesian methods to identify and estimate these two sources of inefficiency under a variety of endogeneity assumptions.

Atkinson and Tsionas (2016) use Bayesian techniques to estimate optimal firm-specific directions for each input and output. This is in contrast to the typical method where multiplicative factors 1 are used for good outputs and -1 are used for inputs and bad outputs. To estimate the directional distance function, the authors estimate it in conjunction with the cost minimization and profit maximization first-order conditions.

Beginning with the usual quadratic function of all inputs and outputs

$$F(z) = \sum_{w=1}^{W} \alpha_w z_w + \frac{1}{2} \sum_{w=1}^{W} \sum_{w'=1}^{W} \beta_{ww'} z_w z_{w'}, \tag{14.8.1}$$

with $z = [z_1, \ldots, z_W]'$ including all of the inputs and outputs, both good and bad, the traditional distance function is defined as

$$\vec{D}(z, g) = \max \left\{ \beta : z + \beta g = (x + \beta g_x, y + \beta g_y) \in T \right\}, \quad (14.8.2)$$

with directions $g_y > 0$ and $g_x < 0$.

Given

$$\beta_w W = - \sum_{w'=1}^{W-1} \beta_{ww'} g_{w'} / g_W, \forall w = 1, \ldots, W, \quad (14.8.3)$$

we now have

$$\vec{D}(z, g) = \frac{z_W}{g_W} + \sum_{w=1}^{W-1} \alpha_w \left(z_w - \frac{g_w}{g_W} \right) + \frac{1}{2} \sum_{w=1}^{W-1} \sum_{w'=1}^{W-1} \beta_{ww'} \left(z_w z_{w'} - \frac{g_w}{g_W} z_w z_W \right).$$

$$(14.8.4)$$

The key difference here is that the directions (g) are not imposed, but rather parameters to be estimated. Using the above distance function and the first-order conditions of the profit function, the authors again suggest an MCMC approach. The authors ultimately find that using non-fixed directions leads to higher estimated firm–specific technical efficiency, technical change, and productivity change when compared to fixed direction analysis.

14.9 ENDOGENEITY, COPULAS, AND STOCHASTIC METAFRONTIERS

A copula is a statistical tool that is used to create a joint distribution with specified marginal distributions. Copulas allow one to model the dependence between non-normal random variables. For example, Smith (2008) used a copula to allow for dependence between statistical noise (normal) and technical inefficiency (half-normal) in a stochastic frontier model. Similarly, in Amsler et al. (2014) a copula is used to model dependence between the levels of technical inefficiency for a given firm over time, in a panel setting. They wanted a firm's level of inefficiency to be correlated, but not perfectly correlated, over time. Correlation of statistical noise over time can be modeled with the multivariate normal distribution, but there is no obvious distribution for correlated half-normals. A technical issue is that the integrals that are needed for the distribution of the composed error are intractable, so estimation is by the method of simulated maximum likelihood (i.e., the likelihood is evaluated by simulation).

Amsler et al. (2016) was the first systematic treatment of endogeneity in stochastic frontier models. Earlier work, notably Kutlu (2010) and Karakaplan and Kutlu (2017a) had allowed correlation between some of the regressors and statistical noise, under the assumption that the errors in the reduced form equations for the endogenous regressors are normal. Amsler et al. (2016) allowed the regressors also to be correlated with technical inefficiency. Once again this requires a copula, and the use of simulated maximum likelihood. This basic model structure has recently been extended by Amsler et al. (2017) to consider "environmental variables" (determinants of inefficiency), a situation also considered by Kutlu but where now the environmental variables are correlated with either statistical noise, the "base level" inefficiency, or both. This raises some difficult and unfamiliar technical issues whose resolution would prove most important in addressing the endogeneity issue.

Amsler et al. (2017) consider endogeneity in a somewhat different light in their work on metafrontiers. Suppose that a firm (or some other cross-sectional unit) chooses one of a set of possible technologies, and the modeler knows which one that is. Each technology is represented by a stochastic frontier model, and the metafrontier is defined as the upper envelope of the technology-specific frontiers. The econometrician wants to measure technical inefficiency (the distance from the technology-specific frontier to observed output) but also the metafrontier distance (the distance from the metafrontier to the technology-specific frontier). Previous work in this literature has typically not respected the stochastic nature of the frontiers in the sense that if each technology-specific frontier is stochastic, then so is the metafrontier. Amsler et al. (2017) show how to calculate the distribution of the metafrontier, and also showed that ignoring its stochastic nature understates the metafrontier distance since it ignores the effect of the "max" operator on the random components of the individual frontiers.

14.10   OTHER TYPES OF ORTHOGONALITY CONDITIONS TO DEAL WITH ENDOGENEITY

Kuosmanen et al. (2015) develop a set of orthogonality conditions for the directional distance function that are based on the axioms of production theory we have discussed in earlier chapters as well as on the basic properties of stochastic distance and directional distance functions that we have also discussed to deal with endogeneity. Their work is particularly interesting in that they are able to show that orthogonality conditions necessary for point identification rest critically on the distance metric for the directional distance function. That is, the direction itself is an identifying condition. They also provide a consistent nonparametric estimator of the directional distance function based on the StoNED model of Kuosmanen and Kortelainen (2012) which satisfies the essential axioms of production theory.

Recent work by Kuosmanen and Johnson (2017), Johnson and Layer (2016), and Johnson et al. (2017) consider alternative methods of establishing point identification in the directional distance function using methods introduced into the econometrics literature by De Nadai and Lewbel (2016) and develop methods to establish orthogonality based on implications of the errors in variables problem for the vector of outputs, treating the errors as correlated, as in De Nadai and Lewbel (2016). Johnson and Layer (2016) and Johnson et al. (2017) are also able to show that the results of De Nadai and Lewbel (2016) and Schennach and Hu (2013) can be used to establish conditions for point identification by utilizing directions and heteroskedastic errors implied by the errors in variables covariance specification as identifying conditions. Much work on these issues remains to be completed and is the focus of intense research activity.

14.11 CONCLUDING REMARKS

This chapter has provided a set of approaches and methods to address endogeneity based on structural and non-structural models of productivity. The issue of how to separate statistical noise from a set of explanatory variables, or to best represent a treatment effect, or to address the sequential timing of firm decisions, all involve identifying restrictions of one form or another. We anticipate that this issue will continue to be the source of many disagreements on how best to model productivity and to be the major factor in how various camps in the productivity research community continue to differentiate their intellectual product market.

14.12 EXERCISES

1. Assume that we want to estimate a translog cost function by using the model of Kutlu (2010) where there are two endogenous input prices. In particular, consider the following cost function:

$$\ln C = \beta_0 + \beta_1 \ln w_1 + \beta_2 \ln w_2 + \beta_3 \ln w_1 \ln w_2 + \beta_4 \ln Q \\ + \beta_5 \ln w_1 \ln Q + \beta_6 \ln w_2 \ln Q,$$

where w_1 and w_2 are endogenous input prices and Q is the output quantity. Let $\ln z_1$ and $\ln z_2$ be proper instruments for $\ln w_1$ and $\ln w_2$. Under the standard assumptions for 2SLS, we would need five instrumental variables to estimate such a model. In the control function/LIML setting of Kutlu (2010), it is possible to estimate this equation by using only two instrumental variables. Under what conditions would this give us consistent parameter estimates?

2. Consider the transformed model of Kutlu et al. (2018). What happens to the distribution of u_{it} after transformation? How does it affect the pre-truncation and the post-truncation parameters of the distribution?

3. Consider the transformed model of Kutlu et al. (2018). Show that the probability density function of vec $(\tilde{\varepsilon}_{i.})$ is given by:

$$f_{\tilde{\varepsilon}_{i.}}(\tilde{\varepsilon}_{i.}) = \left(\left| 2\pi \left(\Omega_\varepsilon \otimes M_{x_{3i}} \right) \right|^* \right)^{-1/2} \\ \times \exp\left(-\frac{1}{2} \text{vec}(\tilde{\varepsilon}_{i.})' \left(\Omega_\varepsilon \otimes M_{x_{3i}} \right)^+ \text{vec}(\tilde{\varepsilon}_{i.}) \right) \\ = (|2\pi\Omega|)^{-(T_i - k)/2} \exp\left(-\frac{1}{2} \left(\Omega^{-1} \tilde{\varepsilon}'_{i.} \tilde{\varepsilon}_{i.} \right) \right),$$

where $\tilde{\varepsilon}_{i.} = M_{x_3}\varepsilon_{i.}$; T is the number of time periods; k is the number of regressors included in $x_{3i.}$; $|.|^*$ denotes the pseudo determinant and the superscript "+"denotes the Moore–Penrose pseudo inverse of a matrix. (**Hint:** For a positive semi-definite matrix A with at least one nonzero eigenvalue, $|A|^*$ is equal to the product of the nonzero eigenvalues.)

4. One can use a two-stage procedure to estimate the models of Kutlu and his coauthors. How can one relax the distributional assumptions on $\left(\text{vec} \left(\varepsilon_{i.}^{*\prime} \right)^{\prime}, v_{i.}^{\prime} \right)^{\prime}$ using two-stage estimation procedures?

5. Intuitively, explain the role of the $(x_{i.} - z_{i.}\Delta)\eta$ term. Also, explain why this term can be used for testing endogeneity of endogenous variables.

CHAPTER 15

Dynamic Models of Productivity and Efficiency

In this chapter, we wish to explore models that differentiate between short-run transitory and long-run persistent inefficiency, possibly due to market pressures, or the lack thereof. With the introduction of the technical efficiency measurement techniques we have discussed in previous chapters, empirical studies of the sources of productive inefficiency using both DEA (Leibenstein and Maital, 1992), and SFA (Caves and Barton, 1992) were taken up relatively quickly by leading scholars in the field of economics and management as software platforms became publically available. In their exhaustive study of 285 US industries, Caves and Barton (1992) found that the degree of competition in the various industries had a measurable effect on the level of efficiency. During this time period in the early 1990s studies of the links between efficiency and market structure were also carried out by public utilities (Reifschneider and Stevenson, 1991), since the dependency between efficiency and competitive pressure has significant regulatory relevance. Button and Weyman-Jones (1992), in their summary of the X-efficiency literature, found similar results that point to a strong link between the level of regulatory oversight in an industry and the efficiency levels. Market structure is a driver of performance and this has long been recognized by economists (Hicks, 1935). Leibenstein (1966) pointed out that, given "proper motivations," firm performance can be enhanced. The empirical studies that have followed to date continue to provide a strong consensus for the existence of such a link.

15.1 NONPARAMETRIC PANEL DATA MODELS OF PRODUCTIVITY DYNAMICS

The foundation for the theory of dynamic adjustment can be broadened by considering the axiomatic approach by Silva and Stefanou (2003), who laid out the set theoretic approach that was then extended in Silva and Stefanou (2007). Elaboration on the foundation for an adjustment cost framework by switching to the dynamic directional distance function approach allowed Silva et al. (2015) to deal with an even broader characterization of efficiency and productivity notions. Building on the Luenberger-based approach (using the dynamic directional distance function), Stefanou and his colleagues develop the relationship between the primal and dual forms of productivity (Lansink et al., 2015). Econometrically implementable frameworks for the dynamic adjustment model that address asymmetric dynamic adjustment appear in the review by Hamermesh and Pfann (1996). Specification and estimation of asymmetric adjustment rates for quasi-fixed factors of production, similar in spirit to the Sickles and Streitwieser (1998) model, are found in Chang and Stefanou (1988), while Luh and Stefanou (1991) provide the modeling set up for estimating productivity growth within a dynamic adjustment framework. Previous efforts for estimating productivity growth in a dynamic adjustment model essentially ignored the adjustment/disequilibrium component of the productivity decomposition. Luh and Stefanou (1991) develop this framework and then econometrically implement it in a dynamic duality framework. This paper is the precursor for much of the work that follows, elaborations and extensions for which can be found in Rungsuriyawiboon and Stefanou (2007).

The ability to capture the dynamic nature of a firm's performance relative to its competitors has important modeling advantages in the productivity literature as static models of inefficiency may be misspecified. The general treatments we gave to such dynamics in Chapters 12 and 13 were leveraged largely by more general treatments of unobserved heterogeneity and not due to any formal structure on the firm effects based on economic theory. In this chapter, we explore such issues, first by revisiting how the output-oriented Farrell technical efficiency estimator can be expressed in an intertemporal setting using both Data Envelopment Analysis (DEA) and Free-Disposable Hull (FDH) specifications of the production technology. We then discuss concepts of cointegration and convergence in the context of this literature. We consider how to test whether or not increasing competitive forces after an industry is deregulated (e.g., the US airline industry) is consistent with the technical efficiency scores of firms moving together in the long run (cointegration), as well as whether or not they move closer together over time (convergence). Evidence of these time series characteristics would be indicative of a greater concern among firms to maintain high relative technical efficiency levels in order to surpass, or at the least to follow, the benchmarks established by the most efficient firms in the industry. We then discuss parametric models of the growth process that include the treatment of efficiency dynamics introduced in Ahn et al. (2000) that allows for the estimation of both short-run and long-run inefficiency and technical change.

15.1.1 Revisiting the Dynamic Output Distance Function and the Intertemporal Malmquist Productivity Index: Cointegration and Convergence of Efficiency Scores in Productivity Panels

As we pointed out in Chapter 8, when a researcher wishes to compare the efficiency scores (or a value of the distance function) for a firm in one period relative to the frontier in a different period, the *output*-oriented Shephard's distance function for an allocation (x_s, y_t) relative to the (estimated) technology for period τ can be estimated via

$$\left(\hat{D}_o^\tau(x_s, y_t)\right)^{-1} \equiv \max_{\theta, z^1, \ldots, z^n} \theta \qquad (15.1.1)$$

s.t.

$$\sum_{k=1}^n z^k y_{m\tau}^k \geq \theta \, y_{mt}, \quad m = 1, \ldots, M, \qquad (15.1.2)$$

$$\sum_{k=1}^n z^k x_{l\tau}^k \leq x_{ls}, \quad l = 1, \ldots, N, \qquad (15.1.3)$$

$$\theta \geq 0, \; z^k \geq 0, \; k = 1, \ldots, n. \qquad (15.1.4)$$

Here we have imposed constant returns to scale.[1] Variable returns to scale can be accommodated by adding the constraint $\sum_{k=1}^n z^k = 1$ and nonincreasing returns to scale can be accommodated by replacing the constraint with $\sum_{k=1}^n z^k \leq 1$. Moreover, since the measurement is based on the allocation (x_s, y_t), the r.h.s. of the constraints involves x at time s and y at time appearing with time-subscript t. Since the technology is measured with respect to the observed best-practice technology in some period τ, the l.h.s. of the constraints uses the data on (x, y) with subscript τ.

The Farrell technical efficiency score can also be estimated using the FDH approach of Deprins et al. (1984). FDH does not require that all convex combinations of the observed production activities be considered in the production set but only those that are observed in practice and those they dominate due to the assumption of the free disposability of all inputs and all outputs. This leads to a characterization of technology being the free disposal hull of the observations on (x, y), hence its name (see Chapter 8 for more details on DEA and FDH). This results in a non-convex stepwise frontier instead of a piecewise linear one and results from the linear program above when the last constraint $z^k \geq 0$ is replaced by the constraint that $z^k \in \{0, 1\}$. Alam and Sickles (2000) used both the DEA and the FDH formulations of the output-oriented Farrell technical efficiency score to examine the cointegration of firms in the US airline industry after deregulation.

15.1.1.1 Cointegration

The possibility that nonstationary series may be related is a bit counterintuitive but quite real. For stationary series, meaningful relationships may

---

[1] In the Alam and Sickles (2000) study applying these methods to the US airline industry, such an assumption was tested and could not be rejected using standard regression-based methods.

be established in a rather straightforward fashion, but going back to at least Yule (1926) and picked up again by Granger and Newbold (1974) almost a half-century later, such relationships may be meaningless when the series are not stationary. However, under certain circumstances it may still be possible to establish a relationship, i.e., a cointegrating relationship, wherein linear combinations of nonstationary series are stationary; that is, they yield a stable long-run solution, or equilibrium, or relationship that keeps the series from moving too far away from each other (Engle and Granger, 1987). A series that is permanently affected by a shock is referred to as integrated up to some order. For example, if a single differencing operation on a nonstationary series yields a stationary series, then we refer to the nonstationary series as integrated up to order 1. A nonstationary series wherein differences in differences of it yield a stationary series is referred to as a series that is integrated up to order 2, and so on. If long-run movements among series are meaningful, then differencing, or differencing the differences, or so on will remove much of the information on which a long-run relationship may rest. Let's say we have a k-vector of possibly nonstationary variables $\{x_t\}$. If there is a corresponding k-vector θ such that $\theta' x_t$ is integrated up to order 0 then θ is the cointegrating vector and we say that the elements in the vector x_t are cointegrated. We do not need to difference away long-run information in order to allow such elements of x_t to have meaningful and non-spurious short-run relationships. Of course, such a cointegrating vector may not be found, in which case the variables would display no long-term links or behaviors.

The concept of cointegration can be used to examine the existence of competitive industry pressures that drive successful firms to comparable levels of efficiency. The long-run dynamics of a competitive market structure would seem to be consistent with the cointegration of the productivities of the firms in the industry, even if the productivities themselves may display nonstationary behaviors. Such behaviors of productivities, their stochastic nature, and their cointegrating behaviors have been found elsewhere in productivity studies at the macro and firm level by, among others, Antras (2004), Atalla and Bean (2017), Duygun et al. (2016), Chambers (2008), Liu et al. (2011), Bos et al. (2016), and Aquino-Chávez and Ramírez-Rondán (2017).

Take as another example the US airline industry after the industry was deregulated in the late 1970s. Industry analysts at the time noted that a variety of business practices were adopted to increase the profitability of the carriers by focusing on cost-saving measures that ultimately compromised the quality of service. Service quality was one of the only forms of competition in which the carriers could engage while the Civil Aeronautics Board regulated the tariffs and routes of the carriers. The technology of the airline industry, the planes, the reservation systems, etc. were largely available to all of the carriers. Thus differential productivity growth among carriers was driven largely by efficiency differences. This was because the airline carriers adopted a business model at the time based largely on the use of technology of service provision that evidenced long-run constant returns to scale. The vast majority of studies of the airline industry at the time concluded that the technology of airline service provision exhibited constant returns to scale. Since new technologies could be appropriated by all the carriers, competition was played out in the arena of firm-specific cost-cutting business practices and thus, the temporal pattern of efficiency scores of firms should be comparable when the airline carriers mimic their competitors' efficiency improvements. Failure to find that a firm's efficiency scores are cointegrated with its competitors would signal that the carrier was unable to take advantage of the best practices employed by its competitors. Evidence of cointegration would be explored by utilizing the standard strategy of first testing for the presence of a unit root in the Malmquist index (after controlling for a variety of heterogeneity controls) using an augmented Dickey Fuller (ADF) test. This would be followed up with a joint test of the existence of a cointegrating vector using a Johansen maximum likelihood procedure or other available multivariate tests (Im et al., 2003; Johansen, 1988; Pedroni, 2004). One could also reverse the null and alternative hypotheses and use the Kwiatkowski–Phillips–Schmidt–Shin (KPSS) test (Kwiatkowski et al., 1992). Shin (1994) extended KPSS to test for evidence of cointegration.

In order to establish that a set of series is cointegrated, it is necessary to test each firm's time series for unit root behavior using standard ADF or KPSS tests. Firms for which neither the unit root nor the trend stationary hypotheses can be rejected are excluded from the cointegration analysis. Next, tests such as the Shin and Johansen tests of cointegration between firms exhibiting unit root behavior are carried out. In the Alam and Sickles (2000) study, results of the Shin test found 66 (92 percent) of the 72 possible pairs of US airline carriers after deregulation did not reject the null hypothesis of cointegration at the 5 percent level using the DEA efficiency estimates and 70 (97 percent) of the possible pairs did not reject the null of cointegration using the FDH efficiency estimator. Pairs cointegrated under the Johansen test were also cointegrated, in at least one direction, under the Shin test. As an example, Continental Airlines and United Airlines were strongly cointegrated under both tests (the null of no cointegration is rejected and the null of cointegration cannot be rejected). However, Delta Airlines and Ozark Airlines were cointegrated under the Johansen test while under the Shin test cointegration was found only when the Ozark Airlines efficiency scores were regressed on Delta Airline's efficiency scores. This situation suggests a one-sided relationship wherein Ozark Airlines is dependent on Delta Airlines but the reverse is not true. Interestingly, they found that when the relationship does not go in both directions, it was always the smaller carrier which was dependent on the larger carrier, indicating that smaller carriers were taking cues from the larger carriers' strategies.

15.1.1.2 Convergence

In Chapter 4, we discussed decomposing the Malmquist Productivity Index into a portion that captured innovation and a portion that captured efficiency

(Färe et al., 1989a, 1992b; Färe et al., 1994c). For a constant to returns production technology this decomposition states that

$$
M_o(x_s, x_t, y_s, y_t) \equiv \left(M_o^s(x_s, x_t, y_s, y_t) \times M_o^t(x_s, x_t, y_s, y_t) \right)^{1/2}
$$

$$
= \left[\frac{D_o^s(x_t, y_t)}{D_o^s(x_s, y_s)} \times \frac{D_o^t(x_t, y_t)}{D_o^t(x_s, y_s)} \right]^{1/2}
$$

$$
= \frac{D_o^t(x_t, y_t)}{D_o^s(x_s, y_s)} \times \left[\frac{D_o^s(x_s, y_s)}{D_o^t(x_s, y_s)} \times \frac{D_o^s(x_t, y_t)}{D_o^t(x_t, y_t)} \right]^{1/2}
$$

$$
= Eff\Delta \times [Tech\Delta_s \times Tech\Delta_t]^{1/2}
$$

$$
= Eff\Delta \times Tech\Delta. \tag{15.1.5}
$$

The first component is an efficiency index that measures the ratio of the efficiency measure in period t to the efficiency measure in period s for a technology expressed in terms of the output distance function. A number greater than unity indicates efficiency improvement between periods s and t. This is the result of an inefficient firm moving toward the frontier. We have referred to this as the catch-up of firms as they converge to the frontier technology over time. This amount in percentage terms is $(Eff\Delta - 1)$. A score that is less than unity means that the firm is becoming less efficient. The second component is a geometric mean of two different measures of technical innovation that compares technologies in two different periods s and t. Again, the technologies are expressed in terms of the underlying output distance function. The first part of this second component uses quantities in the base period s while the second part of this second component uses quantities at period t. As pointed out in Chapter 4, the geometric mean of these two parts of the second component that measures innovation, or technical change, deals in part with the arbitrary choice of the reference period (s or t). The amount of innovation, or technical change, is $(Tech\Delta - 1)$. This measures the rate at which frontier technology is shifting over time. A positive number suggests technical improvement while a negative number suggests technological regress. This measure can be broadened to accommodate panel data using the Malmquist intertemporal productivity index and its components of innovation and catch-up outlined in Chapter 8.

Testing for catch-up or convergence began in the literature on economic growth (Baumol, 1986) and the objective of studies of convergence was to better understand if the gap between less productive (inefficient) and more productive (efficient) countries (or firms) closed over time and what were the mechanisms that could explain this phenomenon. A simple test of convergence can be based on a standard approach taken from the economic development literature (Abramovitz, 1986) which bases convergence findings on the significance of the coefficients in a simple parametric regression of average growth rates on a constant and the initial efficiency levels. High significant inverse correlations are suggestive of convergence, which was the finding of Alam and Sickles (2000) for the US airlines after deregulation supporting the convergence hypothesis that technological advances had become dispersed throughout the industry. An alternative test can be based on the patterns of the firm-specific efficiency change component of the Malmquist productivity index. The efficiency change component, $Eff\,\Delta$, is indicative of how similar the carriers' are becoming over time in their use of a common technology. Alam and Sickles (2000) found that for the industry as a whole efficiency growth only appeared in the pre-deregulation years. Their results also indicated that the relatively smaller carriers, such as Piedmont, Frontier, and Ozark exceeded the efficiency changes by the Big Three carriers – America, Delta, and United – after deregulation. Possibly such larger carriers were not as nimble to take advantage of the added flexibility assured them after the CAB stopped making tariff and routing decisions for them due to longer labor contracts and a less flexible route network.

The implied catch-up times from these convergence and catch-up models can also be analyzed using a duration model. Hultberg et al. (1999) used institutional variables such as political and civil rights, political stability, bureaucratic efficiency, and openness to international trade in explaining catch-up times. Barro (1991) used revolutions and coups as well as the number of assassinations to control for political instability. Knack and Keefer (1995) have criticized the use of such variables to measure political stability and particular institutional environments as they are simply loose proxies for factors that influence the institutions that characterize a country and its economic and social milieu.

Whatever factors are considered to be important determinants of catch-up times can be included in a second-stage analysis using the duration model. Consider a continuous time duration model where the (ln) hazard function for catch-up times t_i for country/sector i is specified by the widely used proportional hazard model as

$$\ln h\,(t_i \mid x_i, \theta_i) = \gamma \ln t_i + x_i \beta + \theta_i. \tag{15.1.6}$$

Here t_i is the continuous time of a completed spell, x_i is a vector of exogenous time-varying or constant covariates, and θ_i is unobserved scalar heterogeneity. Heckman and Singer's (1984) Nonparametric Maximum Likelihood Estimator (NPMLE) can be implemented to avoid parameterizing the unknown mixing distribution for the unobserved heterogeneity θ_i. For a more detailed discussion of this and competing duration models with unobservable heterogeneity see Huh and Sickles (1994) and Sickles and Taubman (1997).

Hultberg et al. (2004) utilized the Weibull specification with and without the NPMLE of Heckman and Singer to analyze catch-up times to close 50 percent of the gap. Their analysis was based on the STAN (structural analysis database) published by the OECD and focused on a modified neoclassical growth model with country-specific inefficiency. Their results indicate a rather robust finding of a relatively elastic effect that bureaucratic efficiency has on reducing the catch-up times and is consistent with most policy-makers, beliefs that a country's institutional arrangements and traditions are major factors in constraining or in promoting economic development and growth. These findings are also consistent with policy recommendations by such international organizations such as the IMF. Structural reforms, such as those that led to Egypt's aborted private sector manufacturing reforms of the 1990s that ushered in a period of productivity and efficiency growth in the Egyptian economy (Getachew and Sickles, 2007) mitigate factors which may give rise to bureaucratic inefficiencies. Dal Bianco (2016) found comparable results for labor productivity using sector-specific data on 28 developed and developing countries during 1980–95. Absolute convergence was found in manufacturing, and convergence tendencies were found to be sector-specific. Their findings suggest that labor productivity convergence is hindered by the suboptimal structural reallocation from non-convergence to convergence activities, which can be interpreted as a sector/country-specific inefficiency and they recommend, among other things, that catching-up strategies to address the inefficiencies be pursued by the countries: just the sort of institutional and trade indicators that Hultberg et al. (2004) found important in their analysis.

15.2 PARAMETRIC PANEL DATA MODELS OF PRODUCTIVITY DYNAMICS

We next turn to the study of a dynamic panel data model that is flexible but that also differentiates between short-run and long-run inefficiencies and allows for the patterns of both short-run and long-run productivity to differ among firms. The model was introduced by Ahn et al. (2000) and has been modified and utilized in studies of Egyptian private sector manufacturing by Bhattacharyya (2012, 2014). The model is best suited to study firms that are unable to immediately adjust their input levels to optimal values because of the quasi-fixed nature of some inputs and/or because of institutional constraints. One source of short-run and long-run variations in technical inefficiency is a firm's tardy adjustment of its inefficiency levels. Another source comes from technical innovations in the industry that are not immediately adopted by firms and thus results in suboptimal choices on input levels.

Inefficiency levels may vary because of prior or current institutional regimes, as we have pointed out in the previous section. For example, in the airline study by Alam and Sickles (2000) discussed above, inefficiencies may persist as there are substantial adjustment costs associated with changing the network structure, with changing union work rules, and with reallocations of aircraft fleets because of changes in slot allocations by the airport authority. The model of Ahn et al. (2000) nests the traditional fixed effects model and the fixed effects model with autocorrelated errors. For this latter model the fixed effects are measures of a firm's long-run technical efficiency level. We now turn to a more detailed discussion of the Ahn et al. (2000) model.

15.2.1   The Ahn, Good, and Sickles (2000) Dynamic Stochastic Frontier

Ahn et al. (2000) first define observed production as

$$y_{it} = \alpha + x'_{it}\beta + \gamma t + v_{it} - u_{it} = x'_{it}\beta + \alpha_{it}v_{it}, \tag{15.2.1}$$

where $u_{it}(\geq 0)$ is technical inefficiency for firm i at time t, v_{it} is the usual disturbance term, and where $\alpha + \gamma t$ is a time-varying component of the frontier technology that each firm shares. If we differentiate between actual production (y_{it}) and frontier production (y_{it}^F) of firm i at time t, then we can similarly differentiate between the actual level of productivity (α_{it}) and the level of frontier technology (productivity) common to all firms (α_t^F) at time t, where discrepancies between the two $(\alpha_{it} = \alpha_t^F - u_{it})$ are due to the firm's inability to utilize the frontier technology common to all firms. Which estimation technique to use in estimating this dynamic model is based on the dynamic evolution assumed for u_{it} (or α_{it}). Ahn et al. (2000) begin with the assumption that a firm's inefficiency follows a simple AR(1) process, although they point out that with rather straightforward modifications of their estimation procedures more general AR specifications can be considered. Given the time-series nature of this model, it is important to be specific as to when information becomes available to the firm. The information set $\Omega_{i,t-1}$ represents information available to firm i at the beginning of time period t. If we let the adjustment speed for firm i's efficiency catch-up be ρ_i and innovations in the AR(1) specification of inefficiency be ξ_{it}, then we can express the dynamic adjustment for a firm's inefficiency level at time t as

$$u_{it} = (1 - \rho_i)u_{i,t-1} + \xi_{it}; \quad E\left(\xi_{it} \mid \Omega_{i,t-1}\right) = \lambda_i \geq 0, \tag{15.2.2}$$

where $(0 < \rho_i \leq 1)$ and ξ_{it} is an iid non-negative random variable. The parameters ρ_i and λ_i vary due to heterogeneity in the quality of a firm's management and labor force. An implicit assumption behind (15.2.2) is that at the beginning of time period t, each firm learns about the level of the inefficiency $(u_{i,t-1})$ it suffered during the last time period, takes actions to mitigate the lost product due to such inefficiency $(\rho_i u_{i,t-1})$, resulting in a firm's current inefficiency level being a function of the unadjusted portion of the last-period inefficiency $(1 - \rho_i)u_{i,t-1}$ and the new arrival of unexpected inefficiency sources ξ_{it}. They consider only cases for which ρ_i is strictly positive to ensure that actual output levels are stationary and that inefficiency levels are bounded.

This AR specification parsimoniously provides an estimate of a firm's long-run average inefficiency level λ_i/ρ_i and has economic intuition as firms in equilibrium will react to random factors such as technology shocks, changes in regulatory oversight, and changes in market pressures that negatively influence efficiency by adjustments to reduce costs and move back to efficient operations given the new environment. However, the inefficiencies are somewhat persistent since adjustment costs are not negligible. Efficient management will tend to remove these inefficiencies and reach the new equilibrium more quickly than inefficient management. A firm with relatively efficient management would

thus be expected to have a ρ_i closer to 1 than a firm with relatively inefficient management. A more general specification would allow inefficiency to
be time-varying, similar to the models we examined in Chapters 12 and 13.
However, Ahn et al. (2000) deal only with a partial adjustment model in the
specification of the dynamic efficient process.

A somewhat more general model was considered by Ahn et al. (2000) with
a modification of the simple AR(1) process above. If one introduces a new
random variable $\eta_{it} (\geq 0)$ as a time-varying inefficiency score for firm i at
time t and assumes that $E(\eta_{it} \mid \Omega_{it}) = \kappa_i \geq 0$, then the productivity level
firm i could adopt were it able to adopt the innovations with no delay could be
defined as $\alpha_{it}^* = \alpha_t^F - \eta_{it} = \alpha + \gamma t - \eta_{it}$. If adjustment is only partial then
$\alpha_{it} = (1 - \rho_i)\alpha_{i,t-1} + \rho_i\alpha_{it}^*$ and thus technical inefficiency $u_{it} = \alpha_t^F - \alpha_{it}$
would be correlated with its lagged levels since

$$u_{it} = (1 - \rho_i)u_{i,t-1} + (1 - \rho_i)\gamma + \rho_i\eta_{it}, \tag{15.2.3}$$

which is (15.2.2) with a simple reparameterization, where $\xi_{it} = (1 - \rho_i)\gamma + \rho_i\eta_{it}$ and $\lambda_i = (1 - \rho_i)\gamma + \rho_i\kappa_i.$[2] The long-run average technical inefficiency
level of firm i is then given by

$$u_i^{LR} = \frac{\lambda_i}{\rho_i} = \kappa_i + \frac{(1 - \rho_i)\gamma}{\rho_i}, \tag{15.2.4}$$

which is finite for $\rho_i > 0$. Here κ_i is long-run inefficiency due to firm i's poor
management while the term $(1 - \rho_i)\gamma/\rho_i$ is long-run efficiency loss due to
the firm's sluggish adoption of technical innovations and is declining in the
adjustment speed ρ_i. This particular endogeneity problem is often overlooked
in productivity studies when dynamic adjustments are not explicitly modeled.
Also, were industry productivity to grow nonlinearly instead of linearly, as has
been assumed here, then u_i^{LR} would be a function of time.

When dynamics are introduced in the evolution of inefficiency using this
relatively simple autoregressive specification, the production model has much
in common with a production function with fixed effects and autocorrelated
errors. We can use a simple reparameterization of the model and let the short-
run deviation of technical inefficiency from the long-run level $u_i^{LR} \equiv \lambda_i/\rho_i$ be
given by $u_{it}^d = u_{it} - u_i^{LR}$, in which case (15.2.1) can be written as

$$y_{it} = x_{it}'\beta + \gamma t + \left(\alpha - u_i^{LR}\right) - \epsilon_{it}, \tag{15.2.5}$$

where $\epsilon_{it} = u_{it}^d - v_{it}$ and $u_{it}^d = (1 - \rho_i)u_{i,t-1}^d + (\xi_{it} - \lambda_i)$. The error term ϵ_{it}
in (15.2.5) will be autocorrelated unless $\rho_i = 1$.

Ahn et al. (2000) point out that least squares dummy variables would provide consistent estimates of the production function (15.2.5) parameters if the

---

[2] We should point out that without further restrictions this dynamic stochastic frontier and the
spatial stochastic frontier discussed in Chapter 13 do not satisfy the scaling property discussed
in Wang (2002), Wang (2003), Wang and Schmidt (2002), and Alvarez et al. (2006).

input variables in x'_{it} were exogenous (predetermined) to ϵ_{it}. Chapter 14 and Ahn et al. (2000) point out why such an assumption may not hold (Ahn et al., 2000, p. 468). To deal with the potential endogeneity of the regressors and ϵ_{it}, which under reasonable assumptions may be a function of the serially correlated error term u^d_{it}, (15.2.5) can be transformed into a nonlinear dynamic function:

$$y_{it} = x'_{it}\beta + (1-\rho_i)y_{i,t-1} + x'_{i,t-1}[-(1-\rho_i)\beta] + \rho_i\gamma t + \rho_i\delta_i - e_{it}, \quad (15.2.6)$$

where $\delta_i = \alpha - u^d_{it} + (1-\rho_i)\gamma/\rho_i$ and $e_{it} = (\xi_{it} - \lambda_i) - [v_{it} - (1-\rho_i)v_{i,t-1}]$. If adjustment is instantaneous for all firms, then $\rho_i = 1$ for all i, (15.2.6) reduces to the usual fixed-effects model with a linear time trend, which is the model considered in Lee and Schmidt (1993) and which we discussed in Chapter 12. When the production frontier is stochastic, e_{it} is MA(1)[3] and $y_{i,t-1}$ is no longer predetermined and nonlinear generalized least squares (NLGLS) would generate biased estimates, which motivates the use of generalized methods of moments (GMM) to estimate the model (15.2.6).

As a practical matter, the number of parameters to be estimated in the model (15.2.6) grows with the number of firms (n). We can deal with this problem by estimating an average adjustment speed ρ for the firms in the industry and assume that deviations among them are iid, in which case (15.2.6) is a dynamic panel data model in which the slope coefficients are the same over different i. Various dynamic panel estimators are available that utilize GMM for the large n and small T datasets often available to productivity researchers (see, for example, Anderson and Hsiao, 1981; Arellano and Bond, 1991; Ahn and Schmidt, 1995, 1997).

15.2.1.1 GMM Estimation of the Ahn, Good, and Sickles (2000) Dynamic Stochastic Frontier

In order to outline the generalized methods of moments (GMM) estimator and tests for the dynamic model (15.2.6), it would be helpful to introduce some standard notational conventions for panel data models. First let the regressors be

$$z_{it} = \left[x'_{it},\, d_i \otimes \left(y_{i,t-1},\, x'_{i,t-1},\, t,\, 1\right)\right]', \quad (15.2.7)$$

where d_i is the $1 \times n$ vector of dummy variables for individual firms. Define $y_i = (y_{i1}, \ldots, y_{iT})'$, $z_i = (z_{i1}, \ldots, z_{iT})'$, and $e_i = (e_{i1}, \ldots, e_{iT})'$. The parameters are contained in $\theta = (\beta', \delta_1, \rho_1, \ldots, \delta_n, \rho_n)'$. Let $\pi_i = (\beta', 1-\rho_i, -(1-\rho_i)\beta', \rho_i\gamma, \rho_i\delta_i)'$ and $\pi(\theta) \equiv (\pi'_1, \ldots, \pi'_n)'$. For the model with the restrictions $\rho_i = \rho$, denote $\theta = (\beta', \rho, \delta_1, \ldots, \delta_N)'$ and $\pi_i = (\beta', 1-\rho, -(1-\rho)\beta', \rho\gamma, \rho\delta_i)'$. This allows the model (15.2.6) to be written as

---

[3] Note that the sum of a MA(1) process and white noise is also MA(1). See Hamilton (1994).

$$y_i = z_i' \pi (\theta) - e_i. \tag{15.2.8}$$

The lagged dependent variable $y_{i,t-1}$ is contained in z_i and thus consistent estimation of the model (15.2.8) requires the use of instrumental variables which are uncorrelated with the error vector e_i. Candidate instruments are two-period (or more) lagged output levels, current and lagged input levels, time (t), dummy variables (d_i) for each of the firms. Let w_{it} be the column vector of instruments; and let $w_i = [w_{i1}, \ldots, w_{i,T}]'$. Define $f_i(\theta) = w_i'(y_i - z_i'\pi(\theta))$ for each i, and $m(\theta) = \sum_i f_i(\theta)$. If the instruments are weakly exogenous, then $E[m(\theta)] = 0$, and this, along with other standard assumptions for the GMM estimator, implies that

$$\frac{1}{\sqrt{nT}} m(\theta) \to N(0, \Lambda), \tag{15.2.9}$$

as $NT \to \infty$. The optimal GMM estimator of θ, $\hat{\theta}_{GMM}$, is obtained by minimizing

$$J(\theta) = \frac{1}{nT} m(\theta)' \Lambda^{-1} m(\theta). \tag{15.2.10}$$

Ahn et al. (2000) discuss robust procedures to estimate Λ. In order to calculate a firm's relative long-run average inefficiencies using the resulting GMM estimates, they utilize the results from Schmidt and Sickles (1984) and estimate the relative size of u_i^{LR} by $\left(u_{max}^{LR} - \hat{u}_i^{LR}\right)$, where $u_{max}^{LR} = \max\{\hat{u}_j^{LR}\}$. The output loss due to sluggish adoption of technical innovations is estimated by $(1 - \hat{\rho}_i)\hat{\gamma}/\hat{\rho}_i$.

15.3 EXTENSIONS OF THE AHN, GOOD, AND SICKLES (2000) MODEL

While Ahn et al. (2000) propose an autoregressive model for technical efficiency that captures the effects of lagged adoption of new technology on efficiency, Bhattacharyya (2012) discusses an alternative dynamic stochastic production frontier incorporating the sluggish adjustment of inputs.

Bhattacharyya (2012) assumes that λ ($0 \leq \lambda \leq 1$) is the speed of adjustment of inputs. Only a portion (λ) of potential output $y_{i,t+1}^*$ in the next period is produced and thus λ represents the portion of the gap between the potential output and the previous period's output the firm is able to close. She represents this dynamic process as

$$y_{i,t+1} = \lambda y_{i,t+1}^* + \lambda(1 - \lambda)y_{it}^*, \tag{15.3.1}$$

where the actual output produced by firm i at time t using a vector of inputs x_{it} is $y_{it} = \lambda y_{it}^*$ and $y_{it}^* = f(x_{it}, \beta)$. The stochastic version of this production model at time t with time-invariant inefficiency is given by

$$y_{it} = (1 - \lambda)y_{i,t-1} + \lambda f(x_{it}, \beta) + v_{it} - u_i, \tag{15.3.2}$$

where $u_i \geq 0$ are the efficiency effects with $E(u_i) = \mu$ and $var(u_i) = \sigma_u^2$. Using the system GMM estimator of Blundell and Bond (1998) and panel data on private sector manufacturing establishments in Egypt, Bhattacharyya (2012) estimates the speed of adjustment of inputs, which is assumed to be comparable to the speed of adjustment of output, and shows that the conventional static model significantly underestimates technical efficiency by ignoring the dynamic adjustment process. For an alternative approach to modeling the technical progress of the Egyptian private sector manufacturing sectors see Getachew and Sickles (2007). In her empirical setting the dynamic model provides more realistic efficiency estimates and rankings of production units, especially for production systems in which sluggish adjustment of inputs is a very plausible phenomenon.

A more general dynamic stochastic frontier model is given in Bhattacharyya (2014) where the speed of adjustment changes over time:

$$y_{it} = (1 - \lambda_t)y_{i,t-1} + \lambda_t f(x_{it}, \beta) + v_{it} - \theta_t f_i, \qquad (15.3.3)$$

where λ_t is the portion of desired change in output that the firm can adjust in time t and $\theta_t f_i$ is the firm-specific technical inefficiency term that varies with time. As discussed by Lee and Schmidt (1993), this structure is less restrictive than those proposed by Kumbhakar (1990) and may also, under certain parameterizations of the pattern of time-varying inefficiency, be less restrictive than those suggested in Cornwell et al. (1990). Bhattacharyya (2014) adapts the method described by Holtz-Eakin et al. (1988) and further extends it to provide estimation method for the time-varying speed of adjustment and technical efficiency of production units. Using the panel data on private sector manufacturing establishments in Egypt, she shows that the conventional static model not only generates biased estimates of technical efficiency and rankings in the presence of sluggish adjustment of inputs, it also fails to capture the detailed temporal variation in the efficiency measures.

15.4 CONCLUDING REMARKS

Much of the modeling of productivity and efficiency is conducted in a dynamic setting in which firms respond to price, quantity, and other market information using the best information available to them. However, their efforts to optimize may be compromised by a number of factors they either recognize explicitly or about which they are unaware, as the best information is costly and is also not shared by all parties in many market transactions. In such a dynamic setting, we have endeavored to present models that can be used in aggregate productivity, industry, and firm-level studies that provide modeling approaches to address these issues, to measure technical change and efficiency change, and to introduce measures of short run and long run of suboptimal production levels, vis-á-vis other more productive and efficient countries or industries, or firms. The dynamic models we have discussed in this chapter are instructive in that they provide benchmarks against which more general and more structural approaches can be compared and evaluated.

15.5   EXERCISES

1. What are the properties of residual-based estimates of productivity growth obtained from the dynamic panel model of Ahn et al. (2000) when the error process is a unit root but the time period is finite?

2. Using the UNIDO data available at the following website estimate the model developed by Duygun et al. (2017) using the CSSWITHIN and the CSSGLS estimators based on the OECD countries during the period 1970–2000 and the Cox proportional hazard model to assess the time to convergence (at the 50 and 90th percentile) of the different OECD countries:

   https://sites.google.com/site/productivityefficiency

3. Based on your estimates from question 2, examine what factors may be inhibiting particular countries from converging as rapidly as others.

4. Use the DEA methods developed by Alam and Sickles (2000) to replicate the model and approach from question 2.

5. Based on your estimates from question 4, examine what factors may be inhibiting particular countries from converging as rapidly as others.

CHAPTER 16

Semiparametric Estimation, Shape Restrictions, and Model Averaging

As the book has pointed out in its earliest chapters, economic theory provides the most reasoned, and often the most powerful and leveraged, guidance for econometric modeling of productivity. The primal and dual relationships that are specified and estimated by functional representations in the form of the production, cost, revenue, and profit functions derive their interpretability from the regularity conditions that were utilized in specifying the production sets, distance functions, and in deriving cost, revenue, and profit functions. These regularity conditions are often difficult to impose with many of the flexible parametric functional forms we discussed in Chapter 6 and may be even more difficult to impose when the functional relationships are specified nonparametrically using kernel smoothers or other classical nonparametric methods. In the production setting monotonicity is often required, analogous to its requirement in models with rational preferences. Concavity of production functions have analogs in convex preferences and risk aversion in utility theory. Demand theory results in downward sloping demand curves for normal goods (Matzkin, 1991; Lewbel, 2010; Blundell et al., 2012), while production theory and duality provide us with implications of profit-maximizing behavior that require profit functions to be concave in output prices. Cost minimization yields cost functions that are monotonically increasing and concave in input prices. Auction theory and optimal bidding strategies that vary across auction formats and bidders' preferences are based on monotonicity in bidders valuations. Derivative pricing models are highly leveraged on convex function estimation (Broadie et al., 2000; Aıt-Sahalia and Duarte, 2003; Yatchew and Härdle, 2006). Such considerations are ubiquitous in economics and it is essential that we address them in the context of the topic that our book in part endeavors to address, empirical productivity analysis.

In this chapter, we discuss several methods to deal with estimation of the primal production function utilizing semi- and nonparametric econometric specifications under monotonicity and curvature constraints. General reviews of this material can be found in Matzkin (1994) and Yatchew (2003, Chapter 6). Work that speaks to relatively recent extensions can be found in Hall and Huang (2001), Groeneboom et al. (2001), Horowitz et al. (2004), Carroll et al. (2011), Shively et al. (2011), Blundell et al. (2012), and Pya and Wood (2015), among others. We first discuss issues of estimation of the functions and then discuss how they can be constrained to possess the monotonicity and curvature properties consistent with the particular regularity conditions used in deriving them and thus required in order to interpret them. In this chapter, we also must keep in mind that in addition to the need for our specified empirical models to comply with economic theory, the functional representations must be flexible enough to be allowed to fit the data, as economic theory unfortunately does not tell us everything about the production environment and its characteristics. The tension between requiring compliance with economic theory and imposing rigid functional forms is an ever–present reality in empirical productivity modeling and the possibility of theoretically implausible predictions being generated from a model that does not negotiate these tensions effectively is an ever–present problem.

The chapter ends with a brief review of model averaging. Discovering the true model might not be possible. Statistical inference based on post-model-selection estimators (Leeb and Pötscher, 2005) might lead to invalid analysis and different selection criteria might give contradictory rank orders. As discussed in Burnham and Anderson (2002), given the interpretation of data as a set of random variables, then a particular data set has its own source of statistical noise and any sample we choose introduces error of often unknown form into the classical model selection paradigm. However, it is never obvious that any best-performing model is indeed the true model. Model selection is a special case of weighting models in which one model is given the entire weight. Buckland et al. (1997) pointed out that statistical inference should not be conditioned on model certainty but that the stochastic environment in which inferences are made should be broadened to include model uncertainty as well. Clear analogues to the model averaging of many competing models with varying degrees of misspecification can be found in finance. Diversified portfolios contain assets whose prices may fall or rise based on the same or different factors but optimal portfolio theory and investment professionals point to their advantages. Consistent with these views is the quote attributed to George Box: "essentially, all models are wrong, but some are useful" (Box and Draper, 1987, p. 424).

16.1   SEMIPARAMETRIC ESTIMATION OF PRODUCTION FRONTIERS

16.1.1   Kernel-Based Estimators

Kneip and Simar (1996) and Fan et al. (1996) suggested using nonparametric kernel regression methods integrated into parametric maximum likelihood, while Adams et al. (1997, 1999) integrated parametric and nonparametric production function specifications into a semiparametric efficient estimator based on a semiparametric likelihood function.

Fan et al. (1996) adopted a three-stage semiparametric pseudo-likelihood estimation. At the very first stage, one proceeds with fully nonparametric estimation of the following average production relationship based on the ALS composed error model

$$y_i = m(x_i) + v_i - u_i = m(x_i) + \varepsilon_i \qquad (16.1.1)$$
$$= m(x_i) + E[\varepsilon_i|x_i] + (\varepsilon_i - E[\varepsilon_i|x_i]) = m^*(x_i) + \varepsilon_i^*,$$

$i = 1, \ldots, n$, where v_i is normally distributed and u_i is truncated normal. $E[\varepsilon_i|x] \neq 0$ due to the one-sided nature of u_i, which creates a bias, correcting for which helps identifying the frontier. Fan et al. (1996) used the Nadaraya–Watson nonparametric estimator for $m^*(x_i)$. These estimates of $m^*(x_i)$ are then employed at the second stage, which is a parametric MLE of the stochastic frontier model, in order to back out an estimate of $E[\varepsilon_i|x_i]$. In the third stage, an estimate of $m(x_i)$ is constructed for each i by correcting $\widehat{m}^*(x_i)$ with the estimate of $E[\varepsilon_i|x_i]$, i.e.,

$$\widehat{m}(x_i) = \widehat{m}^*(x_i) - \hat{E}[\varepsilon_i|x_i], \quad i = 1, \ldots, n. \qquad (16.1.2)$$

Kneip and Simar (1996) considered a panel data model and proposed a similar strategy for correcting for the bias occurring in estimating (16.1.1) nonparametrically, again using the Nadaraya–Watson nonparametric estimator. Adams et al. (1999) considered a panel data model in which the production function took on a semi-nonparametric form, again based on the Robinson (1988) conditional mean estimator, and specified the stochastic frontier using the Schmidt and Sickles (1984) composed error with firm-specific inefficiency and different possible correlation structures between the efficiency effects and the regressors. This was based in large part on the semiparametric efficient estimators developed for the stochastic panel frontier in the series of papers by Park et al. (1998, 2003, 2007) that we discussed briefly in Chapter 13.

In their study of banking efficiency, Adams et al. (1997) utilized a parametric treatment for the stochastic frontier distance function and a nonparametric treatment for the composed error term in the stochastic panel frontier. Adams et al. (1999) utilized a semiparametric model of the stochastic distance function and a nonparametric treatment for the composed error term. As we have discussed in previous chapters, the distance function $D_o(x, y)$ is nondecreasing, linearly homogeneous and concave in y and nonincreasing and quasi-concave in x. Recognizing that some of the elements of x_{it} are outputs, a linearized form of the output distance function can be written as

$$y_{it} = \alpha + x'_{it}\beta + v_{it} - u_i, \quad i = 1, \ldots, n; \ t = 1, \ldots, T, \qquad (16.1.3)$$

or our familiar panel data model

$$y_{it} = \alpha_i + x'_{it}\beta + v_{it}, \qquad (16.1.4)$$

where u_i is the usual technical efficiency term with positive support, $E(u_i) = \mu \geq 0$, v_{it} is a zero-mean iid disturbance, and $\alpha_i = \alpha - u_i$. Here we abstract from a time-varying level of inefficiency. See Chapters 12 and 13 for various ways in which time-varying inefficiency can be introduced. The nonnegative difference $1 - D_o(x, y)$ for a firm can be approximated by $u \approx 1 - \exp(-u)$ for relatively small levels of u and labeled as inefficiency. If the number of outputs (M) is greater than 1 then x will contain outputs, normalized with respect to the output that has been moved to the l.h.s. of the relationship above (label these y^*) as well as inputs and any other controls.

Adams et al. (1999) used the semiparametric efficient estimator of Park et al. (1998) that allowed for correlation between the efficiency effects and endogenous normalized outputs based on the latter's long-run average. This estimator was discussed in Chapter 13. If we label the variables in x that are strictly exogenous as x^*, then we can characterize the density of (α, x^*, y^*) as

$$f(\alpha, x^*, y^*) = h(\alpha, \bar{y}^*)g(x^*|y^*), \tag{16.1.5}$$

where h is the joint distribution of α and $\bar{y}^*$. This assumption simplifies the correlation structure, but it also avoids the curse of dimensionality problem that would arise were we to allow for a more general correlation structure. One can utilize the semiparametric efficient estimation procedure outlined in our earlier Chapter 13 on second-generation panel frontiers to estimate the slope parameters regardless of the nonparametric part of the model, which at this point focuses on the joint distribution of the effects and the (correlated) regressors. We do not outline the procedure here but suggest either a rereading of that section in Chapter 13 or the original papers by Park et al. (1998) and Adams et al. (1999). Under a set of regularity conditions and for large n and T, the adaptive semiparametric efficient estimator of the slope coefficients provide us with consistent estimates of α_i, which we use in the normalization of the most efficient firm: $\max_{j=1,\ldots,n}(\hat{\alpha}_j)$. Relative technical efficiencies are then derived by taking the distance of each firm's α_i from the most efficient firm and the predictor of relative technical efficiencies can then be generated by the approximation

$$TE_i = (\hat{\alpha}_i - \max_{j=1,\ldots,n}(\hat{\alpha}_j)). \tag{16.1.6}$$

The model we just considered was basically the model considered in Park et al. (1998). However, it is relatively straightforward to allow for more flexibility in the functional form by forming a semi-nonparametric function in the spirit of Robinson (1988) to estimate the distance frontier. One possible extension would be to allow for separability between the inputs and outputs and estimate the portion of the distance function involving the inputs with a nonparametric procedure and utilize a specific functional form (perhaps linear in logs or linear in logs and cross products) for the r.h.s. normalized output terms. This would be a middle ground between the fully parametric and the nonparametric methods used by McAllister and McManus (1993) and many others to estimate the technical and cost efficiencies of the banks that utilize a multi-output technology involving providing various types of loans and other intermediation services.

If we reconsider the model above and let $f(x^*)$ be the unspecified function of the inputs then, we can write the output distance frontier as:

$$y_{it} = \psi(x_{it}^*) + y_{it}^{*\prime}\gamma + \alpha_i + v_{it}. \tag{16.1.7}$$

If we can assume that the inputs are not correlated with the effects, then the conditional expectation of the distance frontier can be written as

$$E[y_{it}|x_{it}^*] = \psi(x_{it}^*) + E[y_{it}^*|x_{it}^*]'\gamma, \tag{16.1.8}$$

which provides us with the model to be estimated:

$$y_{it} - E[y_{it}|x_{it}^*] = \left(y_{it}^{*\prime} - E[y_{it}^*|x_{it}]'\right)\gamma + \alpha_i + v_{it} \tag{16.1.9}$$

and

$$\psi(x_{it}^*) = E[y_{it}|x_{it}^*] - E[y_{it}^*|x_{it}^*]'\gamma. \tag{16.1.10}$$

Fan et al. (1996), Kneip and Simar (1996), and Adams et al. (1999) used the Nadaraya–Watson estimator employed by Robinson (1988) to estimate the conditional expectations. Härdle (1990), Scott (1992), and Kneip and Simar (1996), among others, have detailed the estimation and the asymptotic properties and rates of convergence of this and many other nonparametric estimators. We can apply dummy variables or the within estimator to the transformed model to find the parameters, γ, and the firm effects, α_i, can be estimated using the adaptive methods discussed above. Also, with this approach, the correlation between the effects and the outputs is retained, because the within estimator allows for correlation between the regressors and effects.

16.1.2 Local Likelihood Approach

The first use of the local likelihood approach in the stochastic frontier analysis appears to be Kumbhakar et al. (2007b), based on the work of Tibshirani and Hastie (1987) and Fan and Gijbels (1996). The approach is similar to the parametric likelihood approach except that kernel-based weights instead of equal are used for weighting the individual contributions to the likelihood, which makes the estimation local. To be precise, let $f_\varepsilon(\varepsilon, \theta)$ be regression error density, then the local log-likelihood function is given by

$$\ell_n(\theta(x), m_x) = (n|h|)^{-1} \sum_{i=1}^{n} \ln f_\varepsilon(y_i - m(x_i); \theta(x_i))\mathcal{K}_{i,x}, \tag{16.1.11}$$

where m_x models the conditional mean of y given x ($k \times 1$ vector of inputs) and θ is the vector of remaining parameters of f_ε, $\mathcal{K}_{i,x} = \prod_{s=1}^{N} h_s^{-1}\mathcal{K}\left(\frac{x_{is}-x_s}{h_s}\right)$ is the product kernel where $\mathcal{K}(\cdot)$ is any second-order univariate kernel (Gaussian,

Epanechnikov, etc.) and h_s is the smoothing parameter for the sth element of x and is the sth element of h, while $|h| := h_1 \times h_2 \times \cdots \times h_q$.[1]

Kumbhakar et al. (2007b) use a local-linear approximation for the unknown production function $m(x_i)$ and assume local normality for v_i and local half-normality for u_i, where the unknown total variance and the ratio of the variance of inefficiency to the variance of the noise is also modeled as an unknown function of inputs. The resulting log-likelihood is

$$\ell_n = (n|h|)^{-1} \sum_{i=1}^{n} \left[-0.5\sigma_x^2(x_i) - 0.5\varepsilon_i^2 \exp(-\sigma_x^2(x_i)) \right.$$

$$\left. + \ln \Phi \left(-\varepsilon_i \exp(\lambda_x(x_i) - 0.5\sigma_x^2(x_i)) \right) \right] \mathcal{K}_{i,x}, \quad (16.1.12)$$

where $\varepsilon_i = y_i - m_x(x_i)$, $m_x(x_i) = m_0 - m_1'(x_i - x)$, $\sigma_x^2(x_i) = \sigma_0^2 + \sigma_1^{2\prime}(x_i - x)$, and $\lambda_x(x_i) = \lambda_0 + \lambda_1'(x_i - x)$.

Park et al. (2015) point out that the main focus of interest is often related to σ_u and proposed parameterizing the local-likelihood directly in terms of σ_u^2 (and σ_v^2) rather than in terms of their ratio and their sum. Such modeling of σ_u^2 and σ_v^2 as unknown functions of inputs allows inputs to influence both efficiency and the frontier, and explicitly models heteroskedasticity of the noise. In order to impose positivity of σ_u and σ_v throughout the estimation, they parameterized the likelihood in term of $\ln \sigma_v^2$ and $\ln \sigma_u^2$, which also makes it more stable in computations. Park et al. (2015) also outlined the asymptotic theory for modeling categorical regressors using the local-likelihood approach. The local-likelihood function in this case is given by

$$\ell_n(\theta(x^c, x^d), m_{x^c, x^d})$$

$$= (n|h|)^{-1} \sum_{i=1}^{n} \left[-0.5 \ln \left(\exp(\sigma_v^2(x_i^c, x_i^d)) + \exp(\sigma_u^2(x_i^c, x_i^d)) \right) \right.$$

$$- \frac{0.5\varepsilon_i^2}{\exp(\sigma_v^2(x_i^c, x_i^d)) + \exp(\sigma_u^2(x_i^c, x_i^d))}$$

$$\left. + \ln \Phi \left(\frac{-\varepsilon_i \exp(\sigma_u^2(x_i^c, x_i^d)/2 - \sigma_v^2(x_i^c, x_i^d)/2)}{\sqrt{\exp(\sigma_v^2(x_i^c, x_i^d)) + \exp(\sigma_u^2(x_i^c, x_i^d))}} \right) \right] \mathcal{K}_{i,x^c} W^i(x_i^d),$$

$$(16.1.13)$$

where x_i^c is a vector of continuous regressors, x_i^d is a vector of discrete regressors, $\sigma_u^2(x_i^c, x_i^d) = \sigma_{u0}^2 + \sigma_{u1}^{2\prime}(x_i^c - x^c)$, $\sigma_v^2(x_i^c, x_i^d) = \sigma_{v0}^2 + \sigma_{v1}^{2\prime}(x_i^c - x^c)$, and $W^i(x_i^d)$ is an appropriate discrete kernel (see, for example, Aitchison and Aitken, 1976 or its extension). Park et al. (2015) also derived the

---

[1] The distinction between x (any level of input on which we condition) and x_i (the level of an input for observation i) is important here because in the nonparametric approach one estimates at each point of interest (here x), which could be the observed point or some other point (e.g., the mean, quatile, or any other hypothesized value).

asymptotic distribution of the estimator when the discrete kernel is $W^i(x^d) = \prod_{j=1}^k \omega_j^{I(x_{ij}^d \neq x_j^d)}$, i.e., a version of the Aitchison–Aitken kernel, standardized so that the bandwidths for a jth discrete variable, ω_j, are always between 0 and 1, regardless of the number of categories (see Racine and Li, 2004). The theory extends to many other cases of discrete kernels, including adaptive bandwidths, e.g., to allow for bandwidths of some or all continuous regressors to vary across categories of some or all categorical variables (e.g., see Li et al., 2016).

As for any likelihood approach, the estimates of parameters of interests are obtained by maximizing the log-likelihood functions, and standard optimization algorithms can be employed here. Though, as with any nonlinear optimizations, careful choice and multiple trials of initial values are important here to ensure the global rather than local or degenerate optima are reached. Kumbhakar et al. (2007b) described procedure based on the least squares cross-validation, while Park et al. (2015) proposed using maximum likelihood cross-validation.

16.1.3 Local Profile Likelihood Approach

Martins-Filho and Yao (2015) introduced semiparametric profile likelihood to the stochastic frontier paradigm. In the spirit of the class of estimators developed in the panel stochastic frontier literature by Park et al. (1998, 2003, 2007) the profile likelihood estimator of Martins-Filho and Yao (2015) is also semiparametric efficient over a wide class of alternative estimators. The estimator specifies a nonparametric frontier function and a parametric composed error. Adams and Sickles (2007) considered a panel frontier that was parametric but with a composed error that was nonparametric in developing their semiparametric efficient estimator. The extension to a semiparametric estimator for the mean function is relatively straightforward as we will see below.

Consider cross-sectional data on the joint distribution of the iid random variables $\{y_i, x_i\}, i = 1, \ldots, n$. Assume that the joint probability density function is $f(y, x) = f_{y|x}(y) f_x(x)$ and that the conditional density for y given x belongs to a family of distributions known up to a parameter θ. Using the approach of Severini and Wong (1992) rewrite the joint density as $f(y, x) = f_{y|x}(y; \theta, \psi(x)) f_x(x)$ based on a process specified as

$$y_i = \psi(x_i) + \varepsilon_i. \tag{16.1.14}$$

This class of models is referred to as conditionally parametric, since θ and $\psi(x)$ enter only through the conditional density $f_{y|x}(y)$, which is known up to a finite dimensional parameter $\theta \in \Theta$. The class of conditional densities is further restricted by requiring the following conditions:

$$E(y|x) \equiv m(x; \theta, \psi) \equiv \psi(x) - \gamma(\theta), \tag{16.1.15}$$

$$V(y|x) = \upsilon(\theta). \tag{16.1.16}$$

In the ALS model,

$$y_i = x_i'\beta + \varepsilon_i = x_i'\beta + v_i - u_i, \tag{16.1.17}$$

where $v_i \sim N(0, \sigma_v^2)$ and $u_i \sim |N(0, \sigma_u^2)|$ and thus $\psi(x) = x_i'\beta$, $\gamma(\theta) = \sqrt{\frac{2}{\pi}\sigma_u^2}$, and $V(y|x) = \upsilon(\theta) = \frac{n-2}{n}\sigma_u^2 + \sigma_v^2$. Two maximum likelihood estimators for θ and $\psi(x)$ can be pursued. Both are based on the log-likelihood function

$$\bar{\ell}(\theta, \psi) = \frac{1}{n}\sum_{i=1}^{n}\ln\left(f_{y|x}(y_i; \theta, \psi(x_i))\right)$$

$$= \frac{1}{n}\sum_{i=1}^{n}\ln\left(f_\epsilon(y_i - m(x_i; \theta, \psi) - \gamma(\theta); \theta)\right). \tag{16.1.18}$$

The first estimator is based on quasi-maximum likelihood and is a two-stage procedure. It exploits the idea that if we knew ψ, then the parametric estimator for θ would be straightforward using standard maximum likelihood methods. Since ψ is not known the log-likelihood $\bar{\ell}(\theta, \psi)$ is approximated by $\bar{\ell}(\theta, \hat{m}+\gamma(\theta)) = \frac{1}{n}\sum_{i=1}^{n}\ln(f_\epsilon(y_i-\hat{m}(x_i)-\gamma(\theta); \theta))$, where $\hat{m}$ is an estimate for $m(x_i; \theta, \psi)$, leading to the estimator

$$\hat{\theta} \equiv \underset{\theta}{\operatorname{argmax}} \, \bar{l}_n(\theta, \hat{m} + \gamma(\theta)). \tag{16.1.19}$$

The second estimator, motivated by Severini and Wong (1992), jointly estimates $\{\theta, \psi\}$ in two-stages as well, using the log-likelihood

$$\bar{\ell}(\theta, \psi)_n = \frac{1}{n}\sum_{i=1}^{n}\ln f_\varepsilon(y_i - \psi_x(x_i); \theta)\frac{1}{h_n}\mathcal{K}\left(\frac{x_i - x}{h_n}\right), \tag{16.1.20}$$

where $\varepsilon = v - u$, $\psi_x(x_i) = \alpha(x) + \beta(x)(x_i - x)$, $\mathcal{K}$ is a kernel and h_n is the bandwidth associated with $\mathcal{K}$.

In the first stage, define $\hat{\alpha}_\theta(x)$ and $\hat{\beta}_\theta(x)$ for fixed x and θ as

$$\left(\hat{\alpha}_\theta(x), \hat{\beta}_\theta(x)\right) \equiv \underset{\alpha(x),\beta(x)}{\operatorname{argmax}} \, \bar{\ell}(\theta, \psi_x). \tag{16.1.21}$$

The estimator for θ is then defined in the second-stage as

$$\tilde{\theta} \equiv \underset{\theta}{\operatorname{argmax}} \, \bar{\ell}_n(\theta; \hat{\alpha}_\theta). \tag{16.1.22}$$

With this estimator of θ in hand, one can now define the estimator of $\psi(x)$. The usual efficiency measures based on the Aigner et al. (1977) estimator can be constructed using the approaches we discussed in Chapters 11–13.

16.1.4   Local Least-Squares Approache

The likelihood-based approaches discussed above have appealing theoretical advantages. They may, however, involve complicated numerical optimization of the local-likelihood function over many parameters, which is computationally burdensome. A much simpler alternative comes from local least-squares methods that involve relatively straightforward and basic matrix operations and thus do not rely on nonlinear optimization, with the exception of bandwidth selection. For cross-sectional data (or pooled panel data) Simar et al. (2017) (SVKZ) provide nonparametric and semiparametric generalizations of the corrected ordinary least squares (COLS) estimator of Olson et al. (1980) as well as the asymptotic properties of their estimators. Although earlier chapters have discussed possible shortcomings of the cross-sectional stochastic frontier model, it is nonetheless an iconic estimator that has been studied extensively and used in a wide variety of empirical studies, as well as in industry as the basis for setting public utility rates. Cross-sectional stochastic frontier models tend to be special cases of panel stochastic frontier models, but they also have their own specific challenges, specifically how the terms in the composed error that is a combination of inefficiency effects (u) and statistical noise (v) can be decomposed. The problem of distinguishing these two sources of error in the cross-sectional stochastic frontier model nonparametrically has yet to be solved. However, there are other measures of the technology, e.g., elasticities of expectations of inefficiency levels conditional on inputs (x) and other environmental variables (z), that can be obtained nonparametrically based on conditional independence assumptions involving how x and z can influence u and v and the frontier.

Considered a generalization of (16.1.1) given by

$$y_i = m(x_i, z_i) + v_i - u_i = m(x_i, z_i) + \varepsilon_i, \tag{16.1.23}$$

where, as before, $m(\cdot, \cdot)$ is the unknown production frontier, x is input vector, z is a vector representing environmental factors, and v and u are the usual random terms in the ALS stochastic frontier model representing statistical noise and inefficiency, respectively. The focus on this particular nonparametric model of the production frontier is the nonparametric treatment of the environmental variables that do not directly contribute to production via the technology but rather influence it and possibly the inputs as mediating factors that affect the level of efficiency. Further assumptions that are used to characterize the role of the environmental factors z are

1. $(u_i|x_i = x, z_i = z) \sim \mathcal{D}^+(\mu_u(x, z), \sigma_u^2(x, z))$, where $\mathcal{D}^+(\cdot, \cdot)$ is a positive random variable from a skewed distribution with mean $\mu_u(\cdot, \cdot)$ and some variance $\sigma_u^2(\cdot, \cdot) \in (0, \infty)$;
2. $(v_i|x_i, z_i) \sim \mathcal{D}(0, \sigma_v^2(x, z))$, where $\mathcal{D}(0, \cdot)$ is a real-valued random variable with a symmetric distribution around zero and some variance $\sigma_v^2(\cdot, \cdot) \in (0, \infty)$;
3. u_i and v_i are independent random variables, conditionally on (x_i, z_i).

Although $E[\varepsilon_i|x, z] = -E[u_i|x, z] = \mu_u(x, z) \neq 0$, after recentering, one can write

$$y_i = m(x_i, z_i) + v_i - u_i + E[u_i|x_i, z_i] - E[u_i|x_i, z_i] = m^*(x_i, z_i) + \varepsilon_i^*, \tag{16.1.24}$$

where $m^*(x_i, z_i) = m(x_i, z_i) - E[u_i|x_i, z_i]$ and $\varepsilon_i^* = \varepsilon_i + E[u_i|x_i, z_i]$.

SVKZ suggested several stage of estimation. At the first stage, one can estimate $m^*(x_i, z_i)$ via local-polynomial least-squares, calling it $\widehat{m}^*(x_i, z_i)$.[2] In the second stage, SVKZ use the moment conditions implied by the assumptions on u_i and v_i:

$$E[\varepsilon^*|x, z] = 0, \tag{16.1.25}$$

$$E[(\varepsilon^*)^2|x, z] = \sigma_u^2(x, z) + \sigma_v^2(x, z), \tag{16.1.26}$$

$$E[(\varepsilon^*)^3|x, z] = -E\left[(u_i - E[u_i|x, z])^3 \, |x, z\right]. \tag{16.1.27}$$

Note that these are generalizations of moment conditions from Olson et al. (1980) to the heteroskedastic and nonparametric context and SVKZ proposed to estimate the last two via the local-polynomial methods, utilizing the residuals $\widehat{\varepsilon}_i^* = y_i - \widehat{m}^*(x_i, z_i)$ from the first stage in place of the true but unknown realizations of ε^*, i.e., obtain

$$\widehat{m}_2(x, z) = \sum_{i=1}^{n} \omega_i(x, z)\widehat{\varepsilon}_i^2, \tag{16.1.28}$$

and

$$\widehat{m}_3(x, z) = \sum_{i=1}^{n} \omega_i(x, z)\widehat{\varepsilon}_i^3, \tag{16.1.29}$$

where $\omega_j(x, z)$ vary depending on the type of the local smoothing.

If the level of the frontier is of interest then the (local) parametric distributional assumptions for u_i is required. Moreover, note that if the moments of u_i do depend on x_i or z_i, then the frontier correction will also depend on x_i and z_i implying that any properties of the frontier (such as marginal productivity and marginal rate of transformation, the returns to scale, etc.) may depend on the distribution of u_i. One, therefore, must either assume a distribution for u_i or accept a kind of separability assumption, such as $E[u|x, z] = E[u|z]$. Specifically, for the normal-half-normal framework with heteroskedasticity, generalizing Olson et al. (1980), SVKZ show that

$$\widehat{\sigma}_u(x, z) = \max\left\{0, \left[\sqrt{\frac{\pi}{2}}\left(\frac{\pi}{\pi - 4}\right)\widehat{m}_3(x, z)\right]^{1/3}\right\}, \tag{16.1.30}$$

$$\widehat{\sigma}_v^2(x, z) = \widehat{m}_2(x, z) - \widehat{\sigma}_u^2(x, z)\left(\frac{\pi - 2}{\pi}\right). \tag{16.1.31}$$

One can then use these estimates, at the third stage, to obtain the efficiency estimates for each observation, by generalizing Jondrow et al. (1982) to the

---

[2] Under fairly mild conditions and appropriate choice of the bandwidths, local-polynomial least-squares have appealing statistical properties (Fan and Gijbels, 1992), such as consistency, asymptotic normality, etc.

semiparametric and heteroskedastic case involving $E[u_i|\varepsilon_i, x_i, z_i]$ instead of $E[u_i|\varepsilon_i]$. These estimates of efficiency scores are predicted values conditional on the unobserved ε_i replaced with its estimate for the specific realization i. Therefore, their confidence intervals are usually fairly wide (see Simar and Wilson, 2010 for related discussion in a parametric context).

A consistent estimator for $E[u|x, z]$ is

$$\hat{E}[u|x, z] = \widehat{\mu}_u(x, z) = \sqrt{\frac{\pi}{2}} \widehat{\sigma}_u(x, z), \qquad (16.1.32)$$

which can be used to consistently estimate the level of the frontier, $m(x, z)$, at a point of interest (x, z), using

$$\widehat{m}(x, z) = \widehat{m}^*(x, z) + \widehat{\mu}_u(x, z). \qquad (16.1.33)$$

SVKZ noted that if the influence of z or x on the conditional mean of efficiency is of interest, then the expression for $E[u|x, z]$, can be calculated with no parametric assumptions, even for the distribution of u_i, if willing to accept that u_i belongs to the one-parameter scale family of distributions. They prove that the elasticity measure of $E[u|x, z]$ wrt an element of (x, z), defined as

$$\xi_{\psi_\ell}(x, z) = \frac{\partial \mu_u(x, z)}{\partial \psi_\ell} \frac{\psi_\ell}{\mu_u(x, z)}, \qquad (16.1.34)$$

where ψ_ℓ is an element of (x, z), and assuming that $\mu_u(x, z) \neq 0$, can be consistently estimated via

$$\widehat{\xi}_{\psi_\ell}(x, z) = \frac{1}{3} \frac{\widehat{\partial m_3}(x, z)}{\partial \psi_\ell} \frac{\psi_\ell}{\widehat{m}_3(x, z)} \ , \ \text{if } \widehat{m}_3(x, z) \neq 0, \quad (16.1.35)$$

where $\widehat{m}_3(x, z)$ and $\widehat{\partial m_3}(x, z)/\partial \psi_\ell$ are the estimates from the local polynomial estimator for the particular point of interest (x, z), obtained at the second stage. The asymptotic distribution for the elasticity measure of $E[u|x, z]$ wrt an element of (x, z) is shown to be

$$(nh^{p+d+2})^{1/2}\big(\widehat{\xi}_{\psi_\ell}(x, z) - \xi_{\psi_\ell}(x, z)\big) \longrightarrow N(0, s^2_{\xi_\ell}(x, z)). \quad (16.1.36)$$

For more details about these and other kernel-based approaches for SFA and well as related challenges in using these methods, see a comprehensive review by Parmeter and Zelenyuk (2018) and references therein.

16.2 SEMIPARAMETRIC ESTIMATION OF AN AVERAGE PRODUCTION FUNCTION WITH MONOTONICITY AND CONCAVITY

We now consider how the semiparametric approaches we have just discussed for the stochastic frontier, and which have been discussed in earlier chapters for the deterministic frontier, can be augmented by monotonicity and concavity constraints, which may be needed to ensure that it is a well-defined technology that is being estimated. We base this section on recent work by Wu and Sickles (2018). Their method utilizes transformations of the underlying semiparametric function via particular forms of differential equations. Their approach has the benefit of being in compliance with a priori shape constraints while at the same time utilizing methods that transform a constrained problem into an unconstrained one. The flexible functional forms we use for specifying the particular functional representation nonparametrically are based on penalized splines. We exploit the relative ease of embedding smoothers into nonlinear functionals and of thus imposing structures in multiple regression models. Recall that penalized splines, which are special cases of general sieve estimators (Chen, 2007), were used to specify the time–varying and firm–specific efficiency terms in the Kneip et al. (2012) panel stochastic frontier model. Here we use variants of that approach to specify the entire mean function. Although it is straightforward to introduce inefficiency into the approach we outline below, we will discuss it in the context of an average production (cost) function.

16.2.1   The Use of Transformations to Impose Constraints

We introduce a few examples of the use of transformations to restrict a function. Let us begin with a range restriction on a function. For example, we may wish to specify a function that is nonnegative. If this is the case then we can use a standard approach such as specifying the function as $f(x) = (r(x))^2$ or $f(x) = \exp(r(x)) \implies f(x) \geq 0$. In order to constrain the function to take on values between 0 and 1 we can specify it as $f(x) = \frac{1}{1+\exp(r(x))} \implies 0 < f(x) < 1$. A more general range restriction that restricts the function to lie in an interval (a,b) is $f(x) = a + \frac{b-a}{1+\exp(r(x))} \implies a < f(x) < b$. The advantage of this transformation approach is to transform a constrained problem, which in this case is the modeling of the function f, into an unconstrained problem. In these examples the unconstrained problem is the modeling of r. Such transformations allow us to maintain global compliance with constraints as opposed to observation-specific compliance typically secured when using the kernel-based methods of Mukerjee (1988) and Mammen (1991). Hall and Huang (2001) utilized penalized kernel-smoothers as did subsequent applications and generalizations of their methods by Henderson et al. (2012), Blundell et al. (2012), Ma and Racine (2013), and Du et al. (2013).

Monotonicity constraints can be imposed through integration transformation procedures. We can start with a smooth monotone function and with no loss of generality let $x \in [0, 1]$. Ramsay (1998) noted that the function $f(x)$ can be represented as:

$$f(x) = \int_0^x \exp(r(s))ds. \tag{16.2.1}$$

This integral transformation allows us to model the function $r(x)$ free of constraints. Monotonicity and concavity can be imposed by noting that such properties require that $f'(x) = \exp(r(x)) > 0$ and that $f''(x) = f'(x)r'(x) < 0$. Thus $r'(x) < 0 \implies f''(x) < 0$ and the solution is to apply the integration transformation to r as

$$f(x) = \int_0^x \exp\left(\underbrace{-\int_0^s g(t)dt}_{r(s)}\right) ds, \qquad (16.2.2)$$

where $f'(x) = \exp\left(-\int_0^x g(t)dt\right) > 0$ and $f''(x) = -f'(x)g(x)$. If the function $g(x)$ satisfies $g(x) > 0$, then $f''(x) < 0$ for all x. A positiveness constraint is relatively straightforward. Possible choices include $g = x^2$, $g = \exp(x)$, among others. This means that the two constraints, monotonicity and concavity, are able to be imposed via a simple nonnegativity constraint on $g(x)$.

An alternative motivation for the transformation approach can be based on the following linear differential equation

$$g(x) = -f''(x)/f'(x), \qquad (16.2.3)$$

where g is the relative curvature of f with respect to its slope. This is also the Arrow–Pratt absolute risk aversion if f is a utility function. In this case the general solution becomes

$$f(x) = \beta_0 + \beta_1 \int_0^x \exp\left(-\int_0^s g(t)dt\right) ds, \qquad (16.2.4)$$

where of course the constant and the slope parameters are needed to identify the function $f(x)$.

16.2.2 Statistical Modeling

Modeling the average production, cost or other dual productivity relationships, which we have generically referred to as the function $f(x)$, requires data. Assume that the data come to us as iid draws of $\{y_i, x_i\}_{i=1}^n$ and that our goal is to require that the average production function $f(x)$ is a monotone and concave function in x.[3]

Given the data generating process we have just described, we can then write

$$f(x) = E(y|x), \qquad (16.2.5)$$

---

[3] Wu and Sickles (2018) did not specifically address the use of curvature restrictions on a stochastic frontier production function but their method can easily be modified to allow for a composed error containing a normal and a half normal (skew-normal) random error. If we let $\varepsilon_i = v_i - u_i$ be the skew-normal, then we can utilize either a variant of a MOLS or a COLS after estimating the model using the transformation given in the example below and base our conditional efficiency estimates on the Jondrow et al. (1982) efficiency estimate. Of course with panel data we can adopt a method that allows for the consistent estimation of firm-specific efficiency that is not conditional on stochastic error based on the methods we discussed in Chapters 12 and 13.

and the transformation-based model becomes

$$y_i = \beta_0 + \beta_1 \int_0^{x_i} \exp\left(-\int_0^s g(t)dt\right) ds + \varepsilon_i. \tag{16.2.6}$$

Here ε_i is the iid error with mean zero and finite variance. In this transformation-based model, $g(x) > 0$ for all x, which ensures that the function is concave.

A goal of productivity measurement is to ensure that what we have specified and measured is consistent with the conditions required for ensuring that what we have specified and measured is meaningful. The only way this is possible is if the regularity conditions are met. However, this may also sacrifice the flexibility required of the functional relationships we have discussed in Chapter 6. The flexible functional forms provide the basis of what is referred to as Diewert flexibility. Thus we also must keep in mind that however the restrictions are imposed we wish to ensure flexibility. To this end let $g(x) = g(h(x))$, e.g., $g(x) = (h(x))^2$. We can model h, free of constraints, using splines. A spline is simply another nonparametric function and is piecewise polynomial smoothly connected at its joints (knots). For example, polynomial splines with degree p can be expressed as

$$\varsigma(x) = \underbrace{(1, x, \ldots, x^p}_{\text{power series}}, \underbrace{(x - k_1)_+^p, \cdots, (x - k_M)_+^p)^T}_{\text{piecewise power series}}, \tag{16.2.7}$$

where $(x)_+ = \max(x, 0)$ and $k_1 < \cdots < k_M$ are spline knots. Spline approximations are in the form of $h(x) = c'\varsigma(x)$, which is a linear combination of spline basis with c being the spline coefficients. Examples of a method to specify a general production model with time-varying and cross-sectionally varying productivities are given in Chapter 13 in Kneip et al. (2012). Such power series determine the overall shape of the function and a piecewise spline basis captures local variations on each interval. Combinations of small p and relatively large M offer robustness and flexibility.

Penalized spline estimation is the basis of the Kneip et al. (2012) model and in the context of our generic average production model example gives us the following parameterization of the model:

$$y_i = \beta_0 + \beta_1 \int_0^{x_i} \exp\left(-\int_0^s g(c'\varsigma(t))dt\right) ds + \varepsilon_i \tag{16.2.8}$$

$$= f(x_i; \beta, c) + \varepsilon_i.$$

The penalized nonlinear least squares estimator is:

$$\min_{\beta, c}\left(\underbrace{\frac{1}{n}\sum_{i=1}^n (y_i - f(x_i; \beta, c))^2}_{\text{goodness of fit}} + \underbrace{\lambda D(f)}_{\text{roughness penalty}}\right), \tag{16.2.9}$$

where $D(f) > 0$ measures roughness in f and the smoothing parameter λ governs the trade-off between the goodness-of-fit and smoothness to avoid over-fitting. The roughness penalty shrinks the spline coefficients toward zero. A common choice of penalty is the integrated squared derivatives

$$D(f) = \int_0^1 (f^{(q)}(x))^2 dx, \ q = 1, 2, \ldots, \tag{16.2.10}$$

although a model-based penalty also can be specified based on a careful selection of D, and this can simplify the estimation and reduce bias.

Heckman and Ramsay (2000), e.g., suggest a natural choice for the penalty for relative curvature for the function f, where $g(x) = -f''(x)/f'(x) > 0$ to be

$$D(f) = \int_0^1 g(x)dx. \tag{16.2.11}$$

Technical assumptions for consistency and asymptotic normality of the average production function's parameters are given in Wu and Sickles (2018).

16.2.3 Empirical Example using the Coelli Data

An example of the usefulness of this method is given below using the Coelli and Perelman (1996) benchmark data for the output of 60 firms along with capital and labor. Output is supposed to be monotone and concave in either input, but of course such an assumption is not necessarily maintained for a non-parametric functional form given to the production relationship. Let's assume that production is modeled as an additive model of two inputs and thus given by the following additive form:

$$y_i = f_1(x_{i1}) + f_2(x_{i2}) + \varepsilon_i, \tag{16.2.12}$$

where y is output, x_1 is capital, and x_2 is labor. Assume that the ε_i are iid disturbances with zero mean. We want the functions f_j, $j = 1, 2$, to be monotone and concave and hence we want $f_j > 0$ and $f_{jj} < 0$ for j = 1, 2. Wu and Sickles (2018) estimated this model using their back-fitted transformation spline estimator, the details of which we do not repeat here and can be found in Wu and Sickles (2018). Figure 16.1 shows the surface and contour plots of the estimated production function as well as the positive and marginally decreasing contribution of capital and labor. The bottom figure illustrates the additive component associated with capital and labor respectively and the results indicate that the marginal productivity of capital of the firms levels off gradually while that of labor persistently increases.

16.2.4 Nonparametric SFA Methods with Monotonicity and Shape Constraints

Ensuring that insights from models of productivity and efficiency are robust to the various assumptions that may plague these models, whether the assumptions are made on the specification of the production function itself, or how

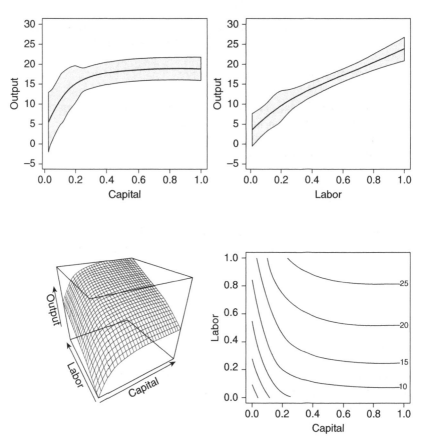

Figure 16.1 Surface and contour plots of capital and labor: Coelli data using the Wu–Sickles Estimator.

efficiency enters the model, are two of the main motivating factors for semi-nonparametric and nonparametric econometric modeling approaches. This chapter has briefly discussed these issues and we also have touched on the topic in several other previous chapters. These issues have direct consequences on the measurement of productivity of the firm. Parmeter and Racine (2013) demonstrate how to estimate a production function nonparametrically, while ensuring that standard axioms of producer theory hold. This involves extending the work of Fan et al. (1996) by using the constrained kernel regression estimator of Du et al. (2013) instead of the approaches of Wu and Sickles (2018) that we have just discussed. Additionally, Parmeter et al. (2014) extend the work of Du et al. (2013), but in the parametric setting. Interestingly, they find few differences in estimating theoretically restricted and unrestricted translog estimates of returns to scale. Such axioms and their use in specifying and modeling production technologies are also distinguishing features of models developed by Timo Kuosmanen and his colleagues and are probably best represented in his work on stochastic non-smooth envelopment of data (StoNED, Kuosmanen and Kortelainen, 2012). Yagi et al. (2018) have recently introduced a Shape Constrained Kernel-weighted Least Squares (SCKLS) estimator and have explored their estimator's asymptotic properties. Not only can this estimator impose monotonicity and convexity/concavity constraints, but it can also be used to test the specification of the shape constraints. Although their model set up and empirical results focus on productivity without a further decomposition into its innovation and efficiency components, it would appear that this decomposition may be a possible extension to their model.

16.3 MODEL AVERAGING

The discussion below summarizes work from a series of papers on model averaging and productivity measurement by Sickles et al. (2014), Sickles et al. (2015), Sickles et al. (2016), Duygun et al. (2017), and Isaksson et al. (2018). We begin with motivations for model averaging and then discuss various specific methods to construct optimal estimators based on the model averaging concepts that have been used in many empirical settings in econometrics and time-series forecasting.

16.3.1 Insights from Economics and Statistics

There are many insights that one can draw from economics and statistics for combining information from alternative models or agents' choices. One motivation for model averaging comes from the economics literature via theoretical treatments in majority voting. It is well known in the literature of social choice theory (see Moulin, 1980) that majority voting tends to result in median outcomes. Replacing the preferences of voters with the preferences of modelers (that is, which estimator based on which specification do they choose to use) and assuming a symmetric distribution, the aggregated estimator, i.e., the median, will be the simple average. Another motivation for model averaging is the rent-seeking game of Tullock (1980). Assume that a decision maker needs to decide on a choice among several competing models. Each model gives an estimate. The decision maker tries to make a decision based on her preferences and that her preference is to avoid a loss and thus the minimization of a loss function is the goal. The probability of winning the decision maker's favor can be compared to the rent-seeking game described by Tullock (1980). With, e.g., two bidders, bidder 1 has bid x ($x \geq 0$) and bidder 2 has bid y ($y \geq 0$). The situation is analogous to an all-pay auction, where all bidders pay and the highest bidder wins. It is common practice to use the Tullock contest function in such an auction format where every bidder with positive bid has a positive probability of winning the auction. Let π be the probability of winning, where

$$\pi(x, y) = \frac{1}{2}, \text{ if x, y} = 0,$$

$$\pi(x, y) = \frac{x}{x + y}, \text{ otherwise.} \tag{16.3.1}$$

The Tullock contest functions can be connected to our model averaging example if the decision-maker chooses the model with a bigger R^2 corresponding to the model with the smallest loss (the R^2 for each model is x and y) and the probability of winning is the R^2 weight. The expected estimate from this process is thus

$$\pi(x, y) \times \text{"estimate 1"} + (1 - \pi(x, y)) \times \text{"estimate 2"}, \tag{16.3.2}$$

and this is just the R^2 weighted estimates we consider later in this section, along with other weights in the model averaging exercise. Other insights to combining information to develop a consensus estimate can be based on the treatments to combine forecasts in the statistics literature. With whatever method one chooses, however, the statistical noise introduced by errors in model selection is no less important than the standard statistical noise we introduce via the disturbance term in our usual regression analyses (Duygun et al., 2017) or because of other modeling defects (Hjorth, 1993).

The key issue in model averaging, to which we now turn, is how to choose the weights that we use to combine the estimates. Although we do not discuss Bayesian Model averaging (BMA), it was developed in parallel with model averaging under the classical framework (Raftery et al., 1997; Hoeting et al., 1999; Koop et al., 2007). One way to proceed is to average the estimates. It might not always be reasonable to assume that every model should be given the same weights, but rather different weights based on how well the model fits the data. Many statistical criteria are developed to assess the information content of alternative models, e.g., the Akaike Information Criterion (Akaike, 1973) (AIC), Mallows' CP (Mallows, 1973), and the Bayesian Information Criterion (Schwarz, 1978) (BIC). Buckland et al. (1997) used two of these information criteria, the Akaike and Schwarz, as weights in their model averaging exercise. Hansen (2007) showed that the model average estimator using Mallows' weights has optimality properties in large samples and is often a better criterion on which to base the weights than either the AIC or the BIC. Hansen and Racine (2012) considered situations in which candidate models are non-nested and proposed a jackknife model averaging estimator, which they showed is asymptotically optimal in the sense that it approaches the lowest possible expected squared errors. Parmeter et al. (2017a) have begun to assess the finite sample properties of this estimator via Monte Carlo simulations.

There are several common assumptions in the application of model averaging (as well as meta-analysis) that may be difficult to justify and that is independence among studies in the case of meta-analysis or independence of estimators in the case of model averaging. It is rather unlikely that researchers whose expertise is similar and thus publish in the same sub-discipline would not use common sources, such as standard references, updated and current

Internet postings, and presentations at academic conferences they have jointly attended, not to mention shared academic advisors, co-authors, etc.

16.3.2 Insights from Time-Series Forecasting

As we have mentioned above, another averaging approach involves the combining of time-series model predictions. Newbold and Harvey (2002) and Bates and Granger (1969), among others, have urged researchers to use a combined forecast when there exist separate and reliable forecasts. Diebold and Lopez (1996) argued that these could serve to link short-run and long-run forecasts. Machine learning algorithms also have been utilized to choose weights and address problems with missing observations (Lahiri et al., 2016). Two important points are raised in both Clement (1989) and Timmermann (2006) in regard to forecasting combination methods. One is that smaller error forecasts may be obtained via weights that are based on simplified assumptions, such as by ignoring the correlation between models. Another is that oftentimes a simple average of the forecasts dominates more complicated weighting techniques (Lahiri et al., 2016). Additional insights can also be found in a series of studies by Lahiri and Sheng (2010), Lahiri et al. (2010).

16.3.3 Frequentist Model Averaging

Like other statistical techniques, model averaging methods can be classified into Frequentist Model Averaging (FMA) and Bayesian Model Averaging (BMA). In general, the BMA approach first assigns to each candidate model a prior probability, which is updated through the observed data, and the updated posterior probability is then used as the weight. A tutorial on the basics of the BMA approach can be found in Hoeting et al. (1999). Choosing the prior probabilities is the first step in the BMA method, which is problematic because we do not know what priors are the most appropriate, and priors can be in conflict with each other.

The FMA approach, on the other hand, does not need such *ex ante* assumptions of probabilities, and thus avoids finite sample problems associated with the BMA approach. As part of the growing literature discussing FMA methods, Buckland et al. (1997) proposed to assign weights according to an information criterion of each candidate model m:

$$I_m = -2\ln\mathscr{L}_m + l. \tag{16.3.3}$$

Here $\mathscr{L}_m$ is the maximized likelihood function of the mth model, and l is some penalty function. The weights based on this criterion are calculated as

$$w_I = \frac{\exp(\frac{1}{2}I_m)}{\sum\limits_{m\in M} \exp(\frac{1}{2}I_m)}, \tag{16.3.4}$$

where M is the set of all competing models. If $l = 2k$, where k is the number of parameters in the model, the information criterion I_m is the AIC score.

If $l = k \cdot \ln(n)$, and n represents the number of observations, then I_m is the BIC score. It is straightforward to base the weights on such model evaluating criteria, but we lack a method to measure the effectiveness of these weighting schemes. Moreover, it is also difficult to tell by how much they can improve the quality of the estimators. Other weighting schemes have been proposed in recent years. Leung and Barron (2006) considered assigning the weights to a set of least squares estimators based on their risk characteristics. Hansen (2007) proposed to select the weights by minimizing a Mallows criterion, which works in a set of nested linear models with homoskedastic errors. If one constrains oneself to a finite number of possible models, then Hansen (2007) proved that in large samples the lowest squared error is achieved by an estimator using his Mallows-weight-based model average estimator. Based on the work of Hansen (2007), Wan et al. (2010) relaxed the assumptions that candidate models should be nested based on certain ordering of regressors. They also provided a proof of the optimality of Mallows criterion in a continuous weight set. Wang et al. (2009) also reviewed important developments in FMA methods.

16.3.4   The Hansen (2007) and Hansen and Racine (2012) Model Averaging Estimators

We next consider two model averaging methods that can be used to combine inferences from various linear but not necessarily nested models that are used to estimate productivity. Many of these models are discussed in the chapters on panel methods in SFA modeling. We begin with the method proposed by Hansen (2007) and examined by Sickles et al. (2016).

16.3.4.1   The Hansen (2007) Model Averaging Estimator

To illustrate this approach one first specifies a (nested) unrestricted model. Such a model can be written as

$$y_{it} = \sum_{j=1}^{k} \beta_j x_{itj} + \sum_{r=0}^{\infty} \delta_r t^r + \varepsilon_{it}, \qquad i = 1, \ldots, n; \; t = 1, \ldots, T.$$

$$(16.3.5)$$

Here $\varepsilon_{it} \sim \mathcal{N}(0, \sigma_\varepsilon^2)$ and is iid Let $z_{it} = (x_{it1}, \ldots, x_{itk}, 1, t^2, t^3, \ldots)'$ be the vector of regressors with associated parameters $\gamma = (\beta_1, \ldots, \beta_k, \delta_0, \delta_1, \ldots)'$. The model can be compactly expressed as

$$y_{it} = z_{it}'\gamma + \varepsilon_{it}. \qquad (16.3.6)$$

There are a finite number of nested models M, indexed by $m = 1, \ldots, M$.[4] We order the parameters $p < k_1 < k_2 < \ldots < k_M$ and represent the mth model as

$$Y = Z_m \Gamma_m + \epsilon. \tag{16.3.7}$$

Estimates of the coefficients in the mth model are $\hat{\Gamma}_m$. The weight vector for the Hansen model averaged estimator is given by $w = (w_1, \ldots, w_M)$, is model specific, and is assumed to lie on the unit simplex. Thus $w_m \in [0, 1]$ and $\sum_{m=1}^{M} w_m = 1$. The unrestricted model average estimator is then

$$\hat{\Gamma} = \sum_{m=1}^{M} w_m \begin{pmatrix} \hat{\Gamma}_m \\ 0 \end{pmatrix}. \tag{16.3.8}$$

Further defining $k(w) = \sum_{m=1}^{M} w_m k_m$, the optimal weights are then obtained by numerically minimizing the Mallows criterion

$$C(w) = (Y - Z_M \hat{\Gamma})'(Y - Z_M \hat{\Gamma}) + 2\sigma^2 k(w). \tag{16.3.9}$$

16.3.4.2 The Kneip–Sickles–Song Model to Nest Competing Models

One candidate unrestricted model is the Kneip et al. (2012) factor model. The model allows for very general pattern effects that vary with time and with the cross section. In their empirical study of the US Commercial Banking Industry, Kneip et al. (2012) interpret the normalized effects as unobserved productivity effects. Their model is specified as

$$y_{it} = \beta_0(t) + \sum_{j=1}^{k} \beta_j x_{itj} + u_{it} + v_{it}, \quad i = 1, \ldots, n; t = 1, \ldots, T, \tag{16.3.10}$$

where $\beta_0(t)$ is some average function. In this model u'_{it}s represent unobserved effects that vary with time and with the cross-section and are assumed to take on a factor structure given by

$$u_{it} = \sum_{r=1}^{L} \theta_{ir} g_r(t), \quad i = 1, \ldots, n. \tag{16.3.11}$$

$\beta_0(t)$ is eliminated by using the centered form of the model

$$y_{it} - \bar{y}_t = \sum_{j=1}^{k} \beta_j (x_{itj} - \bar{x}_{tj}) + \sum_{r=1}^{L} \theta_{ir} g_r(t) + v_{it} - \bar{v}_i, \quad i = 1, \ldots, n;$$

$$t = 1, \ldots, T, \tag{16.3.12}$$

---

[4] In our discussion of model averaging we adopt the notation used in that literature to represent the set of models as indexed by $m = 1, \ldots, M$. In previous chapters we have used M to be the number of outputs in the technology set.

where $\bar{y}_t = \frac{1}{n}\sum_i y_{it}$, $\bar{x}_{tj} = \frac{1}{n}\sum_i x_{itj}$, and $\bar{v}_{ti} = \frac{1}{n}\sum_i v_{it}$. If we denote $\tilde{y}_{it} = y_{it} - \bar{y}_t$ and $\tilde{x}_{itj} = x_{itj} - \bar{x}_{tj}$, then we can use the following general form to estimate various panel productivity models as

$$\tilde{y}_{it} = \sum_{j=1}^{k}\beta_j \tilde{x}_{itj} + \sum_{r=1}^{L}\theta_{ir}g_r(t) + \tilde{v}_{it}, \qquad i = 1,\ldots,n;\ t = 1,\ldots,T.$$

(16.3.13)

This model effectively nests several specifications in stochastic frontier analysis. For example, if $g_r(t) = t^{r-1}$ and $L = 3$, then the model collapses to the productivity model of Cornwell et al. (1990). Recall the Kumbhakar (1990) model

$$y_{it} = x'_{it}\beta - u_{it} + v_{it},$$

(16.3.14)

where u_{it} is assumed to be an exponential function of time given by $u_{it} = (1 + \exp(bt + ct^2))^{-1}\tau_i$ and where the distribution of τ_i is assumed to be iid $\mathcal{N}^+(0, \sigma_\tau^2)$. One can replace u_{it} with a Taylor-series expansion for some finite degree of polynomial in time (L_1) after suitable normalizations on τ_i and t and rewrite the model as

$$y_{it} \simeq x'_{it}\beta + \sum_{r=0}^{L_1}\delta_{ir}t^r + v_{it}.$$

(16.3.15)

The Battese and Coelli (1992) model also can be nested within the KSS model using the same argument. For the Battese and Coelli (1992) model the effects are parameterized as

$$u_{it} = \{\exp[-\eta(t - T)]\}\tau_i.$$

(16.3.16)

Again, after suitable normalizations on τ_i and t, we can approximate the u_{it} with a polynomial of degree L_2, resulting in the model

$$y_{it} \simeq x'_{it}\beta + \sum_{r=0}^{L_2}\delta_{ir}t^r + v_{it}.$$

(16.3.17)

It is shown in Kneip et al. (2012) that both the fixed effects and random effects estimators also are special cases of the KSS estimator.

16.3.4.3 *The Hansen and Racine (2012) Jackknife Model Averaging Estimator*

Hansen and Racine (2012) considered a more general situation in which the candidate models can be non-nested and have heteroskedatic errors. The proposed estimator is termed the "jackknife model averaging" (JMA) estimator and is obtained by minimizing a leave-one-out cross-validation criterion. We review below this estimator and its use in productivity studies based on recent work by Isaksson et al. (2018). The JMA estimator is shown by Hansen and Racine to be asymptotically optimal in the sense that it approaches the lowest possible expected squared errors as the sample size approaches infinity (for a panel data of n individuals and T time periods). To simplify the setup let the (M) competing models be written as

$$y_i = \mu_i + \epsilon_i, \qquad i = 1, \ldots, M. \qquad (16.3.18)$$

Here $\mu_i = E(y_i|x_i)$ and x_i is the vector of regressors. ϵ_i is the error term with zero mean conditional on x_i. The conditional variance of ϵ_i is allowed to vary across observations. That is:

$$E(\epsilon_i|x_i) = 0, \qquad (16.3.19)$$

$$E(\epsilon_i^2|x_i) = \sigma_i^2. \qquad (16.3.20)$$

Suppose that for each candidate model m, we have a linear estimator, denoted as $\hat{\mu}^m = P_m y$. The estimator is linear in the sense that P_m is not a function of y. This definition covers a fairly broad class of estimators that contains standard OLS, ridge regression, nearest neighbor estimators, series estimators, etc. The jackknife averaging estimator is then calculated as the weighted average of all the candidate models. The weights are calculated using the following steps. First denote, for each model m, the jackknife estimator $\tilde{\mu}^m = (\tilde{\mu}_i^m, \ldots, \tilde{\mu}_n^m)'$, where $\tilde{\mu}_i^m$ is the estimate of y_i with the parameters estimated after the ith observation is deleted (leave-one-out cross-validation). The jackknife residual is then computed as $\tilde{\varepsilon}^m = y - \tilde{\mu}^m$. The weights are assumed to be nonnegative and sum to one, thus requiring that the weight vector lie on the $\mathfrak{R}^M$ unit simplex:

$$\mathcal{H}_M = \{w \in \mathfrak{R}^M : w^m \geq 0, \sum_{m=1}^{M} w^m = 1\}. \qquad (16.3.21)$$

Given a specific weight vector w, the averaged estimator is

$$\tilde{\mu}(w) = \sum_{m=1}^{M} w^m \tilde{\mu}^m = \tilde{\mu}w \qquad (16.3.22)$$

and the averaged residual is

$$\tilde{\varepsilon}(w) = y - \tilde{\mu}(w) = \tilde{\varepsilon}w. \qquad (16.3.23)$$

The jackknife or leave-one-out cross-validation criterion is

$$CV_n(w) = \frac{1}{n}\tilde{\varepsilon}(w)'\tilde{\varepsilon}(w). \qquad (16.3.24)$$

The next step then obtains the jackknife weights by minimizing this criterion over the weight $\mathcal{H}_M$

$$w^* = \underset{w \in \mathcal{H}_M}{\operatorname{argmin}} \, CV_n(w). \qquad (16.3.25)$$

The jackknife averaging estimator is thus $\hat{\mu}(w^*) = \hat{\mu}w^*$. Depending on different specifications of the model setting, the applicable weight space might be only a subset of $\mathcal{H}_M$.

16.3.5 Other Model Averaging Approaches to Develop Consensus Productivity Estimates

Robust considerations for the many different possible specifications of the stochastic frontier model have also been considered recently by Parmeter et al. (2017a), who develop several stochastic frontier model averaging estimators based on Frequentist model averaging insights. Their work is a direct extension of the work by Sickles (2005), who first proposed model averaging to study productivity. While Sickles (2005) admittedly used a simple approach to average across different productivity estimators, Parmeter et al. (2017a) formalize many of the insights of Sickles (2005) and propose several avenues to average different objects in a stochastic frontier exercise, depending upon the interests of the researcher. Recent work referenced at the beginning of this section on model averaging by Sickles et al. (2014, 2015, 2016), Isaksson et al. (2018), and Duygun et al. (2017), continues to build on the work of Sickles (2005), both in applied and theoretical treatments using variants of the methods discussed in this chapter.

In our discussion of model averaging we have focused on issues that, although seldom discussed in classical regression and economic theory courses, are becoming more and more acceptable and have become common practice for practitioners and for forecasters. Exacting theoretical concerns that are leveraged on one "true" model, while ignoring the possibility that a true model is often a fiction in economics and productivity measurement, are becoming a thing of the past. Big data and the computing power and information processing technology that has made its analysis possible will continue to offer options for optimal predictions and forecasts to be made from a variety of formal models, not necessarily nested and not necessarily linear. The chapter has just scratched the surface on how this new technology can be utilized to develop consensus estimates for productivity and efficiency levels and growth rates.

16.4 CONCLUDING REMARKS

Semiparametric and nonparametric methods to analyze productivity have become an essential part of the productivity and efficiency researcher's toolkit. Available software and developments in simulation and bootstrapping methods have also aided the applied researcher in implementing the many methods available in the semiparametric and nonparametric literature. It is often the case, however, that the researcher may find that restrictions needed in order to interpret results based on various dual forms to the production technology are not as easily imposed when estimating such models of productivity. We have pointed out the difficulties inherent in imposing meaningful economic restrictions on functional representations of productivity models and suggested methods that can be adopted to address this issue.

Moreover, as analyses of productivity and its determinants becomes more model and data-intensive, it is clear that new approaches to display and summarize results across a broad spectrum of potential models and model specifications must be adopted in order that robust conclusions can be made. Much of the current literature on productivity and the broader empirical literature in economics has adopted an approach that simply provides a list of results based on different specifications, along with summary diagnostics. The material in this chapter has focused on scientific ways to develop a consensus estimate from the many models and specifications that an econometrician can use and that have various advantages and disadvantages. When such results are assessed via model averaging, it allows the researcher or policy analysts to summarize results based on a coherent and statistically valid set of methodologies. Much work is underway to generalize these approaches to a broad set of modeling scenarios and we anticipate that such model averaging methods as we have discussed in this chapter will become the accepted approach to summarizing future results in the productivity literature.

16.5 EXERCISES

1. Discuss how the Moulin model of the median voter and the Tullock model of rent-seeking behavior can be viewed as an averaging estimator of preferences.
2. Weights assigned to a model m according to the information criterion $I_m = -2 \ln \mathcal{L}_m + 2k$ for each candidate model can be expressed as

$$w_I = \frac{\exp(\frac{1}{2}I_m)}{\sum_{m \in M} \exp(\frac{1}{2}I_m)},$$

where $\mathcal{L}_m$ is the maximized likelihood function of the mth model, and I indexes the models. Derive this expression for the weights based on Buckland et al. (1997) and the Akaike information criteria. Here k is the number of parameters in the model.
3. What is the basis function and what is the number of factors under which the KSS estimator collapses to the random and fixed effect estimator for the panel stochastic frontier model with time–invariant efficiency (the Schmidt and Sickles, 1984 estimator).
4. The jackknife procedure utilized in Hansen and Racine (2012) uses a "leave-one-out" procedure. Discuss alternatives to this approach and the potential numerical advantages of the standard jackknife with other bootstrapping-type methods to develop weights for the model-averaging estimator.

5. The Hansen and Racine estimator can be shown to minimize the asymptotic mean-squared error for a set of potentially non-nested linear models when the number of alternative models is finite. Can you conjecture on how the conditions might be altered to address certain nonlinear models, such as a structural model of productivity that is based on the framework given in Olley and Pakes (1996)?

CHAPTER 17

Data Measurement Issues, the KLEMS Project, Other Data Sets for Productivity Analysis, and Productivity and Efficiency Software

In this chapter we briefly discuss some of the issues that arise when using standard index numbers as input quantity or price measures, as well as particular data sets that can be used in productivity research. In regard to the latter, we focus first on the World KLEMS project data and recent studies using it. These studies are based on modern approaches to productivity measurement using largely neoclassical approaches that assume perfectly competitive markets and frontier behaviors by firms, industries, and countries. We discuss in our summary of these papers how concepts we have put forth in our book speak to the topics and approaches used in these studies and how, in many ways, their frameworks and methods are closely aligned with modeling approaches and scenarios we have discussed in our earlier chapters. We then provide a short description of many other public use datasets and information on how to access them. Of course, it is important to be able to have accessible and easy to use software to analyze such data using methods we have discussed in this book. The software is detailed in the last section of this, our concluding chapter.

17.1   DATA MEASUREMENT ISSUES

The accurate modeling and measurement of the productivity growth determinants and their contributions in an aggregate economy, in its component industries, and in particular firms, has advanced considerably since the Jorgenson and Griliches (1967) seminal treatise on the measurement problems inherent in assessing productivity growth. However, the problems that Jorgenson and Griliches pointed out over 50 years ago are still with us, as noted in Chapter 4. Although major improvements in data collection and methodology have been incorporated in government and private-sector data collection protocols through the efforts of Jorgenson and Griliches and their many collaborators and colleagues, variations in the quality of data still affect the measurement and analysis of productivity growth. Such issues tend not to be discussed in applied work. Griliches (1994) summarized the potential measurement issues pertaining to productivity analysis, listing the following general problems and questions: 1. Coverage issues, definition of the borders of a sector, and the relevant concept of "output" for it. For example, is illegal activity included? Are pollution damages counted against the "output" of an industry?; 2. The difficulty in measuring "real" output over time as prices and the quality of output change; 3. Improper measurement of inputs over time when there are changes in the skill-mix of the labor force, changes in the quality of the machinery and equipment used, and changes in the utilization of the labor force and of the existing capital stock; 4. Exclusion of certain inputs involving such items as research and development and of public infrastructure expenditures in the total input concept; 5. Missing data on hours worked by people, machines, and other specific inputs; 6. Improper "weights" used to construct a particular index which often ignore the divergence of market prices from "shadow prices" and the impact of various disequilibria; 7. Formula differences, the unknown shape of the underlying production possibilities frontier, and gross versus net concepts; 8. The consequences of aggregation over heterogeneous individuals and industries.

In their development of a new hedonic price index for airline travel for the BLS, Good et al. (2008) pointed to the importance of these issues and the need for continued vigilance by serious researchers at universities and statistical offices. The measurement issues are highly problematic, costly, and often subject to serious controversies. These issues affect how productivity is measured and what are the legitimate contributors to its growth. Often it is not one of these issues but a combination of them that influence the determinants of productivity growth. Their importance varies across countries, industries, and time. Therefore, it is extremely important to continue and accelerate the efforts of US governmental data collection agencies to improve the quality of the data that is the source of many productivity studies. As Griliches (1994) noted, major problems have been associated with measurement of real output and real input growth because of incorrect measurement of prices and associated adjustments for quality changes. Measurement of capacity utilization of capital and labor is a measurement issue in the context of the short run comparisons while in the long run, the quality improvement of the labor force through education and experience, the amount of resources devoted to discovery of new knowledge through R&D effort, and organizational restructuring of industries and productive units to absorb new and advanced production techniques are likely to be both major sources of true productivity growth and also present a continuous and major challenge for analysts of productivity behavior. These issues had particular currency in the classic pronouncements and policy recommendations from the Boskin Commission (Boskin et al., 1996) and in related work by commission members and their colleagues (Boskin et al., 1997; Boskin and Jorgenson, 1997; Boskin et al., 1998).

Although their focus was on measurement issues pertaining to the Consumer Price Index (CPI) the issues addressed by the Boskin Commission continue to have currency in stressing the importance of accurate measurement of prices and quantities in general and thus to measurement issues we encounter in productivity analysis. All serious empirical work in production analysis requires accurate measurement of prices and quantities. Abraham et al. (1998) responded to the commission report with initiatives for government data collection agencies aimed at addressing these shortcomings and the inaccuracies they generated. A number of changes were initiated, including the use of geometric means instead of arithmetic means to mitigate the impact of substitution bias, superlative chained indexes such as the Divisia index instead of the Laspeyres and Paasche indexes. Deaton (1998) and Diewert (1998), among others, have pointed out the problematic issues associated with quality changes and argued for the greater use of quality adjustments that could be implemented using hedonic regression techniques.

Many of the aforementioned issues and the proper methods and data protocols to address them have been the theme behind the enormous effort by Dale Jorgenson and his colleagues in developing the World KLEMS database, to which we now turn.

17.2 SPECIAL ISSUE OF THE INTERNATIONAL PRODUCTIVITY MONITOR FROM THE MADRID FOURTH WORLD KLEMS CONFERENCE: NON-FRONTIER PERSPECTIVES ON PRODUCTIVITY MEASUREMENT

The World KLEMS project lead by Dale Jorgenson has highlighted a number of issues in the study of international productivity trends and determinants that have been a boon to researchers and policymakers. The detailed sector-specific analyses made possible by this pioneering project are too numerous to cover in this book. Instead, we direct the interested reader to recent studies, many of which were presented in the 2016 World KLEMS Conference in Madrid, published in the Special Issue from the Fourth World KLEMS Conference in the International Productivity Monitor (2017, Centre for the Study of Living Standards, Ottawa, Ontario). These papers provide a perspective on productivity modeling and measurement that represents the very best of the National Bureau of Economic Research's perspectives on productivity measurement and we would be remiss were we to exclude this from our treatment of productivity and performance. Although the studies do not explicitly model productivity and efficiency using exactly the same models and methods as we have explored in the book, it is often relatively straightforward to frame these studies in the context of the generic models we have discussed in previous chapters that have focused on dynamics, endogeneity, panel methods, unobserved factors, and the modeling of innovation and efficiency change. When appropriate, we will point the reader to earlier chapters that have detailed issues addressed in these studies as well as commonalities in the generic models we have discussed and the particular approaches these distinguished researchers have pursued.

We begin with the contribution to the Special Issue by Jorgenson (2017) and discuss each of the ten papers in turn.[1]

17.2.1   Productivity and Economic Growth in the World Economy: An Introduction

Jorgenson (2017) noted in his introduction to the Special Issue of the International Productivity Monitor from the Madrid Fourth World KLEMS Conference that three regional organizations – European Union KLEMS, Latin American KLEMS, and Asia KLEMS – were actively represented in this volume and discussed the role of each in his contribution. The European Union (EU) KLEMS initially applied international standards to 25 members of the EU and showed similar data when applying the standards to Australia, Canada, Japan, and the United States. The main findings of studies that have utilized the EU KLEMS data is that the European economy has had a slow recovery after the US Great Recession began. The resulting lack of investment in human capital, IT, and R&D contributed to low growth in employment and productivity, creating an even larger gap in growth between Europe and the United States. An important update of the EU KLEMS took place in 2016 by the European Commission that applied the European System of Accounts 2010 to 34 industrial sectors to recalculate value added. Van Ark and Jäger (2017) used an updated version of the database to show that a weak recovery in the European economy has taken hold, although substantial variations continue to exist in major European economies. Perez and Benages (2017) look into the differences between Spain and other EU countries relative to the USA and show that some investments in capital negatively impacted *TFP* growth.

The Latin American (LA) KLEMS was organized by the Economic Commission for Latin America and the Caribbean (ECLAC), an agency of the UN, and produced industry-level production accounts for major Latin American countries. Early studies based on LA KLEMS found no *TFP* growth in the leading LA economies in the past two decades. Specifically, a report based on Mexico KLEMS shows that Mexican debt crisis, the US dotcom crash, and the Great Recession were drags on the Mexico's economy since the late 1990s. Using Argentina KLEMS, Coremberg (2017) reveals that official statistics were manipulated by the former Argentine government, and shows consistent results using Argentina KLEMS with those using reconstructed national accounts under the current government.

The Asia KLEMS includes the Japan Industrial Productivity database, supported by the Research Institute for Economy, Trade and Industry (RIETI), which also supports the China Industrial Productivity database, and is used to analyze the sources of economic stagnation in Japan. The India KLEMS, supported by the Reserve Bank of India, is used to compare China and India's growth and productivity by Wu et al. (2017), the first study using this

---

[1] The authors wish to thank Shasha Liu for her contribution to this section.

industry-level data. The study by Miyagawa et al. (2017) on intangible investments in Japan shows that the rate of return to capital is positively related to intangibles such as R&D, human capital, and IT.

As investment in human capital is becoming increasingly important, Christian (2017) uses a lifetime income approach to measure the value of human capital and the impact on labor incomes. He shows that human capital per capita has been stagnant in the USA because the aging population offsets the positive effect of increased educational levels. Investment in IT has also been important in productivity research. Byrne and Corrado (2017) show in their study of ICT prices and services in the USA that the benefits from ICT investments and ICT services in terms of growth are greater than those based on the official US government estimates. The third important focus is international trade. Timmer (2017) decompose production of final demand into separable stages of value added production. Their method offers an extension to the traditional growth accounting in the world of integrating production.

The three regional organizations of KLEMS are contributing important research results to productivity study. Labor and capital continue to be the primary drivers of economic growth, and *TFP* growth is still an important determinant of economic growth in both developed and developing countries.

17.2.2 Recent Trends in Europe's Output and Productivity Growth Performance at the Sector Level, 2002–2015

Using the most recent EU KLEMS database, van Ark and Jäger (2017) discuss sectoral productivity in Europe. They note that the financial crisis of 2008–9 and the ensuing Euro Area recession of 2011–12 greatly impacted the economic growth of Europe. They also analyzed post-crisis growth rates up to 2015, focusing on 12 European countries which accounted for 90 percent of the EU's nominal GDP in 2015. An important change in the methodology of the current EU KLEMS database involves the measurement of capital stocks and capital services. By using capital stocks by industry and type of asset instead of calculating capital stocks by the perpetual inventory method the updated EU KLEMS database tries to minimize deviations from official capital stock estimates. They first discuss estimates of output and labor productivity growth, which show that EU-12 (The original member states of the European Union when it was established November 1, 1993) experienced a substantial drop in output growth from an average 2 percent per year in 2002–7 to −0.6 percent per year in 2008–10, recovering slightly to a meager 1 percent growth rate per year in 2011–15. Hours worked were the main driver in the output recovery since 2011.

They next decompose growth in output into growth in labor hours, labor composition, ICT capital, non-ICT capital, and total factor productivity on a national level as well as sector levels. Their estimates confirm that the two recessions harmed the growth of total labor hours, especially in the manufacturing sector. Slow employment growth, stagnant capital input growth, and

TFP growth all contributed to the slow recovery of European economies. Capital showed slow growth after the crisis, reflecting weak investment strength. The manufacturing sector lost significant productivity growth and was in decline in terms of output, investment, and labor productivity growth. The services sector recovered faster than the manufacturing sector and by the end of the sample period had recovered to the *TFP* growth rates before the financial crisis. However, by 2015 output and labor productivity growth rates were still only half of the pre-crisis rates in this sector.

When looking at the five largest European economies, Germany was found to have recovered more rapidly from the crisis. The authors argued that this was due to labor market reforms which happened in the early 2000s and to efforts in knitting the manufacturing sector into global value chains, a topic taken up later in the volume by Timmer (2017), which we discuss below. However, Germany still had much lower labor productivity growth compared to its pre-crisis level. By contrast, France experienced much stronger labor productivity growth because of the shrinking share of hours worked in manufacturing. Spain and Italy had the worst drop in manufacturing output growth. In the services sector, the UK had the highest output growth after the crisis (3 percent compared to average 1.6 percent). In the service sector, Germany had much stronger *TFP* growth than France from 2011 to 2015 (1 percent vs. −0.2 percent), again due possibly to the proactive German policies that focused on the integration of global value chains. Spain's and Italy's service sectors recovered much more slowly.

Recall that in our Chapter 4 we discussed the theoretical underpinnings of index number decompositions such as those discussed in this paper and the conditions under which such decompositions are valid for particular index numbers, such as those also used in the paper.

17.2.3   The Role of Capital Accumulation in the Evolution of Total Factor Productivity in Spain

Perez and Benages (2017) focus their attention on Spain's stagnant *TFP* growth in the last three decades and the role of both labor productivity and capital productivity in explaining this pattern of stagnant growth while taking into account the effects of improvements made in the measurements of both of these factor inputs. Decomposing long-term *TFP* growth into the growth of factor inputs, the study finds both stagnant labor productivity growth and declining capital productivity. Even though Spain invested heavily, to the extent that net capital stock per employed person (or capita) has caught up the USA and EU, capital accumulation has not translated into increased labor productivity. This lack of monotonicity between capital investment and productivity is an interesting empirical finding given the role of such monotonicity relationships in identifying the Olley–Pakes class of structural models and related extensions. An implication of this negative relationship is that resources are used less efficiently in Spain. When the authors look at the changes in the composition of labor, they see an improved level of education among the employed. However, labor productivity has not progressed proportionally after accounting for the labor quality improvements and thus there has been deceleration of the growth in the stock of human capital and its capacity to generate value added. Capital productivity has declined by almost 50 percent if they look at the productive capital and capital services, which capture the quality improvements in capital stock and thus account for changes in the capital composition. The capital productivity decline in Spain is the direct consequence of the increase in the productive capital. However, the greatly increased level of productive capacity is not utilized to fully capture the benefits from the improved production factors, and it does not generate the value added commensurate with the level expected. Moreover, the increased capital–output ratio has not improved labor productivity and appears to have further slowed down *TFP* growth. Overall, Perez and Benages (2017) find that capital productivity contributes more to the decline in *TFP* growth than does labor productivity, at least since the 2000s. Output growth, however, does appear to be significant and appears due to the improved quality of labor and capital.

Perez and Benages (2017) empirically test three hypotheses for the causes of capital productivity decline: (1) heavy real estate investment has crowded out investment in other assets that have more weight in productive capital; (2) short-term profitability drives up investments in non-residential real estate assets which turn out to be unproductive; (3) the composition of the producing sector (e.g., weight of large firms, traditional sector and intangibles assets) does not foster capital productivity. Evidence indicates that investment driven by short-term profitability, rather than long-term productivity of assets, harms capital productivity. In terms of the composition of the producing sector, small-sized businesses, which make up the majority of Spanish companies, are not efficient compared to other business sizes. In addition, Spain has a much lower level of intangible assets (6.49 percent) compared to the USA (14.16 percent) and other European countries. The low level of investment in intangible assets in Spain may contribute to the under-utilization of physical capital, which explains the under-utilized capacity and low capital productivity of the Spanish economy.

Perez and Benages (2017) argue that policies to improve *TFP* performance should enhance the interlink between improvements in labor and capital productivity. They note that improved labor quality can contribute to better capital productivity and vice versa and that companies could better allocate human capital to optimize the use of human resources by, for example, assigning leadership positions to those with higher ability. Spanish government and businesses should also reduce misallocation of investments such that labor productivity can be improved.

The use of monotonicity restrictions as an identifying assumption of the Olley–Pakes class of structural models was discussed in part in Chapter 14. Moreover, the differentiation between output-based and input-based inefficiency, referred to above, was discussed at length in Chapter 3. Also, topics of dynamics and sluggish adjustment as a source of productive (technical inefficiency) was presented in Chapter 15.

17.2.4   Sources of Productivity and Economic Growth in Latin America and the Caribbean, 1990–2013

Hofman et al. (2017) study the growth of 23 Latin American and Caribbean countries from 1990 to 2013 using two methods to measure different components of GDP growth. They begin by pointing out that production is a function of factor inputs and the efficiency with which those inputs are used. The authors use efficiency here to mean *TFP* and thus define *TFP* in terms of the standard Solow-residual measure. They begin with the traditional growth accounting decomposition of GDP growth into growth in labor, capital, and *TFP*, where the capital stock is measured at constant prices using the perpetual inventory method and labor is measured as the total number of hours worked. They then modify the labor input by controlling for different education levels and adjusting for their respective rates of return. The capital measure is also adjusted into different asset classes based on the user cost before being aggregated into the capital service index. Results from these two methods show that traditional approaches underestimate the contribution of capital and generate faster *TFP* growth compared to the adjusted method. *TFP* growth becomes negative when labor quality and capital services are accounted for in the input measures. In general, capital plays an important role in the GDP growth process and the increased capital contribution generates higher levels of *TFP*. The increase in the labor contribution has different impacts on *TFP* growth. They also conduct a study focusing on the five largest Latin American countries (Argentina, Brazil, Chile, Colombia, and Mexico) and use the new LA-KLEMS database, which provides more detailed information on the inputs by breaking down the labor factor into hours and quality and the capital factor into ICT and non-ICT capital. It also provides information by sector. Again *TFP* growth is found to be negative in general in this subsample of five countries and nine industries using the more disaggregate approach. Analysis shows that sectoral GDP growth is higher in the tertiary sector (services) than in the primary (agriculture, livestock, and mining) and secondary sectors for all countries except Brazil.

Regarding capital, non-ICT capital is the largest component of the capital contribution. The largest contribution to the growth in total value added is investment in non-ICT capital, which also explains the growth in transport and communications, the fastest-growing industry. Regarding labor, hours worked explained most of the growth of value added. Both labor and *TFP* have procyclical patterns in the contributions to GDP growth. Growth in labor quality has had an unexpected minimal impact on economic growth.

When comparing the five largest Latin American countries with the seven largest developed countries (France, Germany, Italy, Japan, Spain, the United Kingdom, and the United States) from 1995 to 2007, Hofman et al. (2017)

find that, in addition to a wide gap in labor productivity growth between the two groups of countries, the Latin American countries have higher variation in industry productivity than the developed countries used as the benchmark. This can be explained by greater production inefficiencies in some industries.

Based on the empirical evidence presented in the paper, Hofman et al. (2017) argue that macroeconomic policies should be targeted to accomplish three main goals: (1) counter economic downturns by maintaining a level of capacity that sustains labor productivity; (2) improve labor productivity and *TFP* in certain industries, such as removing barriers to production or increasing access to credit for small businesses; and (3) keep tradable industries competitive such that increased productivity can be more likely to be materialized.

Growth accounting and its various decompositions were discussed in Chapters 4 and 15.

17.2.5 Argentina Was Not the Productivity and Economic Growth Champion of Latin America

Coremberg (2017) shows that Argentina's GDP growth was overstated during the Kirchner administration from 2002–15. The Kirchner administration manipulated official data, such as the CPI, to hide inflation. This led to what was believed to have been an upward bias in the reported Argentine real GDP growth rate due to the downward bias in, among other price indices, the CPI used to deflate nominal GDP. The contribution of each detailed industry to the total difference between the INDEC and the INDEK (the indices manipulated by Kirchner's administration) real GDP growth rates between 2007 and 2015 indicates a simple distortion by INDEK in the reported numbers prepared by INDEC, and not methodological bias, was what generated the upward bias in GDP estimates.

Several findings by Coremberg (2017) disprove the statistics shown by the Kirchner administration. First of all, real GDP growth during 2002–15 was lower than during 1990–8 as evidenced by the new INDEC and AR-KLEMS estimates. Further, GDP growth during 2002–15 was 69.1 percent and 76.2 percent by AR-KLEMS and the new INDEC statistics, compared to 97.4 percent by INDEK. The high INDEK estimates make Argentina the country with the second largest GDP growth after Peru, while AR-KLEMS and new INDEC show that Argentina experienced medium GDP growth. Second, the commodities boom accelerated GDP growth during 2002–7 when "Chinese rates" appeared to be GDP growth rates for Argentina. After 2007, Argentina experienced significant GDP growth slowdown, with only 2.2 percent annual growth. Third, Argentina's GDP growth was the lowest among the Latin American countries in 1998–2015, excluding Venezuela. The GDP increase during 1998–2015 was 39.4 percent and 43.9 percent according to the AR-KLEMS and the new INDEC estimates, while it was reported to be 61.2 percent by

INDEK. The low GDP growth is a direct result of the large impact of large economic recession in Latin America during 1998–2002. Argentina suffered the greatest loss from the economic recession, along with Venezuela and Uruguay. The substantial impact of economic shocks on Argentina was largely due to fiscal deficits, large debt ratios and the decision by the Currency Board to let the Argentine peso float. Lastly, GDP growth in Argentina during 2002–15 was the result of factor accumulation, not total factor productivity.

The overestimation of GDP growth by INDEK had a predictable effect of causing an upward-biased *TFP* growth rate since 2007, the year the Kirchner government intervened in falsifying official statistics. The new INDEC and AR-KLEMS estimations show that capital and labor, not *TFP* growth, have contributed greatly to the GDP growth. The low *TFP* growth, thanks to the price boom, was of course not sustainable – in direct opposition to the claims the Kirchner government maintained at the time.

It is clear from this paper, and of our professional engagement in productivity research and research in general, that politics must be taken out of the statistical agencies – data is only as important as the political will to report it. This of course applies not only to the data itself but also to the methods to analyze it.

17.2.6 How Does the Productivity and Economic Growth Performance of China and India Compare in the Post-Reform Era, 1981–2011?

China and India experienced relatively rapid GDP growth from a set of market reforms they began to implement in the 1980s. However, the two countries' relative productivity performances have often been ignored or, it is argued by Wu et al. (2017), incorrectly analyzed in the literature. Wu et al. (2017) conduct a comprehensive study on growth and productivity of the two countries.

To allow for different contributions to aggregate productivity growth by industries, Wu et al. (2017) use an industry-level production function and an aggregate production possibilities frontier (Jorgenson et al., 2005) with Domar (1961) aggregation, in order to parse the contributions of individual industries to aggregate growth and reallocation effects of inputs on total factor productivity growth.

They begin with an industry gross output function

$$y_{it} = f_i(K_{it}, L_{it}, M_{it}, t), \; i = 1, \ldots, n; \; t = 1, \ldots, T, \qquad (17.2.1)$$

where n is the number of industries (27 in each study), y is output, K is capital services, L is labor services, M is intermediate inputs, and t is a time trend to account for technological change. Using the standard assumptions of full utilization of inputs, competitive factor markets, and constant returns to scale, and assuming the production function is translog, the output growth is written as

$$\Delta \ln y_i = \bar{s}_i^K \, \Delta \ln K_i + \bar{s}_i^L \, \Delta \ln L_i + \bar{s}_i^M \, \Delta \ln M_i + T\dot{F}P_i, \qquad (17.2.2)$$

where the time subscript is dropped to maintain notational clarity and $\bar{s}_i^{input}$ is a two-period average of nominal weights of an input where, e.g., $\bar{s}_i^K = \left(\frac{w_{it,K} K_{it}}{p_{it,y} y_{it}} + \frac{w_{i,t+1,K} K_{i,t+1}}{p_{i,t+1,y} y_{i,t+1}} \right) / 2$.

They rewrite the growth of the input by including type-specific, two-period average cost weights. Total labor growth in industry i, for example, can be expressed as a Törnqvist quantity index based on sub-aggregates of different types of labor:

$$\Delta \ln L_i = \sum_h \bar{s}_{hi} \Delta \ln H_{h,i}, \tag{17.2.3}$$

where $\Delta \ln H_{hi}$ is the growth of hours worked by labor type h. The other input factor growth equations can be written in a similar form.

The growth rate in value-added output is then shown to be

$$\Delta \ln y_i = \bar{s}_i^V \Delta \ln V_i + \bar{s}_i^M \Delta \ln M_i, \tag{17.2.4}$$

where s_i^V is the share of value-added (nominal) in the output of industry i, and V_i is real value-added in industry i. The growth in the value-added in an industry can be derived as

$$\Delta \ln V_i = \frac{\bar{s}_i^K}{\bar{s}_i^V} \Delta \ln K_i + \frac{\bar{s}_i^L}{\bar{s}_i^V} \Delta \ln L_i + \frac{1}{\bar{s}_i^V} T\dot{F}P_i. \tag{17.2.5}$$

The growth of aggregate value-added by the aggregate production possibilities frontier is the weighted industry value-added:

$$\Delta \ln V = \sum_i s_{V,i} \Delta \ln V_i, \tag{17.2.6}$$

where $s_{V,i}$ is the ratio of an industry's value-added to aggregate value-added. They combine the two equations for the growth in aggregate and industry value-added and derive an expression for the growth in aggregate value-added in terms of weighted capital growth, labor growth and *TFP* growth. Assuming the same marginal productivity for inputs across all industries, growth in aggregate *TFP* is defined as

$$T\dot{F}P \equiv \sum_i \bar{s}_{V,i} \Delta \ln V_i - \bar{s}^K \Delta \ln K - \bar{s}^L \Delta \ln L. \tag{17.2.7}$$

By allowing inputs to have different marginal productivities among industries, the aggregate *TFP* growth can be traced to the sources of industry-level *TFP* growth. These expressions are given in Wu et al. (2017) and decompose aggregate *TFP* growth into weighted industry *TFP* growth and the effects of reallocation of capital and labor in industries.

The data sets for China are reconstructed using the KLEMS principles. Since the Indian industries were already consistent with the EU KLEMS standard, the Chinese industries are reclassified in line with their Indian counterparts. The industries were then categorized into ten groups and the sample time period divided into four sub-periods accounting for policy regime shifts. Empirical results show that China experienced a 9.4 percent growth in value-added while India only had 6.1 percent growth. However, China's *TFP* growth was 25 percent less than India's over the last three decades. China and India, the two countries which experienced different political shifts and governments, had different growth paths during the sub-periods in which major political and economic reforms took place. China experienced a larger loss in *TFP* growth during the Financial Crisis from 2007 to 2010. When they look at GDP growth in different sectors, they find that manufacturing accounted for 50.3 percent and 22.4 percent in China and India respectively, while services accounted for 29 percent and 56.2 percent respectively. The contributions of the two sectors to the *TFP* growth in India were consistent with their GDP growth. China, however, had an abnormally high contribution by manufacturing and a negative contribution by services, which may be explained by large capital reallocation costs that impacted *TFP* growth and is consistent with the distortions engendered by government intervention in allocating resources and in building up institutional barriers to factor mobility.

We have already mentioned the chapters focusing on index number construction and growth accounting (Chapters 4 and 15), but here our discussion in Chapter 5 of aggregation issues would be particularly relevant for this study to consider.

17.2.7   Can Intangible Investments Ease Declining Rates of Return on Capital in Japan?

The Japanese growth experience since the end of the bubble economy in the 1990s has been well-documented. Contributions of capital to Japanese economic growth have been considerably lower than in the USA and in Asian countries with similar growth paths since the 1990s. Moreover, the real gross rate of return on capital in Japan has been falling since the 1990s, measured by the marginal rate of return and the real rate of return on capital. Miyagawa et al. (2017) study the long-term changes in rates of return on capital from 1985 to 2012 using the Japan Industrial Productivity (JIP) database, which includes 92 industries. Assuming a constant returns to scale Cobb-Douglas production function, they express the marginal rate of return on capital (MRK) as the capital share α divided by the capital/output ratio. Looking at the capital–output ratio and capital share in the market sector, IT industries and non-IT industries, the paper finds variations in rates of return on capital among the industries. This motivates the authors to conduct analysis on rates of return by each industry.

The formal analysis begins by linking the first of their two types of real gross rates of returns on capital (MRK) with a firm-level Cobb–Douglas production function. Assuming cost-minimization – that is, assuming no inefficiency – they can derive the following expression for the return to capital as

$$\ln(\text{MRK}_t) = \ln r_t = const + \alpha w_t + bA_t, \tag{17.2.8}$$

where w_t is the real wage, and A_t is technical progress, or productivity change, as firms and input markets are assumed to be fully efficient. The technological factor is unobservable and assumed to be Hicks neutral. Miyagawa et al. (2017) treat it much as Corrado et al. (2009) treat it – as an intangible factor in production – and use it as a linear measurement equation expressed in terms of logs of capital stocks in software-based information technology (IT), R&D, and human resources (HR), normalized by stocks of tangible assets (in an additional specification they consider interactions among these variables), as well as industry value-added and as industry and time fixed effects. Thus, MRK can be modeled by the real wage rate and innovative factors that improve productivity.

Besides the fixed effect estimation, they also use a GMM estimation to account for endogeneity. For the market sector, their results confirm with one's expectation that the higher the real wage rate the lower the rate of return is. The IT capital stock positively and significantly impacts the rates of return on capital when estimating the model with interactions to address possible complementarities. Interestingly, the R&D capital stock is significantly and negatively related to the real rates of return to capital across most of their model specifications. The HR capital stock is found to have a positive and significant impact on the real wage and there appears to be strong IT/HR complementarities. IT and HR contribute greatly to increased rates of return on tangible capital.

Miyagawa et al. (2017) then examine industry groups divided between IT and non-IT industries and obtain quite comparable results for the IT industries as those from the market sector. An exception is that complementary effects between IT and R&D are all positive and significant. In non-IT industries, IT investment no longer has a stable contribution to a higher profit rate and the coefficient accounting for the interaction between IT and R&D becomes negative and significant. They explain these findings by arguing that many declining industries in non-IT industries have no incentive to invest in IT, which results in the decline in R&D efficiency. One of the important implications of the study is that Japan can improve the rate of return on capital by increasing IT investments in industries with higher accumulated IT stock. Another important finding is that HR investment can substantially improve the rate of return in any industry. Complementary effects are also likely to raise the profit rate when HR capital is involved, suggesting that governments should increase investments in HR as well as other intangibles, especially in IT-intense industries.

Unobserved efficiency effects can be thought of as a placeholder for intangibles and thus our Chapters 12 and 13 have special importance as a vehicle for framing the issues of measuring intangibles in this study. Also, the authors utilize essentially a two-step procedure for identifying the determinants of intangibles and such issues are discussed in depth in Chapters 12 and 14.

17.2.8 Net Investment and Stocks of Human Capital in the United States, 1975–2013

Human capital is an important aspect of measuring long-term productive capacity. It is a strong indicator of a nation's productivity and economic growth. Christian (2017) develops a framework to estimate human capital based on the approach of Jorgenson and Fraumeni (1989, 1992), and further disaggregates human capital by age, sex and education. In addition, the paper also uses a cost-based approach to compare the investment in education from the two approaches.

The income-based approach of Jorgenson and Fraumeni is the most common method to measure human capital. The idea is to use the discounted value of lifetime earnings to calculate the stock of human capital. Average lifetime income is computed among different groups by age, sex, and education at the oldest age at which human capital is supposed to stop accumulating. Then it works backwards. The oldest age is set at 80 in this study. At 80 and older, and assuming an infinite series, Christian (2017, p. 131) specifies lifetime income as

$$i_{y,s,80+,e} = [1 - (1 + \delta)^{-1}(1 + g)sr_{y,s,81+}]^{-1} yi_{y,s,80+,e}, \quad (17.2.9)$$

where

$i_{y,s,a,e}$ = lifetime income in year y of persons of sex s, age a, and years of education e;

$yi_{y,s,a,e}$ = yearly income in year y of persons of sex s, age a, and years of education e;

$sr_{y,s,a}$ = survival rate in year y of persons of sex s from age $a - 1$ to a;

δ = discount rate;

g = income growth rate.

At all other ages, lifetime income is

$$i_{y,s,a,e} = yi_{y,s,a,e} + (1 + \delta)^{-1}(1 + g)sr_{y,s,a+1}$$
$$\times [enr_{y,s,a,e} i_{y,s,a+1,e+1} + (1 - enr_{y,s,a,e}) i_{y,s,a+1,e}],$$
$$(17.2.10)$$

where $enr_{y_{s,a,e}}$ is school enrollment rate of population of sex s, age a, and education e in year y.

To compute lifetime market income, Christian (2017) defines yearly market income as average wage, salary, and self-employment earnings before taxes by each group (age, sex, and education). Yearly non-market income is defined as the average wage after taxes multiplied by the time in household production. The data sets used are the October and March supplements of the Current Population Survey from 1975 to 2014. The stock of human capital at year y then becomes

$$hc_y = \sum_s \sum_a \sum_e (pop_{y,s,a,e} \times i_{y,s,a,e}), \quad (17.2.11)$$

where $pop_{y,s,a,e}$ is the yearly population of different sex and age cohorts with different levels of education. A slight transformation makes it possible to decompose changes in nominal human capital into net investment and revaluation as

$$hc_{y+1} - hc_y = \sum_s \sum_a \sum_e [(pop_{y+1,s,a,e} - pop_{y,s,a,e}) \times i_{y,s,a,e}]$$
$$+ \sum_s \sum_a \sum_e [pop_{y+1,s,a,e} \times (i_{y+1,s,a,e} - i_{y,s,a,e})].$$

$$(17.2.12)$$

The paper shows that the market value of human capital stock has been steadily increasing from 1975–2014 with acceleration during the 1990s. The real human capital stock can be decomposed across the population by age, sex, and education. The total growth in human capital can be decomposed into population change, population change by sex, population change by age within sex, and population change by education within age and sex. Christian (2017) also finds that the main driver of human capital growth from 1975 to 2014 was population growth. The second driver was an improvement in education that has a positive impact on human capital growth. The third important force was an aging population that negatively impacts human capital growth. Overall, growth in the human capital stock did not change significantly due to the cancellation effect between an improved education level and an increased working age in the population.

17.2.9 ICT Services and Their Prices: What Do They Tell Us About Productivity and Technology?

Byrne and Corrado (2017) extend a multi-sector growth model to include purchased ICT services. The framework for two sectors, an ICT sector and a general non-ICT sector is

$$Y = C + I = Y_T + Y_N, \qquad (17.2.13)$$
$$Y_T = C_T + I_T, \qquad (17.2.14)$$
$$Y_N = C_N + I_N, \qquad (17.2.15)$$

where Y is the final demand consisting of consumption and investment, T is the ICT sector, and N is the non-ICT sector. Sectoral production, assuming that only sector N produces for final demand is

$$Q_T \equiv Y_T + M_T^N = A_T f^T(K_N^T, K_T^T, M_T^T, L^T), \qquad (17.2.16)$$
$$Q_N \equiv Y_N = A_N f^N(K_N^N, K_T^N, M_T^N, L^N), \qquad (17.2.17)$$

where A_i is the technology used in the production, K_i^j is sector j's capital input from investment of type $i (i = T, N)$, M_T^j is sector j's use of ICT services, and L is labor. The value of each sector's factor revenue is

$$P_i Q_i = r_N K_N^i + r_T K_T^i + w L^i + p_T M_T^i, i = T, N, \qquad (17.2.18)$$

with factor shares

$$S_{K_T} = \frac{r_T(K_T^T + K_T^N)}{PY}, \tag{17.2.19}$$

$$S_L = \frac{w(L^N + L^T)}{PY}, \tag{17.2.20}$$

$$S_T^N = \frac{p_T M_T^N}{PY}. \tag{17.2.21}$$

Here S_T^N is the share of ICT services purchased by sector N in total income.

Assuming $A_T > A_N$, constant returns, and same input quantities in both sectors, the model shows that relative ICT prices can be a proxy for relative productivity of the sector: $\dot{p} = \frac{\dot{P_L}}{P_N} = A_N - A_T < 0$. A further derivation for the contribution of ICT to the growth in output per hour leads to

$$\frac{S_{K_T} + S_T^N}{S_L}(-\dot{p}) + \frac{p_T Y_T}{PY}(-\dot{p}), \tag{17.2.22}$$

which decomposes the contribution of ICT to output growth into the effect of ICT use and the effect of ICT production. The first term describes use and productivity (diffusion) effect, and the second term is production effect.

Two types of ICT services are considered. The first is ICT-capital intensive. The value of this type of ICT services using quality-adjusted real prices is

$$p^{S_T} M_T^N = \left((\rho + \delta_T)p^{I_T} K_T^T\right)u, \tag{17.2.23}$$

where p^{S_T} is the price of ICT services adjusted for quality, p^{I_T} is the price of ICT investment adjusted for quality, ρ is the real rate of return to investment in the steady-state, δ_T is the constant depreciation rate of ICT capital, and u represents the efficiency of ICT services. The model predicts that the price of ICT services is impacted mostly by real prices of ICT investment or efficiency.

The other type of ICT services is system design service within firms in the non-ICT sector. The model derives the value of this type of ICT services to be

$$r_T^N K_T^N = (\rho + \delta_T)p^{I_T} K_T^N, \tag{17.2.24}$$

where r_T^N is the real rental price of the ICT services. The industry revenues can be derived as

$$p^{S_T} M_T^N = \alpha r_T^N K_T^N(-\dot{u}_N), \tag{17.2.25}$$

where α is the proportional fee producers will pay for system design services, and $\dot{u}_N$ is the proportional improvement in r_T^N that is given. This equation suggests that improvements achieved by providers will increase the value of ICT services relative to ICT capital income.

Byrne and Corrado (2017) show that ICT R&D investment in the USA has been increasing, especially in software products R&D, which has tripled from the late 1980s to 2014. The model's prediction of substantial growth in ICT services, cloud services, and systems design services accounting for GDP is consistent with empirical evidence. The main driver of price change in ICT services is price change in ICT investments. Declines in the ICT investment price in the past four decades has contributed to growth in output per hour significantly given a weak productivity growth in the recent decade.

17.2.10 Productivity Measurement in Global Value Chains

In his paper, Timmer (2017) takes the position that the traditional approaches to measure productivity are becoming less realistic due to the increasing fragmentation of production as firms outsource and offshore production. Traditional approaches require strong assumptions of separability and the use of a properly measured price for intermediate inputs. Specification of a production process that formerly integrates the global value chain (GVCs) provides a feasible improvement in measuring the productivity growth attributable to such a GVC. GVCs are different production stages utilized in order to produce one unit of final good, also including pre- and post-production phases such as R&D, software, design, and logistics. The approach by Timmer (2017) nets out intermediate inputs by focusing on factor inputs only in both the domestic and foreign sectors. The GVC modeling method emphasizes the increasing role of intangible capital and increasingly specialized skill and capital-intensive activities, and thus helps us understand the various stages of production as an integrated production process.

Moving to the technical exposition, we can see that under market clearing condition, the quantities of a product produced in a sector within a country should equal the quantities of this product used home and abroad:

$$y_i(s) = \sum_j f_{ij}(s) + \sum_j \sum_t m_{ij}(s, t), \tag{17.2.26}$$

where $y_i(s)$ is the output produced in country i sector s, $f_{ij}(s)$ is the product from this sector s to be used in any country j (can be home or abroad), and $m_{ij}(s, t)$ is the product from this sector to be used as an intermediate in sector t, country j (can be home or abroad). The market clearing condition in a matrix form is $\mathbf{y} = \mathbf{f} + \mathbf{A}\mathbf{y}$, which becomes the following after rearranging:

$$\mathbf{y} = (\mathbf{I} - \mathbf{A})^{-1}\mathbf{f}, \tag{17.2.27}$$

where A is the $SN \times SN$ global intermediate input coefficients matrix A with elements $a_{ij}(s, t) = \frac{m_{ij}(s,t)}{y_j(t)}$, each element of which measures the ratio of the output from sector s country i used as intermediates by sector t country j to output from sector t country j. The matrix $(I - A)^{-1}$ is the Leontief inverse. The total factor requirements (labor and capital) of a unit of final output are obtained by taking out the intermediates using the Leontief inverse. Define a row vector l containing all country-sector labor per unit of output and a row vector k for capital in a similar way. Then, they derive the total labor and capital requirements as

$$L = \hat{l}(I - A)^{-1} \tag{17.2.28}$$

and

$$K = \hat{k}(I - A)^{-1}, \tag{17.2.29}$$

where $\hat{l}$ and $\hat{k}$ are diagonal matrices. An element (i, j) of L is the labor requirement in sector j to produce one unit of final output in sector i. The same applies to K. This allows one to define the factor cost shares in GVC of a final product using these factor requirements. Gross value added is defined as total value of output minus the cost of intermediates $p(I - A)$, where p is a vector of product's prices for each country-sector. Since capital compensation and labor compensations equal gross value added in this exercise, we have $p(I - A) = w\hat{l} + r\hat{k}$, where w is the vector of hourly wage rates, and r is the vector of rental rates. After some transformations, this identity turns into an equation for the price of a final product:

$$p = wL + rK. \tag{17.2.30}$$

The factor cost shares in a particular product can then be derived, and the country, as well as the sector from which the factor costs incurred, can also be traced.

Productivity growth then can be measured based on the cost shares and quantities above. Define F as a translog production function for a final output j : $f_j = F_j(l_j, k_j, T)$ where l_j, a vector from the matrix L, is total labor requirements to produce good j (similar for k_j), and T is technology. Assuming constant returns to scale, TFP growth in the production of good j can be defined as

$$T\dot{F}P \equiv -s_j^L \frac{d\ln l_j}{dt} - s_j^K \frac{d\ln k_j}{dt}, \tag{17.2.31}$$

where the share weights sum up to the share of labor in the final product j when summed over all sectors and countries, and similarly for capital.

Applying this GVC method to the production of German cars, the paper is able to empirically implement the measures using synthetic input–output tables. It shows different contributions of factors (within Germany and abroad) to final output growth and TFP growth. The GVC method is considered to supplement the traditional KLEMS approach in the way that the GVC bypasses the empirical difficulties (e.g. data on intermediates, services and intangibles) in traditional analysis. The GVC method also has limits in that it does not model the interaction of the prices and quantities of intermediates inputs. However, it is a first attempt to study the complicated characteristics of globally integrated production systems.

Recall that earlier in Chapter 13 we discuss alternatives to the way supply chains can be treated in our discussion of the spatial productivity literature.

17.2.11 These Studies Speak of Efficiency but Measure it with Non-Frontier Methods

More than sixty times, the terms "efficiency," "inefficiency," "efficient," "inefficient," and "frontier" were used in these ten articles, written by leading productivity researchers. Interestingly, there is not one reference given in this collection of papers to any studies in the literature on measuring productivity and efficiency by other leading productivity scholars whose contributions have been discussed at length in this book. This is a literature focused on measuring the efficiency that was defined and operationalized by the giants of our profession: Gerard Debreu (1951), Tjalling Koopmans (1951b), and Michael Farrell (1957). The term "efficiency," and the many terms closely related to it, are instead used in these ten studies to refer either to productivity or some unobserved factor in the performance of the industry or country, but not as a measurable and distinct part of productivity, such as factors like innovation, reallocation, etc. that are mentioned in these studies. We trust that our treatment of this topic in this book will provide researchers and scholars with methods and justifications for viewing such a factor as efficiency as important in its own right – as a concept and measurable factor that is crucial to our understanding of productivity performance – along with other important factors.

17.3 DATASETS FOR ILLUSTRATIONS

The data set we use for illustrations of the software we introduce below is the World Productivity Database (WPD) developed by the United Nations Industrial Development Organization (UNIDO). These data cover a large set of countries across the globe. The data contain various definitions of capital stock and labor input measures. For the detailed definitions and sources of measures in the WPD, refer to Duygun et al. (2017).

Capital input is hard to measure and the WPD provides three different approaches based on various combinations of the initial capital stock: depreciation rates, depreciation schedules, and the lifetime of the asset. They are labeled K06, Ks, and Keff.

Measures of labor input vary depending on the differences in employee numbers and working hours. Employment (EMP) is the first available measure of labor force (LF) and is a direct measure of employment. The second is obtained by applying unemployment rates on LF data, which results in derived employment (DEMP).

The (Y, X) data can be entered in whatever form the modeler wishes, such as levels (for the linear or quadratic), logs (Cobb–Douglas or translog) or square-roots (for the right-hand-side variables this is done for the generalized Leontief).

We adopted the approach taken by Hulten and Isaksson (2007), who divided all 112 countries in the WPD into six mutually exclusive groups, in accordance with the World Bank classification by income per capita. The groups we considered are the group of Low Income countries (hereinafter LOW), the group of Lower-Middle Income countries (hereinafter LOW-MID), the group of Upper-Middle Income countries (hereinafter UPPER-MID), the group of High-Income countries (hereinafter HIGH), four Old Tigers (the original Asian Four Tigers) and five New Tigers.

As a result of limitations in the availability of data, we used EMP as labor input. K06, Ks, and Keff are the different capital input measures. Thus, every country group contains three input combinations.

17.4   PUBLICLY AVAILABLE DATA SETS USEFUL FOR PRODUCTIVITY ANALYSIS

Below we provide information about a number of other data sets that productivity researchers have used and which are generally publicly available. The list is not exhaustive.

17.4.1   Amadeus

Run by the Bureau van Dijk, a publisher of business information, the Amadeus data set contains information on 21 million European companies. The firm level data provided in Amadeus allows for firm comparisons across nations. Amadeus offers information on the typical information on company financials as well information such as financial strength indicators and outlines of the corporate structure.

www.bvdinfo.com/en-gb/our-products/company-information/international-products/amadeus

17.4.2   Bureau of Economic Analysis

The US Bureau of Economic Analysis (BEA) offers a variety of public use data sets including industry specific data that includes input–output accounts, capital flow, and industry level production accounts. International data is also available through the BEA, and includes information on balance of payments, trade, international services, and international investment.

www.bea.gov/industry/index.htm
www.bea.gov/international/index.htm

17.4.3   Bureau of Labor Statistics

The Bureau of Labor Statistics (BLS) is the statistical and data gathering arm of the US Department of Labor. Its data archives include detailed information on a wide array of economic indicators including inflation and prices, employment, and productivity.

www.bls.gov/data/

17.4.4   Business Dynamics Statistics

Available through the Census Bureau, the Business Dynamics Statistics (BDS) database is publicly available and contains information "aggregated by establishment and firm characteristics." Among the key variables in the data are employment, job expansions, number of establishments, establishment openings and closing, and number of startups and firm shutdowns. The BDS is constructed using the Longitudinal Business Database (LBD), a confidential database also maintained by the US Census Bureau.

www.census.gov/ces/dataproducts/bds/data.html

17.4.5   Center for Economic Studies

Data come from the US Department of Commerce's Economic Census of establishments as well as surveys on establishments and firms. Access to the data at the establishment level is restricted and must be conducted at one of the secure Federal Statistical Research Data Centers.

www.census.gov/ces/rdcresearch/index.html

17.4.6   CompNet

CompNet maintains a firm-level database that links the firm characteristics with productivity. The database includes American companies as well as companies from a number of European countries. CompNet contains variables on "employment, trade, mark-ups, financial constraints," as well as precomputed measures of productivity.

www.comp-net.org/data/

17.4.7   DIW Berlin

The Deutsches Institut für Wirtschaftsforschung (DIW) houses two firm-level databases for researchers. AFiD is the primary database maintained by DIW Berlin; it contains official firm level longitudinal data for German companies. DIW Berlin also maintains the CAMPUS files, an anonymized database intended for teaching purposes.

www.forschungsdatenzentrum.de/en/data_supply.asp

17.4.8   Longitudinal Business Database

The Longitudinal Business Database (LBD) is a restricted use database maintained by the US Census Bureau. Unlike the BDS, the LBD offers longitudinal data at the firm level. Due to the sensitivity of the data, the LBD can only be accessed by approved researchers in Federal Statistical Research Data centers. The LBD contains data on "all industries and all states."

www.census.gov/ces/dataproducts/datasets/lbd.html

17.4.9   National Bureau of Economic Research

The National Bureau of Economic Research (NBER)'s data archives that facilitate productivity research reflect the programmatic initiatives it has promoted through several of its research programs, specifically those in Industrial

Organization, International Finance and Macroeconomics, International Trade and Investment, Labor Studies, and Productivity.

www.nber.org/data/

17.4.10 OECD

The OECD provides detailed economic data for its 35 member countries, as well as for countries like China, India and Brazil. The OECD data has both country- and sector-specific information, including output levels, prices, and employment activity.

https://data.oecd.org/

17.4.11 OECD STAN

The OECD Structural Analysis Database (STAN) includes data on output, labor input, investment, and capital from 1970 to 2015 for 25 OECD countries. Data is organized by industry and is primarily gathered using OECD member countries' national accounts data.

www.oecd.org/sti/ind/stanstructuralanalysisdatabase.htm

17.4.12 Penn World Table

Now in its ninth iteration, the Penn World Table is a vast collection of country-level data that includes information on "relative levels of income, output, input and productivity." Commonly used in productivity studies, the tables go back as far as 1950 and currently cover 182 countries. The Penn World Table is built on national accounts data and price surveys conducted by the International Comparison Program. While many databases use exchange rates to compare countries, the Penn World Table is notable for its use of purchasing power parity for measures of wealth like such as GDP per capita.

www.rug.nl/ggdc/productivity/pwt/

17.4.13 Statistics Canada

Statistics Canada uses Canadian census data and 350 active surveys to provide information on a wide array of Canadian economic activities. Sector-specific data is broken down into about 30 different categories and economic accounts data are provided in detailed formats that include measures of productivity.

http://www.statcan.gc.ca/

17.4.14 UK Fame

Like Amadeus, Fame is maintained by the Bureau Van Dijk and offers a wide variety of information on companies located in the United Kingdom and Ireland. Fame currently has information on 9 million companies, with 2 million in detailed format and 220,000 in a summary format.

https://fame.bvdinfo.com/version-201761/Home.serv?product=fameneo

17.4.15 UK Office of National Statistics

The Office of National Statistics publishes time series data for general economic indicators in the United Kingdom. With measures of sector specific trade, employment and output and productivity, the office of national statistics is a valuable resource for UK-related information.

`www.ons.gov.uk/employmentandlabourmarket/peopleinwork/`
`labourproductivity/datalist?filter=datasets`

17.4.16 UNIDO

The United Nations Industrial Development Organization (UNIDO) maintains databases at different levels of industry aggregation. The INDSTAT2 is organized at the two-digit ISIC level (23 industries) and contains time-series data from 1963 to the present day. UNIDO also hosts the INDSTAT4, which is organized at the three- and four-digit ISIC level and features data on 150 manufacturing categories and dates back to 1990. Both of the databases offer insights into the changes of economies over time.

`www.unido.org/resources/statistics/statistical-data`
`bases.html`

17.4.17 USDA-ERS

The United States Department of Agriculture publishes data on American agricultural productivity. The data set includes information on the adoption of advanced techniques, trade, sales, research funding, productivity measures, and various other statistics.

`www.ers.usda.gov/data-products/`

17.4.18 World Bank

The World Bank provides a wide variety of publicly available economic data on a vast set of countries. In addition to its macro-level data, the World Bank also offers the Micro-data Library which "facilitates access to micro-data collected through sample surveys of households, business establishments or other facilities." Though most of the data is available publicly, some may be subject to restrictions. Data is available either directly through the World Bank website, or through the accompanying API.

`http://data.worldbank.org/`

17.4.19 World Input–Output Database

The World Input–Output Database (WIOD) provide input–output data for 28 EU countries and 15 other major national economies. The data currently spans the period from 2000 to 2014. As of December 2017, WIOD began to publish a Socio-Economic Accounts data set.

`www.wiod.org/database/seas16`

Table 17.1 *Models included in the software.*

Estimator	Reference
FIX, RND	Schmidt and Sickles (1984)
HT	Hausman and Taylor (1981)
CSSW, CSSG, CSSI	Cornwell et al. (1990)
BC	Battese and Coelli (1992)
PSS1	Park et al. (1998)
PSS2W, PSS2G	Park et al. (2003)
PSS3	Park et al. (2007)
KSS	Kneip et al. (2012)
BIE	Almanidis et al. (2014)
JS	Jeon and Sickles (2004)
SZL	Simar and Zelenyuk (2006)
SZB	Simar and Zelenyuk (2007)

17.4.20 World KLEMS Database

Comprised of "output, inputs and productivity" data at the industry level, the World KLEMS database was constructed specifically for growth and productivity studies. The World KLEMS initiative sets standards by which productivity data is collected so that figures are comparable across countries. This includes setting "input definitions, price concepts, aggregation procedures and comparable measures of inputs and productivity."

www.worldklems.net/data.htm

17.5 PRODUCTIVITY AND EFFICIENCY SOFTWARE

We next describe the programs to implement the various models discussed in the previous chapters and the way to set up programs that can be accessed via the publicly available software website found at https://sites.google .com/site/productivityefficiency/.[2] The models introduced below are coded in MATLAB and R. The provided code estimates various efficiency measures using panel data. The programs are for academic uses only and users of the programs should cite this book. Provided codes are for the models listed in Table 17.1.

Let n be the number of firms, T the number of time series and nT the total number of observations, i.e., nT. Input data are configured as follows: y is an $nT \times 1$ column vector of dependent variable and x' is an $nT \times k$ vector of explanatory variables. The first T observations are for the first cross-section, the second T observations are for the second cross-section and so on.

---

[2] This section summarizes the software available to estimate a number of the productivity models discussed in this book that are available on the software website maintained by Dr. Wonho Song of the School of Economics, Chung-Ang University, Seoul, South Korea.

The following results are printed as outputs: Parameter estimates, standard errors, t-values, average technical efficiency, correlation of effects and efficiencies, Spearman rank order correlation of effects and efficiencies, R-squared and adjusted R-squared; "results.out" is the default output filename.

17.6 GLOBAL OPTIONS

This section explains options that apply to more than one estimator in the software.

17.6.1 Model Setup

- Basic model is a linear panel data model with the following form:

$$y_{it} = \alpha + x'_{it}\beta - u_{it} + v_{it}. \tag{17.6.1}$$

  Here, we note that global mean (α) is subtracted in the regression. This demeaning method is applied to FIX, RND, HT, CSS and BC estimators.
- Note that the codes do not allow missing observations or unbalanced panels.
- If tmtr=1, a time trend is included in the regression and if tmtr=2, a time trend and a time trend squared are included in the regression. The first (or first two when tmtr=2) coefficient of FIX, RND, HT, PSS1,2,3, and BC is the one for the time trend. This option does not apply to time-varying effects estimators such as CSS and KSS which flexibly estimate individual effects.
- k1 is the number of variables in X that are not correlated with individual effects. Uncorrelated variables come first in the data set. This option applies to HT, CSSI and PSS1 estimators.

17.6.2 Weighted Averages of Efficiencies

We consider three weighting schemes. Weighting options are as follows: AVE=0 is equal weights (simple average), AVE=1 is AIC-based weights and AVE=2 is BIC-based weights where:

- Equal weights:

$$w_i = \frac{1}{n},$$

- AIC-weights:

$$w_i = \frac{\exp(-AIC_i)}{\sum_{i=1}^{n} \exp(-AIC_i)},$$

- BIC-weights:

$$w_i = \frac{\exp(-BIC_i)}{\sum_{i=1}^{n} \exp(-BIC_i)}.$$

17.6.3   Truncation

In calculating efficiency from the estimated individual effects, there may be outliers which may affect the efficiency measures substantially. Thus, to calculate efficiency scores, estimated effects may be trimmed at the upper and bottom 5 percent level (see Berger, 1993). This does not apply to the BC or DEA estimators.

The method of truncation of the estimated effects is a little complicated. For the time–invariant estimators such as FIX or RND, this method is obvious because we may just delete individuals whose effects are in the upper and bottom 5 percent range of estimated effects. For the time-varying estimators such as CSS or KSS, it is not obvious because an individual's effects may stay in the upper and bottom 5 percent range only for a few periods. In this case, there may exist various ways to delete individuals whose effects are in the upper and bottom of 5 percent range and the method adopted here is as follows.

For example, if we trim by 10 percent then we find the firms whose effects are included in the upper and bottom 5 percent range "at least in one period." Then we exclude these firms from the calculation of efficiency. Thus, practically, we are deleting more than $10(= 5 + 5)\%$ of firms from the calculation. Also, note that the total number of deleted firms varies depending on estimators. In this sense, careful attention should be paid when we compare the efficiencies from the BC estimators with those from the CSS or KSS estimators. trunc1 is for the FIX, RND, HT, PSS, CSS, KSS, and BIE estimators and trunc2 is for the BC and DEA estimators. For example, trunc1=0.05 means that individuals whose effects are in the upper and bottom 5 percent range are excluded in the calculation of efficiency. Pearson and Spearman's rank correlations of effects and efficiencies from the various estimators are calculated only when both trunc1=0 and trunc2=0 are set.

17.6.4   Figures and Tables

The software provides a few options for figures and tables. Select the value 1 to print and 0 to skip the results. For figures, fig1=1 shows the average of efficiencies from the time-variant estimators, fig2=1 all the efficiencies from the time-variant estimators, fig3=1 average of efficiencies from all the time-variant/invariant estimators and fig4=1 weighted average of all the efficiencies. For tables, tab1=1 shows the average of efficiencies from the time-variant estimators, tab2=1 efficiencies from the time-variant estimators and tab3=1 individual effects from all the effects estimators. If firmeff=1, efficiencies of each individual are saved in the file Vxxx.mat where xxx is the name of the estimator. For example, VFIX.mat contains the estimated efficiencies from the FIX estimator.

17.7   MODELS

17.7.1   Schmidt and Sickles (1984) Models

The FR option determines the Schmidt and Sickles (1984) models. FR=1 prints only the results of fixed effects estimator (FIX) and FR=2 displays both the results of fixed and random effects estimators (FIX and RND). R2_choice option determines R-squared results. R2_choice=1 prints Within R-squared, R2_choice=2 Between R-squared and R2_choice=3 Overall R-squared. Estimates of random effects estimator slightly vary depending on the methods used to estimate the variance components. Three different methods are used: Greene's (2002), STATA, and Baltagi's (1995) methods. The software chooses Baltagi's method as default because we can replicate the random effects results using the CSSG estimator with constant effects only, not including time and time-squared. If FR=2, the *p*-value of the Hausman–Wu test statistic is printed.

17.7.2   Hausman and Taylor (1981) Model

The HT option determines the Hausman and Taylor (1981) model. HT=1 prints the results and HT=0 skips the results. The HT estimator allows for correlations between regressors and individual effects. k1 is the number of variables in X that are not correlated with the individual effects and uncorrelated variables come first in the data set.

17.7.3   Park, Sickles, and Simar (1998, 2003, 2007) Models

The PSS1, PSS2, and PSS3 options determine the Park et al. (1998, 2003, 2007) models, respectively. The value of 1 prints the results and 0 skips the results. We find the optimal bandwidth by a data-driven method based on a bootstrap algorithm for a selected grid. NB is the number of bootstrap repetition, gr_st the starting point of the grid search, gr_in the increment of the grid search, and gr_en the end point of grid search. If pss_out=1, we print the bootstrap MSEs for the selected grid. For the PSS1 estimator, k1 is the number of variables in X that are not correlated with the individual effects and uncorrelated variables come first in the data set. Note that the PSS3 estimator does not currently support the model with multiple outputs.

17.7.4   Cornwell, Schmidt, and Sickles (1990) Model

The CSS option determines the Cornwell et al. (1990) models. CSS=1 prints the results of Within (CSSW) estimator, CSS=2 the results of Within and GLS (CSSG) estimators, CSS=3 the results of Within and Efficient IV (CSSI) estimator, and CSS=4 the results of Within, GLS and Efficient IV estimators.

CSS estimators allow time-invariant variables in X and time-invariant variables should be placed at the end of X. zp is the number of time-invariant variables. As in the HT estimator, k1 is the number of time-varying variables in X that are not correlated with individual effects and uncorrelated variables come first in the data set. Similarly, j1 is the number of time-invariant variables in X that are not correlated with individual effects and uncorrelated variables come first.

17.7.5   Kneip, Sickles, and Song (2012) Model

The KSS option determines the Kneip et al. (2012) model. KSS=1 prints the results and KSS=0 skips the results. The KSS estimator needs to find the optimal number of factors. We vary the number of factors from L_{max} to L_{min} and find the first highest number at which the dimensionality test is not rejected. We find the optimal smoothing parameter by the leave-one-out cross-validation for a selected grid. gr_st is the starting point of the grid search, gr_in the increment of grid search, and gr_en the end point of the grid search.

17.7.6   Battese and Coelli (1992) Model

The BC option determines the Battese and Coelli (1992) model. This model permits only same shape of efficiencies for all the firms. For the BC estimator, the log-likelihood value is provided instead of R-squared.

17.7.7   Almanidis, Qian, and Sickles (2014) Model

The BIE option determines the Bounded Inefficiency Model of Almanidis et al. (2014). We choose options for distribution by bie_dist; bie_dist=0 select truncated exponential, bie_dist=1 truncated half normal, and bie_dist=2 doubly truncated normal distributions.

17.7.8   Jeon and Sickles (2004) Model

The JS option determines the Jeon and Sickles (2004) model. This model uses the directional distance function method to analyze productivity growth. It enables us to explicitly examine the effects of undesirable outputs, such as carbon dioxide and other greenhouse gases, on the frontier production process. The production frontier is specified as a piecewise linear and convex boundary function. The variables are y for desirable outputs, b for undesirable outputs and p for inputs. The printed outputs are productivity growth, efficiency change (catching up) and technology change (innovation). The statistical significance of the estimates is calculated using the bootstrap methods. The OECD dataset is provided as an illustration.

17.7.9   Simar and Zelenyuk (2006) Model

This program performs the Li (1996b) test in the context of comparing distributions of efficiency estimated via DEA. LiTestDEA_example.m is the example file which tells us how to use the programs in the package. It provides an example where the Li (1996b) test statistic and corresponding *p*-values are calculated. The example uses the data from Kumar and Russell (2002) which has two inputs and one output. The function `Li_1996_test.m` computes the Li statistic, the function `Silv_h_Robust.m` computes the bandwidth, and the bootstrap loops are performed by the function `Li_Test_Naive_Boot.m`. For moderate dimensions of the DEA model relative to the sample size, the Li (1996b) test, adapted via Algorithm II, which smooths boundary estimates by adding uniform noise of order of magnitude less than the order of magnitude of noise added by the DEA estimator, is a reliable tool for testing the equality of distributions of unknown but DEA-estimated efficiency scores.

17.7.10 Simar and Zelenyuk (2007) Model

The program provides a way of constructing reliable confidence intervals and bias corrections for the DEA-estimated aggregate efficiencies of a group and also its two subgroups, as well as propose an appropriate test for comparison of such aggregate efficiencies.

The main program file is `DEA_SubSmpl2smplGWHet_Sh_J_CndX.m`. It calls all other files and produces final results. In particular, it calls `eff = deasel.m` for estimation of DEA individual efficiencies and `DEA_SubSampl_Ag_2_Smpl.m` for bootstrapping (subsampling) of aggregate efficiencies and RD statistic, which in turn calls `resample.m` for subsampling, `deaXNewYNew.m` for DEA reestimation with bootstrapped data and `P_indep_weights.m` for computation of price-independent weights (can be modified to compute other weights) using the bootstrapped data. For solving a linear programming problem, we use the MATLAB function `lp.m` (Copyright (c) 1990–98 by The MathWorks, Inc.). There is a newer version (linprog.m) but it is slower. Densities are estimated using bandwidth due to Sheather and Jones (1991), by calling `Sh_J_Run.m` which in turn calls `Sheth_Jones_h.m`.

X is an $n \times p$ matrix of input(s) and Y an $n \times k$ matrix of output(s). The option `ori='I'` is for input orientation, `ori='O'` for output orientation, `rts='NIRS'` for nonincreasing returns to scale (rts), `rts='NDRS'` for nondecreasing rts, `rts='CRS'` for constant rts, `'VRS'` for variable rts, `prdl='P'` for primal approach and `prdl='D'` for dual approach.

Three example files, `Sim_Ex_1.m`, `Sim_Ex_2.m`, and `Sim_Ex_3.m`, generate the simulated data sets that are used in the paper. These datasets are loaded, one at a time, by the main program. All examples involve data generated from the truncated normal distribution using `TruncNormGenerator.m`. The main file also produces figures that are saved as `Figure1.fig`, `Figure2.fig`, `Figure3.fig`, and `Figure4.fig` where the numbers correspond to the number of figures in the paper. All the final results of bootstrapping (subsampling) from the main file for each example, respectively, are saved in

Ex1_BS_Agg_ppr.mat, Ex2_BS_Agg_ppr.mat, and Ex3_BS_Agg_ppr. mat, where the numbers correspond to the number of examples in the paper.

17.8 CONCLUDING REMARKS

This chapter has provided a more focused treatment of data resources and available software for productivity and efficiency researchers and analysts. We have detailed some of the many empirical studies recently completed using one such data set developed by the World KLEMS Project in order to give the reader some idea of the remarkably fertile insights and approaches that can be generated from such data. The many other data sets that we have briefly discussed are publicly available and the software platforms of MATLAB and R are easily accessed via university, government, or private sector business licenses or are freeware. We hope that a discussion of one of the more high profile data sets from the World KLEMS project, and the many varied questions that researchers using it have addressed in the papers we reviewed at the outset of this chapter, will give readers insights and perspectives on how to pursue similar or extended or completely novel studies using not only the KLEMS data but the many other data sources we have documented.

Afterword

The economic performance of firms and the economic growth of countries have never been more important than in this historical epoch, both in terms of how labor services are being replaced with capital services and artificial intelligence algorithms and how the divergence in compensation to labor and capital services appears to be increasing. The outcome of such a dynamic has not only economic implications but also serious political repercussions, especially in our increasingly globalized and interconnected world.

If effective public policies can be formulated to address the many aspects of economic growth that impact individual welfare, they will be based on the methods and analyses we have detailed in this textbook as well as in the further developments of these methods and analyses as the science of productivity and efficiency measurement continues to advance. Public policies that address income growth and income inequality will need to be economically as well as politically sustainable. This means that they will need to take advantage of market mechanisms and the compatible incentives that drive the functioning and operation of competitive markets. Decision-makers will need to recognize that, for a variety of reasons, firms may not be forced by market mechanisms to make decisions on economic allocations that are optimal relative to standard economic definitions of optimizing behaviors. Whether this is due to long-standing market failures, protected market niches, institutional or other external constraints is not as important as the need for optimizing behaviors to be tested as the alternative hypothesis, not stated as the null hypothesis when conducting economic research. Researchers and scholars will need to understand how the economic well-being of individuals and the wealth of nations evolve and devolve. Practitioners will need to be able to implement methods that allow them to construct the economic measures that tell them if there is an improvement in economic well-being. As with any meaningful empirical measurement of an important public phenomenon such as growth in per capita income levels or growth in a country's income and the distribution of this growth among economic agents, public resources will need to be brought to bear to make accurate measurement possible and transparent.

This textbook provides a coherent treatment on the topic of productivity and efficiency. Measurement cannot rest on an edifice of theoretical rigor that focuses on logical consistency but lacks a firm foundation based on realistic assumptions. We feel that this textbook has provided a balanced perspective on such assumptions.

We hope that this textbook has succeeded in its purpose – to provide students, scholars, and practitioners with a cohesive and integrated source to study the vast area of productivity and efficiency, its theoretical basis, and the various methods that can be utilized to measure it.

Following common tradition, our original plan was to have a Conclusion chapter at this point. However, we realized that after a decade of writing and constantly updating the draft of this book, the ideas in our book cannot possibly be regarded as formal conclusions on a topic as dynamic and ever-changing as the theory and measurement of productivity and efficiency. Instead of concluding we have tried to provide the most comprehensive textbook-style foundation for the new and outstanding research by the contributors to this rather vast literature. So let us not conclude, but rather continue.

Bibliography

Abraham, K. G., Greenlees, J. S., and Moulton, B. R. (1998). Working to improve the consumer price index. *The Journal of Economic Perspectives*, 12(1):27–36.

Abramovitz, M. (1986). Catching up, forging ahead, and falling behind. *The Journal of Economic History*, 46(2):385–406.

Acemoglu, D. (2002). Technical change, inequality, and the labor market. *Journal of Economic Literature*, 40(1):7–72.

Acemoglu, D., Carvalho, V. M., Ozdaglar, A., and Tahbaz-Salehi, A. (2012). The network origins of aggregate fluctuations. *Econometrica*, 80(5):1977–2016.

Ackerberg, D., Benkard, C. L., Berry, S., and Pakes, A. (2007). Econometric tools for analyzing market outcomes. In Heckman, J. J. and Leamer, E. E., editors, *Handbook of Econometrics*, volume 6, chapter 36. Amsterdam: Elsevier, 1st edition.

Ackerberg, D., Caves, K., and Frazer, G. (2006). Structural identification of production functions. Working Paper No. 38349, Munich: MPRA.

Ackerberg, D. A., Caves, K., and Frazer, G. (2015). Identification properties of recent production function estimators. *Econometrica*, 83(6):2411–2451.

Aczél, J. and Dhombres, J. (1989). *Functional Equations in Several Variables*. New York, NY: Cambridge University Press.

Adams, R. M., Berger, A. N., and Sickles, R. C. (1997). Computation and inference in semiparametric efficient estimation. In Amman, H., Rustem, B., and Whinston, A., editors, *Computational Approaches to Economic Problems, Advances in Computational Economics*, pages 57–70. Boston, MA: Kluwer Academic Publishers.

Adams, R. M., Berger, A. N., and Sickles, R. C. (1999). Semiparametric approaches to stochastic panel frontiers with applications in the banking industry. *Journal of Business and Economic Statistics*, 17(3):349–358.

Adams, R. M. and Sickles, R. C. (2007). Semiparametric efficient distribution free estimation of panel models. *Communications in Statistics–Theory and Methods*, 36(13):2425–2442.

Afriat, S. N. (1972). Efficiency estimation of production functions. *International Economic Review*, 13(3):568–598.

Ahn, S. C., Good, D., and Sickles, R. C. (2000). Estimation of long-run inefficiency levels: A dynamic frontier approach. *Econometric Reviews*, 19(4):461–492.

Ahn, S. C., Lee, Y. H., and Schmidt, P. (2001). GMM estimation of linear panel data models with time-varying individual effects. *Journal of Econometrics*, 101(2):219–255.

Ahn, S. C., Lee, Y. H., and Schmidt, P. (2007). Stochastic frontier models with multiple time-varying individual effects. *Journal of Productivity Analysis*, 27(1):1–12.

Ahn, S. C., Lee, Y. H., and Schmidt, P. (2013). Panel data models with multiple time-varying individual effects. *Journal of Econometrics*, 174(1):1–14.

Ahn, S. C. and Schmidt, P. (1995). Efficient estimation of models for dynamic panel data. *Journal of Econometrics*, 68(1):5–27.

Ahn, S. C. and Schmidt, P. (1997). Efficient estimation of dynamic panel data models: Alternative assumptions and simplified estimation. *Journal of Econometrics*, 76(1):309–321.

Aigner, D., Lovell, C., and Schmidt, P. (1977). Formulation and estimation of stochastic frontier production function models. *Journal of Econometrics*, 6(1):21–37.

Aigner, D. J., Amemiya, T., and Poirier, D. J. (1976). On the estimation of production frontiers. *International Economic Review*, 17(2):377–396.

Aigner, D. J. and Chu, S.-F. (1968). On estimating the industry production function. *American Economic Review*, 58(4):826–839.

Aıt-Sahalia, Y. and Duarte, J. (2003). Nonparametric option pricing under shape restrictions. *Journal of Econometrics*, 116(1):9–47.

Aitchison, J. and Aitken, C. G. G. (1976). Multivariate binary discrimination by the kernel method. *Biometrika*, 63(3):413–420.

Akaike, H. (1973). Information theory and an extension of the maximum likelihood principle. In *2nd International Symposium Information Theory*, pages 267–281. Budapest: Akademiai Kiadó.

Alam, I. M. S. (2001). A nonparametric approach for assessing productivity dynamics of large US banks. *Journal of Money, Credit and Banking*, 33(1):121–139.

Alam, I. M. S. and Sickles, R. C. (2000). Time series analysis of deregulatory dynamics and technical efficiency: The case of the US airline industry. *International Economic Review*, 41(1):203–218.

Allais, M. (1943). *Traitè D'Èconomie Pure*, volume 3. Paris: Imprimerie Nationale.

Allen, R., Athanassopoulos, A., Dyson, R. G., and Thanassoulis, E. (1997). Weights restrictions and value judgements in data envelopment analysis: Evolution, development and future directions. *Annals of Operations Research*, 73:13–34.

Allen, R. G. D. (1938). *Mathematical Analysis for Economists*, London: Macmillan and Co. Ltd, 1–571.

Almanidis, P., Karagiannis, G., and Sickles, R. C. (2015). Semi-nonparametric spline modifications to the Cornwell–Schmidt–Sickles estimator: An analysis of US banking productivity. *Empirical Economics*, 48(1):169–191.

Almanidis, P., Qian, J., and Sickles, R. C. (2014). Stochastic frontier with bounded inefficiency. In Sickles, R. C. and Horrace, W. C., editors, *Festschrift in Honor of Peter Schmidt: Econometric Methods and Applications*, pages 47–82. New York, NY: Springer.

Almanidis, P. and Sickles, R. C. (2012). The skewness problem in stochastic frontier models: Fact or fiction? In Van Keilegom, I. and Wilson, P. W., editors, *Exploring Research Frontiers in Contemporary Statistics and Econometrics: A Festschrift in Honor of Léopold Simar*, pages 201–227. New York, NY: Springer.

Alvarez, A., Amsler, C., Orea, L., and Schmidt, P. (2006). Interpreting and testing the scaling property in models where inefficiency depends on firm characteristics. *Journal of Productivity Analysis*, 25(3):201–212.

Amsler, C., O'Donnell, C. J., and Schmidt, P. (2017a). Stochastic metafrontiers. *Econometric Reviews*, 36(6–9):1007–1020.

Amsler, C., Prokhorov, A., and Schmidt, P. (2014). Using copulas to model time dependence in stochastic frontier models. *Economic Reviews*, 33(5–6):497–522.

Amsler, C., Prokhorov, A., and Schmidt, P. (2016). Endogeneity in stochastic frontier models. *Journal of Econometrics*, 190(2):280–288.

Amsler, C., Prokhorov, A., and Schmidt, P. (2017b). Endogenous environmental variables in stochastic frontier models. *Journal of Econometrics*, 199(2):131–140.

Amsler, C. and Schmidt, P. (2017). Distinguishing heterogeneity and inefficiency in a panel data stochastic frontier model. Unpublished manuscript, East Lansing, MI:: Michigan State University.

Anderson, N. H., Hall, P., and Titterington, D. M. (1994). Two-sample test statistics for measuring discrepancies between two multivariate probability density functions using kernel-based density estimates. *Journal of Multivariate Analysis*, 50(1): 41–54.

Anderson, T. W. and Hsiao, C. (1981). Estimation of dynamic models with error components. *Journal of the American Statistical Association*, 76(375):598–606.

Andrews, D., Criscuolo, C., and Gal, P. N. (2015). Frontier firms, technology diffusion and public policy: Micro evidence from OECD countries. Technical report, The Future of Productivity: Main Background Papers. Paris: OECD.

Antras, P. (2004). Is the US aggregate production function Cobb–Douglas? New estimates of the elasticity of substitution. *Contributions to Macroeconomics*, 4(1):1–34. Article 4.

Appelbaum, E. (1979). On the choice of functional forms. *International Economic Review*, 20(2):449–458.

Aquino-Chávez, J. and Ramírez-Rondán, N. R. (2017). Estimating factor shares from nonstationary panel data. Working Paper No. 89. Lima: Peruvian Economic Association.

Arellano, M. and Bond, S. (1991). Some tests of specification for panel data: Monte Carlo evidence and an application to employment equations. *Review of Economic Studies*, 58(2):277–297.

Arrow, K. J. (1962). The economic implications of learning by doing. *Review of Economic Studies*, 29(3):155–173.

Arrow, K. J., Chenery, H. B., Minhas, B. S., and Solow, R. M. (1961). Capital-labor substitution and economic efficiency. *Review of Economics and Statistics*, 43(3):225–250.

Ashley, R. A. and Parmeter, C. F. (2015). Sensitivity analysis for inference in 2SLS/GMM estimation with possibly flawed instruments. *Empirical Economics*, 49(4):1153–1171.

Atalla, T. and Bean, P. (2017). Determinants of energy productivity in 39 countries: An empirical investigation. *Energy Economics*, 62:217–229.

Atanackovic, T. N. and Guran, A. (2000). *Theory of Elasticity for Scientists and Engineers*. New York, NY: Springer.

Atici, K. B. and Podinovski, V. V. (2015). Using data envelopment analysis for the assessment of technical efficiency of units with different specialisations: An application to agriculture. *Omega*, 54:72–83.

Atkinson, S. E. and Tsionas, M. G. (2016). Directional distance functions: Optimal endogenous directions. *Journal of Econometrics*, 190(2):301–314.

Aw, B. Y., Chen, X., and Roberts, M. J. (2001). Firm-level evidence on productivity differentials and turnover in Taiwanese manufacturing. *Journal of Development Economics*, 66(1):51–86.

Azzalini, A. (1985). A class of distributions which includes the normal ones. *Scandinavian Journal of Statistics*, 12(2):171–178.

Azzalini, A. (2013). *The Skew-Normal and Related Families*, volume 3. New York, NY: Cambridge University Press.

Bada, O. and Liebl, D. (2014). The R-package phtt: Panel data analysis with heterogeneous time trends. *Journal of Statistical Software*, 59(6):1–33.

Bădin, L., Daraio, C., and Simar, L. (2010). Optimal bandwidth selection for conditional efficiency measures: A data-driven approach. *European Journal of Operational Research*, 201(2):633–640.

Bădin, L., Daraio, C., and Simar, L. (2012). How to measure the impact of environmental factors in a nonparametric production model. *European Journal of Operational Research*, 223(3):818–833.

Badinger, H. and Egger, P. (2011). Estimation of higher-order spatial autoregressive cross-section models with heteroscedastic disturbances. *Papers in Regional Science*, 90(1):213–235.

Badunenko, O. (2010). Downsizing in the German chemical manufacturing industry during the 1990s. Why is small beautiful? *Small Business Economics*, 34(4):413–431.

Badunenko, O., Henderson, D. J., and Zelenyuk, V. (2008). Technological change and transition: Relative contributions to worldwide growth during the 1990s. *Oxford Bulletin of Economics and Statistics*, 70(4):461–492.

Badunenko, O., Henderson, D. J., and Zelenyuk, V. (2017). The productivity of nations. In Grifell-Tatjé, E., Lovell, C. A. K., and Sickles, R. C., editors, *The Oxford Handbook of Productivity*, chapter 24, pp. 781–815. New York, NY: Oxford University Press.

Badunenko, O. and Kumbhakar, S. C. (2017). Economies of scale, technical change and persistent and time-varying cost efficiency in Indian banking: Do ownership, regulation and heterogeneity matter? *European Journal of Operational Research*, 260(2):789–803.

Badunenko, O. and Tochkov, K. (2010). Soaring dragons, roaring tigers, growling bears. *Economics of Transition*, 18(3):539–570.

Bai, J. (2009). Panel data models with interactive fixed effects. *Econometrica*, 77(4):1229–1279.

Bai, J. and Ng, S. (2002). Determining the number of factors in approximate factor models. *Econometrica*, 70(1):191–221.

Balk, B. M. (1998). *Industrial Price, Quantity, and Productivity Indices: The Micro-Economic Theory and an Application*. Boston, MA: Kluwer Academic Publishers.

Balk, B. M. (2004). Decompositions of Fisher indexes. *Economics Letters*, 82(1):107–113.

Balk, B. M. (2008). *Price and Quantity Index Numbers: Models for Measuring Aggregate Change and Difference*. New York, NY: Cambridge University Press.

Balk, B. M. and Althin, R. (1996). A new, transitive productivity index. *Journal of Productivity Analysis*, 7(1):19–27.

Balk, B. M. and Diewert, W. E. (2001). A characterization of the Törnqvist price index. *Economics Letters*, 72(3):279–281.

Balk, B. M. and Diewert, W. E. (2010). The Lowe consumer price index and its substitution bias. In Diewert, W. E., Balk, B. M., Fixler, D., Fox, K. J., and Nakamura, A. O., editors, *Price And Productivity Measurement*, volume 6, chapter 8, pages 187–196. Bloomington, IN: Trafford Press.

Balk, B. M., Färe, R., Grosskopf, S., and Margaritis, D. (2005). The equivalence between the Luenberger productivity indicator and the Malmquist productivity index. Unpublished manuscript, Rotterdam: Erasmus University.

Ballivian, M. A. and Sickles, R. C. (1994). Product diversification, economies of scope and risk avoidance: An application to Indian agriculture. *Journal of Productivity Analysis*, 5(3):271–286.

Baltagi, B. H. (1995). *Economic Analysis of Panel Data*. New York, NY: Wiley.

Baltagi, B. H. (ed.) (2014). *The Oxford Handbook of Panel Data*. New York, NY: Oxford University Press.

Baltagi, B. H. and Griffin, J. M. (1988). A general index of technical change. *The Journal of Political Economy*, 96(1):20–41.

Banker, R. D. (1993). Maximum likelihood, consistency and data envelopment analysis: A statistical foundation. *Management Science*, 39(10):1265–1273.

Banker, R. D., Charnes, A., and Cooper, W. W. (1984). Some models for estimating technical and scale inefficiencies in data envelopment analysis. *Management Science*, 30(9):1078–1092.

Banker, R. D. and Morey, R. C. (1986a). Efficiency analysis for exogenously fixed inputs and outputs. *Operations Research*, 34(4):513–521.

Banker, R. D. and Morey, R. C. (1986b). The use of categorical variables in data envelopment analysis. *Management Science*, 32(12):1613–1627.

Banker, R. D. and Natarajan, R. (2008). Evaluating contextual variables affecting productivity using data envelopment analysis. *Operations Research*, 56(1):48–58.

Banker, R. D. and Thrall, R. M. (1992). Estimation of returns to scale using data envelopment analysis. *European Journal of Operational Research*, 62(1):74–84.

Barnett, W. A. (1983). New indices of money supply and the flexible Laurent demand system. *Journal of Business & Economic Statistics*, 1(1):7–23.

Barnett, W. A. and Lee, Y. W. (1985). The global properties of the minflex Laurent, generalized Leontief, and translog flexible functional forms. *Econometrica*, 53(6):1421–1437.

Barro, R. J. (1991). A cross-country study of growth, saving, and government. In Bernheim, D. and Shoven, J. B., editors, *National Saving and Economic Performance*, pages 271–304. Chicago, IL: University of Chicago Press.

Bates, J. M. and Granger, C. W. (1969). The combination of forecasts. *Journal of the Operational Research Society*, 20(4):451–468.

Battese, G. E. and Coelli, T. J. (1988). Prediction of firm-level technical efficiencies with a generalized frontier production function and panel data. *Journal of Econometrics*, 38(3):387–399.

Battese, G. E. and Coelli, T. J. (1992). Frontier production functions, technical efficiency and panel data: With application to paddy farmers in India. *Journal of Productivity Analysis*, 3(1–2):153–169.

Battese, G. E. and Coelli, T. J. (1995). A model for technical inefficiency effects in a stochastic frontier production function for panel data. *Empirical economics*, 20(2):325–332.

Battese, G. E., Rao, D. S. P., and O'Donnell, C. J. (2004). A metafrontier production function for estimation of technical efficiencies and technology gaps for firms operating under different technologies. *Journal of Productivity Analysis*, 21(1):91–103.

Bauer, P. W. and Hancock, D. (1993). The efficiency of the Federal Reserve in providing check processing services. *Journal of Banking & Finance*, 17(2–3):287–311.

Baumol, W. J. (1986). Productivity growth, convergence, and welfare: What the long-run data show. *American Economic Review*, 76(5):1072–85.

Baumol, W. J. and ten Raa, T. (2009). Wassily Leontief: In appreciation. *The European Journal of the History of Economic Thought*, 16(3):511–522.

Behrens, K., Ertur, C., and Koch, W. (2010). "Dual" gravity: Using spatial econometrics to control for multilateral resistance. *Journal of Applied Econometrics*, 27(5): 773–794.

Behrman, J. R., Lovell, C. A. K., Pollak, R. A., and Sickles, R. C. (1992). The CET-CES-generalized Leontief variable profit function: An application to Indian agriculture. *Oxford Economic Papers*, 44(2):341–354.

Belotti, F., Daidone, S., Ilardi, G., and Atella, V. (2013). Stochastic frontier analysis using Stata. *Stata Journal*, 13(4):718–758.

Belotti, F. and Ilardi, G. (2012). Consistent estimation of the "true" fixed-effects stochastic frontier model. Working Paper No. 231. Rome: Centre for Economics and International Studies.

Bera, A. K. and Sharma, S. C. (1999). Estimating production uncertainty in stochastic frontier production function models. *Journal of Productivity Analysis*, 12(3):187–210.

Beran, R. and Ducharme, G. R. (1991). *Asymptotic Theory for Bootstrap Methods in Statistics*. Montréal, QC: Centre de Recherches Mathématiques.

Berg, S. A., Førsund, F. R., and Jansen, E. S. (1992). Malmquist indexes of productivity growth during the deregulation of Norwegian banking 1980–1989. *Scandinavian Economic Journal*, 94:211–228.

Berger, A. N. (1993). "Distribution-free" estimates of efficiency in the US banking industry and tests of the standard distributional assumptions. *Journal of productivity Analysis*, 4(3):261–292.

Berndt, E. (1991). *The Practice of Econometrics: Classic and Contemporary*. Boston, MA: Addison-Wesley Publishing Company.

Berndt, E. R. and Hesse, D. M. (1986). Measuring and assessing capacity utilization in the manufacturing sectors of nine OECD countries. *European Economic Review*, 30(5):961–989.

Berndt, E. R. and Khaled, M. S. (1979). Parametric productivity measurement and choice among flexible functional forms. *The Journal of Political Economy*, 87(6):1220–1245.

Bhattacharyya, A. (2012). Adjustment of inputs and measurement of technical efficiency: A dynamic panel data analysis of the Egyptian manufacturing sectors. *Empirical Economics*, 42(3):863–880.

Bhattacharyya, A. (2014). Adjustment of inputs and measurement of time-varying technical efficiency: A dynamic panel data analysis. *Journal of Quantitative Economics*, 12(1):31–50.

Bickel, P. J. and Freedman, D. A. (1981). Some asymptotic theory for the bootstrap. *Annals of Statistics*, 9(6):1196–1217.

Bickel, P. J. and Sakov, A. (2008). On the choice of m in the m out of n bootstrap and confidence bounds for extrema. *Statistica Sinica*, 18(3): 967–985.

Birnbaum, Z. W. (1950). Effect of linear truncation on a multinormal population. *Annals of Mathematical Statistics*, 21(2):272–279.

Bjurek, H. (1996). The Malmquist total factor productivity index. *The Scandinavian Journal of Economics*, 98(2):303–313.

Blackorby, C., Lovell, C. A. K., and Thursby, M. C. (1976). Extended Hicks neutral technical change. *The Economic Journal*, 86(344):845–852.

Blackorby, C. and Russell, R. R. (1981). The Morishima elasticity of substitution; symmetry, constancy, separability, and its relationship to the Hicks and Allen elasticities. *Review of Economic Studies*, 48(1):147–158.

Blackorby, C. and Russell, R. R. (1989). Will the real elasticity of substitution please stand up? (A comparison of the Allen/Uzawa and Morishima elasticities). *American Economic Review*, 79(4):882–888.

Blackorby, C. and Russell, R. R. (1999). Aggregation of efficiency indices. *Journal of Productivity Analysis*, 12(1):5–20.

Blaug, M. (1999). The concept of entrepreneurship in the history of economics. In Blaug, M., *Not Only an Economist: Recent Essays*, pages 95–113. Cheltenham, UK: Edward Elgar.

Blazek, D. and Sickles, R. C. (2010). The impact of knowledge accumulation and geographical spillovers on productivity and efficiency: The case of US shipbuilding during WWII. *Economic Modelling*, 27(6):1484–1497.

Bloom, N., Eifert, B., Mahajan, A., McKenzie, D., and Roberts, J. (2013). Does management matter? Evidence from India. *The Quarterly Journal of Economics*, 128(1):1–51.

Bloom, N., Genakos, C., Sadun, R., and Van Reenen, J. (2012). Management practices across firms and countries. *The Academy of Management Perspectives*, 26(1):12–33.

Bloom, N., Lemos, R., Sadun, R., Scur, D., and Van Reenen, J. (2016). International data on measuring management practices. *American Economic Review*, 106(5):152–156.

Bloom, N. and Van Reenen, J. (2007). Measuring and explaining management practices across firms and countries. *The Quarterly Journal of Economics*, 122(4):1351–1408.

Blundell, R. and Bond, S. (1998). Initial conditions and moment restrictions in dynamic panel data models. *Journal of Econometrics*, 87(1):115–143.

Blundell, R., Horowitz, J. L., and Parey, M. (2012). Measuring the price responsiveness of gasoline demand: Economic shape restrictions and nonparametric demand estimation. *Quantitative Economics*, 3(1):29–51.

Bogetoft, P. (1996). DEA on relaxed convexity assumptions. *Management Science*, 42(3):457–465.

Bogetoft, P., Tama, J. M., and Tind, J. (2000). Convex input and output projections of nonconvex production possibility sets. *Management Science*, 46(6):858–869.

Bol, G. (1986). On technical efficiency measures: A remark. *Journal of Economic Theory*, 38(2):380–386.

Bos, J. W. B., Candelon, B., and Economidou, C. (2016). Does knowledge spill over across borders and technology regimes? *Journal of Productivity Analysis*, 46(1):63–82.

Boskin, M. J., Dulberger, E. L., Gordon, R. J., Griliches, Z., and Jorgenson, D. W. (1998). Consumer prices, the consumer price index, and the cost of living. *Journal of Economic Perspectives*, 12(1):3–26.

Boskin, M. J., Dulberger, E. R., Gordon, R. J., Griliches, Z., and Jorgenson, D. W. (1996). Toward a more accurate measure of the cost of living. Final Report to the Senate Finance Committee, Washington DC.

Boskin, M. J., Dulberger, E. R., Gordon, R. J., Griliches, Z., and Jorgenson, D. W. (1997). The CPI commission: Findings and recommendations. *American Economic Review*, 87(2):78–83.

Boskin, M. J. and Jorgenson, D. W. (1997). Implications of overstating inflation for indexing government programs and understanding economic progress. *American Economic Review*, 87(2):89–93.

Boussemart, J.-P., Briec, W., Kerstens, K., and Poutineau, J.-C. (2003). Luenberger and Malmquist productivity indices: Theoretical comparisons and empirical illustration. *Bulletin of Economic Research*, 55(4):391–405.

Boussofiane, A., Dyson, R. G., and Thanassoulis, E. (1991). Applied data envelopment analysis. *European Journal of Operational Research*, 52(1):1–15.

Box, G. P. and Draper, N. R. (1987). *Empirical Model-Building and Response Surfaces*. New York, NY: Wiley.

Brandenburger, A. M. and Stuart, H. W. (1996). Value-based business strategy. *Journal of Economics & Management Strategy*, 5(1):5–24.

Brea-Solís, H., Casadesus-Masanell, R., and Grifell-Tatjé, E. (2015). Business model evaluation: Quantifying Walmart's sources of advantage. *Strategic Entrepreneurship Journal*, 9(1):12–33.

Breusch, T. S. and Pagan, A. R. (1980). The Lagrange multiplier test and its applications to model specification in econometrics. *Review of Economic Studies*, 47(1):239–253.

Briec, W. (1999). Hölder distance function and measurement of technical efficiency. *Journal of Productivity Analysis*, 11(2):111–131.

Briec, W., Chambers, R. G., Färe, R., and Peypoch, N. (2006). Parallel neutrality. *Journal of Economics*, 88(3):285–305.

Briec, W. and Kerstens, K. (2004). A Luenberger–Hicks–Moorsteen productivity indicator: Its relation to the Hicks–Moorsteen productivity index and the Luenberger productivity indicator. *Economic Theory*, 23(4):925–939.

Briec, W. and Kerstens, K. (2011). The Hicks–Moorsteen productivity index satisfies the determinateness axiom. *The Manchester School*, 79(4):765–775.

Broadie, M., Detemple, J., Ghysels, E., and Torrés, O. (2000). American options with stochastic dividends and volatility: A nonparametric investigation. *Journal of Econometrics*, 94(1):53–92.

Brunsdon, C., Fortheringham, A. S., and Charlton, M. E. (1996). Geographically weighted regression: A method for exploring spatial nonstationarity. *Geographical Analysis*, 28(4):281–298.

Brynjolfsson, E. and Hitt, L. (2003). Computing productivity: Firm-level evidence. *Review of Economics and Statistics*, 85(4):793–808.

Buckland, S. T., Burnham, K. P., and Augustin, N. H. (1997). Model selection: An integral part of inference. *Biometrics*, 53(2):603–618.

Burnham, K. and Anderson, D. R. (2002). *Model Selection and Multimodel Inference: A Practical Information-Theoretic Approach*. New York, NY: Springer.

Button, K. J. and Weyman-Jones, T. G. (1992). Ownership structure, institutional organization and measured X-efficiency. *American Economic Review*, 82(2):439–445.

Byrne, D. M. and Corrado, C. A. (2017). ICT prices and ICT services: What do they tell us about productivity and technology? *International Productivity Monitor*, (33):150–181.

Captain, P. F., Good, D. H., Sickles, R. C., and Ayyar, A. (2007). What if the European airline industry had deregulated in 1979? A counterfactual dynamic simulation. In *The Economics of Airline Institutions*, volume 2, pages 125–146. Amsterdam: Elsevier.

Carree, M. A. (2002). Technological inefficiency and the skewness of the error component in stochastic frontier analysis. *Economics Letters*, 77(1):101–107.

Carroll, R. J., Delaigle, A., and Hall, P. (2011). Testing and estimating shape-constrained nonparametric density and regression in the presence of measurement error. *Journal of the American Statistical Association*, 106(493):191–202.

Casadesus-Masanell, R. and Ricart, J. E. (2007). Competing through business models. Working Paper No. 713, Barcelona: IESE Business School.

Casadesus-Masanell, R. and Ricart, J. E. (2010). From strategy to business models and onto tactics. *Long Range Planning*, 43(2):195–215.

Casadesus-Masanell, R. and Ricart, J. E. (2011). How to design a winning business model. *Harvard Business Review*, 89(1–2):100–107.

Casadesus-Masanell, R. and Zhu, F. (2010). Strategies to fight ad-sponsored rivals. *Management Science*, 56(9):1484–1499.

Caudill, S. B., Ford, J. M., and Gropper, D. M. (1995). Frontier estimation and firm-specific inefficiency measures in the presence of heteroscedasticity. *Journal of Business & Economic Statistics*, 13(1):105–111.

Caves, D. W. and Christensen, L. R. (1980). Global properties of flexible functional forms. *American Economic Review*, 70(3):422–432.

Caves, D. W., Christensen, L. R., and Diewert, W. E. (1982a). The economic theory of index numbers and the measurement of input, output, and productivity. *Econometrica*, 50(6):1393–1414.

Caves, D. W., Christensen, L. R., and Diewert, W. E. (1982b). Multilateral comparisons of output, input, and productivity using superlative index numbers. *The Economic Journal*, 92(365):73–86.

Caves, D. W., Christensen, L. R., and Swanson, J. A. (1981). Productivity growth, scale economies, and capacity utilization in US railroads, 1955–74. *American Economic Review*, 71(5):994–1002.

Caves, R. E. and Barton, D. R. (1992). Efficiency in US manufacturing industries. 30(1):185–187.

Cazals, C., Florens, J.-P., and Simar, L. (2002). Nonparametric frontier estimation: A robust approach. *Journal of Econometrics*, 106(1):1–25.

Chamberlain, G. (1980). Analysis of covariance with qualitative data. *Review of Economic Studies*, 47(1):225–238.

Chambers, R. G. (1988). *Applied Production Analysis: A Dual Approach*. New York, NY: Cambridge University Press.

Chambers, R. G. (1996). A new look at exact input, output, and productivity measurement. Working Paper No. 96-05, College Park, MD: University of Maryland Department of Agricultural and Resource Economics.

Chambers, R. G. (2008). Stochastic productivity measurement. *Journal of Productivity Analysis*, 30(2):107–120.

Chambers, R. G., Chung, Y., and Färe, R. (1996b). Benefit and distance functions. *Journal of Economic Theory*, 70(2):407–419.

Chambers, R. G., Chung, Y., and Färe, R. (1998). Profit, directional distance functions, and Nerlovian efficiency. *Journal of Optimization Theory and Applications*, 98(2):351–364.

Chambers, R. G. and Färe, R. (1994). Hicks neutrality and trade biased growth: A taxonomy. *Journal of Economic Theory*, 64(2):554–567.

Chambers, R. G., Färe, R., and Grosskopf, S. (1996a). Productivity growth in APEC countries. *Pacific Economic Review*, 1(3):181–190.

Chambers, R. G., Färe, R., Grosskopf, S., and Vardanyan, M. (2013). Generalized quadratic revenue functions. *Journal of Econometrics*, 173(1):11–21.

Chambers, R. G. and Quiggin, J. (2000). *Uncertainty, Production, Choice, and Agency: The State-Contingent Approach*. New York, NY: Cambridge University Press.

Chambers, R. G. and Quiggin, J. (2002). The state-contingent properties of stochastic production functions. *American Journal of Agricultural Economics*, 84(2):513–526.

Chang, C.-C. and Stefanou, S. E. (1988). Specification and estimation of asymmetric adjustment rates for quasi-fixed factors of production. *Journal of Economic Dynamics and Control*, 12(1):145–151.

Charnes, A., Cooper, W., Golany, B., Seiford, L., and Stutz, J. (1985). Foundations of data envelopment analysis for Pareto–Koopmans efficient empirical production functions. *Journal of Econometrics*, 30(1–2):91–107.

Charnes, A., Cooper, W., and Rhodes, E. (1978). Measuring the efficiency of decision making units. *European Journal of Operational Research*, 2(6):429–444.

Charnes, A., Cooper, W. W., Huang, Z. M., and Sun, D. B. (1990). Polyhedral cone-ratio DEA models with an illustrative application to large commercial banks. *Journal of econometrics*, 46(1-2):73–91.

Charnes, A., Cooper, W. W., Lewin, A. Y., and Seiford, L. M., editors (1994). *Data Envelopment Analysis: Theory, Methodology, and Applications*. Amsterdam: Springer.

Chen, X. (2007). Large sample sieve estimation of semi-nonparametric models. In *Handbook of Econometrics*, volume 6, pages 5549–5632. Amsterdam: Elsevier.

Chen, Y. and Liang, K.-Y. (2010). On the asymptotic behaviour of the pseudolikelihood ratio test statistic with boundary problems. *Biometrika*, 97(3):603–620.

Chen, Y.-Y., Schmidt, P., and Wang, H.-J. (2014). Consistent estimation of the fixed effects stochastic frontier model. *Journal of Econometrics*, 181(2):65–76.

Chesher, A. (1984). Testing for neglected heterogeneity. *Econometrica*, 52(4):865–872.

Chowdhury, H. and Zelenyuk, V. (2016). Performance of hospital services in Ontario: DEA with truncated regression approach. *Omega*, 63:111–122.

Christensen, L. R. and Greene, W. H. (1976). Economies of scale in US electric power generation. *The Journal of Political Economy*, 84(4):655–676.

Christensen, L. R., Jorgenson, D. W., and Lau, L. J. (1971). Conjugate duality and the transcendental logarithmic production function. *Econometrica*, 55(1):255–256.

Christev, A. and Featherstone, A. M. (2009). A note on Allen–Uzawa partial elasticities of substitution: the case of the translog cost function. *Applied Economics Letters*, 16(11):1165–1169.

Christian, M. S. (2017). Net investment and stocks of human capital in the United States, 1975–2013. *International Productivity Monitor*, (33):128–149.

Chung, Y. (1996). *Directional distance functions and undesirable outputs*. PhD thesis, Carbondale, IL: Southern Illinois University at Carbondale.

Chung, Y., Färe, R., and Grosskopf, S. (1997a). Productivity and undesirable outputs: A directional distance function approach. *Journal of Environmental Management*, 51(3):229–240.

Chung, Y. H., Färe, R., and Grosskopf, S. (1997b). Productivity and undesirable outputs: A directional distance function approach. *Journal of Environmental Management*, 51(3):229–240.

Clement, J. (1989). Learning via model construction and criticism. In *Handbook of Creativity*, pages 341–381. New York, NY: Springer.

Cobb, C. W. and Douglas, P. H. (1928). A theory of production. *American Economic Review*, 18(1):139–165.

Coe, D. T. and Helpman, E. (1995). International R&D spillovers. *European Economic Review*, 39(5):859–887.

Coe, D. T., Helpman, E., and Hoffmaister, A. W. (1997). North–South R&D spillovers. *The Economic Journal*, 107(440):134–149.

Coelli, T. (2000). *On the Econometric Estimation of the Distance Function Representation of a Production Technology*. Louvain: Université Catholique de Louvain Center for Operations Research and Econometrics [CORE].

Coelli, T. and Perelman, S. (1996). Efficiency measurement, multiple-output technologies and distance functions: With application to European railways. CREPP Working Paper No. 96/05, Liège: University of Liège.

Coelli, T. and Perelman, S. (1999). A comparison of parametric and non-parametric distance functions: With application to European railways. *European Journal of Operational Research*, 117(2):326–339.

Coelli, T. J. (1995). Estimators and hypothesis tests for a stochastic frontier function: A Monte Cparlo analysis. *Journal of Productivity Analysis*, 6(3):247–268.

Coelli, T. J., Rao, D. S. P., O'Donnell, C. J., and Battese, G. E. (2005). *An Introduction to Efficiency and Productivity Analysis*. New York, NY: Springer.

Colombi, R., Kumbhakar, S. C., Martini, G., and Vittadini, G. (2014). Closed-skew normality in stochastic frontiers with individual effects and long/short-run efficiency. *Journal of Productivity Analysis*, 42(2):123–136.

Colombi, R., Martini, G., and Vittadini, G. (2011). A stochastic frontier model with short-run and long-run inefficiency random effects, Working Paper 1101, Bergamo: University of Bergamo Department of Economics and Technology Management.

Cook, W. and Seiford, L. (2009). Data envelopment analysis (DEA) – thirty years on. *European Journal of Operational Research*, 192(1):1–17.

Cook, W. D., Liang, L., and Zhu, J. (2010). Measuring performance of two-stage network structures by DEA: A review and future perspective. *Omega*, 38(6):423–430.

Cooper, W., Huang, Z., Li, S., Parker, B., and Pastor, J. (2007a). Efficiency aggregation with enhanced Russell measures in data envelopment analysis. *Socio-Economic Planning Sciences*, 41(1):1–21.

Cooper, W. W., Pastor, J. T., Aparicio, J., and Borras, F. (2011a). Decomposing profit inefficiency in DEA through the weighted additive model. *European Journal of Operational Research*, 212(2):411–416.

Cooper, W. W., Seiford, L. M., and Tone, K. (2007b). *Data Envelopment Analysis: A Comprehensive Text with Models, Applications, References and DEA-Solver Software*. New York, NY: Springer.

Cooper, W. W., Seiford, L. M., and Zhu, J., editors (2011b). *Handbook on Data Envelopment Analysis*. New York, NY: Springer.

Coremberg, A. (2017). Argentina was not the productivity and economic growth champion of Latin America. *International Productivity Monitor*, (33):77–90.

Cornwell, C., Schmidt, P., and Sickles, R. C. (1990). Production frontiers with cross-sectional and time-series variation in efficiency levels. *Journal of Econometrics*, 46(1):185–200.

Corrado, C., Hulten, C., and Sichel, D. (2009). Intangible capital and US economic growth. *Review of Income and Wealth*, 55(3):661–685.

Csontos, L. and Ray, S. C. (1992). The Leontief production function as a limiting case of the CES. *Indian Economic Review*, 27(2):235–237.

Cuesta, R. A. (2000). A production model with firm-specific temporal variation in technical inefficiency: With application to Spanish dairy farms. *Journal of Productivity Analysis*, 13(2):139–158.

Curi, C., Lozano-Vivas, A., and Zelenyuk, V. (2015). Foreign bank diversification and efficiency prior to and during the financial crisis: Does one business model fit all? *Journal of Banking and Finance*, 61(S1):S22–S35.

D'Agostino, R. and Pearson, E. S. (1973). Tests for departure from normality. Empirical results for the distributions of b_2 and $\sqrt{b_1}$. *Biometrika*, 60(3):613–622.

Dakpo, K. H., Jeanneaux, P., and Latruffe, L. (2017). Modelling pollution-generating technologies in performance benchmarking: Recent developments, limits and future prospects in the nonparametric framework. *European Journal of Operational Research*, 250(2):347–359.

Dal Bianco, S. (2016). Going clubbing in the eighties: Convergence in manufacturing sectors at a glance. *Empirical Economics*, 50(2):623–659.

Dantzig, G. (1963). *Linear Programming and Extensions*. Princeton, NJ: Princeton University Press.

Dantzig, G. B. (1949). Programming of interdependent activities: Ii mathematical model. *Econometrica*, 7(3):200–211.

Dantzig, G. B. (1955). Optimal solution of a dynamic Leontief model with substitution. *Econometrica*, 23(3):295–302.

Dantzig, G. B. (1982). Reminiscences about the origins of linear programming. *Operations Research Letters*, 1(2):43–48.

Daouia, A. and Simar, L. (2005). Robust nonparametric estimators of monotone boundaries. *Journal of Multivariate Analysis*, 96(2):311–331.

Daraio, C. and Simar, L. (2005). Introducing environmental variables in nonparametric frontier models: A probabilistic approach. *Journal of Productivity Analysis*, 24(1):93–121.

Daraio, C. and Simar, L. (2007a). *Advanced Robust and Nonparametric Methods in Efficiency Analysis: Methodology and Applications*. New York, NY: Springer.

Daraio, C. and Simar, L. (2007b). Conditional nonparametric frontier models for convex and nonconvex technologies: A unifying approach. *Journal of Productivity Analysis*, 28(1):13–32.

Daraio, C. and Simar, L. (2014). Directional distances and their robust versions: Computational and testing issues. *European Journal of Operational Research*, 237(1):358–369.

Daraio, C., Simar, L., and Wilson, P. W. (2018). Central limit theorems for conditional efficiency measures and tests of the "separability" condition in nonparametric, two-stage models of production. *Econometrics Journal*, 21(2):170–191.

Daskovska, A., Simar, L., and Van Bellegem, S. (2010). Forecasting the Malmquist productivity index. *Journal of Productivity Analysis*, 33(2):97–107.

Davison, A. C. and Hinkley, D. V. (1997). *Bootstrap Methods and Their Application*. New York, NY: Cambridge University Press.

De Helguero, F. (1908). *Sulla rappresentazione analitica delle statistiche abnormali*. Rome: Accademia dei Lincei.

De Loecker, J., Goldberg, P. K., Khandelwal, A. K., and Pavcnik, N. (2016). Prices, markups, and trade reform. *Econometrica*, 84(2):445–510.

De Nadai, M. and Lewbel, A. (2016). Nonparametric errors in variables models with measurement errors on both sides of the equation. *Journal of Econometrics*, 191(1):19–32.

Deaton, A. (1998). Getting prices right: What should be done? *The Journal of Economic Perspectives*, 12(1):37–46.

Debreu, G. (1951). The coefficient of resource utilization. *Econometrica*, 19(3):273–292.

Demchuk, P. and Zelenyuk, V. (2009). Testing differences in efficiency of regions within a country: The case of Ukraine. *Journal of Productivity Analysis*, 32(2):81–102.

Denny, M. (1974). The relationship between functional forms for the production system. *Canadian Journal of Economics*, 7(1):21–31.

Deprins, D., Simar, L., and Tulkens, H. (1984). Measuring labour efficiency in post offices. In Marchand, M., Pestieau, P., and Tulkens, H., editors, *The Performance of Public Enterprises: Concepts and Measurement*, pages 243–267. Amsterdam: Springer.

Despotakis, K. A. (1986). Economic performance of flexible functional forms: Implications for equilibrium modeling. *European Economic Review*, 30(6):1107–1143.

DeYoung, R. (1998). Management quality and x-inefficiency in national banks. *Journal of Financial Services Research*, 13(1):5–22.

Diao, X., Rattsø, J., and Stokke, H. E. (2005). International spillovers, productivity growth and openness in Thailand: An intertemporal general equilibrium analysis. *Journal of Development Economics*, 76(2):429–450.

Diebold, F. X. and Lopez, J. A. (1996). Forecast evaluation and combination. In G. S. Maddala, C. R. R., editor, *Handbook of Statistics*, volume 14, pages 241–268. Amsterdam: Elsevier.

Diewert, W. E. (1971). An application of the Shephard duality theorem: A generalized Leontief production function. *Journal of Political Economy*, 79(3):481–507.

Diewert, W. E. (1973). Functional forms for profit and transformation functions. *Journal of Economic Theory*, 6(3):284–316.

Diewert, W. E. (1974a). Applications of duality theory. In Intriligator, M. D. and Kendrick, D. A., editors, *Frontiers in Quantitative Economics*, volume 2, pages 106–171. Amsterdam: Elsevier.

Diewert, W. E. (1974b). Functional forms for revenue and factor requirements functions. *International Economic Review*, 15(1):119–130.

Diewert, W. E. (1974c). A note on aggregation and elasticities of substitution. *The Canadian Journal of Economics*, 7(1):12–20.

Diewert, W. E. (1976). Exact and superlative index numbers. *Journal of Econometrics*, 4(2):115–145.

Diewert, W. E. (1980). *Aggregation Problems in the Measurement of Capital*, pages 433–528. Chicago, IL: University of Chicago Press.

Diewert, W. E. (1981). The economic theory of index numbers: A survey. In Deaton, A., editor, *Essays in the Theory and Measurement of Consumer Behaviour (in Honour of Richard Stone)*, pages 163–208. London: Cambridge University Press.

Diewert, W. E. (1982). Duality approaches to microeconomic theory. In *Handbook of Mathematical Economics*, volume 2, pages 535–599. Netherlands: Elsevier.

Diewert, W. E. (1983a). The measurement of waste within the production sector of an open economy. *The Scandinavian Journal of Economics*, 85(2):159–179.

Diewert, W. E. (1983b). *The Theory of the Output Price Index and the Measurement of Real Output Change*. British Columbia, CA: University of British Columbia, Department of Economics.

Diewert, W. E. (1992a). Fisher ideal output, input, and productivity indexes revisited. *Journal of Productivity Analysis*, 3(3):211–248.

Diewert, W. E. (1992b). The measurement of productivity. *Bulletin of Economic Research*, 44(3):163–198.

Diewert, W. E. (1993). Symmetric means and choice under uncertainty. In Diewert, W. E. and Nakamura, A. O., editors, *Essays in Index Number Theory*, volume 1, pages 355–433. Amsterdam: Elsevier.

Diewert, W. E. (1998). Index number issues in the consumer price index. *The Journal of Economic Perspectives*, 12(1):47–58.

Diewert, W. E. (2002). The quadratic approximation lemma and decompositions of superlative indexes. *Journal of Economic and Social Measurement*, 28(1):63–88.

Diewert, W. E. and Fox, K. J. (2017). Decomposing productivity indexes into explanatory factors. *European Journal of Operational Research*, 256(1):275–291.

Diewert, W. E. and Lawrence, D. (2002). The deadweight costs of capital taxation in Australia. In Fox, K. J., editor, *Efficiency in the Public Sector*, pages 103–167. Boston, MA: Kluwer Academic Publishers.

Diewert, W. E. and Morrison, C. J. (1986). Adjusting output and productivity indexes for changes in the terms of trade. *Economic Journal*, 96(383):659–679.

Diewert, W. E. and Nakamura, A. O., editors (1993). *Essays in Index Number Theory*, volume 1. Amsterdam: Elsevier.

Diewert, W. E. and Wales, T. (1987). Flexible functional forms and global curvature conditions. *Econometrica*, 55(1):43–68.

Diewert, W. E. and Wales, T. J. (1988). A normalized quadratic semiflexible functional form. *Journal of Econometrics*, 37(3):327–342.

Diewert, W. E. and Wales, T. J. (1992). Quadratic spline models for producer's supply and demand functions. *International Economic Review*, 33(3):705–722.

Dirac, P. A. M. (1930). *The Principles of Quantum Mechanics*. New York, NY: Oxford University Press, 1st edition.

Dmitruk, A. V. and Koshevoy, G. A. (1991). On the existence of a technical efficiency criterion. *Journal of Economic Theory*, 55(1):121–144.

Dodgson, M. and Gann, D. (2010). *Innovation: A Very Short Introduction*. New York, NY: Oxford University Press.

Dogramaci, A. and Adam, N. R., editors (1981). *Aggregate and Industry-Level Productivity Analyses*. Hingham, MA: Martinus Nijhoff Publishing.

Dogramaci, A. and Färe, R., editors (1988). *Applications of Modern Production Theory: Efficiency and Productivity*. Boston, MA: Kluwer Academic Publishers.

Domar, E. D. (1961). On the measurement of technological change. *The Economic Journal*, 71(284):709–729.

Dowrick, S. and Nguyen, D.-T. (1989). OECD comparative economic growth 1950–85: Catch-up and convergence. *American Economic Review*, 79(5):1010–1030.

Drucker, P. F. (1954). *The Practice of Management: A Study of the Most Important Function in America Society*. New York, NY: Harper Collins.

Druska, V. and Horrace, W. (2004). Generalized moments estimation for spatial panel data: Indonesian rice farming. *American Journal of Agricultural Economics*, 86(1):185–198.

Du, K., Pham, M. D., and Zelenyuk, V. (2017a). Likelihood ratio test for the 2-stage DEA and truncation regression via bootstrap with application to cross-countries efficiency analysis. Unpublished manuscript, Brisbane: The University of Queensland.

Du, K., Worthington, A. C., and Zelenyuk, V. (2017b). Data envelopment analysis, truncated regression and double-bootstrap for panel data with application to Chinese banking. *European Journal of Operational Research*, 265, 2 (2018):748–764.

Du, P., Parmeter, C. F., and Racine, J. S. (2013). Nonparametric kernel regression with multiple predictors and multiple shape constraints. *Statistica Sinica*, 23(3):1343–1372.

Duygun, M., Hao, J., Isaksson, A., and Sickles, R. C. (2017). World productivity growth: A model averaging approach. Special Issue of the *Pacific Economic Review* on Economic Growth, Productivity and Efficiency, Cliff Huang and Tsu-tan Fu (Guest-Editors), 22(4):587–619.

Duygun, M., Kutlu, L., and Sickles, R. C. (2016). Measuring productivity and efficiency: a Kalman filter approach. *Journal of Productivity Analysis*, 46(2–3):155–167.

Dyson, R. G. and Thanassoulis, E. (1988). Reducing weight flexibility in data envelopment analysis. *Journal of the Operational Research Society*, 39(6):563–576.

Efron, B. (1979). Another look at the jackknife. *Annals of Statistics*, 7(1):1–26.

Efron, B. and Tibshirani, R. J. (1993). *An Introduction to the Bootstrap*. New York, NY: Chapman and Hall.

Eichhorn, W. (1976). Fisher's tests revisited. *Econometrica*, 44(2):247–256.

Eichhorn, W. and Voeller, J. (1976). Theory of the price index. In *Lecture Notes in Economics and Mathematical Systems*. Berlin: Springer.

Elandt, R. C. (1961). The folded normal distribution: Two methods of estimating parameters from moments. *Technometrics*, 3(4):551–562.

Elhorst, J. (2001). Dynamic models in space and time. *Geographical Analysis*, 33(2):119–140.

Elhorst, J., Lacombe, D., and Piras, G. (2012). On model specification and parameter space definitions in higher order spatial econometric models. *Regional Science and Urban Economics*, 42(1):211–220.

Eltetö, O. and Köves, P. (1964). On a problem of index number computation relating to international comparison. *Statisztikai Szemle*, 42:507–518.

Emrouznejad, A., Parker, B., and Tavares, G. (2008). Evaluation of research in efficiency and productivity: A survey and analysis of the first 30 years of scholarly literature in DEA. *Journal of Socio-Economics Planning Science*, 42(3):151–157.

Engle, R. F. and Granger, C. W. J. (1987). Co-integration and error correction: Representation, estimation, and testing. *Econometrica*, 55(2):251–276.

Entani, T., Maeda, Y., and Tanaka, H. (2002). Dual models of interval DEA and its extension to interval data. *European Journal of Operational Research*, 136(1):32–45.

Epure, M., Kerstens, K., and Prior, D. (2011). Technology-based total factor productivity and benchmarking: New proposals and an application. *Omega*, 39(6):608–619.

Ertur, C. and Koch, W. (2007). Growth, technological interdependence and spatial externalities: Theory and evidence. *Journal of Applied Econometrics*, 22(6):1033–1062.

Eubank, R. L. (1988). *Nonparametric Regression and Spline Smoothing*. New York, NY: Marcel Dekker, 2nd edition.

Evans, D. S. and Heckman, J. J. (1984). A test for subadditivity of the cost function with an application to the bell system. *American Economic Review*, 74(4):615–623.

Fan, J. and Gijbels, I. (1992). Variable bandwidth and local linear regression smoothers. *Annals of Statistics*, 20(4):2008–2036.

Fan, J. and Gijbels, I. (1996). *Local Polynomial Modelling and Its Applications*. London: Chapman & Hall.

Fan, Y., Li, Q., and Weersink, A. (1996). Semiparametric estimation of stochastic production frontier models. *Journal of Business & Economic Statistics*, 14(4):460–468.

Fan, Y. and Ullah, A. (1999). On goodness-of-fit tests for weakly dependent processes using kernel method. *Journal of Nonparametric Statistics*, 11(1–3):337–360.

Färe, R., Fukuyama, H., Grosskopf, S., and Zelenyuk, V. (2015). Decomposing profit efficiency using a slack-based directional distance function. *European Journal of Operational Research*, 247(1):335–337.

Färe, R., Fukuyama, H., Grosskopf, S., and Zelenyuk, V. (2016a). Cost decompositions and the efficient subset. *Omega*, 62:123–130.

Färe, R., Grifell-Tatjé, E., Grosskopf, S., and Lovell, C. A. K. (1997a). Biased technical change and the Malmquist productivity index. *The Scandinavian Journal of Economics*, 99(1):119–127.

Färe, R. and Grosskopf, S. (1983). Measuring congestion in production. *Zeitschrift für Nationalökonomie / Journal of Economics*, 43(3):257–271.

Färe, R. and Grosskopf, S. (1985). A nonparametric cost approach to scale efficiency. *The Scandinavian Journal of Economics*, 87(4):594–604.

Färe, R. and Grosskopf, S. (1996). *Intertemporal Production Frontiers: With Dynamic DEA*. Norwell, MA: Kluwer Academic Publishers.

Färe, R. and Grosskopf, S. (2003). Nonparametric productivity analysis with undesirable outputs: Comment. *American Journal of Agricultural Economics*, 85(4):1070–1074.

Färe, R. and Grosskopf, S. (2004). Modeling undesirable factors in efficiency evaluation: Comment. *European Journal of Operational Research*, 157(1):242–245.

Färe, R. and Grosskopf, S. (2009). A comment on weak disposability in nonparametric production analysis. *American Journal of Agricultural Economics*, 91(2):535–538.

Färe, R. and Grosskopf, S. (2010). Directional distance functions and slacks-based measures of efficiency. *European Journal of Operational Research*, 200(1):320–322.

Färe, R., Grosskopf, S., and Li, S.-K. (1992a). Linear programming models for firm and industry performance. *The Scandinavian Journal of Economics*, 94(4):599–608.

Färe, R., Grosskopf, S., Lindgren, B., and Roos, P. (1989a). Productivity developments in Swedish hospitals. Unpublished manuscript, Corvallis, OR: Oregon State University.

Färe, R., Grosskopf, S., Lindgren, B., and Roos, P. (1992b). Productivity changes in Swedish pharmacies 1980–1989: A non-parametric Malmquist approach. *Journal of Productivity Analysis*, 3(1):85–101.

Färe, R., Grosskopf, S., Lindgren, B., and Roos, P. (1994a). Productivity developments in Swedish hospitals: A Malmquist output index approach. In Charnes, A., Cooper, W., Lewin, A. Y., and Seiford, L. M., editors, *Data Envelopment Analysis: Theory, Methodology and Applications*, pages 253–272. Boston, MA: Kluwer Academic Publishers.

Färe, R., Grosskopf, S., and Logan, J. (1983). The relative efficiency of Illinois electric utilities. *Resources and Energy*, 5(4):349–367.

Färe, R., Grosskopf, S., and Lovell, C. A. K. (1985). *The Measurement of Efficiency of Production*. Boston, MA: Kluwer-Nijhoff Publishing.

Färe, R., Grosskopf, S., and Lovell, C. A. K. (1986). Scale economies and duality. *Zeitschrift für Nationalökonomie / Journal of Economics*, 46(2):175–182.

Färe, R., Grosskopf, S., and Lovell, C. A. K. (1994b). *Production Frontiers*. New York, NY: Cambridge University Press.

Färe, R., Grosskopf, S., Lovell, C. A. K., and Pasurka, C. (1989b). Multilateral productivity comparisons when some outputs are undesirable: A nonparametric approach. *The Review of Economics and Statistics*, 71(1):90–98.

Färe, R., Grosskopf, S., and Margaritis, D. (2008a). Efficiency and productivity: Malmquist and more. In Fried, H., Lovell, C. A. K., and Schmidt, S., editors, *The Measurement of Productive Efficiency and Productivity Change*, pages 522–621. New York, NY: Oxford University Press.

Färe, R., Grosskopf, S., Norris, M., and Zhang, Z. (1994c). Productivity growth, technical progress, and efficiency change in industrialized countries. *American Economic Review*, 84(1):66–83.

Färe, R., Grosskopf, S., and Roos, P. (1996). On two definitions of productivity. *Economics Letters*, 53(3):269–274.

Färe, R., Grosskopf, S., and Roos, P. (1997b). Malmquist productivity indexes: A survey of theory and practice. In Färe, R., Grosskopf, S., and Russell, R. R., editors, *Index Numbers: Essays in Honour of Sten Malmquist*, pages 127–190. Amsterdam: Springer.

Färe, R., Grosskopf, S., and Zelenyuk, V. (2004). Aggregation of cost efficiency: Indicators and indexes across firms. *Academia Economic Papers*, 32(3):395–411.

Färe, R., Grosskopf, S., and Zelenyuk, V. (2007). Finding common ground: Efficiency indices. In Färe, R., Grosskopf, S., and Primont, D., editors, *Aggregation, Efficiency and Measurement*, pages 83–95. Boston, MA: Springer.

Färe, R., Grosskopf, S., and Zelenyuk, V. (2008b). Aggregation of Nerlovian profit indicator. *Applied Economics Letters*, 15(11):845–847.

Färe, R., He, X., Li, S. K., and Zelenyuk, V. A (2018). unifying framework for Farrell profit efficiency measurement. *Operations Research*, Accepted. ISSN 1526–5463 (online).

Färe, R. and Karagiannis, G. (2014). A postscript on aggregate Farrell efficiencies. *European Journal of Operational Research*, 233(3):784–786.

Färe, R. and Lovell, C. K. (1978). Measuring the technical efficiency of production. *Journal of Economic Theory*, 19(1):150–162.

Färe, R. and Primont, D. (1995). *Multi-Output Production and Duality: Theory and Applications*. New York, NY: Kluwer Academic Publishers.

Färe, R. and Primont, D. (2006). Directional duality theory. *Economic Theory*, 29(1):239–247.

Färe, R. and Sung, K. J. (1986). On second-order Taylor's-series approximation and linear homogeneity. *Aequationes Mathematicae*, 30(1):180–186.

Färe, R. and Svensson, L. (1980). Congestion of production factors. *Econometrica: Journal of the Econometric Society*, 48(7):1745–1753.

Färe, R. and Zelenyuk, V. (2002). Input aggregation and technical efficiency. *Applied Economics Letters*, 9(10):635–636.

Färe, R. and Zelenyuk, V. (2003). On aggregate Farrell efficiencies. *European Journal of Operational Research*, 146(3):615–620.

Färe, R. and Zelenyuk, V. (2005). On Farrell's decomposition and aggregation. *International Journal of Business and Economics*, 4(2):167–171.

Färe, R. and Zelenyuk, V. (2007). Extending Färe and Zelenyuk (2003). *European Journal of Operational Research*, 179(2):594–595.

Färe, R. and Zelenyuk, V. (2012). Aggregation of scale elasticities across firms. *Applied Economics Letters*, 19(16):1593–1597.

Farrell, M. J. (1957). The measurement of productive efficiency. *Jornal of the Royal Statistical Society. Series A (General)*, 120(3):253–290.

Ferrier, G., Leleu, H., and Valdmanis, V. (2009). Hospital capacity in large urban areas: Is there enough in times of need? *Journal of Productivity Analysis*, 32(2): 103–117.

Filippini, M. and Greene, W. H. (2016). Persistent and transient productive inefficiency: A maximum simulated likelihood approach. *Journal of Productivity Analysis*, 45(2):187–196.

Fisher, F. M. and Shell, K. (1972). *The Economic Theory of Price Indexes*. New York, NY: Academic Press.

Fisher, I. (1911). *The Purchasing Power of Money*. New York, NY: Macmillan.

Fisher, I. (1921). The best form of index number. *Journal of the American Statistical Association*, 17(133):533–537.

Fisher, I. (1922). *The Making of Index Numbers*. Boston, MA: Houghton Mifflin.

Florens, J.-P. and Simar, L. (2005). Parametric approximations of nonparametric frontiers. *Journal of Econometrics*, 124(1):91–116.

Førsund, F. R. (1996). On the calculation of the scale elasticity in DEA models. *Journal of Productivity Analysis*, 7(2–3):283–302.

Førsund, F. R. (1997). The Malmquist productivity index, TFP and scale. Memorandum No. 233, Gothenburg: Department of Economics and Commercial Law, Göteborg University.

Førsund, F. R. (2009). Good modelling of bad outputs: Pollution and multiple-output production. *International Review of Environmental and Resource Economics*, 3(1):1–38.

Førsund, F. R. (2010). Dynamic efficiency measurement. *Indian Economic Review*, 45(2):125–159.

Førsund, F. R. (2017). Productivity measurement and the environment. In Grifell-Tatjé, E., Lovell, C. A. K., and Sickles, R. C., editors, *The Oxford Handbook of Productivity*, chapter 8. New York, NY: Oxford University Press.

Førsund, F. R. and Hjalmarsson, L. (1979). Generalised Farrell measures of efficiency: An application to milk processing in Swedish dairy plants. *The Economic Journal*, 89(354):294–315.

Førsund, F. R. and Hjalmarsson, L. (2008). Dynamic analysis of structural change and productivity measurement. Working Paper No. 2008,27, Oslo: University of Oslo Department of Economics.

Førsund, F. R. and Sarafoglou, N. (2002). On the origins of data envelopment analysis. *Journal of Productivity Analysis*, 17(1):23–40.

Foster, L., Haltiwanger, J., and Syverson, C. (2008). Reallocation, firm turnover, and efficiency: Selection on productivity or profitability? *American Economic Review*, 98(1):394–425.

Fox, K. J. (1998). Non-parametric estimation of technical progress. *Journal of Productivity Analysis*, 10(3):235–250.

Fox, K. J. (2003). An economic justification for the EKS multilateral index. *Review of Income and Wealth*, 49(3):407–413.

Frantz, R., Chen, S.-H., Dopfer, K., Heukelom, F., and Mousavi, S., editors (2017). *Routledge Handbook of Behavioral Economics*. New York, NY: Routledge.

Frantz, R. S. (1997). *X-Efficiency: Theory, Evidence and Applications*. Norwell, MA: Kluwer Academic Publishers, 2nd edition.

Frantz, R. S. (2007). Empirical evidence on X-efficiency, 1967–2004. In Frantz, R., editor, *Renaissance in Behavioral Economics: Essays in Honour of Harvey Leibenstein*, pages 221–227. New York, NY: Routledge.

Fried, H. O., Lovell, C. A. K., and Schmidt, S. S. (2008). *The Measurement of Productive Efficiency and Productivity Growth*. New York, NY: Oxford University Press.

Frisch, R. (1930). Necessary and sufficient conditions regarding the form of an index number which shall meet certain of Fisher's tests. *American Statistical Association Journal*, 25(172):397–406.

Frisch, R. (1936). Annual survey of general economic theory: The problem of index numbers. *Econometrica*, 4(1):1–38.

Fu, X. M. and Heffernan, S. (2009). The effects of reform on China's bank structure and performance. *Journal of Banking & Finance*, 33(1):39–52.

Fukuyama, H. (2000). Returns to scale and scale elasticity in data envelopment analysis. *European Journal of Operational Research*, 125(1):93–112.

Fukuyama, H. (2003). Scale characterizations in a DEA directional technology distance function framework. *European Journal of Operational Research*, 144(1):108–127.

Fukuyama, H. and Weber, W. (2009). A directional slacks-based measure of technical inefficiency. *Socio-Economic Planning Sciences*, 43(4):274–287.

Funke, H. and Voeller, J. (1978). A note on the characterization of Fisher's "ideal index". In Eichhorn, W., Henn, R., Opitz, O., and Shephard, R. W., editors, *Theory and Applications of Economic Indices*, pages 177–181. Heidelberg: Physica-Verlag.

Fuss, M., McFadden, D., and Mundlak, Y. (1978). A survey of functional forms in the economic analysis of production. In Fuss, M. and McFadden, D., editors, *Production Economics: A Dual Approach to Theory and Applications*, volume 1, chapter 4, pages 219–268. Ontario: McMaster University Archive for the History of Economic Thought.

Fuss, M. A. and McFadden, D., editors (1978). *Production Economics: A Dual Approach to Theory and Applications*, volume 1. Amsterdam: North-Holland.

Gallant, A. R. (1981). On the bias in flexible functional forms and an essentially unbiased form: The Fourier flexible form. *Journal of Econometrics*, 15(2): 211–245.

Gallant, A. R. (1982). Unbiased determination of production technologies. *Journal of Econometrics*, 20(2):285–323.

Gallant, A. R. (1984). The Fourier flexible form. *American Journal of Agricultural Economics*, 66(2):204–208.

Gallant, A. R. and Golub, G. H. (1984). Imposing curvature restrictions on flexible functional forms. *Journal of Econometrics*, 26(3):295–321.

Gao, W., Hartley, P. R., and Sickles, R. C. (2009). Optimal dynamic production from a large oil field in Saudi Arabia. *Empirical Economics*, 37(1):153–184.

Georgescu-Roegen, N. (1951). The aggregate linear production function and its applications to von Neumann's economic model. In Koopmans, T., editor, *Activity Analysis of Production and Allocation*. New York, NY: Wiley.

Getachew, L. and Sickles, R. C. (2007). The policy environment and relative price efficiency of Egyptian private sector manufacturing: 1987/88–1995/96. *Journal of Applied Econometrics*, 22(4):703–728.

Getis, A. and Aldstadt, J. (2004). Constructing the spatial weights matrix using a local statistic. *Geographical Analysis*, 36(2):90–104.

Gijbels, I., Mammen, E., Park, B. U., and Simar, L. (1999). On estimation of mono-tone and concave frontier functions. *Journal of the American Statistical Association*, 94(445):220–228.

Gini, C. (1931). On the circular test of index numbers. *Metron*, 9(9):3–24.

Glaister, K. W. (2014). The contribution of management to economic growth: A review. *Prometheus*, 32(3):227–244.

Glass, A., Kenjegalieva, K., and Paez-Farrell, J. (2013). Productivity growth decomposition using a spatial autoregressive frontier model. *Economics Letters*, 119(3):291–295.

Glass, A., Kenjegalieva, K., and Sickles, R. C. (2014). Estimating efficiency spillovers with state level evidence for manufacturing in the US. *Economics Letters*, 123(2):154–159.

Glass, A., Kenjegalieva, K., Sickles, R. C., and Weyman-Jones, T. G. (2018). The spatial efficiency multiplier and random effects in spatial stochastic frontier models. RISE Working Paper No. 16–002, Houston, TX: Rice Institute for the Study of Economics, Rice University.

Glass, A. J., Kenjegalieva, K., and Sickles, R. C. (2016). A spatial autoregressive stochastic frontier model for panel data with asymmetric efficiency spillovers. *Journal of Econometrics*, 190(2):289–300.

Good, D. H., Nadiri, M. I., and Sickles, R. C. (1997). Index number and factor demand approaches to the estimation of productivity. In Pesaran, M. H. and Schmidt, P., editors, *Handbook of Applied Econometrics*, volume II - Microeconometrics, chapter 1, page 14. Reprinted as NBER Working Paper No. 5790 Cambridge, MA: National Bureau of Economic Research.

Good, D. H., Röller, L.-H., and Sickles, R. C. (1995). Airline efficiency differences between Europe and the US: Implications for the pace of EC integration and domestic regulation. *European Journal of Operational Research*, 80(3):508–518.

Good, D. H., Sickles, R. C., and Weiher, J. C. (2008). A hedonic price index for airline travel. *Review of Income and Wealth*, 54(3):438–465.

Gordon, R. J. (2017). The Rise and Fall of American Growth: The US Standard of Living since the Civil War. Princeton, NJ: Princeton University Press.

Granger, C. W. J. and Newbold, P. (1974). Spurious regressions in econometrics. *Journal of Econometrics*, 2(2):111–120.

Greene, W. H. (1980a). Maximum likelihood estimation of econometric frontier functions. *Journal of Econometrics*, 13(1):27–56.

Greene, W. H. (1980b). On the estimation of a flexible frontier production model. *Journal of Econometrics*, 13(1):101–115.

Greene, W. H. (1990). A Gamma-distributed stochastic frontier model. *Journal of Econometrics*, 46(1):141–163.

Greene, W. H. (2002). Alternative panel data estimators for stochastic frontier models. Unpublished manuscript, New York, NY: New York University.

Greene, W. H. (2004). Distinguishing between heterogeneity and inefficiency: Stochastic frontier analysis of the World Health Organization's panel data on national health care systems. *Health Economics*, 13(10):959–980.

Greene, W. H. (2005a). Fixed and random effects in stochastic frontier models. *Journal of Productivity Analysis*, 23(1):7–32.

Greene, W. H. (2005b). Reconsidering heterogeneity in panel data estimators of the stochastic frontier model. *Journal of Econometrics*, 126(2):269–303.

Greene, W. H. (2007). The econometric approach to efficiency analysis. In Fried, H. O., Lovell, C. A. K., and Schmidt, S. S., editors, *The Measurement of Productive Efficiency: Techniques and Applications*. New York, NY: Oxford University Press.

Greene, W. H. (2010). A stochastic frontier model with correction for sample selection. *Journal of Productivity Analysis*, 34(1):15–24.

Greenwald, B. C. and Stiglitz, J. E. (1986). Externalities in economies with imperfect information and incomplete markets. *The Quarterly Journal of Economics*, 101(2):229–264.

Greenwood, J., Hercowitz, Z., and Krusell, P. (1997). Long-run implications of investment-specific technological change. *American Economic Review*, 87(3):342–362.

Grifell-Tatjé, E. and Lovell, C. (1995). A note on the Malmquist productivity index. *Economics letters*, 47(2):169–175.

Grifell-Tatjé, E. and Lovell, C. A. K. (1999). A generalized Malmquist productivity index. *Top*, 7(1):81–101.

Grifell-Tatjé, E. and Lovell, C. A. K. (2004). Farrell's technical efficiency measurement. In Segura, J. and Braun, C. R., editors, *An Eponymous Dictionary of Economics: A Guide to Laws and Theorems Named after Economists*, page 75. Cheltenham: Edward Elgar.

Grifell-Tatjé, E. and Lovell, C. A. K. (2005). *An Eponymous Dictionary of Economics*, chapter Michael James Farrell, page 75. Cheltenham: Edward Elgar Publishing Ltd.

Grifell-Tatjé, E. and Lovell, C. A. K. (2013). Advances in cost frontier analysis of the firm. In Thomas, C. R. and Shughart, W., editors, *The Oxford Handbook of Managerial Economics*, pages 1–18. London: Oxford University Press.

Grifell-Tatjé, E. and Lovell, C. A. K. (2014). Productivity, price recovery, capacity constraints and their financial consequences. *Journal of Productivity Analysis*, 41(1):3–17.

Grifell-Tatjé, E. and Lovell, C. A. K. (2015). *Productivity Accounting*. New York, NY: Cambridge University Press.

Grifell-Tatjé, E., Lovell, C. A. K., and Sickles, R. C. (eds.) (2018). *Oxford Handbook of Productivity*. New York, NY: Oxford University Press.

Griffin, J. M. (1977). The econometrics of joint production: Another approach. *The Review of Economics and Statistics*, 59(4):389–397.

Griffin, J. M. (1978). Joint production technology: The case of petrochemicals. *Econometrica*, 46(2):379–396.

Griffin, R. C., Montgomery, J. M., and Rister, M. E. (1987). Selecting functional form in production function analysis. *Western Journal of Agricultural Economics*, 12(2):216–227.

Griffiths, W. E. and Hajargasht, G. (2016). Some models for stochastic frontiers with endogeneity. *Journal of Econometrics*, 190(2):341–348.

Griliches, Z. (1994). Productivity, R&D, and the data constraint. *American Economic Review*, 84(1):1–23.

Griliches, Z. (1996). The discovery of the residual: A historical note. *Journal of Economic Literature*, 34(3):1324–1330.

Griliches, Z. and Mairesse, J. (1995). Production functions: The search for identification. NBER Working Paper No. 5067.

Groeneboom, P., Jongbloed, G., and Wellner, J. A. (2001). Estimation of a convex function: Characterizations and asymptotic theory. *Annals of Statistics*, 29(6):1653–1698.

Gronberg, T. J., Jansen, D. W., and Taylor, L. L. (2011). The impact of facilities on the cost of education. *National Tax Journal*, 64(1):193–218.

Grosskopf, S. (1986). The role of the reference technology in measuring productive efficiency. *The Economic Journal*, 96(382):499–513.

Grosskopf, S. and Self, S. (2006). Factor accumulation or TFP? A reassessment of growth in Southeast Asia. *Pacific Economic Review*, 11(1):39–58.

Guan, Z., Kumbhakar, S. C., Myers, R. J., and Lansink, A. O. (2009). Measuring excess capital capacity in agricultural production. *American Journal of Agricultural Economics*, 91(3):765–776.

Guilkey, D. K., Lovell, C. A. K., and Sickles, R. C. (1983). A comparison of the performance of three flexible functional forms. *International Economic Review*, 24(3):591–616.

Gunning, T. S. and Sickles, R. C. (2011). A multi-product cost function for physician private practices. *Journal of Productivity Analysis*, 35(2):119–128.

Gunning, T. S. and Sickles, R. C. (2013). Competition and market power in physician private practices. *Empirical Economics*, 44(2):1005–1029.

Hadjicostas, P. and Soteriou, A. (2010). Different orders of one-sided scale elasticities in multi-output production. *Journal of Productivity Analysis*, 33(2):147–167.

Hadjicostas, P. and Soteriou, A. C. (2006). One-sided elasticities and technical efficiency in multi-output production: A theoretical framework. *European Journal of Operational Research*, 168(2):425–449.

Hafner, C. M., Manner, H., and Simar, L. (2016). The "wrong skewness" problem in stochastic frontier models: A new approach. *Econometric Reviews*, 37(4), 380–400.

Hajargasht, G., Coelli, T., and Rao, D. S. P. (2008). A dual measure of economies of scope. *Economics Letters*, 100(2):185–188.

Hall, M. J., Kenjegalieva, K. A., and Simper, R. (2012). Environmental factors affecting Hong Kong banking: A post-Asian financial crisis efficiency analysis. *Global Finance Journal*, 23(3):184–201.

Hall, P. (1984). Central limit theorem for integrated square error of multivariate nonparametric density estimators. *Annals of Statistics*, 14(1):1–16.

Hall, P. (1992). On bootstrap confidence intervals in nonparametric regression. *Annals of Statistics*, 20(2):695–711.

Hall, P. and Huang, L.-S. (2001). Nonparametric kernel regression subject to monotonicity constraints. *Annals of Statistics*, 29(3):624–647.

Hall, P. and Marron, J. S. (1991). Local minima in cross-validation functions. *Journal of the Royal Statistical Society. Series B (Methodological)*, 53(1):245–252.

Hall, R. E. and Jones, C. I. (1999). Why do some countries produce so much more output per worker than others? *The Quarterly Journal of Economics*, 114(1):83–116.

Haltiwanger, J. C., Lane, J. I., and Spletzer, J. R. (1999). Productivity differences across employers: The roles of employer size, age, and human capital. *American Economic Review*, 89(2):94–98.

Hamermesh, D. S. and Pfann, G. A. (1996). Adjustment costs in factor demand. *Journal of Economic Literature*, 34(3):1264–1292.

Hamilton, J. D. (1994). *Time Series Analysis*, volume 2. Princeton, NJ: Princeton University Press.

Hampf, B. (2015). Estimating the materials balance condition: A stochastic frontier approach. Darmstadt Discussion Papers in Economics No. 226, Darmstadt: Darmstadt Universiy of Technology, Department of Law and Economics.

Han, J., Ryu, D., and Sickles, R. C. (2016a). How to measure spillover effects of public capital stock: A spatial autoregressive stochastic frontier model. In Fomby, T. B.,

Hill, R. C., Jeliazkov, I., Escanciano, J. C., and Hillebrand, E., editors, *Spatial Econometrics: Qualitative and Limited Dependent Variables*, volume 37 of *Advances in Econometrics*, chapter 9, pages 259–294. Bingley: Emerald.

Han, J., Ryu, D., and Sickles, R. C. (2016b). Spillover effects of public capital stock using spatial frontier analyses: A first look at the data. In Greene, W. H., Sickles, R., Khalaf, L., Veall, M., and Voia, M.-C., editors, *Productivity and Efficiency Analysis: Proceedings from the 2014 North American Productivity Workshop*. New York, NY: Springer.

Han, J. and Sickles, R. C. (2019). Estimation of industry-level productivity with cross-sectional dependence by using spatial analysis. RISE (Rice Initiative for the Study of Economics) Working paper # 19–002, Rice University.

Hanoch, G. (1970). Homotheticity in joint production. *Journal of Economic Theory*, 2(4):423–426.

Hanoch, G. (1971). CRESH production functions. *Econometrica*, 39(5):695–712.

Hanoch, G. (1975). The elasticity of scale and the shape of average costs. *American Economic Review*, 65(3):492–497.

Hansen, B. E. (2007). Least squares model averaging. *Econometrica*, 75(4):1175–1189.

Hansen, B. E. and Racine, J. S. (2012). Jackknife model averaging. *Journal of Econometrics*, 167(1):38–46.

Hao, G., Wei, Q. L., and Yan, H. (2000). A game theoretical model of DEA efficiency. *The Journal of the Operational Research Society*, 51(11):1319–1329.

Härdle, W. (1990). *Applied Nonparametric Regression*. Cambridge: Cambridge University Press.

Hardy, G., Littlewood, J., and Pólya, G. (1934). *Inequalities*. Cambridge: Cambridge University Press.

Haskel, J. and Westlake, S. (2018). *Capitalism Without Capital: The Rise of the Intangible Economy*. Princeton, NJ: Princeton University Press.

Hausman, J. A. and Taylor, W. E. (1981). Panel data and unobservable individual effects. *Econometrica*, 49(6):1377–1398.

Heckman, J. J. (1976). Sample selection bias with continuous and discrete endogenous variables and structure shifts. In Goldfield, S. and Quandt, R. E., editors, *Studies in Non-Linear Estimation*, pages 235–272. New York, NY: Harper Collins.

Heckman, J. J. (1979). Sample selection bias as a specification error. *Econometrica*, 47(1):153–161.

Heckman, J. J. and Singer, B. (1984). A method for minimizing the impact of distributional assumptions in econometric models for duration data. *Econometrica*, 52(2):271–320.

Heckman, N. E. and Ramsay, J. O. (2000). Penalized regression with model-based penalties. *Canadian Journal of Statistics*, 28(2):241–258.

Henderson, D. J., Tochkov, K., and Badunenko, O. (2007). A drive up the capital coast? Contributions to post-reform growth across Chinese provinces. *Journal of Macroeconomics*, 29(3):569–594.

Henderson, D. J., Kumbhakar, S. C., Li, Q., and Parmeter, C. F. (2015). Smooth coefficient estimation of a seemingly unrelated regression. *Journal of Econometrics*, 189(1):148–162.

Henderson, D. J., List, J. A., Millimet, D. L., Parmeter, C. F., and Price, M. K. (2012). Empirical implementation of nonparametric first-price auction models. *Journal of Econometrics*, 168(1):17–28.

Henderson, D. J. and Parmeter, C. F. (2015). A consistent bootstrap procedure for nonparametric symmetry tests. *Economics Letters*, 131(C):78–82.

Henderson, D. J. and Russell, R. R. (2005). Human capital and convergence: A production-frontier approach. *International Economic Review*, 46(4):1167–1205.

Henderson, D. J. and Zelenyuk, V. (2007). Testing for (efficiency) catching-up. *Southern Economic Journal*, 73(4):1003–1019.

Hicks, J. R. (1932). *The Theory of Wages*. London: Macmillan.

Hicks, J. R. (1935). Annual survey of economic theory: the theory of monopoly. *Econometrica*, 3(1):1–20.

Hicks, J. R. (1961). Measurement of capital in relation to the measurement of other economic aggregates. In Hague, D. C., editor, *Theory of Capital*. New York, NY: Springer.

Hicks, J. R. and Allen, R. G. D. (1934). A reconsideration of the theory of value. Part II. A mathematical theory of individual demand functions. *Economica*, 1(2):196–219.

Hjalmarsson, L., Kumbhakar, S. C., and Heshmati, A. (1996). DEA, DFA and SFA: A comparison. *Journal of Productivity Analysis*, 7(2):303–327.

Hjorth, J. S. U. (1993). *Computer Intensive Statistical Methods: Validation, Model Selection, and Bootstrap*. New York, NY: CRC Press.

Hoch, I. (1958). Simultaneous equation bias in the context of the Cobb–Douglas production function. *Econometrica*, 26(4):566–578.

Hoeting, J. A., Madigan, D., Raftery, A. E., and Volinsky, C. T. (1999). Bayesian model averaging: A tutorial. *Statistical Science*, 14(4):382–401.

Hofman, A., Aravena, C., and Friedman, J. (2017). Sources of productivity and economic growth in Latin America and the Caribbean, 1990–2013. *International Productivity Monitor*, (33):51–76.

Holtz-Eakin, D., Newey, W., and Rosen, H. S. (1988). Estimating vector autoregressions with panel data. *Econometrica*, 56(4):1371–1395.

Horowitz, J. L. (2002). Bootstrap critical values for tests based on the smoothed maximum score estimator. *Journal of Econometrics*, 111(2):141–167.

Horowitz, J. L., Mammen, E., et al. (2004). Nonparametric estimation of an additive model with a link function. *Annals of Statistics*, 32(6):2412–2443.

Horrace, W. C. (2005). On ranking and selection from independent truncated normal distributions. *Journal of Econometrics*, 126(2):335–354.

Horrace, W. C. and Parmeter, C. F. (2018). A Laplace stochastic frontier model. *Econometric Reviews*, 37(3):260–280.

Horrace, W. C. and Schmidt, P. (1996). Confidence statements for efficiency estimates from stochastic frontier models. *Journal of Productivity Analysis*, 7(2–3):257–282.

Horrace, W. C. and Schmidt, P. (2000). Multiple comparisons with the best, with economic applications. *Journal of Applied Econometrics*, 15(1):1–26.

Horrace, W. C. and Wright, I. A. (2017). Stationary points for stochastic frontier models. Center for Policy Research Working Paper No. 196, Syracuse, NY: The Maxwell School, Syracuse University.

Hsieh, C.-T. and Klenow, P. J. (2009). Misallocation and manufacturing TFP in China and India. *The Quarterly Journal of Economics*, 124(4):1403–1448.

Huang, T.-h. and Wang, M.-h. (2004). Comparisons of economic inefficiency between output and input measures of technical inefficiency using the Fourier flexible cost function. *Journal of Productivity Analysis*, 22(1–2):123–142.

Huh, K. and Sickles, R. C. (1994). Estimation of the duration model by nonparametric maximum likelihood, maximum penalized likelihood, and probability simulators. *The Review of Economics and Statistics*, 76(4):683–694.

Hultberg, P. T., Nadiri, M. I., and Sickles, R. C. (1999). An international comparison of technology adoption and efficiency: A dynamic panel model. *Annales d'Economie et de Statistique*, (55/56):449–474.

Hultberg, P. T., Nadiri, M. I., and Sickles, R. C. (2004). Cross-country catch-up in the manufacturing sector: Impacts of heterogeneity on convergence and technology adoption. *Empirical Economics*, 29(4):753–768.

Hulten, C. R. and Isaksson, A. (2007). Why development levels differ: The sources of differential economic growth in a panel of high and low income countries (No. w13469). Cambridge, MA: National Bureau of Economic Research.

Im, K. S., Pesaran, M. H., and Shin, Y. (2003). Testing for unit roots in heterogeneous panels. *Journal of Econometrics*, 115(1):53–74.

Inanoglu, H., Jacobs Jr, M., Liu, J., and Sickles, R. C. (2016). Analyzing bank efficiency: Are "too-big-to-fail" banks efficient? In *The Handbook of Post Crisis Financial Modeling*, pages 110–146. New York, NY: Palgrave Macmillan.

International Labour Office, Internatonal Monetary Fund, Organisation for Economic Co-operation and Development, Statistical Office of the European Communities (Eurostat), United Nations, World Bank (2004). *Consumer Price Index Manual: Theory and Practice*. Geneva: International Labour Office.

International Productivity Monitor. (2017). Special Issue from the Fourth World KLEMS Conference, 33 (Fall). Ottawa: Centre for the Study of Living Standards.

Isaksson, A., Shang, C., and Sickles, R. C. (2018). Non-structural analysis of productivity growth for the industrialized countries: A jackknife model averaging approach. Unpublished manuscript, Houston, TX: Rice University.

Jeon, B. M. and Sickles, R. C. (2004). The role of environmental factors in growth accounting. *Journal of Applied Econometrics*, 19(5):567–591.

Jeong, S.-O. and Simar, L. (2006). Linearly interpolated FDH efficiency score for nonconvex frontiers. *Journal of Multivariate Analysis*, 97(10):2141–2161.

Jiang, C., Yao, S., and Zhang, Z. (2009). The effects of governance changes on bank efficiency in China: A stochastic distance function approach. *China Economic Review*, 20(4):717–731.

Johansen, S. (1988). Statistical analysis of cointegration vectors. *Journal of Economic Dynamics and Control*, 12(2-3):231–254.

Johnson, A. and Layer, K. (2016). Direction selection in stochastic directional distance functions. Unpublished manuscript, College Station, TX: Texas A&M University.

Johnson, A., Layer, K., and Sickles, R. C. (2017). Modeling noise and estimating of the directional distance function. Unpublished manuscript, College Station, TX: Texas A&M University.

Jondrow, J., Lovell, C. A. K., Materov, I. S., and Schmidt, P. (1982). On the estimation of technical inefficiency in the stochastic frontier production function model. *Journal of Econometrics*, 19(2–3):233–238.

Jones, C. I. (2012). Misallocation, economic growth, and input-output economics. In Acemoglu, D., Arellano, M., and Dekel, E., editors, *Advances in Economics and Econometrics*. New York, NY: Cambridge University Press.

Jones, C. I. (2015). Pareto and Piketty: The macroeconomics of top income and wealth inequality. *The Journal of Economic Perspectives*, 29(1):29–46.

Jorgenson, D. W. (2002). *Econometrics: Economic Growth in the Information Age*, volume 3. Cambridge, MA: MIT Press.

Jorgenson, D. W. (2017). World KLEMS: Productivity and economic growth in the world economy: An introduction. *International Productivity Monitor*, (33):1–7.

Jorgenson, D. W. and Fraumeni, B. M. (1989). The accumulation of human and nonhuman capital, 1948–1984. In Lipsey, R. E. and Tice, H. S., editors, *The Measurement of Saving, Investment and Wealth, Studies in Income and Wealth*, volume 52, pages 277–282. Chicago, IL: University of Chicago Press.

Jorgenson, D. W. and Fraumeni, B. M. (1992). The output of the education sector. In Griliches, Z., editor, *Output Measurement in the Services Sector, Studies in Income and Wealth*, volume 55, pages 303–338. Chicago, IL: University of Chicago Press.

Jorgenson, D. W. and Griliches, Z. (1967). The explanation of productivity change. *Review of Economic Studies*, 34(3):249–283.

Jorgenson, D. W. and Griliches, Z. (1972). Issues in growth accounting: A reply to Edward F. Denison. *Survey of Current Business*, 52(5, Part II):65–94.

Jorgenson, D. W., Ho, M. S., and Stiroh, K. J. (2005). *Productivity, Volume 3: Information Technology and the American Growth Resurgence*, volume 3. Cambridge, MA: MIT Press.

Jorgenson, D. W. and Lau, L. J. (1974). The duality of technology and economic behaviour. *Review of Economic Studies*, 41(2):181–200.

Jorgenson, D. W. and Lau, L. J. (1979). The integrability of consumer demand functions. *European Economic Review*, 12(2):115–147.

Jorgenson, D. W. and Nishimizu, M. (1978). U.S. and Japanese economic growth, 1952–1974: An international comparison. *Economic Journal*, 88(352):707–726.

Jovanovic, B. (1982). Selection and the evolution of industry. *Econometrica*, 50(3):649–670.

Kalirajan, K. (1981). An econometric analysis of yield variability in paddy production. *Canadian Journal of Agricultural Economics/Revue Canadienne D'Agroeconomie*, 29(3):283–294.

Kalirajan, K. P., Obwona, M. B., and Zhao, S. (1996). A decomposition of total factor productivity growth: The case of Chinese agricultural growth before and after reforms. *American Journal of Agricultural Economics*, 78(2):331–338.

Kantorovich, L. V. (1960). Mathematical methods of organizing and planning production. *Management Science*, 6(4):366–422.

Kao, C. (2009a). Efficiency decomposition in network data envelopment analysis: A relational model. *European Journal of Operational Research*, 192(3):949–962.

Kao, C. (2009b). Efficiency measurement for parallel production systems. *European Journal of Operational Research*, 196(3):1107–1112.

Kao, C. (2014). Network data envelopment analysis: A review. *European Journal of Operational Research*, 239(1):1–16.

Karagiannis, G. (2015). On structural and average technical efficiency. *Journal of Productivity Analysis*, 43(3):259–267.

Karagiannis, G. and Lovell, C. A. K. (2015). Productivity measurement in radial DEA models with a single constant input. *European Journal of Operational Research*, 251(1):323–328.

Karakaplan, M. and Kutlu, L. (2017a). Handling endogeneity in stochastic frontier analysis. *Economics Bulletin*, 37(2):889–901.

Karakaplan, M. U. and Kutlu, L. (2017b). Endogeneity in panel stochastic frontier models: An application to the Japanese cotton spinning industry. *Applied Economics*, 49(59):5935–5939.

Karlin, S. (1959). *Mathematical methods and theory in games, programming, and economics*, volume 2. Reading, MA: Addison Wesley.

Katona, G. (1951). *Psychological Analysis of Economic Behavior*. New York, NY: McGraw-Hill.

Kelejian, H. and Prucha, I. (1998). A generalized spatial two-stage least squares procedure for estimating a spatial autoregressive model with autoregressive disturbances. *The Journal of Real Estate Finance and Economics*, 17(1):99–121.

Kelejian, H. H. and Prucha, I. R. (2010). Specification and estimation of spatial autoregressive models with autoregressive and heteroskedastic disturbances. *Journal of Econometrics*, 157(1):53–67.

Kendrick, J. W. (1961). *Productivity Trends in the United States*. Princeton, NJ: Princeton University Press.

Kenjegalieva, K., Simper, R., Weyman-Jones, T., and Zelenyuk, V. (2009). Comparative analysis of banking production frameworks in Eastern European financial markets. *European Journal of Operational Research*, 198(1):326–340.

Keynes, J. M. (1936). *General Theory of Employment, Interest and Money*. London: Palgrave Macmillan.

Kiefer, N. M. (1982). A remark on the parameterization of a model for heterogeneity. Working Paper No. 278, Ithaca, NY: Cornell University Department of Economics.

Kim, J.-I. and Lau, L. J. (1994). The sources of economic growth of the East Asian newly industrialized countries. *Journal of the Japanese and International Economies*, 8(3):235–271.

Kim, M., Kim, Y., and Schmidt, P. (2007). On the accuracy of bootstrap confidence intervals for efficiency levels in stochastic frontier models with panel data. *Journal of Productivity Analysis*, 28(3):165–181.

Kim, M. and Schmidt, P. (2008). Valid tests of whether technical inefficiency depends on firm characteristics. *Journal of Econometrics*, 144(2):409–427.

Kim, S. and Lee, Y. H. (2006). The productivity debate of East Asia revisited: A stochastic frontier approach. *Applied Economics*, 38(14):1697–1706.

Kim, S., Park, J. H., and Sickles, R. C. (2008). Is East Asia growth productivity-driven? A production frontier with group-specific time varying technical efficiency. Unpublished manuscript, Gwangju: Honam University.

Klein, L. R. (1953). *A Textbook of Econometrics*. Evanston, IL: Row, Peterson, and Co.

Klump, R., McAdam, P., and Willman, A. (2012). The normalized CES production function: Theory and empirics. *Journal of Economic Surveys*, 26(5):769–799.

Knack, S. and Keefer, P. (1995). Institutions and economic performance: Cross-country tests using alternative institutional measures. *Economics & Politics*, 7(3):207–227.

Kneip, A., Park, B. U., and Simar, L. (1998). A note on the convergence of nonparametric DEA estimators for production efficiency scores. *Econometric Theory*, 14(6):783–793.

Kneip, A. and Sickles, R. C. (2011). Panel data, factor models, and the Solow residual. In Van Keilegom, I. and Wilson, P. W., editors, *Exploring Research Frontiers in Contemporary Statistics and Econometrics: A Festschrift in Honor of Léopold Simar*, chapter 5, pages 83–114. New York, NY: Springer.

Kneip, A., Sickles, R. C., and Song, W. (2004). Functional data analysis and mixed effect models. In *COMPSTAT 2004-Proceedings in Computational Statistics*, pages 315–326. New York, NY: Springer.

Kneip, A., Sickles, R. C., and Song, W. (2012). A new panel data treatment for heterogeneity in time trends. *Econometric Theory*, 28(3):590–628.

Kneip, A. and Simar, L. (1996). A general framework for frontier estimation with panel data. *Journal of Productivity Analysis*, 7(2–3):187–212.

Kneip, A., Simar, L., and Wilson, P. W. (2008). Asymptotics and consistent bootstraps for DEA estimators in nonparametric frontier models. *Econometric Theory*, 24(6):1663–1697.

Kneip, A., Simar, L., and Wilson, P. W. (2011). A computationally efficient, consistent bootstrap for inference with non-parametric DEA estimators. *Computational Economics*, 38(4):483–515.

Kneip, A., Simar, L., and Wilson, P. W. (2015). When bias kills the variance: Central limit theorems for DEA and FDH efficiency scores. *Econometric Theory*, 31(2):394–422.

Kneip, A., Simar, L., and Wilson, P. W. (2016). Testing hypotheses in nonparametric models of production. *Journal of Business & Economic Statistics*, 34(3):435–456.

Kolm, S.-C. (1976). Unequal inequalities. II. *Journal of Economic Theory*, 13(1):82–111.

Kolmogorov, A. (1933). Sulla determinazione empirica di una legge di distribuzione. *Giornale dell'Instituto Italiano degli Attuari*, (4):83–91.

König, M. D., Lorenz, J., and Zilibotti, F. (2016). Innovation vs. imitation and the evolution of productivity distributions. *Theoretical Economics*, 11(3):1053–1102.

Konüs, A. A. (1939 [1924]). The problem of the true index of the cost of living. Translated into English and published in 1939. *Econometrica*, 7(1):10–29.

Konüs, A. A. and Byushgens, S. S. (1926). K probleme pokupatelnoi sily deneg. *Voprosy Konyunktury*, 2(1):151–172. English translation of Russian title: "On the problem of the purchasing power of money."

Koop, G., Poirier, D. J., and Tobias, J. L. (2007). *Bayesian Econometric Methods*. New York, NY: Cambridge University Press.

Koop, G., Steel, M. F., and Osiewalski, J. (1995). Posterior analysis of stochastic frontier models using Gibbs sampling. *Computational Statistics*, 10:353–373.

Koopmans, T. (1951a). *Activity Analysis of Production and Allocation*. New York, NY: Wiley.

Koopmans, T. (1957). *Three Essays on The State of Economic Science*. New York, NY: McGraw-Hill.

Koopmans, T. C. (1951b). Analysis of production as an efficienct combination of activities. In Koopmans, T. C., editor, *Activity Analysis of Production and Allocation*, volume 13, pages 33–37. New York, NY: Wiley.

Kopp, R. J. (1981). The measurement of productive efficiency: A reconsideration. *The Quarterly Journal of Economics*, 96(3):477–503.

Kopp, R. J. and Mullahy, J. (1993). Least squares estimation of econometric frontier models: Consistent estimation and inference. *The Scandinavian Journal of Economics*, 95(1):125–132.

Korostelev, A., Simar, L., and Tsybakov, A. B. (1995a). Efficient estimation of monotone boundaries. *Annals of Statistics*, 23(2):476–489.

Korostelev, A., Simar, L., and Tsybakov, A. B. (1995b). On estimation of monotone and convex boundaries. *Publications de l'Institut de Statistique des Universités de Paris*, 39(1):3–18.

Krein, M. and Smulian, V. (1940). On regulary convex sets in the space conjugate to a Banach space. *Annals of Mathematics*, 41(2):556–583.

Krugman, P. (1994). The myth of Asia's miracle. *Foreign Affairs*, 73(6):62–78.

Kumar, S. and Russell, R. R. (2002). Technological change, technological catch-up, and capital deepening: Relative contributions to growth and convergence. *American Economic Review*, 92(3):527–548.

Kumbhakar, S. and Lai, H. (2017). Endogeneity in panel data stochastic frontier model with determinants of persistent and transient inefficiency. Unpublished manuscript, Binghamton, NY: State University of New York.

Kumbhakar, S. C. (1987). The specification of technical and allocative inefficiency in stochastic production and profit frontiers. *Journal of Econometrics*, 34(3): 335–348.

Kumbhakar, S. C. (1990). Production frontiers, panel data, and time-varying technical inefficiency. *Journal of Econometrics*, 46(1):201–211.

Kumbhakar, S. C. (1994). A multiproduct symmetric generalized McFadden cost function. *Journal of Productivity Analysis*, 5(4):349–357.

Kumbhakar, S. C. (1997). Modeling allocative inefficiency in a translog cost function and cost share equations: An exact relationship. *Journal of Econometrics*, 76(1):351–356.

Kumbhakar, S. C. and Heshmati, A. (1995). Efficiency measurement in Swedish dairy farms: An application of rotating panel data, 1976–88. *American Journal of Agricultural Economics*, 77(3):660–674.

Kumbhakar, S. C. and Lovell, C. A. K. (2000). *Stochastic Frontier Analysis*. New York, NY: Cambridge University Press.

Kumbhakar, S. C., Orea, L., Rodríguez-Álvarez, A., and Tsionas, E. G. (2007a). Do we estimate an input or an output distance function? An application of the mixture approach to European railways. *Journal of Productivity Analysis*, 27(2):87–100.

Kumbhakar, S. C., Park, B. U., Simar, L., and Tsionas, E. G. (2007b). Nonparametric Stochastic Frontiers: A Local Maximum Likelihood Approach. *Journal of Econometrics*, 137(1):1–27.

Kumbhakar, S. C., Parmeter, C. F., and Tsionas, E. G. (2013). A zero inefficiency stochastic frontier model. *Journal of Econometrics*, 172(1):66–76.

Kumbhakar, S. C. and Tsionas, E. G. (2016). The good, the bad and the technology: Endogeneity in environmental production models. *Journal of Econometrics*, 190(2):315–327.

Künsch, H. R. (1989). The jackknife and the bootstrap for general stationary observations. *Annals of Statistics*, 17(3):1217–1241.

Kuosmanen, T. (2005). Weak disposability in non-parametric production analysis with undesirable outputs. *American Journal of Agricultural Economics*, 87(4):1077–1082.

Kuosmanen, T., Cherchye, L., and Sipiläinen, T. (2006). The law of one price in data envelopment analysis: Restricting weight flexibility across firms. *European Journal of Operational Research*, 170(3):735–757.

Kuosmanen, T. and Johnson, A. (2017). Modeling joint production of multiple outputs in StoNED: Directional distance function approach. *European Journal of Operational Research*, 262(2):792–801.

Kuosmanen, T., Johnson, A., and Parmeter, C. (2015). Orthogonality conditions for identification of joint production technologies. Available at SSRN: http://dx.doi.org/10.2139/ssrn.2602340.

Kuosmanen, T. and Kortelainen, M. (2012). Stochastic non-smooth envelopment of data: Semi-parametric frontier estimation subject to shape constraints. *Journal of Productivity Analysis*, 38(1):11–28.

Kuosmanen, T., Kortelainen, M., Sipiläinen, T., and Cherchye, L. (2010). Firm and industry level profit efficiency analysis using absolute and uniform shadow prices. *European Journal of Operational Research*, 202(2): 584–594.

Kuosmanen, T. and Podinovski, V. (2009). Weak disposability in nonparametric production analysis: Reply to Färe and Grosskopf. *American Journal of Agricultural Economics*, 91(2):539–545.

Kutlu, L. (2010). Battese-Coelli estimator with endogenous regressors. *Economics Letters*, 109(2):79–81.

Kutlu, L. and Nair-Reichert, U. (2018). Efficiency and executive pay: Evidence from Indian manufacturing sector. Unpublished manuscript, Atlanta, GA: Georgia Institute of Technology.

Kutlu, L. and Sickles, R. C. (2012). Estimation of market power in the presence of firm level inefficiencies. *Journal of Econometrics*, 168(1):141–155.

Kutlu, L., Tran, K., and Tsionas, M. (2018). A time-varying true individual effects model with endogenous regressors. Unpublished manuscript, Atlanta, GA: Georgia Institute of Technology.

Kwan, S. H. (2006). The X-efficiency of commercial banks in Hong Kong. *Journal of Banking & Finance*, 30(4):1127–1147.

Kwiatkowski, D., Phillips, P. C. B., Schmidt, P., and Shin, Y. (1992). Testing the null hypothesis of stationarity against the alternative of a unit root: How sure are we that economic time series have a unit root? *Journal of Econometrics*, 54(1–3):159–178.

Lahiri, K., Peng, H., and Sheng, X. (2010). Measuring aggregate uncertainty in a panel of forecasts and a new test for forecast heterogeneity. Unpublished manuscript, Albany, NY: University of Albany, SUNY.

Lahiri, K., Peng, H., and Zhao, Y. (2016). Online learning and forecast combination in unbalanced panels. *Econometric Reviews*, 36(1–3):1–32.

Lahiri, K. and Sheng, X. (2010). Measuring forecast uncertainty by disagreement: The missing link. *Journal of Applied Econometrics*, 25(4):514–538.

Landau, L. D. and Lifshitz, E. M. (1959). *Course of Theoretical Physics Vol 7: Theory and Elasticity*. Oxford: Pergamon Press.

Lansink, A. O., Stefanou, S., and Serra, T. (2015). Primal and dual dynamic Luenberger productivity indicators. *European Journal of Operational Research*, 241(2):555–563.

Laspeyres, E. (1871). Die berechnmung einer mittleren waarenpreissteigerung. *Jahrbücher für Nationalökonomie und Statistik*, 16:296–314.

Lau, L. J. (1976). A characterization of the normalized restricted profit function. *Journal of Economic Theory*, 12(1):131–163.

Lee, L.-F. and Chesher, A. (1986). Specification testing when score test statistics are identically zero. *Journal of Econometrics*, 31(2):121–149.

Lee, S. and Lee, Y. H. (2014). Stochastic frontier models with threshold efficiency. *Journal of Productivity Analysis*, 42(1):45–54.

Lee, Y. H. (1991). *Panel Data Models with Multiplicative Individual and Time Effects: Applications to Compensation and Frontier Production Functions*. PhD thesis, East Lansing, MI: Michigan State University.

Lee, Y. H. (1996). Tail truncated stochastic frontier models. *Journal of Economic Theory and Econometrics*, 2:137–152.

Lee, Y. H. and Schmidt, P. (1993). A production frontier model with flexible temporal variation in technical efficiency. In Fried, H. O., Lovell, C. A. K., and Schmidt, S. S., editors, *The Measurement of Productive Efficiency: Techniques and Applications*, pages 237–255. New York, NY: Oxford University Press.

Leeb, H. and Pötscher, B. M. (2005). Model selection and inference: Facts and fiction. *Econometric Theory*, 21(1):21–59.

Leibenstein, H. (1966). Allocative efficiency vs. "X-efficiency". *American Economic Review*, 56(3):392–415.

Leibenstein, H. (1975). Aspects of the X-efficiency theory of the firm. *The Bell Journal of Economics*, 6(2):580–606.

Leibenstein, H. (1987). *Inside the Firm: The Inefficiencies of Hierarchy*. Cambridge, MA: Harvard University Press.

Leibenstein, H. and Maital, S. (1992). Empirical estimation and partitioning of X-inefficiency: A data-envelopment approach. *American Economic Review*, 82(2):428–433.

Leontief, W. (1925). Die bilanz der russischen volkswirtschaft - eine methodologische untersuchung. *Weltwirtschaftliches Archiv*, 22(2):338–344.

LeSage, J. P. (2004). A family of geographically weighted regression models. In Anselin, L., Florax, R. J., and Rey, S. J., editors, *Advances in Spatial Econometrics*, pages 241–264. New York, NY: Springer.

Leung, G. and Barron, A. R. (2006). Information theory and mixing least-squares regressions. *IEEE Transactions on Information Theory*, 52(8):3396–3410.

Levinsohn, J. and Petrin, A. (2003). Estimating production function using inputs to control for unobservables. *Review of Economic Studies*, 70(2):317–341.

Levkoff, S. B., Russell, R. R., and Schworm, W. (2012). Boundary problems with the "Russell" graph measure of technical efficiency: A refinement. *Journal of Productivity Analysis*, 37(3):239–248.

Lewbel, A. (2010). Shape-invariant demand functions. *The Review of Economics and Statistics*, 92(3):549–556.

Li, D., Simar, L., and Zelenyuk, V. (2016). Generalized nonparametric smoothing with mixed discrete and continuous data. *Computational Statistics and Data Analysis*, 100(C):424–444.

Li, Q. (1996a). Estimating a stochastic production frontier when the adjusted error is symmetric. *Economics Letters*, 52(3):221–228.

Li, Q. (1996b). Nonparametric testing of closeness between two unknown distribution functions. *Econometric Reviews*, 15(3):261–274.

Li, Q. (1999). Nonparametric testing the similarity of two unknown density functions: Local power and bootstrap analysis. *Journal of Nonparametric Statistics*, 11(1–3):189–213.

Li, Q. and Racine, J. S. (2007). *Nonparametric Econometrics: Theory and Practice*. Princeton, NJ: Princeton University Press.

Li, S.-K. and Cheng, Y.-S. (2007). Solving the puzzles of structural efficiency. *European Journal of Operational Research*, 180(2):713–722.

Li, S.-K. and Ng, Y. C. (1995). Measuring the productive efficiency of a group of firms. *International Advances in Economic Research*, 1(4):377–390.

Liang, L., Wu, J., Cook, W. D., and Zhu, J. (2008). The DEA game cross-efficiency model and its Nash equilibrium. *Operations Research*, 56(5):1278–1288.

Lieberman, M. B., Lau, L. J., and Williams, M. D. (1990). Firm-level productivity and management influence: A comparison of US and Japanese automobile producers. *Management Science*, 36(10):1193–1215.

Liu, J., Sickles, R. C., and Tsionas, E. G. (2013). Bayesian treatments to panel data models. Unpublished manuscript, Houston, TX: Rice University.

Liu, J., Sickles, R. C., and Tsionas, E. G. (2017). Bayesian treatments to panel data models with time-varying heterogeneity. *Econometrics*, 5(33):1–21.

Liu, Y., Shumway, C. R., Rosenman, R., and Ball, V. E. (2011). Productivity growth and convergence in US agriculture: New cointegration panel data results. *Applied Economics*, 43(1):91–102.

Lovell, C. A. K. (2013). Lecture on imperfect optimization. In *Workshop in Honor of Professor C. A. Knox Lovell*. Belgium: University of Liege.

Lovell, C. A. K. and Sickles, R. C. (1983). Testing efficiency hypotheses in joint production: A parametric approach. *The Review of Economics and Statistics*, 65(1):51–58.

Lovell, C. A. K. and Sickles, R. C. (1999). Causes and consequences of expert disagreement: Methodological lessons from the U.S. v. AT&T debate. In Slottje, D., editor, *The Role of the Academic Economist in Litigation Support*, pages 189–206. Amsterdam: North-Holland.

Lovell, C. A. K. and Sickles, R. C. (2010). In memoriam: John W. Kendrick. *Journal of Productivity Analysis*, 34(1):1–2.

Lovell, C. A. K., Travers, P., Richardson, S., and Wood, L. (1994). Resources and functionings: A new view of inequality in Australia. In Eichhorn, W., editor, *Models and Measurement of Welfare and Inequality*, pages 787–807. New York, NY: Springer.

Lozano, S. (2012). Information sharing in DEA: A cooperative game theory approach. *European Journal of Operational Research*, 222(3):558–565.

Lozano, S., Hinojosa, M. A., Mármol, A. M., and Borrero, D. V. (2016). DEA and cooperative game theory. In *Handbook of Operations Analytics Using Data Envelopment Analysis*, pages 215–239. New York, NY: Springer.

Lucas, R. E. (1988). On the mechanics of economic development. *Journal of Monetary Economics*, 22(1):3–42.

Luenberger, D. G. (1992). Benefit functions and duality. *Journal of Mathematical Economics*, 21(5):461–481.

Luh, Y.-H. and Stefanou, S. E. (1991). Productivity growth in US agriculture under dynamic adjustment. *American Journal of Agricultural Economics*, 73(4):1116–1125.

Ma, S. and Racine, J. S. (2013). Additive regression splines with irrelevant categorical and continuous regressors. *Statistica Sinica*, 23(2):515–541.

Magnus, J. R. (1979). Substitution between energy and non-energy inputs in the Netherlands, 1950–1976. *International Economic Review*, 20(2):465–484.

Mallows, C. L. (1973). Some comments on CP. *Technometrics*, 15(4):661–675.

Malmquist, S. (1953). Index numbers and indifference surfaces. *Trabajos de Estadistica*, 4(2):209–242.

Mammen, E. (1982). *The Increase of Information Due to Additional Observations in the Case of Asymptotically Gaussian Experiments*. Stuttgart: University of Sonderforschungsbereich.

Mammen, E. (1991). Estimating a smooth monotone regression function. *Annals of Statistics*, 19(2):724–740.

Mammen, E. (1992). Bootstrap, wild bootstrap, and asymptotic normality. *Probability Theory and Related Fields*, 93(4):439–455.

Mammen, E. (1993). Bootstrap and wild bootstrap for high dimensional linear models. *Annals of Statistics*, 21(1):255–285.

Mammen, E. and Thomas-Agnan, C. (1999). Smoothing splines and shape restrictions. *Scandinavian Journal of Statistics*, 26(2):239–252.

Marschak, J. and Andrews, William H., J. (1944). Random simultaneous equations and the theory of production. *Econometrica*, 12(3–4):143–205.

Martins-Filho, C. and Yao, F. (2015). Semiparametric stochastic frontier estimation via profile likelihood. *Econometric Reviews*, 34(4):413–451.

Mastromarco, C. and Simar, L. (2015). Effect of FDI and time on catching up: New insights from a conditional nonparametric frontier analysis. *Journal of Applied Econometrics*, 30(5):826–847.

Materov, I. S. (1981). On full identification of the stochastic production frontier model. *Ekonomika i Matematicheskie Metody*, 17:784–788.

Matzkin, R. L. (1991). Semiparametric estimation of monotone and concave utility functions for polychotomous choice models. *Econometrica*, 59(5): 1315–1327.

Matzkin, R. L. (1994). Restrictions of economic theory in nonparametric methods. In Engle, R. F. and McFadden, D. L., editors, *Handbook of Econometrics*, volume 4, pages 2523–2558. Amsterdam: Elsevier.

Mayer, A. and Zelenyuk, V. (2014a). Aggregation of Malmquist productivity indexes allowing for reallocation of resources. *European Journal of Operational Research*, 238(3):774–785.

Mayer, A. and Zelenyuk, V. (2014b). An aggregation paradigm for Hicks–Moorsteen productivity indexes. CEPA Working Paper No. WP01/2014, Queensland: Center for Efficiency and Productivity Analysis, School of Economics, University of Queensland.

McAllister, P. H. and McManus, D. (1993). Resolving the scale efficiency puzzle in banking. *Journal of Banking & Finance*, 17(2):389–405.

McCloskey, D. N. (1985). The industrial revolution 1780–1860: A survey. In Mokyr, J., editor, *The Economics of the Industrial Revolution*, pages 53–74. Lanham, MD: Rowman and Littlefield.

McFadden, D. (1978). Cost, revenue, and profit functions. In McFadden, D. and Fuss, M. A., editors, *Production Economics: A Dual Approach to Theory and Applications*, volume 1: The Theory of Production, chapter 1. Amsterdam: North-Holland.

McMillen, D. P. and McDonald, J. F. (2004). Locally weighted maximum likelihood estimation: Monte Carlo evidence and an application. In Anselin, L., Florax, R. J., and Rey, S. J., editors, *Advances in spatial econometrics*, pages 225–239. New York, NY: Springer.

Meeusen, W. and van den Broeck, J. (1977). Efficiency estimation from Cobb–Douglas production functions with composed error. *International Economic Review*, 18(2):435–44.

Melitz, M. J. and Polanec, S. (2015). Dynamic Olley–Pakes productivity decomposition with entry and exit. *The RAND Journal of Economics*, 46(2):362–375.

Mester, L. J. (1993). Efficiency in the savings and loan industry. *Journal of Banking & Finance*, 17(2–3):267–286.

Miyagawa, T., Takizawa, M., and Tonogi, K. (2017). Can intangible investments ease declining rates of return on capital in Japan? *International Productivity Monitor*, (33):114–127.

Mizobuchi, H. (2017a). Productivity indexes under Hicks neutral technical change. *Journal of Productivity Analysis*, 48(1):63–68.

Mizobuchi, H. (2017b). A superlative index number formula for the Hicks–Moorsteen productivity index. *Journal of Productivity Analysis*, 48(2–3):167–178.

Mizobuchi, H. and V. Zelenyuk (2018) "Measuring Productivity by Quadratic-mean-of-order-r Indexes" CEPA Working Paper No. WP06/2018.

Mokyr, J. (1985). The industrial revolution and the new economic history. In Mokyr, J., editor, *The Economics of the Industrial Revolution*, pages 1–51. Lanham, MD: Rowman and Littlefield.

Moorsteen, R. H. (1961). On measuring productive potential and relative efficiency. *The Quarterly Journal of Economics*, 75(3):151–167.

Morrison, C. (1987). Capacity utilization and the impacts of pollution abatement, capital regulation and energy prices. In Moroney, J. R., editor, *Advances in the Economics of Energy and Resources*, volume 6, pages 17–61. Grenenwhich, CT: JAI Press.

Moulin, H. (1980). On strategy-proofness and single peakedness. *Public Choice*, 35(4):437–455.

Mugera, A. and Ojede, A. (2014). Technical efficiency in African agriculture: Is it catching up or lagging behind? *Journal of International Development*, 26(6):779–795.

Mukerjee, H. (1988). Monotone nonparametric regression. *Annals of Statistics*, 16(2):741–750.

Mundlak, Y. (1988). Endogenous technology and the measurement of productivity. In Capalbo, S. M. and Antle, J. M., editors, *Agricultural Productivity: Measurement and Explanation*, chapter 11, pages 316–331. Washington DC: RFF Press.

Murphy, K. M. and Topel, R. H. (1985). Estimation and inference in two-step econometric models. *Journal of Business & Economic Statistics*, 3(4):370–379.

Mussard, S. and Peypoch, N. (2006). On multi-decomposition of the aggregate Malmquist productivity index. *Economics Letters*, 91(3):436–443.

Mutter, R. L., Greene, W. H., Spector, W., Rosko, M. D., and Mukamel, D. B. (2013). Investigating the impact of endogeneity on inefficiency estimates in the application of stochastic frontier analysis to nursing homes. *Journal of Productivity Analysis*, 39(2):101–110.

Nakabayashi, K. and Tone, K. (2006). Egoist's dilemma: a DEA game. *Omega*, 34(2):135–148.

Nallari, R. and Bayraktar, N. (2010). Micro efficiency and macro growth. The World Bank Policy Research Working Paper No. 5267, Washington, DC: The World Bank.

Neary, J. P. (2004). Rationalizing the Penn World Table: True multilateral indices for international comparisons of real income. *American Economic Review*, 94(5):1411–1428.

Nelson, R. R. and Wright, G. (1992). The rise and fall of American technological leadership: The postwar era in historical perspective. *Journal of Economic Literature*, 30(4):1931–1964.

Nemoto, J. and Goto, M. (2004). Technological externalities and economies of vertical integration in the electric utility industry. *International Journal of Industrial Organization*, 22(1):67–81.

Nerlove, M. (2001). Zvi Griliches: 1930–1999. In *Biographical Memoirs*, volume 80, pages 1–29. Washington, DC: The National Academy Press.

Nesterenko, V. and Zelenyuk, V. (2007). Measuring potential gains from reallocation of resources. *Journal of Productivity Analysis*, 28(1–2):107–116.

Newbold, P. and Harvey, D. I. (2002). Forecast combination and encompassing. In *A Companion to Economic Forecasting*, pages 268–283. Oxford: Blackwell Press.

Newson, R. (2006). Confidence intervals for rank statistics: Somers' D and extensions. *Stata Journal*, 6(3):309–334.

Nishimizu, M. and Page, J. M. (1982). Total factor productivity growth, technological progress and technical efficiency change: Dimensions of productivity change in Yugoslavia, 1965–78. *Economic Journal*, 92(368):920–936.

O'Donnell, C. J. (2010). Measuring and decomposing agricultural productivity and profitability change. *Australian Journal of Agricultural and Resource Economics*, 54(4):527–560.

O'Donnell, C. J. (2012a). An aggregate quantity framework for measuring and decomposing productivity change. *Journal of Productivity Analysis*, 38(3):255–272.

O'Donnell, C. J. (2012b). Nonparametric estimates of the components of productivity and profitability change in U.S. agriculture. *American Journal of Agricultural Economics*, 94(4):873–890.

O'Donnell, C. J. (2014). Econometric estimation of distance functions and associated measures of productivity and efficiency change. *Journal of Productivity Analysis*, 41(2):187–200.

O'Donnell, C. J. (2016). Using information about technologies, markets and firm behaviour to decompose a proper productivity index. *Journal of Econometrics*, 190(2):328–340.

O'Donnell, C. J., Chambers, R. G., and Quiggin, J. (2010). Efficiency analysis in the presence of uncertainty. *Journal of Productivity Analysis*, 33(1):1–17.

Oks, E. and Sharir, M. (2006). Minkowski sums of monotone and general simple polygons. *Discrete and Computational Geometry*, 35(2):223–240.

Olley, G. S. and Pakes, A. (1996). The dynamics of productivity in the telecommunications equipment industry. *Econometrica*, 64(6):1263–97.

Olson, J. A., Schmidt, P., and Waldman, D. M. (1980). A Monte Carlo study of estimators of the stochastic frontier production function. *Journal of Econometrics*, 13(1):67–82.

Orea, L. and Kumbhakar, S. C. (2004). Efficiency measurement using a latent class stochastic frontier model. *Empirical Economics*, 29(1):169–183.

Orea, L. and Steinbuks, J. (2012). Estimating market power in homogenous product markets using a composed error model: Application to the California electricity market. EPRG Working Paper No. 1210/CWPE Working Paper No. 1220. Cambridge: University of Cambridge.

Paasche, H. (1874). Über die preisentwicklung der letzten jahre nach den hamburger börsennotirungen. *Jahrbücher für Nationalökonomie und Statistik*, 23:168–178.

Pachkova, E. V. (2009). Restricted reallocation of resources. *European Journal of Operational Research*, 196(3):1049–1057.

Pagan, A. and Ullah, A. (1999). *Nonparametric Econometrics*. New York, NY: Cambridge University Press.

Pagan, A. R. and Hall, D. (1983). Diagnostic tests as residual analysis. *Econometric Reviews*, 2(2):159–218.

Panzar, J. C. and Willig, R. D. (1977a). Economies of scale in multi-output production. *The Quarterly Journal of Economics*, 91(3):481–493.

Panzar, J. C. and Willig, R. D. (1977b). Free entry and the sustainability of natural monopoly. *The Bell Journal of Economics*, 8(1):1–22.

Park, B. U., Jeong, S.-O., and Simar, L. (2010). Asymptotic distribution of conical-hull estimators of directional edges. *Annals of Statistics*, 38(3):1320–1340.

Park, B. U., Sickles, R. C., and Simar, L. (1998). Stochastic panel frontiers: A semiparametric approach. *Journal of Econometrics*, 84(2):273–301.

Park, B. U., Sickles, R. C., and Simar, L. (2003). Semiparametric-efficient estimation of AR(1) panel data models. *Journal of Econometrics*, 117(2):279–309.

Park, B. U., Sickles, R. C., and Simar, L. (2007). Semiparametric efficient estimation of dynamic panel data models. *Journal of Econometrics*, 136(1):281–301.

Park, B. U. and Simar, L. (1994). Efficient semiparametric estimation in a stochastic frontier model. *Journal of the American Statistical Association*, 89(427): 929–936.

Park, B. U., Simar, L., and Weiner, C. (2000). The FDH estimator for productivity efficiency scores: Asymptotic properties. *Econometric Theory*, 16(6):855–877.

Park, B. U., Simar, L., and Zelenyuk, V. (2008). Local likelihood estimation of truncated regression and its partial derivatives: Theory and application. *Journal of Econometrics*, 146(1):185–198.

Park, B. U., Simar, L., and Zelenyuk, V. (2015). Categorical data in local maximum likelihood: Theory and applications to productivity analysis. *Journal of Productivity Analysis*, 43(2):199–214.

Parmeter, C., Sun, K., Henderson, D. J., and Kumbhakar, S. (2014). Estimation and inference under economic restrictions. *Journal of Productivity Analysis*, 41(1):111–129.

Parmeter, C., Wan, A., and Zhang, X. (2017a). Model averaging estimators for the stochastic frontier model. Working Paper No. 2016–09. Coral Gables, FL: University of Miami Department of Economics.

Parmeter, C. and Zelenyuk, V. (2018). Combining the virtues of stochastic frontier and data envelopement analysis. Operations Research, accepted.

Parmeter, C. F. and Racine, J. S. (2013). Smooth constrained frontier analysis. In Chen, X. and Swanson, N. R., editors, *Recent Advances and Future Directions in Causality, Prediction, and Specification Analysis*, pages 463–488. New York, NY: Springer.

Parmeter, C. F., Wang, H.-J., and Kumbhakar, S. (2017b). Nonparametric estimation of the determinants of inefficiency. *Journal of Productivity Analysis*, 47(3):205–221.

Pastor, J. T. and Lovell, C. A. K. (2007). Circularity of the Malmquist productivity index. *Economic Theory*, 33(3):591–599.

Pedroni, P. (2004). Panel cointegration: Asymptotic and finite sample properties of pooled time series tests with an application to the PPP hypothesis. *Econometric Theory*, 20(3):597–625.

Perez, F. and Benages, E. (2017). The role of capital accumulation in the evolution of total factor productivity in Spain. *International Productivity Monitor*, (33):24–50.

Petersen, N. C. (1990). Data envelopment analysis on a relaxed set of assumptions. *Management Science*, 36(3):305–314.

Peyrache, A. (2013a). Hicks–Moorsteen versus Malmquist: A connection by means of a radial productivity index. *Journal of Productivity Analysis*, 41(3):435.

Peyrache, A. (2013b). Industry structural inefficiency and potential gains from mergers and break-ups: A comprehensive approach. *European Journal of Operational Research*, 230(2):422–430.

Peyrache, A. (2013c). Multilateral productivity comparisons and homotheticity. *Journal of Productivity Analysis*, 40(1):57–65.

Peyrache, A. (2015). Cost constrained industry inefficiency. *European Journal of Operational Research*, 247(3):996–1002.

Pham, M. D. and Zelenyuk, V. (2018). Slack-based directional distance function in the presence of bad outputs: Theory and application to Vietnamese banking. *Empirical Economics* 54, 1:153–187.

Pham, M. D. and Zelenyuk, V. (2019). Weak disposability in nonparametric production analysis: A new taxonomy of reference technology sets. *European Journal of Operational Research*, https://doi.org/10.1016/j.ejor.2018.09.019.

Pilyavsky, A. and Staat, M. (2008). Efficiency and productivity change in Ukrainian health care. *Journal of Productivity Analysis*, 29(2):143–154.

Pitt, M. M. and Lee, L.-F. (1981). The measurement and sources of technical inefficiency in the Indonesian weaving industry. *Journal of Development Economics*, 9(1):43–64.

Podinovski, V. V. (2004). Production trade-offs and weight restrictions in data envelopment analysis. *Journal of the Operational Research Society*, 55(12):1311–1322.

Podinovski, V. V. (2015). Dea models with production trade-offs and weight restrictions. In Zhu, J., editor, *Data Envelopment Analysis: A Handbook of Models and Methods*, pages 105–144. New York, NY: Springer.

Podinovski, V. V. and Bouzdine-Chameeva, T. (2013). Weight restrictions and free production in data envelopment analysis. *Operations Research*, 61(2):426–437.

Podinovski, V. V., Førsund, F. R., and Krivonozhko, V. E. (2009). A simple derivation of scale elasticity in data envelopment analysis. *European Journal of Operational Research*, 197(1):149–153.

Podinovski, V. V. and Kuosmanen, T. (2011). Modelling weak disposability in data envelopment analysis under relaxed convexity assumptions. *European Journal of Operational Research*, 211(3):577–585.

Politis, D. N. and Romano, J. P. (1994). Large sample confidence regions based on subsamples under minimal assumptions. *Annals of Statistics*, 22(4):2031–2050.

Politis, D. N., Romano, J. P., and Wolf, M. (2001). On the asymptotic theory of subsampling. *Statistica Sinica*, 11(4):1105–1124.

Pollak, R. A., Sickles, R. C., and Wales, T. J. (1984). The CES-translog: Specification and estimation of a new cost function. *The Review of Economics and Statistics*, 66(4):602–607.

Pya, N. and Wood, S. N. (2015). Shape constrained additive models. *Statistics and Computing*, 25(3):543–559.

Qian, J. and Sickles, R. C. (2008). Stochastic frontiers with bounded inefficiency. Unpublished manuscript, Shanghai: Shanghai Jiao Tong University.

Quiggin, J. and Chambers, R. G. (2006). The state-contingent approach to production under uncertainty. *Australian Journal of Agricultural and Resource Economics*, 50(2):153–169.

Raa, T. T. (2011). Benchmarking and industry performance. *Journal of Productivity Analysis*, 36(3):285–292.

Racine, J. and Li, Q. (2004). Nonparametric estimation of regression functions with both categorical and continuous data. *Journal of Econometrics*, 119(1):99–130.

Raftery, A. E., Madigan, D., and Hoeting, J. A. (1997). Bayesian model averaging for linear regression models. *Journal of the American Statistical Association*, 92(437):179–191.

Ramsay, J. O. (1998). Estimating smooth monotone functions. *Journal of the Royal Statistical Society: Series B (Statistical Methodology)*, 60(2):365–375.

Ray, S. C. (2004). *Data Envelopment Analysis: Theory and Techniques for Economics and Operations Research*. New York, NY: Cambridge University Press.

Reifschneider, D. and Stevenson, R. (1991). Systematic departures from the frontier: A framework for the analysis of firm inefficiency. *International Economic Review*, 32(3):715–723.

Reiss, P. and Wolak, F. A. (2007). Structural econometric modeling: Rationales and examples from industrial organization. In Heckman, J. J. and Leamer, E. E., editors, *Handbook of Econometrics*, volume 6. Amsterdam: Elsevier, 1st edition.

Rezvanian, R., Ariss, R. T., and Mehdian, S. M. (2011). Cost efficiency, technological progress and productivity growth of Chinese banking pre- and post-WTO accession. *Applied Financial Economics*, 21(7):437–454.

Richmond, J. (1974). Estimating the efficiency of production. *International Economic Review*, 15(2):515–521.

Rissanen, J. (1973). Algorithms for triangular decomposition of block Hankel and Toeplitz matrices with application to factoring positive matrix polynomials. *Mathematics of Computation*, 27(121):147–154.

Robbins, L. (1932). *An Essay on the Nature and Significance of Economic Science*. New York, NY: Macmillan.

Robinson, J. (1933). *Economics of Imperfect Competition*,. London: Macmillan, 1933.

Robinson, P. M. (1988). Root-N-consistent semiparametric regression. *Econometrica*, 56(4):931–954.

Röller, L.-H. (1990a). Modelling cost structure: The Bell system revisited. *Applied Economics*, 22(12):1661–1674.

Röller, L.-H. (1990b). Proper quadratic cost functions with an application to the Bell system. *The Review of Economics and Statistics*, 72(2):202–210.

Romer, P. M. (1986). Increasing returns and long-run growth. *Journal of Political Economy*, 94(5):1002–1037.

Rosenbaum, P. R. (2002). *Design of Observational Studies*. New York, NY: Springer.

Rosenberg, N. (1982). *Inside the Black Box: Technology and Economics*. New York, NY: Cambridge University Press.

Rosenblatt, M. (1956). Remarks on some nonparametric estimates of a density function. *Annals of Mathematical Statistics*, 27(3):832–837.

Rothenberg, T. J. and Leenders, C. (1964). Efficient estimation of simultaneous equation systems. *Econometrica*, 32(1–2):57–76.

Rungsuriyawiboon, S. and Stefanou, S. E. (2007). Dynamic efficiency estimation: An application to US electric utilities. *Journal of Business & Economic Statistics*, 25(2):226–238.

Russell, R. R. (1987). On the axiomatic approach to the measurement of technical efficiency. In Eichhorn, W., editor, *Measurement in Economics: Theory and Application of Economic Indices*, pages 207–217. New York, NY: Springer.

Russell, R. R. (1990). Continuity of measures of technical efficiency. *Journal of Economic Theory*, 51(2):255–267.

Russell, R. R. (1998). Distance functions in consumer and producer theory. In Färe, R. S., Grosskopf, S., and Russell, R. R., editors, *Index Numbers: Essays In Honor of Sten Malmquist*. Boston, MA: Kluwer Academic Publishers.

Russell, R. R. and Schworm, W. (2009). Axiomatic foundations of efficiency measurement on data-generated technologies. *Journal of Productivity Analysis*, 31:77.

Russell, R. R. and Schworm, W. (2011). Properties of inefficiency indexes on <input,output> space. *Journal of Productivity Analysis*, 36(2):143–156.

Ruud, P. A. (1997). Restricted least squares subject to monotonicity and concavity constraints. *Econometric Society Monographs*, 28:166–187.

Saal, D. S., Arocena, P., Maziotis, A., and Triebs, T. (2013). Scale and scope economies and the efficient vertical and horizontal configuration of the water industry: a survey of the literature. *Review of Network Economics*, 12(1):93–129.

Saal, D. S. and Parker, D. (2001). Productivity and price performance in the privatized water and sewerage companies of England and Wales. *Journal of Regulatory Economics*, 20(1):61–90.

Saal, D. S., Parker, D., and Weyman-Jones, T. (2007). Determining the contribution of technical change, efficiency change and scale change to productivity growth in the privatized English and Welsh water and sewerage industry: 1985–2000. *Journal of Productivity Analysis*, 28(1–2):127–139.

Sahoo, B. K., Luptacik, M., and Mahlberg, B. (2011). Alternative measures of environmental technology structure in DEA: An application. *European Journal of Operational Research*, 215(3):750–762.

Samuelson, P. and Swamy, S. (1974). Invariant economic index numbers and canonical duality: Survey and synthesis. *American Economic Review*, 64(4): 566–593.

Scheel, H. (2001). Undesirable outputs in efficiency valuations. *European Journal of Operational Research*, 132(2):400–410.

Schennach, S. and Hu, Y. (2013). Nonparametric identification and semiparametric estimation of classical measurement error models without side information. *Journal of the American Statistical Association*, 108(501):177–186.

Schmidt, P. (1976). On the statistical estimation of parametric frontier production functions. *Review of Economics and Statistics*, 58(2):238–239.

Schmidt, P. and Lin, T.-F. (1984). Simple tests of alternative specifications in stochastic frontier models. *Journal of Econometrics*, 24(3):349–61.

Schmidt, P. and Lovell, C. A. K. (1979). Estimating technical and allocative inefficiency relative to stochastic production and cost frontiers. *Journal of Econometrics*, 9(3):343–366.

Schmidt, P. and Sickles, R. C. (1984). Production frontiers and panel data. *Journal of Business & Economic Statistics*, 2(4):367–374.

Schneider, R. (1993). *Convex Bodies: The Brunn-Minkowski Theory*. New York, NY: Cambridge University Press.

Schubert, T. and Simar, L. (2011). Innovation and export activities in the German mechanical engineering sector: An application of testing restrictions in production analysis. *Journal of Productivity Analysis*, 36(1):55–69.

Schuster, E. F. (1985). Incorporating support constraints into nonparametric estimators of densities. *Communications in Statistics – Theory and Methods*, 14(5):1123–1136.

Schwarz, G. (1978). Estimating the dimension of a model. *The Annals of Statistics*, 6(2):461–464.

Scott, D. W. (1992). *Multivariate Density Estimation: Theory, Practice, and Visualization*. New York, NY: Wiley.

Seiford, L. M. and Zhu, J. (2002). Modeling undesirable factors in efficiency evaluation. *European Journal of Operational Research*, 142(1):16–20.

Seitz, W. D. (1970). The measurement of efficiency relative to a frontier production function. *American Journal of Agricultural Economics*, 52(4):505–511.

Serletis, A. and Feng, G. (2015). Imposing theoretical regularity on flexible functional forms. *Econometric Reviews*, 34(1–2):198–227.

Serletis, A. and Shahmoradi, A. (2007). A note on imposing local curvature in generalized Leontief models. *Macroeconomic Dynamics*, 11(2):290–294.

Serra, T., Lansink, A. O., and Stefanou, S. E. (2011). Measurement of dynamic efficiency: A directional distance function parametric approach. *American Journal of Agricultural Economics*, 93(3):752–763.

Severini, T. A. and Wong, W. H. (1992). Profile likelihood and conditionally parametric models. *Annals of Statistics*, 20(4):1768–1802.

Shane, S. (2009). Why encouraging more people to become entrepreneurs is bad public policy. *Small Business Economics*, 33(2):141–149.

Shang, C. (2015). *Essays in the use of duality, robust empirical methods, panel treatments, and model averaging with applications to housing prices index construction and world productivity growth*. PhD thesis, Houston, TX: Rice University.

Sheather, S. J. and Jones, M. C. (1991). A reliable data-based bandwidth selection method for kernel density estimation. *Journal of the Royal Statistical Society. Series B (Methodological)*, 53(3):683–690.

Shee, A. and Stefanou, S. E. (2015). Endogeneity corrected stochastic production frontier and technical efficiency. *American Journal of Agricultural Economics*, 97(3):939–952.

Shephard, R. W. (1953). *Cost and Production Functions*. Princeton, NJ: Princeton University Press.

Shephard, R. W. (1970). *Theory of Cost and Production Functions*. Princeton studies in mathematical economics. Princeton, NJ: Princeton University Press.

Shephard, R. W. (1974). Indirect production functions. In *Mathematical Systems in Economics*, volume 10. Meisenheim am Glan: Verlag Anton Hain.

Shin, Y. (1994). A residual-based test of the null of cointegration against the alternative of no cointegration. *Econometric Theory*, 10(1):91–115.

Shiu, A. and Zelenyuk, V. (2012). Production efficiency versus ownership: The case of China. In Van Keilegom, I. P. W. W., editor, *Exploring Research Frontiers in Contemporary Statistics and Econometrics*, pages 23–44. Heidelberg: Springer.

Shively, T. S., Walker, S. G., and Damien, P. (2011). Nonparametric function estimation subject to monotonicity, convexity and other shape constraints. *Journal of Econometrics*, 161(2):166–181.

Sickles, R. C. (1985). A nonlinear multivariate error components analysis of technology and specific factor productivity growth with an application to the US airlines. *Journal of Econometrics*, 27(1):61–78.

Sickles, R. C. (2005). Panel estimators and the identification of firm-specific efficiency levels in parametric, semiparametric and nonparametric settings. *Journal of Econometrics*, 126(2):305–334.

Sickles, R. C. and Cigerli, B. (2009). Krugman and Young revisited: A survey of the sources of productivity growth in a world with less constraints. *Seoul Journal of Economics*, 22(1):29–54.

Sickles, R. C., Good, D., and Johnson, R. L. (1986). Allocative distortions and the regulatory transition of the US airline industry. *Journal of Econometrics*, 33(1–2):143–163.

Sickles, R. C., Good, D. H., and Getachew, L. (2002). Specification of distance functions using semi-and nonparametric methods with an application to the dynamic performance of Eastern and Western European air carriers. *Journal of Productivity Analysis*, 17(1–2):133–155.

Sickles, R. C., Hao, J., and Shang, C. (2014). Panel data and productivity measurement: An analysis of Asian productivity trends. *Journal of Chinese Economic and Business Studies*, 12(3):211–231.

Sickles, R. C., Hao, J., and Shang, C. (2015). Productivity and panel data. In Baltagi, B., editor, *Handbook of Panel Data*, chapter 17, pages 517–547. New York, NY: Oxford University Press.

Sickles, R. C., Hao, J., and Shang, C. (2016). Productivity measurement, model averaging, and world trends in growth and inequality. In Greene, W. H., Khalaf, L., Sickles, R. C., Veall, M., and Voia, M.-C., editors, *Productivity and Efficiency Analysis*, Springer Proceedings in Business and Economics, pages 305–323. New York, NY: Springer.

Sickles, R. C. and Schmidt, P. (1978). Simultaneous equations models with truncated dependent variables: A simultaneous tobit model. *Journal of Economics and Business*, 31(1):11–21.

Sickles, R. C. and Streitwieser, M. L. (1992). Technical inefficiency and productive decline in the US interstate natural gas pipeline industry under the Natural Gas Policy Act. *Journal of Productivity Analysis*, 3(1–2):119–133.

Sickles, R. C. and Streitwieser, M. L. (1998). An analysis of technology, productivity, and regulatory distortion in the interstate natural gas transmission industry: 1977–1985. *Journal of Applied Econometrics*, 13(4):377–395.

Sickles, R. C. and Taubman, P. (1997). Mortality and morbidity among adults and the elderly. In Rosenzweig, M. R. and Stark, O., editors, *Handbook of Population and Family Economics*, volume 1, chapter 11, pages 559–643. Amsterdam: Elsevier.

Silva, E., Lansink, A. O., and Stefanou, S. E. (2015). The adjustment-cost model of the firm: Duality and productive efficiency. *International Journal of Production Economics*, 168:245–256.

Silva, E. and Stefanou, S. E. (2003). Nonparametric dynamic production analysis and the theory of cost. *Journal of Productivity Analysis*, 19(1):5–32.

Silva, E. and Stefanou, S. E. (2007). Dynamic efficiency measurement: Theory and application. *American Journal of Agricultural Economics*, 89(2):398–419.

Silverman, B. W. (1986). *Density Estimation for Statistics and Data Analysis*. London: Chapman and Hall.

Simar, L. (1992). Estimating efficiencies from frontier models with panel data: A comparison of parametric, non-parametric and semi-parametric methods with bootstrapping. *Journal of Productivity Analysis*, 3(1):171–203.

Simar, L. (1996). Aspects of statistical analysis in DEA-type frontier models. *Journal of Productivity Analysis*, 7(27):177–185.

Simar, L. (2007). How to improve the performances of DEA/FDH estimators in the presence of noise? *Journal of Productivity Analysis*, 28(3):183–201.

Simar, L., Van Keilegom, I., and Zelenyuk, V. (2014). Nonparametric least squares methods for stochastic frontier models. CEPA Working Paper No. WP03/2014, Queensland: Center for Efficiency and Productivity Analysis, School of Economics, University of Queensland.

Simar, L., Van Keilegom, I., and Zelenyuk, V. (2017). Nonparametric least squares methods for stochastic frontier models. *Journal of Productivity Analysis*, 47(3): 189–204.

Simar, L. and Vanhems, A. (2012). Probabilistic characterization of directional distances and their robust versions. *Journal of Econometrics*, 166(2):342–354.

Simar, L., Vanhems, A., and Wilson, P. W. (2012). Statistical inference for DEA estimators of directional distances. *European Journal of Operational Research*, 220(3):853–864.

Simar, L. and Wilson, P. W. (1998). Sensitivity analysis to efficiency scores: How to bootstrap in nonparametric frontier models. *Management Science*, 44(1):49–61.

Simar, L. and Wilson, P. W. (1999). Of course we can bootstrap DEA scores! But does it mean anything? Logic trumps wishful thinking. *Journal of Productivity Analysis*, 11(1):93–97.

Simar, L. and Wilson, P. W. (2000a). A general methodology for bootstrapping in nonparametric frontier models. *Journal of Applied Statistics*, 27(6):779–802.

Simar, L. and Wilson, P. W. (2000b). Statistical inference in nonparametric frontier models: The state of the art. *Journal of Productivity Analysis*, 13(1):49–78.

Simar, L. and Wilson, P. W. (2001). Testing restrictions in nonparametric efficiency models. *Communications in Statistics-Simulation and Computation*, 30(1):159–184.

Simar, L. and Wilson, P. W. (2002). Non-parametric tests of returns to scale. *European Journal of Operational Research*, 139(1):115–132.

Simar, L. and Wilson, P. W. (2007). Estimation and inference in two-stage, semiparametric models of production processes. *Journal of Econometrics*, 136(1):31–64.

Simar, L. and Wilson, P. W. (2008). Statistical inference in nonparametric frontier models: Recent developments and perspectives. In Harold Fried, C. A. K. L. and Schmidt, S., editors, *The Measurement of Productive Efficiency*, pages 421–521. New York, NY: Oxford University Press, 2nd edition.

Simar, L. and Wilson, P. W. (2010). Inferences from cross-sectional, stochastic frontier models. *Econometric Reviews*, 29(1):62–98.

Simar, L. and Wilson, P. W. (2011a). Inference by the m out of n bootstrap in nonparametric frontier models. *Journal of Productivity Analysis*, 36(1):33–53.

Simar, L. and Wilson, P. W. (2011b). Two-stage DEA: Caveat emptor. *Journal of Productivity Analysis*, 36(2):205–218.

Simar, L. and Wilson, P. W. (2013). Estimation and inference in nonparametric frontier models: Recent developments and perspectives. *Foundations and Trends in Econometrics*, 5(3–4):183–337.

Simar, L. and Wilson, P. W. (2015). Statistical approaches for nonparametric frontier models: A guided tour. *International Statistical Review*, 83(1):77–110.

Simar, L. and Zelenyuk, V. (2003). Statistical inference for aggregates of Farrell-type efficiencies. Unpublished manuscript, Louvain: Institute of Statistics, UCL.

Simar, L. and Zelenyuk, V. (2006). On testing equality of distributions of technical efficiency scores. *Econometric Reviews*, 25(4):497–522.

Simar, L. and Zelenyuk, V. (2007). Statistical inference for aggregates of Farrell-type efficiencies. *Journal of Applied Econometrics*, 22(7):1367–1394.

Simar, L. and Zelenyuk, V. (2011). Stochastic FDH/DEA estimators for frontier analysis. *Journal of Productivity Analysis*, 36(1):1–20.

Simar, L. and Zelenyuk, V. (2017). Central limit theorems for aggregate efficiency. *Operations Research* 166, 1 (2018):139–149.

Simon, H. A. (1957). *Models of man; Social and Rational*. New York, NY: Wiley.

Smirnov, N. V. (1939). Estimate of deviation between empirical distribution functions in two independent samples. *Bulletin of Moscow University*, 2(2):3–16.

Smith, M. D. (2008). Stochastic frontier models with dependent error components. *The Econometrics Journal*, 11(1):172–192.

Smolny, W. (2000). Sources of productivity growth: An empirical analysis with German sectoral data. *Applied Economics*, 32(3):305–314.

Solow, R. M. (1956). A contribution to the theory of economic growth. *The Quarterly Journal of Economics*, 70(1):65–94.

Solow, R. M. (1957). Technical change and the aggregate production function. *Review of Economics and Statistics*, 39(3):312–320.

Sonis, M. and Hewings, G. J. D. (1999). Economic landscapes: Multiplier product matrix analysis for multiregional Input-Output systems. *Hitotsubashi Journal of Economics*, 40(1):59–74.

Starr, R. M. (2008). Shapley-Folkman theorem. In Durlauf, S. N. and Blume, L. E., editors, *The New Palgrave Dictionary of Economics*, pages 317–318. Basingstoke, UK: Palgrave Macmillan.

Stefanou, S. E. (2009). A dynamic characterization of efficiency. *Agricultural Economics Review*, 10(1):18–33.

Stevenson, R. E. (1980). Likelihood functions for generalized stochastic frontier estimation. *Journal of Econometrics*, 13(1):57–66.

Stigler, G. J. (1976). The Xistence of X-efficiency. *American Economic Review*, 66(1):213–216.

Stiroh, K. J. (2001). What drives productivity growth? *Economic Policy Review*, 7(1):37–59.

Su, L., Shi, Z., and Phillips, P. C. B. (2016). Identifying latent structures in panel data. *Econometrica*, 84(6):2215–2264.

Suárez, C. and de Jorge, J. (2010). Efficiency convergence processes and effects of regulation in the nonspecialized retail sector in Spain. *Annals of Regional Science*, 44(3):573–597.

Sueyoshi, T., Yuan, Y., and Goto, M. (2017). A literature study for DEA applied to energy and environment. *Energy Economics*, 62:104–124.

Swan, T. W. (1956). Economic growth and capital accumulation. *Economic Record*, 32(2):334–361.

Szulc, B. (1964). Indices for multiregional comparisons. *Przeglad Statystyczny*, 3:239–254.

Taube, R. (1988). *Möglichkeiten der Effizienzmessung von öffentlichen Verwaltungen*. Berlin: Duncker & Humblot.

Thaler, R. H. and Sunstein, C. R. (2009). *Nudge: Improving Decisions About Health, Wealth, and Happiness*. London: Penguin.

Thanassoulis, E., Portela, M. C., and Allen, R. (2004). Incorporating value judgments in DEA. In Cooper, W., Seiford, L. M., and Zhu, J., editors, *Handbook on Data Envelopment Analysis*, pages 99–138. Boston, MA: Kluwer.

Thompson, G. D. (1988). Choice of flexible functional forms: Review and appraisal. *Western Journal of Agricultural Economics*, 13(2):169–183.

Thompson, R. G., Langemeier, L. N., Lee, C.-T., Lee, E., and Thrall, R. M. (1990). The role of multiplier bounds in efficiency analysis with application to Kansas farming. *Journal of Econometrics*, 46(1–2):93–108.

Tibshirani, R. and Hastie, T. (1987). Local likelihood estimation. *Journal of the American Statistical Association*, 82(398):559–567.

Timmer, C. P. (1971). Using a probabilistic frontier production to measure technical efficiency. *Journal of Political Economy*, 79(4):776–794.

Timmer, M. (2017). Productivity measurement in global value chains. *International Productivity Monitor*, (33):182–193.

Timmer, M. P., Dietzenbacher, E., Los, B., Stehrer, R., and de Vries, G. J. (2015). An illustrated user guide to the world input-output database: The case of global automotive production. *Review of International Economics*, 23(3):575–605.

Timmer, M. P., Erumban, A. A., Los, B., Stehrer, R., and de Vries, G. J. (2014). Slicing up global value chains. *Journal of Economic Perspectives*, 28(2):99–118.

Timmermann, A. (2006). Forecast combinations. In Elliot, G., Granger, C. W. J., and Timmermann, A., editors, *Handbook of Economic Forecasting*, volume 1, pages 135–196. Amsterdam: Elsevier.

Tone, K. (2001). A slacks-based measure of efficiency in data envelopment analysis. *European Journal of Operational Research*, 130(3):498–509.

Tone, K. and Tsutsui, M. (2010). Erratum to "network DEA: A slacks-based measure approach". *European Journal of Operational Research*, 202(1):308–309.

Tone, K. and Tsutsui, M. (2014). Dynamic DEA with network structure: A slacks-based measure approach. *Omega*, 42(1):124–131.

Törnqvist, L. (1936). The Bank of Finland's consumption price index. *Bank of Finland Monthly Bulletin*, 16(10):1–8.

Tran, K. C. and Tsionas, E. G. (2013). GMM estimation of stochastic frontier model with endogenous regressors. *Economics Letters*, 118(1):233–236.

Tran, K.C. and E.G. Tsionas (2015), "Endogenous Stochastic Frontier Models: Copula Approach without External Instruments." *Economics Letters*, 133(8):85–88.

Triantis, K. (2011). Engineering applications of data envelopment analysis. In Cooper, W. W., Seiford, L. M., and Zhu, J., editors, *Handbook on Data Envelopment Analysis*, chapter 14, pages 363–402. New York, NY: Springer.

Triantis, K. (2014). Network representations of efficiency analysis for engineering systems: Examples, issues and research opportunities. In Cook, D. W. and Zhu, J., editors, *Data Envelopment Analysis: A Handbook on the Modeling of Internal Structures and Networks*, chapter 22, pages 569–584. Boston, MA: Springer.

Triantis, K. (2016). Efficiency performance measurement for transportation systems: A primer using an empirical frontier perspective. In Teodorovic, D., editor, *Routledge Handbook of Transportation*, chapter 28, pages 428–436. New York, NY: Taylor and Francis Group.

Triebs, T. P., Saal, D. S., Arocena, P., and Kumbhakar, S. C. (2016). Estimating economies of scale and scope with flexible technology. *Journal of Productivity Analysis*, 45(2):173–186.

Trinh, K. D. T. and Zelenyuk, V. (2015). Productivity growth and convergence: Revisiting Kumar and Russell (2002). *CEPA Working paper*. No. WP11/2015.

Tsionas, E. G. (2002). Stochastic frontier models with random coefficients. *Journal of Applied Econometrics*, 17(2):127–147.

Tsionas, E. G. and Kumbhakar, S. C. (2014). Firm heterogeneity, persistent and transient technical inefficiency: A generalized true random-effects model. *Journal of Applied Econometrics*, 29(1):110–132.

Tulkens, H. (1993). On FDH efficiency analysis: Some methodological issues and applications to retail banking, courts, and urban transit. *Journal of Productivity Analysis*, 4(1):183–210.

Tullock, G. (1980). Efficient rent seeking. In Buchanan, J. M., Tollison, R. D., and Tullock, G., editors, *Toward a Theory of the Rent-Seeking Society*, chapter 6, pages 97–112. College Station, TX: Texas A&M University Press.

Tyteca, D. (1996). On the measurement of the environmental performance of firms – a literature review and a productive efficiency perspective. *Journal of Environmental Management*, 46(3):281–308.

Tyteca, D. (1997). Linear programming models for the measurement of environmental performance of firms – concepts and empirical results. *Journal of Productivity Analysis*, 8(2):183–197.

Uzawa, H. (1962). Production functions with constant elasticities of substitution. *Review of Economic Studies*, 29(4):291–299.

van Ark, B. and Jäger, K. (2017). Recent trends in Europe's output and productivity growth performance at the sector level, 2002-2015. *International Productivity Monitor*, (33):8–23.

Van Beveren, I. (2012). Total factor productivity estimation: A practical review. *Journal of Economic Surveys*, 26(1):98–128.

Van Praag, C. M. and Versloot, P. H. (2007). What is the value of entrepreneurship? A review of recent research. *Small Business Economics*, 29(4):351–382.

Varian, H. R. (1983). Non-parametric tests of consumer behaviour. *Review of Economic Studies*, 50(1):99–110.

Varian, H. R. (1992). *Microeconomic Analysis*. New York, NY: W. W. Norton.

Vogt, A. (1980). Der zeit und der faktorumkehrtests als "finders of test". *Statistiche Hefte*, 21(1):66–71.

von Bortkiewicz, L. (1924). Zweck und struktur einer preisindexzahl. *Nordisk Statistisk Tidskrift*, 1(3):208–251.

von Neumann, J. (1938). On infinite tensor products. *Composite Mathematics*, 6:1–77.

von Neumann, J. (1945). A model of general equilibrium. *Review of Economic Studies*, 13(1):1–9.

Waldman, D. M. (1982). A stationary point for the stochastic frontier likelihood. *Journal of Econometrics*, 18(2):275–279.

Wales, T. J. (1977). On the flexibility of flexible functional forms: An empirical approach. *Journal of Econometrics*, 5(2):183–193.

Wan, A. T. K., Zhang, X., and Zou, G. (2010). Least squares model averaging by Mallows criterion. *Journal of Econometrics*, 156(2):277–283.

Wang, H., Zhang, X., and Zou, G. (2009). Frequentist model averaging estimation: A review. *Journal of Systems Science and Complexity*, 22(4):732–748.

Wang, H.-J. (2002). Heteroscedasticity and non-monotonic efficiency effects of a stochastic frontier model. *Journal of Productivity Analysis*, 18(3):241–253.

Wang, H.-J. (2003). A stochastic frontier analysis of financing constraints on investment: The case of financial liberalization in Taiwan. *Journal of Business & Economic Statistics*, 21(3):406–419.

Wang, H.-J. and Ho, C.-W. (2010). Estimating fixed-effect panel stochastic frontier models by model transformation. *Journal of Econometrics*, 157(2):286–296.

Wang, H.-J. and Schmidt, P. (2002). One-step and two-step estimation of the effects of exogenous variables on technical efficiency levels. *Journal of Productivity Analysis*, 18(2):129–144.

Wang, W. S., Amsler, C., and Schmidt, P. (2011). Goodness of fit tests in stochastic frontier models. *Journal of Productivity Analysis*, 35(2):95–118.

Wang, W. S. and Schmidt, P. (2009). On the distribution of estimated technical efficiency in stochastic frontier models. *Journal of Econometrics*, 148(1):36–45.

Weill, L. (2008). On the inefficiency of European socialist economies. *Journal of Productivity Analysis*, 29(2):79–89.

Wheat, P., Greene, W. H., and Smith, A. (2014). Understanding prediction intervals for firm specific inefficiency scores from parametric stochastic frontier models. *Journal of Productivity Analysis*, 42(1):55–65.

White, H. (1980). Using least squares to approximate unknown regression functions. *International Economic Review*, 21(1):149–170.

White, H. (1984). *Asymptotic Theory for Econometricians*. New York, NY: Academic Press.

Wikström, D. (2015). Consistent method of moments estimation of the true fixed effects model. *Economics Letters*, 137:62–69.

Winsten, C. B. (1957). Discussion on Mr. Farrell's paper. *Journal of the Royal Statistical Society, Series A*, 120:282–284.

Wolff, H., Heckelei, T., and Mittelhammer, R. C. (2010). Imposing curvature and monotonicity on flexible functional forms: An efficient regional approach. *Computational Economics*, 36(4):309–339.

Wooldridge, J. (2013). *Introductory Econometrics: A Modern Approach*. Mason, OH: South-Western, 5th edition.

Wu, C. F. J. (1986). Jackknife, bootstrap and other resampling methods in regression analysis. *Annals of Statistics*, 14(4):1261–1295.

Wu, H. X., Krishna, K. L., Das, D. K., and Das, P. C. (2017). How does the productivity and economic growth performance of China and India compare in the post-reform era, 1981–2011? *International Productivity Monitor*, (33):91–113.

Wu, X. and Sickles, R. C. (2018). Semiparametric estimation under shape constraints. *Econometrics and Statistics*, 6(2):74–89.

Yagi, D., Chen, Y., Johnson, A. L., and Kuosmanen, T. (2018). Shape constrained kernel-weighted least squares: Estimating production functions for Chilean manufacturing industries. *Journal of Business & Economic Statistics*. Forthcoming.

Yao, S., Han, Z., and Feng, G. (2008). Ownership reform, foreign competition and efficiency of Chinese commercial banks: A non-parametric approach. *The World Economy*, 31(10):1310–1326.

Yatchew, A. (2003). *Semiparametric Regression for the Applied Econometrician*. New York, NY: Cambridge University Press.

Yatchew, A. and Härdle, W. (2006). Nonparametric state price density estimation using constrained least squares and the bootstrap. *Journal of Econometrics*, 133(2):579–599.

Ylvinger, S. (2000). Industry performance and structural efficiency measures: Solutions to problems in firm models. *European Journal of Operational Research*, 121(1):164–174.

Young, A. (1992). A tale of two cities: Factor accumulation and technical change in Hong Kong and Singapore. In *NBER Macroeconomics Annual*, volume 7, pages 13–64. Chicago, IL: University of Chicago Press.

Young, A. (1995). The tyranny of numbers: Confronting the statistical realities of the East Asian growth experience. 110(3):641–680.

Yule, G. U. (1926). Why do we sometimes get nonsense-correlations between time-series?–A study in sampling and the nature of time-series. *Journal of the Royal Statistical Society*, 89(1):1–63.

Zelenyuk, N. and Zelenyuk, V. (2015). Productivity drivers of efficiency in banking: Importance of model specifications. CEPA Working Paper No. WP08/2015, Queensland: Center for Efficiency and Productivity Analysis, School of Economics, University of Queensland.

Zelenyuk, V. (2002). *Essays in efficiency and productivity analysis of economic systems*. PhD thesis, Corvallis, OR: Oregon State University.

Zelenyuk, V. (2006). Aggregation of Malmquist productivity indexes. *European Journal of Operational Research*, 174(2):1076–1086.

Zelenyuk, V. (2013a). A scale elasticity measure for directional distance function and its dual: Theory and DEA estimation. *European Journal of Operational Research*, 228(3):592–600.

Zelenyuk, V. (2013b). A note on equivalences in measuring returns to scale. *International Journal of Business and Economics*, 12(1):85–89.

Zelenyuk, V. (2014a). Directional vs. Shephard's distance functions. *Optimization Letters*, 8(8):2185–2189.

Zelenyuk, V. (2014b). Scale efficiency and homotheticity: Equivalence of primal and dual measures. *Journal of Productivity Analysis*, 42(1):15–24.

Zelenyuk, V. (2014c). Testing significance of contributions in growth accounting, with application to testing ict impact on labor productivity of developed countries. *International Journal of Business and Economics*, 13(2):115–126.

Zelenyuk, V. (2015). Aggregation of scale efficiency. *European Journal of Operational Research*, 240(1):269–277.

Zelenyuk, V. and Henderson, D. J. (2007). Testing for (efficiency) catching-up. *Southern Economic Journal*, 73(4):1003–1019.

Zelenyuk, V. and Zheka, V. (2006). Corporate governance and firm's efficiency: The case of a transitional country, Ukraine. *Journal of Productivity Analysis*, 25(1):143–157.

Zellner, A., Kmenta, J., and Drèze, J. (1966). Specification and estimation of Cobb–Douglas production function models. *Econometrica*, 34(4):784–795.

Zhou, P., Ang, B. W., and Poh, K. L. (2008). Measuring environmental performance under different environmental DEA technologies. *Energy Economics*, 30(1):1–14.

Zieschang, K. D. (1984). An extended Farrell technical efficiency measure. *Journal of Economic Theory*, 33(2):387–396.

Subject Index

Author Index